POPULAR OPINION AND POLITICAL
DISSENT IN THE THIRD REICH

BAVARIA 1933-1945

POPULAR OPINION
AND
POLITICAL DISSENT
IN THE
THIRD REICH

BAVARIA 1933–1945

Ian Kershaw

CLARENDON PRESS · OXFORD

OXFORD
UNIVERSITY PRESS

Great Clarendon Street, Oxford OX2 6DP

Oxford University Press is a department of the University of Oxford.
It furthers the University's objective of excellence in research, scholarship,
and education by publishing worldwide in
Oxford New York
Athens Auckland Bangkok Bogotá Buenos Aires Cape Town
Chennai Dar es Salaam Delhi Florence Hong Kong Istanbul Karachi
Kolkata Kuala Lumpur Madrid Melbourne Mexico City Mumbai Nairobi
Paris São Paulo Shanghai Singapore Taipei Tokyo Toronto Warsaw
with associated companies in Berlin Ibadan

Oxford is a registered trade mark of Oxford University Press
in the UK and in certain other countries

Published in the United States
by Oxford University Press Inc., New York

© Ian Kershaw 1983

First published 1983
New Edition first published in paperback 2002

The moral rights of the author have been asserted
Database right Oxford University Press (maker)

British Library Cataloguing in Publication Data
Data available

Library of Congress Cataloging in Publication Data
Data available

ISBN 0–19–925111–8

1 3 5 7 9 10 8 6 4 2

Printed in Great Britain
on acid-free paper by
Biddles Ltd.,
Guildford and King's Lynn

For Betty, David, and Stephen

Preface to the Second Edition

It is an interesting, but also salutary, feeling to be offered the opportunity to look back and reflect on one's own book from a distance of some years. The distance provides a detachment that it is scarcely feasible to attain at the time of writing. It is, indeed, in some respects a humbling experience to see one's own work as the product of a particular time and a specific set of circumstances, and even more so to realise that it is not a finished product, but merely a contribution to a continuing, and wider, debate that, like a mighty river swallowing a rivulet, consumes it and flows on unabated.

It is twenty years since I wrote the preface to the original edition. I would not want to alter that preface, especially the remarks I made then about how I felt about writing as a non-German describing the position of ordinary people living under the Nazi regime. Equally unchanged are my expressions of personal gratitude to all those to whom I am still indebted for their help and encouragement. But it is appropriate to add a few further comments in this preface to a new edition, on the ways historiography in the area covered by the book has evolved in the twenty-six years or so that have passed since I began the research on which it is based, where the book fits into that historiography, and how my own views have been affected by subsequent research.

I began the research that culminated in the book with what I can perhaps most charitably describe as a refreshing naivety. Since my historical training had been as a medievalist, and I had been fully engaged until then with research and teaching in medieval history, I had familiarity with neither the sources for research on Nazi Germany, nor with the complexities of the historiography. Prompted by a short period living in a small Bavarian town not far from Munich in the early 1970s, and the curiosity about how people in such places had behaved in the Nazi era, I had in mind a purely empirical piece of work based on a local case-study. William S. Allen's pioneering study of a single town's path into the Third Reich, published in the 1960s, had made a deep impression on me.[1] But

---

[1] William Sheridan Allen, *The Nazi Seizure of Power. The Experience of a Single German Town 1930–1935*, Chicago, 1965. In the revised second edition, New York, 1984, Allen extended the period covered to that of 1922–1945.

Allen had not systematically studied society in the Lower Saxon town of Northeim (or 'Thalburg', to use the pseudonym he deployed in the original edition) *after* the initial phase of the Nazi takeover of power. *That* was what I originally had in mind for my project.

Had I remained a medievalist, probably nothing would have come of it. However, much to my own astonishment, I found myself in 1975 with the offer of a lectureship in modern history at Manchester University, enabling me henceforth to concentrate on teaching nineteenth- and twentieth-century European history, instead of medieval history, and to embark on the research on the Third Reich to which, though ill-equipped, I now felt myself committed. Within the space of that same *annus mirabilis* I was also invited to work with the team at the famous Institut für Zeitgeschichte in Munich that was just commencing an important and extensive research project on 'Bavaria in the Nazi Era. Resistance and Persecution, 1933-1945' ('Bayern in der NS-Zeit. Widerstand und Verfolgung 1933-1945').[2] My own immersion in the approaches to research and historiography of the Nazi era rapidly followed, and was strongly influenced by the indispensable help and encouragement I received from Martin Broszat and his team engaged on the 'Bayern-Projekt', and from his colleagues at the incomparable Institut für Zeitgeschichte, who gave me all the benefit of their unparalleled expertise on the Third Reich.

My own intentions of writing a comprehensive study of the development of popular opinion in Bavaria under Nazi rule gradually turned into two separate, but linked, studies.[3] As the original Preface explains, one study looked to the reasons for the popularity of many aspects of Nazism, and focused on the way Hitler was seen by ordinary people, on the creation and reception of the Führer image. This was published first in German and later appeared in a reconstructed and extended English edition.[4] The second study, the one presented here, concentrated on the opposite side of the picture, on what ordinary people found to *criticise* in the Nazi regime, how they had to adjust to new demands on their lives, and how different the recoverable attitudes were from the images of unity and conformity portrayed by Nazi propaganda.

---

[2] For the central publications arising from the project, see Martin Broszat et al. (eds.), *Bayern in der NS-Zeit*, 6 vols., Munich/Vienna, 1977–1983.

[3] The connection between the two volumes was clearly grasped in a perceptive review by Jeremy Noakes, 'Focusing on the Führer', *Times Literary Supplement*, 1 July 1983, p. 689.

[4] Ian Kershaw, *Der Hitler-Mythos. Volksmeinung und Propaganda im Dritten Reich*, Stuttgart, 1980 (new, revised, German edn., *Der Hitler-Mythos. Führerkult und Volksmeinung*, Stuttgart, 1999); *The 'Hitler Myth'. Image and Reality in the Third Reich*, Oxford, 1987.

Prior to undertaking the research for the book, I had, as I came to realise, uncritically swallowed images of the monopolistic control of society in 'totalitarian' states and based my assumptions on them. I remember how struck and excited I was, therefore, by reports, not just by opponents of the regime but coming from the Nazi authorities themselves, which made it plain that there were often very shallow limits to the penetration of propaganda. They showed, too, how ingrained, highly conservative traditions could prove resistant to Nazi ideological inroads in specific areas where they were directly affected, as, for example, in the attacks on the Christian Churches, while at the same time finding other areas of such ideology which they could very easily accommodate.

The three themes around which I structured the book – dissent arising from socio-economic policies, from the assault on the Christian Churches, and from the persecution of the Jews – were devised to reflect my initial hypotheses and findings. Contrary to my own naive assumptions – that the ideological preoccupations of the regime corresponded broadly to those of the mass of the population – what struck me so forcefully from the sources was how little a part seemed to be played in the formation of opinion by the anti-Jewish policy which was so central to the regime, and how large a part by contrast was shaped by resentment at interference in daily 'bread and butter' issues, and at attacks on religious tradition and practice. The shortest chapter in the book, the final chapter on 'popular opinion and the extermination of the Jews', was meant to reflect what I saw to be an extraordinary unimportance in contemporary popular opinion of events of such centrality to the regime's leadership, and of such obvious meta-historical significance, compared with matters far more mundane and insignificant, but which, unlike the extermination of the Jews, affected people's everyday lives, and preoccupied people so much.

This brief description of how the book came to be written, and what it set out to do, suffices to highlight the areas of historiography in which it might be said to find a place. The first area is, broadly speaking, that of 'resistance' (seen in its widest sense), and the related issues of conformity, consensus, and collaboration. The second touches on the problems of social change under Nazism, and the continuities or discontinuities of 'everyday life'. And the third, in some ways historiographically semi-detached from the other two, is the genesis of the Holocaust – specifically the issue of antisemitism in German society and popular reactions to the persecution of the Jews. I will try in what follows to provide a brief (and doubtless superficial) indication, as I see it, of the ways in which

historiography has developed in these areas since my book was initially published, and how my own thinking has been influenced by subsequent research.

I

As the Introduction explains, I chose the term 'dissent' specifically to distinguish from organised forms of resistance the entire gamut of attitudes and actions, often spontaneous and even coming from people who supported much of what the regime stood for, indicating criticism or rejection of any aspect of National Socialism. This very distinction, however, touches upon a central feature of the way the historiography on resistance was developing at the time the book was written, and has developed since. I have dealt with the historiographical issues at length in a chapter of my *Nazi Dictatorship*.[5] I need do no more here, therefore, than underline the most important issues.

At the time in the mid-1970s that I began working on popular opinion in Bavaria in the Nazi era, research into and the conceptualisation of German resistance to National Socialism was entering a new phase. Leaving aside the unchanging monolithic approach in the German Democratic Republic, there had been two previous discernible phases in the Federal Republic. Between the end of the war and the 1960s, the emphasis had been placed heavily upon conservative resistance, and the heroism of 'the men of the 20 July' – those individuals involved in the 1944 plot against Hitler. In the 1960s, much more attention was paid to working-class resistance, though this concentrated mainly on institutional and organisational studies of socialist and communist underground resistance groups. The new phase that began in the 1970s, into which my book fits, widened the perspective much further, to embrace the behaviour of the mass of ordinary Germans, how they reacted to Nazi rule and were affected by it, their usually partial, less heroic, more 'normal', kinds of 'everyday' opposition to the elements of regime policy that most directly touched them.

The most important breakthrough in this direction came, indeed, from the 'Bayern-Projekt', out of which my own work emanated, and which raised empirical research into spheres of conflict between regime and society on to an entirely new plane. The project team defined resistance as

[5] Ian Kershaw, *The Nazi Dictatorship. Problems and Perspectives of Interpretation*, 4th edn., London, 2000, chapter 8.

'every form of active or passive behaviour which allows recognition of the rejection of the National Socialist regime or a partial area of National Socialist ideology and was bound up with certain risks'.[6] It will be readily appreciated that this greatly widened the scope of what might be classed as 'resistance' since it included many forms of minor civil disobedience that flouted the 'total claim' of the regime but fell far short of fundamental rejection of Nazism. Methodologically, the 'Bayern-Projekt' concerned itself less with motivation than with effect, less with intention than with function, seeking to elucidate the ways in which Nazi attempts at social or ideological penetration were in practice blocked, or dented in their impact. The director of the project, the late Martin Broszat, tried to encapsulate this aim by using a new term '*Resistenz*' to imply not actual 'resistance' ('*Widerstand*' in German) but relative 'immunity', as in the usage of the term 'resistance' in medicine.[7] Though Broszat distinguished *Resistenz* from *Widerstand*, the linguistic proximity of the former term to 'resistance' in several European languages (if not in German), while purporting to mean something quite different, has made it in practice confusing and difficult to use.

The historiographical debate on German resistance might be said to have reached its peak around the fortieth anniversary of the 1944 bomb plot.[8] The debate was spurred by the widening of the understanding of resistance that the 'Bayern-Projekt' had prompted, and by the new interest in 'everyday history' (*Alltagsgeschichte*) which had led to a flurry of local and regional studies, and studies of particular social groups, that tended to emphasise political nonconformity.[9] The extension of 'resistance' to

[6] Harald Jaeger and Hermann Rumschöttel, 'Das Forschungsprojekt "Widerstand und Verfolgung in Bayern 1933–1945"', *Archivalische Zeitschrift*, 73(1977), p. 214.

[7] Martin Broszat, 'Resistenz und Widerstand', in *Bayern in der NS-Zeit*, vol.4, pp. 691–709.

[8] For excellent surveys of the many different approaches to the problem of German resistance to Nazism, see Jürgen Schmädeke and Peter Steinbach (eds.), *Der Widerstand gegen den Nationalsozialismus*, Munich/Zurich, 1985 (a volume arising from a major Berlin conference on the fortieth anniversary of the Stauffenberg assassination attempt on Hitler in 1944); Peter Steinbach and Johannes Tuchel (eds.), *Widerstand gegen den Nationalsozialismus*, Bonn/Berlin, 1994; and Hartmut Mehringer, *Widerstand und Emigration. Das NS-Regime und seine Gegner*, Munich 1997.

[9] Detlev Peukert, *Volksgenossen und Gemeinschaftsfremde. Anpassung, Ausmerze und Aufbegehren unter dem Nationalsozialismus*, Cologne, 1982 (Engl.: *Inside Nazi Germany. Conformity, Opposition and Racism in Everyday Life*, London, 1987) provides an excellent summary of the potential of the 'Alltagsgeschichte' approach, and makes good use of some of the large body of local and regional studies as well as those on particular social groups that started to emerge in the late 1970s. An extremely well-informed update of two decades of research on 'Alltagsgeschichte' is provided by Mary Nolan, 'Work, Gender and Everyday Life: Reflections on Continuity, Normality and Agency in Twentieth-Century Germany', in Ian Kershaw and Moshe Lewin (eds.), *Stalinism and Nazism. Dictatorships in Comparison*, Cambridge, 1997, pp. 311–42.

embrace all aspects of partial conflict with the regime at the grass roots of society was, however, contentious.[10]

On the one hand, it was claimed that the notion of 'resistance' had been expanded so far that it covered everything short of positive enthusiasm for the regime;[11] that the type of 'immunity' meant by the term 'Resistenz' could hardly be said to have dented Nazism's ability to wage war and carry out genocide; and that superficial manifestations of discontent were placed on the same level as fundamental and highly courageous opposition to the evil of the regime.[12] On the other hand, it was argued that no inflexible definition of 'resistance' would do justice to the variety of forms of opposition, some partial, some total; that precisely an understanding of the ability to block Nazism's demands in certain spheres (such as the fight to retain Crucifixes in school classrooms, dealt with in Chapter 8 below) helps an understanding of why the regime was so easily able to implement other policies (such as the persecution of the Jews); and that there were instances, such as the mounting unrest among the industrial working class, which, it was argued, did put the regime under pressure.[13] A number of typologies of resistance were developed, indicating its myriad, and often interlocking, forms. One, for example, envisaged a pyramid of nonconformity, rising through refusal of cooperation and public protest to a narrow pinnacle of fundamental resistance.[14] But the term 'resistance' was nevertheless used as the umbrella term to cover *all* forms, thus raising again the problem that the uniform concept may be used to bracket together forms of behaviour which were *quite essentially different*; that there does appear to be a major qualitative distinction between *fundamental opposition* and spheres of *partial conflict*.

It was precisely to avoid the conceptual problems raised by the term 'resistance' (and '*Resistenz*') that I preferred to use the notion of '*dissent*' to cover the *passivity* of much oppositional feeling (often not resulting in any action), and attitudes, often spontaneously expressed, which were in any

[10] For the varying interpretations, see Kershaw, *The Nazi Dictatorship*, 4th edn., pp. 198 ff.

[11] Richard Evans, 'From Hitler to Bismarck: "Third Reich" and Kaiserreich in Recent Historiography', *The Historical Journal*, 26 (1983), p. 1013.

[12] See the comments of the Swiss historian, Walter Hofer, in Schmädeke and Steinbach, pp. 1120–2.

[13] The classic work here is that of Timothy W. Mason, *Arbeiterklasse und Volksgemeinschaft*, Opladen, 1975. See also Michael Voges, 'Klassenkampf in der "Betriebsgemeinschaft"', *Archiv für Sozialgeschichte*, 21 (1981), pp. 329–84.

[14] See Peukert, *Volksgenossen und Gemeinschaftsfremde*, p. 97; and Gerhard Botz, 'Methoden- und Theorieprobleme der historischen Widerstandsforschung', in Helmut Konrad and Wolfgang Neugebauer (eds.), *Arbeiterbewegung-Faschismus-Nationalbewußtsein*, Vienna/Munich/Zurich, 1983, pp. 145ff.

way at all critical of Nazism.[15] As already indicated, I had not conceived my book as dealing with 'resistance' (meaning fundamental opposition to the Nazi regime) at all. It was meant to illustrate areas of grass-roots conflict and tension, seldom if at all leading to outright resistance, between regime and society. I was, in fact, anxious to emphasise the divisions of opinion, the weakness and partial nature of dissent, and the overlapping areas where there was widespread approval of regime policy. Hence, the study was able to suggest why the regime usually succeeded in implementing policy without claiming that this was merely the consequence of terror and repression (though I was certainly not trying to play down the very real role of fear in producing compliance).

This points to a possible way of looking at the otherwise intractable debate about the concept of 'resistance'. The division of interpretation between those advocating a *fundamentalist* approach, defining resistance in a narrow sense and looking to organised attempts to bring down the regime, and those working from a *societal* approach, with a wide definition aimed at highlighting aspects of conflict between regime and society, can be seen as largely a matter of differing perspectives, each in itself valid. The second, within which my own work can be placed, has been undeniably fruitful in opening up the investigation of grass-roots behaviour under Nazism. The first, it might be claimed, is intellectually more sterile, but emotionally and morally still of prime importance. Moreover, there is certainly much to be said for distinguishing the distinguishable in historical research. And putting a bomb under Hitler's table or running an illegal Communist cell were indubitably actions of a wholly different kind, both in the fundamental nature of the opposition and in the draconian retribution it provoked, to protests about Nazi interference with Corpus Christi Day processions or complaints about the farm policy of the Reich Food Estate (*Reichsnährstand*). Since it is plainly impossible to separate the term 'resistance' (*Widerstand*) from the normative values attached to it, it seemed best to me to devise an entirely different concept to cover the wide variety of minor forms of behaviour that did not fit the narrow confines of regime conformity. That is why I preferred, and still do prefer, the term *'dissent'*.

---

[15] I outlined my position (other than in the first pages of the Introduction to Popular Opinion and Political Dissent) in my contribution to the Schmädeke-Steinbach collection (pp. 779–98): '"Widerstand ohne Volk". Dissens und Widerstand im Dritten Reich'. For a recent work which uses the concept to assess the choices and compromises that ordinary German were compelled to make, see Adam Lebor and Roger Boyes, *Surviving Hitler. Choices, Corruption and Compromise in the Third Reich*, London, 2000.

Dealing with *dissent* in the way I have attempted here not only brings into focus critical attitudes and behaviour of the population but, at the same time, illustrates the areas where the regime could depend upon a wide swathe of *consent*. In other words, consent and dissent exist together, often in the same person, and are part of the same problem of understanding and interpretation. What I have called the 'fundamentalist' and 'societal' approaches do not need to remain irreconcilable opposites. In fact, it could be claimed with some justification that *only* an exploration of the contradictions of 'everyday' behaviour revealed by the societal approach opens up the possibility of a fuller understanding of the social and ideological isolation of fundamental resistance, and thereby of the reasons for its failure.

It is crucial to recognise, and not to forget, the sacrifice that many courageous and selfless individuals made to combat Nazi tyranny. But the moral lessons of German resistance, important though they continue to be, cannot suffice on their own. They almost inevitably lead to a monumentalisation and heroisation of resistance which can often stand in the way of a historical understanding of its all too human failings and frailties, and of the political and ideological 'grey areas' that signally helped contribute to its ineffectiveness and failure.[16] Moreover, the heroism itself tends to lose its impact with the passing of the years. What is necessary is to locate that fundamental and heroic leadership in the context of the society which produced it, to view it amid patterns of behaviour which were far less heroic, far less fundamental in their opposition. What I hope my book demonstrates is that the history of dissent, opposition, and resistance in the Third Reich is at the same time the history of consent, approval, and collaboration.

II

David Schoenbaum's classic study, *Hitler's Social Revolution*, has remained highly influential ever since its publication in the mid-1960s.[17] Yet the thesis, embodied in the book's title, that Nazism had indeed brought about a social revolution in Germany, is one which is as contentious

[16] See Martin Broszat, *Nach Hitler. Der schwierige Umgang mit unserer Geschichte*, Munich/Vienna, 1986, 110–12, 169–71.

[17] David Schoenbaum, *Hitler's Social Revolution*, London, 1966. More than thirty-five years after the publication of Schoenbaum's classic work – if, in my view, a flawed classic – we at last have a fine study of German society in the Third Reich in Pierre Aycoberry, *The Social History of the Third Reich*, New York, 1999.

today as when Schoenbaum wrote, and one which continues to play a central role in any attempt to deal with the position of the Third Reich in long-term social development in twentieth-century Germany. The question of social continuities across the 1945 divide remains a pivotal issue of historiography. And this is inseparable from the related central question of whether, intentionally or indirectly, Nazism stimulated the modernisation of German society.

My own book did not address this question directly, nor attempt to deal with it theoretically.[18] But, as a few remarks in the Conclusion indicate, what I was trying to do was to investigate empirically the validity of Schoenbaum's assertions about the transformation of consciousness which he claimed the Nazis had brought about. The evidence he presented did not seem to me to be sufficiently compelling to justify generalised conclusions about 'a society united like no other in recent German history', or 'the classless reality of the Third Reich'.[19] My own research into the attitudes of different social groups in Bavaria during the Third Reich led me to conclusions that conflicted directly with Schoenbaum's interpretation, and seemed to me to throw into doubt the extent to which one might speak of a 'social revolution' in the Third Reich.

The findings I was able to present suggested that the united 'national community', much trumpeted by Nazi propaganda, amounted to a myth; that beneath the surface veneer of a nation pulling together behind its Fuhrer, socio-economic realities, affecting the daily lives of ordinary Germans, revealed a remarkably disunited and discontented society.[20]

Nowhere, I suggested, was the alienation deeper than among the industrial working class. As the late Tim Mason had argued, the regime feared the working class's potential for producing another '1918', and combined repression with blandishments in the attempt to try to win over and

---

[18] I have discussed the problem and the scholarly debate at greater length in *The Nazi Dictatorship*, ch. 7.

[19] Schoenbaum, Anchor Books edn., New York, 1967, pp. 283, 285–6.

[20] On the ways Nazi propaganda portrayed the 'national community' and how such propaganda was received in the population, see Norbert Frei, *Der Führerstaat. Nationalsozialistische Herrschaft 1933 bis 1945*, 6th revised edn., Munich, 2001 (Engl. *National Socialist Rule in Germany. The Führer State 1933–1945*, Oxford/Cambridge, Mass., 1993); Norbert Frei, 'People's Community and War: Hitler's Popular Support', in Hans Mommsen (ed.), *The Third Reich between Vision and Reality. New Perspectives on German History 1918–1945*, Oxford/New York, 2001, pp. 59–77; Aycoberry, ch.2; Peter Reichel, *Der schöne Schein des Dritten Reiches. Faszination und Gewalt des Faschismus*, Frankfurt am Main, 1993; and Bernd Stöver, *Volksgemeinschaft im Dritten Reich. Die Konsensbereitschaft der Deutschen aus der Sicht sozialistischer Exilberichte*, Düsseldorf, 1993.

integrate workers into a 'national community'.[21] In Mason's view, with which I agreed (and still do agree), the attempt was an overwhelming failure. I concurred less with the conclusions Mason drew from his findings.

Mason argued that this meant a most serious limitation on the regime's autonomy of action at its very heart: the ability to prepare for, and wage, total war. His thesis was that, even without trade union representation, *unorganised* forms of working-class behaviour – such as absenteeism from work, refusing to increase the tempo of work along with the regime's demands, exploiting the labour shortage through high wage demands, or moving without permission from one job to another for better pay and conditions – exacerbated the structural economic problems of the regime. These culminated by the late 1930s in a mounting general crisis, determining that the regime had to go to war earlier and less well prepared than it would have wished to be. And even in the war it did not feel confident enough to depress living standards sufficiently to engage in all-out, total war until Germany was facing the prospects of military defeat. In this way working-class unrest had contributed to the weakness of the regime at its very heart, in the key area of war preparation.

My own findings went nowhere near as far as this. Though the evidence seemed to me to point to the inability of the regime to win over the industrial working class, it did, I argued, succeed in neutralising it.[22] Resignation and apathy, rather than rebelliousness and opposition, characterised, so far as I could see, the stance of most industrial workers on the eve of war.

The position of the industrial working class has been less the focus of recent research on social groups in the Third Reich than was the case in the 1960s and 1970s.[23] Mason's interpretation, linking worker industrial opposition with economic crisis limiting the regime's war plans, has generally met with little favour.[24] And there has been greater readiness than

[21] The arguments and evidence are presented at length in his study *Arbeiterklasse und Volksgemeinschaft*.

[22] Mason later seemingly came to accept this. See his excellent essay 'Die Bändigung der Arbeiterklasse im nationalsozialistischen Deutschland', in Carola Sachse et al., *Angst, Belohnung, Zucht und Ordnung. Herrschaftsmechanismen im Nationalsozialismus*, Opladen, 1982, pp. 1153.

[23] Two more recent works add, nevertheless, significantly to an understanding of the stance of industrial workers towards Nazism: F.L. Carsten, *The German Workers and the Nazis*, London, 1995; and Timothy Kirk, *Nazism and the Working Class in Austria. Industrial Unrest and Political Dissent in the 'National Community'*, Cambridge, 1996.

[24] Mason's arguments, and criticisms of them, are summarised in Kershaw, *The Nazi Dictatorship*, 4th edn., pp. 62 n.47, 88–90, 140, 200. For Mason's reply to his critics, see Tim Mason, *Nazism, Fascism and the Working Class*, ed. Jane Caplan, Cambridge, 1995, pp. 295–322.

was formerly the case to accept that certain spheres of Nazi propaganda did penetrate the working class, so that one could at least speak of partial integration into the regime.[25] I had, in fact, acknowledged this in the sections of *Popular Opinion and Political Dissent* that dealt with workers, and even more so in my study of *The 'Hitler Myth'*. More recent work has tended to stress much more than I did (or would still do) the success of 'Strength through Joy', Volkswagen saving schemes (tapping a latent consumerism), and social welfare policy in gaining working-class approval.[26] It has been suggested that, even if 'national community' propaganda could not destroy class and religious loyalties, it *was* able to create a 'new heightened national awareness', providing greater political stability and social integration. 'The obvious danger of citing examples of social dissent (as opposed to resistance)', it has been said, 'is that this may be at the expense of stressing the significance of *Volksgemeinschaft* in terms of integration and stability'.[27]

The difficulty with such arguments is that they ultimately depend upon a rather uncritical reading of the *claims* of Nazi propaganda, more than detailed analysis of its *effects*. Also, they do not give sufficient attention to the *parcellised* and *fragmented* nature of political attitudes in a system which prevented alternatives to the Nazis' own moulding of opinion through propaganda. Thus, the same worker who was thoroughly resentful about working conditions, living standards, social inequality, and the power and corruption of bosses backed by the might of the state, might perfectly well enjoy a works outing to a concert organised by 'Strength through Joy', would probably approve of the recovery of the Rhineland, and could perhaps think of Hitler as a great leader. Once one accepts this, there is no great difficulty in accepting that Nazism's 'national community' propaganda was seen by much of the working class as largely a sham, but that this did not prevent workers, like other social groups,

---

[25] See, for example, Gunther Mai, ' "Warum steht der deutsche Arbeiter zu Hitler?" Zur Rolle der Deutschen Arbeitsfront im Herrschaftssystem des Dritten Reiches', *Geschichte und Gesellschaft*, 12 (1986), pp. 212–34; and for a balanced appraisal of the state of research on the German working class under Hitler, Ulrich Herbert, 'Arbeiterschaft im "Dritten Reich". Zwischenbilanz und offene Fragen', *Geschichte und Gesellschaft*, 15 (1989), pp. 320–60. See also Ulrich Herbert's briefer assessment, ' "The Real Mystery in Germany". The German Working Class during the Nazi Dictatorship', in Michael Burleigh (ed.), *Confronting the Nazi Past. New Debates on Modern German History*, London, 1996, pp. 23–36; and Alf Lüdtke, 'The Appeal of Exterminating "Others". German Workers and the Limits of Resistance', in Christian Leitz (ed.), *The Third Reich*, Oxford/Malden, Mass., 1999, pp. 155–77.

[26] David Welch, 'Manufacturing a Consensus: Nazi Propaganda and the Building of a "National Community" (*Volksgemeinschaft*)', *Contemporary European History*, 2 (1993), pp. 1–15.

[27] Welch, 'Manufacturing a Consensus', p. 11.

being integrated into the central aims of the regime—war and expansion. To this extent, Peter Hüttenberger's comment remains apposite: 'Whatever the perceptible reserve and discontent of the workers, sections of the middle class, and the peasantry, the fact cannot be ignored that the leadership of the Third Reich largely succeeded in producing such a degree of conformity, indeed readiness to collaborate, that its plans, especially preparation for war, were not endangered from within'.[28]

It is in the nature of things difficult to arrive at hard and fast generalisations about mentalities, attitudes, and political consciousness. But now, as when I wrote the book, it appears to me that the evidence is not remotely strong enough to speak of a transformation of mentalities needed to comply with claims that a 'social revolution' had taken place in the twelve years of Nazi rule. What does perhaps seem likely, supported by some oral-history findings since my book was published, is that one effect of Nazism was to break down to some extent traditional working-class solidarity and replace it increasingly – and especially among younger workers – by the individualistic, performance-related attitudes to work which came to fruition in the post-war 'economic miracle'.[29] In this way, some of the political and social 'moorings' of working-class behaviour were changed under Nazism. The massive turnover of workers during the war, and the large-scale replacement of Germans by 'foreign workers' in many industries, also helped to disrupt and break down older loyalties.[30] Of course, to some extent the same was true of other sections of society as well as of the industrial working class. It was, naturally, far from the case that Nazism left society unaltered. But the changes did not amount in my view to a transformation that could be fittingly described by the term 'social revolution'. And the most far-reaching social change came, in fact, not as a direct consequence of Nazi social policy, but with the military defeat and collapse of the regime, and the immense upheaval which followed.

The same point could be made about the related question of Nazism as a modernising regime. My book did not deal directly with this issue,

---

[28] Peter Hüttenberger, 'Nationalsozialistische Polykratie', *Geschichte und Gesellschaft*, 2 (1976), p. 440.

[29] See Lutz Niethammer (ed.), *'Die Jahre weiß man nicht, wo man die heute hinsetzen soll'. Faschismuserfahrungen im Ruhrgebiet*, Berlin/Bonn, 1983; and Peukert, *Volksgenossen und Gemeinschaftsfremde*, pp. 230, 280–8, 294.

[30] On 'foreign workers', the definitive work is that of Ulrich Herbert, *Fremdarbeiter. Politik und Praxis des 'Ausländer-Einsatzes' in der Kriegswirtschaft des Dritten Reiches*, Berlin/Bonn, 1985 (Engl.: *Hitler's Foreign Workers. Enforced Foreign Labor in Germany under the Third Reich*, Cambridge, 1997).

though indirectly my position on Schoenbaum's thesis of a social revolution gave a hint of my views on the modernisation issue, which I have subsequently addressed elsewhere.[31] While Schoenbaum and, in somewhat different fashion before him, the sociologist Ralf Dahrendorf had seen Nazism as unwittingly having a modernising effect through its contradictory policies and destructive impact on established structures, rather than by choice or intention,[32] some subsequent interpretations – though they remained highly controversial – claimed that the Nazi leadership (and Hitler in particular) actually wanted to modernise Germany and intended to bring it about after a successful war for European hegemony.[33] Again, it seems unnecessary to go over ground that I have covered in a chapter of my *Nazi Dictatorship*.[34] Suffice it to say here that the argument rests heavily upon reading Hitler's social ideas, as expressed in newspaper articles, speeches, or comments to his immediate entourage, as firm intentions for a revolutionary restructuring of society. The same applies to suggestions that the head of the Labour Front, Robert Ley, had ideas for and developed policies aimed at pushing Germany into a more modern society.[35]

Such views, though emphasising the 'positive' rather than the gross inhumanity of Nazism, were advanced by genuine scholars, and were not in any sense meant to imply an apologia for the regime. But it is easy to see how they might be interpreted in such a way. Leaving aside the moral dimension, however, they seem to me to miss the point about Nazism as a historical phenomenon: they come close to turning the racial essence of Nazism, the drive for racial purity and racial empire, into a mere vehicle to bring about a revolutionary modernisation of German society. A balanced approach to what the Nazis actually *did*, rather than merely what they said they would do following a victorious genocidal war to subjugate Europe, would certainly be able to point to some areas where modernising change, wittingly or unwittingly, was pushed along in the Third Reich. Technological change for example, was doubtless forced along as

---

[31] See *The Nazi Dictatorship*, ch.7.

[32] Ralf Dahrendorf, *Society and Democracy in Germany*, London, 1968, pp. 402–18.

[33] See especially Rainer Zitelmann, *Hitler. Selbstverstandnis eines Revolutionärs*, Hamburg/Leamington Spa/New York, 1987 (Engl.: *Hitler. The Politics of Seduction*, London, 1999). See also Michael Prinz and Rainer Zitelmann (eds.), *Nationalsozialismus und Modernisierung*, Darmstadt, 1991.

[34] See *The Nazi Dictatorship*, 4th edn., pp. 241–8.

[35] Ronald Smelser, *Robert Ley. Hitler's Labour Front Leader*, Oxford/New York/Hamburg, 1988, p. 305 and note 3. See also Ley's postwar views, shortly before his suicide in 1945, in Richard Overy, *Interrogations. The Nazi Elite in Allied Hands, 1945*, London, 2001, p. 546.

XX PREFACE TO THE SECOND EDITION

a consequence of preparation for, then actually fighting, a major war. But the same would apply, if perhaps in differing degrees, to every other belligerent country. What is important about Nazism is not the features it has in common with other modern and modernising economies, but the murderousness which sets it apart from them.[36]

In any case, an overall check-list would not lead to the conclusion that Nazism brought about, or sought to bring about, Germany's 'modernising revolution'.[37] Though the Nazis claimed they were modernising Germany, propaganda should not be confused with reality.[38] Most importantly, the issue of modernisation has to be seen in its correct perspective. German mastery of a 'racially cleansed' Europe was what Nazism was about.[39] Whether or not, in this or that area, the Third Reich was 'modernising' is, compared with explaining the enormity of the Holocaust, not really an issue of the first importance.

III

The third strand of my enquiry was an attempt to make a small contribution towards answering the most important question of all: how was it possible for a civilised society to come to see the killing of every single member of an ethnic minority, on grounds of race alone, as a major national priority? My conclusion, put very baldly, was that, for the majority of the German people, killing the Jews never was a priority. But widespread passive antisemitism and tolerance of increasingly savage discrimination against a disliked minority presented, of course, no obstacle to the escalating radicalism of those power-groups in the Nazi state for whom finding a 'final solution to the Jewish Question', even if it meant killing all the Jews of Europe, *was* a priority.

[36] This is a point made by Charles Maier, *The Unmasterable Past: History, Holocaust, and German National Identity*, Cambridge, Mass., 1988, p. 96.

[37] Jens Albers, 'Nationalsozialismus und Modernisierung', *Kölner Zeitschrift für Soziologie und Sozialpsychologie*, 41(1989), pp. 346–65. See also Manfred Rauh, 'Anti-Modernismus im nationalsozialistischen Staat', *Historisches Jahrbuch*, 108 (1987), pp. 94–121; Norbert Frei, 'Wie modern war der Nationalsozialismus?', *Geschichte und Gesellschaft*, 19 (1993), pp. 367–87; and Hans Mommsen, 'Noch einmal: Nationalsozialismus und Modernisierung', *Geschichte und Gesellschaft*, 21 (1995), pp. 391–402.

[38] Hans Mommsen, 'Nationalsozialismus als vorgetäuschte Modernisierung', in Walter H. Pehle (ed.), *Der historische Ort des Nationalsozialismus. Annäherungen*, Frankfurt am Main, 1990, pp. 11–46.

[39] This is stressed by Michael Burleigh and Wolfgang Wippermann, *The Racial State. Germany 1933–1945*, Cambridge, 1991. Michael Burleigh repeats the emphasis in *The Third Reich. A New History*, London, 2000.

Of course, I was only looking at one aspect of any attempt to explain this enormous catastrophe for humankind. And in some ways, as my own argument tends to suggest, the attitudes and behaviour towards the Jews of ordinary Germans in one part of the country constituted only a minor aspect. I concluded the first of the two chapters I devoted to the persecution and extermination of the Jews by remarking that, on the evidence I had considered, the reasons for the radicalisation of anti-Jewish policy ought not to be sought in the demands of popular opinion, which provided no block on aggression towards the Jews but did not cause it. 'The road to Auschwitz was built by hate, but paved with indifference', was the way I put it.

I did not, of course, mean by this conclusion to offer any type of apologia for the behaviour of ordinary Germans towards Jews in the Third Reich. What I was trying to do, in the way I structured the book, was to *compare* the strength of feeling of 'ordinary' Germans – that is, people not acting as members of Party formations, or in positions of even low-level leadership – on 'the Jewish Question', with their behaviour and attitudes on a range of socio-economic questions of direct material relevance to them and on the conflict of the regime with each of the main Christian Churches. The term 'indifference' (which does not necessarily mean 'neutral' but can have negative connotations), was meant to suggest that, in a ranking of priorities, most people would have regarded the 'Jewish Question' as less important than 'bread-and-butter' issues, and than attacks on their Church practices, traditions, and institutions. This was even more the case during the War, when people – living under a hail of bombs and fearing for the lives of their loved ones at the front – obviously faced increased worry, anxiety, and hardship of their own, and, it seemed to me, had even less interest in the fate of a tiny, disliked, minority that had by then been removed from Germany. The saying, 'out of sight, out of mind', struck me as I was writing that chapter as characteristic of this mentality.

Of course, this is hardly morally commendable. But nor is it altogether incomprehensible. And nor could it be said to have caused the Holocaust. Indeed, far from offering any apologia for the way ordinary people behaved, it seemed to me that what I was suggesting was more worrying – and had possible wider application to cases beyond Germans and Jews – than the presumption that they had been indoctrinated by Nazi propaganda into becoming ideological antisemites. For these people, *without* being fanatical Jew-haters, could so easily condone barbarous discrimination and persecution. They witnessed what was happening to the Jews before their eyes for eight years before the deportations to the east began. Few were concerned enough to do anything. That in itself is unsurprising. They had seldom been concerned to do anything about anti-Jewish outrages even under the liberal democracy of the Weimar era.[40] It was hardly likely that they would do more in conditions of a terroristic dictatorship. Yet in numerous instances I was able to document, such as the attempt to remove Bishop Meiser or the Crucifix issue, or, in a central humanitarian issue, that of the 'euthanasia action', opposition could, even in the conditions of the Third Reich, be mobilised to some extent. So fear and repression cannot be the whole explanation. The very indifference – the lack of concern – in the case of the Jews seemed to me to have provided the moral vacuum in which the radicalisation could take place. Apathy, moral indifference, and latent antisemitism were sufficient, I argued, to accommodate the 'dynamic' hatred of the genocidal forces in the Nazi regime.

My line of argument was in essence little different from that taken by Marlis Steinert and Lawrence Stokes, earlier pioneers of research into popular opinion.[41] And just as I was finishing the book, an essay by William Sheridan Allen on attitudes of the German public to the so-called *Reichskristallnacht* nationwide pogroms against the Jews on 9–10 November 1938 moved, on the basis of this case-study, to not dissimilar conclusions.[42] Allen argued that reactions to the pogroms demonstrated the low ranking of antisemitism in the scale of values of ordinary Germans, and the inability of Nazi propaganda to persuade people that open shows of brutality against Jews were acceptable forms of public behaviour.

[40] Surprisingly little has so far been written on the social history of antisemitism during the Weimar Republic (other than in general terms in connection with the rise of Nazism). A work of some significance, however, in showing the levels of prejudice, discrimination, and violence towards Jews before the Nazis took power, is Dirk Walter, *Antisemitische Kriminalität und Gewalt. Judenfeindschaft in der Weimarer Republik*, Bonn, 1999. A further study which well illustrates, on a regional basis, the virulently anti-Jewish climate long before Hitler became well known, is that of Michael Wildt, '"Der muß hinaus! Der muß hinaus!" Antisemitismus in deutschen Nord- Und Ostseebädern 1920–1935', *Mittelweg 36*, 10 (2001), pp. 3–25.

[41] Marlis G. Steinert, *Hitlers Krieg und die Deutschen*, Düsseldorf, 1970, pp. 236–63; Lawrence D. Stokes, 'The German People and the Destruction of the European Jews', *Central European History*, 6 (1973), pp. 167–91. For an update of research in this area, see Otto Dov Kulka, 'The German Population and the Jews: State of Research and New Perspectives', in David Bankier (ed.), *Probing the Depths of German Antisemitismus. German Society and the Persecution of the Jews, 1933–1941*, New York/Oxford/Jerusalem, 2000, pp. 271–81.

[42] William Sheridan Allen, 'Die deutsche Öffentlichkeit und die "Reichskristallnacht" – Konflikte zwischen Werthierarchie und Propaganda im Dritten Reich', in Detlev Peukert and Jürgen Reulecke (eds.), *Die Reihen fast geschlossen. Beiträge zur Geschichte des Alltags unterm Nationalsozialismus*, Wuppertal, 1981, pp. 397–411.

My own account of reactions to *Reichskristallnacht* in Chapter 6 below suggests, nevertheless, that the motives for criticising Nazi violence towards the Jews were very mixed, and were frequently far from humanitarian. I saw the criticisms of the pogroms less than Allen did as an outright rejection of the Nazi policy; people indeed often castigated the methods used, but apparently also approved the aim to rid Germany of its Jews. So I would not go to the lengths of Allen's far too undifferentiated conclusion 'that Hitler and his henchmen murdered the Jews from Germany and other parts of Europe against the will of the German people'.[43] At the same time, it seems plain that the secrecy with which the Nazi leadership veiled the 'Final Solution' reflected their awareness that popular support for anti-Jewish measures had its limits.[44]

A more balanced appraisal than Allen's was presented by Hans Mommsen who, accepting a 'relative indifference' of the majority of the population towards the 'Jewish Question', argues that the regime overestimated the extent that it had been able to bring about antisemitic indoctrination. However, such indoctrination was not necessary, given the absence of any checks on the radicalising drive of the fanatical minority pushing for a 'solution to the Jewish Question'. Mommsen went on to argue that as, ultimately during the war, many, perhaps most, Germans came to learn something (though far from everything) about the terrible events in the east, without being able to grasp the enormity of the crimes being committed in their name, they consciously or subconsciously attuned to the collective suppression of all knowledge of it which the regime itself demanded.[45]

Even more problematical in terms of its benevolent judgement of the behaviour of ordinary Germans towards Jews than Allen's assessment

[43] Allen, 'Die deutsche Öffentlichkeit und die "Reichskristallnacht"'p. 409.

[44] A point made by Michael R. Marrus, *The Holocaust in History*, Penguin edition, London, 1989, p. 94.

[45] Hans Mommsen, 'Was haben die Deutschen vom Völkermord an den Juden gewußt?', in Walter H. Pehle (ed.), *Der Judenpogrom 1938. Von der 'Reichskristallnacht' zum Völkermord*, Frankfurt am Main, 1988, pp. 176–200, here esp. pp. 184, 199–200; Hans Mommsen and Dieter Obst, 'Die Reaktion der deutschen Bevölkerung auf die Verfolgung der Juden 1933–1943', in Hans Mommsen and Susanne Willems (ed.), *Herrschaftsalltag im Dritten Reich*, Düsseldorf, 1988, pp. 374–485, here esp. pp. 385, 420–1. See also my article, 'German Popular Opinion during the "Final Solution". Information, Comprehension, Reactions', in Asher Cohen, Joav Gelber, and Charlotte Wardi (eds.), *Comprehending the Holocaust: Historical and Literary Research*, Frankfurt am Main/Bern/New York/Paris, 1988, pp. 145–58. This article makes use, among other evidence, of a telling example of what it was possible to learn – and understand – of the killings from the striking diary entries in Herbert and Sybille Obenaus (eds.), *'Schreiben, wie es wirklich war!' Aufzeichnungen Karl Dürkelfäldens aus den Jahren 1933–1945*, Hanover, 1985.

was a study by Sarah Gordon suggesting (on the basis of a small sample of courtcases analysed, arising from the files of the Düsseldorf Gestapo) a relatively high level of sympathy for Jews and opposition to their persecution.[46] Gordon's assessment of her own evidence was found wanting by Robert Gellately, whose meticulous analysis of the Würzburg Gestapo files relating to racial policy revealed a quite contrasting picture of a population for the most part willing and keen to collaborate with the police in the process of discrimination and persecution against their Jewish neighbours.[47] Gellately's findings have more recently been significantly amplified by Eric Johnson's impressive study of the behaviour of ordinary Germans, as reflected in Gestapo files, towards Jews in Rhineland towns.[48]

What is obvious is that outright sympathy for Jews, let alone actual opposition to Nazi anti-Jewish policy, came from only a tiny minority of the population.[49] My own work was not so much concerned with this highly courageous though, unfortunately, miniscule and unrepresentative section of the population, but with the great mass of the ordinary population who tended to look on, sometimes no doubt with disapproval, and even more frequently to look away.[50] Probably, had I been a German living at the time, I would have been one of them. Their very passivity, from motives ranging from tacit approval to fear of what might happen to them for signs of supporting the Jews, is, I was arguing, both understandable in itself and necessary to an explanation of how the radicalism of another minority – though certainly a far larger one than the opponents of racism; and with all the power of the state at its disposal – could so easily gather pace.

[46] Sarah Gordon, *Hitler, Germans, and the 'Jewish Question'*, Princeton, 1984.

[47] Robert Gellately, *The Gestapo and German Society. Enforcing Racial Policy 1933–1945*, Oxford, 1990. Gellately has extended his emphasis on a society supportive of the Nazi persecution of Jews and other ethnic minorities in his later study, *Backing Hitler. Consent and Coercion in Nazi Germany*, Oxford, 2001. Gellately's interpretation is, however, far more nuanced than the oversimplistic view of the Germans as, almost uniformly, 'eliminationist antisemites' represented in the highly contentious book of Daniel Jonah Goldhagen, *Hitler's Willing Executioners*, New York, 1996. For a reassessment of the Gestapo's role, see Gerhard Paul and Klaus-Michael Mallmann (eds.), *Die Gestapo. Mythos und Realität*, Darmstadt, 1995.

[48] Eric A. Johnson, *Nazi Terror. The Gestapo, Jews, and Ordinary Germans*, New York, 1999.

[49] Konrad Kwiet and Helmut Eschwege, *Selbstbehauptung und Widerstand. Deutsche Juden im Kampf um Existenz und Menschenwürde 1933–1945*, Hamburg, 1984, pp. 42ff, sensibly divide German society into a tiny minority showing solidarity with the persecuted Jews, a far larger (and powerful) minority of aggressors, and the vast mass of the passive and indifferent.

[50] See on 'bystanders' Raul Hilberg, *Perpetrators, Victims, Bystanders. The Jewish Catastrophe 1933–1945*, New York, 1992; and Marrus, ch.8.

The implications of my research were, I thought, particularly well summarised by one reviewer who wrote: 'While it was always frightening to imagine a nation swept away and dominated by the Nazis, it is surely no less frightening to consider that the Nazis were able to accomplish most of what they set out to do without acquiring unquestioning allegiance or imposing complete control. . . . For the Nazi state to thrive, its citizens had to do no more than go along, maintaining a clear sense of their own interests and a profound indifference to the suffering of others'.[51]

Though moral indifference to the terrible persecution inflicted on a minority of citizens, already before the deportations to the east and an even worse fate began in 1941, seemed to me a serious enough condemnation of the behaviour of Bavarians (and other Germans) in the Third Reich, some critics thought the judgement not harsh enough. Michael Kater thought I had downplayed the extent and pervasive nature of popular antisemitism after 1933.[52] Otto Dov Kulka and Aron Rodrigue, in a thoughtful if critical review article, felt that 'indifference' – which they took to mean simple lack of interest, rather than the implied lack of moral concern that which I had intended to convey – was a misleading term. They suggested 'passive complicity' in the persecution (and extermination) of the Jews more aptly summarised the behaviour of the mass of Germans.[53] I conceded, in a paper largely stimulated by this criticism, that I might in places have underplayed the interest shown by ordinary Germans in aspects of anti-Jewish policy.[54] And certainly there was blatant self-interest in the way some Germans welcomed the deportation of their Jewish neighbours in their anxiety to grasp the opportunity to acquire their possessions and move into the homes they were vacating. But I saw no reason to abandon the basic tenor of my argument, nor the usage of the term 'indifference' to denote a point which Kulka and Rodrigue accepted, namely that the 'Jewish Question' was not high on the scale of priorities of the German people during the Nazi era. The alternative concept of 'passive complicity' struck me as difficult to use, and more moral-normative than behavioural-descriptive in connotation – attempting to assign guilt more than look for explanation. In the end,

---

[51] James J. Sheehan, 'National Socialism and German Society. Reflections on Recent Research', *Theory and Society*, 13(1984), pp. 866–7.

[52] Michael Kater, 'Everyday Anti-Semitism in Prewar Nazi Germany: The Popular Bases', *Yad Vashem Studies*, 16 (1984), pp. 129–59.

[53] Otto Dov Kulka and Aron Rodrigue, 'The German Population and the Jews in the Third Reich', *Yad Vashem Studies*, 16 (1984), 421–35.

[54] Ian Kershaw, 'German Popular Opinion and the "Jewish Question", 1939–1943: Some further Reflections', in Arnold Paucker (ed.), *Die Juden im nationalsozialistischen Deutschland 1933–1943*, Tübingen, 1986, pp. 365–86.

however, the difference in interpretation, whatever the disagreement over concepts, turned out to be minimal.

And I suspect that Otto Dov Kulka and Aron Rodrigue can accept just as easily as I can the conclusion, which on a broader source base amplifies and extends rather than contradicts our own findings, arrived at by David Bankier in his excellent synthesis on opinion towards the 'Jewish Question' in Nazi Germany that takes the subject empirically probably about as far as it can go: 'Since most Germans were "traditionally" anti-semitic and did not reject persecution of Jews on principled grounds, their level of resistance to genocidal means was very low'.[55]

Perhaps most of all, research on popular antisemitism and reactions to the persecution of the Jews has revealed, nevertheless, how difficult such broad generalisations are, how variegated the responses of ordinary people turned out to.[56] This has been emphasised, too, in some local studies which arrive at quite diverse conclusions about the level of antagonism shown to Jews in the Nazi era and the importance of antisemitism in the local community.[57] In itself, the difficulty of arriving at hard-and-fast broad generalisations about attitudes in such an important sphere of Nazi policy testifies to the inability of the Nazis, however great the barrage of propaganda, to instil in the mass of the population ideological tenets central to the heart of the regime. The model of the 'totalitarian mass society' falls down at such a key point.[58] What, finally, the research demonstrates is that popular antisemitism in Germany, while a precondition for genocide, cannot be regarded as its cause. That has to be sought in the structures of the Nazi state, the centrality to the regime's elites (not confined to Hitler) of the limitless quest for 'racial purification', and the emerging possibilities of implementing a 'final solution to the

---

[55] David Bankier, *The Germans and the Final Solution. Public Opinion under Nazism*, Oxford, 1992, quotation p. 156.

[56] See the summary of Marrus, *The Holocaust in History*, p. 94.

[57] In a well-researched study, *Die Juden in Gaukönigshofen/Unterfranken (1550–1942)*, Stuttgart, 1988, Thomas Michel demonstrates a poisonous anti-Jewish atmosphere and active participation of the local inhabitants in the pogrom of November 1938. By contrast, Frances Henry's – admittedly far less thoroughly researched – study (based entirely on later recollections) of a small Rhineland town (which she calls 'Sonderburg') distinguishes between the antisemitic drive of a minority of the inhabitants, who were Party activists, and the largely apathetic and passive behaviour of the great majority of the townspeople. – Frances Henry, *Victims and Neighbors. A Small Town in Nazi Germany Remembered*, South Hadley, Mass., 1984.

[58] Since the demise of the Soviet Union the concept of totalitarianism has undergone a renaissance. For an anthology of some of the recent writing on the concept, see Eckard Jesse (ed.), *Totalitarismus im 20. Jahrhundert. Eine Bilanz der internationalen Forschung*, 2nd. edn., Bonn, 1999. The concept was consciously adopted, invoking works of the 1950s, as a main platform of his interpretation by Michael Burleigh in his *The Third Reich. A New History*.

Jewish Question'. For Germany's singularity lay not in the antisemitism of its society, but in the attainment of power over a modern state by a genocidal elite determined to remove with all ruthlessness, and ultimately to eradicate physically, all Jews under its control.[59]

The total obliteration of human rights in Nazi Germany marks the nadir even in the twentieth century's dismal record of assault on human dignity and life. The circumstances which gave rise to Nazism were historically unique. Even recognising the uncertainties and perils that lie ahead, and not minimising the resurgence of racial violence in many countries of Europe, it is highly improbable that, short of unforeseeable conditions which might follow a major war engulfing the continent, anything on the scale of the horrors perpetrated by the Nazi regime is likely to be experienced again. Even so, it seems to me that the attempt to understand – taking full account of all the difficulties of the historical evidence – the behaviour of ordinary people in Nazi Germany, in conditions of a regime consciously seeking to mould ideological conformity and prepared to stoop to the utmost violence against its own citizens to bring it about, still retains importance and relevance today. After all, we need only look to the territory of the former Yugoslavia for an example, uncomfortably close to home, of how rapidly a combination of radical and fundamentalist ethnic nationalism and war for 'ethnically cleansed' land can eradicate all traces of humane and civilised values.[60] We *can* learn from history – at least what should be ruled out of the present and future, and never again ruled in. The study of society in Nazi Germany helps us in some ways to learn those lessons – even if we are not very good at implementing them.

My book was, of course, written as a piece of historical analysis, not as a moral tract for today. Like all historians looking back at their own work after a period of time, I would now write some things differently, and was tempted to do so for a new edition. Certainly, and in the nature of things, it would be in many ways a different book if I were to start it now. However, I think it is better, as I said at the beginning, that books written at a particular time are seen as a product of that time, with all their

---

[59] I place the emphasis on the early years of the Weimar Republic in the creation of a potentially genocidal leadership corps of the Nazi Party in my essay 'Antisemitismus und die NS-Bewegung vor 1933', in Hermann Graml, Angelika Königseder, and Juliane Wetzel (eds.), *Vorurteil und Rassenhaß. Antisemitismus in den faschistischen Bewegungen Europas*, Berlin, 2001, pp. 29–47.

[60] For the mass killing in the former Yugoslavia, placing the 'ethnic cleansing' there in the context of genocidal actions throughout the twentieth century, see the thought-provoking analysis by Norman N. Naimark, *Fires of Hatred. Ethnic Cleansing in Twentieth-Century Europe*, Cambridge, Mass., 2001, Ch.5.

flaws and limitations. I am simply happy, therefore, that the book will now appear in this new edition, and even happier if it contributes in some small way to provoking thought on the weighty issues it was trying to address.

Ian Kershaw
September 2001

Preface to the First Edition

A year ago I published one part of my researches on Bavarian society during the Third Reich in a study which explored predominantly the *acclamatory* side of popular opinion — the integratory effects of the mass adulation of Hitler (*Der Hitler-Mythos. Volksmeinung und Propaganda im Dritten Reich*, Stuttgart, 1980). The present book, while forming an entirely integral and independent study, was conceived alongside the *Hitler-Mythos* volume and provides in my view the necessary completion of the picture by concentrating upon the critical, nonconformist, *dissenting* strands of opinion, falling for the most part well short of real opposition let alone resistance to Nazism but setting nevertheless the acclaim for Hitler and for certain Nazi aims and policies in perspective. The study offers, too, an antidote to the Nazis' own propaganda image of a society united behind its rulers — an image which probably at the time found greater resonance abroad than inside Germany and which is not without echo and even appeal today. Though the book examines opinion and political behaviour in Bavaria only, I am more than ever convinced on the basis of comparable sources I have studied for other parts of Germany that the picture painted — with all due attention to the peculiarities of Bavarian society and politics — has a relevance which extends beyond the geographical limits imposed upon the study. This is quite apart from the advantages of a much deeper level of analysis and differentiation which a regional concentration allows.

For an outsider, a non-German who never experienced Nazism, it is perhaps too easy to criticize, to expect standards of behaviour which it was well-nigh impossible to attain in the circumstances. I have consciously strived to avoid making over-simplistic, moralizing judgements. And where I have been critical, I have still tried above all to understand sympathetically the position of ordinary people living under

such a regime, to recognize the art of the possible. There are
not many villains and even fewer heroes in the story. It is not
about Nazi leaders, nor about the non-Nazi élites, whose sins
of omission and commission are grave. My admiration for the
courageous minority — overwhelmingly communist workers —
who fought uncompromisingly against the Nazis, usually
paying the price in liberty and even life, is boundless. But
my book is not about them either. It is about the muddled
majority, neither full-hearted Nazis nor outright opponents,
whose attitudes at one and the same time betray signs of
Nazi ideological penetration and yet show the clear limits
of propaganda manipulation. The picture painted is not a
simple, straightforward, and clear-cut one. But I would
claim it accords much more than most depictions of Nazi
society with the unclear attitudes and inconsistent behaviour
of ordinary Germans during the Nazi tyranny. I should like
to think that had I been around at the time I would have
been a convinced anti-Nazi engaged in the underground
resistance fight. However, I know really that I would have
been as confused and felt as helpless as most of the people
I am writing about.

It is a great pleasure to be able to record here my thanks to
friends and colleagues without whom this book could not
have been written. Among British experts on modern German
history who have given me great encouragement, provided
invaluable support, and influenced my thinking through
their own excellent work I would like to thank in particular
my good friend and close colleague in the History Department at Manchester University, John Breuilly, along with
Alan Milward, Jeremy Noakes, Tim Mason, Bill Carr, and
Dick Geary. Among historians in Germany the greatest
single influence upon the development of my work has been
Professor Martin Broszat of the Institut für Zeitgeschichte,
Munich. To him and to Elke Fröhlich, Falk Wiesemann, and
Peter Hüttenberger, all of whom helped in shaping my ideas
and guiding my research, I offer my sincere thanks.

I am most grateful for the expert guidance and patient
attention I received from the archivists in all the Bavarian
State Archives, where the bulk of the research was carried

out, and also in the non-Bavarian record repositories where I worked. My thanks are also owing to the *Landratsämter* of Amberg, Friedberg, Neumarkt in der Oberpfalz, Obernburg am Main, Schongau, and Traunstein for permission to use files still in their possession.

Concentrated work for long spells in German archives would for British scholars be impossible without financial support, and here too I have been extremely fortunate. My greatest thanks goes to the Alexander von Humboldt-Stiftung, whose grant allowed me to spend a sabbatical year in Munich in 1976-7. At other times, for this and other research work in Germany, I have been generously supported by the Deutscher Akademischer Austauschdienst, the British Academy, the Twenty-Seven Foundation, the Nuffield Foundation, and the Area Studies Grants of Manchester University. I am delighted to have the opportunity of thanking these institutions publicly for their indispensable support.

My last debts are personal ones. More than anyone else, Traude Spät has helped me in the conception, creation, and execution of this study. She is very much a part of it, and I am more grateful to her than I can say.

Finally, my wife and my two sons have had to suffer not only my long absences in Germany, but also long absences at home — while I have been at my typewriter working rather than kicking a football on the street with the boys or finding time to do various jobs about the house. I cannot think the end product is a worthwhile substitute to them, but I offer it none the less in dedication to Betty, David, and Stephen.

Manchester,   Ian Kershaw
December 1981

Acknowledgement

I am grateful to Oldenbourg-Verlag, Munich and Vienna, and the Institut für Zeitgeschichte, Munich, for granting me permission to use a slightly amended form of the map in *Bayern in der NS-Zeit*, vol. i, and to include in the present text a shortened and partially restructured version of my essay which appeared in *Bayern in der NS-Zeit*, vol. ii.

I. K.

Contents

List of Tables   xxxv
Note   xxxvi
Map: Bavaria, 1933 (excluding the Palatinate)   xxxvii
Introduction   1

Part One: A Sense of Social Unity? The
'National Community', 1933-1939.   31

1. Peasant Opinion and the 'Coercive Economy'   33
   (i) The Tightening Grip of the State   40
   (ii) The Agricultural Labour Crisis   55
2. Repression and Demoralization in the Working Class   66
   (i) The Shadow of Mass Unemployment   72
   (ii) Full Employment and Labour Shortage   95
3. Petty-bourgeois Complaint and Compliance   111
   (i) The Middle-Class Base of Nazi Support, 1933   114
   (ii) Disenchantment Sets in: the Nature of
        Middle-Class Discontent, 1934-6   120
   (iii) Opinion in the 'Productive' Middle Class
        during the Armaments Boom, 1937-9   132
   (iv) The 'Non-productive' Middle Class: Opinion
        among Civil Servants and Teachers, 1938-9   140
   (v) Features of Middle-Class Opinion during the
        Last Years of Peace   148
4. The Disillusioning of the Protestants   156
5. The Alienation of the Catholics   185
   (i) Clergy and Catholic Population   194
   (ii) Popular Opinion and the Anti-Church Measures
        of Party and State   205
6. Reactions to the Persecution of the Jews   224
   (i) Boycott and Terror, 1933-8   231
   (ii) The Influence of the Clergy on Attitudes to
        the Jewish Question   246
   (iii) 'Crystal Night'   257

*Part Two: Social Unity through War? The
    'Community of Fate', 1939–1945.*   279

  7. The Economic Pressures of War   281
        (i) The Peasantry   282
        (ii) The Working Class   296
        (iii) The Middle Class   315
  8. Nazism and the Church: the Last Confrontation,
        1941   331
  9. Popular Opinion and the Extermination of
        the Jews   358

Conclusion   373

List of Abbreviations and Glossary of German Terms
    and Names used in the Text   387
Archival Sources   394
List of Works Cited   398
Select bibliography   413
Index   420

Tables

I. Population Distribution into Main Economic
    Sectors, 1925–39   12
II. Regional Distribution of Employment Groups
    into Main Economic Sectors, 1933   14
III. Regional Distribution of Population according
    to Religious Affiliation   17
IV. Reichstag Elections in Bavaria, 1919–33   19
V. Proportion of Votes (%) gained by the SPD and
    KPD in Reichstag Elections between 1928 and
    1933 in Bavarian Administrative Regions   22
VI. Proportion of Votes (%) gained by the BVP in
    Reichstag Elections between 1928 and 1933
    in Bavarian Administrative Regions   24
VII. NSDAP Proportion (%) of Total Vote,
    1924–33   25
VIII. Proportion of Party Members in the Population   28
IX. Size of Agricultural Holdings, 1933   33
X. Regional Distribution of Agricultural Holdings,
    1933   35
XI. Proportion of Unemployed among the
    Working Population of Bavaria, 1933   68
XII. Political Attitudes of Five Bavarian Workers,
    1937   96–7
XIII. White-Collar, Self-Employed, and Civil Servants
    (including Teachers) in the Nazi Party in
    Bavaria, 1933–5   119
XIV. The Jewish Population of Bavaria, 1933   227

Note

Unless otherwise stated, 'Bavaria' refers throughout this study to the province 'right of the Rhine' comprising the administrative regions of Upper Bavaria, Lower Bavaria and the Upper Palatinate, Swabia, Upper and Middle Franconia, and Lower Franconia, but excluding the Palatinate.

Lower Franconia
Mellrichstadt
Neustadt a. d. Saale
Rodach (Stadt)
Neustadt b. Coburg (Stadt)

Upper Franconia

Brückenau
Kissingen
Königshofen
Coburg
Kronach
Naila
Hof
Hammelburg
Hofheim
Stadt-steinach
Münch-berg
Rehau
Selb (Stadt)
Ebern
Staffel-stein
Echenhausen
Kulmbach
Wunsiedel
Marktredwitz (Stadt)

Alzenau
Aschaffen-burg
Lohr
Gemünden
Schweinfurt
Haßfurt
Bayreuth
Kemnath
Tirschenreuth

Opernburg
Karlstadt
Gerolzhofen
Ebermann-stadt

Marktheidenfeld
Würzburg
Kitzingen
Bamberg
Pegnitz
Eschenbach
Neustadt a. d.
Weiden (Stadt)

Miltenberg
Ochsen-furt
Scheinfeld
Höchstadt d. Aisch
Fochheim
Waldnaab
Vohenstrauß

Upper Palatinate

Uffenheim
Neustadt a. d. Aisch
Erlangen
Lauf
Hers-bruck
Sulz-bach
Amberg
Nabburg
Oberviechtach
Wald-münchen

Rothenburg o. d. T.
Fürth
Nürnberg
Neumarkt i. d. Opf
Burglengen-feld
Neunburg vorm Wald

Middle Franconia
Feuchtwangen
Ansbach
Schwabach
Roding
Cham
Kötzting

Dinkelsbühl
Weißenburg
Hilpolt-stein
Beilngries
Parsberg
Schwandorf (Stadt)
Vechtach
Regen

Nördlingen
Eichstätt
Rieden-burg
Regensburg
Bogen
Deggendorf
Grafenau
Wolfstein

Donauwörth
Ingolstadt
Kelheim
Mallersdorf
Straubing
Landau
Vilshofen
Passau
Weg-scheid

Neuburg a. d. Donau
Rotten-burg
Main-burg
Dingolfing

Dillingen
Schroten-hausen
Freising
Landshut
Vilsbiburg
Eggenfelden
Griesbach

Lower Bavaria

Günzburg
Aichach
Erding
Mühldorf
Pfarr-kirchen
Altötting

Neu-Ulm
Augsburg
Schwab-münchen
Friedberg
Dachau
Wasserburg

Krumbach
Fürstenfeld-bruck
München
Ebersberg

Illertissen
Mindelheim
Landsberg
Aibling
Laufen

Memmingen
Kaufbeuren
Wolfrats-hausen
Rosenheim
Traunstein
Bad Reichenhall (Stadt)

Swabia
Kempten
Markt Oberdorf
Weilheim
Miesbach
Berchtesgaden

Lindau
Füssen
Tölz

Sonthofen
Garmisch

Upper Bavaria

——— Boundaries of administrative regions (*Regierungsbezirke*)

o   Towns/cities

——— Boundaries of administrative districts (*Bezirksämter*, from 1939 *Landkreise*)

Bavaria, 1933 (excluding the Palatinate)

Introduction

(i) Aims, Methods, Sources

Nazi social aims were extraordinarily ambitious. They amounted to no less than a revolution in attitudes and values, a transformation of subjective consciousness more than of objective realities.[1] The German people were to be mobilized in the cause of the nation through the replacing of all class, religious, or regional allegiances by massively intensified national self-awareness. Given the depth of the cleavages in German society, only briefly overcome in the patriotic euphoria of 1914, a movement aiming to 'educate' national unity into the people would inevitably have to employ a high level of manipulation coupled with an even higher degree of repression of unbending, 'nonconformist' attitudes. Such a movement was not going to be satisfied with the mere outward *Gleichschaltung* of institutions already largely achieved within the first few months of 1933. As Hitler himself emphasized in September 1933, ideological movements – in contrast to 'ordinary parties' – 'see in the achievement of political power only the prerequisite for the beginning of the fulfilment of their real mission'.[2]

The vagueness of the Nazi *Weltanschauung* was no hindrance. On the contrary: *Weltanschauung* meant for most Nazi sympathizers in 1933 nothing more precise than the engendering of a new spirit of sacrifice and struggle, necessary to combat the internal and external enemies of the German people in the interests of national unity and harmony. That this new 'spirit' was in large part based upon existing petty-bourgeois values does not detract from the revolutionary intent of the assault on existing mentalities. A comfortable,

[1] Cf. M. Broszat, *The Hitler State*, London, 1981, p. 18.
[2] *Documents on Nazism*, ed. J. Noakes and G. Pridham, London, 1974, p. 333. Cf. also J. Noakes (ed.), *Government, Party, and People in Nazi Germany*, Exeter, 1980, pp. 1–2.

materialist, petty-bourgeois existence was not the end in view, but the moulding of a people in the image of an army — disciplined, resilient, fanatically single-minded, obedient to death for the cause. The intention, it has been aptly said, was a permanent recreation of the experiences of 1914.[3] The revolution in attitudes which was to condition the German people for the inevitable future show-down with the nation's ideological enemies was embodied in the word *'Volksgemein-schaft'* — the sense of 'national community'. The creation of the 'national community' meant the supremacy of the nation above all else. Loyalties to social class, to region, to Church, must disappear.[4] Given the strength of such loyalties before 1933, the Nazis had a job on their hands, though according to some influential interpretations the level of success they attained was not inconsiderable.[5]

The present work is an empirical study of the political mentality and attitudes of 'ordinary Germans' in one part of Hitler's Reich. How the people of Bavaria reacted to change instigated by Nazi policy and ideology is the subject of en-quiry. Through an examination of popular opinion, with the main emphasis upon those aspects of Nazi rule which pro-voked expressions of political dissent, I hope to explore the extent to which Nazism was able to transform social and political values. 'Interpreted' rather than 'objective social reality' is what is at stake.[6] The aim is to understand not necessarily what was happening to these 'ordinary Germans', but what they *thought* was happening to them (and to others).

The terms of reference require a brief comment. I have preferred the notion of 'dissent' to 'opposition' or 'resistance' as more satisfactorily embracing the entire spectrum of opinion as well as action which was non-approbatory towards any aspect of Nazism. If the meaning of 'resistance' is not to

[3] T.W. Mason, *Sozialpolitik im Dritten Reich*, Opladen, 1977, p. 26.
[4] Cf. R. Dahrendorf, *Society and Democracy in Germany*, London, 1968, p. 404. For Nazism 'as a form of integration consisting of the triumph of one sub-community over all others', see W.S. Allen, 'The Appeal of Fascism and the Problem of National Disintegration', in H.A. Turner (ed.), *Reappraisals of Fascism*, New York, 1975, pp. 44-68, (here p. 61).
[5] Cf. Dahrendorf, pp. 402-18 and D. Schoenbaum, *Hitler's Social Revolution* (Anchor Books edn.), New York, 1967, esp. pp. 272-3, 280-1, 283-6.
[6] For these terms cf. Schoenbaum, pp. 285-6.

be wholly diluted, it seems sensible to restrict it to active participation in *organized* attempts to work against the regime with the conscious aim of undermining it or planning for the moment of its demise.[7] 'Opposition', while including 'resistance', can be seen as a wider concept comprising many forms of action with partial and limited aims, not directed against Nazism as a system and in fact sometimes stemming from individuals or groups broadly sympathetic towards the regime and its ideology. Organized 'resistance' in the narrow sense of the political underground or conspiracies against the regime forms no part of this study. On the other hand, certain forms of 'popular opposition', particularly related to the 'Church struggle', do fall within the scope of our enquiry. We are concerned with the reasons why, in certain circumstances, a sense of injustice or outrage leads to 'opposition'; but equally, why 'opposition' so rarely occurs, why quiescence prevails even where the sense of grievance is widespread, and whether the level of intimidation and repression is sufficient explanation for compliance. The term 'dissent' seems therefore better to cover the voicing of attitudes, frequently spontaneous

---

[7] Not everyone would agree. For other definitions of 'resistance', some of them far wider in scope, cf. e.g., P. Hüttenberger, 'Vorüberlegungen zum "Widerstandsbegriff"', in J. Kocka (ed.), *Theorien in der Praxis des Historikers*, Göttingen, 1977, pp. 117–39; F. Zipfel, 'Die Bedeutung der Widerstandsforschung für die allgemeine zeitgeschichtliche Forschung', in *Stand und Problematik der Erforschung des Widerstandes gegen den Nationalsozialismus (Studien und Berichte aus dem Forschungsinstituts der Friedrich-Ebert-Stiftung)*, Bad Godesberg, 1965; H. Bretschneider, *Der Widerstand gegen den Nationalsozialismus in München 1933 bis 1945*, Munich, 1968, p. 6; H. Beer, *Widerstand gegen den Nationalsozialismus in Nürnberg 1933–1945*, Nuremberg, 1976, pp. 5–9; T. W. Mason, 'The Workers' Opposition in Nazi Germany', *History Workship Journal*, xi (1981), 120; M. Broszat, 'Resistenz und Widerstand', *Bayern IV*, pp. 691–709. The last-named essay sums up the results of the major Bavarian research project on 'Resistance and Persecution in Bavaria 1933–1945' ('*Widerstand und Verfolgung in Bayern 1933–1945*'), which took as its definition of 'resistance' (*Widerstand*) 'every form of active or passive behaviour which allows recognition of the rejection of the National Socialist regime or of a partial area of National Socialist ideology and was bound up with certain risks' – H. Jaeger and H. Rumschöttel, 'Das Forschungsprojekt "Widerstand und Verfolgung in Bayern 1933–1945"', *Archivalische Zeitschrift*, lxxiii (1977), 214. Good recent historiographical surveys of the extensive literature on 'resistance' can be found in R. Mann, 'Widerstand gegen den Nationalsozialismus', *Neue politische Literatur*, xxii (1977), 425–42, and D. Peukert, 'Der deutsche Arbeiterwiderstand 1933–1945', *Aus Politik und Zeitgeschichte (Beilage zur Wochenzeitung 'das Parlament')* 14 July 1979, pp. 22–36.

and often unrelated to any intended action, which in any way whatsoever ran counter to or were critical of Nazism. 'Dissent' could become 'opposition', but did not necessarily do so. The heroic minority engaged in the underground illegal 'resistance' organizations were also obviously dissenting, but in a way qualitatively different from the mass of those whose opinions and behaviour were reactive, spontaneous, ill-defined expressions of discontent — often 'political' only because the regime defined them as political. The emphasis placed on dissenting forms of opinion and behaviour in this study ought also to be seen in the context of the elements of Nazism which made for cohesion and integration. Such elements are considered in the chapters which follow as part of the explanation for the lack of opposition and the success of some aspects of Nazi policy and propaganda. They also formed the main thread of a separate study, published in 1980, in which I examined the development of popular attitudes towards Hitler and the Nazi Party.[8]

The term 'popular opinion' also needs a word of explanation at the outset. '*Public* opinion', in the sense of opinion publicly held and expressed, was after 1933 almost wholly that of the Nazi regime, or at least of rival sections within the ruling élites. Yet the survival of an inchoate ground-swell of spontaneous, unorchestrated attitudes beneath the surface of the apparently monolithic unity, which was the regime's propagated image, was recognized by the regime itself, which set up its own apparatus to test, probe, and keep check on opinion, if only to be able to steer propaganda more effectively. In distinction to 'public opinion' — a term by and large applicable only to societies where there exists a plurality of freely and publicly expressed opinion — it seems sensible to designate such attitudes and responses — unquantifiable, often unspecific, diffuse, and ill-coordinated, but real for all that and held by large if indeterminate sections of society even though not normally publicly articulated — as 'popular opinion'.[9]

[8] I. Kershaw, *Der Hitler-Mythos. Volksmeinung und Propaganda im Dritten Reich*, Stuttgart, 1980.

[9] The concept of 'popular opinion' in the context of the Third Reich and the strengths and weaknesses of the source material on which any analysis of it must rest are discussed in M.G. Steinert, *Hitlers Krieg und die Deutschen*, Düsseldorf,

The chapters which follow make no pretence at providing a comprehensive analysis of the myriad forms of popular opinion in the Third Reich. Rather, they attempt to indicate the main lines of development of *three* central aspects, especially concentrating on the formative period before the war, and each aspect relating to the intended remodelling of social attitudes and political mentality. In the first section we explore the differing responses of the peasantry, the working class, and the petty bourgeoisie to Nazi social and economic policies and the extent of penetration of the idea of the 'national community'. The second aspect of opinion considered concerns the effect of the Church-State conflict upon the churchgoing population, both Protestant and Catholic, and the extent to which the religious and social values attached to the traditions and institutions of the Christian Churches could withstand the Nazi assault. Thirdly, we turn to examine racial anti-Semitism, the central ideological mainspring of Nazism, in terms of its impact on popular opinion, seeking to understand how far the Nazis, in this fundamental issue from their point of view, were able either to build upon or to transform existing attitudes and feelings. Though this is necessarily a selective treatment of limited aspects of popular opinion, the evidence presented below provides a mass of contemporary comment on what, taking the three 'layers' together, amounts to an important slice of social reality under Nazism.

The task of reconstructing trends in popular opinion in any society before the introduction and general use of opinion surveys (and sometimes even then) is a difficult one, even when one can work with pluralistic expressions of opinion through political parties, interest groups, trade unions, and the mass media. An attempt to recapture the structure of opinion in a climate of ideological dictatorship with systematic and draconian repression of noncomformist opinion and attempted steerage of opinion by means of a comprehensively organized propaganda machine backed up by the coercion and control of Party and State, is faced with some obvious and daunting problems.

1970, pp. 17-48, and A.H. Unger, *The Totalitarian Party*, Cambridge, 1974, pp. 221-62.

One of the greatest general difficulties in trying to establish patterns of development in political attitudes during the
Third Reich is that direct, authentic expressions of opinion in
their original form are few and far between. In the pervading
climate of fear and repression, frank political comment in
diaries, papers, and letters of private individuals was naturally
sparse. Reconstruction of opinion in the Third Reich has to
rely upon *reported* opinion, in sources moreover which were
compiled for particular administrative and political purposes
and contain their own heavy internal bias and colouring.
There is also the obvious point that the draconian repression
of critical opinion and the accompanying fear of denunciation
produced a web of deceit and mendacity in which spoken
words concealed real feelings; where people frequently neither
said what they meant nor meant what they said; where out of
fear they even more frequently said nothing at all. We can
safely claim, therefore, that the reported comment hostile to
the regime was but the tip of the iceberg. Finally, we have to
face the fact that there is no possibility of quantifying opinion
on the basis of the surviving evidence. After 1933, when the
curtain falls on free and open expression of opinion, the
development of popular attitudes towards Nazism can only
be reconstructed impressionistically. Interpretation can never
take full cognizance of the multiplicity of individualistic
motives for supporting or rejecting a particular measure or
policy. Conclusions must remain, for the most part, tentative
and suggestive. And yet, if we are to penetrate at all the
relationship between the Nazi leadership and the German
people, it seems important to establish at least in broad terms
areas in which Nazi policy alienated considerable sections of
society or succeeded in gaining wide popular support. This
can only be achieved by deducing general patterns of opinion
from sources which have a strong internal bias, are subjective
appraisals of the situation, and allow no possibility of quanti-
fication. If used in a differentiated and critical way, such
material as survives can, despite difficulties of interpretation,
provide many insights into popular mentality and behaviour
in the Third Reich.

Two types of source material are of overwhelming importance for a reconstruction of trends in popular opinion: the

confidential reports on opinion and morale compiled by agencies of the regime (Party, State, Police, Justice, SD etc.); and the reports smuggled out of Germany by opposition groups to the exiled leadership of former left-wing parties, the most valuable of which are the detailed and lengthy reports which reached the leadership of the exiled SPD, the *Sopade* as it now called itself. There are obvious problems to be encountered in dealing with each of these groups of sources, but at the same time there is a rich potential to be exploited.

The regular 'Situation-' and 'Morale-Reports' (*Lage- und Stimmungsberichte*) submitted by the Nazi authorities themselves are for all their interpretational difficulties a source of prime importance for the social history of the Third Reich.[10] Analysis of this type of material faces a number of problems. One such problem is the uneven survival of the reports, both in quality and quantity. Bavaria is the only part of Germany where continuous reports span the whole of the Third Reich, but even there at the district and local level some areas are much better covered than others.[11] However, despite the disappearance or unavailability of so many reports, a daunting mass has survived, so that there is an obvious difficulty in ensuring that reports and comments used are representative. The problem of intimidation, of people being unprepared to say what they really thought, is more serious. The Nazi authorities were themselves only too aware of the difficulty of probing genuine opinion and pointed out on occasion the

---

[10] Selections of this type of report have been published in: *Bayern I; Pommern 1934/35 im Spiegel von Gestapo Lageberichten und Sachakten*, ed. R. Thévoz et al., Cologne/Berlin, 1974; *Volksopposition im Polizeistaat*, ed. B. Vollmer, Stuttgart, 1957; *Nationalsozialismus im Alltag*, ed. F.J. Heyen, Boppard-am-Rhein, 1967; *Verfolgung und Widerstand unter dem Nationalsozialismus in Baden*, ed. J. Schadt, Stuttgart, 1976; and for the wartime period *Meldungen aus dem Reich*, ed. H. Boberach, Neuwied, 1965.

[11] For the value of the reports of the Government Presidents, which cover the entire period of the dictatorship for all five administrative regions of Bavaria in an unbroken series, cf. H. Witetschek, 'Die bayerischen Regierungspräsidentenberichte 1933–1943 als Geschichtsquelle', *Historisches Jahrbuch*, lxxxvii (1967), 355–72. Since Witetschek wrote, the reports for the final two years of the Third Reich have been discovered. For evaluations of the local reports, see the introductions of the various contributions in *Bayern I*.

reluctance of people to speak openly. The silences of the reports are, in fact, sometimes more evocative than what is actually said in them: reading between the lines is a necessary part of the source criticism. It is astonishing, none the less, how many people *were* ready to express open criticism in spite of the climate of intimidation, and how often the reports record such critical comments in evidently faithful fashion. Finally, the subjectivity and bias of the report-compilers is again a problem which can only be tackled through familiarity with both the broad mass of reports and also with the style and preoccupations of individual reporters. The structure, character, and purpose of the different series of reports have also to be taken into account. And in some cases they can serve as a check on each other. The reports must be treated with great caution, but it would be remiss to discard them out of hand for their lack of cold objectivity: used with care they can tell us a great deal about the society they are depicting. Though the higher authorities tended to water down their statements, the earthy, unrefined style of many local reporters often provides a direct and blunt commentary on the opinions they heard expressed around them. The chapters which follow will, I hope, indicate something of the value of this material. And while there are no easy or straight-forward ways of avoiding some of the pitfalls mentioned, acquaintance with the complete mass of documentation emanating from widely differing localities and regions does provide clear indicators of some basic common trends and patterns of opinion.

Surprisingly, there has been no systematic study to date based on the *Sopade* reports, yet this rich material is of extraordinary value both for work on popular opinion and on the society of the Third Reich in general.[12] Though particularly informative on the working class, these reports contain a wealth of material on other sections of society as well as on aspects of Nazi policy such as the persecution of the Jews and the 'Church struggle'. And since the material is drawn

---

[12] A complete reproduction of the *Deutschland-Berichte der Sopade 1934–1940* in seven volumes has just been published by the Verlag Petra Nettelbeck Zweitausendeins, Frankfurt, 1980.

from many different parts of Germany, it provides for both detailed regional study and for comparison of broad trends of opinion. The central *Deutschland-Berichte* (*Germany Reports*) which the *Sopade* produced in Prague from 1934 to 1938, then in Paris until 1940, were based on reports sent in each month or sometimes more frequently by the 'Border Secretaries' (*Grenzsekretäre*) stationed across the borders all round Germany. The two Border Secretaries for northern and southern Bavaria, Hans Dill and Walter von Knoeringen, were posted in the Sudetenland and were provided with a flow of detailed information filtered out of the Reich by their contacts in the underground SPD resistance.[13] The vast accumulation of assembled information and comment in the Border Secretaries' reports includes many details which it was felt dangerous to mention in the central *Sopade* digests.

Whereas the reports of the internal authorities generally imply conformity and support for the regime, whatever the specific criticisms alluded to, the *Sopade* emphasis is naturally upon opposition, alienation, and widespread rejection of the regime — able to keep going only on the strength of massive repression and terror. The impression is conveyed of a regime which throughout has only minimal popular support. However, the *Sopade* analysts, both on the borders and especially in Prague, were anxious to avoid simple over-generalizations. Their reports are filled with qualifications, point to the subjectivity and patent untrustworthiness of some accounts, and to the variegated and differentiated political attitudes in all sections of the population, even in the working class where one might have expected the internal bias to have laid stress simply on the heroic struggle of a militant working class, as the reports of the exiled KPD were wont to do. The result is a most nuanced assessment of the patterns of popular opinion in the Third Reich. Taken in conjunction with the internal evidence, and given a critical approach towards the evident

---

[13] For details of the Bavarian Border Secretaries' reports, their biases, and their sources of information, cf. Beer, pp. 175-209; L. Eiber, *Arbeiter unter der NS-Herrschaft. Textil- und Porzellanarbeiter im nordöstlichen Oberfranken 1933-1939*, Munich, 1979, pp. 6, 93, 106, 108 ff., 138 ff., 186; G. Hetzer, 'Die Industriestadt Augsburg. Eine Sozialgeschichte der Arbeiteropposition', in *Bayern III*, pp. 187-200; Bretschneider, pp. 95-121.

weaknesses of each, many similarities can be seen in the broad trends of political opinion and behaviour.

Other sources — newspaper accounts which despite their pro-regime bias often provide unwitting indications of prevalent expressions of critical opinion, letters and correspondence of the central State authorities, spontaneous comments of persons indicted before the Nazi 'Special Courts' (*Sondergerichte*), scurrilous remarks by writers of anonymous letters or the purveyors of rumours, and anti-regime jokes — often lend additional testimony and support to the evidence drawn from the reports. The picture remains impressionistic, but the material is often so direct and expressive that there can be little mistaking the broad lines of mood and opinion. In what follows, the sources will be given full scope to speak for themselves, so that the full force of their contemporary comment can be seen.

(ii) Bavaria on the Eve of the Third Reich

A study which is regionally based, in particular one which takes as its area of analysis a region with such singular characteristics as Bavaria, can obviously make no claim to be typical of Germany as a whole. Still, it would be far too simple to ascribe the framework of opinion and dissent outlined in subsequent chapters to the peculiarities of the Bavarians, who are themselves often over-ready to emphasize how different they are from other Germans. Though in some ways Bavaria raises special problems in the relationship of its population to the National Socialist regime, it is easy to exaggerate the specifically Bavarian nature of these problems. Often, the issues — even the conflict between the Catholic Church and the State — also had a strong resonance in other parts of the Reich. Unless and until comparable work is carried out in other regions, it is difficult to be sure exactly how 'typical' or 'untypical' Bavaria was. In any case, there is often an exaggerated importance attached to 'typicality' or 'representativeness'. Studies carried out at Reich level, generalizing with scant regard for regional or local nuances, are not necessarily dealing with genuinely 'typical' trends. And no region accords wholly with the fictional 'norm' of 'typicality' imposed abstractly from outside. Would regional studies of, for example, Saxony, Mecklenburg, East Prussia, the Rhineland, Thuringia, or the Mosel Valley be necessarily more 'typical'? In each case, analysis would reveal issues which were apparently common to most or the whole of Germany, and others which had a distinctive local or regional flavour. Part of the richness of regional studies is that they bring out patterns of behaviour which testify to the diversity rather than to the uniformity of society. The fact that we are not invariably handling issues affecting all Germans or all regional areas, or even all parts of Bavaria, is not, therefore, of prime importance. The evidence presented below has in its diversity as well as in its representativeness a relevance to the relationship between government and people in other parts of Germany, even too for the nature of conflict and political dissent in other types of repressive authoritarian state. Even so, we need to preface our consideration of Bavarian popular opinion in the Third Reich by glancing briefly at what sort of place Bavaria was on the eve of the Nazi dictatorship, rapidly sketching in the socio-economic, religious, and political structure of the province before the Nazis came to power.

(a) *Socio-economic Structure*

Bavaria in 1933 was still predominantly rural in character. In accordance with the general pattern of economic development in Germany, there had been since the middle of the nineteenth century a continued fall in the proportion of the population whose livelihood came directly from agriculture and a corresponding rise in the industrial population. But of the almost eight million inhabitants of Bavaria (here including the Palatinate) in 1933, 31.5 per cent compared with only 21 per cent of the whole German population still depended primarily upon agriculture for a living.[14] Conversely, the industrial development of Bavaria still lagged behind much of the rest of Germany: 33.6 per cent of the Bavarian population

---

[14] 'Bayerns Volk und Wirtschaft nach dem Stand der Jahre 1933 und 1934', *Beiträge zur Statistik Bayerns*, cxxiii (1935), 27; 'Berufsgliederung der bayerischen Bevölkerung 1933', *ZdBSL*, lxvi (1934), 202.

TABLE I: Population Distribution into Main Economic Sectors, 1925–39 (incl. Palatinate)

Economic sector	1925		1933		1939	
	No.	%	No.	%	No.	%
Agriculture and forestry	2,575,077	34.9	2,419,352	31.5	2,187,694	27.2
Industry and crafts	2,539,374	34.4	2,582,116	33.6	2,910,329	36.1
Trade and commerce	971,146	13.2	1,024,449	13.3	1,090,788	13.5
Public and private services	440,632	5.9	533,128	6.9	755,167	9.4
Domestic service	149,471	2.0	151,604	2.0	142,254	1.8
Non-dependants without occupation	703,894	9.6	970,935	12.7	964,241	12.0
Totals	7,379,594	100.0	7,681,584	100.0	8,050,473	100.0

Sources: 'Bayerns Volk', pp. 27–39; 'Berufsgliederung', pp. 199–202; 'Die bayer. Bevölkerung', pp. 174–224; *StJBB* (1936), 11–13.

compared with 38.8 per cent of that of the Reich gained its living from industry and crafts, mainly working in the small and middling concerns which characterized the industrial scene in the province.[15] Table I breaks down the Bavarian population into the main economic sectors, showing, too, the clear pattern of change during the peace-time years of the Third Reich: the sharp drop in the agricultural sector, rise in the industrial, and above all the substantial growth in the service sector, trends mirroring those in the Reich as a whole.

Bavaria was divided before 1933 into seven administrative regions apart from the Palatinate, each with its distinctive economic structure as illustrated in Table II. The dominant role of agriculture stands out. Other than those fully engaged in agriculture and forestry, it was estimated that a further 150,000 persons earned a subsidiary part of their income through farming, so that some 1.8 million persons in all were occupied in agricultural production. Lower Bavaria and the Upper Palatinate were overwhelmingly agrarian regions, Lower Franconia and Swabia somewhat less so. In Upper Bavaria, above all because of the commercial and administrative importance of the capital city, Munich, and because of the economic significance of tourism, the commercial, service, and domestic employment sectors of the economy were over-represented. Outside the Palatinate, the highest proportion of persons employed in industry was to be found in Middle and Upper Franconia, especially in the Nuremberg area and the textile and porcelain districts of north-eastern Bavaria around Hof and Selb.

The building trade was the largest single branch of industry in Bavaria, employing almost 225,000 persons according to the 1933 census, though by that date 39 per cent of them were without work.[16] More important, however, in the Bavarian context were the consumer goods industries. Taken together, the mainly small and medium-sized concerns of the clothing and food production industries accounted for some 27 per cent of industrial employees. In these relatively inelastic industries, unemployment was running in 1933 at 15

[15] 'Bayerns Volk', p. 27.
[16] Ibid., p. 29.

TABLE II: Regional Distribution of Employment Groups into Main Economic Sectors, 1933 (incl. Palatinate)

Region	Persons with registered primary occupation, 1933	percentage in following economic sectors				
		(a)	(b)	(c)	(d)	(e)
Upper Bavaria	810,047	36.7	25.7	20.6	11.6	5.4
Lower Bavaria	378,449	68.0	16.3	7.7	5.2	2.8
Upper Palatinate	289,728	59.1	21.4	10.3	6.4	2.8
Palatinate	385,843	35.6	38.6	14.6	7.5	3.7
Upper Franconia	360,700	43.6	36.9	11.4	5.5	2.6
Middle Franconia	449,797	37.6	32.7	17.1	8.8	3.8
Lower Franconia	380,582	54.0	24.2	11.6	7.1	3.1
Swabia	453,046	51.0	27.1	12.0	6.6	3.3
Bavaria	3,508,192	46.4	27.8	14.2	7.9	3.7

(a) Agriculture and forestry
(b) Industry and crafts
(c) Trade and industry
(d) Public and private services
(e) Domestic service

Source: GStA, Reichsstatthalter 562, p. 7.

per cent.[17] Almost 'pre-industrial' conditions prevailed in some crafts, such as the ubiquitous wood-carving workshops, whose many 'home workers' often lived in miserable conditions and great poverty. Modern industrial production, on the other hand, was relatively under-developed and chiefly concentrated in the large urban complexes of Augsburg, Nuremberg, and Munich. The machine-building and motor car industries, for example, employed only 7 per cent of the total industrial work-force in 1933, the chemical industry only 3.6 per cent, and the electro-technical industry only 2.6 per cent.[18] The textile industry, with 88,000 employees (6.5 per cent of the work-force in 1933), was largely confined to Augsburg and to parts of Upper Franconia. Unemployment, at 12.5 per cent in 1933, was lower than in any other branch of industry, but this hides the fact that many of the workers — around half of them women — were on short time. The depressed condition of the industry, in fact, prevailed long after other sectors of industry had profited from the Third Reich's rearmament-led boom.[19]

The dominant features of Bavaria's industrial structure were its small-scale production — smaller on average than in the Reich as a whole — the concentration on production of finished products such as ceramics, toys, wood-carvings, etc., and the significant role played by consumer industries, prominent among them the brewing trade.[20] Though industry became somewhat more concentrated in the 1920s and large concerns like BMW car works in Munich and MAN machine works in Augsburg and Nuremberg grew in size and importance, Bavaria remained on the eve of the Third Reich still very much the land of small industry, characterized by workshops run by independent craftsmen and their assistants, and by branches such as textiles, clothing, food production, and the toy industry which employed a high proportion of female

[17] Ibid., p. 29. Unemployment rates in the iron, steel, and metal production industry were given as 33 per cent, in the stone industry as 31 per cent, and in wood-working as 30 per cent.

[18] Calculated from figures in ibid., pp. 27, 29. Cf. also *Bayern I*, pp. 202-3.

[19] Cf. Fritz Blaich, 'Die bayerische Industrie 1933-1939, in *Bayern II*, pp. 252-4. Figures for the employment structure of the textile industry based on 'Bayerns Volk', pp. 27, 29.

[20] Cf. GStA, Reichsstatthalter 475, pp. 6, 37-8; Blaich, pp. 238-9.

labour — amounting overall to just short of a quarter of the industrial and crafts work-force.[21]

Clearly, a substantial proportion of the Bavarian population — even many of those not directly engaged in agriculture — lived and worked in an essentially rural setting. Urbanization in the province had not gone very far. Excluding the Palatinate, only four cities had a population of over 100,000: Würzburg had 101,000 inhabitants, Augsburg 177,000, Nuremberg 410,000, and Munich 735,000.[22] Of these, only Nuremberg and Augsburg were in a real sense industrial cities. Just under a fifth (19.5 per cent) of the population lived in the cities. A further 11 per cent lived in towns of between 20,000 and 100,000 inhabitants, 19.6 per cent in small towns and market-centres of between 2,000 and 20,000 inhabitants, and almost a half of the population (49.6 per cent) in the 7,586 communities of fewer than 2,000 inhabitants.[23] In all, 35 per cent of Bavaria's population were ascribed to towns by the census-makers, the other 65 per cent to rural districts.[24]

(b) *Denominational Structure*

Of crucial importance in shaping the relationship between the Bavarian population and the Nazi regime was the religious factor, in which the province again reveals some singular features.

Of the Reich population of 1933, 62.7 per cent belonged at least nominally to the Protestant faith while 32.5 per cent were Roman Catholics.[25] These proportions were more than reversed in Bavaria, where 69.9 per cent of the population were Catholic and only 28.7 per cent Protestant. Leaving aside

[21] For the size and composition of the variegated industrial structure, see 'Bayerns Volk', p. 29; *StJBB* (1936), 13; 'Die bayerische Bevölkerung nach Wirtschaftsabteilungen und nach der Stellung im Beruf auf Grund der Berufszählung vom 17. Mai 1939', *ZdBSL*, lxxiv (1942), 190–1. Only 5 per cent of Bavarian industrial concerns employed more than 200 persons in 1936 as against 15 per cent employing between 51 and 200 and as many as 80 per cent employing fewer than 50 persons — Blaich, p. 239.
[22] *StJBB* (1936), 8.   [23] Ibid., p. 9.   [24] Ibid., p. 8.
[25] *Sozialgeschichtliches Arbeitsbuch III. Materialien zur Statistik des Deutschen Reiches 1914–1945*, ed. D. Petzina *et al.*, Munich, 1978, p. 31.

the Palatinate, which in fact weights these proportions slightly in favour of the Protestant sector, the dominance of Catholicism was complete in all administrative regions apart from Middle and Upper Franconia, as Table III shows.

TABLE III: Regional Distribution of Population according to Religious Affiliation (incl. Palatinate)

Region	Roman Catholic		Protestant	
	% of popn.	% of popn. in rural districts	% of popn.	% of popn. in rural districts
Upper Bavaria	89.5	95.8	8.8	3.8
Lower Bavaria	98.8	99.3	1.1	0.7
Upper Palatinate	92.2	93.2	7.5	6.7
Palatinate	42.1	43.6	55.7	55.3
Upper Franconia	39.7	41.7	59.7	58.0
Middle Franconia	28.5	25.2	68.7	74.2
Lower Franconia	80.6	83.7	18.0	15.4
Swabia	86.1	90.9	13.2	8.8
Bavaria	69.9		28.7	

Source: Hagmann, pp. 22–7; StJBB (1936), 9.

In Upper Franconia, the division of the population was more equal than anywhere else, with Catholic enclaves above all in the south-west of the region, centring on Bamberg, and the Protestant strongholds especially prominent in the northeast. Middle Franconia was the one region where Protestantism reigned supreme, giving the Protestant faith there the peculiarly intense piety characteristic of a diaspora. Even here the vagaries of earlier seignorial rule left significant Catholic minorities in some districts and heavy Catholic majorities in two localities — Hilpoltstein (76 per cent Catholic) and Eichstätt (98 per cent Catholic), the seat of a Catholic bishopric and, as a Catholic island in Protestant Franconia, itself exuding a particularly fervent brand of traditional Catholicism and close links between Church and people.

As Table III also shows, the Catholic religion was even more dominant in rural than in urban districts, apart from Middle Franconia where exactly the same point can be made of the Protestant faith. In most districts of Lower Bavaria there was hardly a non-Catholic to be found. In many rural districts of Middle Franconia (e.g. Ansbach, Hersbruck, Neustadt an der Aisch, Rothenburg, Uffenheim) only between 5 and 7 per cent of the population was not Protestant.[26] The social cohesiveness of religious allegiance in communities such as these was a point of no little significance in affecting the relationship of the population to the National Socialist regime.

Long before the Nazis came on the scene, in fact, religion had played a vital role in influencing political allegiances in Bavaria, and we must now turn briefly to charting the political map of the province before the Nazi 'seizure of power'.

(c) *Political Structure*

The World War and the Revolution of 1918 left deep scars on the Bavarian political scene. Anti-Prussian resentments, greatly intensified during the last years of the war, combined with the fear and alarm stimulated by the November Revolution in Bavaria and heightened by the short-lived *Räterepublik* of April 1919 to produce a political climate almost paranoiacally anti-Marxist and at the same time fervently nationalist, based on a strong desire to retain Bavaria's special character and to save Germany from its internal enemies.[27] This peculiar political atmosphere not only gave strong nourishment to the many mushrooming *völkisch* groups, but also inculcated the politics of all but the left-wing parties with particularly strong nationalist, anti-Marxist sentiments and imbued Bavarian political and social relations with a bitterness which had scarcely eased before being resurrected in the conditions of the Depression.

Table IV summarizes the electoral pattern in Bavaria during the Weimar Republic. Before the arrival of the Nazis, the voting population divided into three main blocks: the socialist and communist Left, the Catholic BVP, and the group of

[26] M. Hagmann, *Der Weg ins Verhängnis*, Munich, 1946, pp. 22-7.
[27] Cf. A. Nicholls, 'Hitler and the Bavarian Background to National Socialism', in A. Nicholls and E. Matthias (ed.), *German Democracy and the Triumph of Hitler*, London, 1971, pp. 99-128 (here esp. p. 113).

TABLE IV: Reichstag Elections in Bavaria (without Palatinate), 1919–33
(percentage)

Political grouping	1919	1920	May 1924	Dec. 1924	1928	1930	July 1932	Nov. 1932	1933
Catholic Party (BVP)	35.7	40.6	36.2	35.6	31.7	32.0	33.7	32.8	27.9
Left/Worker Parties (SPD/KPD)	36.9	30.7	24.7	25.3	27.4	25.9	25.0	26.3	21.1
Bourgeois and Economic Parties (DNVP, DDP, DVP, BBB, Wirtschafts-partei etc.)	27.4	28.7	21.7	33.5	34.0	24.8	10.1	12.3	8.4
Fascist Party (NSDAP)	–	–	17.4[a]	5.6[a]	6.9	17.3	31.2	28.6	42.6 ·
Totals	100	100	100	100	100	100	100	100	100

[a] *Völkischer Block*

Sources: Thränhardt, p. 133; Hagmann, p. 16*.

'bourgeois' and 'interest-group' parties. Of this latter group, the so-called 'liberal' parties (DVP, DDP) were in decline from 1920 but the DNVP, the conservative nationalist party, was able to win much of their support and to increase its overall backing to a high-point of 15.8 per cent of the vote in December 1924, retaining 11 per cent in 1928. The instability of this block, as at the Reich level, was shown in the 1930 election when, apart from the successes of the Nazis, economic-orientated, interest-group and splinter parties were able to win 11.1 per cent of the vote.[28] With one exception, these parties all found the bulk of their electoral backing in the Protestant regions of Bavaria. The exception was the *Bauernbund* (BBB), which can be distinguished from other economic interest-group parties in that its long tradition of support came exclusively from overwhelmingly Catholic areas of Lower Bavaria and Swabia where the leading rival party was the BVP, and in that, like the BVP, it was a specifically Bavarian party. In rural Lower Bavaria the BBB picked up as much as 27.5 per cent of the vote in 1924, 35.3 per cent in 1928, and still held on to 29 per cent in 1930. Only after that date did voter support rapidly dwindle. In Swabia the BBB had its high-point of 23.8 per cent in 1928.[29] During the years of the Depression, however, the BBB support, despite coming from Catholic areas, collapsed along with that of other interest-group parties and was swallowed up by the NSDAP. As Table IV clearly demonstrates, the NSDAP gained its main electoral benefit, as in the Reich as a whole, from the demise of the bourgeois and economic-interest parties.

The Nazis were, of course, much less successful in penetrating the other two electoral blocks of the Left and of political Catholicism.

Taken together, the parties of the Left were able to retain a high proportion of their support during the spectacular growth of the NSDAP, despite the fact that, in contrast to heavily industrialized areas such as the Ruhr or Saxony, they were in a comparatively weak position in Bavaria[30] as shown

[28] D. Thränhardt, *Wahlen und politische Strukturen in Bayern 1848–1953*, Düsseldorf, 1973, p. 133.
[29] Hagmann, pp. 17*–18*.
[30] Cf. Thränhardt, pp. 145–51 and also G. Pridham, *Hitler's Rise to Power: the Nazi Movement in Bavaria, 1923–1933*, London, 1973, pp. 114–15.

in Table V. The predominantly rural and Catholic character of much of the province, the limited industrial development and prevalence of small businesses, and not least the widespread virulent anti-communism all mitigated against the worker parties which, in contrast to the Prussian north, were confined to lasting opposition in Bavarian State politics during the Weimar period. Apart from their relative strength in the large cities of Munich, Augsburg, and Nuremberg, and in Fürth and Erlangen in the Nuremberg conurbation, the greatest support for the parties of the Left lay in the smaller industrial towns and semi-rural areas of Upper and Middle Franconia and in oases of industrial production such as the glass-blowing area of Regen in Lower Bavaria and the mining localities of Penzberg and Hausham in Upper Bavaria.

The two worker parties proved as elsewhere in Germany more resistant than any other political grouping (except the Catholic Centre Party/BVP) to the pull of Nazism. Though the SPD lost 164,000 votes in Bavaria between 1928 and 1932, these were almost exclusively garnered by the KPD, which gained 237,000 votes in the same period.[31] In the radicalized conditions of the Depression, the KPD was able not only to win support away from the SPD — in extreme cases in the poverty-stricken industrial districts of Lower Bavaria and Upper Franconia the SPD lost half its support to the communists — but evidently made some inroads into the ranks of previous non-voters, presumably above all among the young unemployed.[32] The falling percentage of the combined left-wing vote (shown in Table IV) conceals, indeed, the fact that the absolute number of votes cast for them increased by almost 70,000 between 1928 and the July election of 1932, and that even in 1933 the worker parties in Bavaria 'right of the Rhine' received 900 more votes than they had done in 1928.[33]

The BVP, the party of conservative political Catholicism, was the 'state party' of Bavaria during the Weimar Republic. It headed Bavaria's government and formed the largest party in the province practically throughout the entire period. And

[31] Calculated from the data in Hagmann, p. 19*.
[32] Cf. *Bayern I*, p. 205.
[33] From data in Hagmann, p. 19*.

TABLE V: Proportion of votes (%) gained by the SPD and KPD in Reichstag Elections between 1928 and 1933 in Bavarian Administrative Regions

	Percentage of workers in popn. (1925)	SPD					KPD				
		1928	1930	July 1932	Nov. 1932	1933	1928	1930	July 1932	Nov. 1932	1933
Upper Bavaria	37	24.5	21.1	16.4	16.0	15.4	5.3	6.9	10.3	13.9	8.2
Lower Bavaria	29	14.0	11.3	8.8	8.7	7.4	1.9	4.0	8.5	10.0	5.3
Upper Palatinate	34	17.4	14.5	13.5	12.5	11.5	2.6	5.6	7.9	8.7	5.1
Upper Franconia	39	31.3	27.5	21.8	20.9	20.0	2.8	4.6	6.1	7.8	4.7
Middle Franconia	39	32.1	29.4	24.2	23.3	23.2	4.0	5.2	7.9	9.5	5.5
Lower Franconia	29	20.7	17.2	16.0	14.8	13.4	2.4	4.2	6.6	7.7	4.5
Swabia	34	19.1	15.4	13.3	12.6	11.1	2.2	4.4	5.8	7.3	4.5
Bavaria (incl. Palatinate)	37	24.5	20.9	17.1	16.4	15.5	4.0	5.9	8.3	10.3	6.3

Sources: Hagmann, pp. 17*–19*, 21, 27; 'Berufsgliederung', pp. 200–1; Bayern I, p. 204.

in contrast to the Left, regarded as the main political and ideological enemy, the BVP, most immune of all electoral blocks to the blandishments of Nazism, was at its strongest in the countryside, especially in areas where it had no challenge for the votes of the farming population from the *Bauernbund*. In the rural districts of Lower Franconia, for example, the BVP could corner an absolute majority of votes in every election down to March 1933, when it still managed 48 per cent. The picture was little different in the BVP-dominated Upper Palatinate. In the urban constituencies of these regions, however, the level of BVP support was considerably lower than in the countryside.[34] In countless rural districts the position of the BVP's local party dignitaries and control of local politics was practically unassailable before the rise of the NSDAP, which became the prime challenge to the BVP establishment. Only in the Protestant parts of Franconia was the BVP's influence negligible. Here, the resentment at the perpetual control of Bavarian politics by the BVP-dominated Catholic south provided one of the attractions of Nazism. Table VI shows the regional distribution of the BVP vote between 1928 and 1933.

The voting impact made by the Nazis in the various regions of Bavaria is illustrated in Table VII. The first electoral successes of the NSDAP in the May election of 1924 bore largely the character of a protest vote, as the steep decline by the time of the December election, held in conditions of much greater economic and political stability, demonstrates. In the extraordinary political climate of post-war Munich, the Nazis were able to win an impressive level of support in the city itself. Outside Munich, however, the main areas paying heed to the Nazi message were already located in Franconia. In most parts of Bavaria, the levels of support for the Nazis in 1924 were not again reached or surpassed until 1930, in Middle and Upper Franconia not before 1932. From 1930 the Nazis were not only able to win back most of the voters they had lost since 1924, but gained the support of many new voters and converts mainly from the 'bourgeois' parties. Nevertheless the hold of political Catholicism in most

[34] Hagmann, pp. 15, 19.

TABLE VI; Proportion of Votes (%) gained by the BVP in Reichstag Elections between 1928 and 1933 in Bavarian Administrative Regions

	% of Catholics in popn. (1933)	1928	1930	July 1932	Nov. 1932	1933
Upper Bavaria	89.5	32.2	32.9	36.2	35.3	28.7
Lower Bavaria	98.8	37.2	38.4	43.2	41.3	31.6
Upper Palatinate	92.2	50.6	49.1	52.7	52.8	44.1
Upper Franconia	39.7	24.4	22.6	21.4	21.4	19.6
Middle Franconia	28.5	11.6	11.2	11.0	10.8	9.8
Lower Franconia	80.6	48.4	48.6	47.9	47.7	43.6
Swabia	86.1	32.9	35.2	37.5	35.8	29.6
Bavaria (incl. Palatinate)	69.9	31.1	31.1	32.4	31.4	27.2

Source: Hagmann, pp. 21, 27.

TABLE VII: NSDAP Proportion (%) of Total Vote, 1924-33

	May[a] 1924	Dec.[a] 1924	1928	1930	Jul. 1932	Nov. 1932	1933
Munich	28.5	9.1	10.9	21.8	28.9	24.9	37.8
Upper Bavaria	19.0	5.7	7.2	17.2	25.8	22.1	38.8
Lower Bavaria	10.7	3.1	3.6	11.6	21.1	19.0	44.0
Upper Palatinate	9.8	2.9	3.6	12.4	19.7	17.9	34.0
Palatinate	5.7	1.9	5.8	22.8	43.7	42.6	46.5
Upper Franconia	24.5	9.3	11.1	23.9	44.4	41.3	48.7
Middle Franconia	24.7	9.1	10.5	23.8	47.7	42.3	51.6
Lower Franconia	10.1	3.3	4.0	12.3	23.7	22.6	33.9
Swabia	12.9	2.8	4.5	14.3	29.8	29.7	45.5
Bavaria (incl. Palatinate)	16.0	5.1	6.8	17.9	32.9	30.5	43.1
Germany	6.6	3.0	2.6	18.3	37.3	33.1	43.9

[a] *Völkischer Block*
Sources: Thränhardt, p. 136; Hagmann, pp. 17*-19*.

Bavarian regions was such that after 1928 the pro-Nazi vote in the province always lagged behind the Reich level.

By the end of 1932 the Nazis had still not succeeded in achieving the decisive breakthrough in the traditionally Catholic areas of Bavaria. Not only the BVP, but the Catholic 'sub-culture' itself proved relatively resistant to Nazism.[35] In the Reichstag election of July 1932 (Reich average Nazi vote 37.3 per cent), seventeen Bavarian rural districts with overwhelmingly Catholic populations gave the Nazis fewer than 15 per cent of the vote. In the November election (Reich average 33.1 per cent), twenty-four rural districts fell well below 15 per cent.[36] All Catholic constituencies fell below the Reich average Nazi vote.[37] By contrast, the

[35] Thränhardt, pp. 179-80.
[36] Hagmann, pp. 21*-22*; cf. Thränhardt, p. 181.
[37] Election statistics in Hagmann, pp. 16*-24*, 22-7, and for the varied electoral patterns within Catholic regions cf. Thränhardt, pp. 162-80.

Protestant regions of northern Bavaria, where in earlier years the now decimated bourgeois, liberal, and right-radical *völkisch* parties and groupings had enjoyed a fickle and shifting electoral support, revealed themselves as the true homeland of Nazism.[38] Apart from the lack of firm political anchorage of much of the population in the Protestant north of Bavaria, a further contributory cause of the success of the Nazis, whose absolute strongholds were in the rural districts, was the support the NSDAP won from Protestant pastors and others who saw in Nazism not only the possibility of a new start politically and economically, but also of a moral-ethical renaissance for Germany which would put a halt to the forward march, as they saw it, of moral decline, decadence, secularism, and atheism. Finally, many people in the Protestant 'diaspora' saw in Nazism a national force not least directed against Catholic BVP-dominated Bavarian State politics.[39]

Following the drop in the Nazi vote in Bavaria as in the rest of Germany in November 1932, the decisive breakthrough in Catholic areas seemed farther away than ever. However, in the five weeks between Hitler becoming Chancellor on 30 January and the Reichstag election on 5 March 1933 an astonishing swing to the Nazis took place in Catholic rural districts. Nationally, the Nazis improved their proportion of the vote from 33.1 to 43.9 per cent. In Catholic rural districts of Bavaria a doubling, even a trebling, of the Nazi vote was no rarity.[40] Everywhere the growth rate was greater in the countryside than in the towns, though in Upper and Middle Franconia, where practically the whole electoral potential had already been realized by July 1932, the increase was in fact below the national average. In Lower Franconia, too, the increase was less spectacular even though the region was mainly Catholic and rural. The relatively high

---

[38] Cf. Thränhardt, pp. 152–62; Hagmann, pp. 16*–21*. For the spread of Nazism in northern Bavaria, see the comprehensive study by R. Hambrecht, *Der Aufstieg der NSDAP in Mittel- und Oberfranken (1925–1933)*, Nuremberg, 1976.

[39] Cf. Hambrecht, pp. 4–5.

[40] Cf. Hagmann, pp. 12–27 for voting figures; and see also Thränhardt, pp. 181–3.

percentage of workers in some districts produced a correspondingly high SPD-vote, and the relative stability of the BVP inhibited the progress of the NSDAP in this region. Above all in Catholic southern Bavaria the increases were seismic, amounting in rural districts of Lower Bavaria to a leap in the Nazi vote from 18.5 to 44.9 per cent.[41] The bitterness and black despair of many peasants, the feeling that Hitler and the NSDAP ought to be given a chance — that they could certainly do no worse than previous governments, that Hitler was the last hope for recovery — coupled with the new respect accruing to Hitler as Chancellor and not least the massive assault on the political Left by the new government, all helped to counter the aversion shown by the Catholic Church towards the NSDAP and to bring about the dramatic increase in the pro-Nazi vote in Catholic districts.

The weakness of the Nazi Movement in Catholic areas, where the conversion of the population in early 1933 was clearly superficial, is revealed by the structure of the Party membership. While not all fervent Nazis were Party members, the relative strength of the membership provides an indicator of the level of activist Nazi support, as illustrated by Table VIII.

Of the five Bavarian *Gaue* (leaving out the Palatinate), only Franconia with 1.30 per cent Party members as a proportion of the population matched the Reich average of 1.29 per cent. All other *Gaue* fell below the average, the Bavarian *Ostmark* (Lower Bavaria, the Upper Palatinate, and Upper Franconia — the 'Eastern Marches' of Bavaria) and Main Franconia (Lower Franconia, the Main basin) way below. These 'weaker' *Gaue* showed, on the other hand, above-average increases in membership following the 'seizure of power' as many ambitious or fearful opportunists jumped on the bandwagon. Main Franconia demonstrates this at its clearest: in last place among all *Gaue* in the Reich in terms of the numbers of 'Old Fighters' of the Movement (*Alte Kämpfer*), it leapt to top place in membership of the 'March converts' — those hastily joining the Party after Hitler had become Chancellor. In many localities of Bavaria, the Party membership remained well below average even long after the 'take-over

[41] Hagmann, p. 23.

TABLE VIII: Proportion (%) of Party Members in the Population

Gau	Party members on 30.1.33	Party members in 1935	Party members entering by 30.1.33.	Party members entering after 30.1.33.
Bavarian Ostmark	0.94	3.43 (24)	27.2 (24)	72.8 (9)
Franconia	1.30	3.67 (18)	35.6 (13)	64.4 (20)
Main Franconia	0.66	5.46 (3)	11.9 (32)	88.1 (1)
Munich/Upper Bavaria	1.07	3.32 (26)	32.4 (17)	67.6 (16)
Swabia	1.00	3.98 (11)	25.3 (27)	74.7 (6)
Reich	1.29	3.78	34.0	66.0

Source: Parteistatistik (Stand: 1935), ed. Reichsorganisationsleiter der NSDAP, Munich, 1935, i. 12–36.
Note: The figures in brackets refer to the respective placings of the Bavarian Gaue among the 32 Gaue of the Reich.

of power'. This was particularly so in Catholic rural districts. The problems confronting the Nazis in some such areas were highlighted by a report from Hilpoltstein, a Catholic outpost in Middle Franconia, in July 1933:

It will take years of work so emphatically to communicate the meaning and content of National Socialism to the broad masses of hitherto BVP voters that these sections of the population become conscious and convinced bearers of the new idea of the State. Several areas of the district are still absolute new territory for Hitler's idea. Propaganda is made difficult through the atomization of the population in dwarf settlements. The 84 local authorities of the district break down into more than 200 villages. The poverty of the population often means that no newspapers are read. For the same reason, in numerous places there is not a single radio-set, so that the most effective form of propaganda — bringing the best speakers to the broad masses of the people — is also ruled out.[42]

Most converts to Nazism had been won not through an idea or Weltanschauung, but through their bitterness at the course of Weimar politics and through the expectation that their self-interest would be best served by a Nazi government. Hopes rested on the vague notion of a political, economic,

[42] GStA MA 106677, RPvOF/MF, 19 March 1933.

and social 'new start' for Germany encapsulated in the Nazi jargon of the *Volksgemeinschaft* — a 'national community' which all groups in society hoped would function directly in their own interests. The NSDAP was faced with two major tasks after it had become the State Party of the Third Reich — even without having captured the hearts and imagination of half the population: it had to serve as an instrument of social control, and at the same time it had the much harder job of ideological 'education'. How far the Nazis succeeded in this latter task, in instilling new social and political attitudes into the people, must be assessed in the light of the experience of everyday reality in the Third Reich and of the degree to which Nazism clashed or coincided with existing behaviour, beliefs, and mentalities. This is attempted in the chapters which follow.

PART ONE
A SENSE OF SOCIAL UNITY?
THE 'NATIONAL COMMUNITY',
1933–1939

'The conviction will grow, that this National Community is not an empty concept, but something really alive', *Hitler, 13 Sept. 1933.*

'They've got to give us bread and water in Dachau, and we haven't more than that at home', *Apprentice Glass-worker during a strike in 1935.*

'Never was the National Community less of a reality than now', *Report from the Protestant Deanery of Kitzingen, 1939.*

1. Peasant Opinion and the 'Coercive Economy'

Peasant farming dominated Bavarian agriculture, which was predominantly mixed in character, though specialized production flourished in the viticulture of Lower Franconia, the hop-growing of parts of Middle Franconia, and the dairy-farming of the alpine reaches of Upper Bavaria and Swabia. As Table IX shows, 77.5 per cent of agricultural concerns in

TABLE IX: Size of Agricultural Holdings, 1933 (incl. Palatinate)

	No. of holdings	Percentage of holdings	Percentage of agricultural area
Smallholdings (*Parzellen-wirtschaften*) (under 2 ha.)	124,701	22.4 (30.5)[a]	3.1 (3.6)[a]
Small peasant farms (2 to 5 ha.)	160,128	28.8 (27.0)	13.1 (10.2)
Medium-sized peasant farms (5 to 20 ha.)	234,914	42.3 (34.3)	55.0 (38.4)
Large peasant farms (20 to 100 ha.)	35,523	6.4 (7.6)	25.9 (29.5)
Large-scale concerns (*Großbetriebe*) (more than 100 ha.)	656	0.1 (0.6)	2.9 (18.3)
Totals	555,922	100 (100)	100 (100)

[a] Figures in brackets are the corresponding percentages for the Reich as a whole.
Source: GStA, Reichsstatthalter 562, p. 9.

Bavaria (here including the Palatinate) were classed in the 1933 census as peasant farms of various sizes, compared with 68.9 per cent in the Reich as a whole. Most typical of the Bavarian rural economy was the medium-sized peasant holding, a tendency strengthened even further if we omit the Palatinate where, in a region of predominantly partible inheritance, three-quarters of all concerns were small peasant farms or smallholdings. Of the administrative regions of Bavaria proper, only Lower Franconia, where partible inheritance was also common, had a disproportionately high ratio of small peasant enterprises and smallholdings. For the rest, as Table X indicates, a half or more of all agricultural units was made up of medium-sized peasant farms with a fair sprinkling of larger farms, especially in southern Bavaria where many of the large peasant holdings were to be found in the alpine foothills.

The peasant holdings were run for the most part as family concerns. It was calculated in 1933 that 84 per cent of labour on Bavarian farms was provided by the farmer and his family.[1] Naturally, the larger the farm the more important proportionately was the part played by outside labour. On concerns of over a hundred hectares paid labour accounted for 92 per cent of the work carried out, on larger peasant holdings for 40 per cent, and on medium-sized holdings − the characteristic Bavarian peasant farm − for 13.5 per cent. In all, 46.5 per cent of paid employees worked on such medium-sized holdings and 36.5 per cent on larger peasant farms.[2] It was mainly these farms, bearing in mind their numerical dominance in Bavaria, which were chiefly affected by the chronic labour shortage of the later 1930s.

Political attitudes of Bavarian peasants had, since the Second Reich, been shaped primarily by religious allegiance and above all by their economic position in an increasingly industrial society.[3] The progressively negative stance of the peasantry during the First World War − the mood in the countryside was being described by 1917 as 'wretched'[4] −

[1] GStA, Reichsstatthalter 562, p. 11.
[2] Ibid., pp. 10–11.
[3] Cf. I. Farr, 'Populism in the Countryside: the Peasant Leagues in Bavaria in the 1890s', in R.J. Evans (ed.), *Society and Politics in Wilhelmine Germany*, London, 1978, pp. 136–59, and W.K. Blessing, 'Umwelt und Mentalität im ländlichen Bayern. Eine Skizze zum Alltagswandel im 19. Jahrhundert', *Archiv für Sozialgeschichte*, xix (1979), 1–42.
[4] K.-L. Ay, *Die Entstehung einer Revolution. Die Volksstimmung in Bayern während des Ersten Weltkrieges*, Berlin, 1968, p. 114.

TABLE X: Regional Distribution of Agricultural Holdings, 1933 (incl. Palatinate)

	Percentage of farms in the following size categories:					
	under 2 ha.	2–5 ha.	5–20 ha.	20–100 ha.	over 100 ha.	Total
Upper Bavaria	17.09	23.05	46.99	12.66	0.21	100
Lower Bavaria	17.88	31.02	41.77	9.24	0.09	100
Upper Palatinate	15.61	30.51	44.97	8.78	0.13	100
Palatinate	44.26	32.42	22.36	0.92	0.04	100
Upper Franconia	24.70	28.55	43.15	3.54	0.06	100
Middle Franconia	18.23	30.33	45.68	5.70	0.06	100
Lower Franconia	29.92	33.00	35.31	1.66	0.11	100
Swabia	12.33	22.96	57.53	6.99	0.19	100
Bavaria	22.43	28.80	42.26	6.39	0.12	100

Source: GStA, Reichsstatthalter 562, p. 10.

was a product of the greatly increased burden which the farmer had to carry in the war years, the stresses of which were sharply accentuated by the labour shortage. This in turn fed feelings of exploitation by the big city populations, captains of industry, and war profiteers — all associated with the hated Prussians — and deep resentment at what the peasant regarded as unnecessary interference in his affairs by the State. Increasing State regulation of the rural economy made the peasant feel that he could no longer run his land as he saw fit, and the price controls together with the labour shortage amounted in his mind to the exploitation and disadvantaging of the hard-working farmer in the interests of profiteers, financiers, and industrialists.[5] This hatred of the *Zwangswirtschaft*, the 'coercive economy', was to linger long in peasant consciousness.

The establishment of the Republic did little to change this situation in the eyes of the peasantry. Protest against tariff levels, price controls, the burden of taxation, and social legislation and expenditure was bitter. And many of the war-time restrictions were retained. Reports from peasant districts in the early years of the Republic emphasized the lack of satisfaction of the peasantry with the achievements of the Weimar State and the longing for a return to the circumstances prevailing before the war. Reports also spoke of peasant disinterest in any political matter not directly affecting the interests of farmers, as well as their increased readiness to defend these interests.[6] Hostility towards the Republic was sharpened by the threat which the apparently dominant forces of the Left seemed to pose to property.[7] Distaste towards the policies of a 'Marxist' or 'Jewish' Republic in which peasant interests were felt to be sacrificed permanently to those of workers and capitalists provided the basis for the potential radicalization of the peasantry long before the onset of the Depression.[8]

---

[5] Ibid., pp. 109-22, 148-52. Cf. also K.-L. Ay, 'Volksstimmung und Volksmeinung als Voraussetzung der Münchner Revolution von 1918', in K. Bosl (ed.), *Bayern im Umbruch. Die Revolution von 1918, ihre Voraussetzungen, ihr Verlauf und ihre Folgen*, Munich/Vienna, 1969, pp. 345-86, esp. 368-74.

[6] *Bayern I*, pp. 331-2.

[7] Ibid., p. 332.

[8] For a local illustration of the struggle between the BVP and BBB to show

Though the rural economy benefited in the short-term from the economic upheavals of the inflation, a serious drop in agricultural prices by 1927-8 heralded the commencement of an economic crisis in agriculture which plummeted to its nadir in 1932-3. The collapse of agricultural prices led to a great shortage of capital, high interest-rates, and consequently to a serious indebtedness, bankruptcies, and forced sales of farms. By 1932, the height of the economic crisis, the number of forced sales in Bavaria (1,923 cases) showed an increase of more than 50 per cent on the previous year's total.[9] By 1927 the Bavarian government had been told that the peasantry was putting the blame for its post-war disappointments on to the parliamentary democratic system.[10] By 1932 there was clearly little love lost for the Republic and all that it stood for.

The NSDAP was relatively slow in recognizing the electoral potential in the countryside. It was not until 1930 that the appointment of a recognized agrarian expert, Walther Darré, as adviser on agricultural matters to the Reich leadership of the NSDAP signified a serious attempt by the Party to exploit the growing rural unrest. By 1932 Darré's 'Agrarian Apparatus' had developed its own extensive bureaucracy, had penetrated the existing peasant organizations, and had become a weapon of the first importance in the fight by Nazism to capture the rural vote.[11] By that time it seemed undeniable to many Bavarian observers that increasing numbers of farmers were beginning to fall prey to the lure of the Nazis.[12] In remote farming districts the visit of a leading

themselves as the Party best upholding and representing peasant interests, see Z. Zofka, *Die Ausbreitung des Nationalsozialismus auf dem Lande*, Munich, 1979, pp. 22-9, which provides an intensive study of the situation in Günzburg (Swabia). Some of the propaganda ploys used by the BVP are mentioned on p. 24, n. 2 and p. 25, n. 1.

[9] *Bayern I*, p. 332.

[10] J.E. Farquharson, *The Plough and the Swastika. The NSDAP and Agriculture 1928-45*, London, 1976, p. 26.

[11] Cf. ibid., pp. 13 ff.; C.R. Lovin, 'German Agricultural Policy, 1933-1936', Univ. of North Carolina Ph.D. thesis, 1965, pp. 14-27; H. Gies, 'The NSDAP and Agrarian Organizations in the Final Phase of the Weimar Republic', in H.A. Turner (ed.), *Nazism and the Third Reich*, New York, 1972, pp. 45-88.

[12] For good concrete examples of the advances the Nazis were able to make in specific rural areas, cf. Zofka, pp. 30-62 and esp. pp. 93-132, and *Bayern I*, pp. 39-63.

Party speaker could prove a sensation, and the ceaseless campaigning of the NSDAP was something quite new in such areas.[13] The Nazis made special efforts to improve their image in the countryside. Farmers were brought in as Party speakers, and Party training courses in farming and agricultural management were set up in some places. Peasants were told that their property would remain untouched in the coming Third Reich, and that agriculture would be aided through reductions in social burdens and taxes and through the removal of marketing uncertainties. No peasant would be driven from his land, mortgage debts would be taken over by the State, interest would be abolished: such were the promises made by Nazi speakers, who emphasized that only the Nazi Party could still help the peasant.[14] Little wonder, then, that, as reports were pointing out, Nazi gains often followed from the naïve expectations of farmers that 'if Hitler gets into the government, liquidation of debts, tax relief, and interest-free credit will be granted'.[15] In broad terms, most farmers wanted a state which placed the interests of agriculture at the top of its list of priorities. These interests were seen as lying in rescue from indebtedness, release from excessive financial burdens, and higher prices for farm products. Global hopes apart, farmers did have some concrete expectations from a Nazi government. Some are listed in a catalogue of demands of the Bavarian Christian Peasant Association in 1933. The Association sought significant tax reductions (and abolition of some forms of tax), the inclusion of parts of Bavaria in the 'Eastern Aid' rural subsidy programme, the reduction of interest to 4 per cent, tackling of the debt problem, and cuts in farming expenditure to be attained by reductions in fertilizer prices and social burdens.[16]

By the end of 1932, however, most farmers probably had little clear conception of where the answer to their problems lay. The scale of the crisis more than possible solutions

---

[13] Cf. *Bayern I*, p. 43.
[14] GStA, MA 102138, RPvOB, 20 Jan. 1932, 5 Feb. 1932, 22 Feb. 1932, 4 Mar. 1932.
[15] GStA, MA 102149, RPvS, 5 Mar. 1932.
[16] A. von Saldern, *Mittelstand im 'Dritten Reich'. Handwerker — Einzelhändler — Bauern*, Frankfurt am Main, 1979, p. 67.

dominated the mood in the countryside. The bitterness at the inability of successive governments to come to terms with the crisis is a continuing hallmark of the Bavarian reports in 1932. According to a report from Lower Bavaria in January 1933, 'all attacks on the government find a lively echo among the peasants; the more caustic the language, the more pleasant it sounds in their ears.'[17] The bitterness was compounded by newspaper reports in the same month of the scandalous distribution of the 'Eastern Aid', which was in practice going into the pockets of the large landholders in the East Elbian regions — news which not unnaturally provoked 'a storm of anger among farmers fighting hard for their very existence'.[18]

Only a complete reordering of politics could, in the eyes of these peasants, bring about any improvement. In the existing climate, however, they initially held out little hope of the new Hitler government. The appointment of Hitler as Chancellor on 30 January 1933 did little to move them: according to contemporary reports, they were in such despair that they were completely apathetic towards the latest change of government and towards 'every political event'.[19] Nevertheless, the conviction grew that this government *was* different from its predecessors, that the coming election would be the last for a long time, and that Hitler must be given a chance to save farmers, as he had promised. The Government President of Lower Bavaria and the Upper Palatinate accurately registered the changing mood in the middle of the election campaign in his report of 20 February 1933: 'Especially among *Bauernbund* supporters the view is apparently gaining ground that Hitler is the right man and that the NSDAP should be given the chance to show what it can do towards improving the economy.'[20] Similar voices were reported elsewhere. The Government President of Upper Bavaria spoke of a shift of opinion in favour of the NSDAP among the peasantry, and attributed it to the slight rise in wood and cattle prices — already marked down as a success of the new government.[21] Farmers' hopes were tentatively raised, though, despite little

---

[17] GStA, MA 106672, RPvNB/OP, 19 Jan. 1933.
[18] Ibid., 3 Feb. 1933.   [19] Ibid., 3 Feb. 1933.
[20] Ibid., 20 Feb. 1933.   [21] GStA, MA 106670, 4 Mar. 1933.

noted hostility to the new regime among the peasantry, the general air was one of scepticism and 'wait and see'.[22] And outside Franconia, where large sections of the peasantry formed a fervent Nazi following, three-fifths of the Bavarian peasantry still did not vote for the NSDAP even in March 1933.

(i) The Tightening Grip of the State

The Nazi answer to the massive problems of the rural economy amounted to an attempt to build a comprehensive set of controls for the regulation of the pricing and marketing of agricultural produce, to wipe out indebtedness and protect peasant farms against land speculation, to stimulate agricultural production, and finally to give peasants a new confidence by according them a prized social and ideological status as the backbone of the new Germany. Darré's ideological conceptions of the peasant radical stock providing the 'source of life' of the German people were combined with a more prosaic aim: to maximize farm production in order to make Germany as self-sufficient as possible in foodstuffs. The instrument of agricultural reconstruction was the immense organization with the archaic-sounding name of the Reich Food Estate (*Reichsnährstand*), set up under Darré in September 1933 and aiming at the direction and regulation of all facets of agriculture and rural life.[23]

Between 1933 and 1936 the National Socialist regime succeeded in part in overcoming the worst effects of the agricultural crisis. In its main lines, the agricultural policy of the regime undoubtedly did bring about some substantial improvements in the well-being of the peasantry, which was able to better its position in relation to other producer groups. Guaranteed higher prices for farm products, measures to reduce indebtedness, and tax and interest reductions all helped stimulate rising agricultural surpluses in the first two years of the Third Reich compared with constant decline in

---

[22] Ibid., 20 Feb. 1933. And see the reports, clearly reflecting this mood, from the *Gendarmerie* stations in the Ebersberg district of Upper Bavaria for 11-12 Feb. and 24-26 Feb. 1933 in StAM, LRA 76887.

[23] Cf. Farquharson, pp. 57-106 and Lovin, pp. 57-89 for the principles and policies of the Reich Food Estate.

the last years of Weimar.[24] Incomes were rising at the same
time that expenditure was being held steady or even slightly
reduced. Farm income rose in absolute terms from 4.2 to
5.6 million RM between 1933 and 1937 — substantially
faster than the growth of income generally. Relatively, however, agriculture was already slipping: farm income amounted
to 8.7 per cent of the national income in 1933, but only 8.3
per cent in 1937; while profits in trade and industry had risen
by 88 per cent, farm income had increased by only 33 per
cent; and after an initial growth rate of about 17 per cent in
the first two years of Nazi rule, farm income almost stag-
nated while the growth rate in national income continued at
upwards of 6 per cent a year.[25] Farmers had, in other words,
profited disproportionately in the first years of the regime,
but by the time of the Four Year Plan in 1936 were rapidly
losing ground to other sectors of the economy. In all this the
Bavarian peasantry fared no differently from the peasantry in
other parts of the Reich.

The improvement in the economic position of farmers had
not been achieved without the imposition of numerous
biting restrictions on the farmers' freedom of action. Difficult
to assess though they are, the subjective feelings of the
peasantry for Nazism hardly matched the benefits which
farming had derived from the regime in the early years of
the dictatorship. Nor did they correspond closely to the
image of the contented and grateful *Bauer*, pillar of the revitalized Germany, which the propaganda machine was busy
cultivating. Peasant discontent was reflected in reports emanating from all parts of Bavaria, and such indications as there
are from other regions of Germany point to similar responses
of the farming community to the agricultural policies of the
National Socialist regime.[26] Peasant grievances revolved chiefly
around three interrelated aspects of the restructuring of
agriculture: the *Reichserbhofgesetz* (Reich Entailed Farm

[24] Farquharson, pp. 66-7.
[25] Ibid., pp. 66-7; Schoenbaum, p. 163; von Saldern, pp. 113-15.
[26] Cf. e.g., the reports printed in *Pommern*, in *Volksopposition im Polizeistaat*,
in *Nationalsozialismus im Alltag* (which contains only a fraction of the ex tensive
reports for the 1934-6 period kept in StA Koblenz), and the brief survey by
Steinert, pp. 63-5.

Law); increased intervention in regulating production and marketing (and closely connected with it the price-structuring of farm produce); and, of rapidly mounting significance, the growing shortage of rural labour. For most farmers, all this added up to the tightening grip of the State on their domain, to their subjection to the remorseless demands of the 'coercive economy'.

The Reich Entailed Farm Law, brainchild of Walter Darré and promulgated in September 1933, was the keystone of Nazi agricultural policy. It sought 'by upholding the old German custom of entailment . . . to retain the peasantry as the blood-spring (*Blutquelle*) of the German people'. Peasant farms were to be protected from heavy indebtedness and division through inheritance. The law affected holdings of between 7.5 and 125 hectares which, henceforth, were to pass on undivided to a single heir. Rights of coheirs were limited to the movables of the peasant and any additional property. The farm itself was inalienable, and the essence of the law was thus to release the peasant holding from the capitalist market economy.[27]

The law potentially affected almost 200,000 peasant farms in Bavaria (here including the Palatinate) — in all, some 36 per cent of the total of 556,000 agricultural concerns of 1933.[28] Those concerns ineligible for enrolment as entailed farms (*Erbhöfe*) were mainly small peasant farms and smallholdings.[29] Already by mid-1935 some three-quarters of eligible farms in Bavaria had been enrolled, so that the process of enrolment was by this early date well on the way to completion.[30] The distribution of entailed farms was uneven: 28 per cent were located in Lower Bavaria and the Upper Palatinate, 23 per cent in Upper Bavaria, 22 per cent

[27] Text in *Documents on Nazism*, pp. 384–5. For the best analysis of the law and its effects, cf. F. Grundmann, *Agrarpolitik im Dritten Reich. Anspruch und Wirklichkeit des Reichserbhofgesetzes*, Hamburg, 1979.

[28] GStA, Reichsstatthalter 562, p. 9, 12–13; Farquharson, p. 267.

[29] Of the 555,922 agricultural concerns in Bavaria (incl. Palatinate) in 1933, 160,128 (28.8 per cent) were classed as small peasant farms of two to five hectares and 124,701 (22.4 per cent) as smallholdings of under two hectares — GStA, Reichsstatthalter 562, p. 9.

[30] Cf. the figures for the regional court districts of Bamberg, Munich, and Nuremberg in Farquharson, pp. 268–9.

in Upper and Middle Franconia, 19 per cent in Swabia, but only 6 per cent in Lower Franconia and 2 per cent in the Palatinate.[31] Apart from the latter two regions, the prevailing inheritance custom in Bavaria was already almost entirely descent to a single heir, and since medium-to-large peasant farms predominated Bavaria was seen as a classic area for the introduction of entailed farms. Even so, the 142,525 entailed farms registered by 1 January 1937 amounted to only 25.6 per cent of all agricultural concerns in the province.[32]

For many peasants the Entailed Farm Law was an intensely unpopular measure. And as the first spectacular step in the regime's agricultural policy it provoked among those affected controversy, criticism, and in no small measure feelings of insecurity.[33] Negative responses to the law were encountered in all parts of Bavaria. Peasants, it was reported, saw in the law both economic disadvantage and a serious intrusion into their freedom. There was widespread feeling that it would now become impossible for peasants to obtain credit, especially cash loans. Even more worrying were the implications for marrying off daughters who now had no hope of coming into possession of any part of the holding.[34] The law was 'not liked', 'not understood', and 'constantly criticized' by the peasants. Farmers' wives without children believed they would be forced off the farm without compensation on the death of their husbands.[35] According to a report from one locality in Upper Bavaria, the law was reviled and attacked in all the inns of the district. Whatever the merits of the law for north Germany, farmers were convinced it had none for Bavaria: 'the Bavarian peasant is today only the administrator of his property. Nothing belongs to him any longer and he can also no longer give his children anything.'[36] Reports reaching the

[31] Calculated from the figures in GStA, Reichsstatthalter 562, p. 12.
[32] Ibid., pp. 9–12.
[33] Cf. Grundmann, pp. 128 ff.
[34] Cf. LRA Friedberg (Registratur), VII/12/6/R, GS Mering, 12 Oct. 1933; GHS Friedberg, 13 Dec. 1933, 27 Feb. 1934.
[35] StAM 76887, GS Zorneding, 27 Oct. 1933; GS Landsham, 26 Feb. 1934; GS Steinhöring, 26 Feb. 1934; GS Grafing, 12 Feb. 1934; GS Markt Schwaben, 10 Feb. 1934; GS Zorneding, 27 Mar. 1934; GS Aßling, 25 May 1934; GS Ebersberg, 12 Feb. 1934.
[36] Ibid., GS Grafing, 30 Nov. 1934 and cf. also the report for 30 June 1935.

Sopade indicated the same grievances, adding that the title *'Reichserbhofbauer'* (Reich Entailed Farm Peasant) was no substitute to the Upper Bavarian farmer for the rights over his holding which had been taken from him.[37] Lack of clarity about the consequences of the law reinforced the fears and worries of the peasants and left the regime with the problem of 'educating' the rural population. According to a report from one purely rural district of Upper Bavaria in November 1933 there were still many 'agitators' who, without any knowledge of the law, were provoking discontent and spreading direct untruths about it. A month later opinion about the law was said to be divided, though in the main hostile: while many regarded it as 'a great intrusion into their personal rights', others, particularly indebted farmers who had gained relief through the law, enthusiastically welcomed it.[38]

The worries and fears provoked by the law were widespread. Even in areas little affected by the provisions of the law, there was condemnation, often arising from anxiety. From one Lower Franconian district, for instance, where, as a result of partible inheritance, the size of holdings was generally small and most farms were consequently ineligible for enrolment as entailed farms, it was reported that the law was a notable source of complaint and that to put it into effect would cause 'great harm to the National Government'. Fears had been expressed among the peasants that those with small farms would have to disinherit their own children in order to allow their holdings to pass to single heirs. The unease died down once it was realized that most were too small to qualify as entailed farms, but isolated criticism of the law continued until 1936.[39]

At the end of the first year of Nazi rule, the mood among farmers in Bavaria was still mainly one of expectation.

---

[37] DBS, 10 Jan. 1935, pp. A17-18. For detailed comment about the negative attitude towards the Entailed Farm Law among Bavarian peasants cf. also ASD, ES/M63/July 1934, pp. 19-20 and M31/2 Aug. 1934, p. 3.
[38] StAM, LRA 112709, BA Wasserburg, 30 Nov. 1933, 30 Dec. 1933; cf. also GStA, MA 106672, RPvNB/OP, 4. 1. 34.
[39] StAW, Sammlung Schumacher 29, GS Sandberg, 23 Nov. 1933; GS Hollstadt, 13 Oct. 1933; LRA Bad Neustadt 125/1, BA Bad Neustadt, 30 Dec. 1933; LRA Bad Neustadt 125/3, BA Bad Neustadt, 29 Jan. 1936; GS Unsleben, 25 Feb. 1936; GStA, MA 106680, RPvUF, 8 Nov. 1933.

Recorded expressions of opinion to some extent reflect divisions present before the coming of the Nazis. But there is sufficient evidence to indicate that the initial high hopes of the regime among the peasantry were already giving way to a more pessimistic evaluation of the likely benefits for farmers in the Third Reich. The 'thunderous applause' said to have greeted Darré's eulogies about the place of the peasant in the new Germany during his visit to Munich in November 1933 contrasts with the more prosaic reflections of peasant feeling registered in the opinion reports. These leave little doubt about a deterioration in the mood of the rural population, which came more clearly to make itself felt in the early months of 1934, and to which the Entailed Farm Law had contributed in no small measure. By early 1934 there was still hardly a sign, from the vantage point of many Bavarian farmers, of the promised revival of agriculture. The peasants had not gone short on propaganda. But reality appeared rather different.

At this juncture the Reich Food Estate introduced new measures aimed at regulating the price and marketing in particular of eggs and milk products by channelling them into centrally located collecting points (*Sammelstellen*).[40] However rational such measures were — and in part they built upon ordinances introduced in the early 1930s — they provoked a wave of criticism which lasted undiminished throughout 1934 and 1935. The anger expressed in reports from all parts of Bavaria derived in part from the feeling that the peasants themselves would be economically disadvantaged as a result of the ordinances. Farmers in the Bayreuth area, for example, complained that they would have to settle at the collection point for 8 Pf. less per litre than they could have got selling direct to the customer. They regarded 'such an incisive measure' as 'incomprehensible' and 'incompatible' with the avowed intention of improving the position of farmers.[41] The ordinances were also seen as a major intrusion

---

[40] Cf. Farquharson, pp. 77–81 and *Chronik der Agrarpolitik und Agrarwirtschaft des Deutschen Reiches von 1933-45*, ed. W. Tornow, Hamburg/Berlin, 1972, pp. 76 ff., 92.

[41] GStA, MA 106677, RPvOF/MF, 19 Jan. 1934, p. 5. The effects of the new ordinance are expounded on pp. 3–6 of the report.

by the State in the freedom of the peasant to carry out his business according to his own wishes. The marketing regulations were strikingly reminiscent of the detested State interventionism during the war, and 'many stated that they preferred the earlier form of trading.'[42] Reports from Bavaria to the *Sopade* also left no doubt about the anger caused by the regulations. They were contributing, claimed the *Sopade*, to a widening gap between the peasantry, which had only voted for Hitler out of selfish motives, and the regime. A 'hidden war' was developing between peasant and government, driving 'the government to even stronger emphasis on its unrestricted power and the peasant to passive resistance.'[43]

The spring and early summer of 1934 were marked by unmistakable signs of growing economic discontent among the peasantry, mentioned in almost all reports of this date. This was proving a difficult time for the Nazi authorities. The typical reaction to the falling confidence of the regime, noted in all parts of the Reich, was to launch a nation-wide campaign against the 'grumblers' and 'miseries' who were regarded as being particularly prominent in rural areas. The campaign, carried out in May and June 1934, aimed at reviving morale through rousing Party meetings and demonstrations which would castigate the mealy-mouthed critics of the regime and employ the tried and tested methods of the *Kampfzeit*, the 'time of struggle' before 1933, to mobilize the whole population 'down to the last village'.[44] The campaign proved a miserable failure, eliciting a very muted response from the people. According to one report, it was only carried out with any energy and skill in south Bavaria, but even there met with no success.[45] The discontent in those parts went so far that the Government President of Swabia felt it necessary to speak of a 'dangerous loss of confidence' among the peasantry.[46] One commentator even inferred that the political mood among the peasantry, revealed 'at a flash' in meetings at which 'everything was criticized which could in any way

[42] Cf. StAM, LRA 76887, GS Steinhöring, 10 Feb. 1934.
[43] ASD, ES/M63/July 1934, p. 21.
[44] *Völkischer Beobachter*, 4 May 1934, as cited in DBS, 26 June 1934, p. A7.
[45] DBS, 26 June 1934, p. A7.
[46] GStA, MA 106682, RPvS, 4 May 1934.

be criticized', forced a comparison with the years 1917 and 1918.[47] This was going altogether too far, as was a report reaching the *Sopade* from the Upper Palatinate in July 1934 which spoke of 'the purest civil war mood' and claimed that market-days, when peasants got together in the towns, resembled political meetings where everyone cursed the corruption of a system in which only the 'big shots' profited.[48] Other *Sopade* reports provided a more realistic and sober assessment. It was pointed out that the diktats from Berlin were indeed hated, but that as usual the Prussians were blamed and north–south antagonisms thereby strengthened: 'What the peasants want to put in the place of the regime cannot be recognized from what they say . . . Most of them don't know themselves.'[49] The general tone of reports reaching the *Sopade* was 'that everywhere the peasants are those who inveigh loudest against the system.' But this was purely a matter of economic self-interest: 'the loss of political rights does not afflict them, does not rouse them to criticism. They believed in Hitler the magician and now they're disappointed.'[50]

Still, the Nazi authorities were aware that economic discontent did have an effect on political attitudes. In Alzenau (Lower Franconia), where peasants had retaliated to the milk marketing ordinances with a delivery strike, poor results (up to 30 per cent no-votes and invalid ballot papers) in the plebiscite of 19 August, acclaiming Hitler as head of state, were directly attributed, among other factors, to peasant anger at the dairy regulations.[51] In Bad Neustadt, another Lower Franconian district, the number of no-votes was again noticeably high especially in places were strong feeling at the dairy ordinances had been expressed.[52] The authorities in

[47] GStA, MA 106765, AA Donauwörth, 11 June 1934.
[48] ASD, ES/M31/2 July 1934, p. 2.
[49] ASD, ES/M63/July 1934, p. 21.
[50] ASD, ES/M31/19 July 1934 (date wrongly given in original as 19 June 1934), p. 4.
[51] StAW, LRA Alzenau 1933–5, BA Alzenau, 26 Aug. 1934.
[52] StAW, LRA Bad Neustadt 125/2, BA Bad Neustadt, 27 Aug. 1934; GHS Bad Neustadt, 23 Aug. 1934. Peasants in Bad Neustadt had been unable to grasp why they should receive only 9 Pf. a litre for produce sold at 22 Pf. and threatened not to deliver any milk unless a price of about 14 Pf. was paid.

rural Lower Bavaria and the Upper Palatinate, where the
mood among the peasantry had already been very depressed
at the start of the summer, also claimed that the significant
increase in no-votes in August 1934 compared with the
previous plebiscite of November 1933 was related in part
to measures of the regime 'with which farmers are not yet
generally in agreement, among which are to be reckoned,
e.g., the Reich Entailed Farm Law and the cereal, butter, and
egg regulation.'[53]

The main problem for Germany's new rulers was how to
break down the stubbornly conservative attitudes of the
peasantry, especially now that the temporary and superficial
mobilization of the initial months of the regime had sagged
into widespread apathy. The peasants confronted the NSDAP
with problems scarcely encountered in other sections of the
population. Their conservatism, lack of adaptability to inno-
vations (except where it suited them), and indifference to
anything not directly affecting their farming interests or
religious beliefs presented the Nazis with an almost impossible
task of mobilization. Communications difficulties made the
task even greater. Many Bavarian peasants did not read a
newspaper, had no radio, did not attend Party meetings, and
were therefore almost inaccessible to Party propaganda. In
the village of Sandberg, near Bad Neustadt (Lower Franconia),
for example, an estimated 10 per cent of the population took
a newspaper, so that 'national education' was said to be
absent in the district. For the broadcast of President Hindenburg's funeral in August 1934 communal loudspeakers were
set up, as in neighbouring villages. But it was to no great avail.
Attendance was miserably poor; in one place nobody turned
up at all. Nor were the chances of winning over the peasantry
enhanced by the organizational and numerical weakness of
the Nazi Party and its affiliations in the district.[54] The
Government President of Lower Bavaria and the Upper
Palatinate summed up the problem in the following way:

---

[53] GStA, 106672, RPvNB/OP, 6 Sept. 1934. For the depressed mood of the
rural population during the summer, cf. ibid., 20 June 1934.
[54] StAW, LRA Bad Neustadt 125/2, GS Sandberg, 22 Aug. 1934.

Further progress in bringing the people to National Socialist thinking will still have to overcome some resistance in the countryside. This is due partly to earlier personal and political enmities and partly to the self-interest and indifference of the rural population. It is hard to get through to these circles since they do not attend meetings which would enlighten them and do not read the National Socialist press.[55]

Frustrated Nazi local leaders put the Party point of view more bluntly. The leading Party functionary in the Upper Franconian village of Erkersreuth stated:

Among the peasants there are still few National Socialists. They are probably nationalists, but they don't have a trace of socialism. To enlighten them is almost impossible since they almost always keep away from meetings of the NSDAP. Naturally, they latch on only to individual mistakes and never see the great thread running through the government measures to save the entire people.[56]

The staccato style of the District Leader of Wasserburg in Upper Bavaria was even more dismissive: 'The peasant to great extent still egoist – has interest only in what affects him personally . . . Peasant can in practice never be made happy – egoist!'[57]

The mood in the countryside showed signs of a slight improvement during 1935. One reason was the higher price of agricultural produce, resulting in fewer complaints about price levels than in 1934.[58] The farmers were, in fact, the main beneficiaries of the growing food shortages which caused such anger among consumers in 1935–6. Beneath the surface, however, the old grievances continued to rankle. One *Gendarmerie* Officer noted sourly that the discontent among farmers meant that the 'national revolution' was being held responsible even for the weather and for crop-yields.[59] Complaints about the Entailed Farm Law, unsatisfactory price levels, bureaucratization, compulsion, and State intervention in the marketing of farm produce, and the exploitation of the hard-working farmers by the parasitic upper class droned on.

[55] GStA, 106672, RPvNB/OP, 19 July 1934.
[56] StAB, M33/410, Ogrl. Erkersreuth, Apr. 1934.
[57] StAM, NSDAP 127, KL Wasserburg, 7 July 1934, 17 Sept. 1934.
[58] Cf. GStA, MA 106672, RPvNB/OP, 7 June 1935, 9 Aug. 1935; MA 106682, RPvS, 6 July 1935; MA 106680, RPvUF, 7 May 1935.
[59] LRA Friedberg (Registratur), VII/12/6/R, GS Mering, 29 Aug. 1935.

50   PEASANT OPINION AND THE 'COERCIVE ECONOMY'

One Nazi local leader commented resignedly: 'The peasant
is of such a disposition that he thinks only he has to work
and the others earn their money for nothing.'[60] And still,
from the other perspective, came the peasants' complaints
that 'the free peasantry has now ceased to exist', that 'this is
no longer a free economy but a system based on coercion.'[61]
The Bavarian peasant did not merely feel economically
hemmed in by Nazism. It must often have seemed to him
that all the traditional props of his world were under threat
of demolition. But he was not necessarily prepared to let all
this happen without a fight. For example, the Nazis' attempt
to do away with the age-old custom of decorating the large
maypole in each village in the traditional Bavarian colours of
white and blue resulted in what the Government President of
Upper Bavaria called an 'unflinching little war'. Breaches of
the peace were caused by the forcible removal of Bavarian
white-blue flags by Hitler Youth and SA groups. In one case
the flag was provocatively thrown into a cesspit. Peasants
retailiated by sawing down maypoles painted in the new
colours of the Nazi Reich.[62] Far more serious was the attack
on the peasant's traditional religion. The 'Church struggle'
contributed massively to the feelings of resentment fuelled
by economic disappointment. Though in this study we are
compelled to deal separately with these two 'layers' of
opinion, economic and religious antagonisms often went together, forming complementary strands of political alienation.

One outward manifestation of peasant feeling was the poor
level of participation at the 1935 Harvest Thanksgiving ceremonies, noted in numerous reports. According to a report
published in an anti-Nazi source, the émigré broadsheet of
the '*Volksfront*' in Paris, one Franconian village even put up
a notice stating that 'the Harvest Festival celebration 1935
. . . will not take place because of the lack of interest and
passive resistance of the peasantry.'[63] Nazi authorities themselves interpreted the poor attendance at the ceremonies 'as
undoubtedly a measure of the present mood among the

[60] StAB, M33/410, Stpl. Unterweißenbach, 27 Sept. 1935.
[61] StAM, LRA 76887, GS Steinhöring, 1 Nov. 1935.
[62] GStA, MA 106670, RPvOB, 8 May 1935, 11 June 1935, 9 July 1935.
[63] WL, *Deutsche Informationen*, 28 May 1936.

peasantry', and one Lower Franconian *Gendarmerie* Officer drew the logical conclusion, that if participation was to be regarded as a test of peasant feeling, 'then one must describe the mood in this sector of the population as very poor.'[64] A report from a rural district of Upper Bavaria also recognized 'that the enthusiasm for the Third Reich among the peasants' had 'quite significantly declined, and frequently among those who had earlier been very keen supporters.' The causes were seen as the Entailed Farm Law, the intrusion by the State in the peasant's domain, and economic disappointment. Among the latter, added the *Gendarmerie* reporter sarcastically, were that taxes had not been reduced, beer had not become cheaper, and that the peasants had not effortlessly had their purses filled with money overnight following the 'take-over of power'.[65] As the Bavarian Political Police (BPP) noted towards the end of 1935, agriculture was objectively speaking much better off than it had been at the 'seizure of power', and yet one still had the impression 'that the peasant is frequently not conscious of his responsibility in the framework of the entire people.' Despite all the benefits they had received from the National Socialist State, 'a large number of farmers have still not grasped the idea of the *Volksgemeinschaft*.'[66]

One direct consequence for the rural economy of the consumer crisis of early 1936 was the introduction of new measures aimed at securing a rational distribution of food products. The reorganization of milk marketing, in particular, had despite the unpopular measures of 1934 proved less than successful. The sixty-three Milk Provisioning Associations set up in the Reich in 1934 to provide an intermediate stage between dairy farmers and the fifteen Dairy-farming Associations were now abolished and the peasants were henceforth to deliver all their saleable produce direct to the latter, which were given sole rights over the marketing and distribution of

[64] StAW, Sammlung Schumacher 29, GS Bischofsheim, 23 Oct. 1935. Cf. also GS Oberelsbach, 24 Oct. 1935; GS Steinach, 21 Oct. 1935, and LRA Bad Neustadt 125/4, BA Bad Neustadt, 29 Oct. 1935.
[65] StAM, LRA 78887, GS Steinhöring, 31 Jan. 1936.
[66] StAN, Pol.-Dir, Nürnberg-Fürth 431, BPP, 1 Dec. 1935, p. 43, 1 Jan. 1936, p. 25.

dairy produce. The rights of farmers to sell their own dairy products direct to the customer were thereby done away with.[67] The so-called 'milk delivery duty' imposed on peasants provoked much hostility and some opposition. Refusals to deliver milk led, in fact, in the short term to even greater shortages and price increases for butter. The BPP reported that police sanctions to break peasant resistance — confiscation of butter from the farm, or in some cases arrest and detention in 'protective custody' — had initially proved less than wholly effective, and that peasants were exploiting the shortages by turning them into 'propaganda hostile to the State' and explaining to buyers 'that they *could* deliver enough butter, but were not allowed to do so.'[68]

Peasant anger at the new ordinances, especially the 'milk delivery duty', is voiced in reports from all areas affected by the changes. One such report, from a dairy-farming locality in Swabia, stated:

The rural population in this district is greatly embittered, especially about the dairy-farming measures. They see in these measures a complete deprivation of rights — the effects of the Entailed Farm Law are in fact still lingering on — and from their comments one has to infer not only ill-feeling but also a turning-away from the path of National Socialism. In the compulsion to milk and butter delivery many farmers see the realization of the long-witnessed plans of the large dairies aiming at the exclusion of the peasant.[69]

The bitterness had still not subsided several months later, when some farmers were considering testing the 'milk delivery duty' in court 'because they thought that there was no regulation or law about it, and that they could not be compelled to deliver.' After the arrest and punishment of a few peasants for their defiance, 'a significant improvement' was said to have taken place in milk delivery.[70]

[67] Cf. *Chronik der Agrarpolitik*, pp. 79–81. A good description of the complex structure and changes in milk marketing introduced in 1934 and 1936 is provided by Lovin, pp. 76–80.

[68] StAN, Pol.-Dir. Nürnberg-Fürth 431, BPP, 1 Dec. 1935, p. 43, 1 Jan. 1936, p. 26.

[69] LRA Friedberg (Registratur), VII/12/6/R, GS Mering, 31 Jan. 1936. Farmers in a neighbouring district declared that they would 'not submit to the coercive economy': ibid., GS Eurasburg, 30 Jan. 1936.

[70] Ibid., GS Mering, 30 Aug. 1936; GHS Friedberg, 31 Dec. 1936.

Talk of a 'coercive economy' was now common. Peasants threatened to produce only sufficient milk for their own needs, or to convert to beef farming and use their milk as fodder. In the view of one Party functionary, the dairy measures had in their impact on morale 'brought about the opposite of what the Production Battle was striving after.'[71] In some areas there were outright refusals to deliver. The Mayor of one village in the Upper Franconian district of Ebermannstadt, faced with peasant resistance, sought to get them to declare in writing that they would faithfully carry out their 'delivery duty', but only three peasants were willing to sign such an undertaking. From five villages in the district no butter at all was delivered. The collection point for cream was boycotted. And the 'delivery duty' could only be imposed under threat of arrest and punishment.[72] Reports published by the 'Volksfront' in Paris claimed an increase in the number of cases in which peasants were defying or ignoring the delivery compulsion and were continuing to sell their dairy products privately.[73]

By 1936 resentment at the 'coercive economy' had largely come to replace the criticisms of the Entailed Farm Law as the main focus of peasant discontent. Though the latter remained a sensitive point, its diminishing role in shaping peasant opinion was probably due both to the fact that the Inheritance Courts, which determined whether a farm should be classed as an entailed farm, in practice often fitted their decisions to local traditions,[74] and to the effective completion of the enrolment of the vast majority of entailed farms by 1936.[75] In any case, by this date the central issue in the

[71] StAB, M33/153, KL Kronach, June 1936.
[72] StAB, K8/III, 18470, BA Ebermannstadt, 3 July 1936; GS Heiligenstadt, 30 June 1936; GS Waischenfeld, 26 Sept. 1936; K8/III, 18472, BA Ebermannstadt, 30 Nov. 1936; GS Waischenfeld, 26 Oct. 1936; GS Muggendorf, 27 Nov. 1936.
[73] WL, Deutsche Informationen, 14 May 1936.
[74] Bayern I, pp. 329-30.
[75] The reports of the OLG-Munich (StAM, OLG 127), extant from Dec. 1935 to Oct. 1936 provide a clear indication of continuing criticism of the Entailed Farm Law, stemming especially from difficulties in obtaining credit and restrictions on the peasant's freedom to dispose of his property. The report of the OLGP Munich from 4 Jan. 1936 commented that the setting-up of the entailed

countryside was shifting to the question of the growing
labour shortage.

Reports from all over Bavaria in late 1936 tell much the
same story: that after four years of Nazi rule morale in the
farming community still left a great deal to be desired. The
BPP continued to attack farmers who had 'apparently a
special conception of *Volksgemeinschaft* . . . which in their
opinion only came into play if benefits were to be gained
for themselves', a point illustrated by the miserly contributions from farmers to the Winter Aid, which some boycotted altogether.[76] Participation at the Harvest Thanksgiving
was again poor in rural districts, and was seen as a reflection
of peasant feeling about the labour shortage and the economic
measures of the regime.[77] The Government President of
Upper Bavaria warned in February 1937 that it would be a
grave mistake to ignore the possible consequences of peasant
discontent. Summarizing the economic factors shaping the
opinion of farmers, according to all the reports which he had
been receiving, he listed the labour shortage, low produce
prices, increased expenditure, high prices for fertilizers,
massive profits of fertilizer manufacturers, grain mills, and
dairies, milk controls, and the bureaucratization of marketing
procedures as main bones of contention.[78]

Four years of Nazism had left, in the eyes of the peasant,
the promised utopia as far away as ever. Instead of the special
place granted to him in the new 'national community', he
felt increasingly hounded and hemmed in by the stranglehold
of the State. As the Government President of Lower Franconia put it in January 1937, the economic system still could
not find favour with a large section of the peasantry 'because
it does not allow them freedom in pricing and the exploitation of the price boom. The political education in particular

---

farm enrolment ought to be completed by March 1936. The figures in Farquharson, pp. 266–9 show little difference in the percentage of potential entailed farms
enrolled in Bavaria in mid-1935 and in 1938.

[76] GStA, MA 106688, BPP, 1 Nov. 1936, p. 2.
[77] GStA, MA 106672, RPvNB/OP, 7 Nov. 1936.
[78] GStA, MA 106670, RPvOB, 10 Feb. 1937, pp. 7–9, repeated with minor
alterations by the Munich office of the Gestapo in GStA, MA 106689, Gestapo
München, 1 Mar. 1937, pp. 82–3.

of the rural population urgently needs to be further promoted.'[79] As the apparent decline in the proportion of farmers in the Party membership by 1937[80] and the difficulties which the Party had in building a membership at all in some rural areas also suggest, the Nazis had by no means achieved the breakthrough in the countryside by the time that farmers were coming to be increasingly preoccupied with the issue which dominated all else in the last peace-time years: the labour shortage.

(ii) The Agricultural Labour Crisis

Agriculture was assigned 16 per cent of the total expenditure estimated under the Four Year Plan – roughly double the level of previous agricultural subsidies. Reductions in fertilizer prices, subsidies for land reclamation and farm mechanization, and improvements in the housing of farm labourers announced by Göring in March 1937 were generally welcomed as positive measures to assist agriculture and to improve the position of farmers. In reality, however, the Four Year Plan began a new period of intensified pressure on farmers which lasted until and beyond the outbreak of war.[81] In this period German agriculture found itself in the midst of a progressively deepening crisis, part of a mounting broader economic problem which was the inevitable outcome of a policy seeking to combine forced rapid rearmament with the satisfaction of consumer demands while avoiding inflation.[82] The root of the difficulties of agriculture as of industry was an increasingly acute shortage of labour which by 1938 was

[79] GStA, MA 106680, RPvUF, 8 Jan. 1937.
[80] Cf. M.H. Kater, 'Sozialer Wandel in der NSDAP im Zuge der nationalsozialistischen Machtergreifung', in W. Schieder (ed.), Faschismus als soziale Bewegung, Hamburg, 1976, pp. 25–67, here esp. p. 50; von Saldern, p. 162.
[81] Cf. Farquharson, pp. 169–81.
[82] For the rapidly worsening economic problems facing Germany in 1938–9 cf. especially T.W. Mason, 'Innere Krise und Angriffskrieg 1938/1939', in F. Forstmeier and H.-E. Volkmann (ed.), Wirtschaft und Rüstung am Vorabend des Zweiten Weltkrieges, Düsseldorf, 1975, pp. 158–88. Mason's thesis of a 'general crisis' of the Nazi system in the years 1938–40 (cf. his Sozialpolitik, p. 41) has been attacked by L. Herbst, 'Die Krise des nationalsozialistischen Regimes am Vorabend des Zweiten Weltkrieges und die forcierte Aufrüstung. Eine Kritik', VfZ, xxvi (1978), 347–92.

threatening to undermine entirely the advances achieved under the 'Production Battle' — advances themselves attained in no small measure by squeezing more work out of the already hard-pressed German farmer. The fine weather and bumper grain crop of 1938 hid strains in agriculture which were endangering the whole drive to intensified production. In fact, although grain yields reached record levels in 1938, milk and butter production was already falling, as were returns in other more labour-intensive sectors of farming. The shortfalls had to be made up through greater imports and use of precious currency reserves.[83] A serious foot-and-mouth epidemic played its part in worsening dairy production in 1938, but the essence of the problem was seen by all contemporary observers to be the critical labour shortage in agriculture. After a brief interlude during the Depression, when the 'flight from the land' slowed down greatly, the impact of Nazi economic policies had been to create such demand for industrial labour that by the time full employment was reached in 1937 the greater mobility, better working conditions, and far higher wages in industry, especially armaments, were draining all labour sources from the rural economy. 'Flight from the land' had been a source of complaint by German farmers for generations, and was also common to farmers in other industrialized countries. Nevertheless, the scale of the labour shortage in the Third Reich amounted to a new phenomenon — quantitatively and qualitatively — and one which, embracing the whole of Germany, formed a major source of worry to Nazi leaders who saw in a threat to agricultural production the shaking of the entire economic and ideological base of the Third Reich. Reports from the central office of the SD in 1938 and 1939 indicated that 'a certain limit' had been reached in the economy and that further intensification was likely to result in falling production and in dangerous inflationary pressure. The problem was outlined as being particularly acute in agriculture, with productive capacity almost completely exhausted. Recourse to less labour-intensive forms of agriculture

[83] Mason, *Sozialpolitik*, pp. 226 ff.; Farquharson, pp. 176 ff., 196–7 and ch. 12 *passim*.

was seen as an inevitable consequence of the labour scarcity, with 'the highpoint of the Production Battle . . . obviously reached' and the 'flight from the land' rolling on with 'in-exorable force into a growing avalanche' and threatening 'not only agricultural production but above all the substance of the nation.' The SD concluded that 'the problem of the flight from the land has been recognized in 1938 as a problem of enormous significance for the whole nation.'[84]

In contrast to the position in northern and eastern Germany, where non-family farm labour was normally supplied by farm-hands on daily or weekly wages, Bavarian peasants depended upon agricultural servants called *Dienstboten*, who were usually youngish, unmarried, and were hired for a year each Candlemas (2 February), during which time they were given board and lodging in the farmhouse. The dependance on this age-old labour provision was most pronounced in Upper and Lower Bavaria, Swabia, and the Upper Palatinate, less prevalent in Upper and Middle Franconia, and insignificant in Lower Franconia.[85] On average, medium-to-large peasant holdings required the labour of between one and three *Dienstboten*. A *Sopade* report of 1939, based on Reich Food Estate sources, argued with some justification that in contrast to the 'flight from the land' before the First World War, when the term had been coined to describe the emigration of landless labourers from Junker estates in eastern Germany, the most serious effects of the labour crisis were now felt not on large estates but on peasant farms of between 5 and 20 hectares, on which there had been a drop of 38 per cent adult male labour and 27 per cent adult female labour between 1935 and 1938.[86]

The future rural labour supply was not regarded as a serious issue in Bavaria in 1933, and the authorities were quietly complacent about the situation.[87] They were rapidly to lose their complacency during the first years of the Third Reich.

[84] BAK, R58/1096, fols. 7, 10–11, and cf. also fols, 3–14, 82, 87–90, and R58/717, fols. 140–7, 187–90.
[85] GStA, Reichsstatthalter 562, p. 12; *Bayern I*, p. 330 and n. 10; M. Spindler (ed.), *Handbuch der bayerischen Geschichte, Band IV, Das Neue Bayern 1800–1970*, Munich 1974–5, pp. 756 ff.
[86] DBS, 12 July 1939, pp. A59–61.
[87] GStA, Reichsstatthalter 562, p. 12.

In the Reich as a whole the number of persons employed on the land fell by close on one and a half million between 1933 and 1939.[88] According to Bavarian census returns, farm-workers expressed as a percentage of all workers in the province declined from 23.3 in 1925 to 20.7 in 1933, and to only 13.6 by 1939.[89] Bavarian farmers, like those elsewhere, were in no position to compete with the attractions of high industrial wages. Despite stringent police measures, *Dienstboten* left the land in droves, often quitting without notice or demanding impossible wages and conditions as their price for staying. German agriculture was very labour-intensive, but increased mechanization of farming was in practice ruled out by the poverty of farmers, the lack of rural credit available, and the meagre subsidies offered by a State which could not afford to build tractors when it needed to build tanks.[90] Immediately effective remedies were sought after and adopted. Attempts to combat the labour scarcity by drafting in squads of Labour Service men or *Wehrmacht* units offered valuable short-term assistance in getting in the harvest, but could hardly counter the deeper structural problems. The introduction of the 'Duty Year' for girls was less than a success: it was clear that girls would do all they could to avoid the back-breaking work on the farm by volunteering for domestic service, despite the picture of the rural idyll presented by Nazi propaganda. The influx of foreign workers *en masse* seemed the only possible way of stemming the tide. From 1937 onwards there was a steady stream of Italians, East Europeans, Austrians, and Sudeten Germans being

---

[88] Mason, *Sozialpolitik*, p. 226; Farquharson, p. 187.

[89] Figures for 1925 and 1933 from 'Berufsgliederung', *ZdBSL*, lxvi (1934), 200–1; for 1939 from 'Die bayerische Bevölkerung nach Wirtschaftsabteilungen', *ZdBSL*, lxxiv (1942), 187. The data given are for people technically in gainful employment (*Erwerbspersonen*), not counting temporarily unemployed. As a percentage of workers together with their families (*Berufszugehörige*), the figures were 17.0 per cent (1925), 15.3 per cent (1933), and 9.8 per cent (1939).

[90] The so-called 'Siebert Programme' theoretically offered Bavarian farmers subventions for acquiring agricultural machinery. There was no shortage of applications: according to a report in July 1939, 362 applications requesting in all 201,375 RM had come from only three districts in Upper Bavaria. The amount available for the three districts totalled, however, only 12,900 RM – GStA, MA 106671, RPvOB, 10 July 1939, p. 5.

directed into rural labour. According to the SD, peasants were clamouring for the foreigners 'irrespective of the proven racial (*bevölkerungspolitisch*) dangers'.[91] The serious plight of Bavarian agriculture in the spring of 1939 was made abundantly clear in a lengthy memorandum of Reich Governor Epp. A 'substantial drop in production' in one of the main agricultural regions of Germany could be reckoned with if Bavarian farming did not receive aid as quickly as possible. Epp estimated the overall loss of labour at 120,000 persons. Wages for farm labour had doubled and often trebled since 1930, and there was a veritable 'struggle for the worker' among peasant employers. The scale of the problem was demonstrated by concrete local examples. In the Bayreuth area there had been a drop of a third in the number of agricultural labourers between 1935 and 1939. In one Swabian village where there had been 120 *Dienstboten*, there were now only twelve. In another village the last farmhand was auctioned off to the highest bidder. A milkmaid who advertised her services in a newspaper received 130 offers of employment.[92] The monotonous recitation of the gravity of the problem and its manifestations in report after report from all parts of Bavaria was a reflection of its deep and widespread impact. And all commentators were in agreement that not only the economic consequences, but also the effect on peasant morale was giving cause for anxiety.

In early 1937 reports were coming in that the farming population of Lower Bavaria and the Upper Palatinate was 'in a depressed mood' because of the labour shortage and the rising agricultural wages.[93] Peasants blamed the State for providing no legal base for the punishment of defecting *Dienstboten*. Though it was correct that no formal law prevented *Dienstboten* leaving their employment without due notice — the old Bavarian police ordinances had been abolished in 1918 — the State authorities and the BPP had in fact used draconian methods from 1935 onwards, even

---

[91] BAK, R58/717, fol. 145.
[92] GStA, Reichsstatthalter 563, pp. 1–8. For examples of wage rises for *Dienstboten* of between 175 and 280 per cent in 1938–9, see StAN, BA Lauf 560, 'Fragebogen über die Lage der Landwirtschaft'.
[93] GStA, MA 106672, RPvNB/OP, 5 Feb. 1937.

going as far as internment in concentration camps, in an un-
availing attempt to keep wayward *Dienstboten* in employment.[94] Given the cut-throat competition between farmers
for the dwindling supply of labourers, the Bavarian offices of
the Reich Food Estate had to admit disconsolately in July
1938 that none of these measures was much help.[95]
Peasants' attention was directed towards the problem particularly in February each year, when the *Dienstboten* were
hired for the following twelve months. The Government
President of Swabia stressed the deep gloom of farmers in
February 1938, adding that, as a result of the shortage of
labour, farmers and their wives were becoming overwrought
in a way he had never before witnessed.[96] Observers in
different rural areas thought that the deep preoccupation
with the shortage of agricultural labour was helping to make
farmers almost wholly indifferent to political events. It was
ruefully admitted that after five years of incessant Nazi
propaganda the political mobilization of the peasantry was
almost impossible: the peasant judged everything as he
always had done — according to his own economic criteria.[97]
Despite the good harvest prospects in the summer of 1938
the prevailing mood among the peasantry was one of deep
dejection due to the labour shortage — heightened by the
impact of the raging foot-and-mouth epidemic.

The increasingly urgent tone of the reports provides an
indication of the serious deterioration in the labour supply
position and in the morale of the peasantry between 1937
and 1939. The SD's annual report for 1938, generalizing
about the Reich as a whole, spoke of a 'mood close to complete despair'. The drain of labour from the land 'gave the
peasant the feeling of being crushed and produced a mood
which turned partly into resignation and partly into an attitude

---

[94] Cf. F. Wiesemann, 'Arbeitskonflikte in der Landwirtschaft während der
NS-Zeit in Bayern 1933-1938', *VfZ*, xxv (1977), 573–90; Farquharson, pp.
185–6.

[95] Wiesemann, 'Arbeitskonflikte', p. 590.

[96] GStA, MA 106683, RPvS, 7 Mar. 1938. Cf. also his report of 7 Jan. 1939
for a full description of the depressed mood of farmers and the reasons for it.
See also Farquharson, pp. 188–91.

[97] StAM, NSDAP 983, NSLB Erding, 22 Feb. 1938; NSLB Traunstein, 25
Jan. 1938.

of downright revolt against the Peasant Leadership.'[98] A few months later the SD reported a further worsening of the mood among peasants, claiming that the disappointment over the regime's inability to fulfil its promise of a rapid and drastic improvement in the labour situation had strongly affected the will to work. In peasant eyes, the solution lay naïvely in the State taking steps to bring agricultural wages into line with those in industry.[99]

Almost without exception Bavarian reports in 1939 allude to the anxious, depressed, and embittered mood of the peasants. Bombarded with a mounting file of such reports, Reich Governor Epp, in the memorandum cited earlier, pointed out the danger as he saw it arising from the 'chronic' and 'catastrophic' labour shortage:

The present position of Bavarian farmers is producing among them an ever more edgy mood. I regard it as necessary to point this out for this reason, that the extent and volume of farm work is dependent in the first instance on the willingness of the farmer to work, which up to now has not been lacking.

Epp went on to cite as support for his view a report of the Provincial Farm Leader of Bavaria to the head office of the Reich Food Estate, illustrating the mood among farmers:

The mood of the peasants has risen to boiling point. Alongside demonstrations in front of Employment Offices and the buildings of the District Peasant Offices a demonstration has now for the first time, on the 2.2.1939, taken place in front of the Provincial Peasant Office of Bavaria in Munich. The peasants declare in unambivalent, vehement terms that they will do away with their cattle and will not cultivate their holdings.[1]

The mood of peasants 'who could not come to terms at all with the labour shortage' was described by an Upper Bavarian District Leader in spring 1939 as 'fatalistic'.[2] Indeed, in July 1939, as the whole of Germany held its breath under the growing threat of war, it was reported that for Bavarian

[98] BAK, R58/1096, fols. 9–10.
[99] BAK, R58/717, fol. 142.
[1] GStA, Reichsstatthalter 563, pp. 13–14 (and original also in the file).
[2] StAM, NSDAP 126, KL Landsberg am Lech, Jan.–Mar. 1939. Cf. also the reports in particular of KL Altötting and KL Aichach for the same period contained in the file.

peasants 'economic worries, above all getting in the coming corn harvest with so few farm hands, take first place.'[3] Political attitudes of Bavarian peasants in the last years before the war seem to have fitted largely into a spectrum running from apathy to downright hostility to the Nazi Movement. 'In the rural population one can above all find fault with the indifference and lack of interest in political affairs' was the typical comment of one report from Upper Bavaria.[4] 'In several villages there are still no Party members; inwardly the population in some places is wholly indifferent to the Movement', ran another report from a farming district in the same region.[5] 'Many, who earlier set about the matter with great keenness are today listless and uninterested', lamented another reporter.[6] Problems of organization and communication remained acute in the countryside. One survey of newspaper readership in Upper Bavaria came up with shocking results in 1939. In the rural parts of the district of Rosenheim, for example, 45 per cent of families in late 1939 were still not taking a newspaper. In the *Gau* of Munich-Upper Bavaria there were an estimated 86,000 non-readers of newspapers, chiefly in country districts.[7] Party meetings were often avoided by peasants even when they dealt specifically with farming issues. And even when they turned up, the farmers' apathy was usually apparent. One Nazi functionary in the Upper Palatinate stated dejectedly that most people, especially in the countryside, did not even notice when an attack was being made on the Nazi ideology or on the Party: 'they are just indifferent.'[8]

This indifference went beyond the customary peasant aloofness from politics. It was a reflection of the growing disaffection of large sections of the peasantry with Nazi economic policies. Since the Four Year Plan, the position of

[3] GStA, MA 106671, RPvOB, 10 July 1939.
[4] StAM, NSDAP 983, NSLB Gauwaltung München/Oberbayern, 5 March 1938.
[5] StAM, LRA 99497, BA Aichach, 1 July 1938.
[6] StAM, NSDAP 983, NSLB Traunstein (Abschnitt Engelsberg), 9 Dec. 1938.
[7] StAM, NSDAP 277, KL Rosenheim, 9 Dec. 1939. In contrast, every family in the town of Rosenheim itself took a newspaper.
[8] IfZ, Db.05.04, Hauptamt für Kommunalpolitik, Vertrauliche Berichtsauszüge, Gauamt für Kommunalpolitik Bayerische Ostmark, 1 Nov. 1937.

the peasantry in the Nazi State had objectively worsened – a deterioration inevitable given the need to squeeze the agricultural sector in the interests of rearmament. According to one calculation, peasants were having to work up to three hours a day longer in 1939 than they had done in 1929, with an average working day of fifteen to sixteen hours,[9] and at a time when farm income as a proportion of national income was declining and farmers were facing new problems of indebtedness. Furthermore, the deterioration in the objective position of the peasantry had been accompanied by unprecedented interference in the farmer's freedom of action and a thorough regimentation of agriculture which made the instrument of Nazi control, the Reich Food Estate, an object of widespread detestation in peasant circles. In the shadow of the labour crisis, the bureaucratization, regimentation, and overt lack of individual freedom in the agricultural economy were felt more acutely and resented even more bitterly in the later 1930s than in the period before the Four Year Plan. Reports from Bavaria and from other parts of Germany reaching the left-wing exile organizations confirm the picture derived from internal sources. Widespread peasant discontent, an openly hostile stance towards the Reich Food Estate and the 'Production Battle' – often resulting in the open flouting of regulations and active opposition to specific measures – continued conflict over the Entailed Farm Law, boycotts of the Winter Aid, grievances about the replacement of earlier peasant representatives by Nazis, and comments that conditions resembled those in Russia, all belonged to the picture painted of the position of the peasantry in the later 1930s.[10] Paradoxically, of course, the peasants who continued to decry the oppressive coercion of the State were most vehemently demanding State action and intervention in regulating an abundant supply of agricultural labour.

This was only one aspect of a deeper ambivalence in the political attitudes and behaviour of the peasantry under Nazi

[9] F. Wunderlich, *Farm Labour in Germany 1810-1945*, Princeton, 1961, p. 229.
[10] DBS, 18 Sept. 1937, pp. A34-77; WL, *Deutsche Informationen*, 20 April 1937, 31 July 1937, 23 July 1938, 20 Oct. 1938, 7 Jan. 1939; *Deutschland-Informationen der KPD*, Mar. 1937, pp. 49-51, June 1937, pp. 7-8, 27-8.

rule. A *Sopade* assessment of peasant attitudes in 1937 differentiated between the great discontent among older farmers,
who compared conditions with the time before Hitler and
remembered the great promises which drew peasants to
Nazism before the 'seizure of power', and the younger generation of farmers, who were more influenced by Nazi propaganda and could hope to find advancement in the 'gigantic
hierarchy' of the Reich Food Estate. Furthermore, as the
report pointed out, the 'coercive economy' had in reality not
been altogether disadvantageous to the peasant: while it had
taken away his freedom to exploit favourable market conditions, it had also given him the price stability and sales
guarantees which hedged him against the effects of a slump.
On the one hand, therefore, there was — in the circumstances
of the police State — remarkably free expression of great discontent, especially among older farmers:

It not infrequently comes to incensed protests of farmers in peasant
meetings in the presence of Nazi big-wigs. If the peasants are intimidated like all other sections of the population by Nazi terror, they are
none the less able to risk more than others, especially than workers, in
giving voice to their sentiments through verbal abuse because the
regime cannot afford to bring the peasants to silence with the same
brutality that it uses on the workers.[11]

On the other hand, the divisions within the peasantry and the
undoubted benefits accruing to some farmers through Nazi
policies meant, as the report put it, that the angry discontent
of the peasants was 'without great political significance' and
was the reflection only of material considerations.[12] The reported comments of a Bavarian peasant, a former BVP
supporter with a medium-sized holding, added to this diagnosis the acute fear and hatred of communism among the
peasantry. Between the devil and the deep blue sea, many
feared 'that Bolshevism will take away their land and property, and prefer to come to terms with the Nazis who only
half-expropriate them.'[13]

The same Bavarian farmer concluded, very likely with
some personal bias, that 'the peasants are more embittered

---

[11] DBS, 18 Sept. 1937, pp. A34-5.
[12] Ibid., pp. A35, 42.   [13] Ibid., p. A40.

by the struggle of the regime against Christianity than by economic troubles, for religious questions bother them greatly.'[14] We have been concerned in this chapter only with economic influences on peasant opinion. The response to the Nazi attack on the traditional religious framework of peasant life is, however, a subject to which we will return in later chapters.

[14] Ibid., p. A40.

2. Repression and Demoralization in the Working Class

'Workers' and their families comprised 40.3 per cent of the Bavarian population according to the 1933 census. Seventy per cent of these workers were employed in 'industry and crafts', 15 per cent in agriculture, just under 12 per cent in trade and commerce, and 3 per cent in the public and private service sector.[1] Industrial workers are our concern in this chapter. If not synonymous with 'the working class' as a whole, it was certainly this group which the Bavarian authorities implied when they spoke in their reports of *'die Arbeiterschaft'*.

No more than a quarter of Bavaria's industrial workers lived in large cities, of which only Augsburg, where 56 per cent of the inhabitants were classed as 'workers' in 1936, Nuremberg (51 per cent), and Munich (43 per cent), could in any sense be regarded as industrial centres.[2] Just over a third of the workers belonged to trade unions in 1930, more than half of these in Augsburg, Nuremberg, and Munich.[3] The milieu of the Bavarian worker was often that of the small town or industrial village rather than the large city, and that of the small business or workshop rather than the large factory.

As we saw in the Introduction, the worker parties (SPD and KPD) were weak in Bavaria when compared with the heavily industrialized regions of Germany. Though remarkably successful in holding on to the allegiance of their supporters when challenged by the growth of Nazism, they were unable to exhaust the electoral potential of the working class. The passivity and hesitancy of the SPD in the face of Brüning's deflationary policies, and the inability of the party to offer any direct alternative to the government's anti-socialism, drove some of its followers into the arms of the communists.

[1] Calculated from data in *StJBB* (1936), 11–12 and 'Berufsgliederung', *ZdBSL*, lxvi (1934), 200–1.
[2] GStA, MA 106731, p. 7; cf. *Bayern I*, p. 203.
[3] *Bayern I*, pp. 199, 202.

The KPD's impact was, however, greatest among the young and unemployed. Within factories, the party's influence was limited: in 1932 it numbered only 11,000 members in Bavaria of whom a mere 15 per cent were currently employed in factories.[4] As in the rest of Germany, few of those workers who had regularly voted for left-wing parties found their way to the NSDAP. While there was unquestionably some seepage, especially from the KPD, to the NSDAP (most likely among young, unemployed, ex-non-voters who in the radicalized climate of 1932 had cast their lot in with the communists before lurching into the Nazi camp), Nazi gains among the industrial working class came predominantly from 'non-organized' workers, often in the 'fringe' industrial zones where the hold of the left-wing parties was weak, and from others who had formed no attachment either to a trade union or to a party of the Left.[5]

The condition of the industrial working class in Bavaria during the Depression differed in degree but not in substance from that in other parts of Germany. The rate of unemployment was somewhat below the national average and substantially lower than in Germany's prime industrial regions. Even so, the approximately half a million unemployed in the province in 1932 amounted to 6 per cent of Bavaria's population, 12 per cent of its working population, and 27 per cent

[4] Ibid., p. 205.
[5] Ibid., p. 205, n. 26; for the limited working-class support for the NSDAP in Bavaria, see also: Pridham, pp. 186-8; Eiber, pp. 40, 55; Zofka, pp. 177-87; Hambrecht, pp. 305-7; Beer, pp. 38-45; F. Wiesemann, *Die Vorgeschichte der nationalsozialistischen Machtübernahme in Bayern 1932/1933*, Berlin, 1975, pp. 266-7. The general weakness of Nazism's appeal to the working class before 1933 is dealt with in Mason, *Sozialpolitik*, pp. 62-78 and has most recently been argued by D. Geary, 'The Failure of German Labour in the Weimar Republic', in M. Dobkowski and I. Wallimann (eds.), *Towards the Holocaust*, New York, 1982. In contrast to that of the Nazi Party, however, the social base of the SA was undoubtedly more heavily proletarian, containing a relatively high proportion of unemployed workers: cf. C. Fischer, 'The Occupational Background of the SA's Rank and File Membership During the Depression Years, 1929 to Mid-1934', in P. Stachura (ed.), *The Shaping of the Nazi State*, London, 1978, pp. 131-59. The debate provoked by Fischer's article can be followed in *Social History* iv (1979) and v (1980), but it does not seem to me that Richard Bessel and Mathilde Jamin, Fischer's antagonists, seriously dented the thrust of his argument. For the latest survey of recent work on the social base of Nazism, see P. Stachura, 'Who were the Nazis? A Socio-Political Analysis of the National Socialist *Machtübernahme*', *European Studies Review*, xi (1981), 293-324.

of industrial workers (Table XI). A third of the unemployed lived in the big cities, though compared with the norm for

TABLE XI: Proportion of Unemployed among the Working Population of Bavaria, 1933 (incl. Palatinate)

Economic group	Working population	Unemployed	As % of working population
Agriculture and forestry	1,651,839	25,189	1.5
Industry and crafts	1,325,389	357,624	27
Trade and commerce	563,660	64,618	11.5
Administration and service sector	294,087	17,410	6
Domestic service	147,117	17,104	11.5
Total	3,982,092	481,945	12

Source: Calculated from figures in StJBB (1936), 13.

Germany's cities, only Nuremberg was especially hard hit. Substantially above-average unemployment was experienced in the building trade and the stone, wood, and metal industries with the lowest ratings in the clothing, food, and textile industries.[6] Less than half of the total unemployed were in receipt of the main unemployment insurance benefit or the State-paid 'crisis relief'. Almost as many were dependant on the 'welfare support' paid by the local government offices, a pittance which has been aptly described as providing 'too little to live and too much to starve'.[7] It has been estimated, in fact, that as many as 20 per cent of Bavaria's registered un-

---

[6] Data from 'Bayerns Volk', p. 29; StJBB (1936), p. 13.
[7] Eiber, p. 30; cf. also Bayern I, p. 204. For the collapse of the unemployment insurance system, see: L. Preller, Sozialpolitik in der Weimarer Republik, Düsseldorf, (1949) 1978, pp. 418-53; and C.W. Guillebaud, The Social Policy of Nazi Germany, Cambridge, 1941, pp. 13-14. Figures for the growth of unemployment and the proportions of unemployed workers covered by the different forms of relief are given in Geschichte der deutschen Arbeiterbewegung, ed. W. Ulbricht et al., vol. ix, Berlin, 1968, pp. 131-2.

employed received no support whatsoever, quite apart from the many (mainly young) workers who had even given up bothering to register at the employment offices.[8] In addition, thousands were reduced to short-time working. In some places, the number of workers on short time greatly exceeded the total unemployed, though only those who lost three days or more a week qualified for the minimal financial support available.[9] Even such levels of support, reducing workers to begging and even to suicide, were savagely cut in the notorious von Papen Emergency Decree of June 1932.[10] Meanwhile, those fortunate to remain in work had to undergo drastic wage reductions and lost practically all the social rights and benefits which workers had attained since the Revolution.[11]

Many workers refused to capitulate meekly to the disastrous worsening of their position. In Germany as a whole there were only 22 per cent fewer strikes registered in the years 1930-2 than in the years 1927-9, though the strikes were on the whole smaller and far shorter, with fewer than half the days lost.[12] The available strike statistics are notoriously incomplete and inaccurate, and a recent detailed local study of the working class in northern Bavaria has revealed numerous small-scale short strikes (mainly unsuccessful) aimed at combating wage cuts.[13] Nevertheless, the massive unemployment among trade unionists, which greatly disrupted worker organization within factories, the unwillingness of the SPD-affiliated union leadership to engage in open battle with the Brüning government, and the general dilemma

---

[8] Eiber, p. 219, n. 148. Cf. also T.W. Mason, *Arbeiterklasse und Volksgemeinschaft*, Opladen, 1975, p. 25; and J. Kuczynski, *Die Geschichte der Lage der Arbeiter unter dem Kapitalismus*, vol. v, Berlin, 1966, p. 197.

[9] Eiber, p. 19, and cf. also pp. 14, 29, 288; Mason, *Arbeiterklasse*, p. 25; Kuczynski, p. 198.

[10] Preller, p. 448; Eiber, pp. 29-30. The Papen decree limited main unemployment benefit to six weeks before being subjected to a rigorous means test and cut the levels of relief by 23 per cent for main benefit and by 10 per cent for crisis and 15 per cent for welfare support.

[11] For wage reductions, see Mason, *Sozialpolitik*, pp. 90-1 and *Sozialgesch. Arbeitsbuch III*, p. 98; and for the situation specifically in north Bavarian industries, see Eiber, pp. 15-36.

[12] *Sozialgesch.Arbeitsbuch III*, p. 114.

[13] Eiber, pp. 20-36. Cf. also *Gesch. d. dt. Arbeiterbewegung*, ix, pp. 161-3.

into which the SPD manoeuvred itself, all hindered working-class militancy. Only the KPD, through its 'Revolutionary Trade Union Opposition', was prepared valiantly to engage in uncompromising struggle.[14] The disunited, weakened, and dispirited working class had already suffered a major defeat even before Germany fell into the clutches of the Nazis.

Though a workers' party in name, and though allegedly aiming to unite all sections of society in a genuine 'people's party' (*Volkspartei*), the NSDAP made little serious effort in Bavaria during the Depression to win over the factory-employed working class. By contrast with some other areas of Germany, its 'socialist' propaganda was extremely muted.[15] Recent local studies have emphasized the total insignificance of the NSBO in Bavaria and the lack of weight which the Nazis themselves attached to the organization. They have pointed, too, to the deliberate avoidance of worker districts in holding election meetings and other propaganda activities, and to the lack of interest in worker problems, especially those concerned with labour relations.[16] To have adopted the social demands and concerns of the working class would in any case have put at risk the allegiance of the peasantry and petty bourgeoisie, whose anti-Marxism, anti-socialism, and anti-trade-unionism (which amounted in Bavaria to much the same thing), coupled with their own self-centred economic interests, had been greatly accentuated in the crisis conditions of the Depression.[17] The whole tenor of the propaganda of the left-wing parties shows that workers attached to these parties, readers of the socialist press, or those attending political meetings held by these parties, could have been in little doubt about the anti-socialism of the Nazi Movement and about its transparently negative aims with regard to the working class should it gain power.

Repression set in with full force and draconian severity in Bavaria immediately following the *Gleichschaltung* of the Bavarian State government on 9 March 1933. Some 10,000

[14] Cf. Eiber, pp. 22–4, 32–6.
[15] Pridham, p. 188.
[16] Eiber, pp. 24–5, 55–6; Zofka, p. 194 & n. 4.
[17] Cf. Zofka, p. 194, n. 5; pp. 121–5.

persons, overwhelmingly functionaries and members of the left-wing parties, especially of the banned KPD, were interned in March and April 1933, and with a second major wave of arrests following the destruction of the trade unions and the outlawing of the SPD in May and June the total number taken into 'protective custody' in 1933 has been put at between 15,000 and 20,000 — the vast proportion of them workers.[18] The savage repression, centring on though by no means confined to the large cities, certainly intimidated, but it was hardly suited to endearing workers whose representatives, friends, and relatives had been arrested by the new regime. Moreover, the experience of repression was not confined to witnessing the arrest and hearing of the maltreatment of party activists and functionaries. The threat of instant dismissal and of being ignored in the distribution of Winter Aid and unemployment benefit was a constant sword hanging over the head of any worker who felt tempted to show his disapproval of the way things were being run. The dismissal of known former activists and internees brought lasting deprivation upon themselves and their families, who sometimes found their only assistance in clandestine payments they received through the underground opposition. Industrial workers, far more than any other social class, were now subjected to continual surveillance, harassment, and intimidation by the Nazi authorities. More than any other group they felt the pressure of the police State.[19]

Nazi social ideology aimed at crushing Marxism but winning over workers and integrating them in the new, united 'national community'. This ideal combined negative goals (largely accomplished within half a year) and extremely ambitious 'positive' aims. In practice, however, despite Hitler's promise of a 'new deal' for workers,[20] and despite the propaganda preoccupation with the worker's elevated status in the supposedly egalitarian society of the Third

[18] Eiber, pp. 117, 258, n. 211; Bayern I, pp. 209, n. 30; 240-1.
[19] Cf. R. Mann, 'Everyday Life in National Socialist Germany. Popular Protest and Regime Support', unpubl. paper, 1978, p. 17. For the surveillance of workers in northern Bavaria, cf. Eiber, pp. 114-26.
[20] Hitler. Reden und Proklamationen 1932-1945, ed. M. Domarus, Wiesbaden, 1973, p. 192. Cf. Schoenbaum, pp. 44-6.

Reich, the negative 'control' and repression element dominated throughout, whereas the winning of the workers became increasingly a half-hearted and cynical exercise.
The effect of the Nazi triumph in 1933 was to reduce the
working class, its strength already greatly sapped during the
Depression, to complete disarray. Resentment was felt
against SPD party leaders who had gone into exile leaving
others within Germany to bear the lash of repression and the
sense of desertion. A tiny minority sought to keep alive the
fight from within, entering the heroic, desperately perilous
world of the underground resistance groups, overwhelmingly
communist, which sprang up in Bavarian cities as elsewhere in
Germany within weeks of the first waves of terror in spring
1933, the odds stacked hopelessly against them.[21] The rest,
broken and demoralized, some cherishing only the illusion
of an early end to Nazi rule, for the most part bowed to the
inevitable and prepared to continue their grey lives under the
drastically changed social order of the new Germany, keeping
out of trouble and conforming as necessary. Deprived of their
leaders and organizations and exposed to a constant and unprecedented degree of intimidation, German workers, in the
conditions of mass unemployment which prevailed until
1936, were in no position to influence the nature of labour
relations and industrial policy. Though their feelings were no
longer articulated by trade unions or political parties, sufficient evidence survives to make possible an attempt to reconstruct their reactions to their position in the 'national
community', to explore the survival of worker consciousness
and possible areas of Nazi penetration of that consciousness,
and to assess the impact of the condition of Bavarian industrial workers upon their political attitudes during the Third
Reich.

(i) The Shadow of Mass Unemployment

Industrial workers, certainly those who had been associated
with the SPD and KPD before 1933, were in a position of

---

[21] For the penetration and effective destruction of communist resistance
organization in Bavarian cities between 1934 and the beginning of 1937, cf.
Bretschneider, pp. 30–73; Beer, pp. 140–3; Hetzer, pp. 159–61, 173–4.

exposed isolation after the Nazi 'seizure of power', outsiders in the wave of national exultation which swept through Germany. Little sympathy was felt for the communist and socialist functionaries who were the main target of Nazi terror. The assault on the Left was widely welcomed and helped bolster the popularity of Hitler and his government in the first months of Nazi rule.[22] Even many non-Nazis regarded the setting up of concentration camps — the first of which, at Dachau, ten miles from Munich, was established in mid-March 1933 — as not an unreasonable way of dealing with 'outsiders', 'trouble-makers', and 'revolutionaries' — a 'class apart'.[23]

Among workers themselves the cataclysmic events of 1933 left, once the dust had begun to settle, a mixed legacy of helpless anger with the leadership of the former worker parties, especially of the SPD, ideological disorientation, and above all the dull resignation which accompanied the all-pervading fear and intimidation. *Sopade* reports from southern Bavaria in December 1933 and the first months of 1934 reveal something of the impact of the Nazi establishment of power on SPD members left in Germany. The destruction of the organization was, it was said, as good as complete in Munich and even more thorough in the provinces after a year of Nazi rule. Former comrades had adopted a realistic approach towards the regime. They expected no revolution and had no great hopes of opposition from those disappointed by what the National Socialist State had to offer them. As long as the mass of the population were firm believers in the miracle-worker Hitler there was little that could be done. No opposition was noticeable in factories, where many workers were amenable to the Nazi message, held Hitler in high regard, and accepted the need for the restoration of Germany's colonies if the country's economic problems were to be solved. Though there was wide discontent with the

---

[22] Cf. Kershaw, *Hitler-Mythos*, pp. 48–50.

[23] This appears to have been the response of the bourgeois population of the town of Dachau itself to the early inmates of the nearby concentration camp. T. Barta, 'Living in Dachau, 1900–1950', unpubl. paper, p. 14. Mr Barta (Univ. of La Trobe, Australia) is engaged in a sociological study of the people of the town of Dachau from the turn of the century onwards.

current situation, commented the Border Secretary's informants, this did not amount to placing any hope in the SPD, which would find it difficult to regain any popular support. Illegal work in the factories was not easy. Workers were for the most part accepting the system as something unchangeable.[24] The immense gulf between the exiled SPD leadership and the rank and file of workers under Nazi rule was made strikingly clear to the two Bavarian Border Secretaries when, at Whitsuntide 1934, they had a meeting with two workers from Augsburg – later prominent members of the SPD's underground organization in the city[25] – who were making their first journey outside Germany since the Nazi takeover. For Hans Dill, Border Secretary for Northern Bavaria, a former Reichstag Deputy, and closely associated with the former SPD leadership and with their tactics in exile, it was a devastating experience, as the tone of his report shows. He found it 'shattering' to see 'how fourteen months of Goebbels's propaganda had affected even these people'. Their criticism of the SPD leadership was unrestrained. They claimed that 'none of us wants to hear any more of that parliamentary stuff' and the 'old story' of workers' rights, people's representatives, and so on; people in their circle did not 'want to know any more of the old Weimar Republic' or 'to hear the name Social Democracy. They only laugh about it.' Nor was there any interest in the Sopade's underground literature: 'the workers don't want news about maltreatment in the concentration camps, they want more fundamental matters.' The two workers denied that they had become communists and were scornful of communist tactics, but had no constructive thoughts whatsoever to offer (in Dill's view) and no concept of how the future might develop. The bitter conclusion drawn from the lengthy discussion was that these workers had become 'nationalist as a result of the Hitler propaganda without knowing it . . . The problem for them today is: what have the old leaders done wrong, not, what is Hitler doing wrong?'[26]

[24] ASD, ES/M63/22 Nov. 1933, Jan./Feb. 1934, 30 Mar. 1934.
[25] Cf. Hetzer, pp. 191-200.
[26] ASD, ES/M31/2 July 1934 and 23 May 1934 (letter of Hans Dill to Hans Vogel); ES/M63/May 1934. Cf. also Hetzer, pp. 193-4.

Worker attitudes in southern Bavaria in the spring of 1934 were summarized in a report of the Border Secretary for that area, Waldemar von Knoeringen, to the *Sopade* leadership. Workers complained about low wages, he reported, but many were at the same time glad at least to have employment again; they were not favourably disposed towards the Nazis, but kept their opinions to themselves; 'viewed generally, workers seem to be stuck at present in a condition of uncertainty and waiting' There was little inclination towards communism – though ome did see the only hope lying in Russia – but a 'very sirong emotional rejection of the concept of Social Democracy'. A pervasive feeling of uncertainty 'in which many are bogged down today' could also be widely observed. Most depressing of all from a socialist point of view was the Nazi conquest of the youth – fanaticized and wholly unamenable to socialist underground propaganda.[27] The Führer cult was another major area of Nazi penetration. Hitler enjoyed much veneration even among workers, and in fact gained in popularity through his savage destruction of the SA leadership in June 1934.[28] On the basis of disguised 'verbal questionnaires' with workers in Swabian factories in summer 1934, observers made 'in some cases the extraordinary discovery, that workers actually believe in the success of a German imperialist war, that through a militarily superior Germany they expect an improvement in their living conditions.' Even so, the same report pointed out that 'Fascism' was not finding the conquest of the working class an easy task and the Nazi idea of the *Volksgemeinschaft* was encountering no success: 'the majority of our workers are not for Hitler. They just don't speak out about it because they would feel the repercussions immediately. The interest in events which are damaging to the Regime is very great.'[29]

The indicators of worker dissent multiply during 1934. The dissent scarcely amounted to active opposition, but confirmed the essentially negative attitude towards Nazism which

[27] ASD, ES/M63/May 1934, pp. 1-5. Cf. also ES/M64/Jahresbericht 1934, pp. 11-15.
[28] ASD, ES/M63/May 1934, p. 5; July 1934. Cf. Kershaw, *Hitler-Mythos*, p. 76.
[29] ASD, ES/M63/Sept. 1934, pp. 1-3.

was widespread in the working class. This seems clear despite the fact that – as reports from the Nazi authorities as well as from the *Sopade* point out – workers, in view of the massive intimidation, were less forthcoming in their open criticism of the regime at this date than every other sector of the population.[30] Not only acute fear of physical recrimination and arrest, but anxiety about losing their jobs kept workers quiet in this period. Reports from different parts of Bavaria point out the impossibility, despite anger at their conditions, of workers defending themselves against 'starvation wages', their unwillingness to engage in any political activity, and their lack of interest in the underground work of the SPD and KPD (despite the latter's increased agitation at this time).[31]

Occasionally there were overt reflections of worker feeling and the strength of discontent. As in many parts of Germany, the first elections to the newly created 'Council of Trust' in the factories proved an embarrassment to the regime. In Weiden (Upper Palatinate), for example, almost three-fifths of the voters in one of the porcelain factories rejected the Nazi candidates. Typically, the result was completely ignored and the Nazi candidates declared elected by a majority. That feeling against the new regime ran high is no surprise when conditions in the factory are considered. Though 1,300 workers were again employed for the first time since 1928, the vast majority of them were now women working up to sixty-five hours a week compared with forty-eight hours earlier, with overtime paid at the flat rate. Many skilled workers were still on short time, but some were now working longer hours than before yet had suffered up to 50 per cent wage cuts. Holidays had to be requested, though in practice workers were too frightened about losing their jobs to ask for them. The few who were actually offered holidays were compelled to take them on 'Strength through Joy' trips into the border area 'to demonstrate to the distressed population how much better workers are already faring'.[32]

[30] Cf. ibid., May 1934, July 1934; DBS, 26 June 1934, pp. A8–10, B23.
[31] ASD, ES/M63 reports for May, June, and July 1934; ES/M31/2 July 1934, 25 Sept. 1934.
[32] ASD, ES/M31/30 Apr. 1934.

Another indicator of worker attitudes was the low turnout at 'factory assemblies', which amounted simply to propaganda sessions. In one Munich factory with a staff of 1,200 persons, only twenty-seven turned up at one meeting. In the Hof-bräuhaus brewery in Munich, employing 800 persons, where the Christian unions had previously been strong, the NSBO was very weak, and where despite the lack of interest in illegal work 'an adverse or passive attitude towards the regime was dominant', only seventy-two workers attended a 'factory assembly' at the beginning of May 1934. The meeting had to be cancelled, and the speaker went away accompanied by jeers.[33] A short time later attendance at the meetings (now called 'duty roll-calls') was made compulsory.[34]

The lack of interest in (or rejection of) Nazi propaganda was also reflected in the behaviour of the 400-strong staff of a wood-ware factory in Lauf near Nuremberg, which ignored the command of the Leader of the Council of Trust to march solidly behind the swastika flag for a communal viewing of a film about the Nazi cult-figure Horst Wessel in the local cinema. Only four workers turned up at the factory gate after work ready to accompany him. The rest disappeared and went home. The proposed visit to the cinema was abandoned and the attempt not repeated.[35] At another factory in the same town a collection for a wedding present for the young go-ahead Nazi managing director, who had replaced the popular Jewish former head of the firm at the 'seizure of power', totalled only twelve marks from a staff of around 700 persons.[36]

According to the official statistics, unemployment in Bavaria fell by over 50 per cent in the first two years of Nazi rule. Average unemployment in 1934 was recorded as 3 per cent of the total population.[37] There was not a little sleight of hand in this statistic. Though there had undoubtedly been some genuine revival of the economy and real job creation, much of the 'achievement' was the result of direct coercion and intimidation. Many unemployed workers were forced to

[33] ASD, ES/M63/May 1934, pp. 13–14.
[34] Ibid., June 1934, p. 12.
[35] ASD, ES/M31/19 July 1934 (wrongly dated 19 June 1934), p. 3.
[36] Ibid., p. 4.   [37] StJBB (1936), p. 185.

take up 'unemployment relief work' at wages often less than the benefit they had been receiving. They were then of course struck off the unemployment registers. Others were compelled to live away from home in primitive conditions on the motorway construction sites, performing hard labour for minimal recompense and having to maintain their families at the same time. Often, too, workers were given temporary employment or short time (sometimes only a day a week) and again deleted from the unemployment totals.[38] In some parts of Bavaria, especially the poverty-stricken porcelain and textile areas of Upper Franconia, and the Upper Palatinate and Bayerischer Wald adjacent to the Czech border, unemployment actually rose during the first phase of Nazi rule. In mid-1934 the prospects in Marktredwitz (Upper Franconia), an area with the highest unemployment ratio in Bavaria outside the large towns and cities, looked anything but rosy: 'Porcelain hopeless . . . Textiles fear the worst . . . Stone in recession . . .' Only production of coarse pottery was 'still good'.[39] The mood of the workers, according to the reports of the Employment Office, matched the situation: 'Workers apathetic; feel ignored', ran the June report in 1934. Two months later the mood among the unemployed was 'depressed . . . Skilled workers completely hopeless. Rationing of wool and cotton adds to the despair . . . All very depressed and dejected.'[40] By the end of the year there was little improvement in the mood of the unemployed: 'Great discontent, feel neglected, believe themselves to be completely repressed by the labour market.' Unemployed women were particularly angry at the low rates of unemployment benefit and poor wages. The only hope for many rested in Hitler himself: 'The Führer rouses the masses again and again; should go himself into the badly situated areas . . .' Feeling about the Party and its organizations, on the other hand, was bitter in the extreme.[41]

[38] For a critical analysis of the official statistics on unemployment and work creation, see Mason, *Sozialpolitik*, pp. 124–47.

[39] GStA, MA 106767, AA Marktredwitz, 7 Aug. 1934.

[40] GStA, MA 106765, AA Marktredwitz, 9 June 1934; MA 106767, AA Marktredwitz, 7 Aug. 1934.

[41] GStA, MA 106767, AA Marktredwitz, 10 Jan. 1935; MA 106765, AA

Sopade reports tell the same tale in even more expressive terms. In Vohenstrauß, a desperately poor area of the Upper Palatinate on the Czech border, unemployment in the summer of 1934 was higher than ever before. The only work creation there was a short stretch of road-building which had taken on forty men, of whom twenty had already been laid off again and the other twenty were soon to follow because the credit had run out. Single workers received a miserable wage of 14 RM gross a week for their toil. Not surprisingly, 'the discontent' was said to be 'in general great in the whole area' with 'cursing and criticizing' commonplace on the construction site.[42]

The situation was equally dismal in the Bayerischer Wald in the extreme east of Bavaria. Given the extreme poverty of the area, the promises of the Nazis had fallen on much fertile ground before 1933, not only among business men and the lower middle classes but also among the poorest sections of the population. Many of the predominantly wood- and glass-workers of the region had belonged to neither trade union nor political movement. The SPD had generally found response only among sections of the glass and building workers in the towns of Regen and Zwiesel and was accordingly very weak. It had, in fact, lost much of its vote to the KPD between 1930 and 1932.[43]

Though the Nazis had made efforts to fend off the worst misery through provision of food packets sent from other parts of the Reich and through Winter Aid, the feeling even among Nazi sympathizers was overwhelmingly depressed and despairing. Far too much had been expected overnight of Nazism, according to the *Sopade's* informants, and the consequence was a steep fall in enthusiasm for the new regime, not least among the long-standing Party members still without jobs who complained bitterly about '*Bonzokratie*', the corrupt rule of the Party bosses. The disappointment ran deep, but there were no signs anywhere of resistance: 'the

---

Marktredwitz, 11 Sept. 1934. According to a *Sopade* report, working-class wives in Upper Franconian towns were more vociferous than their husbands in their complaints and criticism of the regime: ASD, ES/M31/25 Sept. 1934.

[42] ASD, ES/M31/2 July 1934.
[43] Hagmann, pp. 14–15.

fear of punishment lies too deeply in the hearts of the people.' Most depressed of all was the mood among the un-employed — still some 10 per cent of the *total* population in the glass-making towns. Groups of unemployed gathered each day in front of the employment office in Zwiesel and engaged in discussions about the government which were 'not exactly suitable for the ears of the Gestapo', though the authorities left them alone. Hardly any of them would raise their arm in the 'Hitler Greeting' when Party functionaries went by. For those lucky enough to find work, conditions in the glass factories were anything but encouraging. Skilled glass blowers in one factory employing 400 men were earning less than half of what they had been paid four years earlier. The factory had been unionized (mainly the SPD-orientated Free Trade Unions), and according to the report the workers had not been shaken from their old attitude. 'The mood of the workers is very depressed. They feel the coercion but have no means of defending themselves against it. If the old freedom of organization could be restored, the free unions would immediately be there again in their old strength.' The wholly incapable NSBO leader in the factory also contributed to the 'inner resistance' to Nazism which was more prevalent than in other factories. Outwardly, however, there was no sign of this: 'the workers show up as uninterested, many of them are completely despondent and apathetic'. In another glass factory, where the 'quite catastrophic' wages were below the level of unemployment benefit, many workers had expected improvements under Nazism but nothing had happened and the 'shameful conditions' remained unaltered. The workers had gone over to the *Stahlhelm* in considerable numbers following the abolition of trade unions, but 'today commu-nist tendencies dominate in this factory', a reflection less of ideological conviction than of the 'enormous distress' accord-ing to the *Sopade*. In a third glass factory many of the equally communist-inclined work-force had joined the SA. It was said in fact that there were more communists than Nazis in the SA. The majority of workers had not even joined the Labour Front. The two Nazi organizations which were favourably received were Winter Aid and 'Strength through Joy'. However, the poverty of the inhabitants precluded the vast majority from affording even the cheap fares offered by the 'Strength through Joy' trips and the main beneficiaries were allegedly the business men of Zwiesel.[44] Some of the worst conditions and greatest discontent were to be found on building construction sites, where those on work-creation schemes were forced to take on arduous jobs road-digging for wages which, as the authorities themselves recognized, did not cover the cost of food and clothing. The mood among such workers was imaginably bitter.[45] Many unemployed had to be coerced into taking work far from home. They were often, as the employment office in Weißenburg (Middle Franconia) commented, only ready 'with a heavy heart' to take on such work and 'many cases of resistance had to be broken'.[46] Some refused outright to go. In one case, in Neu-Ulm (Swabia), the work offered was rejected collectively by 120 men because the question of the necessary supplement for working away from home had not been agreed.[47] The penalty for obstinate refusal was, however, invariably removal from any unemployment benefit whatsoever and in recalcitrant cases a spell of 'education of the work-shy' in Dachau.[48]

Some 13,000 unemployed had by 1934 been put to work on motorway construction sites in Bavaria.[49] Conditions here were deplorable. Workers, uprooted from family, friends, and home environment, were housed in primitive barracks, earned miserable wages for back-breaking work, and if they

[44] Based on an eight-page report in ASD, ES/M64/Oct. 1934. For a graphic internal description of the appalling conditions in the poverty-belt of Lower Bavaria and the Upper Palatinate, see GStA, MA 106672, RPvNB/OP, 8 July 1935. For bitterness among the unemployed towards the regime, cf. DBS, 26 June 1934, pp. A10–11 for various parts of Germany, and 6 Nov. 1934, p. A6 for northern Bavaria.
[45] Cf. e.g., from the reports of the Bavarian employment offices, GStA, MA 106767, AA Bayreuth, AA Regensburg, AA Ingolstadt, AA Pfarrkirchen, AA Weiden, AA Schwandorf, all 9 Aug. 1934; AA Weilheim, 8 Aug. 1934; AA Traunstein, 7 Aug. 1934, 8 Sept. 1934. Cf. also, MA 106682, RPvS, 17 Apr. 1934. For 'Notstandsarbeiter' in general, see Mason, Sozialpolitik, pp. 127–31.
[46] GStA, MA 106767, AA Weißenburg i.B., 11 Sept. 1934.
[47] Ibid., AA Neu-Ulm, 9 Aug. 1934.
[48] Cf. e.g., ASD, ES/M32/14 Jan. 1935, pp. 8–9.
[49] StJBB (1936), p. 184. The figure rose to 22,000 in 1935 and dropped slightly to 19–20,000 in 1936.

were lucky to live near enough could manage to get home for Saturday evening and Sunday. Hostility towards Nazism was recognized by the authorities as being at its most acute among the Autobahn-workers, among whom there was undoubtedly an admixture of socialists and communists who had sometimes been dismissed from skilled jobs and forced as 'punishment' into navvying. Bitter feelings were expressed about the wages paid, the 'Hitler Greeting' was a rarity, trucks were daubed with anti-Nazi slogans, condemnation of the regime was open, and according to numerous reports the prevalent communist agitation found no difficulty in exploiting the anger and disaffection of the work-force.[50] On one site near Münchberg in Upper Franconia a group of thirty workers, allegedly provoked by 'communist elements', downed tools on a pay-day in November 1934 as a protest at not being given the extra mark a day due to workers travelling to the site each day. When threatened with Dachau the workers joined together in a forceful rendering of the Internationale. The 'rebellious workers' were eventually shipped by lorry to prison in Bayreuth, from where twenty were dispatched to Dachau as 'work-shy'.[51] This incident seems to have prompted the further dismissal of 121 workers, of whom the eighty who came from Nuremberg and Fürth refused to leave unless they were paid for the journey home. Eventually, the District Office undertook to pay the travel costs in order to prevent any further disturbance.[52]

A Munich police report in spring 1935 provides a striking picture of the conditions and political attitudes of motorway workers who met up in the beer-halls of the city on Saturday evenings when they returned home for the weekend. There was a lot of talk of politics.

These work-places are described quite frankly as hot-beds of communism . . . For the most part the workers complain about insufficient wages. They do not satisfy the needs of food, clothing, and accommodation because in the rough areas where the sites are placed extra

[50] Cf. GStA, MA 106767, AA Rosenheim, 8 Aug. 1934, 11 Sept. 1934, 10 Jan. 1935; AA Holzkirchen, 9 Aug. 1934; MA 106691, RPvOB, LB, 7 Dec. 1934.
[51] GStA, MA 106767, AA Nürnberg, 10 Jan. 1935, ASD, ES/M32/Jan. 1935, pp. 8–9.
[52] GStA, MA 106677, RPvOF/MF, 9 Jan. 1935.

expenditure is needed during 'most of the year and high prices are charged in the communal boarding-houses and canteens. The people also complain about poor treatment. No consideration is shown for their needs and there is no place where complaints or grievances can be aired. In answer to the question as to whether there is an attempt from any side to stir up the discontent on the building sites, workers from the site near Weyarn explained only a short time ago that this was not the case. Nor was it necessary, for the discontent derives from the insufficient wages, the unfavourable living conditions, and the poor treatment. Investigations have established that the same poor mood arising from the same mentality is to be encountered among most workers on the other construction sites.[53]

The discontent among workers in 1934, real though it was, remained for the most part just below the surface. The most vociferous criticism had by all accounts come from the peasantry and the *Mittelstand*. During 1935 and 1936, however, the picture changed. An increasingly critical shortage of key foodstuffs — butter, fats, eggs, and meat — was compounded by farmers holding back their produce in the hope of selling at inflated prices. The steep rise in food prices — one report spoke of a 33 per cent rise in the price of meat and 25 per cent in the price of white bread in some areas since 1933 while wages had remained stable or had even fallen because of short time[54] — meant a substantial drop in real wages and severe hardship for industrial workers and their families. As is plain both from internal reports and from *Sopade* material, this was reflected in unmistakable signs of growing unrest accompanied by increased militancy among workers, with the discontent reaching a peak of intensity between autumn 1935 and the end of the following year.

Serious unrest among the working class in particular — the section of the population towards which the Nazi leadership felt most sensitive — was registered with concern by the authorities in all regions. They recorded an increase in criticism of the State and Party leadership and new signs of life among opposition groups whose verbal agitation was

[53] GStA, MA 106685, Pd München, 5 May 1935.
[54] GStA, MA 106682, RPvS, 7 Sept. 1935. For the relationship between wages and living costs between 1933 and 1936, cf. Mason, *Arbeiterklasse*, pp. 60-77.

falling on ever more fertile ground in many factories.[55] The sharp increase in voiced hostility to the regime was mirrored in a rise approaching 50 per cent in the cases of the Munich 'Special Court' in 1936. The majority of those indicted were said by the justice authorities to be no longer Marxists as such, but rather people (largely workers) who had previously been little concerned with active politics.[56] The courts were clear that they would have had a much higher number of cases to deal with had not worker solidarity prevented 'for reasons of misunderstood cameraderie and misplaced sympathy with the family of the person concerned' many instances of 'anti-State behaviour' not being denounced.[57] Bitter criticism was expressed of working conditions, of the Labour Front and the Nazi Party, of the lack of social justice in the contrast between the miserable wages of the workers and the fat salaries and dividends of the company bosses, and of the waste of money on Nazi representative buildings when the housing shortage was so acute and living standards falling.[58] In the depressed textile factories of Augsburg the 'Hitler Greeting' as good as disappeared and the NSDAP came under sharp attack for failing to hold to its promise of abolishing high salaries.[59] Winter Aid was seen

[55] StAN, Pol.-Dir. Nürnberg-Fürth 431, BPP, 1 Nov. 1935, pp. 1, 14–15; GStA, MA 106677, RPvOF/MF, 8 Aug. 1935, 9 Sept. 1935, 10 Oct. 1935; MA 106670, RPvOB, 9 Oct. 1935; MA 106672, RPvNB/OP, 9 Aug. 1935. Following the change in strategy for underground work devised at the VIIth Congress of the Comintern and the Brussels Conference of the KPD in 1935, the illegal KPD in Germany made a deliberate attempt to turn its attention to stirring up unrest in factories and within Nazi organizations (the 'Trojan Horse' tactic). The relationship between KPD agitation, in which stress was laid upon verbal propaganda on the shop-floor, and the growth of serious industrial unrest in 1935–6 has not yet been thoroughly analysed. For the change in KPD strategy in 1935, see *Gesch. d. dt. Arbeiterbewegung*, x, p. 126 K. Mammach, *Die deutsche antifaschistische Widerstandsbewegung 1933–1939*, Berlin, 1974, pp. 124–5.

[56] StAM, OLG 127, OLGP München, 4 Jan 1936, 30 Dec. 1936.

[57] Ibid., 4 Nov. 1936.

[58] E.g., GStA, MA 106697, Pd Augsburg, LB, 1 Oct. 1934; MA 106686, Pd Augsburg, repts. for Jan., Apr., May, June, July, Aug., Sept. 1936. GStA, MA 106687, BPP, 1 Feb., 1 Mar. 1936; MA 106688, BPP, 1 Aug. 1936. Cf. also, *Bayern I*, p. 255.

[59] StAN, Pol.-Dir. Nürnberg-Fürth 431, BPP, 1 Jan. 1936, p. 25; GStA, MA 106687, BPP, 1. 2. 36, p. 3; MA 106686, Pd Augsburg, 1 July 1935; and cf. Hetzer, pp. 132–5.

as no more than a sop: workers said they wanted a decent wage, not alms, and strongly criticized its distribution by the Nazi welfare institution, the NSV.[60] And the luxury of the 'well-to-do', especially of the 'big-shots' (*Bonzen*) in the Nazi Party and the Labour Front, was a constant reminder to the workers of the emptiness of the concept of the classless 'national community'.[61] The Augsburg police noted in summer 1936 'rising unrest' among the city's textile workers, whose 'enthusiasm for State and Party' was 'not great' and whose 'bitter comments' placed the blame for their misery not on raw material shortages but on rationalization measures of the bosses.[62] Such a mood was not confined to the particularly hard-hit textile workers, afflicted with renewed short-time. The climate was just as hostile towards the Nazi State among the workers of Augsburg's more prosperous armaments factories.[63]

Given the level of intimidation, any expression of dissent was bound to be the exception not the rule. However, there is no doubt that the incidence of militancy increased in 1935-6. Some reports pointed to a difference between the situation in southern Bavaria, where the Nazis had on the whole failed to establish a strong position, and northern Bavaria, a region of far greater Nazi penetration.[64] Even within northern Bavaria there were important differences. It was claimed that both the material well-being of workers and the way they were treated tended to be better in Upper Franconia than in the Upper Palatinate, though both formed part of the same *Gau*, the Bavarian Ostmark.[65] Whatever these differences, the *Sopade* informants were anxious to stress that anti-Nazi feeling was prevalent in all areas, even

[60] GStA, MA 106682, RPvS, 7 Feb. 1936; MA 106687, BPP, 1 Mar. 1936; MA 106688, BPP, 1 Aug. 1936; StAA, BA Amberg 2398, GS Hirschau, 20 June 1935, 23 June 1936; GS Schnaittenbach, 22 June 1935.
[61] GStA, MA 106688, BPP, 1 Aug. 1936, p. 2.
[62] GStA, MA 106686, PdAugsburg, rept. for July 1936, p. 6; rept. for Aug. 1936, p. 4.
[63] Ibid., rept. for June 1936, pp. 8-9, where in fact it was claimed that the mood among Augsburg's metal workers was worse than among textile employees, despite the far higher pay. Cf. also Hetzer, pp. 106-30.
[64] ASD, ES/M32/25 Mar. 1935.
[65] Ibid., 25 May 1935.

where it could not be openly expressed. One District Officer in the Upper Palatinate was prepared to hazard a guess that 50 per cent of the workers in his district were inwardly still opponents of Nazism, and a less cautious estimate by a *Sopade* reporter suggested that 80 per cent of metal-workers in the Amberg area would reject the regime given the chance.[66] An indication that below the surface little in attitudes had changed was the unsatisfactory result for the Nazis of the 1935 'Council of Trust' election in the iron-foundry Maxhütte in Burglengenfeld (Upper Palatinate), where a third of the 1,460 workers were allegedly still KPD supporters. In the Nuremberg Triumph Works more than a third of the votes cast were invalid; in a Bayreuth textile factory with 1,100 employees only 600 workers voted and as many as 450 ballot-papers were spoilt; in a small Munich building firm with thirty-six workers, twenty-one votes were cast for an ex-communist who was not allowed to stand as a candidate (and was a fortnight later dismissed).[67] Many spoilt ballot-papers were also handed in in the porcelain and glass factories of Weiden (Upper Palatinate) — in terms of the miserable wages, deplorable conditions, and brutal treatment of workers among the worst industrial districts of Bavaria. Strength of feeling here led to boycotts of the 1935 May Day celebrations together with Hitler's speech. And the burial of a former porcelain-worker, an ex-SPD member who had died in Dachau, was turned into a 'silent protest demonstration' as turners from his factory ignored the management's order not to attend, simply downing tools and joining the entire former SPD membership of the town council and an extraordinarily large gathering at the graveside. Big bouquets of red roses were laid on the grave.[68] In Upper Franconia, women textile workers in Hof refused to buy the May Day badges (on more or less compulsory sale in the factory) as a protest at the bad treatment accorded to a fellow worker.[69] At the Rosenthal factory in Selb, formerly a communist

[66] Ibid., 25 Mar. 1935; GStA, MA 106672, RPvNB/OP, 7 June 1935.
[67] GStA, MA 106672, RPvNB/OP, 7 May 1935; DBS, 12 June 1935, p. A19; cf. Hetzer, pp. 112, 133 for the elections in Augsburg factories, and Mason, *Sozialpolitik*, pp. 192, 206 for the results in Germany as a whole 1934 and 1935.
[68] ASD, ES/M32/28 May 1935.   [69] Ibid., 28 May 1935.

stronghold, pottery-firers refused to work when a special bonus for working in the extreme heat was halved, though they had to return when a compromise left the reduction at 25 per cent.[70] Attendance at the Nazi celebrations of the anniversary of the Hitler Putsch in November 1935 met with a poor response in this area, despite intense pressure from local Party leaders. The inability of the Nazis to break through in Selb and surrounding areas led to a stepping up of the repression against 'the Marxists' and their followers in the town, where intimidation reached a massive scale. The *Sopade*'s informant from Selb summed up: 'No trace of enthusiasm, then, so threats with personal recrimination.'[71]

In the southern parts of Bavaria there were equally vivid indications of extreme discontent. Some *Sopade* reports even hinted that the distress and anger were tending to overcome fear. The attitude of workers in the poverty-belt of southeastern Bavaria in particular was developing into open hatred. In one of the glass factories in the Bayerischer Wald, whose appalling conditions were described earlier, there was even a three-day strike in the summer of 1935, an event perhaps unique in its duration in the Third Reich. The 100–120 workers in the Crystal Glass factory at Theresiental had for generations 'been used to hunger and misery', but old workers claimed that they had never known such times before. Wages were abysmal, and despite Nazi promises, which had attracted some at the start, things had got only worse. At the beginning of July the workers had had enough. They called in the workers' representative, declared that they were going on strike, and – including the seventeen SA men in the factory – left the works. A delegation was told by the 'Factory Leader' that a wage rise was out of the question: the firm's financial position would not stand it. The Labour Front District Leader from Regen was called in to address a works meeting. He told the workers that they had committed a serious offence against the State and that the whole work-force would be sent to Dachau if they did not start work again immediately, that strikes were abolished by law and anyone acting against this must take the consequences. Amid

[70] Ibid., 18 Nov. 1935.
[71] Ibid., 18 Nov. 1935.

the disturbance which followed, one apprentice, cheered by the other workers, shouted out that he had no fear from such a threat: 'they have got to give us water and bread in Dachau, and we haven't more than that at home.' The DAF representative and Factory Leader gave the work-force the assurance that they would do everything possible to achieve a wage rise or at least financial relief for the worst-afflicted families. At this the workers returned to the factory. No recriminations followed their defeat, but 'the bitterness among the workers' was 'undiminished'.[72]

An equally extraordinary demonstration of worker feeling took place in the summer of 1936 in an Upper Bavarian cotton-spinning factory in Kolbermoor, near Bad Aibling, where the entire work-force took part in a mass protest about conditions in the factory.[73] Relations of workers and management (said in the *Sopade* account not to be Nazi) had allegedly been good. A number of overseers and foremen, however, were fanatical Nazis and there had been much friction on the shop-floor between them and the workers. One foreman, in particular, exploited his authority in a vicious way, causing numerous disputes which had always been calmed down by the management, especially because of his dogged persecution of one long-standing worker in the factory — the accounts vary as to whether he had worked there for fifteen or twenty-eight years. In one heated exchange the worker threatened to beat up his tormentor if the bullying did not stop. The foreman reported this to the management and the worker — a man with a wife and three children — was dismissed on the spot, went out into the woods, and hanged himself. A works meeting was hastily called — according to the *Sopade* report by the angry workers, according to the

[72] ASD, ES/M64/July 1935. Cf. also DBS, 3 Aug. 1935, pp. A25-6. An earlier reference to the strike, in DBS, 12 June 1935, p. A24, mistakenly placed it in Pirmasens (Palatinate).

[73] The following account is based upon: DBS, 12 Jan. 1937, p. A26; GStA, MA 106670, RPvOB, 9 Sept. 1936; StAM, LRA 47140, BA Bad Aibling, 5 Sept. 1936. Apart from the discrepancies noted, the descriptions basically accord. The version recorded in the KPD's *Deutschland-Informationen* for the end of June 1937, p. 62 (located in the WL) appears to be based on the *Sopade* account, though places the incident, presumably for purposes of camouflage, in northern Bavaria.

internal reports by the factory management — in order to
smooth the matter over. The assembly was riotous. The
managing director was assaulted, the foreman at the root
of the trouble had to flee the hall for his own safety under
cries of 'murderer' and the staff who came to his assistance
were attacked by the workers. The local Party leader who
had come to address the meeting could not make himself
heard. The police were called, but on orders of the Party
District Leadership did not intervene, except to take the
threatened foreman into 'protective custody' for his own
personal safety.

Though the case seems on the surface to have been a
result of personal frictions, escalating suddenly and spontaneously into a major confrontation, there were deeper-
lying causes of unrest in the factory, as the reports of the
Bavarian authorities make clear. The complaints of the
workers, according to the account of the Government President of Upper Bavaria, stemmed from the drastic rationalization in the factory which had brought mass redundancies,
the 'rigorous treatment' of the workers by the young foremen, and deficient contact between management and work-
force.[74] After the incident, the management — encouraged
by the Trustee of Labour, the National Socialist District
Leadership, and the District Officer of Bad Aibling — sought
to make up for lost time in restoring a 'relationship of trust'
between workers and management. They staged a large-scale
outing, taking the entire staff of the factory in thirty buses
for a day in the country which passed off 'in best harmony'.
Beneath the surface, however, the rancour continued. Anonymous letters to the management signed by 'the workers of
the cotton-factory' threatened violence against one of the
under-foremen and demanded his dismissal. The workers
criticized the meeting held by the Trustee of Labour, called
in to encourage a new start to industrial relations, as simply
'a National Socialist rally', and the following month eight
workers were arrested for singing the Internationale.[75] In

[74] GStA, MA 106670, RPvOB, 9 Sept. 1936, pp. 5–6; StAM, LRA 47140, BA
Bad Aibling, 5 Sept. 1936.
[75] GStA, MA 106670, RPvOB, 9 Sept. 1936, pp. 5–6; StAM, LRA 47140,
BA Bad Aibling, 3 Oct. 1936, 4 Nov. 1936; LRA 47138, BA Bad Aibling to BPP,
10 Sept. 1936.

the District Officer's opinion, the workers had gained confidence through their successful demonstration, which they had thought possibly only in times gone by.[76] The mood spread to other nearby factories as word of the Kolbermoor drama went around. In neighbouring Bruckmühl the workers of the blanket factory were said to have hinted 'that they too have a work-force of 600 men, which would be worth considering, and should it come to similar things there they would know what they had to do'.[77]

The spectacular events at Theresiental and Kolbermoor were obviously exceptional. And yet they highlight aspects of industrial unrest which were never far from the surface of the Nazi State even if, in the circumstances, they seldom found open expression. They are indicators, too, of the trend towards greater unrest and militancy in 1935-6 which is strongly suggested both by the Nazi internal reports and by those of the *Sopade* Border Secretaries. Ministers of the Reich Government noted in October 1936 that attempted strikes for wage rises were no longer a rarity, and an incomplete tabulation of strikes listed 192 stoppages in Germany between February 1936 and July 1937.[78] In a circular of October 1936 the Gestapo warned the State authorities of the increase in work-stoppages and strikes, caused in the first instance by labour relations but in essence deriving from 'purely political motives'.[79] This was certainly an exaggeration, though there is no reason to doubt the assessment of the Government President of Swabia in autumn 1936, based on the 'unanimous reports' of the District authorities, that three-and-a-half years of Nazi rule had not produced the hoped-for results and that among workers there was 'growing ill-feeling towards Government and Party'.[80]

Given the nature of the evidence, it is difficult to be specific

[76] StAM, LRA 47140, BA Bad Aibling, 3 Oct. 1936.
[77] Ibid., 5 Sept. 1936.
[78] Mason, 'Workers' Opposition', p. 124. Details of a great number of strikes, if mainly concerning small numbers of workers and of short duration, are contained in a 381-folio file of the *Gestapa* in the Institut für Marxismus-Leninismus/Zentrales Parteiarchiv (Berlin-DDR), St.3/463. The Kolbermoor incident just dealt with is on fol. 248-9.
[79] StAW, Sammlung Schumacher 17, Gestapo-Rundschreiben, 15 Oct. 1936.
[80] GStA, MA 106682, RPvS, 9 Oct. 1936.

about patterns of disaffection. In the first years of the dictatorship antagonism towards the regime appears to have been especially strong among the remaining unemployed, those drafted in for a pittance to the relief schemes, and workers on the motorways and other building sites — noted trouble spots for the authorities. Regionally, the most extreme expressions of dissent seem to have come from the poverty-belt of eastern Bavaria. In this period it seems the tendency to dissent was greatest where conditions were worst, and where workers' defiance arose from abject misery and a profound sense of anger and despair. Politically nonconformist behaviour apparently occurred at this date among radicalized but 'unschooled' workers more frequently than among more 'educated' workers used to subjecting themselves to party or union discipline. By 1936 there are signs that this was changing, that militancy was spreading to the industrial centres and the better-off sections of the working class in the armaments industries, and becoming more and more a matter of rational exploitation of a changing labour market rather than a futile explosion of bitter frustration. Attitudes varied considerably, however, not only among workers in different industries and regions but also among different groups within the same factory. The examples chosen from *Sopade* reports to conclude this section demonstrate some of these variations, though the material allows little sophistication in terms, for example, of skilled–unskilled divisions or size and composition of factories.

A report from the big Krauss-Maffei metalworks in Munich, which was manufacturing components for tanks, claimed to detect, alongside the generally 'fairly unpolitical', indifferent attitude in the works, specific communist, socialist, Nazi, and Catholic sectors of opinion in the work-force. Most of the so-called communists, it was asserted, had little understanding of communism, but were 'simply radicalized' in an anti-Nazi sense and saw communism as the only conceivable successor to Nazism. They had little interest in illegal work, and in fact since communist cells had already been broken three times by the Gestapo agitation had died away and there was no organizational hard core of committed members. The solidarity among the socialist-inclined grouping was said to be greater. Though in view of the intense surveillance underground activity was out of the question, political friendships forged in the network of SPD clubs and in the unions remained intact: these workers 'were all mates' and stuck together. They had 'no ready recipe in their pocket as the communists frequently had, and as a result they were more cautious and more critical.' The Nazis, probably because of their relative weakness in the factory, had lost much of their earlier animosity towards the Marxist-inclined workers. They were often the butt of jokes, but had stopped denouncing their opponents for criticizing the regime and had become 'quite friendly' so that one knew where one was with them. The fourth group, the Catholics, scarcely warranted consideration: they were 'decent and often very good comrades, but from them too nothing can be expected.' Social conditions in the factory had changed little since Hitler's takeover of power, and wages had remained stable. But the workers decried their lack of rights, held the DAF in contempt, and regarded 'Strength through Joy' as 'the only really good innovation' in the Third Reich.[81]

A far lower level of politicization and hostility towards the regime prevailed among the largely female work-force of a large sportswear factory in Upper Bavaria which was fully taken up in manufacturing clothing for the army. Wages here were satisfactory, stated the *Sopade* report. A seamstress earned on average 20–26 RM a week, more than an Autobahn worker or day-labourer on the railway, and piece-work rates could bring total earnings to 40 RM a week. Because of the army orders there was no longer mass dismissal of workers or reduction to short time during the winter months. The women workers had never been so well off. Opinion in the factory was favourable towards the regime. There was little discussion of politics and a lack of interest in the DAF, but the basic attitude of all the workers amounted to praise for the regime's work creation: 'Since Hitler has been there we've always had our work. Nobody

---

[81] ASD, ES/M64/Sept. 1935, pp. 7–9. Cf. GStA, MA 106670, RPvOB, 9 Oct. 1935 for the repeated daubing of lavatory walls in the Kraus-Maffei works with anti-Nazi slogans, including a swastika daubed in human excrement and a drawing of Hitler's head next to a gallows.

can dispute the fact that he has created work.' Such a remark ended all discussion. There was no critical assessment of what lay behind the work creation: 'What is shown in the factory is the purest indifference.'[82]

Confusion and partial inroads of Nazi propaganda were also reflected in the answers given by a coalminer's wife in summer 1937 to a series of thirty-two questions, laid out in the form of a questionnaire, put to her by *Sopade* informants. Neither the miner himself — an Austrian who had lived all his life in Germany — nor his wife had been interested in party politics. The miner had been a member of the Free Trade Unions; his wife was 'the type of orderly housewife taken up in her concern for husband and child'. She was 'absolutely honest, not a Nazi, but confused and led astray through the propaganda. No clear thought about aim and resistance could be found in her. Probably a large proportion of working-class wives think as she does.' Apart from the distribution of an underground pamphlet two years earlier and the arrest on one occasion of two workers from her street for comments about Hitler, she knew nothing of illegal activity. Though the miners complained much about wages, shortage of butter, and other economic deprivations, they were afraid to go any further and there was no sign of any 'spirit of resistance'. In fact, the wives were more open in their criticism than the workers themselves when they were short of butter or other necessities, 'but things always work out again' and in any case nothing could be done about it. Her own complaints were largely confined to rising prices and shortages of fats. The political interest of the workers, she said, was low. Few newspapers were read; occasionally one spoke about the situation with friends and heard the radio news, but her husband said that no one knew where they were any longer. All she knew of the Spanish Civil War was that the Bolsheviks were causing havoc and were responsible for atrocities such as the rape of children. Asked about workers' attitudes towards Russia, she said that things must be even worse there than in Germany: 'at first we didn't really believe that things are so bad there, but now we all know it.' On the prospects of war, she thought

[82] ASD, ES/M64/Sept. 1936, pp. 3–4.

that if Russia left Germany alone there was no need for hostilities. Workers did not want a war, 'but Russia and Czechoslovakia are agitating for a war and treat the Germans like slaves. Germany cannot take that lying down in the long run. Hitler has no interest in a war. Our youth is still too little trained militarily. But when that has happened nobody will be able to attack Germany again.' Questioned about the exemption of Hitler from criticism, she mirrored the views of large sections of the population: 'Hitler means well, but those behind him commit many misdeeds. And he can't be responsible for everything. He knows what he wants and he has always succeeded up to now. At least he's better than the old parties, which never achieved anything and couldn't even create work.' The last question dealt with her attitude towards emigrants. She replied that they were 'nothing but Jews' who could not stay in Germany any longer — and it was better that they went.[83]

The wide variation in political attitudes among the industrial working class was fully recognized by the *Sopade* leadership. In April 1937 the *Deutschland-Berichte* summarized at length the replies of five Bavarian workers of quite different background, family circumstances, age, and occupation to questions about their attitude towards the regime, their assessment of Bolshevism, their opinion on the Labour Front, wage policy, and the class struggle, and their prognosis of the future development of Germany's policies.[84] The replies, summarized in Table XII, revealed a wide spectrum of opinion on these subjects — from reverence for Hitler, swallowing Nazi propaganda on Bolshevism and the Jews, and recognition of the social achievements of the regime to fully-fledged rejection of Nazism in its entirety (from two of the five who had earlier had political functions in the SPD and Free Trade Unions).

The *Sopade* leadership summed up its impressions on the political attitude of the working class towards Nazism in April 1937 as follows:

[83] ASD, ES/M66/Aug. 1937, pp. 24–9. Cf. also ES/M65/Feb. 1937, pp. 1–3 for another illustration of workers' ideological confusion.
[84] DBS, 12 Apr. 1937, pp. A21-6.

One must as ever distinguish between the politically educated minority, which before the upheaval belonged to the trade unions and the party, and which is for the most part still hostile towards the regime and will probably never be won for the regime, and the attitude of the unpolitical mass, which uncritically and without thought goes along with it and continually gives rise to the view that the regime can number its greatest support particularly in the working class. Naturally, attitudes are widely differentiated also within both these groups. Although we constantly press it upon our reporters as a duty to observe and describe the development with as much objectivity as possible, the influence of the subjective attitude of the individual reporter . . . can never quite be excluded.[85]

The *Sopade* did not rate the political significance of worker discontent very highly during the first years of the dictatorship, lived in the shadow of unprecedented repression and continued mass unemployment.[86] But at least with regard to the labour market the climate had altered drastically. We must now briefly turn our attention to worker opinion during the last peacetime years, in the context of a massive labour shortage produced by the overheated armaments economy.

(ii) Full Employment and Labour Shortage

Despite Germany's economic recovery and the rapidly falling unemployment figures, workers had been compelled between 1933 and 1936 to accept a significant decline in real wages as a result of forced wage reductions, increased deductions from the pay packet, higher rents because of the growing housing shortage in the major conurbations, and rising food prices. The brutal reordering of industrial relations brought a deterioration in living standards and conditions of work which the superficial glitter of the 'Strength through Joy' and 'Beauty of Labour' organizations did not hide from most workers, whatever the propaganda appeal for the outside world. Clearly, in those branches of industry already benefiting from rearmament expenditure, wages and conditions

---

[85] Ibid., p. A21.
[86] For pessimistic assessments of the situation and acceptance of partial, damaging breakthroughs by Nazi propaganda, cf. e.g., DBS, 16 Oct. 1935, pp. A1–2; ASD, ES/M32/18 Nov. 1935; ES/M64/Sept. 1935, Dec. 1935, Mar. 1936.

	Worker 1	Worker 2	Worker 3	Worker 4	Worker 5
Personal details:	Building worker, single, aged 30, lives in parental home, unemployed 1932–5, Autobahn worker 1935–, wage 22 RM a week.	Brewery worker, married, five children, 20 years in same firm.	Salesgirl in grocer's shop, aged 20, lives in parental home, engaged to SA man, earns 70 RM a month.	Forty-year old foreman, married, no children, earns 200 RM a month.	Joiner, aged 50, married, three grown-up children.
Political background:	Trade Union, Socialist Youth, father was SPD member.	Trade Union, SPD functionary.	Petty functionary in Central Association of White-Collar Employees.	Works Councillor of Free Trade Unions. Politically knowledgeable though never active.	Formerly in Catholic Trade Union.
(a) attitude towards regime	Negative. Recognizes Hitler has created jobs, but workers no better off. Condemns corruption of regime. Still retains some idea of socialist aims.	Dictatorship of *Bonzen* and capitalists. Incompetents have high posts in State and DAF and live from sweat of people. Absolute hostility to regime. Contemptuous of Hitler.	Sees in system mainly personality of Hitler, whom she reveres as Führer and a super-man (*Übermensch*). No interest in political affairs. Of her earlier activity, merely says things were different then and these are new times.	Fascism's demise inbuilt: inability to overcome differences between capital and labour. Regime is state capitalism with natural tendency to imperialist war. Points to *Bonzokratie*, rigidifying of administrative apparatus, sterility of leadership – all symptoms of decay.	At first saw Hitler as necessary to defeat Bolshevism, though could not stand gutter politics of Party. Has completely altered his view. NSDAP ruthless repressive machine of total State, not even stopping at Church. Impossibility of combating regime makes him seek consolation in Church (which as an organization he criticizes).
(b) assessment of Bolshevism	Anti-Bolshevik and anti-Semitic propaganda has made him uncertain, but not convinced that	Little time for Russian Bolshevism. Opposed in principle to all forms of repression. But not taken in by NS anti-	Fear more than hatred. Believes propaganda, which strengthens rejection of Bolshevism. Hitler will see that	Bolshevism is horror symbol, currently a prop of regime, but will come to be recognized as empty threat. No direct danger.	Bolshevism mainly rejected as Godless movement. Sees parallel in Nazism, which has weak-

	Russia is hostile. Convinced that Bolshevism must follow Hitler in Germany. Has hardly come across illegal communist resistance.	Bolshevism propaganda since he disbelieves everything the regime says.	Bolshevism never comes to power. Absolutely anti-Semitic: Jews embodiment of evil.	if regime collapses, though 'indifferent mass' see it as only successor to regime.	ened his earlier hostility to Bolshevism.
(c) opinion on DAF, wage policy, class struggle	DAF not trade union, merely health insurance scheme. Best part of it is KdF, but no more than a sop. Hardly any Nazis among workmates. Did not believe in *Volksgemeinschaft*. Just new *Bonzen* in addition to old rich.	Sharpest criticism. Unfavourable comparisons with trade unions. Corruption of DAF functionaries. Nazis will never win over workers. Declines even low office in DAF.	DAF a legitimate representative body of workers and employees. KdF great achievement of Third Reich. Saves every year for KdF holiday trip and has already made a trip to Norwegian fjords.	DAF basis of flourishing corruption of *Bonzentum*. Workers reject it. Hardly any see it as representing their interests. Wage policy shows true face of regime and guaranteed to further class struggle in factories. Present indifference in factories will not be sustained indefinitely. Failure of NS ideology, pseudo-socialism now obvious in all factories. Contradictions between Fascism and revolutionary class movement will deepen with time.	Bothers neither with KdF nor anything else in factory. Pays Winter Aid contributions and looks for his pleasure and satisfaction in his allotment.
(d) view of future	No clear conception. Believes war inevitable and that Hitler will lose it. Does not contemplate doing anything active against Nazism. Absolutely passive. Let things take their course.	Sees fall of Hitler only through outside forces: war. Old parties will never return: have made too many mistakes. New leaders to emerge from working class, but what it will be like unclear to him. Sees nothing of illegal underground and thinks it has little point. Matter of waiting for things to pass.	No worries. All the talk of war bothers her a bit, but trusts that Hitler will prevent downfall of Germany.	Too convenient to expect overthrow of Fascism from outside forces in war. German people must develop forces from within from united revolutionary class movement to create a new order.	Convinced that war will come – nobody knows when, and better not to think about it. The more mankind turns away from God, the greater the misfortune it will bring upon itself.

Source: DBS, 12 Apr. 1937, pp. A21-6.

were generally higher than average and the opportunity of regular work without lay-offs and short time meant that the relatively well-paid workers in these industries sometimes showed approval of the regime's policies. However, increased earnings in this period were for the most part solely the result of longer hours worked.

The elimination of all but residual unemployment by the summer of 1936, coupled with the sharp intensification of the armaments build-up which followed the announcement of the Four Year Plan in September that year, gradually brought about a new situation in industrial relations.[87] In view of the rapidly increasing labour shortage in industry, initially of skilled labour and especially in the armaments industries but widening to a general acute labour shortage crisis by 1939, workers were frequently able even without the help of trade unions to exploit their position of relative strength and bargain for higher wages. The result was a growth of worker solidarity and industrial militancy on the one hand and intensified regimentation and surveillance by the regime on the other hand, as it sought to step up production in an increasingly taut industrial climate. It amounted to a serious intensification of industrial conflict. Unlike the conditions of 1935-6, when the manifestations of worker unrest had derived largely from weakness and despair, the signs are that many workers in the 1937-9 period were ready to take advantage of their improved economic bargaining power and to act, individually or collectively, from a position of relative strength. Even so, there can be little doubt that with their organizations behind them workers would have gained higher wage rises than was possible in the police State of the Third Reich. In fact, the regime was remarkably successful in holding down wages in conditions favouring a wages explosion, though the official statistics hardly tell the full story.[88]

Most workers were by 1939 earning more than they had done since the onset of the Depression. But this was still in great measure a result of longer working hours than of higher

[87] Cf. in general, Mason, *Sozialpolitik*, pp. 208-37.
[88] Ibid., pp. 229-30. For wage statistics, cf. *Docs. on Nazism*, p. 454.

rates of pay.[89] During the last peacetime years German workers were made to work harder than ever before and were subjected to such intense stress and a crippling work-tempo that damaging psychological and physical effects were unmistakable, and, as the authorities fully recognized, found reflection in a rising toll of sickness, indiscipline, and absenteeism among workers and a serious threat to Germany's industrial productive capacity (with a significant drop in production already registered in mining).[90]

Analysis of the impact of this changing industrial climate on the working class in Bavaria is made more difficult by the fact that the Border Secretaries of the *Sopade* for north and south Bavaria, stationed in the Sudetenland, were compelled by the growing tension in central Europe to terminate their activities early in 1938. In April that year the *Sopade* had to move its headquarters from Prague to Paris, and, although its perceptive and informative *Deutschland-Berichte* continued to be published, the material arriving from Bavaria was reduced to a trickle. Even so, there is sufficient evidence to allow a sketch of the political attitudes and behaviour of Bavarian workers in the years before the war. Comparison with both *Sopade* and internal reports from other parts of Germany suggests that the conditions and responses of Bavarian workers mirrored in essence those of workers elsewhere in the Reich.

When due consideration has been given to other socio-economic issues which greatly influenced working-class opinion in the years before the war — prominent among them the increasingly appalling housing shortage in many industrial towns[91] — worker attitudes hinged above all on the wages issue. Whereas work stoppages had earlier been (usually unsuccessful) attempts to prevent wage reductions or a further

---

[89] Mason, *Sozialpolitik*, p. 229.

[90] Ibid., pp. 217, 312–22; Mason, 'Workers' Opposition', pp. 127–30.

[91] The shortfall of housing in Augsburg in 1938–9 was estimated at approximately 20 per cent. In October 1938, 8,300 persons were searching for accommodation, of whom 4,500 had no accommodation whatsoever and the rest lived in intolerable circumstances: StANeu, LO A5, KL Augsburg-Stadt, 26 Jan. 1939; BA/MA, RW19/67, fol. 56, summary of WWI reports, 21 Dec. 1938. The situation in Munich and Nuremberg was little better. There is room for considerable research on the social effects of Nazi housing policy.

deterioration in working conditions, they now became more frequent occurrences and were generally aimed at exploiting the labour shortage for improved wages. It was a sign that workers were beginning to regain some self-confidence — though the odds generally remained hopelessly stacked against them — and were beginning to flex their industrial muscles again. Even where a strike achieved absolutely nothing, the act of defiance and solidarity itself, however short-lived, could diametrically alter the mood among the work-force. For instance, an unsuccessful three-hour stoppage about piece-rates of low-paid glass-workers in the Bayerischer Wald in February 1937 was regarded by the workers themselves, according to the *Sopade* account, 'as a moral victory which has given back to them again the feeling of their own strength . . . Nobody cut himself off and no one denounced [a fellow worker] ; the Nazi bosses faced closed ranks which were not shaken by threats.' The political discussions had again become lively, the old lethargy was gone, and the mood was summed up by one worker who allegedly said: 'This lot should just not play about with us. The day will come when we don't give in any longer.'[92]

More often, and increasingly so, bitter wage negotiations within a factory — usually without assistance from either the 'Council of Trust' or the Labour Front representatives — led to improved wages without going as far as an actual stoppage. The most effective method of ensuring a hearing, especially for skilled workers, was the threat of moving to a better-paid job. At the Zündapp-Werke in Nuremberg, for example, all the workers handed in their notice together in summer 1937 — a demonstration which swiftly brought about the retention of the old piece-time rates rather than the announced reduction.[93] The wage contest between M.A.N. and Siemens-Schuchert in Nuremberg to retain their armaments workers was symptomatic of the intensifying competition between firms for the scarce commodity of skilled labour. By late 1938, in fact, many Bavarian firms had entered

[92] ASD, ES/M65/Mar. 1937, pp. 17–19, Apr. 1937, pp. 12–13.
[93] ASD, ES/M34/21 July 1937. Cf. also WL, *KPD-Deutschland-Informationen*, June 1937, pp. 56–7, 59 and Sept. 1937, pp. 20–1 for other instances of workers' actions securing better wages or preventing reductions.

into a type of concordat by which they only took on skilled labour in agreement with the previous employer – a concordat honoured largely in the breach.[94] Those workers left behind in the pay-race – textile workers, for instance, who were often still on short time but who had no skills enabling them to reap the benefits of the armaments workers – were understandably embittered. A DAF speaker addressing a works meeting at a weaving shed in an Augsburg suburb in October 1937 on the subject of the economic revival and the elimination of unemployment found the heckling and disturbances after five minutes of his talk too much for him and had to end his lecture. According to the account which the Border Secretary received of the incident, the disturbance and shouting had largely been the action of those who were formerly apathetic, not of SPD or KPD supporters.[95] In a big worsted spinning-mill in Augsburg itself, pay-day at the end of October was the scene of riotous protest. Reduced wages through short time meant that some workers with families to support were receiving only 18 RM a week. The anger showed openly where the wage packets were received, but when the workers' representative on the 'Council of Trust' arrived, called in to calm the situation, the workers insulted and spat at him. He in turn called in the factory director, who found all the wage packets thrown down in disgust at his feet and was questioned about how he imagined it was possible to live on such a miserable wage. The director pointed to circumstances beyond the control of the factory and extended hope of the imminent revival of the textile industry, and eventually the angry workers took their pay and bitterly made their way home. The report added that the mood of the workers in the factory was explosive and that none of the few Nazis in the works dared open his mouth. The workers' representative pinned up a notice stating that the local Party would take particular note of the circumstances in its distribution of Winter Aid, but the workers' view was that they wanted work and a decent wage, not charity, and 'then they can go to hell with their NSV'.[96]

---

[94] BA/MA, RW19/67, fol. 25, 1 Oct. 1938; RW19/68, fol. 112, 28 Feb. 1939.
[95] ASD, ES/M63/Nov. 1937, p. 15.
[96] Ibid., pp. 15–16; incorporated in DBS, 18 Jan. 1938, pp. A23–4.

During 1938 the labour shortage crisis sharpened markedly and workers' determination to exploit the market in search of better pay increased accordingly. Legal restrictions imposed by the regime on workers' freedom of movement could not solve the problem and had — as the *Wehrmacht* Economic Inspectorate was prepared to recognize — 'very dubious' consequences for the morale of armaments workers.[97] In the fully stretched building trade in particular, hostility towards the government's increasing regimentation of labour was heightened by the introduction of conscription for workers needed at important military sites, especially the *Westwall* (Siegfried Line).[98] Employers who refused to concede workers' demands were faced in the new market conditions with the loss of their workers to other concerns and the consequent inability to complete contracts on time. A construction site near Nuremberg, for example, lost 114 of the 125 workers assigned to it within a few weeks because the employer refused a wage rise. As a result work on the site had to be stopped.[99] In another case, a building firm near Pegnitz in Upper Franconia was forced to release its workers after they had deliberately cut down their rate of productivity. The firm attempted to keep five workers, however, who allegedly then tried to bring about their own dismissal through indiscipline, turning up drunk on the building site, absenteeism, and eventually threatening to go on strike. The five men were eventually arrested, though this scarcely helped the firm. The result was that the buildings could not be completed on time, which in turn had unfavourable consequences for the Pegnitz mines, whose miners could not be persuaded to stay because of the poor living accommodation.[1] The concession of higher wages was in itself no guarantee of a stable labour force. One Bavarian machine factory was by

[97] BA/MA, RW19/41, WWI VII (Munich), 17 Aug. 1938, p. 2. For the restrictions, see Mason, *Arbeiterklasse*, ch. IV, XIII & pp. 961 ff.
[98] Cf. ibid., ch. XIII. BA/MA, RW19/67, summary WWI reports, 1 Oct. 1938, mention the refusal of workers in the Kulmbach area of northern Bavaria to be transported to '*staatspolitische Arbeiten*', and to the growing tension in the labour market, especially in the Ruhr, as a result of conscription to the *Westwall*.
[99] Mason, *Arbeiterklasse*, p. 655 (Doc. 108).
[1] GStA, MA 106678, RPvOF/MF, 8 June 1938; a similar case in ibid., 8 Aug. 1939.

midsummer 1938 paying up to 25 per cent more than the
tariff wage but could still not stop its workers leaving for
better opportunities elsewhere.[2]
Some relief was hoped for from the influx of workers from
Austria (now called the 'Ostmark') and from the Sudetenland.
The hopes were illusory. Austrians arriving at the Bavarian
road-building site at Bayrischzell-Tatzelwurm, directly on the
former border between Upper Bavaria and the Tyrol, and distinguishing themselves initially as out-and-out Hitler supporters, were soon disillusioned and embittered by the low
wages and long hours. Many disappeared on their bicycles
under cover of darkness, before increased police surveillance
clamped down on their mobility.[3] Sudeten Germans assigned
to military construction sites in Bavaria underwent the same
process of rapid disenchantment. Many of them were at first
proud to out-do the 'Reich Germans' by their hard work and
high productivity.[4] Many among them and among the
Austrians, however, were workers who had retained until
only a short time previously contact with Marxist organizations and had not experienced the level of repression which
German workers had had to undergo for more than five long
years. Such workers were evidently not prepared to tolerate
the conditions and wages to which they were subjected in
Germany and added their own contribution to the growing
problems of labour relations in the Third Reich. Following a
series of strikes in Upper and Middle Franconia during the
foreign political tension of September 1938, the Gestapo
established that a large proportion of the 'agitators' and
those refusing to work were Austrians, especially from
Vienna. And of the 238 persons taken into 'protective custody' in this administrative region in December, after the
Sudetenland had come 'home into the Reich', 232 were
described as 'Sudeten German Marxists', who went on to
compromise 449 out of 485 arrests between December 1938
and April 1939.[5]

[2] Ibid., 6 Aug. 1938. Cf. also BA/MA, RW19/67, WWI summary rept., 25
June 1938.   [3] DBS, 10 Oct. 1938, p. A100.
[4] Ibid., 14 Nov. 1938, p. A47. For the rapid disillusionment of Austrian and
Sudeten-German workers, cf. ibid., 14 Apr. 1939, p. A93.
[5] GStA, MA 106678, RPvOF/MF, 7 Oct. 1938, 7 Jan. 1939, 8 Feb. 1939, 7
Mar. 1939, 10 Apr. 1939, 6 May 1939; cf. also Bayern I, pp. 278–9.

Industrial relations deteriorated to a low ebb as Germany's economic problems mounted. Sharpened class-consciousness and increased militancy were countered by sheer coercion of the police State working ever more closely in conjunction with industrial management. Despite the concessions and higher wages which many workers were able to wring out of unwilling employers and an even more unwilling State during these years, the climate was hardly guaranteed to win a new basis of support for the regime among the working class. Indeed the signs are that the DAF, whose meetings continued to be scorned and detested by their captive audiences, was gradually coming to place less emphasis on its propaganda of the 'factory community' as its failure became increasingly apparent, and as the place of propaganda was more and more taken by outright coercion and increased surveillance within factories.[6]

An indication of the growing tension and antipathy towards the regime is the increase in the number of offences of 'malicious' criticism of the National Socialist State and its representatives dealt with by the Munich 'Special Court'. There were more than three times as many such cases in 1938 and 1939 as in 1936 and five times as many as in 1935.[7] At the same time the number of persons taken into 'protective custody' also rose sharply.[8] In both instances the sector of the population most affected was the industrial working class. There is no indication that the increase in these political offences could be attributed to the expanded activities of the illegal worker organizations, whose significance in Bavaria at this date — measured in terms of the extent of their activity — could not be rated very highly.[9] The 'offences' themselves in the 'Special Court' cases seem to have concerned, far more than in earlier years, criticisms of the economic and social policy of the regime, foreign policy, the imminence of war (and Nazi responsibility for it), and the

[6] Cf. DBS, 14 Apr. 1939, pp. A81-5, 10 Dec. 1938, pp. A90-1, 102-3, 113-15; ASD, ES/M66/Oct. 1937, p. 24.
[7] Data now available in P. Hüttenberger, 'Heimtückefälle vor dem Sondergericht München 1933-1939', in *Bayern IV*, pp. 435-526, here pp. 444-5.
[8] *Bayern I*, p. 241.
[9] Cf. ibid., pp. 271-2.

person of Hitler.[10] Though difficult to evaluate in terms of their representativeness for popular opinion, there can be little doubt that the comments of many of the individual workers arraigned before the 'Special Court' were echoing widespread feelings.[11]

Both the reports of the exiled left-wing organizations and those of the German authorities themselves point in the same direction — that higher wages and increased incomes in the later 1930s had not produced a contented working class, nor one which was convinced of the benefits which Nazism claimed to have brought Germany. Despite the obvious internal bias of the reporting, the wealth of information which the *Sopade* reports in particular provide is very persuasive — all the more so because of the nuanced way in which it is treated in the *Deutschland-Berichte*.

Reports from both sources in 1937–8 suggest widespread discontent and antipathy towards the regime. The smashing by workers of the windows of a hall at a small town in the poverty zone along the Czech border where a conference of Party functionaries was taking place, was interpreted by the authorities as a sign of the strength of feeling on the wages issue.[12] Anti-Nazi slogans daubed on walls were a commonplace in many factories.[13] There are frequent reports that the 'Heil Hitler' greeting had disappeared almost completely among workers, whose hostile stance became ever more apparent to the isolated Nazi sympathizers among the workforce and to the management and authorities.[14] Building sites

[10] Cf. Hüttenberger, 'Heimtückefälle', pp. 476–92; also Kershaw, *Hitler-Mythos*, p. 121, n. 47.

[11] The main preoccupation of workers arrested on *'Heimtücke'* charges were: complaints about the job situation (in the early years of the regime), complaints about low wages, and complaints about high and rising prices. Hüttenberger, 'Heimtückefälle', p. 490.

[12] BA/MA, RW19/27, WWI XII (Nuremberg), 15 May 1937, p. 17.

[13] Cf. DBS, 10 Nov. 1938, pp. A91–2 for regular daubings at the MAN works in Augsburg. See also, Hetzer, pp. 117–18. The *Sopade* report pointed out that the painting in red lead paint of 'long live Communism, long live the Red Army' over the doorway in the main foundry could not have been done in less than ten minutes and needed a ladder. The co-operation and approval of workmates was therefore essential.

[14] Cf. e.g., DBS, 18 Jan. 1938, pp. A20–2, 30 June 1938, pp. A86–9, 10 Oct. 1938, pp. A81–4; GStA, MA 106671, RPvOB, 10 Aug. 1938 (for the miners of

continued to pose problems. 'A radical, anti-nationalist spirit' was reported from one site in the Upper Palatinate, where workers from different parts of Germany had been brought together.[15] The 300 Austrians building a barracks in Mittenwald in the Alps of southern Bavaria were said to be mainly Marxists, whose anti-Regime feeling was highlighted by the singing of the Internationale which prompted the arrest of three workers.[16] In Nuremberg, where the extravagant Party buildings were the source of much heated criticism from a working population faced by an appalling housing shortage, cases of direct sabotage were reported from the site of the Party Congress Hall, as when blocks of granite valued at up to 1200 RM were systematically damaged by some of the 900 workers brought in to the site, with the result that the construction could not be completed on time.[17] Cases of suspected sabotage were also no rarity in Augsburg's armaments factories.[18]

The diplomatic tension of 1938 seems to have reawakened the political interest of workers who had formerly been attached to left-wing parties, to have stirred up dormant anti-nationalist feeling, and to have provoked much speculation about the future of the regime. Penzberg miners, whose alienation from the regime had been continually registered by the Government President of Upper Bavaria since 1934, showed during 1938 heightened interest in the fortunes of the Republicans in Spain, in developments in Czechoslovakia, in conditions in Russia, and even in the situation in China.[19] The mood among Augsburg munition-workers witnessed at the mobilization during the Austrian crisis was allegedly one not seen for many years, giving rise to lively discussion and some optimism that the Western powers would not stand idly by, that a war would bring the end of Hitlerism. The interest shown in Russia was, it was claimed,

Penzberg, echoing regular reports during 1937-8); MA 106672, RPvNB/OP, 9 Aug. 1937, 7 Oct. 1937 (for the iron-workers of Burglengenfeld).
[15] StAA, BA Amberg 2399, GS Vilseck, 24 July 1937; BA Amberg 29 July 1937.
[16] GStA, MA 106671, RPvOB, 9 Sept. 1938.
[17] GStA, MA 106678, RPvOF/MF, 8 Apr. 1938.
[18] Hetzer, pp. 118-19.
[19] GStA, MA 106671, RPvOB, 10 Aug. 1938.

also substantial, and the negative impact which the Stalinist show trials had made was beginning to wear off.[20] As one report sent to *Sopade* headquarters pointed out, such sentiments were almost certainly largely confined to a small, ideologically anchored minority of workers.[21] Much more widespread was the horror among workers as among the rest of the population – especially those who had experienced the World War of 1914-18 – of another conflagration. The mood among BMW workers in Munich was reflected in their reported responses after they had discovered hidden exits from the bunker below the factory during an air-raid practice at the height of the tension in September 1938. The workers reportedly left the factory in droves, making for home and saying: 'We don't want a war. If Munich comes to be bombed, then nothing will be any use anyway.'[22] A few days later, during the Munich Conference, a rumour that war had broken out resulted – according to a report in *Deutsche Informationen* – in a work stoppage amid near panic in a big Munich munition factory employing some 4,000 workers, who demanded to be told the truth about the situation by the management and stated that they were not just going to be sent into war as had been the case in 1914. Only when the rumour proved false did the workers return to their machines.[23] More realistic than this suggestion of outright defiance towards involvement in a war was the *Sopade* appraisal of the mood in the Augsburg M.A.N. works, now resembling 'a single war-machine'. Though not Nazi, workers' attitudes here were reported as evolving in a direction not favourable to socialism. The basic mood was one of deep depression and gloom – like a doctor's waiting-room. There was no militancy among the workers. They did not want to think of the future. They were certain that a war was coming and that there was no chance of escaping it, and this made them all the more keen to concern themselves, ostrich-like, with their daily existence and to exclude thoughts of the

[20] DBS, 30 June 1938, pp. A86-7.
[21] ASD, ES/M66/Oct. 1937, pp. 7-8.
[22] WL, *Deutsche Informationen*, 22 Sept. 1938.
[23] Ibid., 17 Nov. 1938. I have come across no internal reports of these incidents described by the *Deutsche Informationen*.

future. There was consequently waxing political indifference. It was even 'boring to talk about the Nazis' since everything was known about them already, and in any case nothing could be changed.[24]

Measured solely in terms of real wages, the position of industrial workers, especially those in the relatively well-paid armaments industry, improved between 1936 and 1939. In the light of the evidence we have seen, however, the view that higher wages and the benefits of Nazi social policy won over workers to Nazism in these years and created 'a general contentment among the working classes'[25] would hardly be tenable. Nor would there seem much to commend the view that 'Hitler's social revolution' produced a situation as regards the working class where 'the loss of liberté was practically linked with the promotion of égalité', which 'from our point of view . . . may have been slavery, but . . . was not necessarily slavery from the point of view of a contemporary.'[26] The glimpses of worker attitudes which we have extracted from a mass of documentation suggest strongly that workers not only *were* unfree, in the Third Reich, but that most of them *felt* they were unfree, exploited, discriminated against, and the victims of an unfair class-ridden society in which wealth and opportunity were unevenly divided. Far from being won over to Nazism during the boom years of 1937-9, the signs are that Nazism was further losing ground among workers during this period.

It would, however, seem equally mistaken to translate workers' determination to exploit their market position and

[24] ASD, ES/M66/Dec. 1937-Jan. 1938, pp. 27-8; incorporated in DBS, 30 June 1938, p. A88.

[25] J. De Courcy, *Searchlight on Europe*, London, 1940, p. 126. This old myth that Hitler created not only employment, but also prosperity and contentment for the working class not only lives on in many present-day popular misconceptions of society in the Third Reich, but is also shored up implicitly by such widely read and much-acclaimed journalistic works as S. Haffner, *Anmerkungen zu Hitler*, Munich, 1978, which speaks of 'Hitler's economic miracle' providing 'the great majority of the six million unemployed that Hitler found' with new employment 'in quite normal civil industries', of the Third Reich — an 'island of prosperity' in Depression-ridden Europe producing 'in reality . . . cannons *and* butter and much else besides', and of a 'socialist side' of Nazism which furthered the progressive breakdown of status privileges and class barriers (pp. 39-42, 48-53).

[26] Schoenbaum, pp. 110-11.

increase their earnings into terms of overt political opposition to Nazism. Shop-floor militancy, which undoubtedly increased in these years, was certainly politicized by the regime. Intent and motivation on the part of the workers seem, however, to have been more often economic than directly political. Whatever their inner feelings towards Nazism, resignation rather than defiance characterized the outward stance of most workers. The practical significance and effectiveness of the illegal KPD and SPD resistance groups were minimal in this period, and their activities found little resonance among the mass of workers. Numerous *Sopade* reports point out that the degree of repression to which industrial workers, more than any other social class, were subjected meant that they were especially reticent in voicing their political views.[27] Such reports, keen though they were to seize upon any expression of working-class hostility towards the regime, repeatedly emphasized the difficulties of arriving at a generalized interpretation of worker attitudes, stressing the composition of the work-force, labour relations in the factory, and the approach of the local Party functionaries as factors which could affect political attitudes in quite different ways.[28] In addition, the partial ideological penetration by Nazism of sections of the working class was reflected in a spectrum of feelings about Nazi policies, including extensive acceptance among workers as in other sections of the population of the necessity and rectitude of Germany's stance in foreign politics and diplomacy.[29]

In a report just before the war, summarizing its conclusions drawn from evidence from all parts of Germany, the *Sopade* pointed out again the overwhelming impression of exhausted, sullen apathy made by so many workers simply going through the motions, resigned in the face of absent alternatives. Contrary to the view of some of its reports, the *Sopade* concluded that falling production in, for example, the mining

[27] E.g., ASD, ES/M34/21 July 1937; ES/M66/Aug. 1937, Dec. 1937–Jan. 1938; DBS, 10 Oct. 1938, pp. A79–80.
[28] DBS, 14 Apr. 1939, pp. A85–6; and cf. ibid., 10 Oct. 1938, pp. A79–80.
[29] Cf. e.g., ASD, ES/M66/Dec. 1937–Jan. 1938, pp. 1–10; DBS, 18 Jan. 1938, pp. A53–4, 12 Mar. 1938, pp. A32–3.

industry was a result above all of physical exhaustion and not of deliberate sabotage or overtly politically motivated action.[30] German workers, repressed by Nazi terror, were demoralized and without clear hope in 1939. They were resigned, but not rebellious.[31] Whatever the internal bias of the *Sopade's* reporting, the conclusion seems inescapable: the working class had not been converted to Nazism; but it had been effectively neutralized as a political force.[32] The success of Nazism, ended the *Sopade* analysis just cited, lay in the atomization of the working class and the destruction of its leadership, which had previously been able to overcome differences and weld disparate groups together. Though this judgement contains more than a trace of an apologetic for the old SPD leadership, the conclusion is not without merit. Nazi repression had deepened the differences which had always existed: 'those who used to think still think today, and those who did not then think, think now even less. Only that the thinkers are today no longer able to lead the nonthinkers.'[33]

---

[30] DBS, 12 July 1939, p. A77.

[31] This corresponds to the impression of the German authorities, whose constant dire prognostications about the economy and worries about worker morale and labour indiscipline generally contained little fear of imminent political trouble or quasi-revolutionary tendencies among the working class, even in big industrial regions, and were coupled with confident assessments by the *Gestapa* of the containment of underground resistance groups. This is the context in which one must place Hitler's comment in November 1939, that the timing of the war was opportune since he had the German people behind him, 'whose morale can only get worse'. *Docs. on Nazism*, p. 575, and cf. Mason, *Arbeiterklasse*, p. 165.

[32] For an excellent analysis of this neutralization, see T.W. Mason, 'The Containment of the Working Class in Nazi Germany', (forthcoming).

[33] DBS, 12 July 1939, pp. A83-4.

3. Petty-bourgeois Complaint and Compliance

An attempt to explore middle-class opinion during the Third Reich faces some obvious difficulties. The first is definitional. Whatever their internal differentiation and stratification, the peasantry and the working class can be seen as relatively homogeneous social groups. The 'middle class', by contrast, embraces numerous, quite disparate sectors of society with widely differing socio-economic interests. The German terms *'der Mittelstand'*, *'das Bürgertum'*, and *'die Mittelschicht'* differ in emphasis from each other and from the English 'middle class', but are hardly more precise.[1] Scarcely less heterogeneous is the composition of the 'lower middle class' or 'petty bourgeoisie' or *'Kleinbürgertum'* — terms which, though they exclude big industrialists, intellectuals, and the higher ranks of management, the professions, and civil service still comprise extremely variegated strata of the population with apparently unrelated group interests. These can, however, be broken down into two broad fractions of the petty bourgeoisie: the sector of small-scale ownership in production and commerce (craftsmen, retailers, small business men) and a 'non-productive' sector of salaried employees, civil servants, and the low ranks of the professions. Economically, these groups have only the negative characteristic in common that they belong neither to the 'upper class' of the bourgeoisie and aristocracy nor to the 'lower class' of the proletariat. It is on the ideological/political plane that the links of class identity are forged.[2] The threat to property

[1] For a particularly clear elucidation and differentiation of these definitional terms, see J. Kocka, *Angestellte zwischen Faschismus und Demokratie*, Göttingen, 1977, pp. 28–31. Cf. also Pridham, p. 184, n. 2. Though I employ the terms 'middle class', 'lower middle class', and 'petty bourgeoisie' arbitrarily and interchangeably in this chapter, the groups which form the subject of my enquiry are those special categories included in the passage immediately following.

[2] My theoretical starting-point here is based on N. Poulantzas, *Fascism and Dictatorship*, London (1974), Verso edn. 1979, pp. 237–58. The subjective expression of petty-bourgeois class identity ought not to be taken as implying an

and status seen in the Marxist doctrine of the working-class movement provided the main unifying force within the German petty bourgeoisie, prompting the politicization of groups which before the last decades of the nineteenth century had not generally been politically active, colouring the anti-Left tendencies of such groups, and exposing them to the ideological gambits of the radical Right.[3] Ideologically, the fear of being crushed by capitalism and the dread of proletarianization furthered the inclination — strongest among civil servants but widespread throughout the petty bourgeoisie — to identify with a strong but 'neutral' State, above classes but supposedly on the side of the petty bourgeoisie, which would ensure 'social justice', 'equality of opportunity', and social mobility based on 'merit' and 'achievement' — all without a revolutionary transformation of society. In a crisis of the magnitude of that of the early 1930s, such an ideology could be translated into a volatile and dynamic, if transient and unstable, political force.

The definitional difficulties associated with the middle class are compounded, for the period of the Nazi dictatorship, by those of the source materials. The peasantry and the industrial working class confronted the Nazi authorities with recognizable social groups, both of them key producing-sectors of the economy. Allergic to any factors so influencing morale that production was likely to suffer, and especially distrustful of Marxist tendencies among workers, the Nazi rulers were anxious to register any vagaries in the attitudes and behaviour of these groups. The middle class, on the other hand, presented the regime neither with a homogeneous social

---

ideological autonomy from the objective class position of the petty bourgeoisie, i.e. the instability of its situation poised between the two 'real' classes of capital and labour. Nor, following from this and as Poulantzas (p. 240) points out, does petty-bourgeois ideology have any independent standing and formed merely a 'sub-ensemble' of the dominant bourgeois ideology. For a perceptive critique of Poulantzas, cf. J. Caplan, 'Theories of Fascism: Nicos Poulantzas as Historian', *History Workshop Journal*, iii (1977), 83–100.

[3] Cf. esp. G. Eley, *Reshaping the German Right. Radical Nationalism and Political Change after Bismarck*, New Haven, 1980, for the rapid growth of imperialist, anti-Marxist mass movements, heavily petty-bourgeois based, in Wilhelmine Germany.

group with a pronounced common consciousness, nor with any conceivable threat either in productive or in political terms which required detailed surveillance. As a result, the sources are far less informative. Moreover, those sections of the middle class — teachers and civil servants — directly dependent on the State were naturally extremely cautious in expressing dissent. The voices of other important middle-class groups are generally heard only through their 'co-ordinated' professional or representational organizations, while other groups, such as white-collar employees who had been prominent in their support for Nazism before 1933 and had benefited disproportionately from the massive expansion of administration and bureaucracy in the Third Reich,[4] leave hardly any traces in the source material after 1933 by which one can begin to chart their political attitudes and behaviour. The restrictions imposed by the sources necessarily limit the reconstruction of opinion attempted in this chapter to certain groups within the petty bourgeoisie.

The difficulties of generalizing about 'the middle class' and the unhelpfulness of the source material are certainly among the reasons why, despite the universal consensus that petty-bourgeois groups formed the backbone of Nazi support before 1933, there have so far been remarkably few empirical studies of the middle class during the period of the dictatorship itself. Such discussion as has taken place has revolved around the extent to which Nazi economic policy — aimed at, or at least functioning in, the interests of 'big business' — betrayed and alienated the class which had been the mainstay of Nazism before the 'seizure of power', but which had now become 'dispensable'.[5] Recent analyses, however, have been

---

[4] The service sector (almost three-quarters of whose employees were *Beamte* or *Angestellte* — 'white-collar workers') expanded by 41.4 per cent in Bavaria between 1933 and 1939. The number of *Angestellte* in all sections of the Bavarian economy rose in this period by 27.9 per cent, the number of *Beamte* by 15.3 per cent, the Bavarian population as a whole by under 4 per cent. Calculated from data in: 'Berufsgliederung', *ZdBSL*, lxvi (1934), 199-202; and 'Die bayer. Bevölkerung', *ZdBSL*, lxxiv (1942), 187.

[5] Cf. esp. H. Winkler, 'Der entbehrliche Stand. Zur Mittelstandspolitik im "Dritten Reich"', *Archiv für Sozialgeschichte*, xvii (1977), 1-40; Schoenbaum, pp. 129-43; R. Saage, *Faschismustheorien. Eine Einführung*, Munich, 1976, ch. 5-6; R. Opitz, 'Die faschistische Massenbewegung', in R. Kühnl (ed.), *Texte zur Faschismusdiskussion I*, Hamburg, 1974, pp. 176-90, esp. p. 183; A. Leppert-

more inclined to stress not the alienation but the integration of the petty bourgeoisie, claiming at least a partial upholding of *Mittelstand* interests, improvement in the position of some, usually the wealthier, sections of the *Mittelstand* which could accommodate themselves to Nazi demands, greater stratification and differentiation within the *Mittelstand*, and not least considerable affinity of interest between the Nazi rulers and the *Mittelstand*.[6]

The examination of middle-class opinion in the following pages has these issues in mind. Despite definitional and source problems, it seemed an attempt had to be made in a study of popular opinion in the Third Reich to include that complex and variegated third of the population, roughly speaking, which had shown itself before 1933 to be markedly open to the blandishments of Nazism.[7]

(i) The Middle-Class Base of Nazi Support, 1933

There is overwhelming recognition that the Nazi Movement, both in its voter support and in the structure of its membership, was heavily reliant upon the petty bourgeoisie, even if a not insignificant proletarian presence in the rank and file of the Party itself and especially within the SA has sometimes

---

Fögen, *Die deklassierte Klasse*, Frankfurt/Main, 1974; cf. also von Saldern, pp. 12–13.

[6] Von Saldern, pp. 234–46; C.-D. Krohn and D. Stegmann, 'Kleingewerbe und Nationalsozialismus in einer agrarisch-mittelständischen Region. Das Beispiel Lüneburg 1930–1939', *Archiv für Sozialgeschichte*, xvii (1977), 41–98. It is worth pointing out that discussion of the petty bourgeoisie in the Third Reich has concentrated overwhelmingly on small-scale producers and traders.

[7] The size of the petty bourgeoisie is difficult to establish with precision. On the basis of the Bavarian census data of 1933 (incl. Palatinate), the self-employed and employed family members (excluding peasantry), civil servants (excluding higher civil servants), skilled, technical, sales, and office white collar (excluding managerial), and certain groups of those without profession, such as pensioners living from their own property and independent resources, retired civil servants, students etc., amount to just under 36 per cent. (Based on data in *StJBB* (1936), pp. 12–13). Theodor Geiger's classification included almost 36 per cent in the old and new *Mittelstand*. However, he counted peasants in this number, though on the other hand included many self-employed in the category (numbering 12.65 per cent) which he dubbed '*Proletaroide*' — T. Geiger, *Die soziale Schichtung des deutschen Volkes*, Stuttgart, 1932, p. 73; cf. also Leppert-Fögen, p. 34 & n. 62.

been too easily overlooked or underestimated.[8] The membership structure of the NSDAP in Bavaria differs only somewhat in degree from the position elsewhere in Germany. The backbone of the Party membership was formed by the three groups of self-employed (excluding the rural self-employed, covered by the category 'peasants' in the Party statistics), white-collar employees, and *Beamte* (civil servants and teachers). Taken together, these three groups ranged from 43.2 per cent of Party members in Swabia to 54.8 per cent in Upper Bavaria — more than double the 23.5 per cent of the Bavarian population which they comprised.[9] The dominance of the middle class over the Party leadership structure, as has often been pointed out, was even more pronounced. Lists of functionaries before the 'take-over of power' show an overwhelming preponderance of the professional middle class — doctors, lawyers, dentists, teachers, civil servants, and business men — with a smattering of tradesmen, craftsmen, white-collar workers and farmers.[10] The extremely high proportion of primary-school teachers and civil servants frequently gave the Party the appearance of being a purely *'Beamtenpartei'*.[11]

Most members of the petty bourgeoisie were, of course, not organized in the NSDAP. As among other social groups there was in part widespread scepticism and hesitancy about the Party, together with considerable criticism and hostility. The fears and worries about the NSDAP most calculated to alienate potential middle-class support were its apparent social radicalism, its unseemly and violent hooligan element, and above all, especially in Catholic areas, the allegations that the Party was in essence anti-Christian. The Nazis worked hard and with some success between 1928 and 1933 at trying to rid themselves of these damaging aspects of their public image, though they proved unable to win over those

---

[8] See above, Chapter 2 note 5.
[9] *Partei-Statistik*, i. 148; population data from *StJBB* (1936), pp. 12–13. The figures for self-employed given in Pridham, p. 187 are misleading in that they include peasants, though peasants are counted as a separate category in the Party statistics.
[10] Cf. Pridham, p. 190 & n. 11; Hambrecht, pp. 307–8.
[11] Hambrecht, p. 308; cf. Pridham, pp. 191–5.

members of the middle class who were closely attached to the BVP. These fears apart, there was little in Nazi ideology to alienate and much in the Party's social promises to attract middle-class support. The more powerless and futile narrow interest-group organizations and small political parties became in the conditions of the Depression, the more attractive the NSDAP appeared to be, as a large and powerful Movement offering to uphold the interests and further the aspirations of small business man, craftsman, white-collar employee, teacher, and civil servant alike. The characteristic components of Nazi ideology — its anti-Marxism, anti-liberalism, anti-Semitism, chauvinistic nationalism, and its central props of the 'leadership principle' and the 'national community' served to legitimize the varied petty-bourgeois expectations of the authoritarian State under the leadership of a Party which in promising to represent all interests appeared to stand above interest in the cause of the nation.[12]

Nazi propaganda played upon middle-class interests more by way of vague though persistent emphasis upon the favoured position which the *Mittelstand* would occupy in the coming Reich than through detailed policy suggestions. From the point of view of the commercial and craft sectors of the middle class, Nazi promises seemed to offer protection, both from the economic threat posed by department stores, consumer associations, mail-order firms, and mass-producing large-scale capitalist enterprises, and from the Weimar State itself, which through the imposition of excessive tax burdens, increased social insurance, and other interventions in the domain of small business had shown itself to be hostile towards the *Mittelstand*.[13] For the non-producing middle class, bitterness about salary cuts — civil servants smarted under a 23 per cent reduction imposed by Brüning in 1931 — and low pay mingled with status concerns and hopes of greater

---

[12] Cf. Zofka, pp. 124–30, 154–6, 346–8; and H. Winkler, 'German Society, Hitler, and the Illusion of Restoration 1930–33', *Journal of Contemporary History*, xi (1976), 10–12.

[13] Zofka, pp. 147–53; von Saldern, pp. 31–2, 58; H. Winkler, *Mittelstand, Demokratie und Nationalsozialismus*, Cologne, 1972, pp. 166–79; Winkler, 'Germ. Society', pp. 10–11; H. Winkler, 'From Social Protectionism to National Socialism: the German Small-Business Movement in Comparative Perspective', *Journal of Modern History*, xlviii (1976), 10.

recognition for their professions (particularly acute among primary-school teachers) after the dawn of the new Reich.[14] The specific interests of every group to which the Nazis appealed found their common denominator in the political, social, economic, and ideological bankruptcy of the Weimar Republic. The Nazis offered the abrupt removal of the source of middle-class misery in the eyes of so many petty-bourgeois followers of the NSDAP.[15] And with the crushing of the enemies of the *Mittelstand* and the creation of the 'national community' would come 'peace and quiet', the upholding of which, according to the Chairman of the General Trade Association in Munich in 1931, was the first duty of the *Bürger*.[16]

The mood of national exultation which enveloped Germany during the first months of Nazi rule had its tone set above all by the middle class. Most middle-class Germans found much to admire and relatively little to condemn in the spring and summer of 1933. The assault on the Left was widely popular. The 'Emergency Decrees' of 28 February 1933, immediately following the Reichstag Fire, which made devastating inroads into the freedom of the individual, gave extensive executive powers to the government, and announced a state of emergency which was in effect to last until the end of the Third Reich, were warmly welcomed. One provincial newspaper in Upper Bavaria certainly echoed much middle-class opinion when it stated that the 'Emergency Decree' had

finally got to the centre of the German disease, the ulcer which had for years poisoned and infected the German blood, Bolshevism, the deadly enemy of Germany . . . This Emergency Decree will find no opponent despite the quite draconian measures which it threatens. Against

[14] Cf. Pridham, pp. 191–5. For white-collar workers cf. esp. J. Kocka, 'The First World War and the "Mittelstand": German Artisans and White-Collar Workers', *Journal of Contemporary History*, viii (1973), 121–3; and J. Kocka, 'Zur Problematik der deutschen Angestellten 1914–1933', in H. Mommsen *et al.* (eds.), *Industrielles System und politische Entwicklung in der Weimarer Republik*, Düsseldorf, 1977, pp. 800–8.

[15] Winkler, 'From Social Protectionism', p. 10; H. Winkler, 'Vom Protest zur Panik: Der gewerbliche Mittelstand in der Weimarer Republik', in Mommsen, *Industr.System*, pp. 789–90.

[16] Cited in Pridham, p. 189.

murderers, arsonists, and poisoners there can only be the most rigorous defence, against terror the reckoning through the death penalty. The fanatics who would like to make a robbers' cave out of Germany must be rendered harmless. The consequences of the most acute struggle against communism have finally been drawn . . . It concerns more than parties, it concerns Germany, in fact the entire Western culture built upon Christianity. And for this reason we welcome the recent Emergency Decree.[17]

As Table XIII shows, the three main middle-class occupational groupings of white-collar employees, self-employed (excluding peasants), and *Beamte* accounted for 48.7 per cent of the Bavarian Party membership at the time of Hitler's elevation to the Chancellorship, falling slightly to 47.4 per cent by the time entry to the Party was temporarily closed in May 1933.[18] In absolute terms, however, their numbers in the Party almost quadrupled in this period, from 32,524 to 116,904. Civil servants and teachers, as elsewhere in Germany, were in the forefront of the rush to be seen as loyal Nazis: 80 per cent of the *Beamte* in the Party by 1935 had joined after the 'seizure of power'.[19] By the end of the Party enrolment in May 1933, 7.2 per cent of Bavarian white-collar employees, 7.2 per cent of the self-employed, and 8.3 per cent of *Beamte* were 'organized' in the NSDAP — apart that is from indeterminate numbers in the SA and other Party formations.[20] This compared with an overall Party membership ratio of 3.78 per cent of the German population (5.1 per cent of the adult population).[21] Party activists and functionaries locally as at higher levels were predominantly middle class.[22]

[17] *Miesbacher Anzeiger*, 2 Mar. 1933.

[18] The category 'others' ('*Sonstige*') in the Party statistics, which in Munich/ Upper Bavaria accounted for as many as 17.5 per cent of the membership in 1933, undoubtedly also contained a sizeable middle-class element, including as it did among other groups pensioners, housewives, and students.

[19] Calculated from the figures for the individual *Gaue* in *Partei-Statistik*, i. 105.

[20] Those failing to apply for Party membership before the closure of the rolls in May 1933 frequently joined the SA Reserve, treating it as an '*Ersatzpartei*': Zofka, pp. 222-4.

[21] *Partei-Statistik*, i. 34, 40.

[22] Cf. Zofka, pp. 294-5; E. Fröhlich and M. Broszat, 'Politische und soziale Macht auf dem Lande. Die Durchsetzung der NSDAP im Kreis Memmingen', *VfZ*, xxv (1977), 558-9; generally on the social composition of the '*politische Leiter*', E. Hennig, *Bürgerliche Gesellschaft und Faschismus in Deutschland. Ein Forschungsbericht*, Frankfurt/Main, 1977, pp. 171-87.

TABLE XIII: White-Collar, Self-Employed, and Civil Servants (including Teachers) in the Nazi Party in Bavaria, 1933-5

A. *Proportion of the Social Group in the Party*[a]

	Total nos. in popn.	% of popn.	% of group in Party	
			1933	1935
White-collar	575,199	7.5	2.5	7.2
Self-employed	763,866	9.9	2.2	7.2
Civil servants	433,252	5.7	1.8	8.3
Totals	1,772,317	23.1	2.2	7.5

B. *Proportion of the Party Membership belonging to the Social Group*[b]

	1933		1935	
	No. in Party	% of membership	No. in party	% of membership
White-collar	11,969	17.9	35,818	14.5
Self-employed	14,001	21.0	49,000	19.9
Civil servants	6,554	9.8	32,086	13.0
Totals	32,524	48.7	116,904	47.4

[a] Figures in this section refer to Bavaria *including* the Palatinate, the area covered by the population statistics. The Party figures here therefore include the membership in *Gau* Pfalz.

[b] The figures in this section are for Bavaria 'right of the Rhine', i.e. excluding the Palatinate. They comprise therefore the Party *Gaue* of Bavaria proper, i.e. Bavarian *Ostmark*, Franconia, Main Franconia, Munich/Upper Bavaria, and Swabia.

Sources: Census returns from *StJBB* (1936), 12-13. 'Self-employed' category excludes agriculture. Party membership figures from *Partei-Statistik*, i. 90-112, 146-51.

Even the majority of those middle-class Germans not organized in the Party were generally sympathetic towards at least some of its propagated aims and supposed intentions, whatever their misgivings about particular aspects of Nazism. And after the initial *Gleichschaltung* phase, the middle class were exposed to direct Nazi influence through the more or less compulsory membership of craft guilds, chambers of commerce, and professional associations, all of them now run by tried and tested National Socialists.[23] By the end of 1933

[23] Cf. von Saldern, pp. 159-60.

the middle class was 'organized' as never before, by a Party grounded on middle-class support, and committed in its 'unalterable' programme to the preservation of a 'healthy *Mittelstand*'.[24] For many members of the middle class, however, the honeymoon with Nazism was not to last long.

(ii) Disenchantment Sets in: the Nature of Middle-class Discontent, 1934–6

Reports reaching the *Sopade* from Bavaria in spring and summer 1934 echoed those emanating from other parts of Germany in their judgement that the most vociferous expressions of discontent came from the *Mittelstand*, especially from the small-business sector. Loud objections were raised at the pressure to contribute to the incessant stream of Party collections, especially since business had not revived as quickly as expected. Those with government orders complained, too, about the slow settlement of debts by the Reich which caused liquidity problems and forced small businesses to incur high interest charges through having to borrow. And little or nothing had been done about the large department stores and consumer co-operatives which remained the chief source of small-business grievance.[25] It was clearly rubbing salt in the wound to give the Jewish department store Uhlfelder in Munich permission to extend its buildings in the city's main shopping thoroughfare. Opposition by the *NS-Hago*, the small-traders' organization, had proved fruitless. In Nuremberg the support given by the Nazi authorities to the town consumer association was said to have provoked 'hatred' among *NS-Hago* members, who were withdrawing their support because of the weakness of the organization and their feeling that the authorities were out of sympathy with them.[26]

---

[24] *Docs. on Nazism*, pp. 38–9.

[25] DBS, 17 May 1934, p. A32; cf. also 26 June 1934, pp. A11–13.

[26] Ibid., 29 Sept. 1934, pp. A38–40. *NS-Hago* reports from the Upper Bavarian mining town in Penzberg also paint a picture of declining morale in 1934, attributable partly to the general economic worries of raw material shortages and fears of inflation and partly to the low purchasing power of the poorly paid Penzberg miners. Many thought that the guilds (*Innungen*) and the *NS-Hago* itself had not lived up to expectations, and dominant opinion was said to favour representatives of the people again being voted into office and not simply nominated – StAM, NSDAP 655, Stimmungsberichte der NS-Hago, 1 June, 6 July 1934.

An indication of the variety of sources of discontent among the commercial, craft, and small-industrial sectors of the middle class between June 1934 and January 1935 is provided by the 'situation reports' of the forty-one Bavarian employment offices. The most prominent complaints concerned continued low demand and consequent poor trade, raw material shortages, lack of government orders and failure to stimulate the economy in particularly depressed areas, interference in the labour market by pressurizing employers to take on unsuitable 'old fighters' of the Party, oppressive taxation with accompanying low profit margins, and indebtedness towards which — in contrast to its benign treatment of the peasantry — the government seemed oblivious. Trade was further hampered, it was felt, by currency and credit restrictions, and those branches of trade and industry depending upon foreign markets were particularly pessimistic and critical of the severity with which the Jewish Question was being tackled because of its consequences for overseas trade. Fears of inflation and war together with general uncertainty about the future, widely reported in 1934 and increasing during the preparations for the Saar plebiscite in January 1935, also sharply affected the mood of the commercial middle class. In addition, the continued thriving of Jewish department stores and 'single-price shops' (*Einheitspreisgeschäfte*) remained a thorn in the flesh for small shopkeepers. In Memmingen tradesmen were saying bitterly that 'such department stores would probably only be closed when the small business men have been robbed of their existence.'[27]

The employment office 'situation reports' also afford a glimpse of some of the factors shaping opinion among the civil servants and white-collar staff of the offices. Beneath the ritual avowals of political reliability and firm trust in the Führer, there were worries about job security, rumours that the employment offices would be run down or taken over by the DAF, complaints about the massive increase in the burden of work, the uncongenial working conditions — one report compared the primitive conditions of the employment

---

[27] GStA, MA 106767, AA Memmingen, 10 Jan. 1935.

office with the significant improvements which the 'Beauty of Labour' organization had brought about in factories — and, finally, the low pay and poor promotion prospects compared both with industry and with administrative careers in the SA and DAF.[28]

Though towards the end of 1934 the inflation fears had died down somewhat, the raw material and foreign currency situation had become a little easier, and the prospect of Christmas trade had brightened the horizon, the gloom in the commercial middle class about Germany's economic position was little abated and there was considerable disenchantment about the lack of progress made in almost two years of Nazi rule. According to one *Sopade* report, some business men were now beginning to deny that they had supported the Nazis and the case was cited of an 'Old Fighter', a shop-owner and former Party activist, who had become one of the biggest critics of the regime, as testimony to how far the disillusionment had extended.[29] In inimitable fashion the District Leader of Wasserburg in Upper Bavaria described the mood of the *Mittelstand* in his district in November 1934 as 'stinking' and as a result of excessive organization and burdensome demands for collection donations 'close to rebellion'.[30]

The massive wave of indignation at the corruption and scandalous behaviour of Party functionaries, the 'little Hitlers', which expressed itself in hopes for a thorough purge of the Party even before the massacre of the SA leadership at the end of June 1934, articulated above all outraged petty-bourgeois sentiments. According to one report sent to *Sopade* headquarters in May 1934, 'the criticism of the comfortable Munich petty bourgeois and *Spießer*, who actually curses loudest of all today, is summed up in the casual way in which a hairdresser recently put it to his customers: "yes, yes, our Adolfi is all right, but that lot round him, they're nothing

---

[28] GStA, MA 106765, AA Ingolstadt, 10 July 1934; MA 106767, AA Pfarr-kirchen, 9 Aug. 1934; AA Regensburg, 9 Aug. 1934; AA Würzburg, 7 Aug. 1934; AA Weißenburg, 11 Sept. 1934; AA Aschaffenburg, 10 Jan. 1935; AA Marktred-witz, 10 Jan. 1935; AA Mühldorf, 12 Jan. 1935; AA Würzburg, 11 Jan. 1935.

[29] DBS, 6 Nov. 1934, pp. A7–8; cf. also 16 Oct. 1935, pp. A12–13.

[30] StAM, NSDAP 127, KL Wasserburg, 6 Nov. 1934.

but rogues." '[31] This was a widely held view in Bavaria in the summer of 1934.[32] It reflected anger and disgust at the stark contrast between the state-sanctioned 'begging' of constant collections, salary deductions for Party formations, and *Eintopf*-Sundays and the squander, luxury-living, and immorality of their leaders and representatives.[33] Such feelings, among other criticisms, were voiced in the 40 per cent or so of Munich 'Special Court' cases in 1934 involving persons with middle-class occupations.

Despite their emphasis on middle-class discontent in 1934, *Sopade* reporters were anxious not to exaggerate its significance. They stressed the superficiality and weakness of middle-class criticism, its lack of ideological coherence and political aim, and its consequent harmlessness for the Nazi regime. Peasants and *Mittelständler*, reported the *Sopade* in autumn 1934, were competing to see who could complain most about the regime — and, unlike the peasantry, the *Mittelstand* had every cause for grievance since all the Nazi promises had been broken. These sections of the population had provided Hitler with his earliest and strongest support, but had now become 'the most uncertain and refractory members of his following'. This was because both peasant and *Mittelständler* had been driven into Hitler's arms almost entirely through egoistic, materialistic considerations. Politically less schooled than the working class and at the same time more materialistic, both groups had chased uncritically after the limitless promises mouthed by the Nazis and were now sorely disappointed. This disappointment, and not political rejection, determined their criticism of the regime: that the consumer associations had not been dissolved, that department stores continued in existence, that taxes still had to be paid — these were the foundation of their discontent.[34] A report emanating from Bavaria in December 1934 was equally disparaging about middle-class oppositional tendencies, regarding them as wholly lacking in political

[31] ASD, ES/M63/May 1934; DBS, 20 June 1934, p. A2.

[32] Cf. Kershaw, *Hitler-Mythos*, ch. 3.

[33] Cf. DBS, 26 June 1934, p. A1; and also ASD, ES/M31/17 Nov. 1934; ES/M32/25 Feb. 1935, for bitter complaints about the Party as a 'pigsty' riddled by massive corruption.

[34] DBS, 29 Sept. 1934, p. A37; 10 Jan. 1935, p. A20.

motivation and purely a reflex of most petty material complaints. Given an improvement in their personal economic situation, fickle critics — commented the report resignedly — changed their opinion of the regime without stopping to ask about the underlying reasons for the improvement and its inevitably short-term duration.[35]

The extent to which opinion was determined by economic circumstances and prospects also runs through the reports from the employment offices. As one assessment from Weißenburg (Middle Franconia) put it, the barometer of opinion was still largely the turnover of trade.[36] The head of the employment office in Regensburg, who constantly bemoaned the 'non-Nazi spirit' of the previously BVP-orientated Regensburg middle class, summarized the division of opinion among owners of small businesses by asserting that they were either 'hurrah-patriots' or 'morale murderers'.[37] The reports suggest, not surprisingly, that pro-regime attitudes were particularly apparent among those sections of business, trade, and industry which were the direct or indirect beneficiaries of government orders. This was especially the case in the metal-working and building trades, where the economic recovery was fast and the attitude of employers correspondingly favourable towards the efforts of the regime to stimulate the economy.[38] On the other hand morale was poor in those branches of business dependent on increased consumer spending, and particularly in export-geared businesses, where bitter complaints were uttered about loss of markets through Nazi economic policy and not least through the foreign boycotts of German goods resulting from the persecution of the Jews.[39] A report from Nuremberg described the mood among owners of export firms, which had suffered a steep decline in

[35] Ibid., 10 Jan. 1935, p. A26; ASD, ES/M64/Oct.-Nov. 1934, p. 3.

[36] GStA, MA 106767, AA Weißenburg, 9 Jan. 1935.

[37] Ibid., AA Regensburg, 9 Aug. 1934; cf. also the reports for 11 Sept. 1934 and 10 Jan. 1935.

[38] E.g., ibid., AA Augsburg, AA Nürnberg, AA Pfarrkirchen, AA Weiden, all 9 Aug. 1934; AA Würzburg, 11 Jan. 1935.

[39] E.g., GStA, MA 106765, AA Lindau, AA Marktredwitz, both 9 June 1934; MA 106767, AA Ansbach, 8 Aug. 1934; AA Weiden, 11 Sept. 1934; AA Marktredwitz, 7 Aug., 11 Sept. 1934; AA Nürnberg, 9 Aug. 1934.

trade, as 'hopeless'.[40] Equally despairing on account of the export position were the porcelain manufacturers of northern Bavaria.[41] In Cham, near the Czech border in the Upper Palatinate, the toy industry remained in a parlous state and the financial difficulties of employers had produced an angry response to the regime's economic programme. Not a few employers in the area allegedly hoped that the government would fail to master the raw material problems, and that there would then be a 'second revolution'. The reporter categorized those holding such views as 'mainly Jew-friends' who were of the opinion that the economy would not recover because the entire export trade had suffered irreparable damage through the severe handling of the Jewish Question.[42] Feelings in this poverty-zone of eastern Bavaria, that the area had been passed over in the provision of government orders and the financing of public works, ran high.[43] In contrast, the business sector in attractive tourist areas, especially the alpine reaches of Upper Bavaria but also areas such as the *Fränkische Schweiz* in Upper Franconia, had no cause to grumble about the economic benefits which the Third Reich had brought them. These areas had shown above-average support for the Nazis before 1933 and the stimulus to tourism provided by economic recovery in general, by the trips of the 'Strength through Joy' organization, and by the closed border with Austria, gave every reason for the broad satisfaction with the regime's economic measures recorded in the tourist regions.[44]

The shallowness of much of this opinion is obvious. The employment office reports are full of comments about the

[40] GStA, MA 106767, AA Nürnberg, 9 Aug. 1934.
[41] E.g., ibid., AA Marktredwitz, 7 Aug. 1934, 11 Sept. 1934; AA Weiden, 11 Sept. 1934; GStA, MA 106765, AA Marktredwitz, 9 July 1934.
[42] GStA, MA 106767, AA Cham, 10 Sept. 1934.
[43] E.g., ibid., AA Passau, 11 Jan. 1935; AA Cham, 9 Aug. 1934.
[44] E.g., ibid., AA Holzkirchen, 31 July 1934; AA Kempten, 9 Aug. 1934; AA Traunstein, 7 Aug., 8 Sept. 1934. For the high level of tourism in south Bavarian resorts, cf. GStA, MA 106670, RPvOB, 17 Jan., 17 Feb., 3 Mar., 19 Apr., 4 June 1934. The number of tourists in Bavaria showed a 34 per cent rise between 1933 and 1934, a 50 per cent increase between 1933 and 1936, and almost doubled by 1938. See H. Hesse, 'Auswirkung nationalsozialistischer Politik auf die bayerische Wirtschaft (1933–1939)', *Zeitschrift für bayerische Landesgeschichte*, xliii (1980), 442-3.

lack of true 'National Socialist spirit', the 'moneybags attitude', the petty-bourgeois '*Spießergeist*', and the 'individual
good before common good' standpoints among owners of
small businesses and workshops.[45] There are also numerous
indications of distaste for Party organizations and their interference in economic affairs — alongside the disgust at corruption in Party circles.[46] But none of this was incompatible
with broad approval of the course the Nazi government was
steering. In any case, there was no obvious alternative in
view. As *Sopade* analysts pointed out, middle-class opinion
was wholly destructive in nature: it consisted of complaints
but nothing more. The materially based disillusionment in
the lower middle class, claimed these reports, was devoid of
political significance. Fear of communism and 'lack of
political education', as one report put it, was sufficient to
ensure further petty-bourgeois approval of the Nazi government despite economic complaints. Passivity and carping
trivial criticism were seen by *Sopade* informants as the main
characteristics of opinion. The great mass of the regime's
opponents, argued the *Sopade*, were ideologically weak,

merely discontents, grumblers whose dissatisfaction has purely economic causes. That is especially so among the *Mittelstand* and the
peasantry. These social strata are least of all ready to fight seriously
against the regime because they know least of all what they should
fight for . . . The anxiety about Bolshevism, about the chaos which in
the opinion of the great mass in particular of the *Mittelstand* and the
peasantry would follow on the fall of Hitler, is still the negative mass
base of the regime.[47]

In addition, there were the undoubted gains which the regime
had made among middle-class youth. The *Sopade* pointed out
that it would be no more than vulgar Marxism to attribute
this purely to economic advantage and to ignore the very real
idealism among the Nazified youth.[48] Finally, there was the

[45] E.g., GStA, MA 106765, AA Weißenburg, 9 June 1934; MA 106767, AA
Cham, 9 Aug. 1934; AA Regensburg, 9 Aug. 1934; AA Weißenburg, 7 Aug.
1934, 11 Sept. 1934, 9 Jan. 1935; AA Würzburg, 11 Jan. 1935.
[46] E.g., GStA, MA 106765, AA Marktredwitz, 9 June 1934; MA 106767,
AA Regensburg, 11 Sept. 1934, 10 Jan. 1935; AA Straubing, 10 Sept. 1934; AA
Cham, 8 Jan. 1935; AA Schwandorf, 10 Jan. 1935; AA Weißenburg, 9 Jan. 1935.
[47] DBS, 26 June 1934, pp. B22-3 and also pp. A1-22, esp. pp. A20-2; ASD,
ES/M63/May 1934.
[48] DBS, 26 June 1934, p. B24; ASD, ES/M63/May 1934, which distinguishes

continued, even increased belief in the 'redeeming power', as one report put it, of the Führer to act as a counter-balance to the distaste for the more unpalatable sides of Party life in the Third Reich.[49] A south Bavarian report put the middle-class dissatisfaction with Nazism during 1934 in context when he pointed out that there were many discontents, but certainly no more than there had been during the Republic.[50]

The easing of the raw-material and foreign-currency situation which had been so threatening in mid-1934, the continued revitalization of the economy stimulating consumer spending, and an increase in government contracts all helped to bring about some objective improvement in the position of small businesses and craft concerns from late 1934 onwards.[51] There are, however, few signs of a matching improvement in middle-class opinion. Economic complaints continued unabated. Compulsory membership contributions to the obligatory guilds, and guild meetings at which directives were simply handed down without any possibility of debate were said to provoke great criticism. And instead of the expected tax reductions, tax regulations had been so tightened up that many small businesses, no longer daring to attempt minor tax frauds, found their net profits reduced. Among craftsmen, there was disappointment that army orders were consistently placed with large concerns which could offer better rates. Small traders, claimed the *Sopade*, were even worse off than *Handwerker* from government interference in the economy, and in many cases were being made arbitrary scapegoats for rising prices.[52] Butchers in particular, exposed to the full brunt of public fury at the meat and fats shortages and closely scrutinized by the authorities, felt aggrieved when, having been forced by farmers to pay more than the regulation price for meat carcasses, they were denounced by angry customers to the police for over-charging and fined or even taken into 'protective custody'. Since notices advertising

---

the criticism among older members of the *Mittelstand* from the pro-Nazi enthusiasm of the youth.
[49] ASD, ES/M63/Jan.–Feb. 1934; May 1934; July 1934.
[50] DBS, 6 Nov. 1934, p. A9.
[51] Cf. von Saldern, pp. 172–4, 279, 288.
[52] DBS, 12 Nov. 1935, pp. A89–108; cf. also 14 May 1935, p. A39.

the shortages and 'sold out' notices were banned, butchers — on occasion prosecuted even for complaining that the situation was so bad that they might as well go out of business — were compelled to buy at high prices in order to obtain any meat at all, but then to sell at the low fixed prices. It was little surprise, then, that bitter criticisms about profit margins were voiced, and that an Augsburg police report could describe the mood among butchers in the city as 'very depressed'.[53] This atmosphere probably contributed to the growth of racial violence involving 'aryan' attacks on Jewish cattle-dealers and butchers in 1935-6.

Sopade informants were adamant that there had been no improvement in middle-class attitudes towards the regime in 1935-6. On the contrary, they pointed out that the most vehement criticisms of the regime were still to be heard from the middle class, who 'because of their economic situation and their disappointed hopes' had become 'passionate grumblers' (*Nörgler*). Munich, in particular, was a hot-bed of criticism, though there was less to be heard in the more ex-posed atmosphere of small towns. Towards the end of 1936, the *Mittelstand* and small traders were said to be falling into 'an ever more disconsolate mood'.[54] Though the *Sopade* often inclined to stretch dissatisfactions with the regime as far as possible, support for its interpretation of middle-class discontent in 1935-6 comes from the reporting of the Nazi authorities themselves.

As consumers, broad sections of the middle class were ex-posed, like workers, to the food shortages and steeply rising prices of 1935-6 and were not slow to voice their anger. The growing unrest resulting from high food prices, butter and meat shortages, and, in addition, foreign currency difficulties and raw material deficiencies were common-place in the reports of the Bavarian authorities in these years.[55] One report in autumn 1935 from an NSDAP Block Leader in

[53] Ibid., 2 Apr. 1936; GStA, MA 106670, RPvOB, 9 Mar., 10 July, 9 Oct., 10 Nov., 11 Dec. 1936; MA 106677, RPvOF/MF, 9 Nov. 1935, 5 Nov. 1936; MA 106686, Pd Augsburg, 1 Sept., 3 Nov. 1936; ASD, ES/M64/Mar. 1936; ES/M34/20 Feb. 1937 (Hof).

[54] DBS, 4 July 1936, pp. A15-17; 9 Dec. 1936, p. A2.

[55] E.g., GStA, MA 106670, RPvOB, 8 Aug., 9 Sept., 11 Nov. 1935; 10 July, 9 Oct. 1936.

Mühldorf (Upper Bavaria) drew a clear distinction between the gratitude towards Hitler and the glowing faith in Nazism which he found among the very poor in his locality and the carping criticism and discontent which he encountered in his normal circle of contacts in the middle-class and business world. He had, he said, previously judged these sections of society to be 'the people' and their opinion to be 'popular opinion'. He was glad to be proved wrong, for otherwise

> I would have had to say that popular opinion is in a sorry state, that the people do not see the deeds of National Socialist Germany but as a talking-point know only about a shortage of butter, meat, or even twine, shut their eyes to the racketeering and dirty business of some circles (monasteries) but with Argus eyes watch out for every movement of our leaders and joyfully want to bring imagined mistakes of these men out into the open. [The poor people, content when they had the minimum to satisfy their modest needs, stood as an] unassailable bulwark against those notorious discontents who complain in the pub about the shortage of meat while in the middle of their leg of veal and their ham sandwiches, and after their sixth half litre of beer bemoan the high price of beer and the heavy taxes on it.[56]

Middle-class opinion was also adversely affected by the affront to bourgeois 'order' caused by the unruly and violent behaviour of Party activists during the summer of 1935. The renewed boycott campaign against the Jews (to which we will return in Chapter 6) formed the backcloth to a wave of elemental violence of activated Party groups, especially in the Hitler Youth, the SA, and the SS, which embraced not only publicly brutal treatment of Jews, but also attacks on Church youth groups, collectors for the Catholic *Caritas* organization, apparently mindless assaults on ordinary citizens, and distasteful scenes of street disorder and hooliganism. A whole series of unsavoury incidents in August and September prompted the Government President of Upper Bavaria to write: 'It is obvious that the mood of the people must suffer greatly from these constant serious outrages, that anxiety and hatred result, and that rumours build up into mountains. The people demand with all their might measures to be taken

---

[56] StAM, NSDAP 494. The reference to monasteries concerned the allegations made by the Nazis in 1935 about currency smuggling and other financial sharp-practices among the religious orders.

against these wrongdoers and their severe punishment.'[57] Disturbances of the peace were particularly frequent in places
with a resident camp of SA or SS men, often refugees from
Austria. Residents of the spa-town of Bad Aibling (Upper
Bavaria) experienced constant trouble from the camp of
Austrian SA men from the spring of 1934 until – to their
great relief – the disbanding of the camp in late 1935. The
behaviour of the SA men had, however, harmful consequences
for the area. Serious disturbances in the summer of 1935 led
to visitors packing their bags and leaving their hotels. The
owner of one of the largest hotels, complaining bitterly about
the effect of the SA's rowdyism on the tourist trade, said his
hotel had never been as empty as during the current summer.[58]
The breaches of the peace and frequent clashes with the
locals of the Austrian inmates of an SS camp in the Ebermannstadt district of Upper Franconia were said to have
soured the attitude of the population towards Nazism and to
have seriously damaged the standing of the Party in the
district. Memories of the trouble were long-lived. Seven years
later, in the middle of the war, hatred of the SS arising from
the earlier conflict was still so strong in the area that recruitment for the Waffen-SS met with a wholly negative
response.[59]

Finally, much antagonism in the middle class was provoked
by the 'Church struggle'. The open conflict which burst out
in the Protestant Church in the autumn of 1934 and the
growth in tension in relations between the Nazi State and the
Catholic Church from 1935 onwards were, as we shall see in
subsequent chapters, overriding factors in shaping political
opinion, not least in the middle class.

The breadth of middle-class discontent in 1935-6 was
clearly considerable. In political terms, however, it posed
even less of a problem to the regime than it had done during

[57] GStA, MA 106670, RPvOB, 9 Sept. 1935; MA 106691, RPvOB, LB, 9
Oct. 1935.
[58] GStA, MA 106670, RPvOB, 9 Sept. 1935.
[59] The saga of the conflict between the local population and the SS men
consistently preoccupied the local authorities during 1935-6 and can be followed
in the reports of the BA Ebermannstadt and GS Waischenfeld and Muggendorf in
StAB, K8/III, 18470-2; the failure of the Waffen-SS to recruit in 1943 is in ibid.,
18475, LR Ebermannstadt, 2 Feb. 1943. Cf. also, *Bayern I*, pp. 95–6, 165–9.

the 'summer of discontent' in 1934. According to one assessment of the situation, the 'all-embracing orgy of abuse' actually concealed a declining interest in domestic politics, itself a consequence of growing resignation and fatalism in the face of the power of the State and the lack of any alternative. The criticism was therefore wholly ineffective.[60] Another *Sopade* report argued that it would be mistaken to regard the general discontent as direct hostility to the regime, pointing out the ready compliance with orders despite the criticism and the frequency with which 'people complain very extensively about conditions and then again shout the loudest when they are fired with enthusiasm by Nazi speakers in some rally or other.'[61] Specific causes of discontent were also countered by approval of the wider implications of Nazi policy, or at least the feeling that Nazism offered the best solution possible, however imperfect. *Sopade* reporters were obliged to admit the effectiveness in bourgeois circles of the massive anti-Bolshevik campaign, the prevalent and deep anti-communism in the middle class, the pro-Hitler feeling, the disarming effect of a coup like the march into the Rhineland, and the grudging admission even in critical intellectual circles that Hitler had been proved right yet again. Finally, it had to be recognized that whatever the criticism it had not resulted in any hankering after the old democracy of the unlamented Weimar Republic.[62] The Border Secretary for south Bavaria illustrated the inconsistency of political attitude among the middle class of Augsburg and Munich with several striking examples. In one case, a house-owner launched into a tirade of petty economic criticisms, but on suddenly hearing marching music forced his way to the front on the pavement, raised his arm in the 'Hitler Greeting', and then surpassed himself in praise of the discipline of the marching SS. The observer of this behaviour commented: 'Anyone who had not heard him cursing just before would think that he had a pure

[60] DBS, 4 July 1936, pp. A16–17.
[61] DBS, 16 Oct. 1935, p. A3. For wild fluctuations and extremes of mood, cf. also ibid., 4 July 1936, pp. A6–7.
[62] Ibid., 16 Oct. 1935, p. A12; 12 Nov. 1935, p. A29; 6 Oct. 1936, p. A6; 10 Nov. 1936, p. A15; 9 Dec. 1936, pp. A5–6, 13–15; 15 Feb. 1937, p. A13; ASD, ES/M64/Mar. 1936; ES/M33/18 Mar. 1936; ES/M65/Feb. 1937.

Nazi before him. It seems that the man cannot think far enough to recognize that the marching SS and the power which so represses him in his daily life are in their final point one and the same.' A young typist, apart from her compulsory membership of the DAF not politically active in any way, astonished the *Sopade* informant travelling on the same tram by jumping out when the tram stopped to let a passing SS column cross the track and again enthusiastically and unsolicited offering the Hitler salute. When reproached with the fact that the show of enthusiasm had been wholly unnecessary, she replied that she had not done it for the SS or the Nazis, but 'from patriotic duty . . . because I am a German.'[63]

In addition to such ideological schizophrenia or utter confusion there were of course those who belonged to the growing caste, predominantly petty bourgeois, of Party apparatchiks and State *Beamte*, of the swollen Party and State bureaucracies, whose fates were inextricably bound up with that of the regime and who formed the basis of the new 'state-supportive bourgeoisie'.[64] By the reopening of the Party membership rolls in 1937, the Party itself had become even more middle class than it had been at the time of the 'seizure of power'.[65]

(iii) Opinion in the 'Productive' Middle Class during the Armaments Boom, 1937–9

On the basis of information reaching it from different parts of Germany, the *Sopade* was, for its part, convinced that the disenchantment within the trading and commercial sector of the middle class remained undiminished in the immediate pre-war years, suggesting in fact that there was an intensification of existing grievances, now aggravated by increased state intervention, restricted room for manoeuvre, and adverse effects of the labour and raw material shortages in the

---

[63] ASD, ES/M65/Feb. 1937.

[64] DBS, 5 Aug. 1936, p. A11. The report which uses this term came from Silesia, though the point is of course equally applicable to the position in Bavaria.

[65] Cf. Kater, pp. 49–53.

pressurized armaments economy. All reports had long agreed, it was stated early in 1937, that the commercial and trading *Mittelstand* was the most discontented sector of the population and complained the loudest. The complaints still amounted in essence to the degree of organizational regimentation and restriction, the decline in profit margins — not least through increased and more efficient taxation, contributions to commercial and professional organizations, and compulsory 'donations' to Party causes — raw material and food provisioning difficulties, and finally the continued existence of department stores and consumer co-operatives. Small traders were said to be the worst affected in Bavaria. Though there had been an increased turnover, profit margins had declined steeply. In the wholesale egg trade they had allegedly fallen from about 10 per cent to only 2 per cent, so that a fivefold increase in turnover was needed to achieve the earlier profit level at stable costs. Since January 1936, it was claimed, ninety cigarette shops and 165 out of 800 butcher concerns had been unable to retain commercial viability and had been forced to close down. Full order-books were not necessarily a cause for rejoicing. The wooden-clog industry, for example, had orders as never before but was unable to carry them out because of the leather shortage which prevented straps being made. Tailors were also well stocked with orders but complained that they were unable to complete many of them because dilatory payments by the Reich for military and government supplies left them short of cash and credit was difficult to obtain.[66]

Two years later the picture was little altered, and what change had taken place had generally been for the worst. The self-employed *Mittelstand*, especially the owners of small concerns, who had initially seen Hitler as their saviour, were now said to be bitterly disappointed and formed the 'main body of grumblers and discontents'. The furthering of large-scale industry at the expense of small business and crafts, the compulsory craft organizations and restrictions on the expansion of retail trade, the raw material shortages which

[66] DBS, 10 Mar. 1937, pp. A56, 69–75; cf. also ibid., 8 July 1937, p. A16, and ASD, ES/M147/Sept. 1937, 'Bericht aus München'.

were throttling small businesses, the extent of bureaucratic state interference, and now the conscription of workers from small workshops — often forcing closure — together with pressure to prevent apprentices becoming masters and forcing them into industry, were all sources of great discontent.[67]

Complaints about high taxation, and especially the problems caused by the raw material and labour shortages, recur frequently in the reports of the Nazi authorities. On the whole, however, the reports of the Bavarian Government Presidents contain little specific comment in the later 1930s on political reactions and attitudes among the commercial branches of the *Mittelstand*. The reports of Party functionaries are somewhat more forthcoming. Exceptional in its optimistic evaluation of middle-class opinion was a report from the Traunstein district of Upper Bavaria, which described the excellent mood in trading circles, for whom the Third Reich had, it was said, brought 'a real boom'. As the first beneficiaries of the economic recovery, small business men in the area were almost wholly grateful and ready to protect the Party, in which they gladly worked, from unjustified attacks (above all from those attached to the Church).[68] Apart from the obvious pro-Party tone of the report, Traunstein was one of the areas of southern Bavaria to profit from the undoubted boost which Nazism gave the tourist industry. In more purely rural and less prosperous districts the outlook was not so rosy. In the hop-growing area of Pfaffenhofen (Upper Bavaria) there were anxious fears among tradesmen about the reorganization and combing-out of small businesses to provide extra labour. Those affected were mildly described as showing 'reserve' towards the Party, and membership in business circles was lower than it ought to have been.[69] The District Leader of Landsberg am Lech (Swabia) pointed out in spring 1939 that despite the major foreign political successes in Czechoslovakia and the Memel region of the Baltic, the mood among craftsmen and small traders was depressed because of the impossibility of getting iron, wood, and other

[67] DBS, 5 Aug. 1939, pp. Λ53–79.
[68] StAM, NSDAP 983, KW Traunstein, Abschn.Haslach, 19 Nov. 1938.
[69] StAM, NSDAP 126, KL Pfaffenhofen, Jan.–Mar. 1939.

building materials – shortages so acute that building in the locality had ground almost to a complete halt. Furthermore, the bureaucracy and red tape involved in trying to acquire raw materials was itself a source of great irritation. The difficulties in the local building trade found forceful expression in the pointed criticisms of the extravagant building programmes of Party and State.[70] The implications for political attitudes of the same problems of the *Mittelstand* were emphasized by the District Leader of Aichach (Upper Bavaria). *Handwerk*, he stated, had up to now been favourably placed in the Third Reich. But the building restrictions were producing 'a special state of distress'. Craftsmen were receiving no government orders and 'were therefore already now standing unemployed in their own workshops.' If the restrictions continued, the 'estate of craftsmen' (*Handwerkerstand*) would be in the same danger as the peasantry: 'in the interests of the preservation of the small craftsmen, who are just as rooted in the soil as the peasantry is, it is urgently requested that the severe regulations be lifted or loosened.' The District Leader added that Party members were proud to help the Führer in this difficult time, but economic worries and anxieties depressed all 'joy of working'. People were only too ready to admire the Führer's mighty deeds, but 'the needs and worries of everyday life are so great that the mood quickly becomes depressed again.'[71] That such experiences were widespread is suggested by the frequent reference to the increasingly acute raw material and labour shortages in the reports of the Government Presidents and of the *Wehrmacht* Economic Inspectorate, whose Nuremberg office pointed out as early as 1937 that 'the gravest mood' was to be encountered among craftsmen since they had been most seriously disadvantaged through the regulated distribution of raw materials.[72] The Munich office added a short while later that the current worries about the raw materials

[70] Ibid., KL Landsberg, Jan.–Mar. 1939.
[71] Ibid., KL Aichach, 1. Vierteljahr 1939.
[72] BA/MA, RW19/33, WWI XIII (Nuremberg), 18 Nov. 1937. The raw material and labour shortages recur with monotonous regularity from late 1936 onwards not only in the WWI reports but also in those of all the Government Presidents.

and labour situation were scarcely less than the concern about lack of orders had been during the Depression.[73]

Among the commercial sector of the middle class, the position of those who earned their living from the tourist trade warrants separate mention. The social and economic structure of the south Bavarian tourist resorts, the depressed state of the tourist trade in the economic crisis of the early 1930s, and expectations of a revival under a Hitler government had contributed to above-average electoral support for Nazism in such areas before 1933.[74] And here, at least, the Nazi regime went a long way towards fulfilling such economic expectations during the first years of the Third Reich. The decision in 1933 to hold the Winter Olympics in 1936 at Garmisch-Partenkirchen brought publicity and trade to the district. Already by January 1934 reports of contented owners of hotels, public houses, and tourist-linked businesses, of hotel reservations taken to the last bed, of the influx of thousands of skiers from Munich, and of the arrival of the first major 'Strength through Joy' trips were reaching the Government President of Upper Bavaria from Garmisch and from other resorts.[75] Easter tourism in Garmisch was 40 per cent higher than in 1933; by the summer it had doubled the previous year's total, and the tricentenary of the Oberammergau Passion Play in 1934 brought 400,000 tourists (including 60,000 from abroad) to the area, encouraged by special travel reductions and offers.[76] Better relations with Austria, opened up by the trade treaty in the summer of 1936, caused worries about the likely effect on tourism, but the borders remained closed and record numbers of visitors — Berchtesgaden was 13 per cent up on the existing record set the previous year — and fully-booked hotels continued to be registered.[77] The year 1937 saw the peak of the pre-war tourist trade.[78] Commercially, the years of the big armaments-stimulated boom in the economy and of the major

[73] BA/MA, RW19/41, WWI VII (Munich), 19 Jan. 1938.
[74] Pridham, pp. 284–5; Hagmann, pp. 23*, 2–3, 12–13, 22.
[75] GStA, MA 106670, RPvOB, 3 Mar. 1934.
[76] Ibid., 19 Apr., 4 June, 4 July, 7 Sept., 8 Oct. 1934.
[77] Ibid., 7 Aug., 9 Sept., 11 Nov. 1936.
[78] Ibid., 9 Aug. 1937.

German diplomatic triumphs were years of decline and worry for the south Bavarian tourist resorts. In 1938 the feared and prophesied consequences of an *Anschluß* with Austria became reality: the elimination of the border and the fascination and curiosity of exploring the new extension to the Reich meant that Garmisch and Berchtesgaden fell very much in the shade of the Tyrol as holiday resorts and were reduced to no more than the profits of overnight stays of people en route for the *Ostmark*.[79] The acute tension in the Sudetenland crisis brought a premature end to the summer season in September 1938, and this was followed by reports of a very poor winter season and a correspondingly depressed mood among hoteliers, many of whom claimed substantial losses through having to accommodate their entire domestic staffs all winter despite the low trade. Transport restrictions did not help matters: the reduction in the number of trains serving pleasure areas contributed to a substantial drop even in the number of day-trippers.[80] In the spring and summer of 1939 tourism fell to a new low. Berchtesgaden registered a 10 per cent drop even on the previous year's reduced figure, and doubts were expressed about the policy of sending KdF trips to the Tyrol instead of southern Bavaria.[81] The new attraction this year, however, was Czechoslovakia, and those parts of northern Bavaria which bordered on the newly acquired Sudetenland found their tourism greatly slackened, as had happened in southern resorts the previous year.[82]

The *Sopade* claimed that those who earned their living from tourism had, like others in the commercial middle class, been deceived by Nazism. Business stood in the shade of war preparations and was receding fast. Foreigners were avoiding

---

[79] GStA, MA 106671, RPvOB, 10 Aug. 1938. Reality was naturally not so bleak as hoteliers made it sound. The number of registrations of visitors to Bavaria reached its pre-war peak of just over four million in 1938, before a drop of a half-million in 1939 to a level still higher than the 1936 total. These figures are nevertheless misleading in that they do not specify length of stay, and in 1938-9 many more visitors were simply passing through Bavaria rather than spending their holiday there. Figures from Hesse, p. 443.

[80] GStA, MA 106671, RPvOB, 10 Oct. 1938, 8 Feb. 1939.

[81] Ibid., 9 May, 10 July 1939.

[82] GStA, MA 106678, RPvOF/MF, 6 May, 8 June, 7 July 1939.

German spas for fear of being caught unawares by a declaration of war, and there had been a reduction too in the number of KdF trips. From the Berchtesgaden area it was reported that the expected boom from having the Führer's residence near by had not materialized. Instead the town was filled with empty hotels. The Upper Bavarian spa town of Bad Aibling had been turned into a depot for bomber crews on exercises in the area and all foreign guests had been required to leave. Hotel owners protested in vain at the loss of trade.[83] The palmy days of the tourist trade were over with the *Anschluß*, and though the relative prosperity of the resorts remained there had been a sharply perceptible decline in their fortunes since 1937. The direction which Nazi economic and foreign policy was taking ran counter to the specific interests of the tourist trade, and those who made their living from tourism had reason enough to feel that the Third Reich had flattered only to deceive.

The view that the interests of the 'productive' sectors of the petty bourgeoisie became increasingly sacrificed to the pressing needs of large-scale capitalist enterprise in the armaments drive has been countered by assertions that the degree of economic and political satisfaction among craftsmen and traders generally reached its height in the later 1930s.[84] The widely varying experience under Nazism even of these sections of the middle class makes generalization hazardous. Polarization of economic fortune and increased stratification within the small-business sector were certainly by-products of Nazi economic policies in these years.[85] If the demise of weaker concerns benefited their immediate rivals, and if (as was usually the case in the Third Reich) the strongest and fittest undoubtedly thrived, large numbers of the smaller craft and retail businesses — and they formed the vast majority of *Mittelstand* concerns[86] — must often have felt on a knife-edge of survival. Measured solely in terms of turnover of trade, small business appears to have prospered during the later 1930s,[87] even if this was largely incidental to the main

---

[83] DBS, 5 Aug. 1939, pp. A74–6.
[84] Cf. von Saldern, pp. 172–4, 176, 234 ff.; Krohn/Stegmann, pp. 74–80.
[85] Von Saldern, pp. 236–8.
[86] Cf. ibid., pp. 97–8.
[87] Ibid., pp. 279, 288.

thrust of Nazi economic policies. But the turnover of trade figures are not an index of *Mittelstand* feeling about its position in the Third Reich. Political attitudes did not necessarily have a direct relationship with economic discontent or satisfaction. The prosperous *Bürger* of Garmisch, for instance, who in economic terms had much to thank the regime for were increasingly antagonistic towards Nazism, not so much on economic grounds as because of the assault on the Catholic Church. But quite apart from such non-economic considerations, the evidence we have seen does not suggest that the degree of *Mittelstand* satisfaction with its socio-economic position in the Third Reich substantially increased in the immediate pre-war years. For committed National Socialists among the lower middle class, the economic problems facing them presumably confirmed their diagnosis of the threat to Germany's (and to their) future which only Hitler and Nazism could combat. For avowed anti-Nazis engaged in craft production and small business, the economic circumstances can only have strengthened their original antipathy towards the regime. For those however — probably the vast majority — who held no utopian views of the future but had hoped for concrete gains from the Third Reich, the years 1937–9 were a period of disappointment, worry, and resignation.

Whatever discontent there was in the lower middle class, the regime did not need to take it very seriously (in contrast to its sensitivity towards unrest among workers and also among peasants). Not only was the *Mittelstand* divided among itself, wholly without political or economic muscle, and incapable of disrupting any sphere of production, but the discontent itself, as *Sopade* reports pointed out, was largely unpolitical in nature.[88] The economic grievances of specific groups seldom hindered compliance with the demands of the Nazi authorities and were perfectly compatible with ideological affinities with Nazism and with approval, sometimes enthusiastic, of the Nazi system as a whole.

[88] DBS, 5 Aug. 1939, p. 68.

(iv) The 'Non-productive' Middle Class: Opinion among Civil Servants and Teachers, 1938-9

The compatibility of sectional grievances not only with resigned acceptance but also with full-hearted support for the regime is illustrated most clearly by the sections of the middle class most closely associated with and dependant upon the State — civil servants and teachers.

For very obvious reasons, civil servants — never greatly prone to open criticism of their employer, the State — were particularly reticent about voicing their opinion during the Third Reich. Apart from odd glimmers casting a veiled reflection of their interests, concerns, and responses, civil servants left few traces in the records of their feelings and attitudes. Contemporary reporters on opinion found it impossible to penetrate the wall of silence. The District Leader of Wasserburg, for example, noted that *Beamte* in his district were 'difficult to see through because too well camouflaged', but was convinced that most had become Nazis only in order to save their own skins.[89] The removal of all former socialist civil servants and the intimidation of the rest was also a major hindrance to reliable information about *Beamte* reaching the *Sopade* information network.[90] The reluctance to step out of line needs no stressing. Whereas workers on the shop-floor of a factory could depend upon a degree of solidarity and be well aware of an anti-Nazi stance among many of their immediate work-mates, the atmosphere in which the civil servant worked was permeated by the need to be seen, as one report put it, as '110 per cent National Socialists'.[91] The pro-Nazi or at least regime-conformist attitude in public buildings such as the Nuremberg employment office, where at the beginning of 1935 a third of the *Beamte* and 40 per cent of the white-collar staff were Party members (a large proportion 'Old Fighters') was all but complete.[92]

Even so, signs of disillusionment among civil servants, many of whom had harboured high expectations of a return to the enhanced status traditionally associated with the

[89] StAM, NSDAP 127, KL Wasserburg, 6 Nov. 1934.
[90] DBS, 6 Feb. 1935, p. A45.
[91] StANeu, LO 66, KL Memmingen, Ogr. Heimertingen, 3 Nov. 1936.
[92] GStA, MA 106767, AA Nürnberg, 10 Jan. 1935.

German civil service as a consequence of the Nazi restoration of an authoritarian State, became increasingly apparent in the later 1930s. Among higher civil servants the disenchantment resulting from the loss of authority brought about by the profusion of overlapping competences and administrative chaos, above all by Party interference, from the loss of status caused by constant denigration by the Party and public ridicule of the 'bureaucracy', from salary reductions said to have reduced the civil service 'to the economic status of the proletariat', and finally from the insecurity through constant exposure to political discrimination is clearly to be seen in the memorandum of the leading Prussian civil servant Fritz-Dietlof, Graf von der Schulenburg, a conservative nationalist who was to be executed following the failure of the plot to kill Hitler in 1944. This memorandum, entitled 'The Civil Service. Crisis and Remedy', contrasts vividly with the optimism von Schulenburg expressed in an earlier memorandum, compiled in 1933, which looked to the Nazi State for the necessary regeneration of the higher civil service.[93] Many of the same problems, in what has been dubbed 'a crisis of morale and effectiveness',[94] troubled 'ordinary' Bavarian civil servants of less exalted grade than von Schulenburg. Party interference and control, and the preference accorded to 'Old Fighters', was strongly resented; insecurity, with positions hinging on the arbitrary concept of 'political reliability', was a cause for constant worry; and the feeling that their heavily increased duties and unparalleled devotion to duty were meeting not only with no public recognition but with open denigration by leaders of Party and State was galling in the extreme.[95] In addition, there was the growing pressure of work itself and the lack of due financial recompense — especially compared with the higher salaries to be earned in the private sector — which became increasingly

[93] The two memoranda are in H. Mommsen, *Beamtentum im Dritten Reich*, Stuttgart, 1966, pp. 137-42, 146-50. Part of the 1937 memorandum is translated in *Docs. on Nazism*, pp. 258-9. For a brief pen-picture of Schulenburg, cf. J. Caplan, 'Recreating the Civil Service: Issues and Ideas in the Nazi Regime', in Noakes (ed.), *Govt., Party, and People*, p. 46.

[94] Caplan, 'Recreating the Civil Service', p. 52.

[95] DBS, 14 Jan. 1936, p. A104; cf. also ibid., 4 July 1936, p. A81; 15 July 1935, p. A75; and 10 May 1939, p. 48.

apparent in the immediate pre-war years. The Government President of Upper and Middle Franconia registered in February 1937 what he regarded as the justified complaints within the civil service of the shortage of personnel and the growing burden of work which could not be mastered.[96] In the summer of the following year he included in his report a long explanation of the discontent among civil servants at the new regulation of their working week, now fixed at fifty-one hours.[97] In spring 1939 he noted the problems of trying to maintain local administration given the heavy burden of work and the greater financial opportunities in the private sector arising from the labour shortage.[98] An NSLB report from the Traunstein district of Upper Bavaria in September 1938 also emphasized the unrest among civil servants and the lassitude which the gap in salaries between civil servants and administrators in the private sector had provoked.[99] A report from the same district two months later stated that civil servants still demanded the repeal of Brüning's emergency decree of 1931, which had drastically reduced the salaries of *Beamte*, both because this had been promised in almost all Party meetings before the 'seizure of power' and because salaries had visibly failed to keep up with rising prices in the past few years. The report went on to lament the fact that lower- and middle-ranking civil servants had, as a result, often fallen heavily into debt and, since their salaries 'often no longer sufficed for an appearance in keeping with their position', were increasingly compelled 'to withdraw from social life'. The report stressed, however, that despite these economic worries civil servants were the 'citizens who most sincerely approved of the Third Reich', as their voluntary work in many honorary posts of the Party proved: 'There was probably not a single civil servant who did not rejoice at the creation of the *Wehrmacht* and Greater Germany. The persecution of the Jews was almost generally

---

[96] GStA, MA 106677, RPvOF/MF, 5 Feb. 1937.

[97] GStA, MA 106678, RPvOF/MF, 7 July 1938.

[98] Ibid., 10 Apr., 6 May 1939. Complaints about a 'paper-war' (*Papierkrieg*) were commonplace among local civil servants.

[99] StAM, NSDAP 983, unnamed NSLB-*Abschnitt* to KW Traunstein, 23 Sept. 1938.

understood and welcomed. Only a few old bureaucrats regretted the measures taken [i.e., in the November pogrom of 1938], especially the use of force by the people.'[1] Even allowing for the internal bias of the reporter and the fact that the feelings expressed were in some measure clearly his own, there seems little reason to doubt the impression of growing dissatisfaction with the Third Reich's treatment of civil servants together with widespread acceptance of the main 'achievements' of Nazism implied in the report.

Worries about status and remuneration were also dominant features of opinion among schoolteachers (themselves classed as *Beamte*) in the later 1930s. Like civil servants, teachers had swarmed into the Party in their thousands in 1933. At the closure of Party entry in May 1933 something like a quarter of Germany's 330,000 teachers had joined the NSDAP — Party membership of the overall adult population at this date was about one in twenty — and by 1937 this had risen to close on a third. In addition, almost a quarter of all male teachers were said to belong to the SA, SS, or NSKK.[2] Membership of the NSLB, the Nazi Teachers' Association, was effectively compulsory and comprised 97 per cent of all teachers. However, the high proportion of teachers anxious to join the Party itself cannot be attributed solely to opportunism. Many had great hopes, like civil servants, that the Third Reich would restore the status and authority of the profession, which they felt had sadly declined during the Republic. The emphasis placed by the Nazi Movement upon order, discipline, authority, and leadership seemed to promise much for the future. In addition, teachers were probably more affected than most by a type of naïve idealism and romanticism furthered by connections with the youth movement and patriotic associations, and which the Nazis, with their appeal to youth and the vital task of teachers in educating the future élite, were well able to exploit. This fervent belief in the 'ideals' of Nazism found its reflection in the fact that teachers formed an extraordinarily high proportion of Party functionaries.[3] As teachers never tired of pointing out,

[1] Ibid., KW Traunstein, Abschn. Haslach, 19 Nov. 1938.
[2] *Bayern I*, pp. 528-9; DBS, 8 July 1937, p. A119.
[3] Fourteen per cent of teachers compared with 6 per cent of civil servants

Party work in the province rested overwhelmingly upon their shoulders. The schoolteacher in one Upper Bavarian village did not hesitate to indicate the extra burdens he carried on behalf of the Party: apart from being District Propaganda Leader of the NSLB, he was the Party Local Group Leader, ran the NSV welfare organization, was parish clerk, and held a further six minor offices. 'Where the teacher is missing, the outlook is usually poor', he concluded.[4] Uncharitable souls hinted that only teachers had time to spare for such things.[5]

The 1930s were, however, a period of growing disillusionment and bitterness for many teachers, and their dismay at the educational trend between 1933 and 1939, in particular at their own declining professional status, is well reflected in the tone of the NSLB reports surviving for Upper Bavaria for the years 1938-9.[6] Whatever the promise and the expectation, it is clear that the reality of the Third Reich amounted for teachers to a serious worsening of their professional status and conditions. Rising numbers of pupils in the primary schools were taught by fewer and fewer teachers so that class sizes increased on average from thirty-nine to forty-five between 1931 and 1939 and the shortage of teachers — reckoned at 600 in Bavaria, as many as 3,000 in Prussia by 1939 — prompted above all by low salaries and poor prospects grew steadily worse.[7] In secondary schools the situation was if anything even worse, while the catastrophic fall in the numbers of students at universities and colleges of education presented the prospect of a calamitous shortage of teachers within the near future.[8]

The recurring grievances in the NSLB reports for 1938 and 1939 revolved mainly around the lack of the public esteem which the teacher felt was no more than due recognition of his onerous, selfless, and idealistic service to the community,

---

belonged to the Party's political leadership corps: R. Grunberger, *A Social History of the Third Reich*, London, 1971, p. 287.

[4] StAM, NSDAP 983, KW Wolfratshausen, 21 June 1938.

[5] Ibid., KW Pfaffenhofen, Jan. 1939.

[6] A selection of the NSLB reports from StAM, NSDAP 983 can be found in *Bayern I*, pp. 527 ff.

[7] Grunberger, p. 291; DBS, 14 Apr. 1939, pp. A39-51; StAM, NSDAP 983, KW Landsberg, 17 Mar. 1939.

[8] DBS, 14 Apr. 1939, pp. A41-52; Grunberger, pp. 293-5.

and the deterioration in his material standard of living and the conditions of his professional life. A report from Altötting, a Catholic stronghold in Upper Bavaria, brought out wholly typical teacher attitudes. Of the 130 teachers in the area, 36 (28 per cent) were Party functionaries, eight of whom held between two and four offices; 84 (65 per cent) were Party members; and 80 (62 per cent) belonged to Party affiliations (twenty of these in a leading capacity). An example was given in the report of conditions in one local school: there were eighty (!) children to a class because of shortage of space, there was hardly any cloakroom space, toilet facilities were deplorable, ventilation was poor, and physical education classes could only be held when the weather was fine. The report turned to the burning questions of status and pay:

A large proportion of the teachers volunteer out of idealism for all possible honorary posts. Especially in the countryside the teacher has already become the maid-of-all-work. As the true servant of the State the teacher has to do all the jobs that other people don't want to do, or carry out only reluctantly. Despite this the opinion is prevalent in one section of the population that 'the teacher has nothing to do'. In fact it is the case that the teacher fills up his entire leisure time with honorary jobs. The reward for this: in assessing his school work this extra work is not in any way taken account of. About the poor remuneration of teachers there can no longer be any doubt among those in high places. This is the main cause of the teacher shortage. It is also in the essence of the teaching profession that it offers no possibilities of advancement! One compares the free professions with this. The teacher used to have his service to the Church (i.e., playing the organ etc.) and his clerical work for the parish as good sources of additional earnings. Now he has instead the honorary offices of the Political Leader, far more onerous and not always well liked by the people. How can the carrying out of service to the Church be reconciled with the activity of the Political Leader?[9]

The shortage of teachers and, from the Party standpoint, the unhealthy dependence of the village schoolteacher on the Church through his side-activity as organist or choir-master were both forcefully advanced as reasons why 'in the interest of the standing of our profession it is absolutely necessary that we are socially better placed.'[10]

[9] StAM, NSDAP 983, KW Altötting, 15 Feb. 1939.
[10] Ibid., KW Pfaffenhofen, 10 Jan. 1939; GW Mü.–Obb., 23 Feb. 1939.

The strength of feeling in the teaching profession about declining material and social status was expressed repeatedly and pointedly by the NSLB *Gau* Administration in its monthly reports to the NSLB headquarters in Bayreuth, never more forcibly than in its comments of February 1939:

The teacher of our time, who from morning until late at night works in school with the German child and out of school in the Party and its formations in the reshaping of the German people according to the wishes of our Fuhrer *is no longer prepared* to accept the repeated, most caustic attacks on his professional honour passively and without reply! The bitterness is growing, and with it a loss of desire to take part in the task of education; discontent and distrust are setting in. The insufficient remuneration prompts even the most idealistic teacher to join in the complaints!! According to rumours, the basic salary of the senior teacher is to be reduced from 5,800 to 5,400 RM. Joyful prospects!!![11]

The final comments referred to the eventually implemented co-ordination of teachers' salaries throughout the Reich with the somewhat lower rates in Prussia — in other words a levelling down as far as Bavarian teachers were concerned. The bitterness about the poor public image of the teaching profession was made doubly galling by the contempt with which Baldur von Schirach, the Hitler Youth Leader, had publicly spoken the previous year about 'pedantic schoolmasters', remarks which created a furore among teachers who stressed their devoted and indispensable service to the Hitler Youth Movement, rewarded only by such unprovoked public slander and lack of appreciation by its leadership.[12] The teachers' anger sharpened, too, their resentment at what they saw as the undermining of their authority in the classroom through the lack of respect for teachers being bred into the Hitler Youth, and at the constant interference with the curriculum through the demands made upon young people's time by the youth formations.[13]

By the outbreak of war, morale in the teaching profession was at a lower ebb than at any other time since the beginning

[11] Ibid., GW Mü.-Obb., 23 Feb. 1939.
[12] Ibid., KW Garmisch, 2 June 1938; KW Aichach, 17 June 1938; unnamed *Abschnitt*, KW Traunstein, 23 Sept. 1938; KW Erding, 25 May 1938; KW Pfaffenhofen, 10 Jan. 1939; GW Mü.-Obb., 1 July 1938, 23 Dec. 1938.
[13] Cf. DBS, 10 Nov. 1936, p. A94; ASD, ES/M34/20 Feb. 1937; 21 July 1937 (Nürnberg).

of the Third Reich. The socio-economic grievances of teachers were more deeply felt and more widespread than they had been even three years earlier. In some measure they were also clearly justified. However, for all their complaints a remarkably high proportion of primary school teachers continued to provide a mainstay of the local Party organizations, retained their enthusiasm for the ideals of Nazism, supported the broad policies of the National Socialist State, and never developed their criticism beyond objections to public statements of Baldur von Schirach and a general cultural pessimism about education and the future of their own profession. And, more ideologically motivated than perhaps any other single section of the population, they could be relied upon to provide solid and dependable backing for Nazi policies if and when necessary. More than that, the NSLB was prepared to take the initiative and lead the way in expressions of support for Nazi policy. Following the outrages against the Jews in November 1938, which popular opinion found largely repellent at least in the methods employed, 84 per cent of Protestant and 75 per cent of Catholic teachers in Upper and Middle Franconia refused to teach religious instruction in schools as a protest at the assassination of the German Legation secretary in Paris by a young Jew.[14] The figures for southern Bavaria are not known, but similar sentiments were expressed there too by teachers. After Education Minister Adolf Wagner had decreed that teachers had, after all, to continue holding religious instruction (in order to prevent priests taking it over), some Upper Bavarian teachers recorded their dissent. According to one comment, teachers could not understand why they still had to teach the Old Testament: they were surely not expected to speak about Moses between eight and nine o'clock and then in the next hour preach the ideas of National Socialism.[15] Certainly these comments were not representative of all teachers, and the high percentages refusing to hold religious instruction in November 1938 have to be regarded in part as the product of

[14] GStA, MA 106678, RPvOF/MF, 7 Jan. 1939; cf. *Bayern I*, p. 547 & n. 23-4.
[15] StAM, NSDAP 983, KW Weilheim, Abschn. Peißenburg, 18 Nov. 1938. For Wagner's decree, cf. *Bayern I*, p. 549, n. 25.

fear at being seen to be nonconformist in the key Jewish Question.[16] On the other hand, the pro-Nazi sentiments of substantial sections of the teaching profession cannot be denied. Given this degree of conformity and acclamation of Nazism, the socio-economic complaints about pay and status were of no political significance.

(v) Features of Middle-Class Opinion during the Last Years of Peace

It is not possible to follow in any detail the responses of other specific sections of the middle class in the years immediately preceding the war. However, during this period the *Sopade* came to pay increased attention to the signs of discontent among the bourgeoisie as an indication of Nazism's alienation of its mass base. Though, as the compilers of the *Deutschland-Berichte* themselves pointed out,[17] some reporters exaggerated the significance of the information they provided, the *Sopade* analysis of the nature of middle-class opinion in the last years of peace is perceptive and balanced.

Three features were repeatedly emphasized as characteristics of predominantly middle-class opinion, if not exclusive to that section of the population: anger at corruption and extravagance within the Nazi Party; greater awareness of the repressive nature of the Nazi State; and an all-pervading sense of insecurity and uncertainty as the danger of war loomed ever larger.

Scathing attacks on the corruption and scandalous high-living of Party bosses were apparently commonplace, and an especially striking feature of middle-class opinion in Munich, headquarters of the Party and styled the 'capital city of the Movement'. A number of reports pointed out that Munich was singular in its atmosphere of relatively free criticism of Nazism.[18] The cabaret comedian Weiß Ferdl was reputed to have exaggerated only marginally when he said that although

---

[16] Hints of the coercion used and of the 'inner division' within the teaching profession over the issue can be seen in the report of the RPvOF/MF, 7 Jan. 1939, GStA, MA 106678.

[17] Cf. e.g., DBS, 8 May 1937, pp. A8–9.

[18] E.g. DBS, 18 Sept. 1937, pp. A7–8.

he knew 98 per cent of the city's population stood behind
the Führer and the government he always had the bad luck
to meet people who belonged to the other 2 per cent![19] Anti-
Party feeling was reportedly most vociferous in the middle
class. It focused above all on the corrupt life-styles of the
Nazi big-wigs, the epitome of whom was the universally
detested city councillor Christian Weber, former hotel page-
boy, close associate of Hitler since the early days, and currently owner of the Munich racecourse, the regional bus
service (which was used for KdF outings), numerous villas,
hotels, petrol-stations, and a brewery, who had set up his
appartments in the *Residenz*, former home of the Kings of
Bavaria. Weber, the 'tyrant of Munich' had allegedly become
'the direct symbol of National Socialism' in the city and had
helped substantially in making the Party the 'object of contempt' which could create respect only through coercion.[20]
Though Munich was particularly sensitive on the subject of
Party corruption, the sentiment was widespread. Corruption
was everywhere a leading component of the Party's image.[21]

As *Sopade* observers recognized, however, this type of
anger and discontent had little political significance, and in
fact highlighted the limited political horizons of the middle
class in particular. As a report from early 1938 pointed out,
'it is not as if Weber is identical with Hitler in popular consciousness. People trust that Hitler will come one of these
days and bump off (*abknallen*) Weber and the other big-shots
just as he once bumped off Röhm. That would be something
which would again bring Hitler the sympathy of broad
sections of the population.' In the power struggle in Munich
between Weber and the Police President Eberstein, thought
generally to be 'a decent man', public sympathy was all on
one side, but the perception of the contest was limited:
people were 'not judging National Socialism as a system of
corruption and barbarism', but merely the personal merits

---

[19] ASD, ES/M147/Sept. 1937. DBS, 12 Apr. 1937, pp. A1, 3–7 pointed out
that such comedians were allowed a fair degree of licence by the regime since
their real role was in defusing anger through humour.
[20] DBS, 18 Sept. 1937, pp. A7–13.
[21] Cf. ibid., 14 June 1937, pp. 8–11 from various parts of Bavaria, and Kershaw, *Hitler-Mythos*, p. 88.

and rivalries of Weber and Eberstein.[22] The divisions and confusion of opinion were revealed when one probed any deeper than the superficial lowest common denominator of opposition to the corrupt rule of the Party bosses. Some pointed out that alongside the Party 'big-shots' were 'good and honest leaders who mean well and are idealists'. Those who thought more carefully quickly realized that the *Bonzen* could not consume all the vast sums themselves, however extravagant. The State needed the money for armaments. The question of armaments immediately, however, provoked differing reactions. The argument was commonly put that Germany needed armaments to put it on a par with its enemies, and that neither Hitler nor the *Bonzen* could be blamed for that. Was it not also right, asked some, that Germany should again have colonies like the other major powers so that food supplies would be secured? And the feeling was that Hitler would get them 'because he has always succeeded up to now in that he has set out to do.'[23]

The inability to see the basic essence of the system, to observe more than its surface phenomena, was attributed by *Sopade* analysts to the growing 'depoliticization' of the population, by which they meant the growing tendency, prompted by the apparent pointlessness of opposition and absence of any alternative, to lapse into political indifference and apathy.[24] This was furthered by the regime's ability to disarm critics, demonstrate the awesome power of the State, and legitimize its authority through grandiose feats of organization and propaganda. Though the cost of the State extravaganzas provoked criticism, 'the drive with which the Nazis always set about things impresses people' and 'the art

[22] ASD, EM/M66/Dec. 1937-Jan. 1938; cf. also DBS, 17 Feb.1938, pp. A15-15c; 24 Aug. 1938, pp. A5, 19-20; 10 Dec. 1938, pp. A1-2.

[23] ASD, ES/M66/Dec. 1937-Jan. 1938.

[24] 'Depoliticization' is employed here in a different context and with a different meaning to its usage by modern political scientists writing (rather prematurely) of the 'end of ideology' and 'a "lightening" of the political subsystem in society' as 'the goals of society shift to economic areas and problems but are pursued with less intensity', which has been interpreted as 'a universal phenomenon associated with modernity in general and economic prosperity in particular' – J.P. Nettl, *Political Mobilization. A Sociological Analysis of Methods and Concepts*, London, 1967, p. 74 & n. 1.

of the Propaganda Ministry in always finding something new and bigger can constantly chalk up successes.' One reporter summed up cynically the fickleness of popular opinion: 'the people curse, stand there, and are dazzled.'[25]

Alongside material concerns, the awareness of the repressive nature of the regime and the loss of individual rights was coming to play an increasing role in shaping middle-class attitudes towards Nazism.[26] A report in February 1939 stated that the decline in morale particularly affected the bourgeoisie, and that not even the foreign political successes of 1938 had been able to divert more than temporarily from the materialistic and idealistic issues influencing middle-class opinion. Matters of direct material concern related above all to the ever-increasing intervention of the State in the economy: 'Private property has not been done away with, but its utilization is becoming ever more extensively regulated by the State. Earnings are good, but the freedom of disposition over the earnings is being more and more restricted.' Worries among businessmen and economic experts about the future had increased considerably since the removal of Schacht.[27] Idealistic factors affecting attitudes towards the regime were said to have gained in importance since the pogrom against the Jews in November 1938 'which had seriously damaged the prestige of the regime, particularly among the bourgeoisie.'[28]

Above all, it was the growing uncertainty about the future and the increasing likelihood of Germany's embroilment in another war which preoccupied middle-class opinion in 1938-9. A report of the *Wehrmacht* Economic Inspectorate for southern Bavaria encapsulates the prevailing popular mood, and while not specifically alluding to the middle class expresses sentiments characteristic of this section of the population:

The theatres are well patronized, the cinemas full, the cafés over-crowded, with music and dancing till the early hours. Sunday excursion

---

[25] ASD, ES/M66/Dec. 1937-Jan. 1938.

[26] Cf. e.g., DBS, 14 June 1937, p. A8.

[27] Ibid., 9 Feb. 1939, pp. A3-4. These comments did not derive from specifically Bavarian sources, but there is no reason to suppose that opinion in Bavaria deviated significantly from such sentiments.

[28] Ibid., p. A1.

traffic is setting record figures. And despite all these symptoms of a good economic situation, the mood in broad sections of the population does not accord with the boom conditions. Either it is largely depressed about the future, or unconcerned about the morrow for the sake of a merry *carpe diem*. This discrepancy between economic situation and popular mood is, however, far from attributable to the worry that the big public orders within and outside the *Wehrmacht* might one day come to an end, and with them work and wages; for the broad mass of the population does not concern itself much with the financial background to the German economic recovery. Rather there exists in the broadest sections of the population the earnest concern that in the long or short run a war will put an end to the economic prosperity and have a terrible end for Germany . . . In the last years there has truly been no lack of high political tension. And as grateful as the people is that not least thanks to the love of peace of the leadership of the Reich this has passed off without explosion, the anxious worry still dominates much of the population that, according to the proverb 'the pitcher keeps on going to the well until it breaks', it could sometime turn out differently and a war bring a sudden end to the fortune and prosperity of the present time.[29]

According to *Sopade* reports from Bavaria, the firm belief 'in bourgeois circles' by late 1938 was that world war was inevitable. While there was much contempt for the western democracies, especially after the way they had handed over the Sudetenland, the feeling was that Britain was playing for time in order to rearm and would in the end be able to hold out longer than Germany, whose provisioning was wholly inadequate in the long run. The prognosis, therefore, was that Germany could not win a war.[30] In spring 1939 the *Sopade* even hinted, in almost Wagnerian terms, at an 'end of the world mood' (*Weltuntergangsstimmung*) in the bourgeoisie. The long-existent discontent, even among those who had profited from the boom, was now overshadowed by the repressive feeling of great uncertainty which had developed over the past few months especially, it went on, in those upper reaches of the bourgeoisie which had long sympathized with Nazism and had welcomed Hitler as the liberator from the growing influence of the labour movement, control of free public opinion, and the restrictions of parliamentary democracy, and now realized that they had jumped from the

[29] BA/MA, RW19/41, WWI VII (Munich), 9 Sept. 1938.
[30] DBS, 10 Dec. 1938, p. A2.

frying-pan into the fire. Thinking that Hitler had rescued them from the threat of Bolshevism, they now saw that Nazism, from their point of view, was nothing more than 'a special sort of Bolshevism'.[31]

To ask whether, between 1933 and 1939, growing alienation from Nazism or increasing integration into the National Socialist State more accurately categorized the political attitudes of the middle class is to pose over-simplistic alternatives. A clear distinction is necessary between integration brought about through the serving of direct material interests and that deriving from ideological identification (which may be only tangential to, indirectly related to, or vaguely thought in the long run to benefit material interest).

Given the heterogeneous nature of 'the middle class' and the range of occupations included within that umbrella term, it is not surprising that the objective position of middle-class individuals varied very widely, that there were many winners as well as losers from the economic offshoots of Nazi policies.[32] It would be a gross exaggeration to speak of the middle class being 'bled white',[33] and not all *Mittelstand* interests were blatantly ignored by the regime. But even so there were obvious grounds for grievance: a large proportion of small retail businesses brought their owners an income lower than that of skilled workers; over a hundred thousand independent artisans became wage-workers between 1936 and 1938; and real wages in the 'non-productive' sector fell by up to 20 per cent whereas those of skilled workers remained fairly stable.[34] The evidence presented in this chapter has reflected the widespread discontent arising from the feeling in middle-class circles that the regime was neglecting *Mittelstand* interests. Whatever the objective reality, these interests were not seen as being upheld. On this plane, the dissatisfaction with Nazism was extensive, and had not

[31] Ibid., 14 Apr. 1939, p. A33.
[32] Von Saldern, pp. 234–46.
[33] As stated by Poulantzas, p. 246. His reference here is to the experience of the petty bourgeoisie in fascist Italy, but from his argument there is no doubt that he would see the fate of the petty bourgeoisie in Germany as an identical one.
[34] Ibid., pp. 283–4; von Saldern, p. 95.

noticeably diminished by 1939. Even the *Sopade*, with its vested interest in emphasizing worker antipathy to the regime, continued in the later 1930s to stress that the most outright criticisms were still to be found in the bourgeoisie.[35]

From the point of view of material self-interest, middle-class identification with the regime reached arguably its lowest level. As is well known, however, the various strands which go to form 'popular' or 'public opinion' are seldom consciously interrelated.[36] The sources cited above have demonstrated the compatibility of dissatisfaction on matters of status and economic self-interest with broad basic consensus in acceptance of the values and ideals of Nazism. On the ideological plane, identification with the regime and its presumed aims remained close. It was closest of all in the accordance with the crushing of Marxism and of labour organizations, in the acclamation of foreign policy triumphs and the construction of an internally and externally strong state, and not least in the adulation of the Führer as the epitome of values with which middle-class Germans could identify. In these spheres in particular Nazi propaganda's success rate was undoubtedly high in playing upon pre-existent middle-class prejudices and in reaffirming widely prevalent notions of an idealized social and political order. The close affinities between Nazi values and those of large sections of the middle class in this ideological realm, which largely existed outside the immediate experience of everyday life, continued to accompany and from time to time to override the disenchantments of unfulfilled material interests. As a consequence, middle-class protest, in the economic sphere at least, was largely individualized and confined to loud grumbling and 'wholly ineffectual cursing'.[37] Not only the organizational potential, but also the will to oppose was lacking. Moreover, the regime continued to find in the ranks of the middle class its highest success rates in the mobilization of plebiscitary support. Middle-class disillusionment with economic reality under Nazism was no barrier to its remaining politically and ideologically the backbone of the regime's support, even if this support was for the most part passive and resigned rather than active and enthusiastic. Complaint and compliance were related characteristics of middle-class life in the Third Reich.

4. The Disillusioning of the Protestants

The acquisition of Franconian territories and of the free Reich cities within its geographical area — the most important of which were Augsburg and Nuremberg — brought the Bavarian State for the first time in the early nineteenth century a sizeable Protestant minority, amounting in 1815 to just less than a quarter of the total Bavarian population.[1] The last major addition to the Protestant population took place in 1920 when the Coburg area, a purely Protestant district of some 70,000 souls though previously more closely aligned to Thuringian than to Bavarian Protestant traditions, became part of Bavaria.[2] By 1933, Protestants formed just under a third of Bavaria's population, though a substantial majority of the population of much of Middle and Upper Franconia.[3]

As a minority in a Catholic-dominated State, the Protestant Church in Bavaria developed during the nineteenth century much sharper identity feelings than existed in most other parts of Germany. The fervent attachment of the Bavarian Provincial Church to orthodox Lutheranism, bolstered by a revivalist movement which was particularly strong in Bavaria during the first half of the nineteenth century and by evangelizing missions from the turn of the twentieth century, promoted the extreme piety and intensity of faith characteristic of Bavarian Protestantism. Despite many internal conflicts, the 'rationalist-liberal' wing of evangelical theology could make little ground in a Bavaria dominated by highly conservative-orthodox Lutheran Protestantism.[4]

By 1918 war, defeat, and revolution had left the Protestant

---

[1] Spindler, p. 884.
[2] Ibid., p. 902.
[3] See Introduction, Table III.
[4] Spindler, pp. 888–900. For a clear account of the historical development of the differing strains of German Protestantism and the varied organizational forms of the Evangelical Church, cf. J.R.C. Wright, *'Above Parties': The Political Attitudes of the German Church Leadership 1918–1933*, Oxford, 1974, pp. 1–10.

Church in Germany in disarray and brought into the open theological and ideological rifts which had never been far from the surface. Liberal theology was now discredited, and a new wave of revivalist fundamentalism led on the one hand to a renewed assertion of the truths of Lutheran orthodoxy, on the other to a dangerous association of Christian and nationalist values coalescing in demands for the revival of Germany's power and strength, both nationally and spiritually, voiced especially by the movement, centring on Thuringia, Saxony, and parts of Prussia, which became known by 1932 as the 'Faith Movement of "German Christians"'.[5]

The 'German Christians' hardly penetrated into Bavaria before 1933. However, the conservative orthodoxy of the Bavarian Provincial Church and its previous close identity with the monarchical state meant that the new Republic found few friends among the Protestant clergy and their parishioners. 'God and the Fatherland' were too closely linked for most to overcome their aversion to the Weimar democracy, its leading party the SPD, and to party rule dominated in Bavaria by the Catholic BVP. Though many Protestant ministers remained sceptical about the advancing Nazi movement in the later 1920s and early 1930s, there was no denying the appeal for others of a spiritual as well as a political revival based upon an alliance of Christianity and the politics of national resurgence.[6]

This synthesis of evangelical piety and *völkisch* nationalism had been present among the Bavarian Protestant clergy from the beginnings of the Weimar Republic, and had been enhanced at that time by the counter-revolutionary thrust against socialism and the short-lived *Räterepublik* in Munich. More than a hundred Bavarian Protestant pastors joined

---

[5] J. Conway, *The Nazi Persecution of the Churches 1933-45*, London, 1968, pp. 9-12; Wright, pp. 91-8; for an extensive description of the Evangelical Church and the *völkisch* movement, cf. K. Scholder, *Die Kirchen und das Dritte Reich*, vol. i, Frankfurt/Main, 1977, Teil I, chs. 1-3, 7-8, 11-12; for Bavaria cf. H. Baier, *Die Deutschen Christen im Rahmen des bayerischen Kirchenkampfes*, Nuremberg, 1968, pp. 27-40.

[6] Spindler, pp. 902-3; *Bayern I*, pp. 371-2; E. Henn, 'Die bayerische Volksmission im Kirchenkampf', *Zeitschrift für bayerische Kirchengeschichte*, xxxviii (1969), 14-15.

the *Freikorps* in the early 1920s, and the mixture of Lutheran theology and *völkisch*-national ideology prompted many war veterans among the clergy to support the *völkisch* movement during the troubled years of 1923-4, when the Nazis were already amassing an impressive vote in the solidly Protestant countryside and small towns of Upper and Middle Franconia.[7] By the Depression years, the Church's attitude towards the rapidly growing Nazi Movement became a central point of discussion in church conferences, and though the Church President, Dr Veit, advised remaining aloof from political discussion in the interests of parochial peace and unity, he found himself in a minority and accused of reactionary attitudes.[8] The Nazi appeal to self-sacrifice, idealism, and to the overcoming of selfish materialism and cultural decadence was evidently attractive to many Protestant ministers. The campaign of Hans Schemm, *Gauleiter* of Upper Franconia, under the slogan 'our religion is Christ, our politics Germany', had distinct success in the ranks of Bavaria's Protestant clergy and contributed substantially to the fact that many Protestant rural districts were casting their votes almost entirely for the Nazis by 1932.[9] For large numbers of Protestants in Bavaria, as elsewhere, Hitler's 'seizure of power' marked a day of liberation, a release from the detested Weimar democracy, a beginning of new hope. Some forty years after the event, a Coburg minister still vividly recalled reactions typical of many Protestants at the outset of the Third Reich as he, along with many others in the streets of Coburg, listened to a broadcast of a Hitler speech: 'Our hearts are deeply moved. It is as if the wing of a great turn of fate is fluttering above us. There was to be a new start.'[10]

The Nazi take-over of power in Bavaria brought swift

---

[7] *Bayern I*, p. 370; Baier, *Die Deutschen Christen*, pp. 30-2.

[8] Baier, *Die Deutschen Christen*, p. 36.

[9] Henn, p. 9; *Bayern I*, pp. 370-1.

[10] H. Rößler, 'Erinnerungen an den Kirchenkampf in Coburg', *Jahrbuch der Coburger Landesstiftung* (1975), 155-6. Rößler gives the date as 30 Jan. 1933 and records listening to Hitler's speech from Königsberg. This particular speech was held by Hitler on 4 Mar. 1933 (*Hitler. Reden und Proklamationen*, p. 216). Hitler did not broadcast a speech on 30 Jan. 1933, though there were celebratory gatherings and processions all over the Reich on that evening following Hitler's appointment to the Chancellorship.

changes to the organization of the Protestant Church there. The new head of the Bavarian Church from May 1933, now given the title of Bishop and endowed with wide executive powers, was Hans Meiser, an arch-conservative orthodox Lutheran who, despite his sympathies for the new regime, proved determined to defend the independence of his Church against the growing forces pressing for a centralized Reich Church and the destruction of the traditional structure of independent, loosely aligned provincial churches.

These, in fact, were the tensions destined to split the Protestant Church in Germany almost before the euphoria surrounding the Nazi take-over of power had died down. Ludwig Müller's appointment in summer 1933 as Reich Bishop had been forced upon the provincial churches by Hitler,[11] and the anti-traditional, extremist pressure by the Nazified 'German Christians' — under the slogan 'the swastika on our breasts, and the Cross in our hearts'[12] — for a sub-ordination of evangelical theology to the needs of nationalist ideology provoked the creation of the 'Pastors' Emergency League', led by the pastor of Berlin-Dahlem Dr Martin Niemöller, devoted to a defence of orthodox Protestant dogma. The League immediately gained wide support and formed the basis of what later crystallized into the 'Confessing Church'. The tension spilled over into Bavaria, though conflict there did not reach its climax, as we shall see, until the autumn of 1934.

The 'German Christians' made some inroads into Franconia during summer 1933, winning the support of between one and two hundred clergymen. Most of these ministers none the less remained loyal to Meiser, and the 'German Christians' in Bavaria accepted at a synod in August the authority of the Bishop and their position as a group existing within the Bavarian Church. Any hope of further success by the 'German Christians' was, however, completely destroyed by the repercussions of the notorious assembly in the Berlin *Sportpalast* on 13 November 1933, when, in the presence of the

[11] Wright, pp. 117–42 offers a good account of the complex circumstances surrounding Müller's appointment.
[12] Conway, p. 45.

Reich Bishop and other leading churchmen, a prominent 'German Christian' speaker denounced the Old Testament 'with its Jewish morality of rewards, and its stories of cattle-dealers and concubines', the whole theology of 'the Rabbi Paul', and demanded the presentation of a 'heroic' Christ rather than the broken figure of the Crucified in order to signify 'that the completion of the Reformation of Martin Luther means the final victory of the nordic spirit over oriental materialism.'[13] This remarkable diatribe, which prompted a heated protest from Meiser, led to the voluntary dissolution of the 'German Christians' Faith Community' in Bavaria and the further consolidation of support behind Meiser. The 'German Christians' only recommenced their activities in the early summer of 1934, when they returned to Bavaria from their base in Thuringia.[14]

A glimpse into the attitudes and beliefs of Protestant ministers and their parishioners between autumn 1933 and spring 1934, before the 'Church struggle' in Bavaria fully exploded but during the period when the fronts were taking shape, is provided by the monthly reports sent in to the 'Special Commissioner for the People's Mission' from the local deaneries.[15]

Evangelizing popular missions in Bavaria had a history reaching back into the nineteenth century. The revival of missionary activity in 1933 took place, however, in the context of the euphoric Christian revivalism which had accompanied the Nazi take-over of power. The idea of a missionary 'special action' was first promoted by the 'German Christians' in the summer of 1933 but by September had been adopted by the official provincial Church Council and its organization placed in the hands of the experienced pastor Helmut Kern, since 1926 head of the Mission Establishment at Neuendettelsau, as 'Special Commissioner'. Kern, later to become

[13] Ibid., pp. 52–3; Scholder, pp. 703–5; *Kirche im Kampf. Dokumente des Widerstands und des Aufbaus in der Evangelischen Kirche Deutschlands von 1933 bis 1945*, ed. H. Hermelink, Tübingen, 1950, pp. 54–61 (cited henceforth as Hermelink).

[14] *Bayern I*, p. 372; H. Baier, *Kirchenkampf in Nürnberg*, Nuremberg, 1973, p. 9.

[15] For the nature of these reports, cf. *Bayern I*, pp. 369–76; for the 'People's Mission', see Henn, *passim*.

one of the leading figures in the Bavarian 'Church struggle', was still at this time sympathetic towards the aims of the 'German Christians', but his unquestioned loyalty to Meiser and growing aversion to the centralizing demands of the 'Reich Church' and its theological vagaries led him by 1934 in the direction of, and in later years to outspoken support for, the 'Confessing Church' — and to persecution by the Gestapo.[16]

'The great idea of the People's Mission', wrote the District Dean of Bayreuth in January 1934, was 'to reach and penetrate the nationally awakened masses now also through the Church.'[17] The reports of the 'People's Mission' reflect clearly the hopes and expectations of many Protestant clergymen of such a close correspondence of political and spiritual resurgence and of Nazism's beneficial influence on Protestant Christianity, as reflected in a report of the Bayreuth Deanery in November 1933:

As regards the influence of the political revolution on the parishes in town and countryside, the expectation that church life would be especially enriched as a result has for the time being not been fulfilled . . . But the time is not yet ripe for a final verdict. One thing I was hoping for is that the social prejudice against the Church among workers and the educated classes will be overcome here and there if God really wants to grant us a National Community, and that in thus becoming a nation a way will also be paved for our church work.[18]

As this and other reports indicate, the social groups most antagonistic towards the Church were the working class and the intelligentsia, whereas its social base, like that of the Nazi Movement itself, was centred upon the peasantry and the petty bourgeoisie.[19]

The 'People's Mission' reports reveal significant differences in the vitality of Protestantism within the Franconian region. Not surprisingly, 'diaspora' areas such as Bamberg or Weiden (Upper Palatinate), where the Protestant population was greatly outnumbered by Catholics, tended to report closely-knit parishes and a good record of church attendance. By

---

[16] For Kern, cf. Baier, *Die Deutschen Christen*, p. 146, n. 109, and esp. Henn, *passim.*
[17] Cited in *Bayern I*, p. 372.
[18] Ibid., p. 395. [19] Ibid., p. 375.

contrast, areas like Hof, with a uniformly Protestant population but sizeable working-class element, and Coburg, a latecomer to Bavaria and with a different, less intense Lutheran tradition, reported low attendance and lukewarm attachment to the Church.[20] Some deaneries were hopeful that the removal of Marxists and groups such as Jehovah's Witnesses, which had allegedly made ground especially among the poorer sections of the population during the Depression, would improve matters; others were more sceptical about the impact of the political change. In all cases, however, the support of the Protestant population for the Nazi regime was emphasized, and the political and spiritual unity of Germany's 'awakening' was reinforced by meetings and sermons held by the Mission on subjects such as 'Luther and Hitler' or 'How will we get an SA of the Church?'[21]

The reports contain, however, many indications that the idealistic hopes placed in Nazism's 'spiritual' revival were, in the shade of the intensifying Church conflict, already in the process of being disappointed. Worries increased in the early months of 1934 about anti-Christian tendencies within the Party and its organizations, especially in the Hitler Youth and the SA.[22] Such concern was not assuaged when, in its notorious 'Ritual Murder Edition' of May 1934, Streicher's newspaper *Der Stürmer* associated the Christian Communion with Jewish ritual slaughter, an allegation which brought a storm of outraged protest from Evangelical (and Catholic) pulpits.[23] A visitation report from the Schwabach deanery in summer 1934 shows how disillusionment was setting in, replacing the early hopes of Nazism:

The church life of our parishes did not remain unaffected by the general great movement. In particular, the church-minded and serious parishioners had for years always been the bearers of the national idea, while the Marxist-infected groups were always anti-Church. From our well-meaning evangelical population in Franconia, the NSDAP has won its best people. Our parishes rejoiced wholeheartedly in the first half of 1933 because it was always said, both in the personal professions of our Führer Hitler and in the Programme of the NSDAP, that the highest

[20] Ibid., pp. 370 & n. 3, 387–8.   [21] Ibid., pp. 389, 391.
[22] Ibid., e.g., pp. 382, 393.
[23] Ibid., p. 384 & n. 17; KLB, ii. 26; Baier, *Kirchenkampf*, p. 12.

State leadership wanted to rear a wholly Christian people. Unforgettable are the divine services of 1 May etc., when the crowds of people came in such numbers into our churches that the Houses of God seemed too small. Disappointment, however, followed this early rejoicing very quickly. The complaints from all parishes became ever more pressing, that attendance at services was being increasingly harmed by Sunday activities of the HJ, SA, SS, and other Party organizations, and above all that the younger generation is being put off attendance at Divine Service. The continued disturbances have also reached as far as Christian instruction, though this is a part of the normal school requirement. Complaints have had some success here and there, but despite all the decrees coming from above there has been no really certain success.[24]

Above all, the damaging effects of the Church conflict itself were gradually coming to create most anxiety and confusion, as voiced in the comments of a Lower Franconian pastor in March 1934, a month after he had been asked to take over the 'ideological schooling' of the SA in his district of Eyrichshof:

Sometimes it seems as if a certain fatalism and bound up with it a tired resignation is gripping the spirits. This is brought about by the complete lack of clarity in the church situation. What part has the Pastors' Emergency League in the confusion? Where are the real friends? Are there not many in the camp of the Emergency League who hide behind the Confession in order to be able to nourish their hostile feelings towards the State? Are there not traitors in our ranks who go blabbing (vorschwätzen) the base lie to the State that all who are distrustful of the Reich Bishop are reactionary? What will the Bavarian clergy do if the Reich Bishop, in the further course of his despotism, deposes our provincial Bishop? Many evangelical ministers have prepared the ground for the Third Reich with dogged passion and even today know no other political goal. Is all that already forgotten and isn't it seen?[25]

The rejection of both polarized wings of the dispute within the Church, the antipathy towards the Reich Bishop, and the despairing feeling that as a result of the conflict the State and the Church were being torn apart, that the clergy might despite their abounding loyalty to the new State wrongly be put to the test of their loyalty to Bishop Meiser, runs through this report and typified the feelings of many Protestant clergymen in Bavaria in the early months of 1934. Such worries formed the background to the 'Church struggle' in

[24] *Bayern I*, p. 406.
[25] Ibid., pp. 383–4.

Bavaria, which by this time was moving inexorably towards its dénouement over the question of the independence of the Bavarian Church from Müller's 'Reich Church'.

By the end of 1933 Reich Bishop Müller, well aware of the Nazi leadership's growing disenchantment with his failure to put the Evangelical Church in order, and of the growing strength of the Pastors' Emergency League, by this time some 7,000 strong, was moving to the offensive. He attempted to ban public discussion of the Church conflict by members of the clergy — suspending numerous pastors who disobeyed his notorious 'muzzle decree' — and stepped up his campaign to amalgamate the remaining independent provincial churches. By late January 1934 Hitler was compelled to intervene in a rapidly worsening situation. Following the disclosure of indiscrete comments about Hitler and Müller by Martin Niemöller, which had been recorded by telephone-tapping, the assembled church leaders, including Meiser, were compromised into humiliating avowals of loyalty to Hitler, to the State, and to Müller, and forced to distance themselves from Niemöller's League. Müller failed to make the most of this unexpected bonus, however, and his continued bullying of the provincial churches further alienated any lingering support he might have enjoyed. However, when the Bishops of the still independent south-German Churches, Wurm of Württemberg and Meiser of Bavaria, protested in an audience with the Führer about Müller's autocratic behaviour, Hitler ended the audience abruptly with a furious verbal assault on the Bishops as 'traitors to the people, enemies of the Fatherland, and the destroyers of Germany'.[26]

Up to the late spring and early summer of 1934 the effects of Church conflict in Bavaria had largely been felt by the clergy and there were few signs of serious disturbance or concern among the laity. The growing pressure on Meiser, however, took the conflict out of the realms of heady theology and ecclesiastical organization on to a plane which every churchgoer could understand. Loyalty to the Bishop and defence of the traditional structure of the Church against outside interference became the clear focus of the struggle.

[26] Conway, pp. 76-7; cf. also Wright, pp. 156-62.

And from the time of the attack on the autocratic Reich Bishop and his policies, read out from many pulpits in early May 1934, the clergy took an active role in involving their parishioners in the dispute, with a consequent growth in unrest and tension.[27] In the view of the Government President of Upper and Middle Franconia, the Church dispute did not amount to a political attack on the regime but was none the less politically highly undesirable because of the great danger of the issue spilling over from a Church affair into the political arena.[28] In August he pointed out that although the Church remained on the whole loyal to the government, the sharp polemicizing from the pulpit against the Reich Bishop and his associates from a clergy wholly behind Meiser was being interpreted by many as an anti-Nazi stance.[29]

On 23 August the Bavarian Provincial Synod unanimously rejected amalgamation with the Reich Church and passed a resolution of solidarity with Meiser. The NSDAP's ban on the announcement of these decisions from the pulpit the following Sunday served only to heighten the tension still further.[30] The Government President of Upper and Middle Franconia saw his fears being realized:

In particular the religiously inclined evangelical circles, which stand behind their Bishop Meiser, could and still can be counted among the most loyal supporters of National Socialism. It is a tragedy that precisely these people have to be upset in the conflict between Reich Bishop and Provincial Church by the State they most gladly acclaimed.[31]

The dispute moved into its climacteric phase with the open attack on Bishop Meiser — accusing him of treason and shameful disloyalty to Hitler and the State — launched on 15 September by the *Fränkische Tageszeitung*, organ of the Franconian *Gau* leadership and edited by Deputy *Gauleiter* Karl Holz.[32] This was immediately followed up with a leaflet and poster campaign in Nuremberg demanding Meiser's ousting. A further attack in the newspaper occurred two days later, and Holz arranged to address a mass meeting the

---

[27] KLB, ii. 25-6.   [28] Ibid., p. 26.
[29] Ibid., pp. 30-1.   [30] Ibid., p. 73 & n. 1; Rößler, p. 161.
[31] KLB, ii. 33.
[32] Baier, *Die Deutschen Christen*, pp. 112–15; Hermelink, p. 156.

same evening in Nuremberg's Market Square (now renamed Adolf-Hitler-Platz). The meeting was effectively sabotaged by Meiser's supporters. On learning that the meeting was to be held in the evening, the Director of the Protestant Preacher Seminary in Nuremberg, Pastor Schieder, cancelled classes and he and his students went into the streets of the city encouraging people to be in the Market Square that evening and to break out into the traditional Lutheran hymn 'A Mighty Fortress is our God' ('*Ein' feste Burg ist unser Gott*') if attacks on the Bavarian Church were made. In the afternoon, the Nuremberg group around Schieder, fearing wire-tapping, telephoned a cryptic message to Church headquarters in Munich: 'Uncle Hans should come to Nuremberg immediately.' The message quickly came back that Bishop Hans Meiser was on his way.[33]

Meiser's arrival in Nuremberg that evening was a triumph. When word went round that he was in the city and would speak in the main churches the crowds streamed away from the meeting in the Market Place and packed the churches. Leaving St. Giles's church the Bishop was greeted with chants of 'Heil Meiser' from the crowd and the singing of hymns. The situation appeared to be getting out of hand, but police intervention was hedged off by a spontaneous rendering by the crowd of '*Deutschland über alles*', at which the police too stood to attention.[34] During the next few days numerous services, all before packed congregations, were held in and around Nuremberg. Public feeling for Meiser was such that the *Gau* leadership of Franconia was forced to withdraw its application for a speaking ban to be placed on Meiser, and he had a tumultuous reception on his appearance to hold sermons in Ansbach and Gunzenhausen.[35] A circular sent to pastors on 24 September commented on the remarkable events:

We witnessed a miracle here in Nuremberg. There was enormous commotion going on in the town, at its strongest on the Wednesday. We only gave out hand notices at twelve o'clock and in the evening sixteen

---

[33] Baier, *Kirchenkampf*, pp. 12–14.   [34] Ibid., p. 15.
[35] KLB, ii. 34–6; Baier, *Die Deutschen Christen*, pp. 120–1; Hermelink, pp. 157–8.

churches were full to bursting. Similar favourable news is coming in everywhere from the preaching trips which our brethren are carrying out throughout the Franconian countryside. Everywhere, often at the most inconvenient times, churches are full. The Gunzenhausen meeting was one single exultant profession of faith in Meiser by thousands of Franconian peasants.[36]

Even these spectacular events were overshadowed, however, by what took place the following month. The immediate attack had been warded off. However Reich Bishop Ludwig Müller and his henchman August Jäger, popularly known as 'Kirchenjäger' ('Church Hunter'), were now set on breaking the intransigence of the still independent provincial Churches and forcing their amalgamation into the Reich Church. On 2 October Meiser and the Provincial Church Council in Bavaria sent an open letter of vehement protest about the attack on the independence of the provincial Churches to the Reich Bishop.[37] Four days later Bishop Wurm of the sister-church in Württemberg was placed under 'protective custody' in his house in Stuttgart. It was clear that an assault on the Bavarian Church was imminent.[38] In a frenzy of activity, Helmut Kern organized contingency plans to counter the awaited take-over. A secret communications network was created to mobilize the clergy and laity on the word that the Provincial Church had been occupied or Meiser dismissed from office. There was to be an immediate summons to attend services of atonement at which carefully devised sermons and readings of Lutheran texts would be accompanied by the ceremonial extinguishing of candle and wearing of black mourning garb. Each parish was to organize its own protest petition to be sent to the Reich Justice Minister and to the Bavarian Reich Governor and Minister President.[39] In the meantime demonstrations in favour of Meiser were

---

[36] Cit. in Rößler, p. 163.   [37] Hermelink, pp. 160–6.
[38] Cf. in general: Conway, p. 99; E.C. Helmreich, 'The Arrest and Freeing of the Protestant Bishops of Württemberg and Bavaria, September–October 1934', *Central European History*, ii (1969), 159–69; Hermelink, pp. 139–53 and P. Sauer, *Württemberg in der Zeit des Nationalsozialismus*, Ulm, 1975, pp. 185–9, for the arrest of Bishop Wurm; Baier, *Die Deutschen Christen*, p. 125, for rumours of an impending attack on the independence of the Bavarian Church.
[39] Henn, pp. 30–1.

still taking place. On the day after Bishop Wurm's arrest, Meiser travelled to Neu-Ulm on the extreme west of Bavaria and immediately adjoining Ulm proper, part of Württemberg. Many Württembergers were in the crowd, estimated at 3,000, which welcomed Meiser. He and his entourage exchanged the 'Hitler Greeting' before entering the church, where Meiser spoke of his need to bear witness in place of Bishop Wurm. The service was transmitted to the crowd outside, which gave Meiser a rousing reception on his reappearance. He told them to stay loyal to the Church; 'Ein' feste Burg' was sung, followed by the Horst-Wessel Song (the anthem of the Nazi Party); cheers of 'Heil Meiser' rang out; and the hero departed.[40]

On 11 October the blow fell. With full knowledge of the civil and Party authorities, Jäger and his accompaniment of strong-arm men forcibly entered and occupied the offices of the Bavarian Church in Munich, declared Meiser deposed and under house-arrest, suspended the Church Council, and placed the Provincial Church — now divided into two administrative districts — under provisional control of clerical commissars.[41] This was the trigger to the unprecedented explosion of outraged protest which followed.[42]

Churchgoers were made aware of the gravity of the situation in a proclamation read out in most churches despite an express ban by the police on 14 October. The proclamation affirmed in emotive terms the loyalty to the Bishop and to his legal authority in the Bavarian Church and denounced in the most vehement fashion the usurpation of the Church's rights: 'We protest before God and the community, we protest before the people and State, we protest before the Führer of the Reich about the breach of loyalty and faith, about the destruction of character and trust.' The proclamation ended by appealing to ministers and parishioners 'to show no obedience towards this unconfessional and unconstitutional church government.'[43]

---

[40] HStA, Sonderabgabe 1/1722, fol. 122, Bericht des Polizeioberkommissars Neu-Ulm, without date but 8 Oct. 1934; cf. also Conway, p. 419.

[41] Hermelink, pp. 167–8; Baier, *Die Deutschen Christen*, pp. 128–31.

[42] Cf. Baier, *Kirchenkampf*, pp. 16–23; Baier, *Die Deutschen Christen*, pp. 136–9, 143–6; Hermelink, pp. 169–78; KLB, ii. 37–40.

[43] Hermelink, p. 170; Baier, *Kirchenkampf*, p. 18.

The clergy of Nuremberg, centre of opposition to the usurpers, demonstrated their solidarity the next day in a special celebration of Holy Communion in the city's St Jakob's Church. A similar service a few days later was attended by over 850 Protestant pastors and their wives from all over Bavaria.[44] Following the lines laid down by Helmut Kern, the forms of protest were designed to make a powerful visual impact. Services were held as Requiems, altars were decked in black, and candles extinguished until the 'imprisoned' Bishop should return. Emotive sermons brought tears and cries of anger from the congregations at Meiser's treatment.[45] Petitions were started, demanding Meiser's restoration to office, and a mass meeting was called for 16 October. Ten thousand people found their way on to the Nuremberg streets that day following packed services in all the city's main churches, and the police could contain the crowds only with difficulty.[46] Public opinion forced *Gauleiter* Streicher, much against his will, to be conciliatory when he met leading Church dignitaries the following day. Through a published ban on Party members involving themselves in attacks on the Church and a denial that the differences of opinion within the Church had anything to do with the NSDAP, he was consciously seeking to repair some of the damage done to the Franconian *Gau* leadership's standing and to extricate the Party from a situation which was becoming daily more embarrassing and politically harmful. *Gauleiter* Hans Schemm attempted the same tactic in Bayreuth.[47]

Such belated intervention by the Party leadership in northern Bavaria was, however, by now completely futile as the protest spread rapidly to the outlying Franconian countryside. It was becoming ever clearer to the authorities that the ecclesiastical issue could not be kept self-contained and separated from wider political questions. According to reports from Protestant parishes in the Upper Franconian district of Ebermannstadt, pastors were consciously or not

[44] Baier, *Kirchenkampf*, pp. 19, 24.
[45] KLB, ii. 39; Baier, *Kirchenkampf*, p. 19; Hermelink, pp. 176–8.
[46] Baier, *Kirchenkampf*, p. 20; Baier, *Die Deutschen Christen*, p. 146.
[47] KLB, ii. 37; Baier, *Kirchenkampf*, pp. 20–3; Baier, *Die Deutschen Christen*, pp. 147–8.

evoking an increasingly distrustful attitude towards the State and their 'agitation' was having the effect of 'political disintegration'. The District Officer warned: 'So much doubt about the State and National Socialism has been conveyed to the population through the Church dispute that, as local mayors have credibly assured me, an election or plebiscite at the present time would show an absolutely devastating result.'[48]

In many parts of the Franconia countryside names were being busily collected for petitions demanding Meiser's reinstatement and preparations were made for deputations to be sent to the Bavarian Minister President and relevant authorities in Berlin, where Franconian peasants attempted in vain to secure an audience with Hitler.[49] Prominent members of the Nuremberg clergy played the central role in organizing and leading these delegations, one of which brought over 800 Nuremberg Protestants to Munich on a chartered train, demanding to see their Bishop.[50] The extent of bitterness caused by the affair and the political gravity of the situation were, not least through these deputations, being made abundantly clear to the highest authorities in Bavaria, as the file on the issue kept by Minister President Siebert shows.[51]

Siebert had already on 15 October conveyed the serious consequences of the conflict for the Party in a report sent to Reich Minister of the Interior Wilhelm Frick. He wrote in alarmed terms that since the deposition of Meiser he had been besieged by 'mountains of telegrams, representations from the deaneries, and entreaties of every sort'. The affair was now passing into the political sphere: Party members who held the Golden Badge of Honour, District Leaders, and Protestant pastors who had fought at the front and were long-standing supporters of the Party had warned that the consequences of the issue for the Party should not be underrated. One Franconian District Leader had reported that his entire work was taken up with trying to stop peasants from

---

[48] StAB, K8/III, 18470, BA Ebermannstadt, 3 Oct. 1934; cf. *Bayern I*, pp. 74–7.

[49] Baier, *Die Deutschen Christen*, pp. 155–6.

[50] Ibid., pp. 153–6; KLB, ii. 40.   [51] GStA, MA 107291.

leaving the Party. A pastor and long-time supporter of the Movement reckoned that 50 per cent of his parishioners, who had all voted '*Ja*' in the plebiscite confirming Hitler as Head of State in August, would leave both Church and Party if Meiser were not reinstated.

Five days later Siebert described at length in a second communication to Frick the latest developments and their serious consequences. He emphasized that the whole question was no longer an inner-Church affair but a matter of State politics which the government must gain control of if 'the most serious internal unrest' were to be avoided. Referring to the demonstrations in Nuremberg he pointed out that the police had only contained the situation with difficulty and that sooner or later would be faced with the decision to use arms in order to disperse the crowds. Both he and Reich Governor Epp had received hundreds of protest declarations promising 'united resistance to the last extreme'.

At least four Franconian deputations made their presentations to Siebert. On 19 October he received a deputation purporting to represent 60,000 peasants of south-west Franconia 'in order to express the truth about the mood of the people in the Evangelical Church dispute.' The deputation made 'wholly the impression of being religious fanatics, solidly determined to take matters as far as possible, to fear no force, and to let themselves rather be stamped as martyrs.' They described the press reports about the Church conflict as open lies and the comments of Deputy *Gauleiter* Holz in the *Fränkische Tageszeitung* as 'deliberately untrue'. They were of the opinion that a man like Holz 'was not suitable and had no right to speak in the name of the Protestants'. One clergyman present stated in no uncertain terms that even Party members with the Golden Badge of Honour were on the point of rebellion and that farmers would give no more to the Winter Aid until the question was settled.[52] An index of feeling was the mass gathering of 6,000 to greet Meiser's visit to Gunzenhausen. The delegation thought that if word had got round quickly enough more than ten thousand would

---

[52] Attempts to boycott the Winter Aid were indeed carried out. Cf. KLB, ii. 38; *Berichte des SD und der Gestapo über Kirchen und Kirchenvolk 1934–1944*, ed. H. Boberach, Mainz, 1971, p. 71.

have turned up, whereas at a Streicher meeting in the same place only the few came who had been ordered to attend.

In trying to calm the members of the delegation, Siebert advised them not to confuse the Church issue with that of their loyalty to National Socialism and the Führer. A Franconian peasant replied: 'The peasants have now only three ideas: the Führer, religion, and land and soil, but will let none of these things be taken from them.' The delegation ended by reiterating its demand for Meiser's reinstatement, saying that 95 per cent of the Franconian peasantry were behind him and that if the issue was not quickly solved in accordance with their wishes the peasants could not be held back from a rebellion and would lose faith politically.

A further delegation, this time 'in the name of 70,000 peasants' from the districts of Windsheim, Rothenburg, and Leutershausen in Middle Franconia claimed in their audience with Siebert on 23 October that only sixty-two out of 1,400 pastors did not support Meiser. They asked Siebert to listen to them 'as National Socialists and Christians', stating that they would not deviate a single foot's breadth from their position, 'for people and Führer rested on Christianity rooted in the soil'.

The consequences for the Party's standing were brought home to Siebert by the final delegation he received, from the Schweinfurt and Haßfurt areas of Lower Franconia, on 29 October. The peasants explained that they came in the interest not just of the Church, but also of the State. The force employed against the Church had aroused enormous bitterness among the people. In the countryside the Church conflict was squarely identified with the Party; people said the arrest of Meiser could only have been brought about through the Party's involvement in the affair, and for this reason no one was willing to contribute to the Winter Aid. It had already gone so far that people were saying one had to be a Bolshevik to be in the SA.

Siebert was already well aware of the danger to the Party's relationship with the Bavarian population. In his second communication to Frick on 20 October he emphasized the effect on the Party as the most serious danger of all. People had been driven into an impossible position of having to choose between loyalty to the Führer and loyalty to the Church. If, as seemed certain, large numbers of resignations from the Party followed, the Party's image would be seriously affected not only abroad but also at home, where oppositional groups would be given new impetus. Siebert ended his letter with the urgent request that the Führer should be comprehensively informed about the situation, and hoped himself for an audience with Hitler and with Frick in Munich, where the issue was such a live one.

Of course, Siebert was anxious above all to calm things down and relieve the tension, which for effect he may well have exaggerated. However, the 'rebellious' sentiments of the Franconian population do not necessarily have to be taken literally to realize that the regime had for the first time on its hands a problem of mass opposition which in its extent and vehemence had taken the authorities completely by surprise.

By this time the mass unrest in Bavaria and Württemberg had become not only a scandal within Germany itself but an embarrassment to the Nazi State in its relations with other countries. Foreign Minister Neurath, in receipt of protests from all over the world, joined in putting pressure on the Führer, who decided the time had come to intervene. On 26 October, the same day that Siebert requested the Bavarian Minister of the Interior Adolf Wagner to lift Meiser's house-arrest, Hitler dismissed the detested Jäger and ordered the release of Bishops Meiser and Wurm and their reinstatement in office. Their rehabilitation was completed in an audience with Hitler on 30 October at which the Führer stressed the neutrality of Party and State in Church affairs and gave bland assurances that the Church would henceforth be ruled according to the constitutional arrangements which had been laid down in July 1933.[53] A day later, a test case in Munich declared the illegality of the Reich Church's intervention in Bavaria,[54] and on 1 November 1934 Meiser resumed office. Popular feeling showed itself in unmistakable fashion three days later when thousands flocked to Nuremberg from all

[53] Conway, pp. 100–1; Helmreich, pp. 164–7; Baier, *Die Deutschen Christen*, pp. 158–63, 167–8.
[54] Ibid., pp. 166–7; Baier, *Kirchenkampf*, p. 23; KLB, ii. 39.

over Bavaria to mark Meiser's reappearance after captivity as a festive occasion. The doors of St Lorenz's Church in Nuremberg, where Meiser was due to speak, had to be closed an hour before the start of the sermon because it was already bursting at the seams.[55]

The high point of the 'Church struggle' in Bavaria had now passed. The period from the unleashing of the attack on Meiser by the Franconian *Gau* leadership to his reinstatement in office had spanned no more than six weeks. Yet in that time Party and State had encountered mass opposition and had suffered an undisguisable major defeat at the hands of popular opinion, steered and orchestrated by the Protestant clergy — a defeat which only a few weeks earlier would have seemed unthinkable. It was a spectacular display of what popular protest could achieve even in the restrictive conditions of a repressive police state. And the regime was given a sharp jolt about the arbitrary use of its power when aimed at the traditional fabric of society. The episode reveals some of the complexities of popular opinion in the Third Reich, and also some of the limitations to the forms of 'popular opposition' and what it could be expected to achieve. Several ingredients were necessary to produce such a mass display of opposition.

Firstly, this was no attack by the Nazi State on a tiny un-loved minority, such as Jews, on a group of 'outsiders' such as gypsies or homosexuals, or on a well-recognized ideological enemy such as the communists. In being seen to back the 'Reich Church' and the 'German Christians', Party and State were in fact this time putting themselves on the side of an increasingly unpopular minority, and were tackling an established traditional power with a wide social base. Nor did the attack remain levelled at abstract institutions and organizations. As long as that was the case, confusion and indifference characterized the response of the laity. It was when the defence of tradition became embodied in the person of Bishop Meiser that popular identity with the cause of the Bavarian Church was assured. In this way, Meiser became the symbol of a conservative defence aimed at the restoration of the former status quo in the Bavarian Church against what

---

[55] Baier, *Die Deutschen Christen*, p. 171.

was seen to be an attack by Nazi radical elements.

Secondly, the anger and disgust over the affair were immediate and widespread, involving and uniting practically everyone attached in any way to the Protestant Church. The decision to take part in any 'nonconformist' action in the Third Reich which might well incur the wrath of the Nazi authorities was never one to be taken lightly, but the danger of recrimination was quite obviously far greater where the person undertaking the action was isolated, unsure of support, and thereby fully exposed to possible denunciation. The weakness of the individual 'nonconformist' in the face of the regime's might needs no stressing. The recollections of Pastor Rößler of Coburg show how important it was not to feel isolated in protest. Unlike the clergy in the rest of Bavaria, pastors in the Coburg area, with its different ecclesiastical tradition and less pronounced devotion to Meiser, proved reluctant to read out the protest proclamation in support of the Bishop on 14 October. Police intimidation here, though not elsewhere, was largely successful. Rößler, one of the few to read out the proclamation in the Coburg district, later explained: 'We had no idea at the time of the announcement that by far the largest proportion of the remaining Bavarian clergy stood united behind Meiser and the emergency church government, and that the State would be unable to depose so many pastors.'[56] The more the affair gathered pace, the more obvious it was that the authorities were not going to resort to mass arrests and exemplary punishments. Being 'one of the crowd' and demonstrating with impunity was assured. Furthermore, of course, the 'demonstrations' were dignified and orderly, not riotous tumults, and took place among sections of the population whose basic loyalty to the Nazi State was not in question.

A third component, closely linked to the second, was that of leadership and organization, however rudimentary and improvised. Clearly the mass protest of lay people would never have attained such a scale without the direction and stimulation of the clergy. Particularly prominent roles were played by several important members of the Nuremberg clergy and the Church Council, and by Helmut Kern, 'Special Commissioner

[56] Rößler, p. 167.

for the People's Mission'.[57] The unity of almost the entire clergy and its energy, initiative, and talent for emotive counter-propaganda (extinguishing candles, black-draped altars, the unexpected arrival of Meiser in Nuremberg at the height of the campaign against him, the communications network based on the Preacher Seminary in Nuremberg which aimed at reaching 20,000 people by direct contact within three hours[58]) played the vital role of simplifying and communicating a complex issue to the mass of the population.

A fourth point links up with this. Mass opposition was possible because the conflict had been reduced to one single issue which everyone could understand and, above all, was *capable of obvious solution*. It was not just an abstract issue, a theoretical point of complexity, or a matter which only affected some and not others. Nor was it a group of interwoven issues on which there could be a multitude of differing opinions. Nor, finally and importantly, was the population faced with a *fait accompli* — however unpopular — which was irreversible. The issue was simply: was Meiser going to be reinstated or not? And the concrete aim — the reinstatement of Meiser — was obviously a realizable one.

The one-dimensional nature of the opposition clearly highlights, however, its weaknesses in terms of political resistance. Indeed, unless an unacceptably wide definition is employed, the opposition in the 'Church struggle' could not for the most part be classed as 'resistance'.[59] Undoubtedly the important though tiny minority among the Protestant clergy whose growing hostility to Nazism was pushing them towards outright rejection of the regime in all its forms were prepared to exploit the situation to encourage anti-regime feeling. For the most part, however, enormously bitter though the affair was, it touched on no other aspect of Nazi policy or ideology and could come to the boil ironically in a region with a very high level of long-standing avid Nazi support. This same area where popular opposition to Nazi Church policy was so

[57] Henn, pp. 30–2; Baier, *Kirchenkampf*, p. 24.
[58] Baier, *Kirchenkampf*, Appendix, Illustration 12.
[59] Cf. Introduction and references cited there (note 7) for the concept of 'resistance'.

vigorous continued, in fact, to prove itself a hotbed of vicious popular anti-Semitism, provided no indication of anything but wholehearted support for the regime's chauvinistic and aggressive foreign policy, and remained a bastion of intense pro-Hitler feeling. The opposition in the Church conflict was overwhelmingly levelled not at the regime itself but merely at one unattractive and — it was felt — wholly unnecessary aspect of its policy. The Government President of Upper and Middle Franconia pointed this out in his report on the conflict in October 1934: 'Perhaps in isolated cases a hidden enmity or grievance against National Socialism plays a part in the dispute. The great majority of Meiser's supporters, however, particularly in Franconia, are to be regarded as loyal National Socialists, in many cases ranking as old Party members.'[60] The singing of the Horst-Wessel Song by demonstrating crowds, the continued use of the 'Hitler Greeting' by Meiser and his supporters in public, and the stirring patriotic language used by the clergy, were all outward signs of support for the regime. The protest was to this extent carried out more in sorrow than in anger that such an issue should destroy the hoped-for unity of Church and National Socialism in the building of a 'new Germany'.

The lack of interest shown by the *Sopade* in the dispute and ensuing popular unrest was a clear reflection both of the perceived sectional nature of the opposition and of its obvious political and ideological limitations. The *Sopade* continued to see the divisions between socialists and Protestants as far wider than those between Protestants and the National Socialist regime. No eye-witness accounts of the dramatic events in Bavaria were included in the *Sopade* reports of autumn 1934.[61] It did, however, provide, under the heading 'Protestantism, Authoritarian State, and Reaction' a harsh evaluation of the significance of the Protestant

---

[60] KLB, ii. 36.

[61] DBS, 6 Feb. 1935, pp. A55-62 included belated reports, among them a short account (pp. A59-60) of events in Bavaria. From 1935 the *Sopade* grew increasingly aware of the major issues at stake and the deepening opposition to the regime in Church circles, especially within the Catholic Church, and compiled extensive reports on the 'Church struggle' on a number of occasions in the years 1935-7.

opposition and its victory over Nazism in the torrid autumn weeks.[62] After a lengthy denunciation of the Evangelical Church's role in Germany before the First World War as a crucial servant and ideological prop of the authoritarian, monarchical State, and in Weimar as a leading element in reactionary thought and politics, the analysis posed the question: 'Amid all the rebellion against *Gleichschaltung*, where is the open revolt (*Empörung*) in the camp of the Protestant opposition against nationalism, against total war armament, against the systematic preparation for war?' The answer was immediately provided: 'It does not exist; for in this point even the "new reformers" are completely in agreement with the Hitler form of authoritarian State.'[63] As far as the affair in South Germany was concerned, the personalities of the 'main actors' showed that there was no issue of opposition to the NSDAP as such at stake:

The Bavarian Meiser can still be regarded today as a convinced personal supporter of Hitler, dating from even as long ago as the Putsch period. Herr Wurm [the Bishop of Württemberg] was formerly a politician decidedly of the Right. He was a German National Landtag member and had also already squarely won his spurs in the view of the Nazi partisans through his passionate hatred of Marxists.[64]

For the *Sopade*, the entire history of the Church dispute proved one thing with utter clarity: 'this was no struggle against the system, but a struggle *within the system* for a share in the domination, power, and booty in the new authoritarian State.'[65] Despite the bitter bias of the report, there was truth in these comments.

At the same time, however, the conflict did change to some extent the relationship between Party and people in the affected parts of Franconia. Things were never quite the same again. Despite the attempt by the Party to play down the issue as an internal Church wrangle and to profess its neutrality, there was no doubt in the mind of the Government President of Upper and Middle Franconia, the most severely afflicted region, that confidence in the Party, and in the State too, had suffered serious damage.[66] He summed up the

---

[62] DBS, 26 Nov. 1934, pp. B10-36.   [63] Ibid., p. B13.
[64] Ibid., p. B33.
[65] Ibid., p. B34.   [66] KLB, ii. 40.

implications of the conflict, in his own view, in a report compiled in early December 1934: 'The danger of profound damage to Party and State, and certainly to the National Community, draws ever closer . . . Struggle in the Church divides the people only too easily.'[67]

It is unnecessary for our purposes to describe in detail the further history of the conflict between the Nazi State and the Evangelical Church in Bavaria. Relevant here are merely its lasting repercussions on popular opinion. The evidence points towards two main legacies of the upheavals of 1934, reinforced in later years, which permanently affected the relationship of the Protestant clergy and people to Party and regime: a heightened sensitivity and grave distrust of the Party in all matters connected with the Church; and a pervading disillusionment which reflected the destruction of the ideal of 1933 — a revitalized Church and a new Germany arising together. Both sentiments combined to produce a feeling of widespread and growing pessimism and resignation among Protestants in the later 1930s.

Clerical disillusionment with the 'new Germany' was expressed clearly in an article written at the end of 1935, a year in which the 'German Christians' succeeded in keeping alive the 'Church struggle' here and there in Bavaria but had by the end of the year become a force of only minor importance,[68] by Julius Schieder, one of Nuremberg's leading pastors and one of Meiser's staunchest defenders the previous autumn:

The cause of the serious position of the Church does not now lie with the German Christians, but elsewhere. We stand at the hour of fate of the German people . . . The German people always desired to be a Christian people. Today the German people is faced with the possibility of no longer wanting that. That is all the more serious since it seemed, two and a half years ago, as if the German people wanted to form a new alliance with its Christian Church. I think of 21 March 1933 ['the day of Potsdam'], that day which most deeply gripped the hearts of every German man and every German woman. On that occasion the

[67] Ibid., p. 43.
[68] For the 'German Christians' in 1935, cf. Baier, *Die Deutschen Christen*, ch. 6. The Bavarian authorities reckoned in April 1935 that only some 2 to 5 per cent of Bavaria's Protestants sympathized with the 'German Christians' — Ibid., pp. 225-6.

men of the new Germany assembled for their first Reichstag. They met in the House of God, in the church of Potsdam. The young Germany proferred its hand to the Church. A new marriage was contracted. Two and a half years this marriage has lasted. Today the battle-cry goes through broad sections of our German people: 'Out from the Church! Away with the Church!'[69]

Such worries were intensified in 1936 by the Nazi assault on the position of denominational schools in Bavaria. This issue, which we will consider more fully in the Catholic context during the next chapter, created enormous conflict and ill-feeling in affected places, and the Party seems consciously to have tried in 1936 not to inflame the situation still further and risk its standing with the population as in 1934. In one instance where a local Nazi speaker unexpectedly launched into a tirade against the clergy and the Christian Faith, the District Leadership of the Party stepped in with an immediate denunciation of the speaker in order to quell the ensuing furore.[70] However, in the context of the increased animosity over the school issue and the news of the Nazi attempt to remove crucifixes and pictures of Luther from schools in Oldenburg (and the subsequent spectacular defeat of the authorities at the hands of popular opinion),[71] 'unrest, discontent, and doubt, even distrust of National Socialism' again characterized the stance of the rural population in particular during the early months of 1937.[72] The widescale arrests of Protestant pastors (including Niemöller) in 1937 and the announcement and eventual postponement of new Church elections — which would have been the first since 1933 — kept the 'Church struggle' in a state of tension throughout the year and sustained the popular unrest which, commentators said, bore within it the undeniable danger of political repercussions.[73] This fear was, as 1934 had shown, grossly exaggerated by local administrators over-sensitive to any manifestation of unease in their region. An official

[69] KLB, ii. 68-9.

[70] StAN, 212/13/II, 654, BA Neustadt an der Aisch, 5 Jan. 1937.

[71] Cf. J. Noakes, 'The Oldenburg Crucifix Struggle of November 1936: a case-study of opposition in the Third Reich', in P. Stachura (ed.), *The Shaping of the Nazi State*, London, 1978, pp. 210-33.

[72] KLB, ii. 131.

[73] Ibid., pp. 172, 183. Cf. Conway, pp. 206-13.

statement which Meiser and the Bavarian Church Council had sent out to members of the clergy in October 1937 summed up the limited concern of the evangelical opposition when it asserted: 'Our Church is not carrying out a political struggle against National Socialism. In truth the Church fights only against the disparagement and undermining of its biblical faith. We reject the substitution of political motives.'[74]

The final two years before the war saw the Protestant Church (like the Catholic Church) defeated on the schools issue. Dominated as they were by foreign tension, these years produced the quietest period in Church affairs since 1933. Two reports from this immediate pre-war period, emanating from parish visitations by rural deans, provide some indication of what six years of conflict and struggle had meant to Protestant parishes and give some insight into the impact of the struggle on political and social attitudes of clergy and laity.

The parishioners of the Lower Franconian village of Frühstockheim in the deanery of Kitzingen had, according to a visitation report of May 1939, rallied round the local pastor as a result of the Church conflict.[75] His position in the community had been greatly strengthened, especially since the village teacher — the opposite pole ideologically — had forfeited all respect and support. Agitation against the Church in the district had been fruitless: 'one would be publicly ashamed to be a German Christian or worse.' Despite such solidarity, people's fear and acceptance of the inevitable when faced with lack of alternative meant the use of force against the Church would encounter little resistance. From age-old experience, continued the report, the villagers regarded those ruling them as their enemies, but still complied with the inevitable consequences of their subjection because they had no alternative. And that would now be the case if the 'flickering ideological struggle' should develop into outright coercion. 'An inner resistance can only be attained by a strong spiritual leadership, and this leadership can very quickly be silenced', reported the Dean resignedly. He was, however, left in no doubt as to the true feelings of his parishioners:

74 KLB, ii. 230.
75 Bayern I, pp. 409–12.

The overwhelming majority of people inwardly reject the Party; many — and these are the best sort of person — see through the ideological intentions of the Party down to the last consequences. The criticism can of course be only carefully expressed. It is first of all levelled at the particular situation in farming . . . The criticism moves from the economic to the spiritual sphere. There it can repeatedly be established that despite all clarification by the pastor it is not important and fundamental factors which shape criticism. Criticism is voiced rather about small detailed matters.

Furthermore, despite the general rallying-round the pastor, exposure to Nazi rule had magnified the divisions within the community:

The growing discontent in the countryside and the accompanying increasing fear of the rulers among many people show another very unpleasant side of parish life: people's distrust of each other and the nasty conflict between entire households and families. Never was the National Community less of a reality than now.

That this depressing picture was not untypical is shown by a summary report of the Provincial Church Leadership, drawn up late in 1939 and based upon 360 deanery visitation reports for 1937 and 1938 from all parts of Bavaria.[76] Though the report spoke of an 'inner deepening' of religious life in some parishes in the light of the 'Church struggle', there had been, it was admitted, generally 'a certain fall-off in church life'. The changes of the years 1936-9 had, it was claimed, posed an even more serious challenge to the religious life of the village than had the developments of the years 1932-5, even the eventful year 1934. Above all, the 'catastrophic changes in the field of school and religious education' in 1938 had had the most serious consequences for the community. Though the 'German Christians' had been fended off and were now merely 'a piece of history', parishes faced a much more sinister enemy 'which is everywhere visibly fighting against Christianity'. The main danger was the threat of advancing resignation and indifference breaking the popular will to defend Church and Faith against a powerful and remorseless enemy:

[76] Ibid., pp. 412-17.

The overwhelming majority of parishes will not willingly be disloyal to their Christian Faith, but they think to a considerable extent that 'anyhow nothing can be done' against the new forces, and become resigned. People do not forget so easily any longer, but nor do they dare so quickly to do anything.

Confidence and lack of concern for the position of the Church had given way to despondency. The especially deep impact made by the 'school question', where a strongly supported traditional structure in village life had despite opposition been removed through Nazi chicanery and replaced by the so-called 'community schools', had left people alert to the danger of anti-Christian forces but feeling that 'they are faced with an "inevitability" in the development'. This feeling, and the lack of co-ordinated opposition on the 'school question' shows how difficult mobilization of opinion had become on issues where, in contrast to the Meiser affair, the matter was more abstract, where opinions were sharply divided, and where there was no concrete focus of the unrest.

The depressed tone of the report also derived from the strong impression that not only the religious community but also the traditional pattern of village life, which had to such an extent revolved around the church, was itself breaking down. The shortage of labour and rural migration had reached a pitch where the farming population was so overburdened and demoralized that they were 'resigned and tired' even in matters concerning the Church. The former unity of church and school in village life was also breaking down. Pastor and village teacher, traditionally the twin bulwarks of the religious and educational framework of village life, were now 'the visible embodiments of two different worlds'. Young teachers especially, with their 'German Faith ideas' often formed a 'foreign body' in the village, causing further dissension and conflict. Their influence on the village youth was among the most pernicious effects. The position of youth constituted in fact the gravest worry about the future. The constant interference of the Nazi youth organizations and the influence of anti-Christian doctrines had drawn many away from the Church and would inevitably lead ultimately to an 'inner alienation' from Christianity of such young Germans. Villages within range of the 'corrupting influence of the town' were particularly exposed to such tendencies. All in all, people felt 'in the new circumstances and the spiritual transformation of the village the disappearance of old customary forms of life and morals; old traditions are decaying and the inner unity of the village is breaking apart.'

Whether the earlier village idyll implicit in such comments had ever existed in reality is not pertinent here. The strong cultural pessimism of the report and the feeling of inevitability about changes which Church and people were powerless to prevent say much about the process of disillusionment that six years of Nazism had brought to sections of the population which had looked initially to the Third Reich as the dawn of a new era.

The crudity of the Nazi attack on the traditional position of the Church turned the initial euphoria for the new State into outraged opposition by autumn 1934 and succeeded for a time only in revitalizing Protestantism. However, the continuing remorseless pressure applied in a variety of forms between 1935 and 1939, none more devastating than the inroads made into the attachment of youth to the Church and especially the forced abolition of denominational schools, transformed attitudes of defiant opposition into despondency and resignation. Protestants had widely misconceived the Nazi phenomenon. Even so, the values which the Protestant population had held in 1933 had not been destroyed or dispelled by the negative experience of Nazism. Hence by 1939 widespread distaste in Protestant circles for the Nazi Party and rejection of its 'totalitarian' claims towards the Church and anti-Christian character of the Party did not stand in the way of continued fervent support for the conservative-national goals and values which after the commencement of war could only with even greater difficulty be separated from the 'specifically Nazi' components of Nazism.[77]

[77] It is true, however, that a section of the 'Confessing Church' had from an early period, and especially from 1936–7, become aware of the real nature of the regime and came to form what has been dubbed a 'reluctant resistance movement' (E. Wolf, 'Political and Moral Motives behind the Resistance', in H. Graml et al., *The German Resistance to Hitler*, London, 1970, p. 209; cf. also Wright, pp. 163–73). The Bavarian Bishop Meiser did not associate himself with this more fundamental opposition to the National Socialist regime.

5. The Alienation of the Catholics

In its relations with the Catholic population of Bavaria, the Nazi Movement faced both before and after 1933 problems of an entirely different order from those which it encountered in its dealings with the Protestant population. Compared with the historical divisions and theological rifts which were features of a critical disunity in the Protestant Church during the Weimar Republic, Catholic institutions and religious life between the foundation of the German Empire and the rise of Nazism were characterized by an extraordinary degree of inner strength, cohesion, unity, and vitality, which rose to a peak in the years of the Republic. The experience of the *Kulturkampf* of the 1870s and the sense of being 'outsiders' in the Bismarckian Reich contributed in no small measure to a hardening of Catholic identity-feeling and the growth of a sub-culture parallel in many ways to that of the socialist working class. The re-foundation of monastic houses and the rapid spread of religious orders provided much of the intellectual stimulus and missionary zeal while the development of a dense network of clubs and associations, welfare and youth organizations, a flourishing and influential Catholic press, and the political articulation of Catholic interests through the Centre Party all assisted in the revitalization of Catholicism and in the sharpening of the contours of the Catholic sub-culture. Ideologically, the key-point was defence of the Catholic faith and institutions not only against the encroachments of the State but also against the threats seen in socialism, liberalism, and atheistic materialism. The chief protection lay, it was felt, in the intensification of pastoral care and especially in the continued propagation of Catholic values through Catholic education — the focus of attack in the *Kulturkampf*. The Revolution of 1918 seemed to make the need to uphold Catholic values all the more urgent. Yet the guaranteeing of freedom of religion by the Weimar Constitution, along with the formal separation of Church and

State though continuance of State subsidies to the Churches, provided the climate in which the Catholic revival reached its apogee. Catholic societies and organizations multiplied, intellectual life thrived, youth associations expanded to a membership of one-and-a-half million, and by the end of the 1920s there was on average one Catholic priest for every thousand souls compared with one pastor for every two-and-a-half thousand Protestants.[1]

Bavaria, overwhelmingly Catholic, played a full part in these developments and was deeply affected socially and politically by the efflorescence of Catholic life. A plethora of educational, social, cultural, and welfare associations sprang up in the late nineteenth century and the dynamic growth continued in the Weimar period, spanning practically every sphere of activity. Student organizations flourished as never before. Parents' associations and Mothers' Unions furthered the vital emphasis laid upon Catholic education and youth work. The 'Catholic Press Association for Bavaria' supplied 660 public libraries in Bavaria with over half a million volumes on Catholic matters, distributed brochures and pamphlets, laid on films and lectures, and shared in the publication of thirteen daily newspapers. Catholic values were also reinforced through an upsurge of popular missionary activity, much of it carried out by the still-expanding religious orders.[2] Compared with the Protestant Church in Bavaria, where — to go by the 'People's Mission' reports[3] — attendance at services and active involvement in church life was sagging and often at a low ebb in the early 1930s, the Catholic Church showed much vitality and the great majority of Bavarian Catholics were still active churchgoers — more so in fact than Catholics elsewhere in Germany.[4]

A number of specific features of Bavarian Catholicism during the Weimar Republic help an understanding of the relationship of Catholics and the Nazi Movement both before and after 1933.

[1] G. Lewy, *The Catholic Church and Nazi Germany*, London, 1964, pp. 4-5.
[2] Spindler, pp. 933-40.
[3] Cf. *Bayern I*, pp. 369 ff. and above, Chapter 4.
[4] Cf. L. Volk, *Der bayerische Episkopat und der Nationalsozialismus 1930-1934*, Mainz, 1965, p. 45.

Unlike the situation in almost all other parts of Germany, Catholicism was in effect the established religion in Bavaria. The eight Bavarian bishops, led by the indomitable Cardinal Faulhaber of Munich-Freising, wielded enormous influence both over the framing of politics and over the shaping of public opinion. Throughout practically the whole of the republican era politics were dominated by the Catholic BVP. Though never commanding an absolute majority in the Bavarian Landtag, between 1924 and 1933 during the premiership of Dr Heinrich Held the BVP dictated the tone of Bavarian politics — extreme conservatism, anti-socialism, and patriotism, all deeply imbued with the upholding of 'white-blue' Bavarian-Catholic values.[5]

Church–State relations in Bavaria were cemented by the signing of a Concordat with the Papacy on 29 March 1924. In contrast to the Weimar Constitution's neutral phrasing of the role of Christian denominations in the State, the Concordat expressed outright the Christian character of the Bavarian State. The rights of the Catholic Church — and, by treaties concluded at the same time, also of the Evangelical Church — of freedom of religion, self-governance, and financial support and protection by the State were thereby anchored in law. Above all, the legal affirmation of the denominational school (*Bekenntnisschule*) as the basic unit of primary education distinguished Bavaria from most German states. The upholding of the denominational school lay at the very root of Catholic pastoral and political aims during the Weimar period and the assault launched against this principle by the Nazis provoked, as we shall see, one of the most bitter spheres of conflict and protest in the Third Reich.[6]

The Concordat met with a cool reception outside Bavaria, and within the province it split opinion diametrically. It was accepted by the Bavarian Parliament in January 1925, but only in the face of the combined opposition of Left and Right — the *Völkischer Block*, SPD, and KPD voting against.[7]

[5] Cf. Pridham, pp. 20-1, 152-3; Wiesemann, *Vorgeschichte*, pp. 20-6, 43-7, 96-7; Spindler, pp. 484-517.
[6] Spindler, pp. 491-4, 937-8, 978-80 outlines the Bavarian Concordat and the place of the denominational school in the Bavarian Constitution.
[7] The vote was 73 for, 52 against — Spindler, p. 494. On the NSDAP's attitude to the Concordat, see Pridham, pp. 163-4.

Many primary-school teachers, from a variety of idealistic motives wishing to see the hold of the Church on education broken, were repelled by the Concordat, eventually finding their way as a consequence directly or indirectly to the NSDAP.[8]

The divisions over the Concordat reflected basic cleavages in Bavarian politics and society. The success of the Held administration in being the first German State to conclude a Concordat with the Vatican was a clear indication of the strength of the BVP-Catholic Church 'establishment' in Bavaria, a dominance which provoked much ideological and political resentment. Anti-BVP feeling was found even within Catholic circles, for the party of political Catholicism was not itself synonymous with the Catholic sub-culture nor with the Church hierarchy. As the 'establishment' in a province where Catholic pre-eminence was assured, in fact, the BVP could rely on the allegiance of fewer Catholics than could the Centre Party on the rest of the Reich. Only 56 per cent of practising Catholics voted for the BVP in 1924 compared with 76 per cent who voted for the Centre Party in the rest of Germany, and it has been estimated that well under a half of Bavaria's total Catholic voting population supported the BVP.[9] At the same time, it was clearly the case that political control was unshakably in the hands of BVP worthies in a great many localities and neither the SPD and KPD on the Left nor the Nazis on the Right could see a way to achieving radical political and social change without breaking the hold of the BVP on its traditional bastions of power.

The two individually most formative influences on the shaping of political opinion in Catholic Bavaria during the Weimar period were the voices of Dr Heinrich Held, Bavarian premier between 1924 and 1933, and Cardinal Michael Faulhaber, Archbishop of Munich-Freising. Their articulation

[8] Wiesemann, *Vorgeschichte*, pp. 92–3. Cf. also the newly-appeared thorough exploration by F. Sonnenberger, 'Der neue "Kulturkampf". Die Gemeinschafts-schule und ihre historischen Voraussetzungen', in *Bayern III*, pp. 235–327, esp. here pp. 253–75; and for a specific local study, E. Kleinöder, 'Katholische Kirche und Nationalsozialismus im Kampf um die Schule. Antikirchliche Maßnahmen und ihre Folgen untersucht am Beispiel von Eichstätt', *Sammelblatt des Historischen Vereins Eichstätt*, lxxiv (1981), esp. 32–7.

[9] Volk, *Der. bayer. Episkopat*, p. 45; Pridham, p. 158 & n. 8–9.

of the Catholic 'establishment' position was instrumental in helping to determine the stance of Bavaria's Catholics towards the growing power of Nazism. The political and ideological views of these two leaders of Catholic opinion illustrate at one end and the same time both the later intransigence of the Catholic sub-culture in the face of Nazi chicanery and 'totalitarian' *Gleichschaltung* pressure, and the possible areas of consensus and *rapprochement* between Catholicism and Nazism. They hint at the future parameters of conformity and opposition among Bavaria's Catholics.

Held, not a Bavarian by birth, was a devout Catholic, an ardent monarchist, a diehard conservative, a fanaticist for legal constitutionalism, and not least a fervent anti-Marxist — and by Marxists he meant mainly the SPD.[10] He abhorred the rabble-rousing populism of the Nazis and saw in the NSDAP not only a threat to public order but also an anti-Catholic, anti-monarchist, and not least anti-Bavarian movement. He exalted the nation and Catholic love of the Fatherland in response to damaging accusations that Bavarian Catholics were 'anti-patriotic', yet repudiated the 'hard-hearted nationalist spirit which produces hostility and hatred'.[11]

Faulhaber was equally scathing about Nazi methods, radicalism, and vulgarity. His criticism of anti-Semitic agitation in 1923 made him even at this early date a target of Nazi abuse. Munich university students dubbed him 'the Jewish cardinal'.[12] However, Faulhaber was also an authoritarian conservative and extreme anti-socialist with a pronounced antipathy for parliamentary democracy and hankering after the monarchical State. In a notorious address to the German Catholic Assembly in 1922 he labelled the Revolution of 1918 'perjury and high treason' which would remain 'tainted and branded with the mark of Cain'.[13] He carried his anti-republicanism and anti-socialism far enough

[10] Pridham, pp. 20–1.
[11] Cf. ibid., p. 153.
[12] Ibid., p. 152. For Faulhaber's political views in general, cf. Volk, *Der bayer. Episkopat*, ch. 1 and esp. L. Volk, 'Kardinal Faulhabers Stellung zur Weimarer Republik und zum NS-Staat', *Stimmen der Zeit*, clxxvii (1966), 173–95.
[13] Volk, 'Kardinal Fäulhabers Stellung', p. 177; Pridham, p. 154.

to forbid church-bells to be rung as a sign of respect for the dead Reich President, Friedrich Ebert, in 1925.[14] His denunciation of the Revolution and vitriolic attacks on communism were frequently alluded to by Nazi speakers who, in their attempts to win Catholic voters and to play down the anti-religious taint attached to the National Socialist Movement, made great play on the common ground shared by the Church and Nazism in working for the defeat of Marxism and the creation of a united German nation.[15]

Under Faulhaber's direction, the eight Bavarian bishops sought in February 1931 to clarify the Catholic position on the Nazi Movement by issuing joint pastoral instructions to the Bavarian clergy. They warned against Nazism 'as long and so far as it proclaims politico-cultural views which are irreconcilable with Catholic teaching', forbade priests any involvement in the Movement, banned any attendance of Nazi formations with flags at Catholic services, and left the question of admission of Nazi members to the sacraments to individual judgement.[16] However, though leaders of Catholic opinion both inside and outside Bavaria shared common concern about the anti-Christian ethos of the Nazi *Weltanschauung*, views on how best to combat the undoubted inroads which the Nazis were making among Catholic voters, and how best to come to terms with a Movement dramatically increasing its strength and including apparently positive aims of anti-Marxism and fervent patriotism, were deeply divided.[17] Catholic leaders were being pressurized to some extent by grass-roots opinion and behaviour. While the BVP (and outside Bavaria the Centre Party) bastions stood remarkably firm even down to 1933 against the Nazi electoral assault, those Catholic voters not anchored in the BVP/Centre were proving less obdurate. Probably some two million Catholic voters helped the Nazis to their electoral triumph in July 1932,[18] and though Catholic areas still proved relatively blind to the attractions of Nazism in the November election,

---

[14] Volk, *Der Bayer. Episkopat*, p. 7.
[15] Pridham, pp. 154–5, 175–83.
[16] Volk, *Der bayer. Episkopat*, pp. 27–9; Lewy, p. 10.
[17] See Lewy, pp. 12–24.
[18] Ibid., p. 19.

precisely such areas registered the greatest swing to the NSDAP in the weeks following Hitler's accession to the Chancellorship.[19] This changing Catholic public opinion had to be taken into account by the hierarchy. In the light of the formal promises made by Hitler, above all in his speech to the Reichstag prior to the passing of the Enabling Act in March 1933, to uphold the rights of the Churches and the provision of denominational education, the Catholic bishops reversed their previous stance in late March 1933. Without repealing their condemnation of 'certain religious and moral errors', they withdrew their previous prohibitions on the Nazi Party and on Catholic participation in it.[20] The Bavarian hierarchy had shown signs of reluctance at issuing such a statement, though its own clarification for the Bavarian clergy contained only minor alterations in content and expression. The Bavarian bishops called for Christian obedience to the new Bavarian government, though acts of injustice and violence were still to be criticized. The role of the priest was to oppose godlessness and immorality, but at the same time to support government measures aimed at the 'spiritual renewal of our national life' and to avoid expressions of disrespect for the government. The Bavarian administration interpreted this as an order to the clergy to support the new regime.[21]

The following months saw the Catholic hierarchy in Bavaria and elsewhere attempting, despite much provocation from the Nazi rank and file, to create a *modus vivendi* with the new regime in a period highlighted by the negotiations for an ambitious Reich Concordat, something which the Weimar State had never achieved. In May 1933 the Bavarian bishops called in a pastoral letter for support for the government's programme of 'spiritual, moral, and economic rejuvenation'.[22] Even in the face of violent attacks on Catholic organizations, youth groups, and clergy in the summer of 1933 and the shock-waves running through Bavaria at the arrest and temporary internment of almost two thousand

[19] Cf. Thränhardt, pp. 182–3.
[20] *Docs. on Nazism*, pp. 192–3; Lewy, pp. 25–41.
[21] Lewy, p. 41.
[22] Cited in ibid., p. 55.

BVP members in late June, Cardinal Faulhaber in particular placed great hope in the prospects of the Concordat, which was eventually concluded on 20 July after the formal dissolution of the BVP and Centre Party.[23] 'What the old parliaments and parties did not accomplish in sixty years, your statesmanlike foresight has achieved in six months', wrote Cardinal Faulhaber in a letter of congratulation to Hitler following the signing of the Concordat.[24]

Such enthusiasm quickly wore off as Nazi anti-Catholic activity continued unabated, and towards the end of the year Cardinal Faulhaber's celebrated Advent sermons, in which in an intimidating atmosphere he offered a pungent theological defence of the Old Testament against the attacks of Nazi anti-Christians and anti-Semites, marked out clear lines of continuing tension between Catholicism and Nazism.[25]

Support for Nazism among Bavaria's Catholic population had been late in coming and was even in 1933 partial and superficial. The problem of breaking down the Catholic subculture was one which the Nazis had not solved. Contrasted with the initial enthuasism of the Protestants, Catholic coolness and reserve towards Nazism was striking. Yet it had to be dispelled if a genuine 'National Community' was to be created. If the strength of the Catholic Church and force of public opinion ruled out total repression as a possible solution to the problem, integration of Catholics through a *rapprochement* similar to that of Mussolini's Italy was in the German context and given the extreme anti-clerical pressures within the Nazi Movement also out of the question. As a consequence, the Third Reich saw a relentless but essentially piecemeal series of attacks on Catholic traditions and customs, on institutions, on the educational structure, and on the Catholic faith as a *Weltanschauung*. In contrast to the rapid explosion of the Protestant church conflict, the Catholic 'Church struggle' was a war of attrition with a period of high tension between 1935 and 1938 and a final flare-up to dramatic confrontation in 1941.

[23] Ibid., pp. 101–4; Spindler, p. 531.   [24] Lewy, p. 104.
[25] M. Faulhaber, *Judentum, Christentum, Germanentum*, Munich, no date (1934); cf. Lewy, p. 111; Spindler, p. 532.

No attempt is made in what follows to offer a description of the generally well-known stages of the 'Church struggle'.[26] I am concerned only with the circumstances in which Bavarian Catholics were prepared to show their dissent, with the forms of their opposition, and with the effect of the 'Church struggle' on Catholic attitudes towards Nazi Party and regime. The framework within which popular opposition could be formed requires a few preliminary remarks. A number of different factors contributed decisively to shaping the nature of Catholic dissent.

Firstly, a point of undoubted importance was the great inherent strength and unity of the Catholic *Weltanschauung*, in no way weakened by internal theological conflict as were Protestant beliefs and exerting through its own 'total' claims upon believers a far stronger doctrinal and behavioural influence over them than did Lutheranism over most Protestants. Secondly, bound up with firmly held Catholic beliefs was a rich tapestry of rituals and customs which represented for Catholics a 'way of life'. It was this traditional world which the Nazis were trying to penetrate and break down. Catholic opposition was therefore on relatively strong ground: it was defending tradition and was at its most vehement where customs of generations were in danger of being swept away. Thirdly, Catholic communities, especially in rural districts, maintained a high degree of attachment to their Church and an extraordinary level of social cohesion. Like the sub-culture of working-class districts, that of Catholics could survive even the breakdown of the rich panoply of associ-- ations and organizations which made up the institutional life of the community. And just as Nazis in the 'factory commu- nity' or in the streets of former SPD or KPD strongholds were an exposed, isolated minority, so were they also 'out- siders' in many Catholic districts – and became all the more so as the 'Church struggle' intensified Catholic bitterness and polarized attitudes. Even some Nazis, registered Party mem- bers but little else, could still be seen to side more with the Church than with the Party, so that the 'real' Nazis in the community were often even more exposed and confined to

[26] Cf. for this esp. the works by Lewy and Conway.

not much more than the local Party leadership and activist core. This meant that hostility to Party and regime in word and in deed could frequently be carried out in relative safety, with no feeling of social or political isolation, with less risk of denunciation. Obviously, in large cities the situation was different. But even here the social cohesion of Catholic churchgoers was a powerful force which furthered the retention and spread of anti-regime feeling.

The fourth point is of at least equal significance: the crucially active role played by the Catholic clergy in giving a lead to their congregations. Catholics were made clearly aware of the direct involvement of the hierarchy in the 'struggle'. They received guidance through frequent pastoral letters, episcopal statements, and sermons of church leaders. There was a strong likelihood, therefore, of at least moral support and sometimes active backing from the bishops for popular opposition to Nazi anti-Church measures. Even more important was the role of the parish priest in shaping and co-ordinating grass-roots opinion. The 'Church struggle' produced in many cases a closer relationship than ever between priest and parishioners, with the priest functioning as the symbol of traditional values, the focus of anti-Nazi feeling, and the counter-pole to the village teacher, so often the arch-exponent of 'progressive' anti-clerical Nazi views. In the First World War Catholic as well as Protestant clergy had served the German government well in upholding national, patriotic values and defending the established order.[27] Before and during the Second World War, the established order meant for the clergy first and foremost the upholding of the position of the Catholic Church, and in the Catholic clergy the Nazi regime made influential enemies. We turn in the following section to a closer consideration of the relationship between clergy and Catholic population and its repercussions for the formation of political opinion.

(i) Clergy and Catholic Population

Many reports from Nazi authorities have an outright anti-clerical tone. Nevertheless, there is no cause to doubt the

[27] Ay, *Entstehung*, pp. 89-94.

truth of their repeated assertions of the continued, even increased, dominance of the clergy over the Catholic population in most country districts especially, and of the consequent difficulty of the Party's task in penetrating Catholic communities. The Government President of Lower Bavaria and the Upper Palatinate attributed in summer 1934 the failure of the Party in mobilizing the Catholic peasants of the region in no small measure to the counter-influence of an unsympathetic clergy.[28] Noted Catholic bastions, where clerical influence was strong, tended to produce high numbers of 'Nein' votes in the plebiscite of August 1934 confirming Hitler as Head of State (though the Catholic vote in general still held up well at this date).[29] Reports from localities in Upper Bavaria the following summer accused the clergy of doing all they could to poison the atmosphere against Nazism among the local peasantry through cleverly hinted attacks in sermons and through visits to individual homes.[30] Priests put up a particularly stern fight in their attempt to keep a hold on Catholic youth. Recruitment to Nazi youth organizations was poor in very Catholic districts. According to one report, the BdM was recruiting only about 3 per cent from Catholic girls' schools, and other reports attributed the frequent resignations from the BdM and *Jungvolk* to the machinations of priests.[31] The clergy were also active and, it seems, successful in seizing on Rosenberg as the epitome of the anti-Christian spirit of Nazism and in emphasizing the connections between Nazism and the 'new heathenism'.[32] Incidents such as the one which took place in the super-pious Eichstätt in 1934, when the Nazi District Leader ordered the replacement of the 'High Cross', a huge crucifix on the hillside above the town, by a *'Thingplatz'* — a Teutonic assembly place related to pagan Germanic sun-worship — naturally played straight into the hands of the clergy and seemed to demonstrate the

[28] KLB, iv. 30, 34.
[29] e.g., KLB, i. 27.
[30] StAM, LRA 79888, Bgm. Glonn, 1 June 1935.
[31] KLB, iv. 50. Cf. also ibid., pp. 72, 97; KLB, i. 143–4; KLB, iii. 74. For a local case-study of the conflict over youth organizations and the role of the clergy, see E. Kleinöder, 'Verfolgung und Widerstand der Katholischen Jugendvereine. Eine Fallstudie über Eichstätt, in *Bayern II*, pp. 175–236.
[32] KLB, iii. 56–7, 96; KLB, iv. 73.

justification of the attack on Rosenberg's 'new heathenism'.[33]

In the Catholic clergy, Goebbels met his propaganda match. The defamation campaign against currency frauds in 1934-5 and the publication of the 'immorality trials' of members of religious orders in 1936-7 were countered effectively by priests pointing out to their congregations not only the patent fabrication of many of the allegations but also the demonstrably much wider prevalence of gross immorality and corruption within the Nazi Party itself.[34] The press reportage, openly denounced by the clergy as lies, was subjected to massive criticism. Catholics were recommended not to read newspapers and to cancel their subscriptions because of the articles on the 'immorality trials', and many of them did precisely that.[35] Clergy also took the lead in many outward signs of nonconformity: demonstrative use of the *'Grüß Gott'* greeting and avoidance of 'Heil Hitler'; omitting to put out the swastika flag on days of official celebration, or continuing to show the banned church flags; and the building up of church feasts into veritable demonstrations of solidarity and defiance — the more so the greater the attempt on the part of the Nazis to interfere with traditional celebrations. The reports of the Nazi authorities are littered with cases of priests being arrested and punished in one form or another for such behaviour.

An example of how a purely ecclesiastical affair was consciously made by the Church into a demonstration of Catholic feeling and solidarity, and by the Nazis authorities into a political act of defiance is provided by the *Primizfeier*. The *Primiz* was the first Mass of a newly ordained priest. When this could be celebrated in the priest's home parish, the village would traditionally make an occasion out of it. In the later 1930s, however, the *Primizfeier* developed its new significance as a Church propaganda weapon until in 1939 the Gestapo eventually banned all festivities outside

[33] E.N. Peterson, *The Limits of Hitler's Power*, Princeton, 1969, pp. 301-5.
[34] KLB, iv. 136. Cf. in general for this Nazi defamation campaign, H.G. Hockerts, *Die Sittlichkeitsprozesse gegen katholische Ordensangehörige und Priester 1936/1937*, Mainz, 1971.
[35] KLB, i. 241; KLB, ii. 207; KLB, iii. 77, 107, 139; KLB, iv. 136; GStA, MA 106680, RPvUF, 10 June 1937.

the church building itself.[36] The Nazi unease at the effect of
the *Primizfeiern* is not hard to understand. The authorities
contrasted the buoyant attendances at the *Primizfeiern* with
the poor record of Party meetings.[37] At one *Primiz* celebration in Oberammergau, a district where attendance at
Party meetings and events was notoriously low, 6,000 people
poured in by train, car, and bicycle to pack the Passion
Theatre and provide what the reporter described as 'a power
display of the Church'.[38] Strong attendance from far afield
was also noted in six *Primiz* celebrations within a month in
the summer of 1938 in the Freising district. The sermons
concentrated deliberately on the person of the priest and
pointed out that although the 'immorality trials' had sought
to destroy his standing, the growing attachment of the population to the priesthood and to the convent nuns (whose
schoolteaching activities had been stopped) showed exactly
the opposite, 'for the priests alone are the leaders appointed
by God, while the leaders of the nation are only appointed
by men.' One preacher caused unrest among his listeners by
hinting that the time would come 'when each Catholic would
have to vote whether he wished to remain a Catholic and still
have a priest.' The Government President cited the report as
an illustration of 'the activity by which the Catholic clergy
knows, by means of old tried and new methods, how to exert
influence on the broad mass of the population.'[39] Intervention by the local police to curtail the *Primiz* celebrations
was in practice extremely difficult. In the Lower Franconian
village of Mömlingen, for instance, the *Primizfeier* held in
March 1937 was said to have been organized as 'a demonstration against the National Socialist State'. Prior to the
service, the ringing of the church-bell gave the prearranged
signal for the villagers to hang out the yellow and white
church flags, whose use on private houses had been expressly
banned by the District Office. When the *Gendarmerie* officer
reminded the inhabitants of the ban, he was told in no

[36] The ban itself led to considerable bitterness. Cf. KLB, i. 310–12.
[37] StAA, BA Amberg 2399, GS Freudenberg, 23 July 1938; KLB, ii. 328;
KLB, iii. 187; KLB, iv. 239.
[38] StAM, LRA 61615, GS Oberammergau, 29 May 1937.
[39] KLB, i. 294.

uncertain terms that the flags would remain out whatever he
had to say about it. Even Party members had hung out
church flags. 'Since', the report went on, 'all the inhabitants
of Mömlingen stood together, intervention on the part of
the *Gendarmerie* was not possible, or at least would not have
proved successful. Consequently, with the permission of the
District Office, nothing was done.'[40]

The personality and energy of individual priests unquestionably influenced the degree of bitterness with which
the 'Church struggle' was contested. How difficult it was for
the Nazis to penetrate a closed Catholic community which
stood under the strong influence of the local priest is shown
graphically in the case of the village of Leidersbach in Lower
Franconia.[41] Before the 'seizure of power' the village had
been a stronghold of the BVP. The mayor himself was an
ex-BVP man who had been given his post only in the complete absence of any alternative possible candidate. Though
now claiming to be standing 'firmly on the ground of the
National Socialist Movement', he had to defend himself
against allegations of siding with the Church against the
Party. He admitted 'that the situation in Leidersbach is
hopeless' and felt that

the resistance which the spread of the Movement in Leidersbach meets
among a section of the inhabitants is due to the fact that these people
think National Socialism is turning on religion . . . Ninety-five per cent
of the residents of Leidersbach used to belong to the Bavarian People's
Party [BVP]. I see my task as bringing over these people who are still
aloof from the Movement to the National Socialist *Weltanschauung*.
Naturally, this needs time. In Leidersbach there are some people for
whom things are not going fast enough. As a result they misunderstand
my mediation and call me a black [i.e. Catholic] and a supporter of
the chaplain.

Mainstays of the Party in the village were the local SA leader
— who had a reputation as an idler and a drunkard — and the

---

[40] LRA Obernburg am Main (Registratur), Sammelakt 'Kirche und Nationalsozialismus', BA Obernburg, 6 Feb. 1937, 12 Mar. 1937; SD-AS Aschaffenburg,
5 Feb. 1937; GS Mömlingen, 8 Mar. 1937.
[41] What follows is based on the documentation in the same 'Kirche und
Nationalsozialismus' file in the archives of the LRA Obernburg am Main. I am
grateful to the local authorities in Obernburg for permission to work on this
material.

head teacher who eventually committed suicide under serious suspicion of indecent assault on schoolgirls.[42]

Real power in the village lay in the hands of the young chaplain (village priest), Josef Fäth, already known to the authorities as a 'hidden opponent of the Movement' and to the population as 'the black *Kreisleiter*'. Even the head of the local police station was said to be completely under his influence and could not be trusted to compile a satisfactory report on him. As a result of the poor reputation of the Party's local representatives and of the intensification of the Party's apparent war against the Church, the position of the chaplain was immeasurably strengthened.[43] His hold over the village community and the impossibility of the Nazi Party's representatives, the real outsiders in the village, to make organizational or ideological headway, is well illustrated in a one-sided but informative account of the situation given by the village schoolteacher on 15 March 1937, after a demonstration of some fifty parents had demanded her removal from the school on the grounds that she no longer possessed the confidence of the parents:

The work of every teacher in Leidersbach has been made difficult for years, but recently positive work on behalf of the National Socialist State and Party has become completely impossible. These conditions can be attributed to the underhand activity hostile to the State of the local cleric Chaplain Fäth (known in this district as the black *Kreisleiter*), who understands in masterly fashion how to keep in the background and push others forward. A few facts serve to characterize the local situation. At the last plebiscite on the 29. 3. 36 Leidersbach had in percentage terms the most 'no-votes' in the whole of Main Franconia; on Church feast-days, such as recently on the 11. 10. 36, despite express ban, some seventy yellow and white [church] flags were hung out; on the appointment of an HJ-leader for Leidersbach, Chaplain Fäth agitated to such an extent among the majority of the population about the planned measures of the HJ-leadership that it came to a commotion in which stones were thrown at the HJ-headquarters and the leaders were loudly and violently abused . . . Chaplain Fäth agitated in the Catholic Mothers' Association against the teacher . . . [i.e. the writer of the report] , saying the teacher hung 'Hitler' at the front of her classroom and the crucifix at the side . . . In the mothers' meeting on the

[42] Ibid., 'Beschwerde gegen den Bürgermeister in Leidersbach', 18 Nov. 1935.
[43] Ibid., BA Obernburg to the BPP, 21 Nov. 1935, 'Verhalten des Kaplans Fäth in Leidersbach'.

28. 2. 37 Chaplain Fäth said that the peasants in Oldenburg had thrown a teacher out because he had got rid of the crucifix. Chaplain Fäth agitates, if in secret, against the youth organizations. This is proved by the fact that despite the greatest recruitment drive the number of BdM and *Jungmädel* at the moment together amounts to seventeen girls while 'his' fledglings in the Congregation of Mary number almost two hundred. This secret sabotage is becoming increasingly unbearable. Chaplain Fäth and the national comrades (*Volksgenossen*) stirred up by him apparently regard themselves as completely safe since they have so far always managed to get away with it. They want to attack the Party, the National Socialist State. In their opinion, further considerations are not necessary; popular risings can now be staged. This time in particular, my own person is the target . . . In this case, too, the brains behind the demonstration is Chaplain Fäth, who up to now has succeeded in getting rid of everything in his path in Leidersbach. He understands in a masterly fashion how to bring popular feelings to the boil.[44]

Though the situation in Leidersbach clearly owed much to the personality of the 'black *Kreisleiter*', this report casts light on repercussions of the 'Church struggle' which had a wider currency: the strengthening of the clergy's position in the community, especially in rural areas; the intense antagonisms between clergy and teachers as opposite poles in an ideological confrontation; and the difficulties facing the Nazi Party's representatives, who were often 'foreign bodies' in such tightly-knit communities. The Government President of Lower Franconia mentioned the Leidersbach incident among others in the general context of extensive discontent among the rural population, fanned above all by the 'Church struggle' which was polarizing opinion to such an extent that it was in his view threatening to become a danger to the solidarity of the nation. Nazi attacks on Church and clergy produced such fierce denunciation 'that the churchgoing population takes at heart the side of the priests and that therefore the support for the clergy becomes greater.'[45] Such generalizations were drawn from the tone of countless local police reports noting resignedly that: 'the influence of the Church on the population is so strong that the National Socialist spirit cannot penetrate'; 'the local population is as ever under

---

[44] Ibid., Report to the BA Obernburg, 15 Mar. 1937. Details and comment were also given in the report of BA Obernburg, 18 Mar. 1937 on her application for transfer of post along with that of two other teachers.
[45] GStA, MA 106680, RPvUF, 8 Mar. 1937.

the strong influence of the clergy and behaves indifferently towards the National Socialist government and its measures'; 'these people much prefer to believe what the priest says from the pulpit than the words of the best speakers.'[46]

The increased solidarity of the churchgoing population with the clergy was repeatedly demonstrated, much to the irritation of the Nazi authorities, by the rapturous ovations which greeted Cardinal Faulhaber and the other Bavarian bishops whenever they set foot in public.[47] Keynote sermons by bishops became major advertisements of Catholic solidarity. Word was spread round well in advance that a significant pronouncement was to be made, and the sermon was invariably held in a church or cathedral bursting at the seams. The political sentiments of the listeners sometimes broke through unmistakably. Faulhaber's pungent denunciation in February 1937 of breaches of the Concordat was interrupted on several occasions by cries of 'down with the dictatorship' and Ex-Crown Prince Rupprecht of Bavaria who had attended the service was given an ovation by crowds thronging the Munich streets chanting 'long live King Rupprecht, Rupprecht is our leader, down with the Antichrist.'[48]

The solidarity was particularly marked when individual local clergymen were under attack by the Nazis. When the popular Munich preacher Father Rupert Mayer, a bitter and outspoken critic of the regime, was imprisoned in 1937 a crowd of 400 persons protested outside the Munich police headquarters at his arrest. According to the Munich police report, some 150 churchgoers then made their way to the Gestapo building in Briennerstraße where it came to 'a scuffle between ideological opponents', following which three persons were arrested and later freed. Another demonstration of 250 persons took place after evening service.[49] The Church

---

[46] StAM, LRA 59595, GS Karlskron, 31 Mar., 29 Apr., 29 Oct. 1937; GS Hohenwart, 28 Oct. 1936, 26 Feb. 1937; GS Berg im Gau, 29 Oct. 1938; KLB, i. 241, 294-5; KLB, iv. 97, 135, n. 22.

[47] E.g., StAN, Pol.-Dir. Nürnberg-Fürth 431, BPP, 1 Nov. 1935, p. 23; KLB, ii. 64, 98; KLB, i. 50, 153.

[48] KLB, i. 198-200; ASD, ES/M65/Mar. 1937.

[49] KLB, i. 244-5. Mayer's evangelizing work and his leadership of the Munich 'Men's Congregation of Mary' had earned him a high reputation throughout

authorities' response, however, was to calm matters down and proceed along the path of strict legality. A declaration read out from all pulpits in the diocese urged Catholics to refrain from street demonstrations and stated that a formal protest against the arrest had been sent to the authorities.[50] In a sermon on 4 July 1937, Cardinal Faulhaber stated:

No greater service could we do the police than to furnish them with means to bring action with cudgels and arrests, with lock-outs and dismissals against the odious Catholics, nowadays more hated and persecuted than the Bolsheviks. You have obeyed Father Mayer's wishes in keeping order and refraining from thoughtless words and deeds. There is a time to be silent.[51]

Whether, given the mood of anger at Mayer's arrest, the dampening of likely civil disobedience was a serious mistake which, through its legalistic emphasis on avoiding conflict with the civil authorities, played wholly into Nazi hands must remain a moot point. At any rate, the Church's legalism could not prevent the trial against Father Mayer going ahead at the Munich 'Special Court' that very month.[52] Mayer was given

---

Bavaria and the appellation of the 'Men's Apostle'. His 'national' credentials were impeccable. He had won the Iron Cross First Class in the War, had lost a leg in action, and had before and after the War been an outspoken opponent of Marxism and Bolshevism. He had even once spoken at the same meeting as Hitler, and had received Hitler's handwritten congratulations on his Silver Jubilee as a priest in 1924. After 1933 he became one of the most vehement and forthright defenders of the Church against Nazi aggression and ignored all warnings to tone down his invariably well-attended sermons. To packed congregations in 1937 he launched into savage criticism of Nazi school policy, the Stürmer, Rosenberg's 'neo-heathenism', Goebbels's anti-Church propaganda, and the regime's breaches of the Concordat. His denunciation of the German press as 'the greatest liar in the world' for its reportage of the 'immorality trials' was interrupted by storms of applause during a sermon in Munich, and was followed by cries of 'down with the persecutors of Christians; Goebbels is the Antichrist!'. His standing and influence were such that the Nazis took a considerable risk in arresting him. For further details on Fr Mayer's person, career, and arrest, cf. O. Gritschneder, 'Die Akten des Sondergerichts über Pater Rupert Mayer S.J.', Beiträge zur altbayerischen Kirchengeschichte (1974), 159–218, and The Persecution of the Catholic Church in the Third Reich (no editor), London, 1942, p. 539. For his sermons, cf. KLB, i. 195, 234, 236; DBS, 18 Sept. 1937, p. A112; Gritschneder, pp. 196–201.
    [50] Persecution, p. 68; KLB, i. 246.
    [51] Persecution, p. 538.
    [52] For the trial, see Gritschneder, passim. Mayer's defence was surprisingly weak and widely felt in Catholic circles as a let-down – Cf. Gritschneder, p. 213; DBS, 18 Sept. 1937, p. A113.

a nominal sentence, but effectively taken out of the political arena for the duration of the Third Reich. His courage and fortitude were exemplary. But his voice was silenced, and that had to count as a victory for the Nazi oppressors.[53]

Just how effectively the hierarchy could call the bluff of the authorities by engaging in active defence of clergy and whipping up popular support for priests is shown by two incidents in the Eichstätt diocese in 1936-7. This diocese, one of the most solidly conservative Catholic parts of Bavaria, was headed at the time by Michael Rackl, the most outspoken of the Bavarian bishops who had declared openly that 'National Socialism is not compatible with the Catholic *Weltanschauung*' and that 'every Catholic must decide whether he will be loyal to his Church or wants to become a National Socialist.'[54] With his equally indomitable lieutenant, *Dompfarrer* Johann Kraus, Rackl had been engaged in a direct confrontation with the Nazis since his consecration as bishop over a year earlier and enjoyed massive popular support in the area.[55]

In April 1937, Rackl publicly defended Kraus — known to the Nazis as 'the most active and dangerous political clergyman in the Eichstätt diocese' — in a courageous sermon which received tumultuous applause from a packed cathedral congregation. Rackl stated that he had ordered Kraus to stay in Eichstätt, despite the fact that the authorities had ordered him to leave — a punishment imposed here, as the Bishop pointed out, on a former World War officer who had served with distinction, of the sort formerly reserved for pimps and procurers. The entire officer class would regard the treatment of Kraus as an insult, all the more so since he was only acting as a loyal soldier of Christ in carrying out his duty. Kraus was no revolutionary, as the State knew, but it was a matter here of a struggle between two ideologies which opposed each other like fire and water. Rackl's defence of

---

[53] The Munich police could feel well satisfied with the way the hierarchy quietly dropped the affair — KLB, i. 253. For the 'severe disappointment' of many Catholics about the passivity of the hierarchy, cf. DBS, 18 Sept. 1937, pp. A114-15.

[54] KLB, ii. 98.

[55] For Rackl and Kraus, cf. Peterson, pp. 309-19.

the highly respected and popular *Dompfarrer*, supported by a petition of 2,582 names protesting at his banning, forced the authorities into retreat. Kraus was allowed to stay.[56] Immediately, Rackl turned to the defence of another priest in his diocese. Father Heinloth of Ochsenfeld had been banned from the diocese by the Gestapo because of alleged comments made about the 'community school'. Before leaving, however, he informed his parishioners that on the Bishop's orders he was taking away the Sacrament and extinguishing the sacred light in the church. A medieval-style interdict was imposed. The church was left without a pastor and no services were held, with the exception of a burial service which Rackl himself held, exploiting the occasion to deliver a powerful graveside attack on the Nazi State. Nine days later, Father Heinloth, still under ban, returned illegally to the parish and the population turned out in force, informing the local police that under no circumstances would they let their priest go again, and providing a guard all night long in front of the presbytery. When, a few days later, Father Heinloth was nevertheless rearrested it was the signal for various forms of localized disorder: threats and abuse hurled at the mayor and police, assemblies of angry villagers, a school strike of parents who refused to send their children to school — leading to some further arrests — and eventually the sending in of SS guards to protect the mayor and teachers for more than a week. The result was a compromise. Father Heinloth was released from prison the day after his arrest, but immediately transferred to another parish. The report of the Government President ends: 'And so the state authority had a complete victory.' However dubious such a claim, the affair had an epilogue which was to the liking of neither Party nor State: the case against Father Heinloth before the 'Special Court' was abandoned for lack of evidence.[57]

Owing in great measure to the personalities of Rackl and Kraus the situation in Eichstätt was extraordinary in its intensity even for Bavaria. There too the highpoint of the conflict was passed by 1938, but the legacy of bitterness

[56] KLB, ii. 175–6.
[57] Ibid., pp. 168–9, 177, 187, 222–3. Cf. also Peterson, pp. 317–18.

remained and the alienation of the vast bulk of the population from Nazism was largely complete.[58]

(ii) Popular Opinion and the Anti-Church Measures of Party and State

Alongside the anti-Church measures of the State, which we shall presently consider, the sporadic but ever-recurring wild violence of radical Party activists assisted immeasurably the efforts of the clergy in retaining the allegiance of their parishioners and deepened the antagonisms between Catholics and Nazis. The violence and sacrilegious hooliganism involved in attacks on Catholic symbols — statues of saints and, increasingly, crucifixes — and the occasional assaults even on priests invoked disgust and anger which sometimes embraced even the more 'moderate' ranks of the Party membership. The disturbances caused by roaming bands of Hitler Youth, SA, and SS in Bavarian cities and towns during the *Caritas* collections in May 1935 caused widespread criticism and resentment and were guaranteed, in the words of the Munich police report, 'to damage in the most acute fashion the standing of the Movement'.[59] In the Ebermannstadt district of Upper Franconia the anti-clericalism and anti-religious vandalism of a local SS camp between 1934 and 1936 had such a lasting effect on political attitudes that the local population was still, years later, 'suspicious over the SS and everything to do with it', regarding it as nothing more than a political organization with the job of the 'brutal extermination of the Christian religions'.[60]

Similarly, the 'crucifix affair' of 1941 — to be examined in a later chapter — has to be partly placed in the context of proliferating attacks on crosses in schools, public houses, town squares, or at the wayside from the end of 1936

[58] Further material about Eichstätt in the Third Reich in Peterson, ch. 5 and Kleinöder, 'Kath. Kirche und Nat. soz.'

[59] KLB, i. 68-71, 73. For similar sentiments, cf. StAM, LRA 76887, GS Hohenlinden, 31 May 1935; GS Zorneding, 31 May 1935; LRA 61613, BA Garmisch, 4 June 1935; GS Oberammergau, 31 May 1935; KLB, iii. 61.

[60] StAB, K8/III, 18475, LR Ebermannstadt, 2 Feb. 1943. Cf. above, Chapter 3 note 59.

onwards. The symbol of Christianity was an obvious target to Nazi vandals; its destruction or removal was guaranteed to produce the greatest strain in relations between Catholics and Nazis.

Rumours circulating in and around Munich that all wayside crosses were to be removed and the setting-up of new crosses prohibited were already in 1935 causing alarm in the rural population. According to the report of the Munich police, the peasantry was particularly susceptible to such scare-mongering because of their superstitious worries about the blessing for the harvest.[61] Though the removal of crucifixes or disrespect shown towards the cross was the focus of a number of isolated incidents in the early years of the dictatorship, it was in the context of the fight for the retention of the denominational school that the crucifix came to acquire symbolic significance as the representation of the continued dominance of *Kreuz* over *Hakenkreuz*. Its removal became increasingly an aim of Nazi radicals. The significance of the crucifix as the central symbolic focus of the struggle was highlighted by the events in Oldenburg in North Germany, where popular opposition to the removal of crucifixes from schoolrooms had produced an embarrassing defeat for Party and State — word of which rapidly spread throughout Catholic Bavaria.[62] Immediately, the clergy suggestively brought the removal of crucifixes into the campaign to defend the denominational school, and parents were reminded that in some of the new 'community schools' crucifixes had been taken from the classrooms and children forbidden to make the sign of the cross.[63] Whereas priests had formerly complained on occasion about the displacement of crosses

---

[61] KLB, i. 75.

[62] For Oldenburg, cf. Noakes, 'The Oldenburg Crucifix Struggle', and *Persecution*, pp. 121–7. For news of the events in Bavaria, cf. KLB, i. 183, 185–6; KLB, ii. 134, 136, 147; KLB, iii. 119–20, 129; KLB, iv. 110–11, 115, 119. One Upper Franconian *Kreisleiter* found it embarrassing that the whole Catholic population of his district was obviously well acquainted with the affair while he himself was completely in the dark about the matter — StAB, M33/153/III, KL Kronach, 4 Jan. 1937. StAW, Sammlung Schumacher 27 contains complete transcripts of documents relating to the successful protest in Oldenburg which were brought to light during the Bavarian 'crucifix affair' of 1941.

[63] KLB, i. 122, 184.

but evidently felt unable to do much about it,[64] and where parents and churchgoers had been upset but had felt equally helpless, the success of the Oldenburg opposition evidently provided hope that the cross could be fought for — a point of enormous significance for the crucifix struggle of 1941. Meanwhile, in the new climate the authorities replaced some crucifixes which had already been taken from schoolrooms.[65] The new concern about the crosses on the part of Church and clergy was, especially in the light of the smarting rebuff in Oldenburg, a provocation for Party activists. Outrages and removals of crosses now proliferated.[66] Great anger was caused among the local population in the Bad Tölz area in early 1937 when the figure of Christ was broken off a field cross — almost certainly, it was thought, by members of the SS Leadership School in Tölz — and thrown onto the street.[67] In a Munich suburb the same month, parents refused to allow their children to attend further Hitler Youth meetings on hearing that the local HJ leader had removed the cross from their assembly-room, declaring 'We have another faith, our faith is Germany.'[68] An incident in Weilheim (Upper Bavaria) soon afterwards, in which the village teacher removed — temporarily it was said — the crucifix from the schoolroom, whipped up feeling to such an extent that fathers of schoolchildren were reported as having gone to the school and given the teacher a beating.[69] In Konnersreuth in the Upper Palatinate a party of seventy persons assembled before the house of the teacher in February 1937 angrily demanding a crucifix which the teacher had removed from the classroom. The gathering, wanting to proceed in solemn procession to the schoolhouse in order to replace the cross, was successfully dispersed by the *Gendarmerie* but the District Officer saw to it that the cross was quietly replaced to avoid further trouble.[70] Similar incidents were occurring in different parts of Bavaria in these early months of 1937.

[64] Cf. KLB, iii. 91.
[65] Cf. StAM, LRA 61615, GBF Garmisch, 2 Feb. 1937; GS Mittenwald, 29 Jan. 1937.
[66] Cf. *Persecution*, p. 544 for incidents in the Munich-Freising Archdiocese.
[67] KLB, i. 196.
[68] Ibid., i. 196.
[69] Ibid., p. 222.   [70] KLB, iv. 117.

Though the cross issue died down again after a while, the threat of the removal of crucifixes cast its shadow over the whole fight for the denominational school, and its legacy remained to provide the stimulus for the explosion in 1941.

The actions of individual Party members or of Party affiliations provoked contempt, anger, and bitterness. They remained, however, more or less random, spasmodic incidents. More generally felt as well as more dangerous in itself was the attack by the State on Catholic institutions and practices. This attack was responsible for the largely complete alienation of the Catholic population between 1935 and 1939.

The most blatant signs of the attempted secularization of public life by the Nazi regime were the restrictions imposed on Church processions and the abolition of important feast days in the Church calendar. Interference with the Corpus Christi procession, traditionally the most important of the Church's public processions with thousands of participants in the big cities, took the form of bans on church flags on public buildings, on participation by civil servants except in a purely personal capacity, on uniforms or insignia of Catholic associations, and the specious re-routing of the procession through back streets because of alleged traffic problems. All this understandably created enormous bitterness. Many of the injunctions were flouted or ignored. After a drop in participation in 1935 and 1936 (when the Bavarian Political Police monitored the processions most carefully[71]), attendances picked up again and by the end of the 1930s were as high as ever. Even when, amid much anger, the ceremony was moved in 1940 from its traditional Thursday to the following Sunday to help the war economy, attendance remained good and on the feast day itself many peasants continued to refuse to work.[72] Abolition of the feast days of All Saints (1 November) and Epiphany (6 January) met with a similar fate

[71] Cf. the telegram demand from BPP, AS-Würzburg, 11 June 1936, for information from the District Offices on the participation of youth, of leading local figures, and on street decoration, behaviour of the public, and any disturbances — LRA Obernburg am Main, Sammelakt 'Kirche und Nationalsozialismus'.

[72] *Persecution*, pp. 212–13; KLB, i. 80–1, 149–50, 241, 293, 318–19; KLB, ii. 58–9, 98, 288, 323, 350, 384–5; KLB, iii. 67, 132–3, 184, 198, 218; KLB, iv. 55, 205, 235–6, 267, 286; DBS, 4 July 1936, pp. A93–4; 18 Sept. 1937, p. A115.

in rural areas, with widespread continuation of the old custom of visiting relatives' graves on All Saints and common treatment of the day as a holiday, amid expressions of great resentment at the attempted interference of the State with such age-old practices.[73] This type of State intervention achieved little. Such surface conformity as accrued from the intimidation and chicanery was attained at a high price of alienation of public sympathy. The attachment of the population to Church and clergy was furthered rather than diminished as a result of such crude aggression.

More serious than the disruption of outward practices and piety, however much this was resented, was the attack on Catholic education which, as the Church well realized, formed the very crux of the struggle for ideological dominance. On this ground above all other the fight for the allegiance of Catholics was carried out.

As we saw earlier, the provision of denominational schools was one of the central points of the Bavarian Concordat of 1924 (and of the accompanying treaties with the Evangelical Church). This followed a law of 1 August 1922 whereby the denominational school was seen as the norm in Bavaria (in distinction from the rapidly spreading non-denominational school, the *Simultanschule* or later, in the Nazi period, the *Gemeinschaftsschule*, in other parts of Germany). In 1928 only 2.7 per cent of Bavarian elementary schools were non-denominational.[74] Another peculiarity of the Bavarian educational scene could be seen in the number of private schools, mainly secondary schools, run by the Church and staffed by clergy, especially nuns.[75] Though the Reich Concordat of 1933 appeared to guarantee the legal continuance of such schools, the Nazis sought from 1934 and especially between 1936 and 1938 to abolish them and to make German school education uniformly non-denominational. The eradication of what was regarded as an altogether reactionary and undesirable control over education by the Catholic Church (and to a lesser extent by the Evangelical Church) had long

[73] KLB, i. 275-7, 303, 315; KLB, ii. 257; KLB, iii. 95, 125, 145, 150, 173, 233; KLB, iv. 158, 174, 218, 276, 300, 325.
[74] Spindler, p. 979.
[75] Ibid., p. 984; *Persecution*, p. 130.

corresponded to the educational idealism of liberals and socialists. However, the fight waged by the Nazis for non-denominational education differed diametrically from such earlier idealism. It aimed categorically not only at the secularization of society, but at the replacement of the Church's hold on youth by a new all-embracing and rigid ideology, a new Nazi faith demanding the rejection of Christian values. The attack on the Catholic school took the form, first of all, of attempts to undermine the Christian character of the schools — interference with the wording of prayers, religious symbols, giving a non-Christian or neo-pagan slant to teaching, and so on; more directly effective was the dissolution of convent schools and the turning-out of all nuns teaching in schools in an onslaught which began in summer 1936; and then the conversion of the schools into 'community schools' (*Gemeinschaftsschulen*), implying the de-Christianization and Nazification of the school environment and curriculum. The final stage was the exclusion of the Church even from the sphere of religious instruction and the severe restrictions placed upon such instruction.[76]

The decisive phase of this process took place in 1936-7, and in these years the entire force of Catholic opposition was mobilized by the hierarchy and clergy. The reactions of the population show clearly how disliked the educational changes were, and what repercussions they had for attitudes towards State and Party.

In Bavaria, the introduction of the 'community school' was combined with the removal of members of religious orders from schools.[77] The dismissal of nuns from teaching posts was announced by the Bavarian Ministry of Education in May 1936, when it was stated that 'the State must be able to exercise a centralized control over all its educational affairs . . . The National Socialist State wants a school, a youth, and a form of education in harmony with the National Socialist spirit. For this reason it can no longer entrust the care of State public elementary schools to religious orders.'[78]

[76] Cf. *Persecution*, pp. 115-86; J. Neuhäusler, *Kreuz und Hakenkreuz*, Munich, 1946, i. 88-105, 115-21, 250-5; R. Eilers, *Die nationalsozialistische Schulpolitik*, Cologne, 1963, pp. 22-8, 85-92.
[77] Eilers, p. 91.   [78] *Persecution*, p. 132.

By mid-1938, 1,200 of the 1,600 nuns engaged in teaching in Bavaria had been dismissed without pension.[79] The Bavarian bishops reacted swiftly and issued a strong denunciation in a pastoral letter which, despite being banned by the BPP, was read out from nearly all pulpits on 21 June 1936.[80]

The anger and dismay felt at the State's action, the sympathy for the dismissed nuns, approval of the hierarchy's protest, and the immediate impact of the pastoral in mobilizing opinion are registered in most reports of the authorities in June and July 1936. In numerous places, especially where nuns taught in schools, the local clergy inspired petitions and protests from the population on behalf of the nuns.[81] An anonymous letter sent to the mayor of Schwandorf in the Upper Palatinate from a one-time Nazi supporter expressed what were certainly not isolated sentiments about the dismissal of the nuns who had, claimed the writer, served the community for seventy years to the complete satisfaction of all:

Which Catholic mother did not weep in the last few days when she was told about it by her children? I happened to be a witness as to how the children cried on the streets for their sisters, and all the grown-ups who came with them. Must the sisters go to make way again for *Bonzen*, or because they are Catholic? In fifty years time the children will still have fond memories of their good sisters, while certainly no one will give a damn about these Nazi *Bonzen* whether they disappear today or tomorrow . . . Heil Hitler! The father of a family . . . [P.S.] Would the wicked communists have attacked us Catholics in such a way?[82]

The Nazi leader of a small Bavarian village reported to his District Leader in Deggendorf that the government decree ordering the dismissal of the teaching nuns had been regarded by a large majority of the population, including some Party members, as unjust, brutal, and a direct attack on religion. It had created anger and great discontent — feelings related

[79] Neuhäusler, p. 100.
[80] KLB, ii. 99 & n. 6; a translation of the text is in *Persecution*, p. 133.
[81] KLB, ii. 106; KLB, iii. 111, 116; StAM, LRA 76887, GS Glonn, 30 May 1936; StAA, BA Vohenstrauß 4674, BA Vohenstrauß, 31 July 1936. A written protest about the dissolution of the convent school in Mühldorf (Upper Bavaria) in spring 1937 was accompanied by a demonstration of between forty and fifty people in front of the District Office — KLB, i. 244.
[82] KLB, iv. 91–2.

to the particular respect in which the local nuns had been
held on account of their teaching and youth work:

As a result of the announced dissolution of the convent schools the
local population had been gripped by a mood of strong depression,
often too an outright antipathy towards the Party. Even several Party
members have openly expressed to me their misgivings about it. I must
report that this measure can in no way be understood by the people,
who are almost a hundred per cent opposed to it, and that confidence
in the Party is as a result considerably diminished.[83]

The government decree caused equal unrest in the Upper
Bavarian village of Glonn, to the east of Munich, which housed
a girls' convent school. The local priest occasioned a protest
petition which, on the intervention of the Party, was confiscated by the District Office. As a consequence of the
announced dissolution of the convent school, it was reported,
'opposition to the NSDAP in Glonn from the Catholic population' had risen, finding reflection in the withdrawal of
seventeen boys from the *Jungvolk*. Feeling ran high against
the' two lay teachers in the village, both Nazis and saddled
with the blame for the attack on the convent school. Overnight, a life-size doll stuffed with straw, wearing a red shirt
and tie, a brown jacket, and a black cap bearing the Soviet
hammer and sickle and insulting remarks about the two
teachers was fastened to the lightning-conductor on the
school building. One slogan ran: 'We won't let our nuns be
driven out, otherwise our children will be heathens.' The
report ends by noting that the BPP had started investigations
and in the meantime all was quiet.[84]

Despite the strong feelings provoked by the dissolution of
convent schools and the repercussions for the standing of the
NSDAP in Catholic areas, sporadic local efforts to raise
petitions or in other ways to protest were no match for the
power of the State. Places without convent schools or teaching
nuns were naturally less affected and showed little inclination
to any direct opposition. And the hierarchy itself, after the
initial pastoral letter of June 1936, did little to keep the issue
on the boil as a general question of principle and, as in other

[83] Cit. by Neuhäusler, p. 102.
[84] StAM, LRA 76887, GS Glonn, 30 May 1936; KLB, i. 143-4.

questions, certainly provided no encouragement for civil disobedience as an attempt to block the measure. By the time the Bavarian episcopacy circulated another pastoral letter, on 4 September 1938, informing Catholics of the effectively completed destruction of conventual secondary education in Bavaria, the issue was as good as dead.[85] On this account, and given the fact that the pastoral was issued amid the grave tension over the Sudetenland, it is not surprising that compared with the 1936 pastoral it hardly raised a whimper.[86]

Even before the eradication of convent schools and of the involvement of religious orders in teaching was announced, the move to replace denominational by 'community' schools had begun. It was a policy which had stood high on the agenda of the NSLB since 1930 and remained dear to the hearts of Nazi educationalists (and a large proportion of primary-school teachers) even after the Reich Concordat had confirmed the rights of denominational schools.[87] In the first stage of their fight against the denominational school, the Nazis extended in typically pseudo-plebiscitary fashion a provision existing since 1919 specifically for the cities of Munich and Nuremberg which allowed an annual vote of the parents to determine the nature of the cities' schooling arrangements. This had been originally intended as a move enabling Catholic parents to demand legally the provision of Catholic education. Now the Nazis turned this on its head by seeking at school registration each year a vote from parents as to whether they wished to retain the denominational school or to introduce the 'community school'. The method was tried out in Munich in 1935. Eighty-four per cent of parents had favoured the denominational school at registration the previous year — a higher figure than at any time since the 1918 Revolution.[88] In 1935 this figure dropped to 65 per cent, as a result of which twenty-five Catholic primary schools were converted into 'community schools'. In the suburbs the trend to the 'community school' was even more pronounced, and the figure of 91 per cent in favour was registered in one place.[89] The following year,

[85] *Persecution*, pp. 140–2.   [86] KLB, i. 298.
[87] Eilers, p. 85; Sonnenberger, pp. 253–83.   [88] *Berichte des SD*, p. 232.
[89] *Persecution*, p. 119; Neuhäusler, p. 88; KLB, i. 55; *Berichte des SD*, p. 232.

1936, saw the proportions voting for the denominational and 'community' schools in Munich exactly reversed: only 35 per cent now supported the former, while 65 per cent now voted for the introduction of the 'community school'.[90] By 1937 96 per cent of parents registering children in Munich voted for the 'community school'.[91] In the case of Nuremberg, a largely Protestant city where attachment to the concept of the denominational school was less strong than in Munich, the swing to the 'community school' came earlier. Already in 1934 there was a drop of 22.5 per cent to only 35.4 per cent for the denominational school, practically the whole drop being accountable by Protestant not Catholic parents.[92] By 1936, 85 per cent of Nuremberg's schoolchildren were registered for the 'community school', and this increased the following year to 91.3 per cent, with 4 per cent still choosing Evangelical denominational schools and 4.7 per cent Catholic schools.[93]

The method was extended beyond Munich and Nuremberg. All over Bavaria similar votes were taken with similar sorts of results. The amount of intimidation to which Catholic parents were subjected, quite apart from the massive Party and State propaganda campaign on behalf of the 'community school', was more than a match for the grim defence of the Church authorities. A forceful, but vain, protest about the illegality of the methods used to enforce conformity and support for the 'community school' was made in a pronouncement by the Munich Diocesan Administration in August 1936, in which it was stated that parents had been threatened with dismissal from their jobs, withdrawal of Winter Aid, and various other disadvantages should they choose — which was legally their right under the Concordat — the denominational school.[94] The chicanery of the voting

[90] *Berichte des SD*, p. 232; KLB, i. 133; *Persecution*, p. 143.

[91] KLB, i. 189; *Persecution*, p. 150.

[92] *Berichte des SD*, p. 24.

[93] KLB, ii. 72, 141. The excellent study by F. Sonnenberger, which appeared after the present work was completed, provides extensive coverage of all aspects of the Nazi gains at school registration in Munich and Nuremberg in *Bayern III*, pp. 280 ff.

[94] KLB, i. 159–60; *Persecution*, pp. 143–4 for the text of the pronouncement

was blatant. In one of countless examples — drawn from Kürmreuth near Amberg in the Upper Palatinate — thirty-eight parents who left the meeting about the 'community school' out of protest before the vote was taken were counted as approving the transfer, so that although in fact only forty-one out of eighty-five parents were in favour of the 'community school' the vote was registered as 92.94 per cent. Other cases were even more patently farcical.[95]

Apart from the use of pastoral letters and the pulpit, distribution of literature against the 'community school' — which was mainly confiscated by the police as soon as it appeared outside church — and private exhortation, the Catholic clergy did try both to sabotage the vote (with effects which, as we have just seen, backfired) by encouraging their parishioners not to participate and also to stage their own ballots revealing the genuine opinion of the parishioners. Many examples of such votes showing a high proportion in favour of the denominational school found their way into the reports of the authorities.[96] In some rural districts, where clerical dominance prevailed and where the local mayor was himself unprepared to enter the lists against the denominational school, the Nazis still found it impossible despite pressure and chicanery to win sufficient plebiscitary backing for the 'community school'. The mayor in Etsdorf in the Upper Palatinate tendered his resignation after the 'community school' had found only one supporter in the local council and none among the parents; the mayor in the neighbouring village of Gressenwöhr also declared that he could not in all conscience support the 'community school'; the mayor in Seugast felt he could not introduce the

---

and pp. 145-50 for the methods used in Munich in 1937; cf. also Neuhäusler, pp. 97-8 and DBS, 18 Sept. 1937, pp. A123-4.

[95] StAA, BA Amberg 3665, Ogrl. Kürmreuth, 6 Dec. 1937, 12 Dec. 1937, together with the note of the *Bürgermeister* (20 Feb. 1938) recording the complaint about falsification, together with the letter of the Diocesan Administration of Eichstätt (9 May 1938) taking up the complaint with the Government President in Regensburg. Other instances of even more blatant rigging of the results are in the same file and in *Persecution*, p. 153; cf. also Eilers, p. 88.

[96] E.g., KLB, iv. 154. In this instance — a vote carried out at the suggestion of the Archbishop of Bamberg in the sacristy of the church in Eschenbach (Upper Palatinate), 182 out of 183 parents favoured the denominational school.

'community school' against the almost unanimous vote of the parents for the retention of the denominational school, and that parents' rights should be respected — adding ominously, however, that he could think of no reason why the 'community school' should not be introduced by fiat from above.[97]

By this time, in any case, abolition of the denominational school by decree rather than by parents' ballot was rapidly becoming the norm. Already in February 1937 Adolf Wagner, the Bavarian Education Minister, stated in a circular to the regional administrations in Bavaria that the decision to introduce the 'community school' belonged to the mayor, and that although there could be a ballot, this was not strictly specified (except for Munich and Nuremberg).[98] Five months later, Wagner was exhorting the other regional governments to follow the lead of Upper Bavaria and the Palatinate, where now only 'community schools' existed. It was to be emphasized repeatedly that religious instruction would be unaffected by the change of status of the school.[99] By February 1938 there were no longer any Catholic schools in Main Franconia, where the administration transformed by decree any remaining denominational schools into 'community schools'; by October 1938 Wagner was announcing in the *Völkischer Beobachter* that throughout the whole of Bavaria denominational schools were now a thing of the past.[1] Within a year thereafter serious reductions in the amount of religious instruction given in schools, long campaigned for by the NSLB, had been pushed through, and the clergy of both major denominations were being forced to self-help in arranging for religious instruction to take place privately outside school hours in the presbytery or church hall.[2] Despite Wagner's promises that nothing would be changed as regards the upholding of religion in the school,

[97] StAA, BA Amberg 3665, BA Amberg, 20 May, 28 June 1938; Bgm. Seugast, 9 May 1938.

[98] A copy of the circular from the 'Staatsministerium für Unterricht und Kultus an die Regierungen', 24 Feb. 1937, is in ibid.

[99] Ibid., 'Staatsministerium für Unterricht und Kultus an die Regierungen', 8 July 1937.

[1] *Persecution*, p. 158.

[2] Ibid., p. 173; KLB, i. 308; KLB, ii. 300, n. 2; *Bayern I*, p. 549, n. 25.

the reality of the Nazi 'community school' was now becoming increasingly apparent.

There can be no doubt that the struggle for the denomi-national school, and not least the blackmail, trickery, force, and repression used by the authorities in getting their way, confirmed and intensified the alienation and hatred of Catholics for the Nazi regime. The effects of the struggle for the school were even seen by the Government President of Lower Bavaria and the Upper Palatinate as responsible for the relatively high (in absolute terms, none the less, trivial) number of 'Nein' votes in the 1938 plebiscite, when Lower Bavaria recorded the greatest deterioration in pro-regime votes in the whole Reich compared with the results of the 1936 plebiscite.[3] However, despite an unprecedented cam-paign by Catholic opinion-leaders, and despite an over-whelming preference for the traditional denominational schools on the part of the parents, the Nazis won the battle and clearly inflicted a resounding defeat upon the Church. It is worth considering why the widespread opposition was so fruitless.

The coercive force of the Nazi authorities is the most obvious reason, but is in itself insufficient explanation. Direct action and civil disobedience had already been shown to pay dividends in forcing concessions from the regime, both in the case of the reinstatement of Bishop Meiser in the Protestant conflict of 1934 and more recently in the well-known Olden-burg crucifix episode relating to the Catholic Church. In 1941 such direct action was to achieve a notable victory of popular opinion over Party and State in the Bavarian crucifix affair. The fight for the denominational school differed, how-ever, in a number of significant respects from these cases of spectacular mass opposition.

In the first place, the unevenness and the lengthy nature of the campaign for the introduction of the 'community school', in which some areas had hardly been affected by the time that others had been completely converted, meant that opposition was mainly localized. Secondly, there was no specific focus upon an individual or a symbol. Obviously, the

---

[3] KLB, iv. 198; cf. Kershaw, *Hitler-Mythos*, p. 117 & n. 26.

school was a visible enough institution and the issue one of evident importance, but it was possible to argue that since the teachers (often loyal Catholics) would in any case remain unchanged and the school's clientele would continue to be uniformly Catholic (as was clearly the position in many localities), the change would be essentially one of nomenclature. Furthermore, the State had given its most solemn guarantees that religion would be left untouched, that the move was simply bringing Bavaria in line with other parts of Germany, and that the fears which the clergy were trying to stir up about the de-Christianization of the schools were simply nonsense.[4] In the light of the extreme pressures of an economic and political nature upon parents to conform, this type of argumentation had at least some impact in splitting Catholic opinion and weakening resolve. Thirdly, the sheer magnitude of the task in attempting to combat the might of the State, the ease with which the State swept aside such puny demonstrations of authentic opinion, ignored petitions of protest, and simply fabricated the results it wanted, produced not unnaturally widespread feelings of deep gloom, despondency, apathy, resignation, and of the lack of alternative to the government's arbitrariness and power. Finally, such feelings were given encouragement by the muted legalism with which the hierarchy sought to conduct the fight against its powerful adversary. Though the bishops, at least on the schools issue, fought strongly and tirelessly through the media of pastoral letters, sermons, and exhortations, they were fatally caught on the horns of a dilemma of their own making: the acceptance of a barrier between the affairs of Church and State which the Nazis themselves were wholly unprepared to accept, and the consequent, unrealistic withdrawal into the sphere of the 'unpolitical' defence of Church institutions and practices while at the same time encouraging general support for the regime. The words of the famous pastoral letter of the Bavarian bishops of 13 December 1936,

---

[4] Cf. *Persecution*, p. 146–7 for Wagner's assurances in January 1937 that 'the community school guarantees religious instruction exactly as the denominational school does', and his attempt to allay fears about the removal of crucifixes from classrooms.

usually cited as a statement of their disillusionment with the regime, make the weakness of the episcopal position apparent and outline clearly the limited parameters of the hierarchy's action:

Nothing could be further from our intentions than to adopt a hostile attitude toward, or a renunciation of, the present form taken by our government. For us, respect for authority, love of Fatherland, and the fulfilment of our duty to the State are matters not only of conscience, but of divine ordinance. This command we will always require our faithful to follow. But we will never regard as an infringement of this duty our defence of God's laws and of His Church, or of ourselves against attacks on the faith and the Church. The Führer can be certain that we bishops are prepared to give all moral support to his historical struggle against Bolshevism. We will not criticize things which are purely political. What we do ask is that our holy Church be permitted to enjoy her God-given rights and her freedom.[5]

Disappointment at the passivity of the Church leadership and hesitant, divided, and resigned opinion among Catholics are suggested by *Sopade* reports emanating from Bavaria in spring and summer 1937. One report described the mood of the Catholic population 'as, without exaggeration, despairing' and claimed that the fighting-spirit brought out by the school struggle had given way to 'general indifference' which had its cause in the passive approach of the higher Church dignitaries. Catholics, it was said, were gravely disappointed by their leaders who had made a great deal of noise about carrying on the fight but always buckled before the threats of some Nazi *Gauleiter* or other.[6] Younger members of the clergy were said to be particularly critical of the tolerance and moderate approach of Church leaders and frequently showed a more militant and less accommodating stance towards Nazism. Active, though small, circles of the laity took the same line.[7] Most churchgoers, however, were passive — at best prepared verbally to defend the Church but no more, and there had been a distinct alienation of the youth from the Church, not least as a consequence of the Church leadership's attitude to Nazism.[8]

[5] *Docs. on Nazism*, pp. 371–2.
[6] DBS, 18 Sept. 1937, pp. A114–15.
[7] ASD, ES/M65/Mar. 1937.
[8] DBS, 18 Sept. 1937, pp. A111–12.

From their Social Democratic background, the *Sopade* reporters had little liking or sympathy for the Catholic Church and their prejudices are easily apparent in the tone of their comments. They were outsiders in the 'Church struggle' and both underestimated the extent of the Catholic opposition, also from the hierarchy, and harboured a naïve conception about the potential achievements of a more militant stance. Even so, the divisions of opinion, extensive resignation, and the frustration of, especially, many younger priests ring true. The signs are that the hierarchy could have made things much more difficult for the Nazis than in the event it did so; that it was hidebound by its own legalism; and that even in Church matters it was not prepared to exploit to the full the extensive support of an angered and embittered churchgoing population, on which it could still depend.

The Nazis had failed to make deep inroads into Catholic communities before 1933, and the years which followed were to reveal unmistakably just how partial, superficial, and limited had been the rapid gains made in Catholic areas immediately after the 'seizure of power'. A brief honeymoon period followed the signing of the Concordat in summer 1933. Despite the continuance of attacks on Church and clergy, it was hoped that the Concordat would create a new basis for positive relations between Church and State. The honeymoon period was already drawing to a close when the Bavarian bishops, in exhorting Catholics to support Hitler's call for peace and for the 'honour and equality of rights of the German people' in the plebiscite of 12 November, emphasized that this was not to be taken as a sign of approval of the disturbing events of the previous months or of the breaches of the Concordat which were still taking place.[9] Even so, the plebiscite results both of November 1933 and of August 1934, in which Catholic areas in Bavaria — less so elsewhere in the Reich — generally provided an above-average vote of support for the regime, showed that the Concordat promise and the pro-regime statements of the hierarchy

---

[9] H. Müller (ed.), *Katholische Kirche und Nationalsozialismus*, Munich, 1965, pp. 224–5; cf. Volk, *Der bayer. Episkopat*, pp. 148–63.

continued to influence Catholic opinion towards Nazism.[10]
The period of mainly sporadic, but increasing, anti-Church
activity in 1934-5 brought a rapid sobering of attitudes towards the regime and a steep slide into open disillusionment
and fulfilment of earlier fears as it became clear that the
Concordat was no protection against attacks on Catholic
practices, traditions, and institutions, especially the youth
organizations which were the central target at this stage. The
years 1936-7 saw the height of the struggle, now waged
above all on the school question, and completed the alienation of the Catholic population from Nazism. Though
some of the heat went out of the confrontation during 1938
and 1939, the die was cast: potential Catholic support for
Nazism had been lost and could not now be regained. In the
event, the advent of war made a shelving of the problem of
Church-State relations a necessity.

The alienation of the Catholics was plain for the authorities to see. It revealed itself in outward forms of behaviour
such as the mode of greeting. Outside the offices of State and
Party, the 'Heil Hitler' greeting became increasingly a rarity
in Catholic areas and was frequently rejected quite demonstratively as a sign of anti-Nazi feeling.[11] Collections were
another outward indicator of feeling. Despite the pressure on
people to contribute to the constant stream of Party collections and the counter-pressure to discourage contributions to
Church funds, there was often for the authorities an embarrassing discrepancy between the miserly response to the
Party's demands and the abundant generosity of support for
Church causes.[12] Difficulties of recruitment for the Party and
its affiliations, and poor attendance at Party meetings and

[10] K.D. Bracher, G. Schulz, and W. Sauer, *Die nationalsozialistische Machtergreifung*, Ullstein edn., Frankfurt/Main, 1974, i. 486-98.
[11] The cases recorded in the reports of the Nazi authorities from a wide
variety of Catholic areas are far too numerous to cite. A *Sopade* report on conditions in Munich in September 1937 pointed out that despite notices in all public
places exhorting people to use the 'German Greeting', 'it strikes every stranger
that one is greeted with "Heil Hitler" probably in no other German city less than
in Munich where, just as in the rest of Bavaria, "Grüß Gott" is once again more
common than ever and very demonstratively so' — ASD, ES/M147/Sept. 1937,
'Bericht aus München'.
[12] E.g., KLB, i. 302; KLB, iii. 114-15; KLB, iv, 109.

functions provided further barometers of opinion.[13] Some Catholic rural areas were practically 'no-go areas' for the Nazis, where the writ of the Party did not run, and where the Party suffered a complete loss of authority as a result of the 'Church struggle'. In Tittmoning, a small town in southeast Bavaria, for instance, there appears to have been practically a running feud between the Party leadership and the local peasants in the summer of 1939. So little authority could the Nazi Local Group Leader muster that he reported dejectedly that he was going to denounce no one else to the police since 'my denunciations have become a laughing-stock'.[14] In the big cities, too, the hostility of much of the population to the Nazi rulers was patently obvious. Catholic Munich, home of the Party, was already rapidly developing the reputation which it was to seal during the war as the most anti-Nazi city in Germany.[15]

When the Government President of Upper Bavaria stated at the beginning of 1938 that 'the Party's work of ideological enlightenment still had a long way to go', and his colleague in Lower Bavaria and the Upper Palatinate affirmed at the beginning of the war that the attitude of the great mass of the population towards the Church had hardly altered at all, they were offering no more than a bland understatement of the truth.[16] However, the comment of a *Landrat* in the latter region about the same time that 'the population is in agreement with all measures of the government, but just does not want the fight against religion and clergy', was also not a wild exaggeration.[17] When Church dignitaries and Nazi authorities spoke from different standpoints about the ideological struggle between Nazism and the Church, they were

[13] Complaints abound, for instance, in the reports from the Garmisch-Partenkirchen area from 1934 onwards about chronically poor support for Party functions (compared with Church affairs). In one pious Catholic district not a single recruit for the SS was forthcoming in 1937 — StAM, LRA 61616, GS Unterammergau, 30 Dec. 1937.

[14] StAM, NSDAP 318, Ogrl. Tittmoning to KL Berchtesgaden, no date (June 1939).

[15] Cf. ASD, ES/M147/Sept. 1937, 'Bericht aus München', though the assertion that 'at least three-quarters of the population are opponents of the system' was a wild illusion.

[16] KLB, i. 284; KLB, iv. 242.

[17] KLB, iv. 243.

speaking in terms of religious, moral, and cultural values and of the incompatibility of the new 'German religion' with Catholicism.[18] When it came to ideological questions touching upon the political and social order, there were points of obvious contact — such as the anti-liberal and anti-Marxist emphasis of both Catholic Church and Nazi regime. There was, too, the legalistic reluctance of the Church authorities to become involved in 'political' questions which were not directly the province of the Church. Even this aloofness from 'politics', as the hierarchy defined it, was one-sided: it meant public avowals of support for Hitler personally, for the regime's anti-Bolshevik campaigns, and for foreign policy revisionism;[19] but — with lamentably few exceptions — silence about civil rights, infringement of personal liberties (except those of priests), and the policies of racial hatred. The alienation of the Catholic population came, therefore, to nothing in terms of wider political issues. On matters directly affecting the Catholic traditional 'way of life' detestation of Nazi interference prompted spectacular opposition. But, as we shall see when we turn next to the persecution of the Jews, the Catholic response on matters of less than immediate concern to the Church was muted in the extreme. The conclusion is difficult to resist that had the Nazi regime held to the letter of the Concordat as, by and large, Mussolini kept to the Lateran Agreement of 1929, it would have encountered little trouble from the Catholic population or clergy.

[18] Cf. the uncompromising comments of Bishop Rackl of Eichstätt, who claimed Christian and Nazi ideologies confronted each other like fire and water — KLB, ii. 264.
[19] Cf. Lewy, esp. chs. 7, 10–12; Kershaw, *Hitler-Mythos*, ch. 4.

6. Reactions to the Persecution of the Jews

The significance of the Jewish Question for the 'broad mass' of the German population in the Third Reich is a complex issue which has prompted frequent speculative generalization but little systematic exploration.[1] Alongside the apologetic, much heard in Germany since the end of the war, that the persecution of the Jews could be put down to the criminal or insane fixations of Hitler and the gangster clique of top Nazis around him in the face of widespread disapproval by the mass of Germans in so far as they knew and understood what was going on, exists the counter-generalization, favoured by some Jewish historians, of a German people thirsting for a 'war against the Jews', in which anti-Semitism, based on a centuries-old tradition of persecution, played a central role in providing Hitler's support from the German people and in motivating the popular adulation of the Führer.[2] According to this interpretation, the central role of anti-Semitism in Hitler's ideology is echoed by its central role in the mobilization of the German people.

Far from emphasizing a more or less spontaneous eruption of popular anti-Semitism in the socio-psychological crisis of Weimar, contrasting interpretations have stressed the conscious manipulative exploitation of anti-Semitism, which thus

[1] The only studies to date which have concerned themselves directly with the problem are: Steinert, pp. 236–63; L.D. Stokes, 'The German People and the Destruction of the European Jews', *Central European History*, vi (1973), 167–91; and O.D. Kulka, '"Public Opinion" in National Socialist Germany and the "Jewish Question"', *Zion*, xl (1975), 186–290 (in Hebrew, documents in German, and with an English summary). There is now also the dissertation by S.A. Gordon, 'German Opposition to Nazi Anti-Semitic Measures between 1933 and 1945, with Particular Reference to the Rhine–Ruhr Area', State University New York/ Buffalo, D.Phil. thesis, 1979. The present chapter is a modified and shortened version of my contribution to *Bayern II*, pp. 281–348. I have attempted to survey also the non-Bavarian evidence in a recent essay, 'The Persecution of the Jews and German Popular Opinion in the Third Reich', *Leo Baeck Institute Year Book*, xxvi (1981), 261–89.

[2] L. Dawidowicz, *The War against the Jews 1933–45*, Harmondsworth, 1977, esp. pp. 77, 209–11.

functioned as a tool of integration and mass mobilization by the Nazi regime, whether in the interests of imperialist finance-capital,[3] or as the cementing element which guaranteed the continuing ceaseless 'negative' dynamic diverting from the inevitable failures of socio-economic policy and holding the antagonistic forces of the Nazi movement together.[4]

This chapter seeks to confront such interpretations with as exhaustive an examination as possible of the empirical evidence from Bavaria for the reactions of 'ordinary' people to the anti-Jewish policies of the Nazi regime. By examining dissent from and approval of various facets of the persecution of the Jews, we are attempting to explore the spheres of penetration of Nazi racial ideology in the consciousness of 'ordinary' Germans, and to ask to what extent anti-Semitism served to integrate the German people and mobilize them behind the Nazi leadership during the Third Reich.

At the outset of our enquiry we can do no more than touch upon the pattern of Jewish settlement in Bavaria, the regional distribution and socio-economic structure of the Jewish population, and the traditional framework of its relations with the non-Jewish sector of the population in Bavaria, all of which helped to shape the context in which the radical anti-Semitism of the Nazis has to be placed.

The regional distribution of Jews in Bavaria was very uneven. As a consequence of Wittelsbach policies in the sixteenth and seventeenth centuries, in which the Jews had been driven out of the Bavarian heartlands, there were few resident Jews in *Altbayern* (Upper and Lower Bavaria and the Upper Palatinate) even deep into the nineteenth century. By contrast, the diversified structure of landownership and lordship in Franconia and Swabia had tended since the sixteenth century to promote settlements of Jewish communities in the countryside and in small towns.[5] Since the early

---

[3] K. Pätzold, *Faschismus, Rassenwahn, Judenverfolgung*, Berlin, 1975, pp. 28–32.

[4] M. Broszat, 'Soziale Motivation und Führer-Bindung des Nationalsozialismus', *VfZ*, xviii (1970), 392–409, esp. pp. 400 ff.

[5] S. Schwarz, *Die Juden in Bayern im Wandel der Zeiten*, Munich, 1963, pp. 57 ff.; B.Z. Ophir and F. Wiesemann, *Die jüdischen Gemeinden in Bayern 1918–1945. Geschichte und Zerstörung*, Munich, 1979, p. 13; *Bayern I*, p. 429.

nineteenth century the Jewish proportion of the total population had been in decline. In 1818, after Lower Franconia
and the Palatinate had been incorporated into Bavaria, the
53,208 Jews accounted for 1.45 per cent of the entire
Bavarian population (including the Palatinate). The restrictive
legislation of 1813, the so-called *Judenedikt*, which severely
limited Jewish mobility, seriously contributed, however, to
continued demographic decline. By the time of German
unification the number of Jews had fallen to 1.04 per cent of
the entire population, by the turn of the century to 0.9 per
cent, and by the beginning of the Third Reich to a mere 0.55
per cent.[6]

As many as 88 per cent of Bavaria's Jews still resided in
1840 in country districts or small towns. Only following the
ending of the restrictive legislation in 1861 did Jewish
migration to the larger towns and cities make great headway, and in so doing help foster the nascent anti-Semitism
of the urban communities. But by 1919 the geographical
distribution of Jews had fundamentally altered: now as many
as 78 per cent lived in the cities and larger towns.[7] The overwhelmingly urban character of the domiciled Jewish population is clearly shown in the results of the census of 1933
provided in Table XIV. One implication of this is obvious:
the population of large tracts of Bavaria had no, or at best
minimal, contact with Jews. For very many, therefore, the
Jewish Question could be of no more than abstract
significance.

As the 1933 census shows, only in Middle and Lower
Franconia was the proportion of Jews in the total population
higher than the Reich average of 0.76 per cent.[8] Almost a
half of Bavaria's Jewish population lived in the four cities

---

[6] J. Toury, *Soziale und politische Geschichte der Juden in Deutschland 1847–
1871*, Düsseldorf, 1977, pp. 12 ff.; Ophir, *Die jüd. Gemeinden*, p. 14; *Bayern I*,
p. 428.

[7] Ophir, *Die jüd. Gemeinden*, p. 14.

[8] The census of 16 June 1933 comprised only those of Jewish faith (*Glaubensjuden*). The number of *Glaubensjuden* in Munich was given as 9,005, though
police registration of Jews on 1 Feb. 1933 amounted to a total of 10,737, a discrepancy of 19.23 per cent. The number of Jews leaving Munich between February
and June 1933 cannot, however, be established. (Police data in HStA, MInn.
73725. Details for areas outside Munich have not survived.)

TABLE XIV: The Jewish Population of Bavaria, 1933
(incl. Palatinate)

A. Distribution of the Jewish population in the Bavarian
administrative regions, 1933

Administrative region	Of Jewish faith (*Glaubensjuden*)	
	Absolute	Percentage of total population
Upper Bavaria	9,522	0.54
Lower Bavaria	293	0.04
Upper Palatinate	1,004	0.15
Upper Franconia	2,133	0.27
Middle Franconia	11,621	1.12
Lower Franconia	8,520	1.07
Swabia	2,359	0.27
Palatinate	6,487	0.66
Bavaria	41,939	0.55

B. Distribution of the Jewish population according to size of
municipality in which domiciled, 1933 (%)

Size of municipality	% of Entire population	% of Jewish population
Under 10,000 inhabitants	66.4 (50.7)[a]	28.4 (15.5)[a]
Between 10,000 and 100,000 inhabitants	13.7 (19.9)	22.1 (13.6)
Above 100,000 inhabitants	19.9 (30.4)	49.5 (70.9)

[a] Figures in brackets are the corresponding percentages for the German Reich.
Sources: 'Die Glaubensjuden in Bayern', pp. 447, 451-2; 'Die Juden im Deutschen Reich', p. 150.

of Munich (9,005), Nuremberg (7,502), Augsburg (1,030), and Würzburg (2,145). Fürth, adjoining Nuremberg, was the other major Jewish community. Even so, the urban concentration of Jews in Bavaria was far weaker than in Germany as a whole.[9] In Lower Franconia the proportion of the Jewish population living in villages and small towns (of less than 10,000 inhabitants) was exceptionally large, at 60 per cent. Alongside the five major Jewish communities of over

[9] Jewish settlement in small towns and in the countryside was particularly a feature of south-western Germany. Cf. 'Die Juden im Deutschen Reich 1816 bis 1933', *Wirtschaft und Statistik*, xv (1935), 150.

1,000 souls there were a further eight communities with between 300 and 1,000 members each (in all 4,116 Jews).[10] The remaining 10,694 Jews in Bavaria — roughly a quarter of the total number — formed in all 186 small, mainly very small, communities or lived as individuals in country districts.[11]

Large stretches of Bavaria had, therefore, no resident Jews. Of the sum total of 293 Jews in the whole of Lower Bavaria, as many as 73 per cent lived in the four provincial towns of Straubing, Landshut, Passau, and Deggendorf. Of the few Jews in the Upper Palatinate, 77 per cent lived in the towns of Regensburg, Weiden, Neumarkt in der Oberpfalz, Amberg, and Schwandorf.[12] Outside Franconia, where, on account of the relatively prominent presence and high population density of the Jews, a history of sporadic animosity, and the effect of the anti-Semitic tirades of Julius Streicher and his following in the 1920s, the Jewish Question acquired a peculiar importance, the non-Jewish population of Bavaria came into contact with Jews mainly in the towns — especially the big cities — in spa and tourist resorts, and in some rural areas where Jews dominated agricultural trade.[13]

Anti-Jewish violence was part of the scene of traditional social conflict in some parts of Bavaria, especially in Franconia, in the nineteenth century. Synagogue arson, the desecration of cemeteries, attacks on Jewish property, the hanging of effigies, and other outrages were prompted not only by economic rivalry or social envy, but reflected, too, still existent religious antagonism of Christian towards Jew. Allegations of ritual murders or well-poisonings and the ancient slur attached to the 'crucifiers of Christ' or 'murderers of Christ' — sentiments sometimes inflamed by comments of Catholic priests or Protestant pastors — all occasioned isolated outbreaks of violence against Jews

[10] Ibid., p. 148; 'Die Glaubensjuden in Bayern auf Grund der Volks- und Berufszählung vom 16. Juni 1933', ZdBSL, lxx (1938), 451 ff.

[11] From data in B.Z. Ophir, Pinkas Hakehillot. Encyclopedia of Jewish Communities from their Foundation till after the Holocaust (Germany-Bavaria), Jerusalem, 1972 (in Hebrew with English introduction), p. XIV.

[12] 'Die Glaubensjuden in Bayern', p. 451.

[13] Expressing the sparseness of the Jewish population in another way, there was on average one non-Jewish citizen of Bavaria for every 0.99 square kilometre, one Jew for every 181.21 square kilometres — Calculated from data in ibid., pp. 447, 451 and GStA, Reichsstatthalter 578.

throughout the nineteenth century.[14] For most people, however, feelings probably did not go much further than an abstract dislike or distrust of Jews and there seems to have been a good deal of indifference to what was already being dubbed the 'Jewish Question'. In 1850, for example, partly at the prompting of the Catholic lower clergy, about 13 per cent of the entire population of Bavaria signed petitions opposing Jewish emancipation. When, however, the State authorities made further investigations into the 'true mood' of the people it turned out that many petitioners were wholly indifferent on the issue, had no contact with Jews, knew little of any Jewish Question, and had often added their signatures only at the prompting of the priest.[15]

Elements of this archaic hostility towards Jews undoubtedly lasted in Franconia into the Third Reich. However, the 'traditional' anti-Semitism was already in the later nineteenth century giving way to or merging with the newer, more strongly ideological currents of the *völkisch*-nationalist, racial anti-Semitism which came to provide the basis of Nazi racial thinking. Above all in the crisis-ridden years following the end of the First World War, the Revolution, and the *Räterepublik*, racial anti-Semitism in Bavaria, especially in the cities of Munich and Nuremberg, found conditions in which it could thrive. Favoured for a time even by the Bavarian government, racial anti-Semitism was the main prop of demagogues such as Streicher in Nuremberg and of course Hitler in Munich, whose speeches in the early 1920s poured forth an unending torrent of anti-Jewish filth, much to the approval of those finding their way to Nazi meetings in Munich's beer halls — prominent among them already sections of the *Mittelstand* and lumpen-bourgeoisie, fearful

---

[14] Cf. E.S. Sterling, *Judenhaß. Die Anfänge des politischen Antisemitismus in Deutschland (1815–1850)*, Frankfurt/Main, 1969, pp. 12, 55–62, 171–4 and *passim*. The notorious Deggendorf popular celebrations of the medieval burning of the town's Jews by pious Catholic citizens as revenge for the alleged defiling of the consecrated host were only abolished in 1969 — Cf. Lewy, pp. 272–3; Ophir, *Die jüd. Gemeinden*, p. 66. Streicher, who — perhaps not just coincidentally — grew up as a schoolboy in Deggendorf, exploited such sentiments in the *Stürmer*. For the disgusting 'ritual murder' issue, cf. ibid., p. 22.

[15] Sterling, pp. 159–62.

of the socialist Left and resentful of the influence of 'Jewish' profiteers and financiers.[16]

'Old' and 'new' anti-Semitism existed side by side and provided mutual support for each other. The 'traditional' hostility only surfaced for the most part where there was an actual physical presence of Jews and where the local population came into direct contact, especially economically, with Jews. The racial-*völkisch* variety, although fuelling appalling outrages against Jews, was in essence capable of existing independent of direct contact with Jews as an 'abstract' racial hatred whose target was only superficially a specific Jewish shop or trader, and in reality Jewry itself.

Following a calmer period in the middle years of the Weimar Republic, the climate for Jews all over Germany obviously worsened dramatically during the period of the Nazis' rapid rise to power. However, research has done much to counter and qualify the notion of a society driven by pathological hatred of the Jews, in which 'generations of anti-Semitism had prepared the Germans to accept Hitler as their redeemer'.[17] Though Hitler himself apparently regarded anti-Semitism as the most important weapon in his propaganda arsenal,[18] it seems in fact, far from being the main motive force in bringing Nazism to power, to have been secondary to the main appeal of the Nazi message. A contemporary Jewish assessment of the spectacular gains in the 1930 Reichstag elections emphasized that millions of Nazi voters were in no sense anti-Semites, adding pointedly however that their rejection of anti-Semitism, on the other hand, was evidently not great enough to prevent them giving their support to an anti-Semitic party.[19] Analysis of the ideological motivation of a selection of 'Old Fighters' in joining the NSDAP suggests anti-Semitism was decisive only in a small minority of cases.[20]

[16] See now the comprehensive collection of Hitler's early speeches and writings edited by E. Jäckel, *Hitler. Sämtliche Aufzeichnungen, 1905–1924*, Stuttgart, 1980.

[17] Dawidowicz, pp. 210–11.

[18] H. Rauschning, *Hitler Speaks*, London, 1939, pp. 233–234.

[19] Cit. in A. Paucker, *Der jüdische Abwehrkampf gegen Antisemitismus und Nationalsozialismus in den letzten Jahren der Weimarer Republik*, 2nd edn., Hamburg, 1969, pp. 194–5.

[20] P. Merkl, *Political Violence under the Swastika. 581 Early Nazis*, Princeton, 1975, pp. 33, 446 ff., and *passim*.

And in his perceptive study of the rise of Nazism in Northeim in Lower Saxony, where the NSDAP polled almost double the national average in 1932, W.S. Allen reached the conclusion that the Jews of the town were integrated on class lines before 1933 and that people 'were drawn to anti-Semitism because they were drawn to Nazism, not the other way round.'[21]

Anti-Semitism cannot, it seems, be allocated a significant role in bringing Hitler to power, though, given the widespread acceptability of the Jewish Question as a political issue — exploited not only by the Nazis — nor did it do anything to hinder his rapidly growing popularity. However, the relative indifference of most Germans towards the Jewish Question before 1933 meant that the Nazis did have a job on their hands after the 'take-over of power' to persuade them of the need for active discrimination and persecution of the Jews. The following pages consider the extent of Nazi success in transforming latent anti-Jewish sentiment into active-dynamic hatred.[22] The first section concentrates on popular reactions to Nazi attempts to oust Jews from economic activity, and to the terror and violence employed in the exercise, between 1933 and 1938. The second part then goes on to consider the role played by the lower clergy — whose crucial part in protests on Church matters we have looked at in the previous two chapters — in influencing opinion on the Jewish Question. In the final section, the varying reactions to the November pogrom of 1938 are examined.

(i) Boycott and Terror, 1933–8

The nation-wide boycott of Jewish shops carried out on 1

[21] W.S. Allen, *The Nazi Seizure of Power. The Experience of a Single German Town*, Chicago, 1965, p. 77. Similar conclusions about the relative lack of importance of anti-Semitism in bringing new converts to Nazism were reached in the excellent study by D.L. Niewyk, *The Jews in Weimar Germany*, Manchester, 1980, pp. 79–81. Cf. now also Gordon, ch. 3, for a thorough survey of the evidence.

[22] Cf. M. Müller-Claudius, *Der Antisemitismus und das deutsche Verhängnis*, Frankfurt/Main, 1948, pp. 76–9, 119, 157 for the equivalent formulation '*statischer Haß — dynamischer Haß*'.

April 1933 was, as is generally known, in Bavaria as elsewhere
in the Reich less than a total success from the Nazi point of
view. If it met with no opposition to speak of, the response
of the public had been markedly cool.[23] A repeat performance
across the whole country was never attempted. Though in
Franconia localized boycotts and attacks on Jews continued
to be an all too prominent feature of the political scene
during 1933-4, elsewhere, in the context of a deteriorating
economic situation and the need to avoid making gratuitous
enemies on the diplomatic front, a relative calm in anti-
Jewish activity set in towards the end of 1933. The calm was
an uneasy one and lasted no more than a year before a new
series of verbal tirades by rabid anti-Semites such as *Gauleiter*
Streicher in Franconia and, outside Bavaria, *Gauleiter* Kube
(Kurmark) and *Gauleiter* Grohé (Köln-Aachen), together
with an intensified campaign of filth in Streicher's paper,
the *Stürmer*, set the tone for the renewed and heightened
violence which afflicted the whole of Germany in 1935. The
renewal of anti-Jewish agitation was in large measure the
reflection of the discontent of the Nazi Party, or the leadership of individual sections of it, with the progress (all too
sluggish in their view) made by the State in solving the Jewish
Question. One aim of their activity was to push the State
much more rapidly in that direction. The new wave of anti-
Jewish violence reached its climax in Bavaria with the anti-
Semitic disturbances in the streets of Munich's city centre in
May 1935, to which we will shortly return.

Before then, quite contrary to the situation in Franconia,
the Jewish Question had played in general an insignificant
role both for the population at large and even for the Nazi
Party in southern Bavaria where, outside Munich, few Jews
were resident. The Government Presidents of the non-
Franconian regions came to include a section of their reports
dealing specifically with Jews only in 1935 (in the case of
Lower Bavaria and the Upper Palatinate in fact only in 1938),

---

[23] Cf. Pätzold, pp. 77-9; K.A. Schleunes, *The Twisted Road to Auschwitz.
Nazi Policy towards German Jews 1933-1939*, Chicago, 1970, pp. 88-9; H.
Krausnick, 'The Persecution of the Jews', in H. Krausnick *et al.*, *Anatomy of the
SS State*, London, 1968, p. 26; and specifically for Bavaria, *Bayern I*, pp. 433 ff.;
P. Hanke, *Zur Geschichte der Juden in München zwischen 1933 und 1945*,
Munich, 1967, pp. 83-6.

and even then had frequently nothing to record.[24] This was a reflection of the fact that most reports from the localities were providing 'nil return' (*Fehlanzeige*) entries on the Jewish Question, since no Jews were resident in their areas. Typical for the situation in much of rural southern Bavaria is the comment, in summer 1935, from Bad Aibling (Upper Bavaria) — a locality which, in common with all other districts, was by this time plastered with advertisements for the *Stürmer*, sported notices put up by the local Party carrying the slogan 'Jews not wanted here', and was experiencing a non-stop campaign of scurrilous agitation against the Jews perpetrated by local activists. All this hardly corresponded with the real concerns of the local population, as the District Officer laconically pointed out: 'Actually, the Jewish Question is not a live issue for the district itself because only one Jewish family of Polish nationality lives in the entire district and among the summer visitors only one long-standing summer guest in Feilnbach and a spa visitor in Aibling have been observed.'[25] The Government President of Upper Bavaria added himself a month later that the Jewish Question was insignificant for the rural areas since outside Munich there were only 602 Jews in his entire region.[26]

The situation was of course different in Munich itself, as well as in the other major city of southern Bavaria, Augsburg, in a number of the Swabian small towns with prominent Jewish minorities, in Upper Bavarian tourist areas like Garmisch or Bad Tölz, and in rural districts where Jews plied the cattle or wood trade. But even here serious cases of violence towards Jews seldom occurred before 1938. Such boycotts and harassment of Jews as took place were invariably instigated by local Party organizations quite irrespective of the interests and wishes of the bulk of the local

[24] Special sections on the Jews were first included in the monthly reports of 11 June 1935 (Upper Bavaria), 6 Nov. 1935 (Swabia), and 8 June 1938 (Lower Bavaria and the Upper Palatinate): GStA, MA 106670, MA 106682, MA 106673.
[25] StAM, LRA 47140, BA Bad Aibling, 3 Oct. 1935; cf. also the reports of 6 June, 6 July, 5 Aug., and 2 Nov. 1935 in which it was stated that the Jewish Question was 'not acute' in the district and played 'no role' at all.
[26] GStA, MA 106670, RPvOB, 11 Nov. 1935.

population.[27] The 'boycott movement' and anti-Jewish agitation of spring and summer 1935 tended in fact to alienate rather than win support for the Nazi Party in Munich and southern Bavaria.

A major exception to the relative absence of outbreaks of open violence against Jews in southern Bavaria in the first years of the Third Reich occurred on 18 and 25 May 1935, when anti-Jewish 'demonstrations' took place in the centre of Munich among the crowds of the city's busy Saturday shoppers. There was nothing spontaneous about the riotous disturbances. They were the culmination of a long campaign, initiated and stirred up by no less a figure than *Gauleiter* Adolf Wagner who, as Minister of the Interior, was actually responsible for order in Bavaria. Wagner, as it later transpired, had used two employees of the *Stürmer*, working in collaboration with sections of the Munich police force, to instigate the action — carried out largely by some 200 members of an SS camp near Munich and by members of other Party affiliations. The response of the public, as the Munich police felt compelled to report, was wholly opposed to this sort of anti-Semitism and strong antagonism was felt in the city and its environs. With the mood in the city very heated, Wagner was forced to denounce in the press and on the radio the 'terror groups' who were the cause of the trouble.[28]

The distaste felt by the Munich public was more probably evoked by the hooliganism and riotous behaviour of the Nazi mob than by principled objections to anti-Semitism, for such primitive violence found condemnation deep into the ranks of the Party itself. Even *Gauleiter* Karl Wahl of Swabia — certainly no friend of the Jews — condemned what he called

---

[27] For a good example of a planned disturbance at the abattoir in Regensburg in 1936, where the Gestapo established that the 'indignation' of the 'aryan' dealers about the presence of Jews had been 'obviously arranged and prepared accordingly in advance' by dealers from Nuremberg without any locals taking part at all, cf. GStA, MA 106411, fols. 84-7.

[28] Cf. *Bayern I*, pp. 442 ff.; Pätzold, pp. 216-21; GStA, MA 106411, fols. 361, 373, 382 for Wagner's press notice about 'terror groups'. Reports and investigations about the affair are contained in: GStA, MA 105618, MA 106411, MA 106685 (Pd München, 26 May 1935), Reichsstatthalter 447. For Wagner's direct implication in initiating the trouble, cf. Berlin Document Center, Personal File of SS-Oberf. Frhr. Hermann von Schade, betr. Adolf Wagner, minutes of a meeting in Munich which took place on 25 Jan. 1936.

the 'aping of Franconian methods'.[29] The anti-Jewish 'boycott' formed in fact only one part of a whole series of disturbances initiated by Party activists in the spring and summer
of 1935. The population reacted even more sharply towards
the attacks on Catholic associations taking place at the same
time, the accompanying disturbance of *Caritas* collections,[30]
and the numerous unruly incidents surrounding the traditional
Bavarian white-and-blue flag during the customary May celebrations in rural areas. Popular feeling was certainly incensed,
but much more as a result of the disturbance of order than
the fact that the Jews had been a target of attack. The outcome was hostility towards the Party rather than sympathy
for the Jews or rejection of the anti-Jewish policies of the
regime. Even so, it seems clear from such reactions that the
aggressive, dynamic hatred of the Jews which the Nazi
formations were trying to foster was not easy to instil in a
population whose feelings towards the Jews went little
further for the most part than traditional antipathy.

In Franconia the situation was different. Leaving aside the
Palatinate, 62.8 per cent of Jews in Bavaria at the time of
the 1933 census were to be found there, especially in Middle
and Lower Franconia. Even before the First World War,
Franconian North Bavaria had been known as prime anti-
Semitic territory, and Streicher was able to play on much
existing resentment in making the Jewish Question a prominent feature of agitatory politics to a far greater extent than
in most other regions of Germany during the Nazi rise to
power.[31] Nuremberg and Coburg in particular developed into
centres of the most vitriolic anti-Semitism during the 1920s
and Jews there, made to bear the brunt of the economic
resentments of small traders or farmers, were already given
during the Depression a foretaste of what was to come.[32]
Following the 'seizure of power', the position of Jews,
especially in Middle Franconia but also to a large extent in

[29] GStA, MA 106411, fol. 394.
[30] Cf. Chapter 5 note 59 for references.
[31] Cf. Hambrecht, pp. 5 ff., 249 ff., 292 ff. and *passim*; Pridham, pp. 237,
244; Ophir, *Pinkas*, p. X.
[32] Cf. Hambrecht, pp. 252-4; Pridham, pp. 242-4; Stadtarchiv Coburg,
A7870, A8521.

the neighbouring parts of Upper and Lower Franconia, was
as bad as anywhere in Germany.

The overwhelmingly Protestant Middle Franconia, heavily
under Streicher's influence, saw the most vicious forms of
anti-Semitism. Although even here the local Party leadership, or alternatively the SA, SS, or HJ, directed and perpetrated almost all the outrages, the notorious Gunzenhausen
pogrom of March 1934 — the worst expression of anti-
Jewish violence in the whole of Bavaria before the horrific
events of 'Crystal Night' in 1938 — showed that in extreme
circumstances a wider public could be whipped up into a
hysterical mood against local resident Jews.[33]

Political conflict in Gunzenhausen — a small provincial
town of 5,600 inhabitants in 1933, among them 184 Jews —
seems to have been particularly bitter before the 'take-over
of power', and the local Nazi Party — according to the comments of functionaries in the post-pogrom investigations —
had built up a store of especial hatred towards the town's
Jews who, supported by 'a certain lack of character of a
broad section of the population in the Gunzenhausen district',
had backed the socialists and communists and had stirred up
feeling against the NSDAP even after the 'seizure of power'.
A whole series of violent outbursts, set in motion and executed by a particularly unsavoury local SA leadership,
punctuated the following months, so that by March 1934,
in the SA's own interpretation, 'the mood of the population
in Gunzenhausen had reached such a pitch that the smallest
incident would be enough to prompt a demonstration against
the Jews.'[34] The incident which turned the small town on
Palm Sunday 1934 into an inferno of murderous hatred
towards its Jewish inhabitants occurred after a young local
leader Kurt Bär, along with other SA men, had entered a
public house run by a Jewish couple, had mishandled and
'arrested' them, and had gratuitously beaten up and badly
injured the couple's son. Bär then addressed the mob which
had begun to gather outside in a hate-filled speech in which

[33] The following account is based upon the extensive description of the
events in HStA, MInn 73708 and the trial of Kurt Bär in GStA, MA 106410. Cf.
also Peterson, pp. 256–9.

[34] HStA, MInn 73708, fol. 15; GStA, MA 106410, fols. 100 f.

he called the Jews 'our mortal enemies' who had 'nailed our Lord God to the Cross' and were 'guilty of the deaths of two million in the World War and the four hundred dead and ten thousand seriously injured in the Movement.' He also spoke of innocent girls who had been raped by Jews. The speech was heard by some 200 bystanders.[35] It lit the touch-paper to the quasi-medieval pogrom which followed. In groups of between fifty and several hundred people, the inhabitants of Gunzenhausen roamed the streets of the town for two hours, going from one Jewish home to another and shouting 'the Jews must go'. In brutal fashion some thirty-five male and female Jews were dragged to the town prison, where some were gravely maltreated by Kurt Bär. One Jew was found hanged in a shed; another stabbed himself in the heart before the bellowing mob could get at him.[36] Between 1,000 and 1,500 people were said to have taken part in the pogrom.[37] If without doubt the ringleaders were SA men, it is none the less clear that in this case a considerable number of non-Party members must also have taken part in the wild orgy of violence. It provided, however, a case unique in its horror even for Middle Franconia: 'In no other administrative district of the fifty-three belonging to my governmental region has such an array of infringements taken place as in Gunzenhausen', wrote Government President Hofmann to the Bavarian Ministry of the Interior after the pogrom. He attributed the peculiarly tense situation in Gunzenhausen, where there had been at least eight more or less serious violent incidents between the 'seizure of power' and the pogrom directly to the agitation of the Special Commissioner,

[35] HStA, MInn 73708, fols. 46 f. Cf. also Peterson, p. 257.

[36] Bär and another eighteen ringleaders, most if not all SA men, were given prison sentences of between three and ten months. The sentences of all except Bär (who received ten months) were quashed on appeal. In mid-July, Bär — obviously still at large — returned to the inn where he had started the original outrages and shot the publican and his son, killing one and badly wounding the other. Bär was sentenced to life imprisonment, but apparently put on probation, and reportedly died in a Russian prison camp — GStA, MA 106410, trial of Bär et al.; Ophir, Die jüd. Gemeinden, p. 190; Peterson, p. 259.

[37] GStA, MA 106410, fol. 210. Another estimate, that of SA-Obersturmbann-führer Karl Bär, made in the late evening towards the end of the pogrom, put the number at 700–800 persons — HStA, MInn 73708, fol. 18.

SA- *Obersturmbannführer* Karl Bär (uncle of Kurt), 'who himself has no sense of discipline and order'.[38]

Most reports from the lower administrative authorities in Middle Franconia in the years 1933-5 contain no critical comments of the population about violence shown towards Jews. This must be juxtaposed with the open anger and protest registered in precisely this part of Bavaria at the Nazi intervention in the running of the Protestant Church in 1934. Obviously, the degree of intimidation in the Jewish Question was acute, as is shown by the arrest of a photographer from Gunzenhausen for allegedly making critical remarks about Kurt Bär, the instigator of the Gunzenhausen pogrom and himself arraigned before a court of law for the offence.[39] The level of intimidation was also largely responsible for the fact that already in spring 1933 few dared to engage in economic dealings with Jews, in contrast to the situation in most parts of Germany.[40] 'Friends of Jews' were exposed to practically the same danger as Jews themselves.

Intimidation, however, does not explain quite everything. Since intimidation itself was closely related to and dependent upon denunciation of neighbours or work-mates for their remarks or actions, its effectiveness presupposes that a considerable proportion of the population were, or were thought to be, in basic agreement with the broad contours of the persecution of the Jews.

An example of the poisoned atmosphere in one mid-Franconian village is provided by Altenmuhr, near Gunzenhausen. There were thirty-one Jews among the 800 inhabitants, and when an elderly Jew died in 1936 the construction of a coffin and transportation of the body to the cemetery, even though permission from the local police had been granted, was refused by the local joiner and undertaker. The coffin had eventually to be made by a cartwright and the corpse carried to Gunzenhausen by a hearse ordered from Nuremberg. As the report says, it had once been usual 'for a fair number of aryan mourners to attend a Jewish funeral. Since the takeover of power this fact has however funda-

---

[38] HStA, MInn 73708, fols. 22 f.
[39] StAN, 212/13/II, 654, BA Neustadt an der Aisch, 2 May 1934.
[40] StAN, 212/8/V, 4266, interrogation of Max Strauß, 16 Dec. 1933.

mentally altered. Today in Altenmuhr it is inconceivable that Germans would pay last respects to a Jew.'[41]

In the second half of 1935 the wild *'Einzelaktionen'* — individual measures taken against Jews without any legal base — declined sharply after being banned by the State authorities, and especially following the promulgation of the notorious Nuremberg Laws in September 1935, which in providing anti-Jewish legislation went a long way towards meeting the aims of the Party's summer anti-Semitic campaign.[42] With one eye on the approaching Olympics and the other on the foreign and economic situation, the regime needed a period of relative calm. In August 1935 Hitler and Deputy Führer Hess had expressly banned 'individual actions' against Jews.[43] Even after the murder of Wilhelm Gustloff, the Leader of the Nazi *Auslandsorganisation* in Switzerland, by a young Jew in February 1936 there were no outbreaks of anti-Jewish violence following another firm ban by the Reich Minister of the Interior, together with Hess, on any prospective sallies against Jewish targets.[44]

The largely negative attitude of the population, especially in South Bavaria, to the open violence of Nazi thugs in the summer of 1935 was perfectly compatible with broad approval of the anti-Jewish legislation passed at the Nuremberg Party Rally in September 1935 by a specially summoned assembly of the Reichstag.[45] Probably the Government President of Upper Bavaria was not far from the mark when he distinguished between rejection of the 'inexpedient' slogans and posters of the 1935 campaign, together with fears of economic repercussions in tourist areas, and approval 'in every respect' of the 'objective struggle against Jewry'.[46] Indifference seems, in fact, to have been the most common response to the Nuremberg Laws.[47] A wide range of reports

[41] GStA, MA 106411, fols. 153 f., GHS Gunzenhausen, 28 Mar. 1936.
[42] Cf. U.D. Adam, *Judenpolitik im Dritten Reich*, Düsseldorf, 1972, pp. 114-31.
[43] *Bayern I*, p. 453, n. 17; Ophir, *Pinkas*, pp. XVIII f.
[44] GStA, MA 106411, fol. 216.
[45] For the chaotic immediate background to the promulgation of the Nuremberg Laws, see Schleunes, pp. 120-5; Peterson, pp. 135-40.
[46] GStA, MA 106670, RPvOB, 11 June 1935.
[47] For varying reactions in different parts of the Reich, cf. Kershaw 'Persecution', pp. 272-3; Kulka, p. XLIII.

from Bavarian localities do not even mention the promulgation of the laws, and the reports of the Government
Presidents, summarizing opinion at the regional level, indicate only in the briefest terms that the legal regulation of
the Jewish Question had been generally welcomed and had
met with the approval of the population, not least in its
contribution towards the elimination of 'the recently prevailing intense disturbance'.[48] However, even where they had
been unpopular, the 'individual actions' had not been without influence on people's attitudes towards Jews. As the
alleged provocation of the disturbances, many were glad to
see the back of the Jews, as a report in December 1936 from
Bad Neustadt, an almost wholly Catholic district of Lower
Franconia which. the Nazis had scarcely penetrated before
the 'seizure of power', shows:

Altogether there has been an almost complete change in the attitude
of the population towards the Jews. Whereas people used to side in
unmistakable fashion with the persecuted Jews, one now hears: 'if
only they would all soon be gone!' Solely from the point of view of the
tax shortfall and thus of damage to communal finances is the departure
of the Jews regarded in Unsleben as unfortunate.[49]

Racial anti-Semitism met its greatest obstacle, and came
up against notable resistance, where the Nazis tried to break
commercial relationships between Jews and the non-Jewish
population. In 1936-7 the Party, together with the Nazified
trade and agricultural organizations, made renewed attempts
to destroy trading contacts with Jews. The revitalized boycott encountered little sympathy, it seems, even in Streicher
territory. Those who stood to gain economically through
trading in Jewish shops, trafficking with Jewish cattle-dealers,
providing accommodation for Jewish visitors to tourist
resorts, or finding work in Jewish-owned firms were not eager
to break off their contact and to boycott the Jews. Economic
self-interest clearly prevailed over ideological correctitude.
Here were obvious limits of Nazi ideological penetration.

---

[48] GStA, MA 106770, RPvOB, 9 Oct. 1935; MA 106672, RPvNB/OP, 8 Oct.
1935; MA 106677, RPvOF/MF, 10 Oct. 1935; MA 106680, RPvUF, 8 Oct.
1935; MA 106682, RPvS, 7 Oct. 1935; StAW, LRA Bad Neustadt 125/3, BA
Bad Neustadt, 29 Sept. 1935.
[49] StAW, LRA Bad Neustadt 125/4, BA Bad Neustadt, 1 Dec. 1936.

Alzenau, a relatively industrialized district on the north-western border of Lower Franconia, provides an example of how the ideological norm preached by the Party came to grief in the face of pragmatic material self-interest of workers at the Jewish-owned cigar factories which dominated local industry. Though the Nazis had made no great headway in this area before 1933,[50] the Party was responsible for not in-frequent acts of violence against Jews and their property in the years after the 'seizure of power'.[51] The 'boycott move-ment' had, as the focus of its attack, the Jewish ownership of the cigar factories. Jews in fact owned most of the twenty-nine factories with a combined work-force of 2,206 women and 280 men.[52] Enquiries into the position of the tobacco firms following allegations that the boycott was threatening their existence and the jobs of their employees met with a more or less unanimous response: the people were glad to have work and did not ask whether the employer was an 'aryan' or a Jew; 'the relationship between the firms and the local residents is a thoroughly good and friendly one; com-plaints about the employers have not been heard so far.'[53]

The boycott problems of the Nazis were even greater in the countryside. Here, the main issue was the remaining dominance in many areas of the Jewish cattle-dealer, the traditional middle-man and purveyor of credit for untold numbers of German peasants. Despite vicious intimidation and ceaseless propaganda, however, the Nazis found it an uphill struggle. Most peasants were unconcerned about the racial origins of the cattle-dealer as long as his prices were good and his credit readily forthcoming. 'Aryan' cattle-dealers, complained many peasants, had little capital and could not offer prices comparable to those of their Jewish rivals. The consequence was that the ousting of the Jewish cattle-dealers made remarkably slow progress. The wholesale

---

[50] The votes had been mainly divided among the BVP (46.7 per cent in March 1933), SPD (20 per cent), and KPD (7.2 per cent). The 25.2 per cent which the NSDAP gained in the March 1933 election was below the average for Lower Franconia — Data in Hagmann, pp. 18 f., 26.

[51] E.g., StAW, LRA Alzenau Bd. 5, BA Alzenau, 26 Oct. 1934.

[52] StAW, GL Mainfranken XII/1, BA Alzenau, 18 Oct. 1935.

[53] Ibid., GS Geiselbach, 2 Oct., GS Schöllkrippen, 2 Oct., GHS Alzenau, 7 Oct. 1935.

cattle trade in the Ebermannstadt area was in 1935 still 'to a good ninety per cent' in Jewish hands, and enquiries in autumn 1936 came to the 'regrettable' conclusion that, especially in the hill-farm districts of the Jura, nothing at all had changed: 'Here the cattle-Jew trafficks just as ever in the farmhouses. When questioned, the peasants explain almost in unison that the Jew pays well, and pays cash, which is not the case with the aryan dealers; in some instances there are no aryan dealers at all in the outlying communities.'[54] Even Party members and village mayors were not adverse to keeping ideological precepts and practical profits separate. There are numerous instances on record of functionaries and local dignitaries trafficking with Jews.[55]

Every form of chicanery, especially the withdrawal of trading permits, was used to bring about the almost complete exclusion of Jewish dealers from Middle Franconia as early as the end of 1934, though that was only possible in the peculiar conditions of Streicher's *Gau*, and even here was not always welcomed by the peasants.[56] Elsewhere in Bavaria the Jews could largely maintain their dominance in the cattle trade, despite harassment, down to the end of 1937. A not untypical report from a village in Lower Franconia shows the position clearly. The mayor stated that it was difficult to provide a list of names of peasants dealing with Jews, as requested, since apart from Party members almost all peasants still carried out their transactions with Jews. Recognition of the necessity of avoiding contact with Jews was hardly existent, and 'the currently expected attitude of rejection of Jews' was therefore lacking. Some peasants stood out in fact

[54] StAB, K8/III/18472, BA Ebermannstadt, 29 Dec. 1936. Cf. also K8/IV/ 1476.

[55] E.g., StAM, LRA 76887, Bgm.Egmating, 31 Aug. 1935, GS Egmating, 31 Aug. 1935; StAW, GL Mainfranken II/41, KL Würzburg, 20 July 1936; StAN, 212/8/V,4241, GS Heidenheim, 15 Nov. 1934.

[56] Cf. e.g., StAN, 212/17/III,8444, GBF Schwabach, 2 Mar. 1936, which mentions expressions of regret because the absence of Jewish tobacco dealers meant lack of competition and low prices. For the exclusion of Jewish dealers in Middle Franconia, see Ophir, *Pinkas*, pp. XXI f., and for the whole question as it affected Bavaria, most recently, F. Wiesemann, 'Juden auf dem Lande: die wirtschaftliche Ausgrenzung der jüdischen Viehhändler in Bayern', in D. Peukert and J. Reulecke (eds.), *Die Reihen fast geschlossen. Beiträge zur Geschichte des Alltags unterm Nationalsozialismus*, Wuppertal, 1981, pp. 381–96.

'on account of their friendliness towards Jews'.[57] Gestapo findings were even more alarming to Nazi eyes. Even as late as 1937 the Gestapo at Munich were forced to concede 'shocking results' arising from their enquiry into relations of peasants and Jews. In Swabia alone there had been 1,500 cases of peasants trafficking with Jews in 1936-7, and although this had been put down to the lack of reliable 'aryan' dealers with sufficient capital, the real reason, claimed the Gestapo, was 'the attitude of the peasants which lacked any sort of racial consciousness.'[58] Part of the problem, in the Gestapo's view, was that numerous peasants, 'who mainly have no idea of the racial problem', were of the opinion that commercial dealings with Jews were in order since the State had given them a trading licence.[59] The withdrawal of trading licences, refusal to insure cattle bought from Jews, expulsion from the Cattle Farming Association and not least exposure of those continuing to traffick with Jews in the pages of the *Stürmer* were all part of an intensified campaign to break the Jewish contact with the farming world, and by the end of 1937 the Nazis were approaching their goal.[60] The reactions of peasants from the Lower Franconia village of Bischofsheim an der Rhön mirror the complaint of many farmers, that their economic situation had deteriorated as a result of the exclusion of the Jews since there was no longer anyone who would buy up the cattle: 'The Jews are not allowed to engage in the cattle trade any longer and there are apart from them no cattle-dealers to speak of resident in this district.'[61]

Peasant attitudes were determined almost wholly by material considerations and economic self-interest. Nazi racial propaganda played no great part. The fourfold increase in sales of the *Stürmer* during the first ten months of 1935, despite the widespread distaste the newspaper provoked, was testimony none the less to the fact that anti-Semitism was

[57] StAW, GL Mainfranken XII/6, Bgm. Dittlofsroda, 19 June 1937; cf. also in the same file Bgm. Schwärzelbach, 18 June 1937; and the commentary of the Government President, GStA, MA 106680, RPvUF, 8 Feb. 1937.
[58] GStA, MA 106689, Gestapo München, 1 June 1937, p. 54; MA 106690, Gestapo München, 1 Aug. 1937, pp. 43 f.
[59] GStA, MA 106690, Gestapo München, 1 Sept. 1937, p. 40.
[60] Cf. Ophir, *Pinkas*, pp. XXII f.
[61] StAW, LRA Bad Neustadt 125/5, GS Bischofsheim, 28 Jan. 1938.

gradually gaining ground in popular opinion.[62] And certainly the fact that peasants continued to trade with Jewish dealers does not make them pro-Jewish. But it does suggest that the racial origins of the purchaser of their cattle was for them a matter of complete indifference: the only question that mattered was the price for the cow.

Negative reactions to anti-Jewish placards and slogans posted at the entry and exit in most villages by the local Nazi Party were probably also prompted more by economic than humanitarian motives. Even Nazis themselves recognized that the anti-Jewish slogans — 'Jews are our misfortune', 'Jews not wanted here', and even more threatening and offensive varieties — were guaranteed to damage the tourist trade. An anonymous letter to Reich Governor Epp in August 1934, allegedly coming from a long-serving Party member who undoubtedly had his own economic interest in the matter, pointed out that the anti-Jewish notices made the worst possible impact on foreigners travelling down the 'Romantische Straße' through Franconia to the Passion Play in Oberammergau, and that as a result the tourist industry in towns such as Rothenburg, Dinkelsbühl, Nördlingen, and Ansbach was suffering greatly.[63] With the massive extension of the notices in 1935 — up to then they had been largely a Franconian speciality — came grave misgivings in other tourist areas such as Garmisch-Partenkirchen, where serious economic consequences were feared.[64] In some rural areas peasants expressed their distaste for the anti-Jewish boards by removing them altogether, or altering the wording to express welcome to the Jews. In one Upper Bavarian village, where some peasants were worried that the anti-Jewish notices set up by the Hitler Youth would deter Jews from coming to buy up their hops, the boards — 'Jews not wanted here' — disappeared for a short time before being replaced with an amended text: 'Jews very much wanted here'.[65]

---

[62] 'How popular was Streicher?' (no author), *Wiener Library Bulletin*, v–vi (1957), 48.

[63] GStA, MA 106410, fol. 91; the Reich Minister of Economics had already in July 1934 sought the banning of notices 'in the interests of preventing further unrest in the economy' (ibid., fol. 28), but without much effect in practice.

[64] GStA, MA 106670, RPvOB, 11 June 1935.

[65] StAM, LRA 76887, GS Glonn, 30 June 1935; LRA 58130, GS Höhenkir-

In its patronage of Jewish shops the rural population in particular was regarded by the authorities as 'ideologically unteachable'. In one report about the boycott of Jewish shops in Cham (Upper Palatinate) in December 1936, it was pointed out that the rural population especially, 'despite repeated and thorough instruction at Party meetings and on other occasions', still preferred to buy in Jewish shops. Even being photographed for the *Stürmer*'s rogues' gallery was not enough to deter them, and many were prepared even to take sides with the Jews.[66] In Munich, the police interpreted the massive success of the annual sales at a leading Jewish clothing store as a sign that many women still 'had not understood, nor want to understand, the lines laid down by the Führer for solving the Jewish Question.'[67] Such complaints were common the length and breadth of Germany in these years.[68]

Nevertheless, in the long run the intimidation did not fail to do its work. As early as December 1935 the Government President of Swabia could provide several examples to show how the economic position of Jewish dealers in Swabia had drastically deteriorated. Ichenhausen, where Jews formed a higher proportion of the population (12.4 per cent) than almost anywhere else in Germany and where commercial life revolved around Jewish trade, was described as 'a dying town', since many no longer wanted to buy in Jewish shops and preferred to travel to Günzburg or Ulm to do their shopping — a process which was also damaging Christian shops, added the report.[69] Not a few 'aryan' businessmen saw in the 'Jewish boycott' a chance to damage or even ruin rivals by reporting their Jewish background to the local

---

chen, 5 Jan. 1936; LRA 72055, GS Hohenwart, 3 June 1935, and HJ-Gefolgschaft to KL Schrobenhausen, 27 May 1935.

[66] GStA, MA 106411, fols. 103 f.; MA 106689, Gestapo München, 1 Jan. 1937, pp. 54 f.

[67] GStA, MA 106697, Pd München, LB, 5 Feb. 1936.

[68] Cf. e.g., the *Sopade*'s reports on continued trading in Jewish shops, DBS, 21 Sept. 1935, A29-37, 16 Oct. 1935, pp. 21-5. This and other evidence is summarized in Kershaw, 'Persecution', pp. 266-7.

[69] GStA, MA 106682, RPvS, 7 Dec. 1935; cf. Ophir, *Die jüd.* p. 472.

Party.[70] Under constant pressure, countless Jewish businesses had by the end of 1937 seen their customers driven away, had sold out or gone into liquidation, had emigrated or moved to larger cities where they could continue a shadowy existence for some time to come on the fringes of society, withdrawn, threatened, and persecuted.

(ii) The Influence of the Clergy on Attitudes to the Jewish Question

Following their detailed enquiries into the continuing commercial contact between peasants and Jewish dealers, the Gestapo attributed the limited penetration of the Nazi *Weltanschauung* in rural areas chiefly to the influence of the Christian Churches. If 'despite enlightenment through the National Socialist Movement' there were still those 'who think they have to stand up for the Jewish people', claimed the Gestapo, this was above all the fault of the clergy. It was often the case in rural parishes in fact, continued the report, that the priest or pastor would represent the Jews as the 'chosen people' and directly encourage the people to patronize Jewish shops:[71]

The enquiries, which are not yet concluded, show already that in exactly those districts where political Catholicism still holds sway the peasants are so infected by the doctrines of belligerent political Catholicism that they are deaf to any discussion of the racial problem. This state of affairs further shows that the majority of peasants are wholly unreceptive to the ideological teachings of National Socialism and that they can only be compelled through material disadvantage to engage in commercial links with aryan dealers.[72]

After more than four years of Nazi rule, then, the Nazi *Weltanschauung*, and in particular racial anti-Semitism, its central feature, had in the view of the Gestapo been able to make little headway among the Catholic rural population,

[70] E.g., GStA, MA 106411, fols. 122–39 for the case of an 'aryan' owner of a sausage grillery in Nuremberg who was driven to ruin by his trade rivals under the cover of the anti-Semitic campaign, since his wife was Jewish. Certificates from the Reich Ministry of the Economy confirming the 'aryan' status of his business were of no help.

[71] GStA, MA 106689, Gestapo München, 1 July 1937, pp. 53 f.

[72] GStA, MA 106690, Gestapo München, 1 Aug. 1937, pp. 42 f.

which had no 'racial consciousness' and was 'deaf' to the 'racial problem'. The tendency of the Gestapo, like the SD, to exaggerate the opposition of the Churches is well known. Even so, as we have seen in the two chapters on the 'Church struggle', there is no doubting the fact that the Christian Churches, especially the Catholic Church, were able to exercise very considerable influence on the population, particularly in rural areas. The Churches remained practically the only non-Nazified bodies in Germany which retained enormous influence upon the formation of opinion and the potential — as the 'Church struggle' shows — to form and foster an independent public opinion running counter to Nazi propaganda and policy. Furthermore, it was evident that the racial theories on which Nazi anti-Semitism was grounded amounted to a hatred of part of mankind which was diametrically opposed to the Christian Commandment to 'love thy neighbour': racism, as the central element of the Nazi *Weltanschauung*, stood in irreconcilable conflict with the Christian basic tenet of the equality of all men before God.

However, the attitude of the Churches and of the leaders of both denominations to racism was highly ambivalent. This ambivalence had deep roots. Against the fundamental rejection of racism stood the Christian tradition of anti-Judaism which, though in decline since the Enlightenment, retained some force as a Christian undercurrent of anti-Semitism well into the twentieth century.[73]

Steeped in such traditions, and also in the contemporary commonplaces of racial prejudice, many Church leaders were unable or unwilling to speak out forcefully and unambiguously against anti-Semitism. Even, on the Catholic side, Cardinal Faulhaber who, as we saw earlier, had in 1923 been labelled 'the Jewish Cardinal' by Nazi sympathizers at Munich University for his criticism of anti-Semitic agitation, shied away from an outright public condemnation of Nazi racism. In his bold and justly famous Advent sermons of 1933, which enjoyed a wide readership outside Germany, he stressed that 'the love of one's own race' ought never to be turned into 'hatred towards other people'. He added, however, that the

[73] Cf. Lewy, pp. 268-74.

Church had no objections to 'racial research' (*Rassenfors-chung*) and 'racial welfare' (*Rassenpflege*), 'nor to the endeavour to keep the individuality of a people as pure as possible and, through reference to the community of blood, deepening the sense of national community.' A year later the Cardinal felt compelled to make clear that in his Advent sermons he had 'defended the old Biblical Scripture of Israel, but not taken a stance on the Jewish Question of today.'[74]

The even more strongly featured nationalist leanings in the Protestant Church allowed racial and anti-Semitic thinking to surface all the more readily — quite apart from the 'German Christians', the thoroughly racist Nazified wing of the Church.[75] Both Churches accepted in essence the principle of racial differentiation, rejecting — again apart from the 'German Christians' — only the outrightly aggressive hatred of Jews by the Nazis. Günther Lewy used sharp but fitting words to emphasize the consequences of such an ambivalent stance in the case of the Catholic Church: 'A Church that justified moderate anti-Semitism and merely objected to extreme and immoral acts was ill prepared to provide an effective antidote to the Nazis' gospel of hate.'[76]

The difference in attitude towards the Jewish Question, which we have already witnessed, between Franconia and South Bavaria certainly had something to do with the denominational divide between Protestant and Catholic areas. The particularly pronounced national feeling in Franconia which was closely coupled with fervent Protestantism undoubtedly tended to foster acceptance of Nazi racial stereotypes, and the piously Protestant rural population of Middle Franconia, which defended its Church and bishop so demonstratively and effectively in 1934, revealed in the same period hardly a trace of opposition to the racial idea. However, it would be easy to take the denominational distinction too far.

---

[74] Faulhaber, p. 116; cf. Volk, 'Kardinal Faulhabers Stellung', pp. 183 ff., and Lewy, pp. 275-6.

[75] Cf. Conway, pp. 10-12, 32, 339-46, 353-7; see also I. Arndt, 'Machtübernahme und Judenboykott in der Sicht evangelischer Sonntagsblätter', in W. Benz *et al.* (eds.), *Miscellanea. Festschrift für Helmut Krausnick*, Stuttgart, 1980, pp. 15-31.

[76] Lewy, p. 274.

The position of the Jews was by no means rosy in the adjacent, and largely Catholic, Lower Franconia. Catholicism provided no protection in itself against anti-Semitism (as of course is plain from the example of Austria and other central European countries). Nevertheless, given the generally stronger social cohesiveness of the Catholic Church's following, the Christian teaching which ran counter to the Nazi doctrine of race hatred certainly played a part in influencing opinion on the Jewish Question in the Catholic regions of Bavaria.

While the ambivalent and hesitant attitude of the Papacy, of the Catholic hierarchy, and of the leadership of the Evangelical Church to the Jewish Question has been the subject of thorough enquiry,[77] the stance adopted by the parochial clergy has been little touched upon. Yet it was the parish clergy, as we have seen in previous chapters, who were most able to exert direct influence upon their congregations. The extent to which they attempted to influence opinion on the Jews is an important one, therefore, requiring detailed examination.

Few clergymen of either denomination seem to have spoken publicly (mainly in sermons) on the 'racial problem' in a fully-fledged Nazi sense. As the Nazi authorities themselves often reported, they were the exceptions. One Protestant pastor — 'a rare bird amongst his sort' according to the Government President of Upper and Middle Franconia — was said to have claimed in a sermon in April 1937 that the Jew had nothing in common with the Christian Church, was a foreign element, and must be regarded as the enemy of the Christian faith. The Jew sought to introduce Bolshevism into the Church and by so doing to destroy the religious community. 'The Jews are the destroyers and deserved to be whipped out', he reportedly concluded.[78] An equally 'honourable exception' was the Catholic Redemptorist from Cham who in April 1939 paid tribute to the Nazi State,

---

[77] E.g., ibid., ch. 10; Conway, *passim*; and, most recently, B. van Schewick, 'Katholische Kirche und nationalsozialistische Rassenpolitik', in K. Gotto and K. Repgen (eds.), *Kirche, Katholiken und Nationalsozialismus*, Mainz, 1980, pp. 83–100.

[78] KLB, ii. 174.

touched on the Jewish Question, and described the Jews as murderers because they had crucified Christ.[79] Another Catholic priest from the Bamberg district, whose pro-Nazi comments in a sermon in March 1939 had caused such offence among his congregation that some thirty people left the Church in protest was said to have called out as they went: 'Let them go, they're nothing but Jew-servers.'[80]

Such unrestrained Nazified remarks seldom occurred. Much more frequent were instances where members of the clergy, while not preaching racial hatred, betrayed signs of a racist attitude and of basic acknowledgement that there was indeed a 'racial problem'. In his well-attended sermons in the *Frauenkirche* in Munich in December 1936, the well-known Jesuit Hermann Muckermann, speaking on the personality of the historic Jesus, drew the conclusion that the teaching of Christ was not Jewish in origin but stood rather in opposition to Jewry. He upheld expressly 'the facts of heredity and race' and stated that the Church approved in principle of the eugenic and racial policies of the government.[81] Muckermann had already formulated his ideas about eugenics and race in spring 1936 in a series of lectures in Bamberg, in which he described a 'healthy racial stock' as 'a lofty, magnificent gift of heaven' and regarded it as Christian duty to uphold and increase the 'home race' (*Heimrasse*). Though not in itself against the Divine Order, mixing the 'home race' with 'alien races' was to be rejected.[82] Muckermann's views were based upon his theoretical concern with racial and eugenic problems, upon which subjects he had written a number of tracts. Other clergymen tended rather to reveal in their comments an unreflected acceptance of racial premises. Such attitudes were also betrayed by the eagerness with which a number of Protestant pastors retaliated in denying the 'calumny' that the clergy was 'Jew-ridden' (*verjudet*).[83] When *Gauleiter* Kube of the Kurmark attacked pastors of the 'Confessing Front' as 'Jews' accomplices' in June 1935, for instance, an array of protest telegrams landed

[79] Ibid., p. 317.   [80] Ibid., p. 314.
[81] KLB, i. 175 ff.
[82] KLB, ii. 90.
[83] Ibid., pp. 195, 227, 231; KLB, iii. 155.

in the offices of the Nuremberg police and protestations were also made during services in and around Nuremberg.[84]

Even such a leading figure in the Protestant Church as Helmut Kern, head of the 'People's Mission', who otherwise described concepts of race, blood, and nationality as no more than secular values and recognized the connections between 'new heathenism', racism, and the attack on Christian values, showed — probably in an unreflecting way — undercurrents of anti-Semitism when, in his campaign against the 'community school', he described it as 'a product of the Enlightenment and of Jewish liberalism', or spoke in the same context of the ideas 'of Jew-ridden Marxism and liberalism'.[85] Though it was not the intention in these or similar instances to attack the Jews directly, such comments of pastors and priests could only help to legitimize and strengthen the existing anti-Semitic climate of opinion.

Far more numerous, however, to go from the report material, were instances where clergy of both denominations — though Catholics more frequently than Protestants — took issue with the racial policy of the regime or even sided openly with the persecuted Jews.

The authorities were informed, for example, of a Protestant missionary preacher in the Weißenburg district of Middle Franconia who, in a sermon in 1935, referred disparagingly to the name of the former SA leader Ernst Röhm, shot in 1934, in connection with the notion of race 'in order to show that the aryan race was not to be regarded as better than any other.'[86] Another Protestant preacher was said to have stated that in a time when race and blood were being elevated to the status of idols people needed above all the badge of faith.[87] During a Catholic mission in Bamberg a speaker was alleged to have declared in a sermon: 'For God there are no *völkisch* matters and no national laws . . . For him there are no racial differences.'[88] A Jesuit, also in Bamberg, was reported as saying that the Catholic Church had no use for a national or racial church 'because it preaches its doctrine to all people, whatever their race.'[89]

[84] KLB, ii. 58.
[85] Ibid., pp. 73, 104–5; KLB, iii. 28.
[86] KLB, ii. 76.   [87] Ibid., p. 237.
[88] Ibid., p. 218.   [89] Ibid., p. 274.

Some clergymen of both denominations supported the Jews publicly and openly condemned their persecution. A Catholic priest in Neustadt an der Saale (Lower Franconia), for example, spoke, following a series of terroristic acts against local Jews, in a sermon in October 1934 about human hatred and lack of charity in connection with anti-Jewish actions, referred to an anti-Jewish song of the Hitler Youth, and commented that 'in this way the hatred towards the Jews is planted in the hearts of young people.'[90] The courageous Father Förtsch, a Catholic priest in the Bamberg district and clever opponent of the regime who had long been a thorn in the flesh of the authorities, declared in sermons in February 1936 'that the Jews also did a very great deal of good and were not therefore to be spurned.'[91] In the same month a Protestant pastor at Hersbruck (Middle Franconia) expressly emphasized that according to the Bible the Jews were 'the chosen people'.[92] *Dompfarrer* Kraus of Eichstätt, whom we last encountered battling with the authorities about the attack on Catholicism,[93] also defended the Jews in one of his sermons and strongly criticized an article in the *Stürmer* entitled 'Why I hate the Jews'.[94] Another known opponent of the regime, the brave Protestant pastor Karl Steinbauer, who paid for his courage by forfeiting his liberty, castigated anti-Semitism and the entire *völkisch* way of thinking in a sermon in September 1935 in which he boldly repeated the biblical words: 'Salvation comes from the Jews.'[95] Other pastors prayed for the Jews, or requested the congregation to pray for them.[96] Even during the war some clergymen were prepared to support the Jews. One Catholic priest in the district of Neustadt an der Aisch in Middle Franconia was served with a summons in summer 1940 for allegedly saying in a sermon that 'the Jews should not be cast out since they too are human beings.'[97] Particularly courageous and note-

[90] StAW, LRA Bad Neustadt 125/2, GHS Bad Neustadt, 24 Oct. 1934, BA Bad Neustadt, 27 Oct. 1934.
[91] KLB, ii. 80.   [92] Ibid., p. 76.
[93] Cf. above, Chapter 5 and Peterson, pp. 309–12.   [94] KLB, ii. 146.
[95] StAN, Pol.-Dir. Nürnberg-Fürth 357, BPP, 1 Oct. 1935, pp. 21 f. For Steinbauer, cf. K. Tenfelde, 'Proletarische Provinz. Radikalisierung und Widerstand in Penzberg/Oberbayern 1900 bis 1945', in *Bayern IV*, pp. 348–56.
[96] KLB, ii. 33, 117, 147, 390.   [97] Ibid., p. 353.

worthy were the remarks of the Catholic priest Josef Atzinger
in Landshut in November 1940, in which he condemned the
racial legislation of the Third Reich as 'godless, unjustified,
and harmful'.[98]

Neither the Catholic nor the Evangelical Church leadership
took any official stance towards the November pogrom of
1938. The undoubted deep disapproval of the bulk of the
clergy of both denominations was voiced therefore only in
the isolated comments of individual priests and pastors.
Their courage in speaking out amid the official silence was
all the greater in that they could expect no support from
above, from their bishops and hierarchies, and little or no
protection from any possible retribution by local Party
activists. Four Catholic and two Protestant clergymen in the
district of Wunsiedel in Upper Franconia, for example, were
the targets of violent attacks because of their alleged pro-
Jewish attitude during the 'Crystal Night'.[99]

Reports of the Bavarian authorities contain several instances where the 'Jewish Action' was openly denounced by
members of the clergy of both denominations. A Protestant
pastor in the Bamberg area, for example, was indicted with
offences against the 'Malicious Practices Act' for saying in
sermons in November 1938 that the actions carried out
against the Jews were from a Christian point of view in no
sense deserving of approval but were rather to be condemned
and stating: 'A Christian person does not do such things.
These were sub-humans (*Untermenschen*).'[1] A priest in
Neumarkt in der Oberpfalz compared those who smashed
Jewish windows with 'the purest Bolsheviks'.[2] Another
priest, from Pfarrkirchen in Lower Bavaria, was arraigned
before the Munich 'Special Court' for allegedly saying to an
eleven-year-old schoolboy following the murder of embassy
official Ernst vom Rath — the spur to the pogrom — that
many innocent Jews had to suffer with the one guilty of
vom Rath's assassination.[3] And at St Lorenz's church in the

[98] KLB, iv. 276.   [99] KLB, ii. 300.
[1] Ibid., p. 309 and cf. also p. 301.   [2] KLB, iv. 224.
[3] Ibid., p. 219; StAM, SGM 4731, GS Tann, 1 Dec. 1938. According to GS
Tann's record of the interrogation of 2 Jan. 1939, the priest nevertheless defended himself with anti-Semitic arguments. He claimed the schoolboy had misunderstood him, that he had meant the German people was punishing all the Jews
for the crime of one person because they did not know 'how many are behind it'.

centre of Nuremberg on the Sunday following the pogrom, all the clergy of the parish followed the pastor's remarks of sympathy for the Jews by chanting the Ten Commandments in unison before the altar.[4]

Further critical remarks of the clergy about the pogrom could not be found in the report material. Most priests and pastors kept silent, yet as in the neighbouring Württemberg their general rejection of the pogrom was easily recognizable by the authorities.[5] This was confirmed by the comment of the Government President of Upper Bavaria about reactions to the pogrom: 'Only those circles influenced by the Church do not yet go along with the Jewish Question.'[6]

Examination of remarks made by members of the Bavarian parish clergy about the Jews suggests that attitudes were divided on the 'race question'. Some clergymen adopted an outright Nazi stance and fully approved of the exclusion of Jews from German society. They were, however, exceptions. Most rejected the Nazi dogma of hate towards part of mankind. Nevertheless, latent anti-Semitic feelings occasionally found expression. There was also some ambivalence in a number of statements which appeared to condemn not discrimination itself but merely the methods of discrimination, the deplorable excesses of the persecution of the Jews. The clearest conclusion of all from the evidence surveyed would seem to be, however, that the parish clergy had on remarkably few occasions anything at all to say on the Jewish Question. The overwhelming majority of priests and pastors, like their superiors, refrained from any public comment and let the persecution of the Jews pass them by in silence. Such comments as have been cited in this chapter were therefore themselves exceptional in being made at all. And the fact that most examples derive from Franconian parishes is itself no accident, again showing that the Jewish Question was for the most part only in this area a live issue.[7]

---

[4] A. Müller, *Geschichte der Juden in Nürnberg 1146-1945*, Nuremberg, 1968, p. 245.

[5] Cf. StA Ludwigsburg, K110 Nr. 44, report of SD-*Abschnitt* Stuttgart, 1 Feb. 1939 for the rejection of the pogrom by the Protestant and Catholic clergy of Württemberg. There are no similar SD reports of this date surviving for Bavaria.

[6] KLB, i. 301.

[7] Comments of the Lower Franconian clergy on the Jewish Question are far

In asking why the clergy commented so rarely on the inhumanities of the persecution of the Jews, we have of course immediately to take into account their exposed position in the Third Reich, the intimidation of the police State, the probability of recriminations, and the general pervading atmosphere of fear and repression. This explains much, but not everything. In other matters, especially when it was a case of defending immediate concerns of the Church against the regime, priests were prepared to act despite the obvious dangers involved. Defence of the Church had its own legitimacy for priests and pastors. The Jewish Question, on the other hand, belonged in the realm of 'politics' which the Church, from its leaders down, conscientiously eschewed from 1933 onwards. Even apart from any principle of non-interference in 'politics', however, there are grounds for strong suspicion that the Jewish Question was not regarded by the clergy as a central theme of interest. The narrower field of denominational issues and defence of the Church's rights and practices consumed in great measure the potential energy of the parish clergy to oppose the regime. In this sphere, the priest was able decisively to influence the opinion and behaviour of the population and to manipulate it in the struggle against the anti-Church measures of the regime. He could generally count on popular support of churchgoers in response to Nazi intervention in Church affairs, and on the maximum backing from his superiors. In the Jewish Question things were different. The clergy encountered mainly indifference or feelings of sullen helplessness, when not a widespread if abstract and latent anti-Semitism even among churchgoers. Whereas the clergy tried actively to influence popular opinion in Church matters, in the Jewish Question they gave little lead and tended to follow and reflect rather than mould popular opinion. As Christians the majority of the clergy rejected the inhumanities of the Nazi regime; but as individuals living amid a climate of opinion hostile to Jews they tended largely to mirror the latent

---

less plentiful than those of priests and pastors in Upper and Middle Franconia. This is probably in the main a reflection of the less detailed nature of the reports of the Government President of Lower Franconia.

anti-Semitism and indifference of their society.

Since the Jewish Question appears to have been relatively unimportant to the Church,[8] and since — as we have seen — the clergy rarely took a direct part in shaping opinion on the Jews, the Gestapo's interpretation, linking the lack of penetration of Nazi racial doctrines in rural areas to the active influence of the clergy, seems a dubious one. The lack of 'racial consciousness' in the Bavarian peasantry which the Gestapo bemoaned was undoubtedly often founded on traditional Christian precepts of basic humanity which continued to stand for many Christians in crass opposition to Nazi barbarity. Of at least equal importance, especially in Catholic rural areas, was the widespread rejection of the Nazi Party, above all for its assault on the Catholic Church itself, which brought with it increased solidarity with the priest and rejection of Nazi values. More important still, however, in explaining the unwillingness of the peasantry to go along with Nazi boycott demands was not so much 'lack of racial consciousness' as direct material self-interest.

Nazism had only limited success in breaking down the conventional mentality of the population, built partly on self-interest, and replacing it with an ideological dogma of hatred towards Jews. Though Christian teaching often provided the basis of the antipathy towards the Nazi *Weltanschauung*, the hierarchy and lower clergy did little directly to foster anti-racist attitudes. Only indirectly, through the closer bonds of the population to the Church as a consequence of the 'Church struggle', was immunity to Nazi ideological penetration reaffirmed. The ambivalent attitude of the Church towards race allowed, however, the retention of anti-Semitic views by the faithful. If, according to the teaching of the Church, Jews were not to be hated and persecuted, they did not necessarily have to be loved. The words of the Catholic preacher cited earlier, that in the eyes of God there

---

[8] An indication of this was the decision of the Fulda Bishops' Conference in summer 1938, faced with alternative draft pastoral letters, the one refuting racial ideology, the other condemning 'the struggle against Church and Christianity', to choose the latter. 'Obviously the majority of the bishops regarded the threat to Christianity as so great, in the summer of 1938, that they preferred a clear word on this issue to a public condemnation of racism' — Van Schewick, pp. 90-1.

were no *völkisch* matters, national laws, or racial differences,[9] denoted an uncompromising attitude adopted by a few clergymen even during the war. Such a stance ran, of course, completely counter to the very core of Nazi ideology. As was implicitly recognized here, the Nazi 'new heathenism' was grounded on the principle of racial inequality, which stood in contradiction to the Commandments of God.[10] The defence against the anti-Church component of Nazism ought theoretically, therefore, to have found one of its central points in the rejection of the concept of race. In practice, however, from the point of view of the Church the ideological struggle was regarded mainly as a struggle for the faith in the narrower sense of the word, and as a defence of Church institutions, in which the racial issue was seldom touched upon, and then only tangentially. The isolated voices of protest raised by a few courageous individuals from both denominations acquired, therefore, no significance within the framework of the 'Church struggle' and found little support from the Church leaderships.

One can hardly avoid the conclusion that the Jewish Question was on the whole a matter of just as much indifference to the clergy as it was to the churchgoing population of Bavaria. The courageous stand taken on denominational issues was never matched by anything like the same fervour on matters of so much greater human significance.

(iii) 'Crystal Night'

Only once in the twelve years of the Third Reich was the German people directly confronted with the full savagery of the anti-Jewish terror. This was on the morning of 10 November 1938, following the so-called 'Crystal Night' (*'Reichskristallnacht'*), the quasi-medieval orgy of destruction, plunder, burning of synagogues, and wild devastation carried out by the Party and the·SA at the call of Propaganda Minister Goebbels — in his words as a 'spontaneous answer' of the population to the killing of Legation Secretary Ernst vom

---

[9] KLB, ii. 218.
[10] Cf. the comments of Helmut Kern, KLB, iii. 28.

Rath by a seventeen-year-old Jewish boy, Herschel Grynsz-pan, in Paris.[11]

After the relative calm of the years 1936–7 the position of the Jews in Germany had worsened visibly since the beginning of 1938.[12] Following the *Anschluß* of Austria, and especially in connection with the Sudeten crisis, serious outbreaks of anti-Jewish violence had occurred in numerous Franconian localities as Party activists exploited the tension and the eventual triumphs of the Nazi State to unleash a wave of terror against the Jews.[13] Seen through Jewish eyes, the situation in Middle Franconia was threatening in the extreme during the weeks before the pogrom:

Already for a few weeks there had been decided signs of unrest among the masses . . . There also appeared on various shops, cinemas etc. the notices: 'Jews not wanted' etc. In Ansbach, seat of the district administration, for example, this notice was to be seen weeks beforehand on every shop of whatever sort without exception. In smaller places and in the countryside conditions were worse still. Through terror acts or by being compelled to sign, people were forced to sell all their belongings for a bargain price within a few hours and to go away. Where to? Naturally, into the next big town. The same question, where to? which now confronts all of them.[14]

According to the report of the District Officer of Alzenau (Lower Franconia) at the end of October 1938, the area had experienced a constant spate of night attacks on Jewish buildings. Windows had been smashed in many houses, the walls smeared with red paint, and two synagogues damaged by stone-throwing.[15] Attacks by Party activists on synagogues were sharply increasing in number long before the pogrom. The tone was set by the festive demolition of the main synagogues in Munich and Nuremberg in summer 1938.[16] In Leutershausen (Middle Franconia) the synagogue was plundered by SA men in mid-October and the windows

---

[11] For details and for the course of the pogrom, cf. among other works, L. Kochan, *Pogrom. 10 November 1938*, London, 1957, and R. Thalmann and E. Feinermann, *Crystal Night: 9–10 November 1938*, London, 1974.

[12] Cf. Adam, pp. 172 ff.; Schleunes, pp. 133 ff.

[13] Cf. Ophir, *Pinkas*, p. XXVII, note.

[14] WL, B155 (without date, but from content written in November 1938 or very shortly afterwards).

[15] StAW, LRA Alzenau Bd. 5/2, BA Alzenau, 31 Oct. 1938.

[16] Ophir, *Pinkas*, p. XXVI; Müller, pp. 236–9; Hanke, pp. 204 ff.

of nearby houses smashed amid tumultous scenes.[17] At the end of the month a tear-gas bomb was hurled into the Ansbach synagogue and slogans daubed on Jewish houses: 'Jew, clear off before 1. 1. 39.'[18] The Government Presidents reported ever increasing numbers of outrages against Jews throughout 1938.[19] Only in Upper Bavaria were conditions relatively quiet in the months before the great pogrom. And in contrast to the situation following the murder of Gustloff in February 1936, the dangerously volatile climate inside the country combined with Germany's new dominance in Europe since the Munich settlement to provide more or less ideal circumstances for the anti-Jewish 'retaliatory measures' of November 1938.

The methodically whipped-up hate campaign of 1938, together with the intensified boycott and exclusion of Jews from certain sections of the economy, had accelerated Jewish emigration, especially from small towns and villages where Jews had been particularly exposed. The relatively high proportion of Bavarian Jews living in such areas as compared with the Reich as a whole was one reason why emigration rates from Bavaria were higher than in Germany in general. Whereas the 370,000 Jews still remaining in Germany (leaving aside Austria and the Sudetenland) on 1 October 1938 represented 74 per cent of the recorded number of 1933, in Bavaria (here including the Palatinate) the Jewish population formed only 67.5 per cent of its 1933 level.[20] There were significant regional differences within Bavaria. In Upper and Middle Franconia there was a drop to 59 per cent and in Lower Franconia to as little as 55 per cent, whereas the inflow from internal migration *to* Munich almost compensated for the city's losses and there was only a slight drop to 95

[17] WL, PIIe/765, pp. 29, 62 f.
[18] WL, 'Der 10. November 1938' (typescript of collected short reports of persecuted and émigré Jews, compiled in 1939 and 1940 by S. Brückheimer), pp. 29 f. The volume contains short descriptions of the pogrom events in seventy-two Bavarian localities, mainly in Lower Franconia.
[19] GStA, MA 106681, RPvUF, 9 Apr. 1938, 10 Oct. 1938; MA 106673, RPvNB/OP, 8 Aug. 1938, 7 Oct. 1938, 7 Nov. 1938; MA 106678, RPvOF/MF, 7 Oct., 7 Nov. 1938; MA 106683, RPvS, 6 Aug., 7 Nov. 1938.
[20] For the Reich figure, cf. BAK, R58/1094, SD-Jahresbericht für 1938, p. 35.

per cent of the 1933 figure. The quarterly statistics of the authorities show clearly the increase in emigration since 1937 following the stepped-up boycott. In the period of almost four years from June 1933 to March 1937 the Jewish population in Bavaria had decreased by about 8,500 persons, in the one-and-a-half years from 1 April 1937 to 1 October 1938 by as much as 5,200 persons.[21]

Even this was not fast enough for the Nazi regime. Towards the end of October 1938 around 17,000 Jews of Polish extract were expelled — among them the parents of Herschel Grynszpan, whose revenge killing of vom Rath[22] triggered off the 'Crystal Night' pogrom, the subsequent temporary internment of some 30,000 Jews in concentration camps,[23] and — as one consequence — the massive acceleration of Jewish emigration.[24] Jews now left Germany in droves. By May 1939 more than 40 per cent of those Jews still in Bavaria on the eve of the pogrom had left.[25]

So far as Goebbels had reckoned with spontaneous popular support for the pogrom, however, he was disappointed. The disapproval of large sections of the population was abundantly clear, even if open protest was in the circumstances hardly conceivable.

Though in accordance with Goebbels's instructions the press carried relatively few details about the nature and scale of destruction — in contrast to the extensive coverage of the 'legal' measures introduced immediately after the pogrom[26] —

[21] From data in HStA, MInn 73725, MInn 73726.

[22] See Thalmann, pp. 45 ff; H. Heiber, 'Der Fall Grünspan', VfZ, v (1957), 139.

[23] Thalmann, pp. 167 ff.; Kochan, pp. 76 ff. Following decrees of 12 Nov. 1938 the Jews were also burdened with payment of one milliard RM as 'atonement' and with the costs of the damage caused by the pogrom. They were also completely ousted from the German economy. Cf. H. Genschel, Die Verdrängung der Juden aus der Wirtschaft im Dritten Reich, Göttingen, 1966, pp. 186 ff.

[24] BAK, R58/1094, SD-Jahresbericht für 1938, pp. 25–34.

[25] The number of Jews resident in Bavaria (excluding the Palatinate) was given as 14,684 in the 1939 census, i.e. 59.7 per cent of the number of Jews (24,580) in Bavaria on 1 Oct. 1938. Cf. Ophir, Die jüd. Gemeinden, p. 24; HStA, MInn 73726.

[26] Cf. BAK, Zsg.102/13, fol. 19 for Goebbels's press directive. There is a translation in Docs. on Nazism, pp. 335–6. The newspapers were allowed to state 'that here and there windows had been broken and that synagogues had gone up in flames' but there were to be no front-page headlines, no pictures, and no collective reports from the Reich.

shocked inhabitants of the cities and larger towns had the
appalling evidence of smashed windows, demolished property, and burnt-out synagogues before their very eyes on the
morning of 10 November.[27] Outside the towns there were
fewer signs of destruction, though word of the devastation
in the cities travelled rapidly. The pogrom was throughout
the Reich largely an urban phenomenon, except in the few
areas where rural Jewish settlement was still prominent,[28]
and the scale of the pogrom corresponded largely to the size
of the resident Jewish population and the level of radicality
of the local Party organizations.

In Upper Bavaria few cases of violence and destruction
were recorded outside the city of Munich. Jews were often
forced to leave their place of residence immediately or within
a few hours, to offer their property for sale, and to sign an
agreement never to return. Many were handed over to the
police and kept in custody.[29] The attitude of the local Party
leadership was crucial in determining the limits of the 'action'.
In Garmisch-Partenkirchen, for example, where Party and SA
hotheads demanded 'energetic action' against the Jews, the
local Party functionaries were able to cool things down,
'avoid excesses', and direct the matter 'into orderly channels'.
The forty or so Jews in the district were summoned by the
District Leader and forced to sign a declaration that they
would depart from the area immediately.[30]

In Lower Franconia, on the other hand, where so many
Jews still lived in the countryside, the pogrom split into a
myriad of local actions in small towns and rural districts.
The population in this area was to a far greater extent witness

[27] For Munich, see Hanke, p. 218; for Nuremberg, cf. F. Nadler, *Eine Stadt
im Schatten Streichers*, Nuremberg, 1969, pp. 10 f.
[28] This was especially the case in Lower Franconia, where on the eve of the
pogrom Jews were still resident in every administrative district, as opposed to
the other regions where large tracts were already being recorded as 'free of Jews'
— HStA, MInn 73726.
[29] GStA, MA 106671, RPvOB, 10 Dec. 1938.
[30] StAM, LRA 61616, BA Garmisch, 10 Nov. 1938. The few Jews still resident in the Berchtesgaden district were similarly ordered to leave the area within
an hour — StAM, LRA 29655, BA Berchtesgaden, 5 Dec. 1938. Cf. also E.R.
Behrend-Rosenfeld, *Ich stand nicht allein. Erlebnisse einer Jüdin in Deutschland
1933–1944*, Hamburg, 1949, p. 69.

to the devastation and many experienced at first hand the merciless fate of the Jews. In Swabia, Lower Bavaria, and the Upper Palatinate the horrific scenes took place, outside Augsburg and Regensburg, mainly in small towns like Memmingen, Altenstadt, Amberg, Straubing, and Neumarkt in der Oberpfalz.[31] In Streicher-dominated Middle Franconia the pogrom was especially brutal. Provisional and incomplete figures listed 42 synagogues, 115 shops or businesses, and 594 residences destroyed.[32] The events in Streicher's own city of Nuremberg were as terrible as anywhere in Germany.[33] In contrast to Munich, where for a big city there was relatively little destruction but widescale arrests of male Jews, in Nuremberg — according to Jewish eye-witnesses — there were few arrests but hundreds of houses and dwellings were laid waste.[34] Four weeks after the pogrom, the Government President of Upper and Middle Franconia could register with satisfaction the fact that the towns of Dinkelsbühl, Eichstätt, Schwabach, Zirndorf, and the rural districts of Hersbruck, Neustadt an der Aisch, Nuremberg, Pegnitz, Rothenburg ob der Tauber, and Staffelstein were 'Jew-free'.[35]

Reports of the Government Presidents which spoke of people's 'disgust', 'indignation', and even 'sheer fury' at the news of vom Rath's murder were probably accurate enough.[36] Even stronger emotions were released, however, by the ensuing pogrom. A broad swell of disapproval, unmistakable despite the intimidation, found muted expression in the comments of reporters. Most people were too afraid to speak openly, but muttered invectives and words of disgust at the

[31] GStA, MA 106683, RPvS, 7 Dec. 1938; MA 106673, RPvNB/OP, 8 Dec. 1938; D. Linn, *Das Schicksal der jüdischen Bevölkerung in Memmingen von 1933–1945*, Stuttgart, 1968, pp. 41–7.

[32] GStA, MA 106678, RPvOF/MF, 8 Dec. 1938.

[33] WL, PIIe/765, B. Kolb, 'Juden in Nürnberg' (typescript), pp. 22 ff., 51 ff.; Müller, pp. 240–5 (largely based on Kolb); Nadler, pp. 11 ff.

[34] WL, B28, 15 Nov. 1938; B65, 22 Nov. 1938; cf. also B74 and PIId/37 for further descriptions of events in Nuremberg. For Wagner's provisional estimates of damage in Munich, see GStA, Reichsstatthalter 823 and MA 106412, fos. 3–6.

[35] GStA, MA 106678, RPvOF/MF, 8 Dec. 1938. Four of these districts had no resident Jews in the weeks preceding the pogrom — HStA, MInn 73726.

[36] GStA, MA 106671, RPvOB, 10 Dec. 1938; MA 106673, RPvNB/OP, 8 Dec. 1938; MA 106683, RPvS, 7 Dec. 1938; MA 106678, RPvOF/MF, 8 Dec. 1938; MA 106681, RPvUF, 9 Dec. 1938.

barbarity of the action and shame and horror at what had taken place could be observed in Munich as in other major German cities.[37] In a smaller town like Memmingen, where the organized destruction of the synagogue and accompanying outrages took place a day later than everywhere else in the Reich, both approving and disapproving voices could be heard from the assembled crowd, though most were careful to hold their tongues.[38] Mixed reactions — partly approval, partly indifference, partly silent sympathy for the Jews — could, it was claimed, be perceived among the inhabitants of Heilbrunn, near Bad Tölz, in Upper Bavaria.[39] The *Gendarmerie* officer in the Upper Palatinate district of Vilseck felt able to establish only a single type of reaction: 'The action carried out a short time ago against the Jews was here ignored and passed over.'[40] This may well have been a not untypical reaction in many districts where the pogrom hardly left a mark.

Goebbels's claim that the pogrom had been the 'spontaneous answer' of the German people to the murder of vom Rath was universally recognized as ludicrous. It was perfectly obvious that the whole affair had been directed and orchestrated by the Party — all the more so where the demolition had been carried out by SA squads brought in from outside.[41] Most 'non-organized' Germans knew nothing about the pogrom until confronted with the debris-laden streets the following morning. If there were no signs of spontaneity, willing helpers from the public were not lacking in some places, usually where radical anti-Semites had held

---

[37] Behrend-Rosenfeld, p. 72; cf. also, R. Andreas-Friedrich, *Der Schattenmann*, Berlin, 1947, pp. 28 ff. for reactions in Berlin, and *Docs. on Nazism*, pp. 472–4 for Leipzig.
[38] Linn, pp. 43 ff.
[39] StAM, LRA 134059, GS Heilbrunn, 26 Nov. 1938.
[40] StAA, BA Amberg 2399, GS Vilseck, 23 Nov. 1938. Many *Gendarmerie* reports from rural areas did not mention the pogrom at all.
[41] Linn, pp. 42 f.; StAW, LRA Bad Neustadt 125/4, BA Bad Neustadt, 28 Nov. 1938. The Government President of Upper Bavaria reported that 'the protest action was widely regarded as organized' — GStA, MA 106671, RPvOB, 10 Dec. 1938. That the whole affair had been seen to be directed and orchestrated by the Party was recognized even by the Nazi Party's Supreme Court in its investigations of murders committed during the pogrom — Cf. H. Graml, *Der 9. November 1938. 'Reichskristallnacht'*, Bonn, 1953, p. 16.

leading positions in the local Party for years and had been able successfully to poison the atmosphere against the Jews.[42] Bystanders were sometimes more than ready to join in the work of destruction and in anti-Jewish abuse which added to the evil climate and spurred on the demolition teams. While the Nuremberg synagogue burned, for instance, 'the hysterical voice of a woman' was heard from the crowd by one eye-witness (a non-Jew) crying: 'Sling the Jewish pack into the fire.'[43] A similar cry of 'throw them in the fire' was said to have come from among the assembled crowd in Kitzingen as the arrested Jews were being led past the still burning synagogue, and schoolchildren showered choruses of scorn and abuse on the unhappy internees all along the way to the prison house.[44] The youth of Memmingen amused themselves by making fun of the Jewish hats removed from the synagogue while groups of spectators spoke approvingly of the demolition of the building, remarking that it should have been carried out long ago.[45]

Some *Gendarmerie* reports went so far as to suggest that the population had for the most part regarded the 'retaliatory measures' against the Jews as wholly justified. Fanatical Party and Hitler Youth members in some Upper Franconian villages were even said to have regarded the 'action' as too mild.[46] In one Lower Franconian district, where people with a macabre curiosity went on sightseeing tours of the wreckage, the local police reported that the attacks on Jews and their property had been 'greeted with joy' by the majority of the population.[47] Some of these reports are barely credible as generalizations and were obviously written with a view to providing superiors with the story it was thought they wanted to hear. In so doing they were justifying too, the propaganda myth of the demonstrated unity of leadership and people in the anti-Jewish 'demonstrations'. What

[42] Graml, *Der 9. Nov.*, pp. 7–14.
[43] Nadler, p. 13, eye-witness report of the Nuremberg journalist Otto Fischer.
[44] WL, 'Der 10. November', p. 14.
[45] Linn, p. 42.
[46] StAB, K8/III/18473, GS Muggendorf, 26 Nov. 1938; GS Waischenfeld, 25 Nov. 1938.
[47] StAW, LRA Bad Neustadt 125/5, GS Sandberg, 28 Nov. 1938.

percentage of the population approved of the deplorable
events is impossible to assess. Critical evaluation of the
reports, however, hardly permits any doubt that few other
than wild fanatics in the Party and its affiliations unreservedly
welcomed the 'Jewish Action'. On the basis of an admittedly
small and unrepresentative sample of Party members, Michael
Müller-Claudius's subtly executed private survey of opinion
suggested in fact that only about 5 per cent fully approved
of the pogrom as against 63 per cent who displayed some
form of disgust or anger and 32 per cent who were reserved
or indifferent in their comments.[48] Bavarian reports support
the view that the torrent of violence and destruction not only
met with little sympathy, but was 'condemned deep into the
ranks of the Party'.[49] According to a report from the Amberg
district of the Upper Palatinate, 'not one person up to now
has said that the Jews got what they deserved.'[50] Reports
from Upper Bavaria indicate that criticism of the violence
employed against the Jews was especially prevalent in Catholic
circles and among the 'upper classes'.[51] Catholic peasants and
the bourgeoisie were said to have regarded the show of violence as an affront to 'culture and decency', going too far
even for those who were glad to see the Jews driven out of
the country.[52] Even in Franconia voices were heard to the
effect that 'the older Jews ought not to have been treated
like that.'[53]

In Franconia too, as Jewish 'eye-witness reports' compiled
soon after the event point out, it was in Catholic rural
districts that the most vociferous condemnation of the barbarity was heard. The Catholic population of Lohr, a small
town in Lower Franconia, was said to have been 'very angry

[48] Müller-Claudius, pp. 162 ff.
[49] GStA, MA 106673, RPvNB/OP, 8 Dec. 1938.
[50] StAA, BA Amberg 2399, GS Freihung, 23 Nov. 1938.
[51] GStA, MA 106671, RPvOB, 10 Dec. 1938; StAM, LRA 29654, GS
Reichenhall, 30 Nov. 1938; GS Markt Schellenberg, 30 Nov. 1938; LRA 29655,
BA Berchtesgaden, 5 Dec. 1938.
[52] StAM, NSDAP 983, KW Traunstein, Abschn. Haslach, 19 Nov. 1938;
Abschn. Marquartstein, 19 Nov., 13 Dec. 1938; LRA 61616, GS Wallgau, 26
Nov. 1938; LRA 113813, GS Feilnbach, 17 Nov. 1938; LRA 47140, GS Bad
Aibling, 20 Nov. 1938.
[53] StAB, K8/III/18473, GS Heiligenstadt, 25 Nov. 1938.

about these atrocities'; one woman protested openly and was threatened with arrest.[54] Many Catholics in Gaukönigshofen made what was described as 'a true pilgrimage' to the burnt-out synagogue on the Sunday after the pogrom, making open show of their disgust. Peasants from the neighbouring villages boycotted a public house in Ochsenfurt when they heard that the son of the owner had taken part in the destruction in Gaukönigshofen.[55] In Höchberg, not far from Würzburg, the peasants protested in vain at the burning of the synagogue by a detachment of sixteen SA men who had been detailed to the village, expressed regret and disgust over what had happened, and viewed the sudden death of one of the participants six months later as a just punishment of God.[56] In Fischbach in Swabia, in the Augsburg area, even the mayor had taken a stance against the intended burning of the synagogue, declaring that 'we are no incendiarists', and was actually able to prevent the destruction taking place. Four days after 'Crystal Night' Jewish services were held there again.[57]

Though Catholic peasants were particularly prominent in their denunciation of the pogrom, critical comments came from members of all social classes, as the records of the Munich 'Special Court' show. A master cobbler from Ruhpolding was denounced by SA men for saying that the demolition of property amounted to robbery of the Jews by the Führer.[58] A salesman, once a Party and SA member, was accused of telling three soldiers in a Munich public house that burning the churches of the Jews was a wrongful act, and that in his view all men were equal.[59] A former Freikorps leader and high-ranking Munich police officer who had fought against the Räterepublik was also denounced for condemning the burning of the synagogues as a scandal.[60] A well-to-do lady from the Füssen area had her letter to a friend in America, in which she referred to the pogrom as a 'cultural disgrace' (Kulturschande) and reported widespread

[54] WL, 'Der 10. November', p. 12; cf. ibid., pp. 6, 33 for Schweinfurt and Bamberg.
[55] Ibid., pp. 18f.
[56] Ibid., p. 26.
[57] Ibid., p. 38.   [58] StAM, SGM 4656.
[59] Ibid., 4700.   [60] Ibid., 4604.

unhappiness about it, intercepted by the border police.[61] The impressions of a Munich Jew who lived through the pogrom confirm the feelings of disgust, apparent in all sections of society. One 'aryan lady of the best social class', previously completely unknown to him, declared herself ashamed to be a German, and 'one of the top Munich bankers' begged him to spread the word abroad 'that 90 per cent of the German people is opposed to these ill-deeds. It is only a small clique which has caused this disaster.'[62] Reports reaching the Sopade and other exiled left-wing groups were also unanimous about the sharp condemnation of the outrages by the great majority of the German people, and eyewitnesses recounted the unmistakable abhorrence and many expressions of sympathy for the Jews.[63] Though the exiled anti-Nazi groups were keen to illustrate a broad popular front against the regime, such comments concur wholly with those from all other sources.

Examples abound, both in the Jewish eye-witness accounts and in the Sopade reports, of expressions of sympathy, abhorrence, and shame coming in particular from members of the bourgeoisie.[64] Many who sympathized with much of what Nazism stood for obviously felt this was going too far. A feeling of 'cultural disgrace' and damage to the German image abroad, as in the examples given above, combined with anger at the senseless destruction of property and with humanitarian feelings. One anonymous letter, apparently from a conservative bourgeois Nazi sympathizer in Schweinfurt and addressed to Goebbels, bitterly attacked the spoliation, plunder, useless waste, and endangering of German farm property in the vicinity of the burning synagogues. The writer also pilloried, however, the gratuitous violence and

---

[61] Ibid., 4655.

[62] WL, B66, eye-witness account of Arthur Berg of Munich, recorded in Amsterdam, 22 Nov. 1938.

[63] DBS, 10 Dec. 1938, pp. A44 ff.; Deutsche Mitteilungen, 19 Nov., 22 Nov. 1938, 7 Jan., 25 Feb. 1939 (copies in WL). The newly published article by W.S. Allen, 'Die deutsche Öffentlichkeit und die "Reichskristallnacht" — Konflikte zwischen Werthierarchie und Propaganda im Dritten Reich', in Peukert/Reulecke (eds.), Die Reihen fast geschlossen, pp. 397–411, makes much use of the Sopade material.

[64] Cf. Kershaw, 'Persecution', pp. 278–9.

inhumane treatment even of the elderly and infirm. Not least he was concerned about the damage to Germany's reputation as a civilized nation. His letter ended:

One could weep, one must be ashamed to be a German, part of an aryan noble people (*Edelvolk*), a civilized nation guilty of such a cultural disgrace. Later generations will compare these atrocities with the times of the witch-trials. And nobody dares to say a word against them, though 85 per cent of the population is angry as never before. Poor Germany, wake up properly at last![65]

Other sources make equally clear that a strong motive for the condemnation of the pogrom in the eyes of many people was the futile destruction of property. According to some reports, people deplored such destruction in the light of the needs of the Four Year Plan and said it would have been better to impose a second milliard Reichsmarks as a 'fine' on top of the milliard which had been 'legally' claimed as retribution for the damage 'caused' by the Jews.[66] Given raw material shortages and intense pressure to save and conserve, the wanton demolition and casual wastage — even to the extent of hurling foodstuffs onto the streets — met with a mixture of incomprehension and rage.[67] As one report put it: 'On the one hand we have to collect silver paper and empty toothpaste tubes, and on the other hand millions of marks' worth of damage is caused deliberately.'[68]

As this and other evidence shows, objections to the spoliation and plunder of 'Crystal Night' were wholly compatible with unreserved approval of the draconian but 'legal' form of 'punishment' which the State itself decreed in the immediate aftermath of the pogrom. The response to the 'legal' measures[69] of 1938 was as positive and uncritical as it had been to the Nuremberg Laws of 1935. The Government President of Swabia reported, for example, that the decrees

[65] GStA, Reichsstatthalter 823.
[66] E.g., StAW, LRA Alzenau Bd.5/2, GS Alzenau, 28 Nov. 1938.
[67] StAW, LRA Bad Neustadt 125/4, BA Bad Neustadt, 28 Nov. 1938; LRA Bad Neustadt 125/5, GS Bad Neustadt, 28 Nov. 1938; GS Oberelsbach, 28 Nov. 1938; GS Sandberg, 28 Nov. 1938; StAB, K8/III/18473, GS Waischenfeld, 25 Nov. 1938; BA Ebermannstadt, 2 Dec. 1938; GStA, MA 106681, RPvUF, 9 Dec. 1938; MA 106673, RPvNB/OP, 8 Dec. 1938; MA 106671, RPvOB, 10 Dec. 1938.
[68] StAA, BA Amberg 2399, GS Hirschau, 23 Nov. 1938.
[69] For these measures cf. *Reichsgesetzblatt* (1938), 1579 ff.

of the government, especially the imposition of the 'expiation payment' and the measures to remove Jews from the economy were 'generally appreciated and — especially the economic measures — approved in principle by ever more national comrades.'[70] In contrast to the pogrom itself, the 'legal' measures against the Jews also found 'fullest understanding' in Lower Bavaria and the Upper Palatinate.[71] In Lower Franconia, where there was also general approval, it was said to be the 'expiation fine' which was particularly welcomed.[72] These generalizations of the Government Presidents find frequent confirmation in the reports of the lower authorities.

A widespread hostility to the Jews, uncritical approval of the anti-Semitic decrees of the government, but sharp condemnation of the pogrom because of its material destruction and the tasteless hooligan character of the 'action' perpetrated by 'gutter elements' characterized the reactions of considerable sections of the population. Even many anti-Semites, including Party members, found the pogrom itself distasteful while approving of the root cause of it and of its consequences.

The picture of responses to the 'Crystal Night' seems for the most part, therefore, a rather dismal one in which material self-interest and legal rectitude prevailed over humanitarian considerations. Yet to leave it there would be to ignore another, more appealing, side of the popular reaction to the pogrom: its rejection on grounds of Christian compassion and common humanity. Jewish eye-witness accounts abound with references to the kindness of 'aryan' and 'Christian' neighbours and are anxious to point out the overwhelming rejection of the pogrom by the vast majority of the population. Even the Government President of Lower Bavaria and the Upper Palatinate had to admit that the pogrom had 'unnecessarily' allowed 'sympathy for the Jews in town and countryside' to emerge.[73] Especially in Catholic country districts it was clear

[70] GStA, MA 106683, RPvS, 7 Dec. 1938.
[71] GStA, MA 106673, RPvNB/OP, 8 Dec. 1938.
[72] GStA, MA 106681, RPvUF, 9 Dec. 1938.
[73] GStA, MA 106673, RPvNB/OP, 8 Dec. 1938. An Upper Bavarian NSLB functionary reported similarly: 'The action against the Jews awakened great

that the Nazi message of racial hatred had made only limited inroads. Numerous witnesses from Lower Franconia and the Catholic parts of Upper Franconia confirm that help and sympathy was afforded Jews by 'aryan' neighbours during and after the night of terror. In Prichsenstadt, for example, a farmer ordered a taxi and accompanied a Jewish lady in his village to Schweinfurt to warn her husband that he was being sought out for arrest. The farmer was denounced by the owner of the taxi and spent a fortnight in prison as a result. In Schweinfurt, 'Christian neighbours' brought the children of a Jewish family fresh milk and bedding. In Burgsinn Jews were given money, fresh clothing, bread, and other foodstuffs by local inhabitants. An 'aryan' in Unteraltertheim near Würzburg prevented the house of a Jewish neighbour from being destroyed by threatening the SA men with a revolver if they did not disappear. They left. Peasants in Nördlingen gave a Jewess, whose husband had been arrested, a sack of potatoes and asked whether she was otherwise well provided for. Even the Nazi leader in Asbach, near Bamberg, was said to have shown concern for the Jews, and in other instances Nazi mayors prevented destruction or offered assistance to Jews.[74] Jews who experienced the pogrom in Munich were lavish in their praise of the sympathetic response they encountered among non-Jewish people, as in the following comment by a Jewish emigrant written a few days later:

The mood among the Christian population in Munich is wholly against the action. I encountered the most expressive sympathy and compassion from all sides. It had been generally presumed that the houses would be attacked on the Friday evening (11 November). Aryan people from the area, unknown to me, offered to accommodate my family for the night. Despite the ban on sales to Jews, grocers asked Jews whether they needed anything, bakers delivered bread irrespective of the ban etc. All Christians behaved impeccably.[75]

There were few occasions, if any, in the Third Reich which produced such a widespread wave of revulsion — much of it

<hr />

sympathy in these [church] circles — the poor Jews' (the last three words underlined in red) — StAM, NSDAP 983, Kreisamtsleiter Erding, 21 Nov. 1938.

[74] WL, 'Der 10. Nov.', pp. 5 f, 8, 28 f, 35 ff.

[75] WL, B66; cf. also Behrend-Rosenfeld, pp. 73, 76 ff. and Hanke, p. 218.

on moral grounds – as the 'Crystal Night' pogrom.[76] Even the SD had to admit in its general retrospective survey that from this point of view the 'actions against the Jews' had been less than successful: 'From a basic liberal attitude many believed they had openly to stand up for the Jews. The destruction of the synagogues was declared to be irresponsible. People stood up for the "poor repressed Jews".'[77] As this and much other evidence indicates, reactions to 'Crystal Night' in Bavaria were little different in essence from those registered all over Germany.[78]

The clumsy alienation of German popular opinion through the pogrom seems to have persuaded the Nazi leadership that such a tactic should never again be tried, and that anti-Jewish measures should take a more 'rational' course. Though, from the regime's point of view, the pogrom was successful in forcing the pace of a solution to the Jewish Question, the hostility which leading Nazis showed towards Goebbels, the instigator of the pogrom, may well have been influenced by the negative public response. Similarly, Hitler's announcement – against the pressure of the radicals – that there should be no public identification badge for Jews was possibly a veiled reflection of the negative reactions to anti-Jewish measures.[79] And a year later, following the attempt on Hitler's life in the Munich *Bürgerbräukeller* in November 1939, on the anniversary of the pogrom, Rudolf Hess specifically prohibited a repetition in order to prevent any unrest in the first critical months of the war.[80]

The influence of popular opinion extended no further. This was in great measure a reflection of the conditions of extreme terror and intimidation in which people lived, and which were of themselves sufficient to deter any *organized* pressure of opinion on the regime. Reports of arrests and

---

[76] Kulka's view that 'most did not denounce the atrocities against the Jews, but protested against the destruction of German property' is, as we have seen, a far too sweeping generalization – Cf. Kulka, p. XLIV.

[77] BAK, R58/1094, fol. 109.

[78] Cf. the evidence surveyed in Kershaw, 'Persecution', pp. 275–81; Allen, 'Die deutsche Öffentlichkeit', pp. 397–411, and Gordon, pp. 184 ff.

[79] Cf. D. Orlow, *The History of the Nazi Party, ii, 1933–1945*, Newton Abbot, 1973, pp. 250–1.

[80] Ibid., p. 265, n. 8.

recrimination for pro-Jewish comments, assistance to Jews, or criticism of Nazi actions abound in the sources.[81] Summarizing the impressions of their reporters, the *Sopade* admitted 'that however great the general indignation might be, the brutalities of the pogrom hordes had increased their intimidation and consolidated the notion in the population that all resistance was useless against the unrestrained National Socialist power.'[82] Moreover, without support *from above* popular opinion was bound to remain inchoate and inarticulate. The one source this could — and arguably ought to — have come from was the leadership of the Christian Churches. Apart from much success in orchestrating popular opposition in the 'Church struggle', the Churches came, in 1941, to lead a victory without parallel for public opinion in halting the 'euthanasia action'. It happened because the Churches made a public cause of concern their own.[83] In the case of the Jews, the Churches took no such stance.

Despite the largely negative response to the pogrom, popular opinion on the Jewish Question remained in any case divided. As the evidence we have examined clearly suggests, the Nazis had been unable to instil an active hatred for the Jews into the bulk of the population — in Müller-Claudius's terminology, to transform the latent 'static hatred' into 'dynamic hatred'[84] — and to this extent had met with less than success in a key area of their ideology. On the other hand, the unceasing barrage of anti-Jewish propaganda had not been without effect. People's minds were increasingly poisoned against the Jews in at least an abstract way; the conviction was spreading that there *was* a Jewish Question.[85] In November 1938, as earlier, it was therefore the method rather than the aim of Nazi policy which most people were condemning. Just as the Nuremberg Laws of 1935 had been widely acclaimed in contrast to the condemnation of the

---

[81] E.g., WL, PIId/760; PIId/40; PIId/528; 'Der 10. Nov.', p. 5.

[82] DBS, 10 Dec. 1938, p. A44 and cf. also p. A46.

[83] Cf. below, Chapter 8.

[84] Müller-Claudius, pp. 76-9, 157 ff.

[85] A *Sopade* report from Berlin in 1936 concluded: 'In general terms one can say that the Nazis have indeed brought off a deepening of the gap between the people and the Jews. The feeling that the Jews are another race is today a general one' — DBS, 11 Feb. 1936, pp. A17-18.

primitive brutality of the 'individual actions', so now approval
for the 'legal measures' was juxtaposed with wide condemnation of the brutality and destruction of the pogrom itself.
'Anti-Semitism − o.k., but not like that'[86] seems to sum up
much of the mainstream response to 'Crystal Night', and to
the chequered course of Nazi radical attempts to solve the
Jewish Question before 1938. Despite the widespread rejection of the archaic 'pogrom anti-Semitism', there was,
therefore, extensive acceptance of the 'rational anti-Semitism' whose victory was sealed by the public reactions to
'Crystal Night'.

Furthermore, dissent at the method of proceeding on the
Jewish Question was also perfectly compatible with general
approval of Hitler's leadership and of the main aims of
German policy under Nazi rule. As one *Sopade* observer
pointed out, the view continued to be expressed that the
extremes of Jewish policy took place against Hitler's wishes.
'Hitler certainly wants the Jews to disappear from Germany,
but he does not want them to be beaten to death and treated
in such fashion': such comments could be frequently heard
and, it had to be admitted, continued to carry weight.[87]
Though this *Sopade* report came from Berlin, the detachment of Hitler from the misdeeds of his underlings was
equally a prime feature of the Führer image in Bavaria as
elsewhere.[88]

However negative the instant reactions to 'Crystal Night'
were, the pogrom had no lasting impact on the formation of
opinion. Reactions to events of major importance, whether
of euphoria or of revulsion, gave way remarkably quickly to
the sullen apathy and resigned acceptance which characterized
the day-to-day existence of most Germans in the Third Reich.
'Daily routine again already' (*Schon wieder Alltag*), the
heading of the December report of the *Sopade*, summed it
up neatly.[89] The Jewish Question was at the forefront of
popular opinion on very few occasions during the Nazi
dictatorship. The most spectacular occasion was 'Crystal

---

[86] Andreas-Friedrich, p. 32.
[87] DBS, 10 Dec. 1938, p. A48.
[88] Cf. Kershaw, *Hitler-Mythos*, esp. ch. 3.
[89] DBS, 10 Dec. 1938, p. A1.

Night'. But everything points to the fact that this event receded within a few weeks into the dim background of people's consciousness.[90] It had not been something which concerned them directly, nor was it of continuing intensity, and it had been perpetrated on a tiny and basically unloved social minority. Increasingly from November 1938 the Jews were forced to emigrate or to retire wholly into isolation on the fringes of society. Either way, Germans saw less and less of Jews. The dehumanization and social isolation of Jews after the November pogrom could, therefore, only increase the extent of the indifference of the German people towards the fate of the Jews, an indifference which had been but momentarily disturbed by the atrocities of 'Crystal Night'.

Popular opinion on the Jewish Question formed a wide spectrum running from the paranoid Jew-baiters at the one extreme, undoubtedly a tiny minority; through a wide section of the population whose existent prejudices and latent anti-Semitism, influenced in varying degrees by the virulence of Nazi propaganda, accepted legal restrictions on Jews amounting to economic exclusion and social ostracism whilst rejecting the blatant and overt inhumanity of the Jew-baiters; and finally embraced another minority imbued with a deeply Christian or liberal-humanitarian moral sense, whose value-system provided the most effective barrier to the Nazi doctrine of race hatred.

In its attempt to infuse the German people with a dynamic, passionate hatred of the Jews, the Nazi propaganda machine was less than successful. Except on isolated occasions when the Jewish Question directly confronted them, most obviously following the 1938 pogrom, Germans seldom had Jews on their mind. The constant barrage of propaganda failed to make the Jews the prime target of hatred for most Germans, simply because the issue seemed largely abstract, academic, and unrelated to their own problems. The result was, for the

[90] Critical comments about the Jewish Question formed only slightly more than one per cent of the *Heimtücke* cases of the Munich 'Special Court'. Of all the cases concerning the Jews, more than two-thirds were begun in 1938-9, almost a half — overwhelmingly related to 'Crystal Night' — in the five months between November 1938 and the end of March 1939.

most part, widespread disinterest in the Jewish Question. Amid the widespread apathy and disinterest, however, the 'dynamic' hatred of the few, whose numbers included some of the leaders of the Third Reich and among them the Führer himself, could flourish. 'Dynamic' Jew-haters were certainly a small percentage of the population; but active friends of the Jews formed an even smaller proportion. Furthermore, even when opinion was widely antagonistic towards Nazi actions, as in November 1938, it was impossible to articulate it. No political party, interest group, trade union, or Church had made it its job before 1933 to combat openly the dangerous growth of anti-Semitism. After 1933 the task was incomparably more difficult — perhaps impossible. Divisions of opinion, including widespread latent anti-Semitism, were reflected in the Churches themselves. But the reluctance of the Church hierarchies, for whatever motives, to oppose the inhumanity towards the Jews in the 1930s at the same time that they were often vigorously and successfully combating Nazi anti-Church measures, did much to prevent any possibility of anti-Semitism becoming an issue.

Where the Nazis were most successful was in the depersonalization of the Jew. The more the Jew was forced out of social life, the more he seemed to fit the stereotypes of a propaganda which intensified, paradoxically, its campaign against 'Jewry' the fewer actual Jews there were in Germany itself. Depersonalization increased the already existent widespread indifference of German popular opinion and formed a vital stage between the archaic violence of the pogrom and the rationalized 'assembly-line' annihilation of the death-camps.

It would go too far to deny anti-Semitism any 'objective function' of diverting from acute socio-economic problems and especially of translating pseudo-revolutionary energy into apparently realizable goals which in turn could keep alive the utopian vision of a German-dominated 'New Order' in Europe. In this sense, perhaps, one can speak of anti-Semitism functioning as an integrating element. But this was mainly within the ranks of the Nazi Movement itself, above all within the SS. Anti-Semitism provided a common denominator, necessary in a movement which was so obviously a loose coalition of interests as the Nazi Party, and which after 1933 was devoid of any real active political role apart from indoctrination and social control. The energies galvanized within the Movement in the so-called 'years of struggle' could not simply be phased out from 1933, and were necessary to retain the dynamism of Nazism and prevent it from sagging into stagnation. This more or less aimless energy could be manipulated and channelled, as in 1935 and 1938, into attacks on the Jews, and the Jewish Question could function, too, in giving ideological purpose to the 'enforcement agency' of the regime — the SS-Gestapo-SD organization. Party activists needed activity: and anti-Semitism went a long way towards providing the SA and, in practical terms, otherwise useless sections of the Party with something to do, at the same time binding them propagandistically more closely to the apparent 'aims' of Führer and Movement.

In the light of the Bavarian evidence and that from other parts of Germany, however, it would be mistaken to translate this functionalist explanation to the relationship between the regime and the broad mass of the German people. There was certainly extensive manipulation of opinion, and Nazi propaganda could claim some success. But the ideological function of anti-Semitism with regard to the mass of the population consisted at most in strengthening the German identity-feeling and sense of national-consciousness by associating the Jews with Bolshevism and plutocracy and otherwise caricaturing the non-German character of Jewry. Popular support for National Socialism was based in ideological norms which had little directly to do with anti-Semitism and persecution of Jews, and which can be summed up most adequately by the sense of social, political, and moral order embodied in the term *Volksgemeinschaft* ('National Community'), ensured by a strong state which would suppress conflict to guarantee strength through unity.[91] While Jews and other minority groups, it is true, found no place in the Nazi concept of this 'national community', their exclusion was hardly a leading feature of the hopes and aspirations of the millions who, in

---

[91] Though couched in populist-nationalist language, the class nature of these sentiments implied by the *Volksgemeinschaft* concept needs no emphasis.

the chaos of the Depression, were prepared to entrust the building of this new Germany to Hitler.

The permanent radicalization of the anti-Jewish policies of the regime can hardly be said, on the evidence we have considered, to have been the product of, or to have corresponded to, the strong demands of popular opinion. It led in 1935 and 1938 to a drop in prestige for the Party, which might even have had repercussions for Hitler's own nimbus had he been seen to have supported and sided with the radicals. The radicalization of the negative dynamism, which formed the essential driving-force of the Nazi Party, found remarkably little echo in the mass of the population. Popular opinion, largely indifferent and infused with a latent anti-Jewish feeling further bolstered by propaganda, provided the climate within which spiralling Nazi aggression towards Jews could take place unchallenged. But it did not provoke the radicalization in the first place. The road to Auschwitz was built by hate, but paved with indifference.

PART TWO
SOCIAL UNITY THROUGH WAR?
THE 'COMMUNITY OF FATE',
1939–1945

'Whatever great suffering should fall on the individual German in the next months or years, it will be easy to bear in the consciousness of the indissoluble community which encompasses and embraces our entire great nation', *Hitler, 19 September 1939*.

'Most people are sick from pure anger in their belly; it's time the swindle stopped', *Opinion in Lower Franconia, 1941, as reported by the SD*.

'There can be no talk of a National Community. Each thinks only of his own advantage', *Report from an Upper Franconian village, 1941*.

7. The Economic Pressures of War

The nub of the Nazi social message was that Germany's former class-ridden society had been replaced by a class- and status-transcending 'national community' (*Volksgemeinschaft*), where the only differences between equal members of the nation were those resulting from ability and achievement. From what we saw in earlier chapters which explored the subjective responses of the peasantry, the working class, and varied sections of the middle class, the most obvious propaganda failure of the Nazis was their inability, in the light of the social and economic reality of the Third Reich, to make this social message sound convincing. Whatever the partial penetration of other aspects of Nazi ideology, the 'National Community' idea had long before the war been exposed for the sham it always was. And though in Nazi mythology war was to be the ultimate experience binding together all classes of society in *Heimat* and *Front* in a 'community of fate' (*Schicksalsgemeinschaft*) engaged in the nation's fight for survival, the years 1939–45 were to demonstrate instead, beneath the superficial veneer of a united *Volk*, the complete bankruptcy of the Nazi social ideal.

In this chapter we examine the response of the Bavarian peasantry, working class, and — more briefly because of the limitations of the source material — sections of the middle class to the growing economic pressures of war. Unlike the situation in Britain, where there was a sharp shift to a wartime economy at the outbreak of hostilities, changes in Germany amounted, before the 'total war' phase from early 1943, largely to a tightening of the screw for a society already bent under quasi-war-economy pressures since 1936 at the latest. The trends in opinion which find expression in the following pages are, therefore, recognizably a continuation of those established by the pre-war framework: they were in the main a product of Nazism more than a direct product of the war itself.

(i) The Peasantry

The war brought no immediate and fundamental alteration in the pattern of German farming.[1] War conditions prompted extensive intervention by the State in the economy of all countries and in the liberties of the individual. The German peasant had, however, already been greatly affected by such changes during the 1930s. By the outbreak of war he had lived and worked for six years within the strait-jacket of Reich Food Estate control and for most of that time had been told he was engaged in a 'battle for production' to secure the nation's food supply. The negative responses among the Bavarian peasantry to the Reich Food Estate, the Nazi Party, and to the regime's agricultural policies were, as we saw in Chapter 1, in large measure shaped by the creeping extension of the 'coercive economy' bringing, as the peasant saw it, intolerable restrictions on his freedom of action, his disadvantages in relation to other social classes, and the hardships resulting from the critical shortage of labour which was casting its shadow over the entire rural economy. In each case the war brought a decided accentuation of an existing problem rather than a completely new situation. There were, however, some new issues which had a bearing on peasant mentality and opinion during the war. Among these were relations with the large numbers of prisoners-of-war and 'foreign workers' (*Fremdarbeiter*) who were compelled to work in the German rural economy; the influx of ever-increasing numbers of evacuees once the obliteration of major north-German cities became an Allied tactic from 1942; and finally, though in smaller measure than during the First World War, the 'black economy' of marketeering and hoarding as townspeople roamed through country districts buying up all they could for themselves or for sale on the black market.[2]

For very many peasants — now including even large numbers of smallholders, where the farmer was called up for

---

[1] Cf. in general Farquharson, ch. 14.

[2] For the massive extent and damaging effects of hoarding during the First World War in Bavaria, see Ay, *Entstehung*, pp. 159-78.

military service — the main problem remained the shortage of labour. Call-ups for the *Wehrmacht* made the existing grave problem even more acute and continued to be among the greatest sources of agrarian unrest. Between May 1939 and May 1943 the number of active men in the German farm economy fell from almost five to only three-and-a-quarter millions. Quantitatively this drop was more than made up by the employment by May 1943 of some 700,000 prisoners-of-war and as many as 1,500,000 'foreign workers' in farming. Qualitatively, however, the often only grudgingly co-operative foreign workers were regarded as no substitute for the loss of labour to the *Wehrmacht*.[3] Just as before the war, mechanization of agriculture to make up for the shortfall of labour was out of the question: steel was needed for tanks, not tractors, and in any case there was no fuel left over for farm machines. The result was a move in the course of the war to more extensive forms of agriculture with a drop in yield per hectare and a reduction of the amount of land sown with crops.[4]

That is not to say that farmers were necessarily badly off during the war. The thriving black market, despite draconian penalties, suggests the profits to be made by peasants exploiting their monopoly of that most precious commodity — food. Compared with most other Germans, the peasant himself had more than enough to eat, experienced no housing shortage, and did not have to live under the daily threat from the skies as did the city dwellers. Even so, much evidence points to a continued acute sense of exploitation among the peasantry, prompting deep antipathy towards Party and regime, aloofness from the 'great events' of the war itself, and overwhelming preoccupation with material self-interest — above all else the difficulties of acquiring sufficient farm labour. The reports create a strong impression, in fact, that for a long time the war simply meant for many peasants the loss of their labourers to the army with attendant increased problems in running the farm. Only in the last years of the war, as its horrors struck home and the German people

---

[3] Cf. Farquharson, pp. 232-7.
[4] Ibid., pp. 238-9.

became directly confronted with the stark reality of total defeat did the peasant become fully aware of horizons wider than those of his own farmyard.

The low morale among the peasantry noted by practically all reporters at the time of the invasion of Poland was immediately worsened by the impact of the new war-economy regulations aimed at securing the provision of fats and milk products. As had been the case with the pre-war regulation of milk marketing, the new measures — for example, restrictions on the sale of whole milk by individuals and the channelling of all sales through dairies — met with anger and bitter complaints about the loss of the farmer's freedom to dispose of his own products and the financial exploitation of the producer as a result of dairies paying prices much lower than could be had on the open market. The *Landrat* of one dairy-farming area in Lower Bavaria reported 'a blow to the mood of the population, the effects of which cannot at all yet be assessed' as a consequence of such measures.[5] This was of course a typical exaggeration. Not all farmers were equally affected by the new regulations, and the anger of those who felt most aggrieved subsided after a short time and in any case led to no political action, such as refusal to co-operate with the measures. Even so, the resentment created smouldered on for months.

More widespread, and more serious for the authorities, were the problems of the labour shortage, now even more sharply highlighted through call-ups for the army in the Polish campaign. Similar reactions were registered on this issue in all parts of Bavaria. According to the Government President of Upper and Middle Franconia, whose comments were representative of the tone of all other reports, the unevenness of conscription and the sluggish demobilization following the short Polish campaign — which took place during the harvest season — caused much grievance. It seemed perverse to many that older men, owners of farms, should be called up for service while younger men were left at home.

[5] GStA, MA 106673, RPvNB/OP, 9 Oct. 1939. Cf. also MA 106671, RPvOB, 9 Oct., 11 Dec. 1939.

Farmers complained that they had been promised early release to attend to their holdings and claimed they could easily have been replaced in Poland by younger able-bodied men. In times of dire need, they said, they were only too willing to fight to the last man 'for people and country', but as it was 'they had to idle away so much time, while at home their labour was so urgently needed.'[6] Such a mood was naturally not greatly improved by soldiers' tales about playing cards for days on end and having nothing at all to do.[7] The question of call-up and release from the armed forces, especially that of categorization as 'reserved occupation' (*uk-Stellung, unabkömmlich gestellt*) and hence ineligibility for service, was throughout the war to be the source of anger, bitterness, envy, and corruption, renting many village communities. Arguments about favouritism of one farmer rather than another and allegations of greater concern for the welfare of the farm than for armed service prompted numerous remarks by the reporting authorities about the 'lack of enthusiasm for war among the rural population' in contrast to the sole motivation of 'self-interest' (*Eigennutz*), and of peasants not displaying a suitable degree of national feeling and awareness of Germany's current position.[8] Not the war so much as the labour question was 'for the rural population the question of the moment'.[9]

The difficulty of mobilizing the peasantry psychologically to play their part in the nation's struggle was still greatly hindered by communications problems. One report demanded urgent measures to make possible a far wider reception of radio broadcasts by the farming population 'in order to get at these groups which are politically and ideologically not easily reachable'. The 'possibilities of influence' were limited, it was pointed out, not only by the absence of radios but also by the shortage of batteries for the many with battery sets.[10]

  [6] GStA, MA 106678, RPvOF/MF, 7 Dec. 1939.
  [7] GStA, MA 106681, RPvUF, 10 Nov. 1939; cf. also ibid., 10 Jan. 1940.
  [8] GStA, MA 106678, RPvOF/MF, 6 Feb. 1940; cf. also ibid., 7 Apr. 1940 and *Bayern I*, p. 136.
  [9] GStA, MA 106671, RPvOB, 8 Mar. 1940. The depressed mood among the peasantry because of the shortage of labour was emphasized in almost all reports from rural areas in the first months of the war.
  [10] GStA, MA 106673, RPvNB/OP, 8 Feb. 1940.

As a result, peasants continued to be apathetic, often failing to raise much enthusiasm even for the victories of the Polish campaign. According to a report from one rural district in northern Bavaria, the general attitude in the locality could be summed up in comments voiced particularly by peasants that 'the war should be ended. We don't need a war.'[11] The lack of engagement of the peasants in this area was just as striking during the triumphant western campaign in May 1940. As one report laconically pointed out, nothing was heard about the war at all, except that there was a growing shortage of farm labourers![12]

The war itself, however, offered a ray of hope to farmers in their all-consuming worry about the labour supply. Austrians, Czechs, Italians, and labourers from other nationalities had been employed spasmodically on farms even before Germany's expansion in 1938-9, but the war now provided a supply of foreign labour inconceivable in peace-time. Already during the Polish campaign the first consignments of Polish prisoners-of-war and conscripted civilian labour were being directed into the German countryside and greeted by many German farmers as an answer to their prayers — 'saviours in a time of need' (*Retter in der Not*), as some reports put it.[13] By the middle of the war more than six million foreign workers (among them almost one-and-a-half million women) and prisoners-of-war made up almost 17 per cent of those employed in the German war economy.[14] In the area covered by the *Gau* Employment Office of Franconia, as many as 42 per cent of those in agricultural employment in 1944 were non-Germans.[15]

[11] StAB, K8/III/18473, GP Aufseß, 26 Oct. 1939; cf. also ibid., 26 Dec. 1939; GKF, 29 Oct. 1939.

[12] Ibid., GP Eggolsheim, 27 May 1940.

[13] GStA, MA 106671, RPvOB, 9 Apr. 1940. The first references to the Polish prisoners-of-war — 'awaited on all sides' — in Lower Bavaria and the Upper Palatinate were of general satisfaction with their work and behaviour.

[14] IWM, FD 847/46, Reichsministerium für Rüstung und Kriegsproduktion, 'Arbeitseinsatz', fol. 2a. By mid-1944 foreign workers and prisoners-of-war made up as much as 21 per cent of the total German labour potential — D. Petzina, 'Die Mobilisierung deutscher Arbeitskräfte vor und während des zweiten Weltkrieges', *VfZ*, xviii (1970), 450.

[15] Calculated from data in IWM, FD 5424/45, Strukturblatt des Gauarbeitsamts Franken [1944], fol. 33.

His new source of labour imposed, however, new quasi-policing and surveillance burdens on the farmer — or, since he was increasingly likely to be away at the Front, on his wife. For their part, the authorities were now expending an extraordinary amount of time and energy in attempting to regulate the contact between Germans and foreign workers, but on farms in particular, where foreign workers often lived in the farmhouse and ate at the same table as their employer, it was a wholly impossible task to uphold the level of apartheid which the authorities wanted. Reports complained of the 'very noble' treatment of prisoners-of-war and of the all too friendly behaviour of many peasants towards their foreign labourers. In some places prisoners-of-war were given new clothes for going to church on Sundays; others were presented with watches and other gifts, as one report cynically put it, 'in order to keep awake their liking for work.'[16] Other farmers, however, treated their foreign workers — especially Poles — much less humanely, complaining loud and long about the ungrateful dissatisfaction of the Poles over their working conditions, wages, and rights. The more stubborn the Poles became about their conditions, the more such farmers responded with punitive measures — which then naturally led to such a deterioration in their treatment that the Poles often refused to work at all, resulting in the police being called in by the farmer. Even the authorities, dealing for instance in Lower Bavaria and the Upper Palatinate in July 1940 with sixty-five such cases of intervention by the Gestapo for work refusal or unlawful quitting of service by Poles, were aware that maltreatment by German farmers was to blame, and that often the same farms were involved on which German labourers had earlier refused to stay.[17]

Farmers' opinion about Poles and other foreign workers varied widely. The crucial determinant was usually, however,

[16] StAW, SD/9, AS Würzburg, 10 Sept. 1940, 8 Nov. 1940; SD/4, AS Ebern, 5 Oct. 1940; GStA, MA 106681, RPvUF, 10 Jan. 1940; MA 106673, RPvNB/OP, 8 Feb. 1940; MA 106678, RPvOF/MF, 8 July 1940.
[17] GStA, MA 106673, RPvNB/OP, 8 July 1940. Cf. also MA 106678, RPvOF/MF, 8 July 1940, where the Government President placed the blame 'for the failure of the Poles' partly on their German employers for physically maltreating their foreign workers.

not a criterion according with Nazi racial schooling about the inferiority of 'Slav *Untermenschen*' but the more mundane yet real question of the economic worth of the foreign workers. Ideological instruction about the correct attitude to 'alien peoples' (*Fremdvölker*) tended to meet with only limited success in rural areas.[18] The SD office at Bayreuth had to admit in 1942 that the peasant attitude to the new influx of forced labour from the USSR was to see 'the Russian in the first instance as labour and not as a member of an alien people.' In general, the report went on, farmers were more friendly than German workers in their approach to the Russians, a feature put down to the close contact and individual nature of farm employment 'which let the human side emerge much more' in contrast to the impersonal nature of the employment of whole phalanxes of foreign workers in industry. In addition, the deep-rooted Christian feelings of the Catholic rural population had to be taken into account. 'For the good Catholic population, the very fact that the Russian is also Catholic and pious' was enough 'to see in him another human being'. The real live Russian was set against the stereotype Bolshevik monster, and the result was a propaganda failure with 'a tendency to a strongly humane evaluation of the Russian' being observed.[19]

Economic pragmatism, overlain with Christian humanitarian values, shaped attitudes to foreign workers much more than did Nazi racial theory. In economic terms, however, the increasing calls of the army and armaments industry meant that the labour supply problem — the central question for most farmers — having been temporarily and partially overcome between 1939 and 1941, once more became acute from the mid-war onwards, with clearly negative consequences for the political attitudes of the peasantry.

The underlying discontent of Bavarian farmers was given new focus in 1941 by a sharp extension of State intervention in controlling the marketing of agricultural produce, by the

---

[18] Cf. StAB, M30/840, propaganda directives for the behaviour of the population of the Bavarian *Ostmark* towards foreign workers and prisoners-of-war, 16 Jan. 1942.
[19] StAB, M30/1049, SD-Abschn. Bayreuth, 20 July 1942. Cf. also *Meldungen*, pp. 286-9; Steinert, pp. 309, 592-3.

worsening of the labour problem through call-ups for the Balkan and Russian campaigns, and — an area which will be dealt with in the next chapter — by dramatic events in the 'Church struggle'. Reports from the spring and summer months speak of 'unrest', 'tension', and 'bitterness' in the rural population and describe the morale of the peasants as very low.[20] The signs of discontent were very wide-ranging and find expression in almost every report from this date emanating from a rural district. The general mood seems, in fact, to have been much worse in the countryside than in the towns. Certainly, the District Leader of Augsburg-Stadt, whose reports were normally more intelligent and more socially conscious than most Party reports, had a shock when he spent a summer holiday in the Bavarian countryside in 1941: 'During my short holiday I had the opportunity to become acquainted with the mood in the countryside and was quite plainly astonished at the completely frank way in which things were criticized there, measures condemned, and how people put themselves on the side of the Church.'[21] Compilers of reports who had close contact with peasants left the authorities in no doubt whatsoever about the scale of the discontent. They made clear that even after eight years of the dictatorship, Nazi ideology was making little headway, that the peasant's world ended at his farm gates and was wholly bound up with his material interests, and that he was more closely attached to the Church than ever.

Reports from the Upper Franconian district of Ebermannstadt, an overwhelmingly agricultural area, provide a particularly candid impression of opinion in farming circles during 1941. In one account, from the village of Aufseß in January 1941, the *Gendarmerie* official began by describing the 'unbelievable enmities among the population' arising from 'reserved occupation' releases from the *Wehrmacht* and the strong suspicion that special favour was being shown to the larger landholders. He went on: 'There can be no talk of a National Community. Each thinks only of his own advantage . . . To the peasants, their Fatherland is only their

[20] E.g., GStA, MA 106671, RPvOB, 10 June 1941; MA 106674, 8 Apr. 1941.
[21] StANeu, LO A5, KL Augsburg-Stadt, 11 Aug. 1941.

own farm.' The peasants were so tied up in their own petty world that they ignored the great events outside. 'Enlightenment' and 'ideological schooling' were lacking, but would in any case be of little help since 'egoism has already overrun patriotism.' The attitude amounted to: 'State pay up and then you'll have our respect. If not, then we have no time for you. That, roughly speaking, describes the situation here.'[22]

The *Landrat* himself, extremely well informed and in touch with grass-roots opinion in the farming community of his district, reported month after month in the frankest terms about the poor mood in the countryside, its economic causes, the disastrous effect of the 'Church struggle', and the political implications of the low morale — dissatisfaction with the regime and with the war leadership, lack of interest in the propagated war aims, and an outspoken desire for peace. In April 1941 he wrote:

We've victories enough already. Now we need peace. That, briefly put, is the feeling among the greatest part of the population. This longing for peace is probably partly based in the difficulties of getting provisions and in restrictions which in a long war are felt to be ever more burdensome. Mostly, however, especially in the purely farming areas, it is rooted in the noticeable shortage of labour. The father, the husband, or the son have been away from the farm all too long.[23]

Three months later, shortly after the beginning of the Russian campaign, his report showed up in unmistakable tones the immense gulf between the ideological aims of the Nazi leaders and the wishes and interests of the peasant. There was 'not the least understanding for the realization of plans for world domination which despite all denials intended for America are ever more surmised. The overworked and exhausted men and women do not see why the war must be carried still further into Asia and Africa.'[24] The extraordinary physical and psychological pressure was, he indicated, creating a depth of bitterness which should not be underestimated.

I have only the one wish [wrote the *Landrat* forlornly in August 1941], that one of the officials in Berlin or Munich . . . should be in my office

[22] StAB, K8/III, 18474, GP Aufseß, 26 Jan. 1941.
[23] Ibid., LR Ebermannstadt, 30 Apr. 1941.
[24] Ibid., 1 July 1941.

sometime when, for example, a worn-out old peasant beseechingly requests allocation of labourers or other assistance, and as proof of his need shows two letters, in one of which the company commander of the elder son answers that leave for the harvest cannot be granted, and in the other of which the company commander of the younger son informs of his heroic death in an encounter near Propoiszk.

Those coming into regular contact with people in such surrounds gained a rather different impression of opinion, he said, than one would otherwise have gleaned from the German press or from the claims of the State's leaders.[25]

Victory announcements from the East were unable to lift morale. For peasants, the war was no more than a 'hard "must"' (hartes Muß).[26] The social consequences of the war pressures completely gave the lie to the propaganda model of a united 'community of fate' fighting for Germany. The 'sense of community' (Gemeinschaftssinn) so 'painstakingly planted by the Party in the last years' was disappearing as 'envy, ill will, hatred, and all similar human weaknesses again flourish' — especially when the neighbouring farmer had been granted 'reserved occupation' status and one's own application had been turned down.[27] There was little sense of 'National Community' too, in relations between the peasants and evacuees from the threatened regions of the north. The unwillingness of evacuated women and children to join in the backbreaking farm work, and at a time when labourers were in such short supply, was guaranteed to bring out the worst social prejudices and resentments against what was regarded as the decadent idleness of these 'ladies' from the town.[28]

Apart from their outspoken tone, there was nothing unrepresentative about these reports from the Ebermannstadt area. Nazi functionaries were themselves fully aware of the Party's problems in attempting to reshape peasant attitudes, as a report from Brückenau-Hammelburg, a poor rural district in the north of Lower Franconia, pointed out towards the end of 1941:

[25] Ibid., 30 Aug. 1941.
[26] Ibid., 30 Sept. 1941; GK Ebermannstadt, 29 Aug. 1941.
[27] Ibid., LR Ebermannstadt, 2 Dec. 1941; cf. also GK Ebermannstadt, 1 Dec. 1941.
[28] Ibid., LR Ebermannstadt, 31 July 1941. Similar reactions were reported from all agricultural regions of Bavaria from 1941 onwards.

People frequently question the necessity of this war. They are not clear about the magnitude of this struggle and its far-reaching significance for the future of the German people, and probably no propaganda will succeed in wholly convincing the rural population of it. People think too egoistically and see what is taking place only from the perspective of small everyday matters.[29]

Propaganda meetings were frequently a complete disaster in which only the few believers and the browbeaten turned up to hear the predictable words of exhortation from the local Party hacks. Functionaries could not but be aware of the wall of hostility which they so often encountered. According to a report which found its way out of Germany to left-wing emigration circles, the bitterness of Bavarian peasants 'against the war and against the Prussianism which is to blame — meaning the Nazi Party — is extraordinary. They suffer financially; they have to give up their traditional way of work and are forced to take emergency measures according to the dictate of the war machine, and they hate it.'[30]

Peasant morale took a sharp turn for the worse in 1941 as a result of the new stringent attempts on the part of the Reich Food Estate to channel and control the few remaining loopholes in the marketing of farm produce, especially dairy products. The negative reactions of the peasants led some Party reporters to fear a drop in agricultural production.[31] Only the threat of heavy sanctions against uncooperative peasants forestalled opposition,[32] though it could not prevent renewed bitter criticism of Reich Food Estate, Party, and State. Dairy-farmers were particularly up in arms at the confiscation in spring 1941 of their butter churns and centrifugal machines, carried out in order to restrict production and sale of butter to recognized dairies and to stop peasants consuming their own products or supplying the black market. There was much avoidance in practice, and chaotic organization which had not provided sufficient containers for the

---

[29] StAW, GL Mainfranken II/5, Kreispropagandaleiter Brückenau-Hammelburg, 26 Nov. 1941.

[30] WL, *Reports from Inside Germany* (*Deutsche Inlandsberichte*), 10 Sept. 1941, p. 14. These reports were issued by the *Neu Beginnen* group.

[31] E.g., StAW, GL Mainfranken II/5, Kreispropagandaleiter Brückenau-Hammelburg, report for May 1941.

[32] Ibid., 23 Dec. 1941 states this expressly.

increased milk flow[33] also helped ensure that the Nazis' aim was only partially realized. The ill-feeling engendered was enormous, as was reflected in reports from almost all rural areas in this period.[34] The resentment against the repressive 'coercive economy' — of a different order from anything the peasants had witnessed even in the First World War[35] — was general. The corresponding alienation from the Nazi regime was as good as completed. The local Party leader and mayor of an Upper Bavarian village, himself a farmer, wrote in September 1941: 'If the present conditions last much longer, we can hang up the *Blut und Boden* slogan on the nail.'[36] In reality, if such a slogan had ever had much significance for the majority of peasants, it had long since become a dead letter.

The economic pressures on the peasantry — and their repercussions on political attitudes — intensified as the war dragged on. At the forefront of concern remained the labour shortage which with the massive increase in call-ups to the *Wehrmacht*, the human losses in combat, and the draining of much foreign labour from the countryside to the hard-pressed war industries was again an unbearable strain and the source of bitter attacks on the government.[37] Equally un-diminished was the acute sense of deliberate exploitation — amounting to what was often termed a 'swindle' — by the State in the interests of the non-productive drones of society, prominent among whom were the Party bosses. Peasant

---

[33] E.g., GStA, MA 106674, RPvNB/OP, 8 Apr. 1941, 8 May 1941; MA 106671, RPvOB, 10 June 1941; WL, *Reports from Inside Germany*, 10 Sept. 1941, p. 15.

[34] E.g., GStA, MA 106671, RPvOB, 10 June, 10 July 1941; MA 106681, RPvUF, 11 Nov. 1941.

[35] This was said, and accurately so, by peasants in Lower Bavaria and the Upper Palatinate in spring 1941 — GStA, MA 106674, RPvNB/OP, 8 Apr. 1941.

[36] StAM, LRA 135114, Ogrl. Aschau to KL Mühldorf, without date (Sept. 1941).

[37] A few examples from many: GStA, MA 106674, RPvNB/OP, 9 Nov. 1942, 10 Oct. 1943; MA 106696, RPvNB/OP, 10 Feb. 1944; MA 106671, RPvOB, 9 Jan. 1943; MA 106695, RPvOB, 15 Nov. 1943, 8 Feb. 1944, 9 May 1944, 7 Oct. 1944, 7 Dec. 1944. Two extreme cases among numerous serious ones of acute labour shortage were described in one report: the first case concerned a farm of 200 *Tagwerk* which, with the call-up of the farmer, was now run solely by three Serbian prisoners-of-war; the second related to a farm of 90 *Tagwerk*, now run only by the mother of the farmer and his eighteen-year-old sister — GStA, MA 106674, RPvNB/OP, 8 Feb. 1942.

bitterness in the middle of the war is well reflected in a report from the SD agency at Kitzingen in Lower Franconia:

The mood of the farming population is very poor at present. The most varied things are complained about and cursed terribly . . . The mood is especially 'charged' among smaller peasants . . . The prices for their products are artificially kept down. But if *they* need anything, then they are fleeced . . . In the countryside the general opinion is that they are playing fast and loose with the peasants. The local peasant leaders, mayors etc. are in a dreadful position. If things go much further they will not be able to pacify the people any longer. One would then have to reckon that anyone not standing aside would be done to death (*erschlagen*). Things have already gone so far that people make no secret of saying: 'it's immaterial to us what happens. If we get another government, we'll back it. Things can't get any worse.'[38]

In the last years of the war the peasant came nearer to a sense of involvement in the fate of his countrymen than at any other time in the Third Reich. News of the death of fathers, sons, and brothers at the Front affected peasant families like all others. The mounting losses — one village reported three times as many dead as during the First World War — had imaginable consequences for the standing of the Nazi Party, whose representatives fought shy of conveying notice of death to bereaved families for fear of the reactions they had to face.[39] The countryside was spared the horrors of the bombing for the most part, though the psychological shock waves had a demoralizing effect.[40] Social tensions in country areas were increased in the latter phase of the war by the unending flood of evacuees quartered in Bavarian villages, and by the ceaseless trek of townspeople on the search, despite the threat of punitive sanctions, for foodstuffs to buy up for themselves or for the black market.[41] Finally, the new optimism of foreign workers as the war drew to its close led to numerous clashes, sometimes of a threatening

[38] StAW, SD/17, AS Kitzingen, 9 Apr. 1943; cf. also SD/23, AS Würzburg, 23 Apr. 1943, and SD/37, HAS Würzburg, 17 Apr. 1943.
[39] GStA, MA 106696, RPvNB/OP, 9 Sept. 1944. Cf. StANeu, LO 30/35, reports of the *Ortsgruppen* Pfuhl, Neu-Ulm-Ost, and Neu-Ulm-Ludwigsfeld to KL Neu-Ulm, early March 1943, for the conveyance of news of death to relatives.
[40] Cf. *Meldungen*, p. 505.
[41] E.g., GStA, MA 106671, RPvOB, 8 Apr. 1943; MA 106674, RPvNB/OP, 9 Nov. 1942; MA 106679, RPvOF/MF, 7 July 1942, 8 June 1943.

nature, with German farmers who, in the face of defeat, were becoming increasingly concerned to avoid the big stick and to show how humanitarian they could be.[42]

Detestation of the Nazi regime was by this time almost universal in country areas, though now as before it had few directly dangerous political or economic consequences in terms of refusal to co-operate with the authorities let alone a revolutionary mood. Incidents such as one in which peasants refused to hand over commandeered hay for horses of the *Wehrmacht* with the blunt comment: 'War soon lost anyway, need hay ourselves',[43] were wholly exceptional. As this episode shows, however, peasant passivity did not derive from patriotism, even less from sympathy for Nazism. The coupling of ceaseless grumbling and cursing with political passivity and inactivity had been an age-old characteristic of peasant behaviour, even allowing for such politicization as saw the emergence of the *Bauernbund* in the nineteenth century or the largely negative radicalization of the countryside in the early 1930s. Many of the complaints about the Nazi State and its institutions differed only in tone and emphasis from peasant criticism of previous governments. Certainly farmers now had no choice whatsoever of alternative parties, organizations, or pressure-groups to fight their battles. But in essence their objections to the Nazi regime were not ideological but purely pragmatic — at least as far as economic issues were concerned. The Nazis had simply not produced the peasant wonderland which they had promised. This was cause enough for bitterness and resentment. But it was insufficient in itself to lead to opposition. If, compared with Stalinist Russia, the coercion in the German countryside was mild, it was more than enough to persuade waverers to comply. And the escalation of repression in the post-Stalingrad phase was sufficient to deter any but the near lunatic. Like most other Germans, however deep their dislike of Nazism Bavarian peasants were anxious in this phase to keep as low a profile as possible, their one end in view being to

---

[42] One of many instances: GStA, MA 106695, RPvOB, 8 Mar. 1944.
[43] Ibid., 7 Oct. 1944.

outlive the regime, experience the end of the war — and to see the Americans arriving before the Russians.[44]

(ii) The Working Class

The evidence we considered in Chapter 2 suggested strongly that the main contours of the relationship between the working class and the Nazi regime were definitively formed during the years 1933–9. It seems clear that Nazi social ideology, centring on the replacement of class allegiance by national allegiance and summed up in the concept of the 'National Community', had been an unmitigated failure among the vast majority of the working class long before 1939. The picture painted, however, was one of growing industrial indiscipline and militancy combined with widespread political apathy and resignation. We turn now to consider to what extent war, a struggle against external enemies which German workers experienced in common with all other Germans, could create the sense of national unity so lacking in the working class before 1939.

The regime's response to the chronic labour shortage, clearly recognized as the crux of the war production problem, was partly to make use of new labour resources — women and foreign workers — and partly to extract more from German workers by increasing hours and holding down wages. Both approaches met with at best only partial success.

The extensive mobilization of women which transformed the work-forces of Britain and the USA during the war did not take place in Germany. Half-hearted efforts to pressurize women into working in the armaments industries in the early war years were singularly unsuccessful. The two Bavarian 'Defence Districts' (*Wehrkreise* VII (Munich) and XIII (Nuremberg)) pointed to lack of incentive on account of high deductions from earnings in explaining the drop in women's employment, experienced all over Germany, between the start of the war and the end of 1939. Pressure from labour

---

[44] For the general climate of opinion in Bavaria towards the end of the war, cf. Kershaw, *Hitler-Mythos*, pp. 192–4 and H. Troll, 'Aktionen zur Kriegsbeendigung im Frühjahr 1945', in *Bayern IV*, pp. 646 ff.

exchanges and from the Party resulted in a rise in the number of women employed by summer 1940, but there was another drop by the end of the year. By the eve of the Russian campaign the numbers employed were scarcely higher than at the start of the war. In Germany as a whole the number of 'economically active' women did not rise above the level of May 1939 until the year 1943.[45]

Far more than on the employment of women, German war production depended upon the influx of foreign labour. By 1944 foreign workers amounted to 21 per cent of the total industrial work-force in Germany.[46] However they did not supply the complete answer, quantitatively or qualitatively, to the labour shortage. The demand for foreign labour and for prisoners-of-war remained greatly in excess of supply, despite the complaints about their lack of discipline and poor productivity. And their numbers in the first phase of the war at least were not great. On the eve of the Russian campaign there were only 1,900 male and 1,000 female foreign workers employed in the armaments industries of the Nuremberg 'Defence District'.[47]

Much rested initially, therefore, on the ability of the regime to extract more labour at a lower price from the native German male work-force. Even under wartime conditions, however, there were limits which the regime could not override if it wanted to retain workers' compliance and co-operation, as the failure to implement the most severe measures under the War Economy Decree of 4 September 1939 indicated. These measures signified an instant deterioration in the living standards of the German worker. They included tax increases and the abolition of holiday benefits and higher rates for overtime, Sunday, and night work. Restriction of job mobility and abolition of limits on the length of the working-day had already been implemented. The freezing of wage rates followed.[48] Worker opposition

---

[45] BA/MA, RW20/13/8, fols. 58–9, 109; RW20/13/9, fols. 142, 175; RW20/7/16, fol. 88. Figures for the whole of Germany in D. Winkler, 'Frauenarbeit versus Frauenideologie', *Archiv für Sozialgeschichte*, xvii (1977), 126.

[46] Petzina, 'Mobilisierung', p. 450.

[47] BA/MA, RW20/13/9, fol. 143.

[48] Mason, *Arbeiterklasse*, pp. 961 ff., 1050 ff., 1196, 1205; text of War Economy Decree translated in *Docs. on Nazism*, pp. 634–6. Cf. also S. Salter,

expressed itself in a wave of industrial indiscipline – absenteeism, refusal of overtime, night-shifts, and Sunday work, and poor work performance – and by December 1939 the government had retracted most of the measures and backed down. By September 1940 full pre-war overtime rates had been reintroduced.[49]

Even so, the material position of German workers, unquestionably worsened after the beginning of the war. The longer working hours remained. Coupled with this was the increased presence of the Gestapo in factories, and the threat of an 'educative' sojourn in a labour camp for the 'work shy'. Food price rises, shortages and maldistribution of foodstuffs, clothing, and workshoes, lack of raw materials for civilian building which exacerbated an already acute housing problem, and the catastrophic coal shortage in the severe winter of 1939-40 all affected disproportionately the poorer classes of industrial cities. The privations of war fell heavily upon the working class even in this early stage of the war. What impact did they have on the formation of working-class opinion, and to what extent were they compensated by the great German victories of the first war years?

Robert Ley, head of the Labour Front, claimed in a rallying-call to the German working population in mid-November 1939 that the morale of the workers was excellent and improving from week to week.[50] Reality looked rather different. The authorities were becoming increasingly aware of the consequences of the great strain imposed on workers by the long hours and intensive production-drive, which in the long run led to a staggering rise in cases of illness (real or feigned) among employees and to a growth in the number of works accidents, in some key industries amid falling rather than rising productivity.[51] Absenteeism, indiscipline, and fatigue were especially commonplace among women and younger

---

'Class Harmony or Class Conflict? The Industrial Working Class and the National Socialist Regime 1933-1945', in Noakes (ed.), *Govt., Party, and People*, p. 88.

[49] Mason, *Arbeiterklasse*, pp. 1086 ff., 1183 ff., 1233-4.

[50] Ibid., p. 1195.

[51] E.g., ibid., pp. 1182-3; cf. also pp. 168 ff. For a specific example in Bavaria, that of the Penzberg miners, cf. Tenfelde, pp. 357-62.

foreign and conscripted workers. 'Defence District XIII' (Nuremberg) noted that complaints about indiscipline among women workers were sharply on the increase during the first months of 1940. In one 'entirely well-managed' explosives factory in Nuremberg employing some 2,000 workers there were regularly 400 or so women missing on Mondays and sometimes Tuesdays too. In another armaments factory 300 women out of a total work-force of 1,800 were absent daily. The reasons for their absence were given as the need to stay below the earnings limit so as not to lose family allowances. The authorities put their own gloss on it: bad will and the effect of 'elements provoking unrest' were among the root causes in their view.[52] By spring 1940 the Nuremberg 'Defence District', worried about the extent and consequences of work-fatigue, especially among women, felt obliged to reduce working hours to avoid a drop in production.[53] Faced with similarly heavy losses among women employees through alleged illness, pregnancy, and time needed for housework and shopping, 'Defence District VII' (Munich) followed suit a year later.[54]

Employers attempted to counter the discontent, poor morale, indiscipline, and low productivity by ever-increasing resort to police coercion. The Nuremberg 'Defence District' claimed, in fact, that in cases of 'malicious behaviour' by workers only 'rigorous and swift measures' on the part of the Gestapo could 'guarantee order in the works and thereby undisturbed further running of the war economy.'[55] Occasional intervention by the Gestapo and temporary internment of troublemakers between Saturday lunchtime and Monday morning proved, it was said, 'very salutary'.[56] As Munich Gestapo reports show, increasing numbers of cases of work indiscipline were being dealt with by the police in the first

[52] BA/MA, RW20/13/8, fol. 59.

[53] Ibid., fol. 60.

[54] BA/MA, RW20/7/17, fols. 52–3. 'Breach of work contract', 'poor performance', absenteeism, and alleged illness, especially among women, were also recorded in the reports of the Government Presidents in the winter of 1940-1. Some Upper Bavarian firms claimed to be regularly missing up to a third of their labour force through 'illness' – GStA, MA 106678, RPvOF/MF, 7 Dec. 1940; MA 106671, RPvOB, 10 Dec. 1940, 10 Feb. 1941.

[55] BA/MA, RW20/13/8, fol. 63.   [56] Ibid., fol. 61.

war years. The Gestapo's own figures for fourteen months between October 1940 and December 1941 give a total number of 6,354 employees reported as involved in work stoppages, refusal to work, absenteeism, breach of contract etc. The figures show a rising trend, especially after the invasion of Russia, with a high point (883 workers) being reached in October 1941. Of the workers concerned, just under a third were arrested. The 2,013 workers arrested comprised 9 per cent Germans, 55 per cent Poles, 8 per cent French, 6 per cent Czechs, 5 per cent Belgians, and 17 per cent other nationalities.[57] These figures reflect a claim made regularly in the reports that the main disciplinary problems were posed by foreign workers, especially Poles. Strikes, invariably of very short duration, were almost always carried out by foreign, not German workers – and usually without any show of solidarity by German workers for the actions of the foreigners.[58] These figures suggest, alongside other impressionistic evidence, that whatever their deepseated aversion to Nazism German workers were far less willing than foreign workers – who faced even more draconian punishment for their actions – to become involved in industrial militancy, let alone outright political protest. The youthful age structure, appalling conditions, and alien environment of the foreign workers could push them towards extreme forms of militancy. Workers schooled in the traditions of the German Left with close on a decade of Nazi repression behind them tended rather to recognize the futility and senselessness of open heroics and to concentrate their efforts on the art of the possible – survival, maintenance of class solidarity, and exploitation of all available opportunities within the industrial process of upholding their own interests.[59]

Hitler and the Nazi leadership were anxious, now as before

[57] Calculated from the daily figures provided in the Tätigkeitsberichte der Gestapoleitstelle München in StAM, Gestapo 58.

[58] Mason, *Arbeiterklasse*, pp. 1063-5, 1172-3 for reports of strikes of foreign workers in Bavaria in the first months of the war; *Bayern I*, pp. 310-11 for the absence of solidarity with foreign workers in later war years. Hetzer, p. 129 makes the same point for Augsburg workers. There are, however, some indicators pointing in the opposite direction. Cf. e.g., Tenfelde, p. 368 and n. 435 for instances of solidarity between Penzberg miners and prisoners-of-war.

[59] Cf. Tenfelde, pp. 368-71, 381; Broszat, 'Resistenz und Widerstand', p. 708.

the war, not to invoke a serious loss of popularity through imposing stringent restrictions on consumption.[60] Worker reactions to such consumer restrictions as they did have to endure suggest that Hitler's concern was well founded.

Clothing and foodstuff shortages, but especially the coal crisis, led to a decline in morale and some signs of tension in the winter months of 1939-40.[61] The mood of Bavarian workers and their pessimistic attitude towards the war were singled out by the SD for comment, and the discontent of Munich workers about food shortages seems to have been common knowledge outside the city.[62] Though the coal crisis subsided as winter turned to spring, the food shortages remained and bitter complaints about rising prices putting butter, sugar, and other edibles out of the reach of the less well-to-do sections of the population, and about the holding down of wages while prices were soaring, were commonplace in the reports.[63] In the summer and autumn of 1940, even following the triumphant conclusion of the western campaign, workers were still preoccupied with the depressing conditions of their everyday existence, to go from the reports of the District Leader of Augsburg-Stadt. The 'heavy claims' being made on workers for war production, the less than satisfactory food provisioning, and difficulties in obtaining shoes, clothing, and other necessities were all having 'a somewhat inhibiting effect' on workers' mood, as he cautiously expressed it — immediately adding that one should not conclude that they were disheartened. In fact, the mood was 'satisfactory', though less than good in some factories on account of the oppressive hours of work and the high-handed

[60] A. Speer, Erinnerungen, Frankfurt/Main, 1969, p. 229. Cf. also T.W. Mason, 'The Legacy of 1918 for National Socialism', in A. Nicholls and E. Matthias (eds.), German Democracy and the Triumph of Hitler, London, 1971, pp. 233 ff.
[61] Cf. e.g., GStA, MA 106671, RPvOB, 8 Mar. 1940; MA 106673, RPvNB/OP, 9 Jan., 8 Feb. 1940; Meldungen, pp. 34–5; L.D. Stokes, 'The Sicherheitsdienst (SD) of the Reichsführer SS and German Public Opinion, September 1939–June 1941', Johns Hopkins Univ., Ph.D. thesis, Baltimore, 1972, pp. 389–91.
[62] Meldungen, p. 36; StANeu, Sammlung Schumacher LO 47, GP Eurasburg, 16 Nov. 1939.
[63] E.g., GStA, MA 106671, RPvOB, 8 Mar., 9 May, 9 Aug. 1940, 9 Apr., 10 June 1941; MA 106681, RPvUF, 10 Jan. 1941; MA 106684, RPvS, 8 May 1941; MA 106678, RPvOF/MF, 7 Dec. 1940; Steinert, pp. 164–5.

behaviour of foremen and managers. Housing conditions in the city, deplorable before the war, were now intolerable and prompted not unnaturally 'general embitterment' and a complete lack of sympathy with the great 'social' propaganda ventures of the regime, 'for in a time when the worker has to fight daily to secure his naked existence he has little understanding for such things.'[64] The District Leader also pointed out the negative impact made by police surveillance and arrests in factories. Circumstances in some armaments factories, he said, were reaching a pitch where workers were openly describing the situation as a 'communist dictatorship'. 'To have people sitting behind lock and key since the beginning of the war for next to nothing, and given over to the arbitrary treatment of leaders or their subordinates in concentration camps', was, he concluded, calculated only to increase the anger and discontent of the workforce and was 'certainly no matter which can contribute to the strengthening of the national community.'[65]

In April 1941 the SD reported on the results of extensive investigations into the morale and discipline of workers throughout Germany. The general tenor of the findings, which drew frequently on evidence from the SD office in Würzburg, was that while absenteeism had reached significant proportions there had been no notable increase in labour indiscipline and there was no good reason to speak of poor worker morale.[66] Such a verdict from the Reich Security Head Office suggests that the leading Nazi authorities did not feel poor discipline and bad industrial relations were a danger to the war effort or to the stability of the regime. But it certainly amounted to an underestimation of anti-regime feeling among workers. The Würzburg SD headquarters, which had supplied material for the central SD summary report, was itself in no doubt on the basis of the reports it

[64] StANeu, LO A5, KL Augsburg-Stadt, 10 Nov. 1940. The *Kreisleiter* advocated at the same time playing down the propaganda line which emphasized the huge class differences in English society, since Augsburg workers were simply pointing out the similarity of conditions in Germany and attacking the luxury-living of the Nazi *Bonzen*.

[65] Ibid.; cf. also the report of 10 Oct. 1940.

[66] *Meldungen*, pp. 135–8; cf. also StAW, SD/34/1, HAS-Würzburg, without date (early 1941), 'Arbeitsmoral', fol. 32.

received from local branches in Lower Franconia about the strength of worker feeling. A report from the SD agency in Würzburg itself in spring 1941, for example, made no bones about worker opinion:

In some sections of the working class there is unrest. There the word 'swindle' can again be heard: the people will have nothing to laugh about even if we win the war; we are being lied to at every turn; what is pointed out as a weakness for England is supposed to be a good thing for us; some are getting fat while others starve; workers' wives are conscripted for service, the wives of high civil servants and especially of officers continue their comfortable life of idleness (*Drohnenleben*) just as before; the 'rubbish' ('*Krampf*') is worse than during the World War; most people are sick from pure anger in their belly; it's time the swindle stopped.[67]

In the absence of *Sopade* reports and other accounts reaching left-wing emigration groups[68] it is difficult to reconstruct worker attitudes towards Nazism as clearly as could be done for the pre-war period. Even so, reports such as the above one from local SD stations make clear that little or nothing had changed in the grass-roots opinion of the majority of workers. Most remained alienated from Nazism. The DAF and Party leadership were heavily criticized; there was much talk of corruption among the Party 'plutocrats'; and 'National Community' was regarded as merely an empty slogan.[69] Bitter anger was expressed about a wage rise for civil servants, continued food price rises, and war profits of armaments industrialists. And the Nazi government was held directly responsible for the blatant unfairness of the social and economic conditions. A Lower Franconian bricklayer put it in picturesque fashion when he said the Nazis had promised workers a hand-up, had missed their grasp, and had grabbed them by the throat instead.[70]

Economic conditions, which shaped the daily lives and

[67] StAW, SD/23, AS Würzburg, 25 Feb. 1941.

[68] The *Sopade* reports continued until April 1940, but the later reports contain very little specifically on Bavaria and the same is true of the *Inside Germany* reports of the *Neu-Beginnen* group. At the same time, the picture provided by non-Bavarian material recorded in these exile sources complements the impressions gleaned from internal material in Bavaria.

[69] StAW, SD/14, AS Bad Neustadt, 14 Mar. 1941; SD/22, AS Schweinfurt, 1 Apr. 1941; SD/23, AS Würzburg, 8 Apr. 1941.

[70] StAW, SD/21, AS Lohr, 25 Mar. 1941.

material existence of workers, remained during the first triumphant phase of the war down to the invasion of Russia of paramount importance in the formation of political opinion — and the Bavarian evidence shows few divergences from the picture elsewhere in the Reich.[71] Prices, wages, working conditions, rationing, and food shortages — from which workers suffered more than any other section of society — were of lasting and major significance. By contrast, the euphoria following the military triumphs was of short duration. Clearly, the victories of 1939-41 were not without impact on the attitudes of workers. Service in the *Wehrmacht* in these stirring times could have its own uplifting effect. And even outright opponents of the Nazis have told subsequently how difficult it was at such times to remain aloof from the enthusiastic victory mood of the masses.[72] Reports from the Armaments Inspectorates recorded an improved mood in summer 1940 among armaments workers, many of whom allegedly regretted having 'reserved occupations' and were pressing to join up.[73] Like the foreign political coups before the war, the victories in the west took the wind completely out of the sails of the organized resistance groups, whose activity now fell to negligible proportions. Some reports even claimed that 'former enemies of the State are deeply impressed by the achievements of our highest leadership and of our soldiers.'[74] The police in Hof reported an 'impeccably patriotic attitude' even among former SPD and KPD supporters who, it was claimed, were now anxious to be called up.[75] If such assertions must be taken with a big pinch of salt, it would be remarkable had not most workers, like other Germans, been affected by the wave of patriotic fervour which engulfed Germany in the summer of 1940. The glitter of the victories, however, merely glossed over for

[71] The reports of the Armaments Inspectorates from all parts of the Reich (in BA/MA Freiburg), and the SD *Meldungen aus dem Reich* (cf. the edition by Boberach and the analyses by Steinert and Stokes) amply support this generalization.
[72] Cf. the comments of Carl Severing, cited in Stokes, 'SD', p. 399 and the recollections of a foreman in the Messerschmidt factory in Augsburg cited by W. Domarus, *Nationalsozialismus, Krieg und Bevölkerung*, Munich, 1977, p. 90.
[73] BA/MA, RW20/7/16, fol. 105.
[74] GStA, MA 106671, RPvOB, 8 June 1940.
[75] GStA, MA 106678, RPvOF/MF, 8 July 1940.

a short time the underlying socio-economic realities of worker existence in wartime Germany. And after 1941 there was less and less glitter, even to act as temporary diversion from the dismal, grey routine of daily life.

From 1941 onwards the pressures imposed by an expanding but increasingly unsuccessful war on all sections of society and all aspects of civilian life greatly intensified. In some ways there was in this period a certain 'levelling down' of class differences. The more keenly the privations of war were felt, however, the more sharply focused workers' subjective class perceptions appear to have become. And under rapidly deteriorating economic conditions coupled with military defeat, exposure to terror bombing, and political bankruptcy, any lingering appeal of Nazism for workers completely dissolved.

Reports from various agencies convey a picture of deteriorating work discipline, falling morale, and growing bitterness among workers. One forthright report on the deterioration of worker morale in the first months of 1942 came from the SD office in Schwabach (Middle Franconia), and was entitled: 'Worsening of the mood of workers'. In conventional language of understatement the SD described the mood of local workers as 'to some extent rather irritated'. Their reaction to exhortations to improve productivity was: 'They should give us something decent to eat, then we could work more.' The Works Leader of the three big munitions factories in the district criticized in particular the work rate of younger workers. The SD added that there was no doubt that a section of the work-force could do more but refrained from doing so, fearing an improvement in productivity would simply bring a reduction in piece-time rates. Their productivity was said, in fact, to be lower than that of the prisoners-of-war. Workers' complaints centred upon the wage-freeze contrasted with the continually rising prices of everyday commodities. They pointed to the increase in tobacco tax, rise in the price of beer, the taxing of textile goods, and a new regulation on beer consumption which distinguished between poor quality, watered-down *Lagerbier* and the much preferred *Spezialbier*. The regulation was so framed, argued the workers, that only the 'big-wigs' (*die*

Großen) could buy the dearer beer whereas workers could not afford it, adding that 'they have to throw a crumb to the big-wigs because they are more inclined to make trouble than the workers'. The workers' 'irritation' showed itself in the refusal of free tickets for a 'Strength through Joy' event.[76]

The complaints of the Schwabach workers about the quantity, quality, and price of food and drink came in fact just before the announcement of further cuts in rations, bringing substantial reductions in weekly allowances — 25 per cent in meat, 33 per cent in margarine, 17 per cent in butter, and 11 per cent in bread rations — for all but those engaged in the heaviest types of work.[77] The central SD report of 23 March 1942 claimed it was reflecting the unanimously hostile reactions to the cuts in all parts of Germany. The effect of the announcement had been 'crushing . . . to an extent such as no other event during the war.' There was no sympathy or understanding at all for the cuts and the unrest was most marked among the working class of the big cities and industrial areas, which had regarded the previous rations as more than insufficient. Among these sections of the population 'the mood . . . has reached a low point never before established during the course of the war.' Bitterly sarcastic criticism was levelled at propaganda about securing adequate food supplies and there were hints that workers would reduce their productivity in return for the ration cuts. Awareness of the class divisions of wartime Germany was again sharpened. Workers in particular, reported the SD, spoke 'with great bitterness' about the 'better-off' managing to overcome the food shortages through recourse to their 'connections' and 'bigger purses', and remarks abounded about individual personalities who despite the shortages still had a ready supply of fowl and venison. Indicating the importance of economic matters in shaping opinion the SD report added that the military events of the previous days had been 'forced almost completely into the background by the announcement of the cuts in foodstuffs.'[78]

[76] StAN, 212/11/VI, 1792, SD-AS Schwabach, 2 Mar. 1942.
[77] *Meldungen*, p. 242, n. 1. For earlier reductions in bread, butter, and meat rations in 1940-1, cf. ibid. pp. 94-5, 111-14, 146-8.
[78] Ibid., pp. 242-3.

The situation in Bavaria accorded wholly with this general picture. People felt strongly that profiteering through the black market would now flourish as never before, and that more than ever there was one law for the poor and another for the rich and mighty. It was commonly said that 'in this war too only the little ones are hanged, the big ones let free', and draconian punishments of the wealthy and influential, or of Party functionaries were said to have a salutary effect on opinion.[79] As an SD report in late March 1942 pointed out, the climate, particularly among the working class, was favourable for an extension of exemplary severe punishment by the courts for any type of war profiteering. In the circumstances it is not surprising, therefore, that the working class seems, according to SD reports, to have favoured the announcement by Hitler, in his notorious speech on 26 April 1942 which undermined the whole basis of judicial independence, of ruthless punishment for offenders irrespective of position or standing.[80]

Alongside the deterioration in food rations, the question of the mobilization of labour was coming increasingly to sharpen working-class resentment and sensitivity to social divisions and privilege. Working-class women in Schwabach felt early in 1942, for example, that the same duty to work for war production 'apparently does not apply to the "fine" people, so not all national comrades can be regarded as equal and with equal duties.'[81] The SD in Schwabach, where a good proportion of the population was employed in armaments factories, regarded the conscription of women for work in the armaments industry as a 'not insignificant factor in the general state of morale'. Many working wives were absent for two or three days a week from their work, allegedly because they had to shop for their husbands and families and stand for hours in queues to obtain fruit and vegetables before

[79] GStA, MA 106671, RPvOB, 9 Apr. 1942; cf. also *Meldungen*, pp. 248–9.

[80] *Meldungen*, pp. 246–50, 259–60. Rumours were circulating just prior to Hitler's speech of the introduction of a sixty- or even seventy-hour working week and a reduction of holidays. The anger about low wages and rising prices was undiminished – GStA, MA 106674, RPvNB/OP, 10 Apr. 1942; MA 106679, RPvOF/MF, 7 Apr. 1942.

[81] StAN, 212/11/VI, 1792, SD-AS Schwabach, 2 Mar. 1942. Cf. in general for the mobilization of female labour, D. Winkler, 'Frauenarbeit', pp. 116 ff.

women from the 'better' sections of society bought up everything:

It still cannot be understood by these working-class women that it is always only 'the little one' who has to bear the sacrifice while the 'better ones' lead lives of idleness. These women could be brought into the work process just as well as the others, all the more so since these 'little ladies' (*Dämchen*) often have no children or only one child whereas the working-class wife frequently has four or more children at home. An alteration would be of extraordinarily great significance in the interest of the entire morale of the people. The objection, that in this connection consideration has to be taken of the mood of the 'better' sectors, is in fact far-fetched and not so decisive for the war as the mood of the working population.[82]

The attempt in early 1943 to mobilize all remaining reserves of labour for deployment in a 'total war' did little to change such attitudes.[83] Few women rushed forward to volunteer their services for the total war effort. Numerous criteria of exemption were created, and many women resorted to personal connections and elaborate pretexts to escape employment. Among those who did work, there was a stream of applications for light desk-jobs while the armaments industries still had difficulties in finding women employees. Of 8.6 million women in employment in Greater Germany at the end of 1942, only 968,000 worked in armaments.[84] Criticisms of 'total war' mobilization in Bavaria were no different from those elsewhere in Germany. To cite the Schwabach SD agency again:

[the] entire business was regarded as laughable by large sections of the population. It is said that on the wireless and in the press they are always talking of total war, whereas the effects are in reality entirely different. While our armies out there are having to fight so hard, here at home the mobilization of labour is taking place in bureaucratic fashion. One worker said that if that is total war and we are expected to manage with these measures against Bolshevism, then we have definitely lost the war already.[85]

Once more it seemed to workers that while they were doing

[82] StAN, 212/11/VI, 1792, SD-AS Schwabach, 2 Mar. 1942.
[83] Cf. D. Winkler, pp. 118–20; Salter, p. 91.
[84] Steinert, p. 356 and cf. also pp. 330–6 and *Meldungen*, pp. 348–52, 359–64.
[85] StAN, 212/11/VI, 1792, SD-AS Schwabach, 6 Apr. 1943.

their duty — and had been all along — the 'better-off' were shirking theirs.

Already before the proclamation of 'total war' and before the traumatic effects of the defeat at Stalingrad in February 1943, the mood of workers was causing the authorities concern. The SD station at Friedberg, just outside Augsburg, claimed to notice a marked change in the 'inner attitude' of armaments workers in the Augsburg area in the late summer and autumn of 1942. Inside the factories, it was even alleged, the mood was increasingly reminiscent of that of the year 1918.[86]

The catastrophe at Stalingrad and the increasing penetration of allied bomber forces — now reaching even the southernmost parts of Germany — brought the horrors of the war home with a vengeance to the entire civilian population from early 1943. Though the 'external' events of the war in many ways affected workers much as they affected other sectors of the population, there are numerous indications that one main effect was to reinforce the already dominant feelings of class underprivilege, with corresponding implications for the shaping of political opinion. SD reports from Schweinfurt in Lower Franconia provide evidence of reactions to their socio-economic position in this period from workers in the main firing-line of repeated allied air raids on the town's key ball-bearing factories during 1943 and 1944.[87]

Months before the first of the bombing raids on Schweinfurt, the SD were recording the poor mood of local workers. In May 1943 'a certain indifference', especially among workers, towards military events contrasted with heated feelings in the large factories about new wage controls. One worker, a long-time SA man, felt National Socialism had let workers down. It had promised a system where earnings were a reward for achievement. But instead the Nazis had introduced an unfair wage structure where workers 'had to produce more to earn just what we used to earn.' He disbelieved propaganda that the wage structure was simply an emergency war measure and was convinced that it would

---

[86] StANeu, Sammlung Schumacher Anh.3, SD-AS Friedberg, 14 Sept. 1942.
[87] Cf. Kershaw, *Hitler-Mythos*, pp. 178–81.

remain in operation when the war was over. Another worker, from his tone perhaps a former sympathizer with Nazism, was of the opinion that the decisive change in the mood of workers had taken place two years earlier. In the factory wash-room, which provided the best barometer of morale, workers used to sing after finishing work. Now no one spoke a word. Or if they did, it was only to curse and swear. Extreme work-fatigue and deteriorating living standards had, it was said, led to resignation, to the feeling of being exploited, and to resentment towards the Labour Front which had done nothing for workers.[88] The sheer exhaustion of the crippling work routine brought its own demoralization. One elderly foreman pointed out that the degree of physical exertion made the worker 'so tired that he thought of hardly anything else except sleep'. Party meetings, factory parades, and other supposedly morale-boosting propaganda stunts were of no avail. The demoralization caused, apart from the excessive physical demands on the worker, by four years of inadequate nourishment and the psychological depression since Stalingrad, intensified by the defeats in North Africa and the 'bombing terror', had gone too far. The consequence was

a certain indifference ... and a certain lack of confidence in the leadership. It is being said: 'In the last war the army was said to have done its duty and the people had failed. This time the *Wehrmacht* has again done its duty. The homeland does all that the leadership demands of it. If things go wrong this time whose fault is it?'[89]

Following the first air raids on Schweinfurt in the summer and autumn of 1943, work-morale was said by the SD to have suffered 'colossally' because of the insufficient provision of safe shelters. Workers vehemently demanded secure bunkers instead of simply having to resort to factory cellars during raids, and they blamed their employers for not providing better safety precautions. From comments of workers, SD informants recorded feelings 'that those up there (*die Oberen*) don't care if some workers and white-collar employees have to die. The main thing is that they get to safety themselves in time.'[90] A worker in one big factory was

[88] StAW, SD/22, AS Schweinfurt, 27 May 1943.
[89] Ibid., 7 May 1943.   [90] Ibid., 25 Oct. 1943.

reported as saying: 'One has the feeling that people are worth less today than the machines.' Other workers added bitterly: 'The German worker might as well go to hell (*verrecken*).' The posting of soldiers at the exits of the factories was interpreted as a reaction to the anger and ill-feeling among workers. Rumours circulated that the soldiers would fire upon any worker attempting to leave the factories during an air-raid alarm. Such rumours had an 'extraordinarily depressing' effect on workers, 'all the more so, since the shelters in individual factories, as is generally known, are wholly inadequate.'[91] Nor were workers slow to notice that Party representatives were loath to make an appearance on the scene following a raid. When a visit by Labour Front leader Robert Ley in the company of local Party big-wigs did take place, critical comments were made about the breakneck speed of the whistlestop tour and workers were left wondering how the Party functionaries, allegedly on the same rations as themselves, could look so well fed — a description 'that certainly can't be held of us workers'.[92]

At the end of May 1944 the SD depicted the mood of the Schweinfurt workers as 'very bad' and felt able to detect from their comments signs of their former political allegiance, in essence unchanged. The working population of Schweinfurt was of the opinion, noted the SD, 'that our government should conclude peace before our entire towns and villages are destroyed, since we can't do anything against it in any case.'[93]

The sources at our disposal are seldom subtle enough to distinguish adequately between types of worker, let alone to quantify their recorded opinion. Differences of age, sex, occupation, skill-level, or previous degree of political commitment are only rarely made explicit in either the reports of the German authorities or those of the emigration groups.[94]

[91] Ibid., 1 Nov., 3 Dec. 1943.
[92] Ibid., undated (between 28 Feb. and 28 Apr. 1944).
[93] Ibid., 27 May 1944.
[94] Statistical analysis of 'protective custody' and 'Special Court' cases allows some such differentiation, but there is no obvious methodological solution to the problem of the relationship of individual cases of 'nonconformist behaviour' to general trends of opinion. Cf. Hüttenberger, 'Heimtückefälle' for the potential of the *Sondergericht München* files. Before his sad death at such an early age, Reinhard Mann was at an advanced stage of a detailed analysis of the massive

THE ECONOMIC PRESSURES OF WAR

Furthermore, in their concentration on worker reactions to the work process alone and on questions of work-morale, the internal reports at any rate have little to offer on other crucial aspects of working-class life in the Third Reich. Above all, perhaps, this type of evidence says nothing about the deep emotions of the working-class political victims of the Nazis, their families, and their friends. Yet the evidence of the reports, subjective and non-quantifiable though it is, still paints a powerful picture of working-class responses to their position under Nazism. And it is perhaps just sufficiently differentiated to suggest the generalization that internal structural differences among workers were less significant in framing political attitudes than the common experience of subjection to the ever-expanding pressure of the industrial war-machine, backed by the full might of the police State.

This common experience produced during the war if anything a heightened and even more acute sense of social injustice among German workers than had existed before 1939. Clearly the unifying force of the war itself was insufficient to overcome the social antagonisms and political antipathies which the pre-war years had defined. Rather the contrary in fact: feelings of injustice, exploitation, and lack of social privilege seem to have been magnified by the pressures of war. As some North German workers put it in March 1945: 'We're always the stupid ones. We have no connections and have to bear all the burdens and duties of the war . . . There's just the same class difference today as before. Nothing has changed in that.'[95]

Strong feelings of injustice, however, as Barrington Moore has argued with direct relevance to the German working class,[96] do not necessarily lead to action. Political unrest, let alone revolution, is in no sense an inevitable corollary or consequence of social injustice even for an organized working-class movement. In fact it could be said to mark a quite exceptional and unusual response in an extreme and rare conjuncture of circumstances.

Düsseldorf *Schutzhaft* files, and his work promised a methodological breakthrough in dealing with this type of material.

[95] Cited in Steinert, p. 556, and cf. also p. 590.

[96] B. Moore, *Injustice: The Social Bases of Obedience and Revolt*, London, 1978, esp. ch. 14.

Social disruption [in Barrington Moore's words] 'may cause nothing more than apathy, confusion, and despair. If it is liable to make a population more malleable, it can make it malleable to new and oppressive forms of authority . . . In fact the complete destruction of existing institutions and habits of co-operation may make resistance impossible, indeed unthinkable, by destroying the basis from which it can start.'[97]

The relevance of these comments to the position of workers in Nazi Germany needs no emphasis, not least in the light of the subjective responses to their experience under Nazism considered here and earlier in Chapter 2. Historians of the German labour movement in the Imperial period have naturally been implicitly or explicitly concerned with explaining the enthusiasm of German workers, in company with other Germans, to march to war in August 1914 and their readiness four years later to topple the Kaiser. Historians of the working class in the Nazi era face almost the reverse problem: why workers, unenthusiastic like most other Germans about the war in September 1939, were apparently so quiescent throughout and showed no signs of revolutionary tendencies in 1944–5. The short and easy answer, and one which obviously has much to commend it, looks no further than the extreme repression of the police state itself. Nazi terroristic repression was undoubtedly the crucial prerequisite for ensuring what Tim Mason has called 'the containment of the working class'.[98] But terror acted in conjunction with other important components in neutralizing the potential anti-Nazi political involvement of workers. Atomization, enhancing existing divisions, was a vital product of the destruction of worker organizations and reduced the working class to its component parts. Workers were also 'bought off' by material concessions — not only the sugaring of the pill by 'Strength through Joy' but also the regime's reluctance, in the light of the experience of 1917–18, to depress living standards too far. And there was also the partial integration of workers into some of the aims of Nazism. Patriotism bolstered by war-service and the needs of national defence, nationalist or racialist feelings towards foreign

[97] Moore, pp. 470–1.
[98] Mason, 'Containment' (as yet unpublished). The ideas in this paragraph owe much to this stimulating article.

workers,[99] anti-British feeling shored up by terror bombing, fear or rejection of Bolshevism, and not least the lingering popularity of Hitler even among many workers, all played their part.[1] Moreover, the Nazis undoubtedly had some success in their attempts to focus resentment upon 'shirkers' and 'idlers'. And, not least, food provisioning — despite complaints — and welfare services never came remotely near plumbing the depths of 1917–18. All this, woven together with the sure knowledge that in the escalating climate of terror in the last months of the war any action seen as challenging the regime would be stamped out with utter brutality was enough to deprive the still-active small resistance groups of any possibility of wider support.[2]

Once the destruction of working-class political organizations had been completed in 1933 and workers had found themselves walled in by the apparatus of the police State, the massive alienation and increasing feelings of social injustice could only seldom be translated into terms of political or ideological alternatives. Only the isolated resistance groups in their political vacuum were now capable of that. Deprived of political space in which to organize,[3] the expression of injustice was mainly apathy, resignation, confusion, and despair. Challenge was out of the question; self-preservation was the name of the game. Typical in all probability were comments of older workers expressed in the middle of the war that they had little concern for the future: that they had had to work hard under the Kaiser, in the Weimar Republic, and in the Third Reich, and had probably no more and no less to expect from Bolshevism than hard work and low wages.[4]

[99] *Bayern I*, p. 310; Hetzer, pp. 129–30; instances of chauvinist or racialist feelings among workers occasionally find their way into reports, as when workers in Schwabach complained that prisoners-of-war were better treated than they were, that foreign workers had no right to travel in the same railway carriages as German workers — at the same time occupying seats while Germans had to stand, and that Poles and Ukrainians were enjoying themselves at a spring fair meant for German workers — StAN, 212/11/VI, 1792, SD-AS Schwabach, 20 May, 23 Dec. 1942.

[1] Cf. Mason, 'Containment', for an excellent analysis of the elements of worker integration into the Third Reich.

[2] For the savage repression of the rising in the mining town of Penzberg in the last days of the war, see Tenfelde, pp. 369 ff.

[3] Moore, p. 483; cf. also Mason, 'Containment'.

[4] *Meldungen*, p. 358; cf. also p. 421.

Certainly the Nazi leadership was more wary of the working class than of any other section of society throughout the Third Reich. The apparatus of internal repression was largely constructed to prevent any possible recurrence of insurrection on the 1918 style, and the authorities continued to keep a watchful eye open for any glimmer of political challenge. Certainly, too, the industrial muscle of workers, even deprived of trade unions, was sufficient to wring concessions from the regime. But this should not be taken too far. Despite labour indiscipline, war production was never seriously threatened, labour productivity *did* rise during the war (if more slowly than in Britain), and wages *were* pinned down, rising by a mere fraction of the growth in Britain.[5] Retaining its curiously ambivalent attitude towards the working class, the Nazi leadership continued to the end to believe that the workers had remained loyal while the real faint-hearts, defeatists, and shirkers were to be found in the petty bourgeoisie.[6] Whether the latter part of this allegation had any foundation, we shall attempt to consider in the final section of this chapter.

(iii) The Middle Class

In the absence of the *Sopade* reports, it becomes even more difficult to isolate middle-class social groups in the wartime period than it was in the pre-war years. We can, therefore, provide only a glimpse of some aspects of middle-class responses to the economic and social pressures of war.

As we saw in Chapter 3, the crafts and trading sectors of the *Mittelstand* can generally be said to have improved their economic position in the pre-war years. Most branches were able to benefit in some measure from the armaments boom. However, shortages of raw materials and labour made it an uneasy period for small concerns and already something of a darwinian struggle was taking place, with weaker concerns 'going to the wall'. We saw, too, that the improvement in the objective position of craftsmen and traders as compared with the Depression period found little positive echo in the

---

[5] Salter, p. 94.   [6] Steinert, pp. 554–5.

subjective responses to their socio-economic situation in the Third Reich: anxiety, depression, and disenchantment rather than optimism and enthusiasm for Nazi social and economic policies determined the tone of *Mittelstand* feeling on the eve of the war.

Even in the first, 'triumphant' phase of the war these anxieties were magnified and the existent pressures sharply intensified. In bald economic terms, the turnover of *Handwerk* in Germany as a whole fell by almost one-sixth between 1938 and 1941. At the same time the number of concerns was also falling — by 104,000 between 1936 and 1938 and a further 107,000 by 1941 — so that individual craftsmen and their firms were not necessarily worse off.[7] There were also considerable variations in the branches of retail trade, some continuing to improve their turnover in the early war years, the majority witnessing a fall after 1939 through remaining at a level higher than that of most of the peacetime years.[8] Official returns, however, scarcely do justice to the extra profits to be won from a thriving black market. As a broad generalization, the upward trend for *Handwerk* and for the retail trade, which had begun in the peacetime years of the Third Reich, stretched well into the war, though by 1942–3 at the latest a sharp downward turn had set in.[9]

Bavarian reports during the first war months emphasize the worsening of the labour shortage, especially in the building and metal trades, and the raw material shortages, again acutely affecting building and also textile concerns. Though larger craft firms, especially those managing to gain cherished *Wehrmacht* orders, were flourishing, call-ups were seriously depleting smaller businesses and already causing the close-down of some one-man concerns. Private building, particularly hard hit by manpower and raw material shortages, came to a complete halt in most areas. Cobblers complained that they had hundreds of pairs of shoes waiting for repair, but could get hold of no leather. Fuel and transport difficulties were also beginning to worry small employers. By the end of 1939 a gradual drop in business was being noted in

---

[7] Winkler, 'Der entbehrliche Stand', pp. 31–4, p. 35, n. 50.
[8] Von Saldern, pp. 111–12.
[9] Ibid., p. 126.

the craft sector. The initial problems of the war economy for small concerns were not, however, insurmountable. Retail trade experienced, in fact, 'a substantial increase in turn-over' in the wake of the outbreak of war through panic buying of durables as a hedge against a feared inflation.[10]

One branch of business which suffered a setback — though it proved a temporary one — in the first war years was the tourist trade. Garmisch-Partenkirchen, Bavaria's leading resort, was exceptional in reporting high numbers of winter tourists in the early months of 1940. Retailers, it was said, were making excellent profits here as trippers bought up everything in sight. Neighbouring resorts were, however, doing less well despite ideal winter sport weather and an absence of coal supply problems while the rest of Germany was freezing. Businessmen in Oberammergau were said to have a 'feeling of indifference' (*Wurstigkeitsgefühl*) because of the drop in income and pessimism about Germany's war economy.[11] A fruit and vegetable dealer in a nearby village was reported to the police for insulting visitors trying to buy up his supplies by saying, 'you've shouted Heil Hitler so long that you've nothing more to eat' — one of the first signs of the growing friction between local shopkeepers and greedy trippers in the tourist areas.[12] Elsewhere in Bavaria the tourist trade was initially affected more than in the Garmisch area. In the *Fränkische Schweiz* district of Upper Franconia the introduction of ration cards was blamed for driving away the tourists. Little resorts, dependent on tourism for their livelihood, had been placing all hope in the autumn trippers after a disappointing summer season. Now, it was reported, all hope was gone; most of the guest-houses were completely empty.[13] In Berchtesgaden the restrictions on travel at Whitsuntide 1940 clouded the mood of all those gaining a living from tourism as they feared a serious drop in their

[10] GStA, MA 106678, RPvOF/MF, 7 Sept., 6 Oct., 7 Nov., 7 Dec. 1939; MA 106673, RPvNB/OP, 9 Oct., 9 Dec. 1939; MA 106671, RPvOB, 9 Nov., 11 Dec. 1939; StAB, K8/III, 18473, LR Ebermannstadt, 30 Sept. 1939.
[11] StAM, LRA 61617, GP Oberammergau, 23 Jan. 1940; Schupo Garmisch, 27 Jan. 1940; LR Garmisch, 29 Feb. 1940.
[12] Ibid., GK Garmisch, 28 Mar. 1940.
[13] StAB, K8/III, 18473, LR Ebermannstadt, 30 Sept. 1939.

income from the collapse of the tourist trade. War restrictions had seriously depleted business and in June the number of tourists was no more than a third of the previous year's figure – itself far from a record.[14] There was a depressed mood, too, in the Garmisch area where business men and guest-house owners feared even worse to come. Increased taxes, problems in obtaining sufficient foodstuffs, and bureaucratic food rationing controls were said to be creating great difficulties for business: 'almost every tradesman and business man worries about the continuance and maintenance of his concern.'[15]

By early 1941 the tourist trade faced different problems. A massive revival of tourism in the summer and winter following Germany's victory in the west in 1940, together with the addition of considerable numbers of evacuated women and children from areas threatened by air-raids, brought high profits but frustration for traders and hoteliers unable to acquire sufficient supplies to cope with demand and hemmed in on all sides by what they regarded as a superfluity of bureaucratic red tape. The large influx of visitors caused great friction with the local inhabitants, who blamed the greed and high living of the tourists for the shortages. Shopkeepers, often only too willing to take advantage of the situation, also came in for a good deal of abuse, frequently responding with a brusque 'take-it-or-leave-it' attitude towards their customers. It was anything but a *Volksgemeinschaft* idyll.[16]

Despite the apparently limitless opportunities for exploiting the war conditions in the 'playground of Germany', the mood among the business fraternity in the Garmisch area apparently left much to be desired. Reports from Mittenwald

[14] StAM, LRA 29655, LR Berchtesgaden, 3 May, 5 June 1940; GStA, MA 106671, RPvOB, 9 May, 8 June, 9 July, 9 Aug. 1940; MA 106683, RPvS, 9 July 1940.

[15] StAM, LRA 61617, GK Garmisch, 29 May 1940; GP Mittenwald, 25 Aug. 1940.

[16] Ibid., GK Garmisch, 29 Dec. 1940; LRA 61618, GK Garmisch, 28 Feb. 1941; Schupo Garmisch, 26 Feb. 1941; LR Garmisch, 31 Jan., 1 Aug., 1 Sept. 1941; GP Mittenwald, 25 Mar., 24 July 1941; StAM, LRA 29656, LR Berchtesgaden, 4 Sept. 1941; GP Marktschellenberg, 29 Sept. 1941; GStA, MA 106671, RPvOB, 9 Jan., 10 Mar., 9 Apr. 1941; MA 106674, RPvNB/OP, 8 Aug. 1941.

in summer 1941 point to the lack of interest in the great military events taking place on the eastern Front. This was put down to increased tax burdens, allegedly removing all incentive to strive for extra profit which would merely be creamed off in tax. It was claimed in business circles that the former free tradesman was being reduced to the level of a simple distributor of consumer goods. Whereas he used to work on a profit basis, he now could only await his consignment, distribute it at set prices, and shut up shop when supplies ran out. They described 'the entire present-day economic system' as a 'nationalization of trade and commerce leading to a lessening of achievement and increased cost of goods.'[17] The mood in the district was assessed by the *Gendarmerie* reporter as 'quite generally . . . bad and tired of war', comparable with the mood of 1917, and determined largely 'by satisfaction of palate and stomach' and by the 'constantly increasing great and small worries of everyday life'.[18] His lengthy report in August 1941 was largely concerned with the economic-based discontent, the negative reactions, and the worries of the trading and craft sectors of the *Mittelstand*. He registered a poor state of morale, disbelief in an early end to the war, and distrust of promises of an improvement in economic conditions once the war was over:

It is feared that after the war the *Mittelstand* of trade and commerce will be completely absorbed by the large concerns. The crafts fear that the labour needed for deployment in the new territories will be taken away from them by the labour exchanges and will have to work for larger concerns and that as a result a return of these workers to the native *Handwerk* will either only take place some years later or will only be possible to a very limited extent. And by then the native *Handwerk* will no longer be viable. The trade sector fears that as a result of the distribution principle their own entire stocks will have to be sold up to pay off their taxes and that the small salesman will have neither stock nor cash and will no longer be able to compete against the large dealers.[19]

The complaints of business circles about bureaucratic interference, worries about supplies and lack of labour, and

[17] StAM, LRA 61618, GP Mittenwald, 24 July 1941.
[18] Ibid., 24 May, 28 Nov. 1941.
[19] Ibid., 23 Aug. 1941.

fears for their future existence recur in differently structured areas. The *Landrat* of Ebermannstadt pointed out how disastrous the effects of the labour shortage were for his own district: 'The few stone quarries and water-powered sawworks still in operation are carrying out a hopeless fight to prevent the workers still left to them by the *Wehrmacht* from being called up by the Police Reserve etc.'[20] At the end of the same month, August 1941, he was writing: 'The general picture still remains more or less the same: one concern after another is condemned to shut down.'[21] A Middle Franconian district reported in February 1942 that only one hairdresser remained in business for a population of 4,000 inhabitants, and that there were only two butchers (one an apprentice) in the area, both due for call-up.[22] A report from the Würzburg SD in 1941 reckoned that the demand for apprentices in *Handwerk* could at best be only half met in the current situation and in the foreseeable future.[23] By early 1942 the demands of the eastern Front were biting even more deeply. The high level of call-ups in February 1942 produced extensive labour shortages in all branches of the economy. The most serious effects for small businesses were felt in the few civilian building firms still operational, in bakery and butchery businesses, and in metal crafts, where only a few apprentices and older workers unfit for active service were left.[24]

The worsening of Germany's military position during 1942 accentuated immeasurably all the pressures on small businesses and handicrafts. Complaints about shortages, lack of labour, falling turnover, and the stifling effect of bureaucratic intervention in the economy mounted on all sides.[25] Despite closures, labour exchanges were now reporting that

[20] StAB, K8/III, 18474, LR Ebermannstadt, 1 Aug. 1941, Wirtschaftlicher Lagebericht.
[21] Ibid., 30 Aug. 1941, Wirtschaftlicher Lagebericht.
[22] StAN, 212/11/VI, 1530, LR Hilpoltstein, 25 Feb. 1942.
[23] StAW, SD/34/8, HAS Würzburg, no date (1941). For figures on the labour shortage in various branches of trade and industry in this area, cf. SD/34/1, HAS Würzburg, no date (early 1941). Most reports of the Government Presidents at this time contain details on the scale of the problem.
[24] GStA, MA 106674, RPvNB/OP, 8 Mar. 1942.
[25] Cf. von Saldern, pp. 173–4.

they were unable to drain further supplies of labour for the armaments industry from small businesses.[26] Even in the still prosperous tourist areas of southern Bavaria the strains of war were now unmistakably telling. Intolerably long hours and overwork for both employees and owners of businesses were reflected in agitated and fractious behaviour towards visitors.[27] The resorts were swimming with visitors, though there was little satisfaction at the fact. Hotels were increasingly given over to providing accommodation for evacuees rather than for authentic tourists, the shortage of foodstuffs was creating enormous frustration and bitterness, and the black market was in full swing. The *Landrat* of Berchtesgaden requested in August 1942 urgent measures from the highest authorities either to reduce the numbers of visitors or to increase the allocation of food products. The SD in Berchtesgaden indicated a serious worsening of the situation, reporting that numerous shops had sought permission to close down because they were unable to obtain any supplies: 'One can listen in where one wants. Everywhere there is cursing and swearing.' The brunt of the unrest, however, was borne less by the government than by the visitors 'who arrive daily in swarms like locusts'.[28]

The closures of small businesses, which had been taking place gradually since the beginning of the war in a 'weeding-out' process aimed at finding military recruits and armaments workers, reached their climax in January 1943 with the closure, by order of the Reich Ministry of Economics, of concerns 'not absolutely necessary for the completion of the tasks of the war economy or securing the provisioning of the population', with a view to releasing labour for the 'total war' effort.[29] The results were less spectacular than envisaged, and the closing-down of commercial rivals was often cause for gladness rather than regret among traders and business men. Nevertheless, the overall impact of the closures was demoralizing and fears for the future of the *Mittelstand*

[26] GStA, MA 106679, RPvOF/MF, 7 July 1942.
[27] GStA, MA 106671, RPvOB, 9 July, 8 Aug., 9 Sept. 1942.
[28] StAM, LRA 29656, LR Berchtesgaden, 2 July, 1 Aug. 1942; GKF Berchtesgaden, 27 May 1942; SD-AS Berchtesgaden, 2 July, 27 July 1942.
[29] Winkler, 'Der entbehrliche Stand', p. 35.

were given new life. Owners of small businesses in Lower Franconia saw themselves 'robbed of their existence' and were of the opinion that a re-opening of their concerns after the war would not be allowed.[30] In Bad Kissingen the closures had a bad effect on morale:

Criticisms can now be heard about them which deviate sharply from the spirit of the fighting community (Kampfgemeinschaft) necessary among the people at the present time. Many people see in these measures purely party political actions . . . The closure and partial re-opening of public houses is regarded as a comedy and it is emphasized that the assessment of individual concerns is devoid of any honest and objective standpoint. The regard for the NSDAP has been gravely damaged by the intervention of the Party in the business closures and labour deployment in the province. According to rumour, national comrades stricken by closures and by loss of relatives have pulled down and smashed pictures of the Führer in their homes.[31]

In Bad Brückenau it was commonly felt that the war, like all others, was 'only a war of capital and a struggle of the great ones. For National Socialism also pursues in the last resort only the aim that after the war there will be just leaders and led — only great and small, and that the Mittelstand will disappear altogether.'[32]

Similar sentiments were expressed, according to the SD, in many parts of the Reich. The 'end of the Mittelstand' was feared in circles of small and medium industry in favour of the already generally perceptible construction of monopoly trusts and 'concentration of forces of a state-capitalist nature' in the interests only of a small ruling class. In the light of the closures, Nazism was said to be increasingly resembling Bolshevism. The SD interpreted such views as testimony to the prevailing worries about the nature of the Reich after the war:

The changes in all walks of life conditioned by the war are so incisive that the old conditions could not possibly be re-established afterwards. From the point of view of the leadership only the idea of the fight for existence or non-existence is emphasized at present. The national comrades want beyond that to know how they should shape their lives if they emerge from this war, in the Führer's term, as 'survivors'.[33]

[30] StAW, SD/36, HAS Würzburg, 15 Mar. 1943.
[31] StAW, SD/13, AS Bad Kissingen, 22 Apr. 1943.
[32] StAW, SD/12, AS Bad Brückenau, 7 May 1943.
[33] Meldungen, pp. 369–70; cf. also pp. 382, 470 and Steinert, pp. 360–1.

According to *Gau* reports reaching the Party Chancellory in May 1943 the mood in business circles was bad all over Germany: 'Business people of every kind openly curse the NSDAP and its leaders. "I didn't vote for Hitler!" has become a sort of catchphrase among business people.'[34]

However difficult it is to isolate the responses of the 'producing' sectors of the middle class during the war, it is even harder to reconstruct opinion and attitudes among the 'nonproductive' professional, white-collar, and civil service groups. Only rarely do the sources emanating from the Nazi authorities in this period offer insight into the reactions of these specific social groups. Something of an exception is provided by the reports of the Presidents of the Higher Regional Courts (*Oberlandesgerichtspräsidenten*, OLGP) based within Bavaria in Bamberg, Munich, and Nuremberg, which contain comment about the position and opinion of civil servants. The remarks are obviously based upon firsthand observation of *Beamte* in the Justice Administration, though much of what is said has wider applicability to most sections of the civil service. What follows is largely based upon the reports of the OLGP Bamberg, by far the most acute, frank, and critical of the three Bavarian heads of regional judicial administration.

The main problem for the administrative agencies, as for the economy, during the early war months was already the acute shortage of personnel. Complaints poured in from the earliest period of the war of the massive overwork of an already stretched administration, which with depleted personnel was now expected to cope with a hugely enlarged administrative load. The extremely long working hours and great stress was, it was claimed, putting considerable mental and physical strain on a civil service which, following the many call-ups of younger members, was overweighted with the elderly and infirm.[35] Apart from the burden of work,

[34] Cited by Steinert, p. 387. The latter comment was attributed specifically to Westphalia. For violent attacks on the Party, *Bonzen, Gauleiter* Hellmuth, and even Hitler among business and bourgeois circles of Lower Franconia, cf. StAW, SD/17, AS Kitzingen, 14 May 1943.

[35] Cf. GStA, MA 106673, RPvNB/OP, 8 Nov. 1939; MA 106678, RPvOF/MF, 6 Mar. 1940; StAB, K8/III, 18473, LR Ebermannstadt, 30 Sept. 1939; BAK, R22/3355, fol. 15v, OLGP Bamberg, 30 Apr. 1940.

two concerns came to dominate increasingly the reactions of civil servants to their wartime position: the feeling of growing deprivation and proletarianization as salaries failed to keep pace with rapid increases in food prices — a feature exacerbated by blockages in mobility and promotion; and even more so, the demoralization prompted by public vilification as Nazi propaganda used civil servants as whipping-boys and scapegoats for popular resentment at parasitic and privileged 'non-producers' and the bureaucratization of all walks of life.

According to the OLGP Bamberg in October 1940, the depressed mood among civil servants was attributable in no small measure to their poor financial straits. Serious indebtedness was not uncommon, and applications for public welfare from employees of the lower groups were often supported by 'credible assurances that they have no more than a single suit and a coat and no means of getting replacements.' It was precisely these groups, too, on whom the major burden of repeated Party and State collections fell. Lower civil servants were 'of the opinion that they must always give more because otherwise they or their children could encounter difficulties in their advancement.' Though salary reductions had not taken place since 1933, a regulated drop in salary would have been preferable in the eyes of many civil servants to the wholly arbitrary imposition of constant collections, backed by real or imagined political sanction.[36] In fact, a partial restoration of civil service salaries to their level before the Brüning cuts of the Depression era did take place in early 1941 — much to the disgust of other sectors of the population — but the increase could not assuage the discontent in civil service quarters. In autumn 1941 civil servants were still said to be suffering greatly relative to other groups in the current economic situation. A rise in salaries was put forward not merely as an aspiration, but as an urgent necessity. A further source of grievance, in particular among civil servants in the Justice Administration, was the unfavourable promotion outlook. The influence of the Party on promotions, the need for 'connections' in order to get anywhere, and the general corruption which pervaded

[36] BAK, R22/3355, fol. 27, OLGP Bamberg, 28 Oct. 1940.

public service were sources of great resentment. Salaries of State employees were contrasted with the higher salaries paid for often less well-qualified Party officials.[37] Loss of privilege and fears of diminished status also plagued civil servants, as when Robert Ley announced at the beginning of 1941 that all class and status distinctions would be abolished in provisions for the aged. Civil servants were disturbed that such measures were aimed at robbing them of their pension rights.[38] Discontent among civil servants was noted by the Würzburg SD office in April 1941 as on the increase, and the Bad Neustadt station registered the numerous complaints about civil servants deliberately not pulling their weight and in some cases revealing an outright oppositional stance towards the National Socialist State. Many were of the opinion that most civil servants were Nazis only on paper, from a sense of compulsion.[39]

Even more demoralizing than the economic worries of low pay and poor promotion prospects was the public contempt for civil servants which turned them by the mid-war period into social pariahs. From the civil servant's point of view this was incomprehensible. He was working harder than ever in the cause of the nation, and his reward was constant public ridicule and vilification. All other sections of society received public praise for their efforts, but the civil service, despite carrying one of the main burdens of the war, was wholly ignored.[40] By summer 1941 the mood of civil servants, though 'generally good', was said to have been influenced by the state of morale of other sectors of the population. The civil servant was prepared to go beyond the call of duty and to accept the considerable extra burdens imposed upon him by the personnel shortages without any thought of extra privileges or recompense. What was, however, most strongly and negatively felt by civil servants was the utter absence of

---

[37] Ibid., fols. 42v, 50v, 60, OLGP Bamberg, 31 Oct. 1941, 28 Feb. 1942; GenStA Bamberg, 1 Aug. 1941; StAW, SD/10/1, HAS Würzburg, 1 Feb. 1941; SD/23, AS Würzburg, 8 Apr., 22 Apr. 1941.

[38] BAK, R22/3355, fols. 30v–31, OLGP Bamberg, 2 Jan. 1941.

[39] StAW, SD/23, AS Würzburg, 22 Apr. 1941; SD/15, AS Bad Neustadt, 14 Mar. 1941.

[40] StAW, SD/10/1, HAS Würzburg, 1 Feb. 1941.

any sort of recognition by leading figures of the State such as that received by other social groups. Upsetting beyond all else was the public defamation of the civil servant as 'mentally and physically lazy' and concerned 'only with looking after himself'.[41]

In the deteriorating domestic conditions of 1942–3 the Nazi propaganda machine found the traditionally unpopular civil servant an easy and useful focus of pseudo-egalitarian resentments. The feelings of anxious insecurity among the civil servants themselves were not assuaged by rumours of a substantial lengthening of the working week, including regular Sunday work.[42] The constant denigration provoked counter-signs of class resentment among *Beamte*. The repeated passing-over of jurists and civil servants for the civilian war-service medal prompted the OLGP Bamberg to write in October 1942: 'It really isn't clear why for instance an urban street-cleaner, whatever his excellent achievements in this field, should be thought relatively more worthy in the war effort of the German people than, say, a proficient judge or lawyer in a responsible position.'[43] Goebbels's 'total war' speech in February 1943, in which 'wholly uncalled-for comments' again laid the blame for the inadequate war effort in great measure at the door of the civil servants, caused extensive alienation and 'strong ill-feeling':

If opinion had previously prevailed that the civil servant was constantly counter-poised to the worker, especially to the armaments worker, simply for propagandistic purposes, the view is now gaining ground that the attacks on civil servants are meant to form the prelude to anti-civil servant measures (abolition of pension and welfare rights). There are serious fears for the survival of the professional civil service.[44]

Apart from the generalized attacks on the civil service, the Justice Administration was of course particularly sensitive to the Nazi assault on the inadequacies of Germany's legal administrators, culminating in Hitler's extraordinary public

[41] BAK, R22/3355, fol. 45, OLGP Bamberg, 3 Sept. 1941.
[42] Ibid., fol. 76, OLGP Bamberg, 29 Oct. 1942.
[43] Ibid., fol. 76v, OLGP Bamberg, 29 Oct. 1942.
[44] Ibid., fol. 83, OLGP Bamberg, 29 Mar. 1943.

onslaught in his Reichstag speech on 26 April 1942.[45] The shocked reactions to the speech, evidently acutely experienced in all sections of the Justice Administration and in wider circles of the civil service, were articulated in the April and June reports of the OLGP Bamberg. He vigorously defended civil servants against Hitler's crude allegations that they were in Germany's critical hour concerned only with upholding their sectional rights, in particular to time off and holidays. He retorted even more vehemently to the Führer's defamation of judges, in which Hitler had castigated their 'wrong verdicts' and threatened instant dismissal for future occurrences. Judges as a group, he argued, certainly emerged in terms of mistakes and inadequacies favourably from any comparison with other professional groups, with the army, or with the Party:

It has therefore wounded the judge most deeply that in the view of the entire world he is threatened with dishonourable dismissal after perhaps an esteemed career lasting decades should one of his verdicts meet with the serious disapproval of the highest authority, whereby from previous experience neither the person concerned nor the Justice Administration has ever the possibility of justification. The position of the judge is all the more oppressive since . . . in some cases even of the most serious criminality a clear indication of what the State leadership wants is not at all recognizable.[46]

The OLGP Bamberg returned even more strongly to this theme in his next report. The attacks on civil servants, he admitted, had met with indifference rather than rejection among the public at large, which made them all the more wounding to civil servants themselves.

One asked oneself generally the question [he wrote] as to what monstrous events could have caused the Führer to defame and show up the civil service in this way before the entire world. All in all, whoever provided the Führer with the information for the domestic part of his speech on 26. 4. 42 and advised him, rendered him and the German people no good service.[47]

---

[45] Text of the speech in *Hitler.Reden und Proklamationen*, pp. 1865-77; partial translation in *Docs. on Nazism*, pp. 662-3; for reactions, cf. *Meldungen*, pp. 256-60; Steinert, pp. 287-94.
[46] BAK, R22/3355, fols. 62c-d, OLGP Bamberg, 30 Apr. 1942.
[47] Ibid., fols. 63a-b, OLGP Bamberg, 29 June 1942.

The last reports of this outspoken OLGP Bamberg between autumn 1943 and spring 1944 contain nothing new in the attitudes and responses of civil servants. Complaints about lack of recognition, overwork, and the strains of the personnel shortages persisted.[48] To the end, however, he continued to uphold the 'unchanged irreproachable bearing of the civil servants'. His final words in the last of his reports were, in fact, devoted to emphasizing the extent of the voluntary duties carried out by civil servants in the Party, in the NSV, and in civil defence work. It could even be said, he went on,

that civil servants look after almost the entire administrative business of the lower and middle Party offices. However the attitude of political circles towards the civil service has hardly altered, even if official discrimination from leading personalities has not occurred recently. That the winning of suitable young talent for a civil service career is encountering ever greater difficulties seems to be largely attributable to this low opinion of the civil service and of the work of civil servants.[49]

These comments indicate the pathetic nature of civil service opinion during the Third Reich, and in particular during the wartime period. Courting the regime, the civil service found itself taken advantage of and then spurned; seeking grace and favour, it met only with vilification and defamation; encountering rejection, its only response was to redouble its efforts to find acceptance. The growing alienation of most civil servants from the regime – as witnessed by the decline in use of the 'Heil Hitler' greeting even in top Bavarian government offices in the later war years[50] – was seldom prompted by ideological aversion. The arbitrary authority and 'egalitarianism' of the regime had not provided the form of authoritarianism which most Beamte would have been happy to accept. Above all, they felt like most Germans but in different ways victims of the regime which had brought them denigration and insult instead of the sort of rewards and status which they had expected and desired.

Beyond this there is little to be gleaned from the sources specifically about middle-class opinion during the war. There

[48] Ibid., fols. 86–86v, OLGP Bamberg, 2 Aug. 1943.
[49] Ibid., fol. 97, OLGP Bamberg, 3 Apr. 1944.
[50] Cf. HStA, MF 66928, Dr. Fritz Siebert an die Gefolgschaftsmitglieder des Finanzministeriums, 29 Mar. 1944.

is much evidence about the intense ill-feeling, anger, and bitterness provoked by food restrictions and other deprivations of war, and it is fair to assume that these feelings were shared by many middle-class German families. Vigorous anti-Nazi feelings were also aroused by the anti-Church measures of 1941, as we shall see in the next chapter, and again many middle-class churchgoers shared such antagonism. But in these matters we are dealing with opinion and behaviour which crossed class boundaries. Such specifically middle-class opinion as we have been able to establish in this chapter suggests that, in terms of reactions to their socio-economic position, the two years or so following the invasion of Russia formed the crucial period in which the middle class turned irredeemably against the Nazi regime. Their alienation from Nazism, rapidly accelerating from this period onwards, so far as it was not rooted in the Church–State conflict was largely pragmatic. Prosperity, stability, and order had proved merely transient, and the war had brought not temporary hardship followed by the bonanza of German hegemony in Europe but rather a tightening screw of State power on the *Mittelstand* posing a greater threat than ever of proletarianization.[51] From 1943 onwards, in the conditions of 'total war', the alienation of the middle class mingled with that of other groups of society to deprive the regime of any extensive base of popular support. The mounting terror of the last war years within Germany was testimony to the fact that the legitimacy of the National Socialist regime had dissolved, even among the section of society which had provided the core of its social base.

The middle-class social base of Nazism had, in fact, been dwindling even in the pre-war years before diminishing very rapidly from about 1942 onwards. Whatever discontent there was among the petty bourgeoisie, however, it was for the most part narrowly sectional in expression and of no great political significance. The regime's leaders were able to ignore the complaints of the middle class (as opposed to those of industrial workers) with total impunity. In this sense, the war revealed how 'dispensable' the middle class had become to

[51] Winkler, 'Der entbehrliche Stand', p. 36.

the Nazi regime.[52] At the same time, it would not be wise to push this point of 'dispensability' too far. Before the end of the war, Hitler had come to regard not only the *Mittelstand*, but German society itself as 'dispensable'.

[52] Ibid., esp. p. 40.

8. Nazism and the Church: the Last Confrontation, 1941

After subsiding into an uneasy partial truce in 1938–9 and continuing to simmer at just below boiling-point during the first war years, Church–State relations erupted again during 1941 as the Nazis launched what was to prove their final all-out offensive against the institutions, traditions, and values of in particular the Catholic community. The opposition of the churchgoing population reveals perhaps more clearly than any other single episode the depth and intensity of antagonism towards Nazism. It shows too the ability of ordinary people, even in the conditions of the police State, in certain circumstances effectively to organize the sabotage of specific measures of the regime. Not least, it demonstrates the reactions of the authorities (typically divided among themselves) to the threat of major popular disturbance, and their willingness to compromise and ultimately to capitulate in the face of hostile opinion. Not only the retreat of the authorities, however, but also the nature and limitations of the opposition itself indicate why such widespread unrest posed the regime so few serious problems.

The tension in the 'Church struggle' had already died away in the months preceding the outbreak of hostilities, and immediately after the start of the war Hitler had in fact ordered that no further measures were to be taken against either the Protestant or the Catholic Church for the duration of the war — itself testimony to the appreciated need to placate the churchgoing population and to retain its positive support during the conflict. Similarly, Hitler ordered in 1940 the suspension of all unnecessary measures which could lead to a worsening of Church–State relations. Given the need for national solidarity, the divisive issues of the 'Church struggle' were obviously both dangerous, and of secondary importance.[1] Nevertheless there followed in 1941, from a background which has never been completely elucidated, a new wave of attacks on the Churches which, as Hitler had rightly feared, led only to a futile alienation of support for the Nazi Party and State and threatened for a while to undermine morale and thus the war effort itself. The divergence between Hitler's cooling-down tactics and the provocative actions of Party activists is striking. It seems more than likely that this new wave of anti-Church agitation was stirred up from below rather than from above, though Martin Bormann at the hub of the Party Chancellory clearly did not find such activity unpalatable and for a time took a leading role in its orchestration. In a confidential circular to all *Gauleiter* in June 1941, Bormann stated categorically that Christianity and National Socialism were wholly incompatible and that the Party must struggle to break the power and eliminate the influence of the Church.[2] The *Gauleiter* and Party activists below them had by that time long taken their own initiatives in this direction and were using the supposed needs of war in an attempt — which backfired disastrously on them — to undermine the continuingly irksome hold of the Churches over much of the population.

Prominent among the new anti-Church measures was the disappropriation of monasteries. Between December 1940 and May 1941 the sequestration took place of the property of some 130 monasteries in Alsace-Lorraine, part of Poland, and in Greater Germany (seven of them in Bavaria), partly on the grounds that the property belonged to enemies of the State and partly to accommodate evacuees or make room for Party offices.[3] Among the dissolved Bavarian monasteries was the Benedictine Abbey of Münsterschwarzach in Lower Franconia, where the impressive new monastic church had only just been completed.[4] The hostility of the local population to the closure of the monastery was abundantly clear to the authorities on the spot. The Government President of Lower Franconia reported that the closure of Münsterschwarzach and rumours about the dissolution of other

---

[1] Conway, p. 232.   [2] Ibid., pp. 259-60, 383-6.
[3] Ibid., p. 257; KLB, ii. 378, n. 6; *Berichte des SD*, p. 484, n. 1.
[4] *Berichte des SD*, p. 313, n. 5.

monasteries had caused 'enormous anger' and had 'endangered the general morale in the most serious way':

Threats of work stoppages among the rural population as the result of anger and vexation over the Church measures are no rarity. Many national comrades want to tell their soldiers at the Front about the closure of the monastery and the circumstances surrounding it. They will certainly also feel the greatest indignation about it. But even those not attached to the Church are of the opinion that a measure such as the closing of the monastery of Münsterschwarzach should at present at all account have been stopped.[5]

Two days after the closure there was even a large protest demonstration of about 500 persons, mainly peasants with pitchforks, in Münsterschwarzach.[6] They were said to have made their sentiments known in no uncertain terms and to have treated the Party District Leader 'in most disrespectful fashion'. Even among Nazis such anti-Church measures were condemned 'because they are suited to cause unnecessary unrest among the people at a time when everything must be done to maintain unity.'[7] Even so, the demonstration met with no success. Few people outside the immediate vicinity probably even knew of the closure of Münsterschwarzach. Most probably scarcely even knew of its existence, and of those who did not a few undoubtedly had some sympathy with the official reasons for the closure.[8]

Though the closure of a monastery had no direct implications for the bulk of the Catholic population, other measures affected them much more directly and were guaranteed to increase the climate of unrest in the first half of 1941. The ban on Church publications, the placing of nurseries under the so-called 'brown sisters' of the NSV instead of under Catholic nuns, the abolition of some Church feast-days and the transfer of other major feasts from weekdays to

---

[5] GStA, MA 106681, RPvUF, 11 June 1941.

[6] *Berichte des SD*, p. 665, n. 2.

[7] BAK, R22/3355, fol. 39, OLGP Bamberg, 25 June 1941.

[8] Cf. the comment of H.W. Flannery, successor to William Shirer as German correspondent of the Columbia Broadcasting System, in his *Assignment to Berlin*, London, 1942, p. 132: 'The effect of the religious war was not apparent to many Germans, since it was not in the open . . . The monasteries and convents also were closed only one by one, and those in one district did not know, because of the controlled press, which was forbidden to mention such incidents, that what happened in their neighbourhood was not an isolated case.'

Sundays, and the attempt to abolish school prayers were all measures which greatly increased the tension in the Bavarian countryside in these months. Rumours circulated to the effect that priests would be required to find new jobs before the end of the year, and that the baptism of children would no longer be permitted. People were asking what was going to happen after the war if such things were already taking place. The authorities were for their part anxious not to underestimate the concern of the churchgoing population. If things went much further there could be a serious threat not only to morale at home, but also among soldiers at the Front.[9]

Meanwhile, a far more serious matter had for months been causing grave and mounting concern among the population, as rumours of a most disturbing and worrying kind were whispered from mouth to mouth. This was the notorious 'euthanasia action' which, though not a specifically anti-Church measure, struck directly at the heart of Christian teaching on the sanctity of human life — as well as affecting Catholic and Protestant patients in Church-run asylums. The 'euthanasia action' was set in motion by a secret written order of Hitler shortly after the beginning of the war.[10] By the time the 'action' was officially halted almost two years later it had accounted for the deaths of more than 70,000 mentally and physically handicapped persons.[11] The halting of the 'action' was the direct consequence of the pressure of 'public opinion' as the growing unease and opposition became articulated by the hierarchies of both Christian denominations in the most honourable episode in the otherwise chequered relations of the Churches with the National Socialist regime.

The regime appears in fact to have taken prior soundings about possible negative reactions of the Churches and their

---

[9] KLB iv. 288-9; KLB, iii. 220-1; KLB, i. 327-8; KLB, ii. 380-1; BAK R22/ 3355, fols. 39-40, OLGP Bamberg, 25 June 1941; R22/3381, fols. 76, 78v, OLGP Nürnberg, 1 July 1941, GenStA Nürnberg, 1 Aug. 1941.

[10] *Docs. on Nazism*, p. 614; B. Honolka, *Die Kreuzelschreiber*, Hamburg, 1961, p. 26.

[11] Honolka, pp. 98-9 estimates a figure as high as 90,000. The 'official' ending of the 'action' did not by any means put a complete halt to the murders, especially in concentration camps, of 'euthanasia' victims.

followers before commencing the 'action',[12] but if this was indeed the case then the response to the seeping out of disturbing rumours about the extermination of the mentally sick had evidently been miscalculated. The very secrecy of the 'action', as later with the 'Final Solution of the Jewish Question', points to the scepticism of the regime about the response of popular opinion. It was also proof of the limited extent to which the central racial-eugenic element of Nazi ideology had gained ground in popular consciousness.

The intended complete veil of secrecy was impossible to maintain, and within a year the signs of growing alarm and unrest in the provinces were common knowledge both to prominent Nazis and to Church leaders. The unrest in Württemberg in summer and autumn 1940, partly taken up in a weakly formulated protest letter to the Reich Minister of the Interior by Protestant Bishop Wurm, was sufficient to persuade Himmler to close down the extermination centre in Grafeneck on the Schwäbische Alb and to move the proceedings to Hadamar in Hesse.[13] More forthright letters of protest were sent to the Reich Chancellory and to the Reich Ministry of Justice by the leaders of the Catholic community, Cardinal Bertram, head of the Fulda Bishops' Conference, and Cardinal Faulhaber of Munich-Freising. Faulhaber, in his letter to Justice Minister Gürtner of 6 November 1940, provided hard evidence of what was taking place, spoke openly and categorically about the immorality of the killing of incurable mental patients and the incompatibility of euthanasia with the Christian moral code, and referred to 'great unrest', 'rumours', and 'panic' among the population.[14]

Reports from the Nazi authorities themselves confirm this impression of widespread grave disquiet among ordinary people in Bavaria by the end of 1940. One extensive report in November called the cover-up attempt 'laughable', pointing

---

[12] G. Sereny, *Into that Darkness. From Mercy Killing to Mass Murder*, London, 1974, pp. 60 ff.
[13] Honolka, pp. 84–90. The local population also became rapidly aware of what was happening in Hadamar, and this sanatorium, too, evoked a (belated) protest from the Catholic Bishop of Limburg in August 1941 — *Docs. on Nazism*, pp. 309–10; A. Mitscherlich and F. Mielke, *The Death Doctors*, London, 1962, p. 256.
[14] Honolka, pp. 90–4.

out that when such frequent notices of death were received from the same sanatorium, often containing exactly the same cause of death, the sham was obvious. Presumably in ignorance that the 'action' had been ordered by the Führer himself, the reporter added:

Whoever gave the advice to carry out these measures in this way must have a poor knowledge of the mentality of the people (*Volksseele*). They are all the more keenly discussed and condemned and destroy as hardly anything else confidence also in the Führer personally . . . The people reject in their feelings the thought that we have the right to gain financial and economic benefit from the elimination of national comrades who are no longer capable of working.

Furthermore, since Party officials were in no way able to satisfy the many complaints, enquiries, and protests which were pouring in, the anxieties about the 'action' were increasingly being directed at the representatives of the Churches.[15]

The reports of the OLGP Bamberg claimed the rumours began in earnest when several lunatic asylums in the area had all their patients transferred, to be followed shortly afterwards by the arrival, one after the other, of letters notifying of the sudden deaths of these former inmates. The concern, according to his reports, did not arise solely out of sympathy for the fate of the unfortunate victims of the 'action', but from the feeling that the arbitrary lawlessness of the measures, 'untenable in the long run in a constitutional state', afforded the individual no protection whatsoever so that the purely administrative definition of what was useful or useless life posed ultimately a threat to every single person.[16] There was some justification for the view that many objected not on principle to 'assistance in dying' (*Sterbehilfe*) for the incurably ill, but only to the fact that there was no legal base or published law for the 'action'.[17] One letter from

---

[15] IfZ, Nbg.-Dok. NO–520, Standartenführer Schiele, München, an Obergruppenführer Jüttner, München, 22 Nov. 1940. Cf. also the reports from two Franconian *Kreisleiter* about the embarrassing mistakes in the sending of death notification and the distrust of the official cause of death in ibid., PS–843, D–906/14; cf. Mitscherlich, pp. 250–2.

[16] BAK, R22/3355, fols. 31–31v, 34–34v, OLGP Bamberg, 2 Jan., 1 Mar. 1941.

[17] Cf. IfZ, Nbg.-Dok., NO–520; Mitscherlik, pp. 257 ff. for complaints about the lack of a law to cover the 'action'. Cf. in general on this aspect, L. Gruchmann, 'Euthanasie und Justiz im Dritten Reich', *VfZ*, xx (1972), 235–79.

a Nuremberg lady, evidently a Nazi sympathizer, captures this feeling. She had received notification of the death of both her sisters on successive days. They had suffered from quite different illnesses and were nine years apart in age. Nobody in the world, she said, could persuade her that this was a coincidence:

I could only find peace if I had the certainty that through a law of the Reich it were possible to release people from their incurable sufferings. This is a good deed both for the patient himself and also for the relatives, and a great lessening of the burden on Reich and people. If you could send me confirmation of an authorization for the release of these sick people, I should be very grateful. I myself and my relatives stand firm on the ground of the Third Reich and we would certainly not go against such an ordinance, since I myself have had to witness the misery of these many years. How often was it my only wish that both sisters would soon be released from their severe suffering. But that this, my most sincere wish, should be fulfilled in two days, that I cannot believe.

Permission was granted by the Reich Ministry of the Interior for the lady tactfully to be informed of the situation, provided she was 'politically reliable' and not attached to the Church. Following her interview with Party officials she professed herself content; she had wanted only to hear from the competent authorities 'that it was not a matter of a case here which dispensed with every form of legal foundation'.[18]

The confusion within the Party about how best to handle the unease among the people is shown in an enquiry from the District Leader of Ansbach to his superiors at the *Gau* Staff Office in Nuremberg about whether the Local Group Leader of Bruckberg, in his district, should be allowed to combat rumours that inmates of a nearby asylum, who had gone round from house to house demonstratively taking their leave from everyone in the village before being shipped off to a distant sanatorium, 'would soon be bumped off (*um die Ecke gebracht*), eliminated, or poisoned'. The District Leader himself took the view that it was better to say nothing at all, and he received strict instructions to this effect from the *Gau* Staff Office immediately on receipt of his letter.[19]

A report from early March 1941 dealing with the transfer of the mentally sick from another asylum in Middle Franconia

[18] IfZ, Nbg.-Dok. D-906/9, D-906/7, D-906/27.
[19] Ibid., D-906/5.

illustrates the clumsily obvious way in which the 'secret action' was carried out, the strong sense of unease and awareness by the distressed local population of exactly what was taking place, the part played by the local priest in stirring up such feelings, and also the fact that popular sentiment was shared even by Party members. Of the several hundred mentally deficient patients accommodated in the monastery of Ottilienheim in Absberg in the Gunzenhausen district, twenty-five had been transferred some time in late 1940 and all but one of these had subsequently died. Now, in the last week of February 1941, the rest of the inmates were to be taken away in buses which, instead of going into the courtyard of the asylum and loading up behind closed gates, stopped in the market-place so that the inmates had to be ordered out and forced into the buses. 'The entire population of Absberg, strongly Catholic, had gathered and watched the scene in tears . . . Among the weeping spectators were even some Party members, and comments were made amid the general uproar which must be classed as irresponsible.' The local priest had allegedly been instrumental in engineering the demonstration of human sympathy for the victims who, as everybody realized, were being taken off to a certain death. He had had all the inmates brought into the church and taken up to communion, the disabled carried to the altar by nuns.[20] The seriousness with which the Nazi authorities took such reports of popular unrest, and at the same time the difficulties in which the intended secrecy of the 'action' placed local functionaries by not allowing them to comment on the rumours, is reflected in the concern with which the Absberg incident was followed up. This included a letter from the Franconian *Gau* Staff Office to the Führer Chancellory requesting permission in future to put the Local Group Leaders in the picture beforehand so that he could arrange matters to avoid causing unrest in the population. Permission was refused.[21]

Most cases of local opposition considered in previous chapters resulted, as we have seen, in little action however strong the popular feeling behind it. This was frequently the

[20] Ibid., D-906/17–18.
[21] Ibid., D-906/3, 10–13; NO-575; PS-1969.

consequence not only of inability to organize opposition, but of the fact that the opposition was not taken up and voiced at a high level, nor the concern of individual sectors of the population widened into general concern. In the case of the 'euthanasia action' we see the exception to this general rule. Though Church leaders were responding to popular opinion as much as leading it, they showed themselves increasingly ready from the summer and autumn of 1940 to articulate the unrest and protest at the destruction of 'useless life'. It was the only time during the Third Reich that Church leaders showed their readiness to channel and direct public opinion in a matter not merely of denominational concern but in a matter of the most basic human right − the right to life. During 1941, as public anxiety deepened, the Church-led opposition to the 'euthanasia action' was brought out into the open. The most famous protest, and the most immediately effective in the prevailing climate, was that of Bishop Galen of Münster in his celebrated sermon on 3 August 1941, in which he publicly attacked euthanasia as a breach of the Fifth Commandment, thunderously denouncing the 'murder' of the mentally sick as opposed both to the Law of God and to the laws of the German State.[22] The Nazi leadership was urged to hang Galen. Goebbels pointed out, however, that 'if anything were done against the bishop, the population of Münster could be regarded as lost to the war effort, and the same could confidently be said of the whole of Westphalia.'[23] The only course of action was, in his opinion, not to challenge the Church as long as the war lasted. Instead, Hitler gave the order to halt the 'euthanasia action'.[24] It was a victory without parallel during the Third Reich for the force of popular opinion in a matter which lay not far from the heart of the Nazi racial-eugenic creed of social darwinism.

Even here the framework of oppositional opinion was limited. In some instances Nazis whose loyalty was beyond reproach were involved. And, as we have seen, the disturbing feature for some protesters was not the destruction of life

---

[22] Honolka, pp. 94–6.
[23] *Docs. on Nazism*, pp. 308–9.
[24] Honolka, p. 96. Cf. Sereny, p. 76, where the importance of the Galen sermon in helping to halt the 'action' is questioned.

itself, but the absence of a law officially permitting the life to be taken. Outside the ranks of churchgoers, especially Catholics, opinion on the justification of euthanasia seems, in fact, to have been quite divided, as the varied responses to the Nazi propaganda film on euthanasia, *I Accuse*, suggested.[25] Moreover, even Church leaders who had articulated the deep unease in the population did not distance themselves entirely from the policies and aims of the Nazi State. In the very same months that the 'euthanasia action' came under such forthright attack, Catholic bishops were helping to legitimize the brutal invasion of the USSR by publicly applauding it as 'truly a crusade, a holy war for homeland and people, for faith and Church, for Christ and his most holy Cross.'[26] The hatred for the Nazi regime of bishops such as Michael Rackl, just quoted, needs no stressing. But the partial identity of their values with the values of the detested National Socialist regime is equally clear.

However widespread the anxieties surrounding the 'euthanasia action' — which appears to have caused less of a stir in Bavaria than in some other parts of the Reich, especially those in the vicinity of the extermination sanatoriums — they provoked nothing like the extent of angry opposition caused by the renewed attack on Catholic traditions and institutions in the summer of 1941, culminating in a remarkable episode which put everything else in the shade: the attempt to remove the crucifixes from Bavarian schools.

We saw in Chapter 5 how emotive an issue the destruction or removal of crucifixes had proved in the pre-war period, especially in 1937 in the wake of the 'crucifix affair' in Oldenburg, and how the introduction of the 'community school' had been coupled with seemingly firm guarantees that the Christian character of Bavarian schools would be

---

[25] *Meldungen*, pp. 207–11.
[26] The words of Bishop Rackl of Eichstätt in a pastoral letter of 5 Oct. 1941 — KLB, ii. 394 ff. Cf. also Galen's expressed feelings of relief at hearing of the attack on the USSR and his prayers for the 'successful defence against the Bolshevik threat to our people', in *Berichte des SD*, pp. 570–1. In general for Catholic bishops' attitudes to the war, cf. Lewy, ch. 8 and G.C. Zahn, *German Catholics and Hitler's War: a Study in Political Control*, London, 1963.

upheld.[27] Apparently quite insensitive towards the depth of feeling on such an obviously provocative issue, Adolf Wagner, in his capacity as Minister of Education in Bavaria, issued on 23 April 1941 the so-called 'crucifix decree', by which the usual school prayer would be replaced by Nazi slogans or songs and crucifixes and Christian pictures were to be removed during the summer holidays and substituted by 'pictures suited to the present time'.[28] Wagner appears to have acted without any consultation with his colleagues in the Bavarian administration, presumably aiming to give effect to the new anti-Church climate in Bavaria, where the continued strength of the Church had been a constant thorn in the side of Nazi activists and radicals. It proved an extraordinary miscalculation of the strength of popular feeling.

Already in the early summer, on the basis of reports reaching them from every part of the province, all the Bavarian Government Presidents were registering their concern about the effect that the 'crucifix decree', coming on top of the measures interfering with Holy Days and other anti-Church pressure, was having on public order and on the morale of the Catholic population. In one Upper Franconian district it was said that no regulation or State decree had shaken confidence as much as the order to remove the crosses. Superstitious voices were saying that the hands and feet of anyone daring to touch a crucifix in a school would rot away. One peasant said he would prefer his three sons to fall at the Front rather than to come home to the even worse religious feuds which would take place after the war. In one place the reaction of the farming community was to cut their butter deliveries drastically. In another place the NSV functionary advised against removing the crucifixes because he feared that there would otherwise be a boycott of Party and State collections. One Local Group Leader said it was impossible

---

[27] Cf. above, p. 218 n. 4 for the assurances given at that time.

[28] Text in KLB, iv. 283, n. 3. The idea behind such a decree was already taking shape by mid-March, when a draft ordinance on removing *Kitsch* from classrooms included the phrase: 'Pictures of saints and other denominational pictures have no justification in the German community school, crucifixes only if they are of artistic value and are not larger than 20–30 cm' – HStA, MK 42584, Entwurf: 'Kitsch und Schule', 15 Mar. 1941.

in practical terms to comply with the decree because his position in the community would then become completely untenable, he would encounter economic boycotts, and any confidence in him would be irredeemably destroyed. Other functionaries agreed that the measure was mistaken and calculated only to heighten disunity and undermine morale. The decree had not only up till then proved ineffective, but its implementation would encounter difficulties and have serious lasting consequences.[29] These comments were taken up by the Government President of Upper and Middle Franconia as representative of the popular mood in his region.[30] Similar responses, reflected in protest demonstrations, petitions, refusal to send children to school, and other disturbances, were recorded in the other administrative regions. In Lower Franconia the decree was said to have affected popular feeling and opinion 'extraordinarily badly' and numerous cases of civil disobedience and public disorder were reported.[31] In Lower Bavaria and the Upper Palatinate the effect on morale was, it was claimed, far more unfavourable than the economic difficulties, and again 'the bitterness of the rural population about the removal of the crucifixes found expression at the beginning of the school year recently in greater or smaller actions in various places.' Local authorities reported their great fears for the continued willing co-operation of the population, the unity of the Party, the impact on WHW collections, and not least the effect on morale at the Front.[32] In Wagner's own *Gau* of Upper Bavaria, where feelings were running just as high and where similar scenes of unrest had taken place, direct reference was already being made — as in a protest petition of 218 parents from a village in the Rosenheim district — to the express guarantees which Wagner himself had given in 1937 at the time of the introduction of the 'community school'.[33]

[29] StAB, K8/III, 18474, GKF Ebermannstadt, 30 June 1941; GP Waischenfeld, 26 June 1941; GP Aufseß, 26 June 1941; GP Ebermannstadt, 27 June 1941; *Bayern I*, pp. 149-50.
[30] KLB, ii. 385.
[31] GStA, MA 106681, RPvUF, 11 July 1941; cf. also 11 June, 13 Aug. 1941.
[32] GStA, MA 106674, RPvNB/OP, 7 Sept., 8 Oct. 1941.
[33] GStA, MA 106671, RPvOB, 10 July 1941; cf. also 9 Aug. 1941.

Wagner's initial reaction to the furore he had provoked was a characteristic one. Instead of yielding to the force of popular opinion, represented in the misgivings of Nazi functionaries and government officials, he attempted in mid-August to step up the 'action' and accelerate the removal of all crosses from classrooms before the end of the summer holidays. Measures were, however, only to be taken in closest collaboration with the competent offices of the Party.[34] Only two weeks later, however, Wagner was forced to introduce a 'stop decree' which, in order to protect his own authority and prevent embarrassment, was to remain secret. Crucifixes already removed were not to be replaced in the school-rooms.[35] The 'stop decree' marked the end of the first phase of the 'crucifix affair'. Though it ought to have brought the entire episode to an end, it was in fact the prelude to even worse disturbances which lingered on until the end of the year. In the total administrative confusion which reigned after the 'stop decree', many local Party functionaries decided on their own authority and only at this stage to remove the crucifixes.[36] This remarkable state of affairs, a reflection of the administrative chaos prevailing in the Nazi State and directly too of the supposed secrecy surrounding the 'stop decree', meant that crucifixes were being removed from some schools precisely at the same time that other crucifixes (despite Wagner's order) were being returned to classrooms; and coinciding as all this did with the start of the new school year it meant that news of the crucifix struggles affected other localities, up to then quiet, which now also began to demand the replacement of the crosses in the schools. The intensity of feeling and nature of the opposition in the second phase of the 'crucifix action', after the 'stop decree', can best be seen through a depiction of events in one specific locality. The developments in the small town and district of Parsberg in the Upper Palatinate, a wholly Catholic area with

---

[34] KLB, iv. 291, n. 1.

[35] Text of 'stop decree' in KLB, iv. 293, n. 2.

[36] The administrative confusion was compounded by the fact that the 'stop decree' was only sent to *Party* offices, whereas the original decree of 23 April and the amendment of 14 August had passed to the school authorities through the usual channels of the local government authorities.

two-thirds of its population — above average for the region — engaged in some aspect of the rural economy, and where the Nazis had done reasonably well before the 'seizure of power' (gaining 44 per cent of the vote in 1933),[37] were not uncharacteristic of the situation in many Bavarian localities in the late summer of 1941.

Between the time of Wagner's original decree on 23 April and the 'stop decree' of 28 August crucifixes had been removed from only seven of the sixty-nine schools of the district. *After* the 'stop decree', the removal took place of a further fifteen crucifixes while at the same time public pressure was forcing the return of the crucifix in eight schools. Removal and replacement was therefore taking place simultaneously. The net result, by mid-September, was that fourteen of the sixty-nine schools had lost their crosses.[38] There had been anger and unrest among the population, but it had not until then resulted in any serious disturbance.

For the District Leader of the Party in the area, who was also the district school officer, the result of the 'crucifix action' was simply not good enough. The *Landrat* advised him strongly against any further action, which would he said have the likely consequence of disturbances, school strikes, and 'passive resistance', all the more so since the mood of the population in the light of the poor harvest weather, the 'catastrophic shortage of labour', and the constant call-ups was 'in any case not especially rosy'. The *Landrat* also informed the District Leader that any further removals could not, since the promulgation of the 'stop decree', be based upon the authority of the State. The District Leader replied that, acting solely in his capacity as District Leader of the Nazi Party and not as School Councillor, he would order the removal of the crosses from all schools as a Party mandate, and would see it through. The *Landrat* went away from their meeting with the strong impression 'that the District Leader

---

[37] Hagmann, pp. 14–15, 23.

[38] LRA Neumarkt in der Oberpfalz (Registratur), LRA Parsberg 939, LR Parsberg, 26 Sept. 1941, 'Vorfälle aus Anlaß der Herausnahme der Kruzifixe aus den Schulräumen'. The following depiction of events in Parsberg is based on documents from this informative file. I am grateful to the local authorities of Neumarkt i.d. Oberpfalz for allowing me to consult it.

greatly underestimated the difficulties with the deeply religious population' of the district. Undaunted, the District Leader ordered, at a meeting of all the teachers of the district but plainly with the authority only of Party District Leader, the removal of all crucifixes from every school in the district. Some teachers pointed out to him that a recent agreement reached between the archdiocese and the Education Ministry had established that the crucifixes should remain in the schools from which they had not been removed, but the District Leader was unshaken in his resolve. In the next few days, partly on the direct personal intervention of the District Leader, crucifixes disappeared from a further nineteen schools.[39]

The situation now became chaotic. In most villages the people gathered together and requested the teachers to replace the crucifixes. In seven places the teachers complied, but elsewhere they refused to bow to the pressure. The inconsistency of treatment helped fan the flames. School strikes began in numerous places and in Parsberg and Velburg, the two small towns of the district, there were public demonstrations of opposition to the District Leader's action.

In Parsberg a sizeable crowd gathered outside the school repeatedly demanding the replacement of the crucifix and threatening to use force if necessary to put the cross back in its place. Inside the school representatives of the crowd argued with the school authorities about why 'at such a time as our husbands are at the Front fighting for the Fatherland against Bolshevism such directives are carried out.' The crowd, swelling in numbers, moved on to the office of the *Landrat* and, finding him absent on business, eventually to the district Party office for a confrontation with the District Leader, where the exchanges became heated. The District Leader attempted to address the crowd but his words were drowned as the tumult grew. He said those who did not want to hear him should leave — at which all the crowd departed. Comments were heard about fighting Bolshevism at the Front and seeing it reared at home, and threats of resignation from the

---

[39] According to a table in the file, crucifixes were removed from forty out of sixty-nine schools (from one school twice).

Party and the women's organization, the *NS-Frauenschaft*, and of boycotting collections were voiced. A casual eye-witness described the scenes as unlike anything she had witnessed before, with civil servants from the *Landrat*'s office and doctors and nurses from the local hospital taking part. That afternoon, ten of 'the most prominent representatives of the Parsberg population' eventually managed to obtain an interview with the *Landrat*, who told them that it was a Party affair and none of his business. They then returned to the District Leader, reminding him of the 'stop decree', but the District Leader claimed he was not governed by this decree. Given the stubbornness of the District Leader, all that transpired from the day's protest demonstration was that one of the people's representatives, himself a member of the *Landrat*'s staff, undertook to compile an 'objective' report on the matter for the 'highest authority' (by which was probably meant the Government President), and that in the meantime the protesting population — and it was claimed that 95 per cent of Parsbergers were up in arms at the crucifix affair — would remain peaceful.[40]

The school strike in Parsberg was ended as a result of this agreement. In neighbouring Velburg the protest was less orderly and peaceful. A crowd estimated at 500 strong assembled there after Mass on 21 September and demanded from the mayor, who as Party Local Group Leader had removed the crosses from the school, the keys to the classrooms in order to replace the crucifixes. On his refusal the crowd pushed menacingly into his house and the mayor, reaching for his pistol, was pinned down. His wife gave out the keys and the protesters promptly replaced the crucifixes and then dispersed. The District Leader, on hearing the news, ordered the closure of the school until the crucifixes were again removed.[41] Even on receiving a directive from the

---

[40] LRA Neumarkt i.d. Oberpf., LRA Parsberg 939, GP Laaber, 20 Sept. 1941, 'Verbreitung von Gerüchten'; report of 19 Sept. 1941, 'Durchführung des Kreuzerlasses in Parsberg', signed by *Gewerberat* Ferstl 'as representative of the Parsberg people' and sent to the Government President of Lower Bavaria and the Upper Palatinate.

[41] Ibid., LR Parsberg, 26 Sept. 1941; GP Velburg, 21 Sept. 1941; KLB, iv. 294.

Bavarian Ministry of Education on 25 September ordering the immediate reopening of the school the *Landrat* felt compelled to hesitate since the District Leader 'understandably sees Velburg as a prestige case' and could give no assurances that he would not immediately remove the crosses again — which would have led 'inevitably to very disquieting and unpredictable commotions'. At the time that the report on the Velburg saga was compiled, the results of deliberations at the Ministry of Education together with further directives of the regional administration were still awaited. Eventually, on 2 October 1941 a confidential order by the Government President empowered the local educational authority to replace crucifixes in the schools. A week later, the District Leader had himself to send a circular to all headmasters permitting the reinstatement of the crosses. It was for him and for the Party a total defeat.[42]

What occurred in Parsberg was happening in the summer of 1941 over much of Bavaria. The peak of unrest was reached in September and October when the spread of the wholly uncoordinated, arbitrary actions of local Party functionaries coincided with the beginning of the new school years. The extent of the civil disobedience during these months was greater than at any previous time during the Third Reich in Bavaria. And the protest was largely spontaneous. It was for the most part initiated and organized by villagers or townspeople themselves and not manipulated or steered from above. Wagner himself, along with some local Party functionaries, was only too ready to lay the blame for the unrest squarely at the door of the clergy who, he said, had exploited the situation to unfold their 'counter-propaganda' in rural areas and 'to stir up protest measures'.[43] This allegation was strenuously denied by the Munich-Freising archdiocese,[44] and close examination of the organization and execution of the protests seems for the most part to bear this out. The

[42] LRA Neumarkt i.d. Oberpf., LRA Parsberg 939, decree of RPvNB/OP, 2 Oct. 1941; KL Parsberg, 9 Oct. 1941, 'Wiederanbringung der Kruzifixe in den Schulen'.

[43] HStA, MK 42584, Staatsminister für Unterricht und Kultus an den Reichsminister für Wissenschaft, Erziehung und Volksbildung, Berlin, 2 Sept. 1941.

[44] Ibid., Ordinariat München/Freising an den Stabsleiter des Bayerischen Staatsministerium für Unterricht und Kultus, 17 Nov. 1941.

authorities were unable directly to implicate priests, whose role seems largely to have consisted of providing tacit sanction and backing to the fight for the crosses while carefully refraining from deliberate provocation of action. Certainly Church leaders were anxious, while staying within the strict bounds of legality, to inform the Catholic population of the gravity of the situation and to remonstrate themselves with the civil authorities. Cardinal Faulhaber issued a powerfully emotive pastoral letter on 17 August in which he contrasted the removal of crucifixes from the schools with the placing of crosses on the graves of fallen warriors, leaving the strong impression that the *Wehrmacht* would be opposed to Wagner's decree.[45] The pastoral made a great impact and was scheduled to be re-read in all churches on 14 September, the Feast of the Elevation of the Holy Cross. So anxious were the Nazi authorities to avoid this re-reading on the very feast of the Cross at a time of such unrest that Wagner's Education Ministry entered into an agreement, amounting to little more than a capitulation, with the archdiocese of Munich-Freising. The 'crucifix decree' would not be mentioned, but as the price for this a form of prayer satisfactory to both sides would be introduced into schools, fifty-nine priests arrested for protesting about Nazi interference with Church holy days would be freed, and the planned dissolution of three junior seminaries would not now take place.[46] Instead of reading out the pastoral as originally planned, many priests referred directly or indirectly to the restoration of crosses in certain schools. One priest pointed out sarcastically that whereas Russia was a country in which the crucifix was banned, Germany was a much more fortunate country and the authorities deserved thanks for allowing the crucifixes to remain in the schools, where one hoped they would stay.[47] Another priest warned the faithful 'to gather around the cross'.[48] Other than providing this type of lead, however, there was no evidence that the clergy were behind the demonstrations and various forms of disturbance which took

[45] KLB, i. 332. [46] KLB, iv. 293, n. 3.
[47] KLB, i. 333.
[48] LRA Traunstein (Registratur), LRA Traunstein IV-7-177, GP Engelsberg, 14 Sept. 1941.

place. So much was, in fact, accepted by Reich Governor Epp, the highest authority in Bavaria, despite Wagner's allegations.[49]

The initiative behind the protests was more often than not taken by mothers of schoolchildren. They generally had little difficulty in persuading others to join them in a swelling body of support for the return of the crucifix. The mothers were more closely in touch with the school, and usually with the Church too, than any other section of the community, and in the context of village society it was often relatively easy to rouse support for such a symbolic cause. The issue was all the more emotive since, as the mothers never tired of pointing out, their husbands were away fighting on the 'crusade' (a frequently used term) against 'godless Bolshevism' while the 'Bolsheviks' at home were removing the crosses from schools. The fact that during the summer of 1941 the first noticeable losses at the Front began to make themselves felt in rural parishes also helped to shape the atmosphere of deep concern and the pent-up tensions among many of the village women-folk, which the removal of the crucifix highlighted. In a significant number of cases the direct action to replace the crucifix was taken in the immediate aftermath of a Mass for a fallen soldier from the village, and the link with the Front was also exploited in persuading young soldiers at home on leave to carry the cross back into the classrooms. In one such instance the soldiers, who had just attended a service for a fallen comrade, left notices chalked on the blackboards: 'Six Front soldiers carried in Christ and joined up with other communities on 29. 9. 41' — a reference to the known fact that the crucifixes had already been replaced in neighbouring villages. A crowd of about thirty people watched and applauded the soldiers. The mayor and *Gendarmerie* came by but refrained from intervening 'since resistance from the soldiers, in which the people would without doubt have participated, had to be reckoned with.' The soldiers — craftsmen and a farmer in civilian life, and nearly all in their twenties — were said to have had little to do with the Church

[49] GStA, Reichsstatthalter 157, Epp to Lammers, 23 Dec. 1941.

before the war.[50] In another case, soldiers — again after a service for a comrade who had fallen in action — seem to have taken the initiative themselves on hearing about the crucifix affair in a public house after Mass. They went out, bought three crucifixes, and entered the school, asking pupils in each class to stand up if they wished the crosses to be replaced. The children, presumably bewildered, did so and the soldiers hung up the crucifixes saying: 'Children, we need a Lord God. We were brought up thus in this house, and you should also be brought up in this way.' The news was said to have been received with joy by the local population.[51] In a village near Berchtesgaden the involvement of three soldiers seems to have been on a commercial basis. One of the local mothers, having collected 190 signatures and 285 RM in cash to pay for new crucifixes during a house-to-house campaign, paid the soldiers 10 RM for their work in replacing the crosses in the school.[52]

In one other obvious but highly effective way the 'mothers' revolt' was able to exploit the supposed unity of *Heimat* and *Front*: women were encouraged to write to their husbands about what was happening, and their replies, citing falling morale and utter dismay among soldiers in the front-line, were used as ammunition in the fight for the crosses. In one such example, the heads of schools in Forchheim, a town in Upper Franconia, received an anonymous letter in which was stated that within two days of hearing about the intention to remove the crucifix at the start of the summer holidays the writer and a hundred other women had written to their husbands at the Front. The letter she claimed to have received back from her husband described the terrible conditions in which they were fighting in Russia. He had not, he said, wanted to tell how bad conditions were, but after receiving his wife's letter about the intention to remove the crucifixes had decided that people ought to know about the realities of life at the Front:

---

[50] LRA Traunstein (Registratur), LRA Traunstein IV-7-177, GP Bergen, 30 Sept. 1941.

[51] Ibid., GP Reit im Winkl, 18 Sept. 1941.

[52] StAM, LRA 31933, GP Piding, 24 Sept. 1941.

I read it out immediately to all comrades. The effect was dreadful. These mud-encrusted, exhausted men cursed and ranted. You have no idea. *No one wanted to fight any longer.* Do we have to endure this unheard-of murder, this terrible struggle, these dreadful hardships, so that we are only skin and bones, just for *Bolsheviks* in the homeland? I only have the one wish: Our Lord should let me just once more back home. I'll sort out these *Heimat heroes*, so help me God. And a soldier keeps his word. Let me know immediately if they remove the cross.[53]

Whether or not the letter was wholly genuine or embellished, the point about declining morale at the Front was not one which was lost on the authorities.

The most frequent tactic used by the activist mothers was to send a delegation to the head teacher, the mayor, the local Party leader, and the *Landrat*, with a threat to remove their children from school until the crosses were replaced. In many instances a school strike began and successfully persuaded the local authorities that the time had come to bow to the pressure. On at least one occasion the children themselves went from house to house arranging a boycott of lessons.[54] Any form of unwillingness to concede on the part of the local authorities led to demonstrations by angry groups or crowds of people, prominent among them the women of the village. The impact on mayors and Party representatives was often compelling. At one village near Traunstein in Upper Bavaria the acting headmaster described the menacing crowd of about 150 men and women which assembled on 14 September in melodramatic terms as reminiscent of the revolutionary scenes of 1918![55] In another village in the same district a farmers' meeting attended by 180 farmers and about twenty women was used as the platform to launch a counter-offensive on the crucifix. The purpose of the meeting was to discuss hay delivery quotas, but as soon as the local peasant leader began his speech he was shouted down in an organized tumult. Immediate action was demanded and even a vote taken, revealing only one person not in favour of the crucifix being reinstated. The peasant

[53] StAB, K9/XV, 280, Bgm. Forchheim, 5 Sept. 1941 (emphasis as in original). Two other insulting anonymous letters are attached.
[54] LRA Traunstein (Registratur), LRA Traunstein IV-7-177, GP Grabenstätt, 17 Sept. 1941.
[55] Ibid., Schule Engelsberg, 18 Sept. 1941.

leader yielded to the mood and a delegation of eight peasants was selected to replace the cross. The local teacher also gave way when the delegation told him that nothing more would be delivered from the village until the crosses were replaced. The report on this incident closes by pointing out that the unevenness in the implementation of the crucifix removal had contributed greatly towards stirring up the mood. It was well known that in neighbouring villages the crucifix had not been removed at all, while in others it had been subsequently reinstated.[56] In the district town of Traunstein itself public disturbances were avoided, but a group of women went round house after house collecting signatories for a petition which, by the time it was sent in to the *Landrat*, numbered 2,331 names and included those of several *Beamte*. The words of the petition ran: 'The sons of our town stand in the East in the struggle against Bolshevism. Many are giving their lives in the cause. We cannot understand that particularly in this hard time people want to take the cross out of the schools. We want our children to be brought up under the sign of the cross.'[57] By the time of the petition, the people of the Traunstein district were well on the way to winning their campaign for the crosses: two-thirds of the crucifixes which had been removed had been put back in the schools.[58]

The unrest prompted quite gratuitously by Wagner's 'crucifix action' lasted deep into the autumn. It gave the Bavarian authorities a genuine shock, as the comments of Minister President Siebert and Reich Governor Epp reveal. Siebert, who had been given no forewarning of the 'crucifix decree' by Wagner, his arch-enemy in the Bavarian administration, attacked the latter's arbitrary action in curt tones in a personal letter to the Education Minister in January 1942. He said the mishandling of the 'crucifix question' had caused extraordinary ill-feeling in town and countryside, creating 'almost a revolutionary mood, which we are in no need of at

---

[56] Ibid., GP Grassau, 21 Sept. 1941.

[57] Ibid., LR Traunstein, 20 Sept. 1941, 13 June 1942, and entire petition in file (Heft 2).

[58] Ibid., LR Traunstein, 25 Sept. 1941; HStA, MK 42584, 'Übersicht über die Zahl der Schulorte . . . nach dem Stande am 4. 10. 1941'.

this time.'[59] Epp had already sent extracts from the reports of the Government Presidents to Lammers, head of the Reich Chancellory, in August 1941 in order to give him the flavour of responses to the 'crucifix decree', pointing out however that they provided 'only a weak, official picture of the true mood of the population as I perceive it on the basis of numerous complaints sent directly to me.'[60] In a further letter to Lammers in December 1941 Epp returned to the disastrous effects of the crucifix affair. The first rule of responsible leadership, believed Epp, was the preservation of morale in the *Heimat* during the hardships of war and the avoidance of unnecessary strains on that morale since, as every participant in the First World War was aware, morale at home could lift or depress morale at the Front:

State Minister Wagner wanted in his way to give visible effect to the teaching handed down by *Reichsleiter* Bormann, that National Socialism and Christianity are irreconcilable opposites. By so doing he has provoked demonstrations, school strikes, and unrest in the entire province . . . Much worse, the inner devastation of the people and with it the erection of a front of psychological resistance (*einer geistigen Widerstandsfront*) has remained.[61]

The 'crucifix affair' was a clear defeat for the Nazi administration in Bavaria and — within the scope of this limited issue — a triumph for popular opinion, which had devised its own rough and ready though very effective ways of countering the might of the police State and getting its way. A table compiled in Wagner's ministry gives an indication of the extent of the success in terms of the numbers of crucifixes removed from and retained in schools in Upper Bavaria. There were striking differences between one district and the next. In the Mühldorf district, for example, the crosses were removed from all forty-three schools, but by the date of the report (4 October 1941) only one cross had not been replaced. In the Ebersberg district, on the other hand, not a single crucifix had been removed at all. Much depended upon the keenness of the district Party office. In all, crucifixes had

[59] GStA, MA 105248, Siebert to Wagner, 29 Jan. 1942 (draft).
[60] GStA, Reichsstatthalter 157, Epp to Lammers, 15 Aug. 1941.
[61] Ibid., 23 Dec. 1941.

been removed from 389 of the 977 primary schools in Upper Bavaria (or 39 per cent). By 4 October 1941 only 107 crosses (11 per cent) were still missing from the schools, and the final tally was certainly much lower even than this figure.[62] The position of the Catholic Church was clearly strengthened as a consequence of the affair. The Nazis were now increasingly anxious to avoid any further confrontation for the duration of the war, and the Church was left in relative peace. The ease with which the Catholic Church was able to re-establish its position and authority in Bavaria immediately after the war is testimony in itself to the victory which it could ultimately claim in the hard struggle with Nazism, symbolized by the defiance of the 'crucifix decree' through the sturdy conservatism of the Catholic population. Party functionaries were only too well aware that the unprecedented success of the Church had badly affected morale within the Party and had confirmed that the hope of breaking down Catholic strongholds and replacing the world of Catholic tradition by Nazi values had now disappeared. The District Leader of Augsburg-Land even spoke of a 'change of role' between Church and Party compared with the 'time of struggle' before 1933, with the Church now going over to the offensive and using methods once employed by the Party to extend support.[63]

The increased isolation of Party representatives, especially in the countryside, was the opposite side of the Church's victory. Respect for local Party officials disappeared overnight; the position of many teachers — usually outspoken proponents of the Party's position on the crucifix — became quite untenable; Wagner's reputation was rock-bottom throughout Bavaria. An anonymous letter to Epp from 'some worried Party comrades' from Rosenheim in September 1941 points to a probably not untypical view of Wagner's action even in Party circles:

There really is no point sending us Party comrades to our national comrades with every conceivable task if on the other hand such stupid

---

[62] HStA, MK 42584, 'Betr. Entfernung der Kruzifixe aus den Schulen. Übersicht über die Zahl der Schulorte . . .' Cf. KLB, i. 334–5 for crucifixes replaced in Upper Bavarian schools after the date of the compilation of these figures.
[63] StANeu, LO A5, KL Augsburg-Stadt, 10 Sept. 1942.

things are going to be done which destroy every type of propaganda, agitation etc. At the present time, when the popular mood — unfortunately not particularly first-rate — needs every encouragement and pepping up, we find trampling about like a bull in a china shop not only bloody stupid (*geradezu saudumm*), pardon the language, but sabotage of the equally important job of constantly maintaining the will to hold out in the *Heimat* whatever happens.[64]

A similar assessment may well have been made by Hitler himself, whose popularity — not least because he was himself 'at the Front' and 'leading his soldiers in the fight against Bolshevism' — was left remarkably unscathed by the affair.[65] Hitler is said to have berated Wagner personally for his stupidity, and threatened to send him to Dachau should anything of the sort occur again.[66]

Despite the real enhancement of the Church's position and the enormous loss of face for the Nazi Party in the province, it is necessary to retain a sense of perspective about the nature and scale of popular opposition to the 'crucifix action'. Above all this has to be seen as a conflict *within* the parameters of Nazi rule. Distaste for Wagner's measures was widespread even within the Party and among many government officials. The hard core of Party activists were isolated at this level too and disowned by those who regarded themselves as every bit as good National Socialists but more shrewd in their political assessment of the state of opinion. Furthermore, it is also fully apparent from the reports on the affair that at the local level the mayors and even the teachers (though not usually the head teachers) often sympathized with the Church and saw the 'crucifix decree' as something which, regrettably, they had to carry out but which was wholly unnecessary. Such people were often still unwilling to recognize the innate anti-Christian essence of Nazism and were happy to support practically all Nazi aims except those of the few hotheads who maintained the uncalled-for attack on the Church. The participation in the opposition to the decree by many good Nazis, 'Old Fighters' and recipients of the Golden Badge of the Party, proud owners of the 'Mother's Cross', *Frauenschaft* members, Hitler Youth leaders, and others who,

[64] In: GStA, Reichsstatthalter 644.
[65] Cf. Kershaw, *Hitler-Mythos*, pp. 155–7.
[66] Peterson, p. 219.

apart from the Church question, had no objections to Nazism, demonstrates again the limited political and ideological framework of an opposition whose very narrowness of aim — replacement of the crosses and the upholding of religion in schools — was the key to its success. Though undoubtedly for many, perhaps for most, of the participants there was deep and genuine detestation of the Nazi Party as portrayed by its local representatives and by Wagner, the fervent belief in the 'anti-Bolshevik crusade' on the eastern Front and the condemnation of the 'Bolsheviks' at home itself demonstrates the narrowness of the divide between the ideology of the Catholic opposition and that of the Nazis in crucial spheres of Nazi policy. The violent anti-communism of the protestors finds expression time and time again, as (less frequently) do Nazified racial sentiments, in comments such as: 'The campaign against Jewish Bolshevism is in our eyes a crusade . . . The Catholics of Bavaria', on an anonymous postcard which landed on the desk of Minister President Siebert.[67] The continued support for Hitler, despite strong anti-Party feeling, is a further symptom of the ambivalent stance of many Catholics.[68]

The success of the opposition to the 'crucifix action' suggests the circumstances in which such opposition could be carried out. The sense of unity which the outrage against the symbol of Christianity created among the inhabitants of small villages in Bavaria was such that intimidation was ineffective. The fact that the 'revolt' prominently featured women, especially mothers of small children, further embarrassed the authorities. The issue was also clearly a highly charged, emotive one of quite a unique sort, and took place against the background of the Russian campaign and the mounting dead in the cause of the 'war against Bolshevism'. The opposition had, finally, not only a limited, but an *achievable* aim. Had Wagner unleashed a blitz assault on crucifixes in schools, in which they all disappeared overnight, opposition might have been negligible. The unevenness of the 'action'

---

[67] HStA, MK 42584, Der bayerische Ministerpräsident an das Staatsministerium für Unterricht und Kultus, 20 Aug. 1941.
[68] Kershaw, *Hitler-Mythos*, pp. 156–7.

meant that opposition could build up. At first it occurred in only a few places. But as more and more people learned that opposition could prove successful, so the tempo of opposition accelerated. Finally, and most important of all, the opposition to the removal of the crosses was successful because even for most leading Nazis the issue was wholly subordinate to the primary cause of preserving morale for the war effort. In the particular climate and given an issue which was hardly central to the main pursuits of the regime at that time, there was far too much at stake to risk alienating support and destroying soldiers' morale by attempting to enforce an unpopular measure for which the returns in terms of the war effort would be wholly negative.

Even so, the spectacular display of public protest against the 'crucifix action' does demonstrate the extent to which, even in the Nazi police State, popular opinion could be mobilized *against* measures of the regime. Evidently, on the issue of the crosses people were prepared to an unprecedented degree not only to think critically of the government, but actually to engage in protest action. Denominational issues were, it seems, the *only* matters which could so stir up antagonistic feeling. Certainly the depth of feeling and extent of action in this narrow denomination question contrast starkly and depressingly with the absence of strong feeling on the Jewish Question, even allowing for the higher degree of intimidation attached to racial issues. Popular opinion and the fate of the Jews in the war years is the subject of the next, and final, chapter.

9. Popular Opinion and the Extermination of the Jews

The fate of Bavarian Jews after 'Crystal Night' mirrors closely that of Jews from other parts of the Reich. By the beginning of the war, following the massively accelerated emigration after the pogrom, some 10,000 Jews – less than a third of the Jewish population of 1933 – remained in Bavaria (excluding the Palatinate).[1] The social isolation of these Jews was all but completed during the first war years. The physical presence of the Jew in the countryside or in small towns was now – except for certain parts of Swabia and Lower Franconia – largely a memory of the past, as the persecuted outcasts found their way to the slightly greater security of Jewish communities in the big cities of Munich, Nuremberg, Augsburg, and Würzburg. Following the law of 30 April 1939, preventing Jews and non-Jews from living in the same tenement blocks, the social isolation was increased by the creation of 'Jew houses' and the formation of ghettos in the large cities.[2] Munich provides an example of what was happening.[3] Between May and December 1939 some 900 Jewish dwellings were confiscated, the best of which were given over to Party functionaries, civil servants, or officers. At the start of the war, the city's Jews (numbering about 4,000) had to make room in their increasingly cramped accommodation for several hundred Jews moved to Munich from Baden. From 1939, too, Munich's Jews, like Jews elsewhere, were compelled to perform hard labour in a variety of degrading jobs, frequently as quasi-slave work-parties in armaments factories. By early 1941 many were put to work constructing ghetto barracks for the 'Jewish settlement' in the north of the city. By October that year the barracks were

[1] Ophir, *Die jüd. Gemeinden*, pp. 24–5, 27.
[2] Ibid., p. 27.
[3] Ibid., pp. 27, 54–5; cf. pp. 213–16 for Nuremberg.

accommodating 412 of Munich's Jews, eventually holding
1,376 persons although it was only meant to house a maximum of 1,100. The Milbertshofen Jewish settlement served
from November 1941 as a collecting point for the deportation of Munich's Jews to the death-camps of the east.
The depiction of Jews as the pariahs of the 'National
Community' found its symbolic expression in the introduction of the compulsory wearing of the yellow 'Star of
David' in September 1941. Only the actual physical removal
of the Jews from the sight of Germans now remained. This
was not long delayed.[4] The first deportations of 1,820 Jews
to Riga from collection points in Munich, Nuremberg, and
Würzburg took place in late November 1941. In Spring 1942
further deportations of almost 3,000 Jews to the Lublin area
of Poland followed, and during the remainder of 1942 and
the first half of 1943 another three-and-a-half thousand Jews
were transported to Auschwitz and (the large majority) to
Theresienstadt. In all, 8,376 Jews were deported from
Bavaria, almost all of them by September 1943. Their fate
in the camps of the east merged with that of the other
Jewish victims of the Nazis from within and outside Germany.
Those deported to Riga were most likely among the vast
numbers shot by the *Einsatzkommandos* of the *Sicherheitspolizei* between February and August 1942; those sent to
Lublin probably perished in the gas-chambers of Sobibor and
Belzec; very few survived the war. The post-war Jewish
communities in Bavaria (numbering 5,017 Jews in 1971) have
no direct line of continuity with the historic communities
extinguished by Nazi terror.

How did the Bavarian population, which as we have seen
was capable in the war years of significant expressions of
popular feeling and opposition to Nazi measures, react to the
persecution and deportation of the Jews? What did they
know of the horrors taking place in the occupied territories
of Poland and the Soviet Union?

Remarkable as it may sound, the Jewish Question was of no
more than minimal interest to the vast majority of Germans
during the war years in which the mass slaughter of Jews

[4] Ibid., pp. 28-9.

taking place in the occupied territories. The evidence, though surviving much more thinly for the war years than for the pre-war period, allows no other conclusion.

Above all, the war seems to have encouraged a 'retreat into the private sphere'[5] as regards political opinion in general and the Jewish issue in particular. Such a retreat into concerns of private interest and welfare to the exclusion of all else in conditions of crisis and danger is neither specific to Germany nor to societies under dictatorial rule, but the level of repression and the increasingly draconian punishment for politically nonconformist behaviour enhanced this trend in the German population during the war. Under the growing pressures of war, the worries about relatives at the Front, fears about bombing raids, and the intensified strain of daily existence, great concern for or interest in a minority social group was unlikely to be high. Moreover, the Jews, a generally unloved minority, had become, as we have just seen, almost totally isolated from the rest of German society. For most people, 'the Jew' was now a completely depersonalized image. The abstraction of the Jew had taken over more and more from the 'real' Jew who, whatever animosity he had caused, had been a flesh-and-blood person. The depersonalization of the Jew had been the real area of success of Nazi policy and propaganda on the Jewish Question. Coupled with the inevitable concern for matters only of immediate and personal importance, mainly the routine day-to-day economic worries, and the undoubted further weakening that the war brought in questions of moral principle, it ensured that the fate of the Jews would be far from the forefront of people's minds during the war years.

During the first two years of the war mention of the Jewish Question hardly occurs in the opinion reports of the Nazi authorities. SD informants in Bad Kissingen overheard conversations after the Polish campaign in late 1939 about the planned 'settlement' of Polish, Czech, and Austrian Jews in the Lublin area 'from which there would be no return', and from where it was presumed that the Jews concerned would go or be sent to Russia. This was said to have been

[5] Steinert, p. 242.

THE EXTERMINATION OF THE JEWS 361

'welcomed by Party comrades and by a great proportion of
the national comrades, and suggestions were heard that the
Jews who still live in Germany should also set out on their
march into this territory.'[6] Such comments clearly emanated
from Party circles. They are practically the sole recorded
comments about the Jews from Bavarian sources during the
first phase of the war. A more positive account, though from
a non-Bavarian source, of a Rabbi written towards the end of
1940, went so far as to claim that the Jewish Question had
become less important during the war, and that anti-Jewish
feeling among the ordinary population had declined. He
pointed to the active clandestine help which thousands of
Jews living in their ghetto-like conditions still received daily
from ordinary Germans.[7]

Whether or not this account was over-generous to the state
of opinion towards the Jews, there is no doubt that conditions
for the tiny Jewish minority deteriorated drastically following
the invasion of Russia in June 1941. Apart from the introduction of the 'Yellow Star' in September, a whole series of
new restrictions in the autumn deprived Jews of telephones,
newspapers, and ration cards for meat, milk, fish, white
bread, and many other consumer items. Jewish living conditions were reduced to a level far beyond the tolerable in
the same months that the first mass deportations to the east
got under way. This combination of anti-Jewish measures
occurred in one of the few short periods in the war when
public reactions found a muted and distorted echo in the
reports of the authorities.

According to a report of the Mayor of Augsburg, the
decree ordering the wearing of the 'Yellow Star' brought
expressions of 'great satisfaction among all national comrades'. A ban imposed in December on Jews attending
Augsburg's weekly market was, it was claimed, equally
welcomed.[8] Similar reactions to the introduction of the

StAW, SD/11/1, HAS Würzburg, 27 Nov. 1939.
[7] WL, PIIa/625, cited in A. Rodrigue, 'German Popular Opinion and the Jews
under the Nazi Dictatorship', Univ. of Manchester, B.A. thesis, typescript, 1978
(copy in WL), p. 43.
[8] GStA, MA 106683, RPvS, 8 Oct. 1941; 12 Jan. 1942; BAK, NS 26/1410,
Oberbgm. Augsburg, 6 Jan. 1942.

'Yellow Star' were recounted in the central SD report of 9 October 1941.[9] Summarizing responses, a later SD report emphasized that the decree had met a long-cherished wish of large sections of the population, especially where Jews were numerous, and that many were critical of the exceptions made for Jewish wives of 'aryans', saying this was not more than a 'half-measure'. The SD added that 'for most people a radical solution of the Jewish problem finds more understanding than any compromise, and that there existed in the widest circles the wish for a clear external separation between Jewry and German national comrades.' It was significant, it concluded, that the decree was not seen as a final measure, but as the signal for more incisive decrees with the aim of a final settlement of the Jewish Question.[10] It seems difficult to accept such comments as they stand. The tone is redolent only of the overtly Nazi element of the population, and it is more than likely that the SD was in this case as in other instances repeating comments made by Party members as general popular opinion. Understandably, those critical of the measure were far less open in their comments, though the SD reports themselves point out that 'isolated comments of sympathy' could be heard among the bourgeoisie and Catholics — the two groups most vociferous in their condemnation of earlier anti-Jewish measures — and 'medieval methods' were spoken of.[11] Almost certainly, those condemning the 'Yellow Star' decree were in a minority, as were those openly lauding the public branding of Jews. For the majority of the population, the decree passed without comment, and very likely without much notice.[12]

The deportations, beginning in autumn 1941, were also apparently accompanied by remarkably little attention of the non-Jewish population. Most reports fail to mention any reactions, confining their comments to a cold, factual account of the 'evacuations'.[13] In one or two instances stereotype

[9] Steinert, pp. 239–40.
[10] Ibid., p. 240; *Meldungen*, pp. 220 ff.
[11] Steinert, p. 239.
[12] Cf. ibid., p. 240, where it is pointed out that *NS-Frauenschaft* reports from different parts of the Reich mention reactions to the decree in only two areas, Hesse and Berlin (both of which still had relatively sizeable Jewish communities).
[13] Cf. *Bayern I*, pp. 484 ff.

'approval', 'satisfaction', or 'interest' of the local population is mentioned. The Nuremberg population was said to have 'noted approvingly' the first deportations from the city on 15 November 1941, and 'a great number' of Forchheim's inhabitants allegedly followed the departure of eight Jews from the town 'with interest and great satisfaction'.[14] Such generalized statements of approval, sceptical though one must be of their representative value, practically exhaust the Bavarian evidence on reactions to the deportations. For the rest, the silence is evocative.[15] The absence of registered reactions in the sources is probably not a grotesque distortion of popular attitudes. Not only intimidation but widespread indifference towards the remaining tiny Jewish minority explains the lack of involvement in their deportation. And where real interest was awakened on the part of the non-Jewish population it was less a product of human concern or moral principle than self-interest and the hope of material advantage. Such was the case when a complainant in Fürth near Nuremberg wrote to the Reich Governor of Bavaria in 1942 on behalf of the co-tenants of her apartment block protesting at the sequestration of Jewish property by the local Finance Office when so many were crying out for it. 'Where is the justice and *Volksgemeinschaft* in that?', she lamented.[16]

Such blatant self-interest existed alongside the widespread passivity and emotionless acceptance of the deportations. There can be little doubt that strong reactions would have left their mark in the reports of the authorities. Such reports contain a mass of comment critical of the regime. And at the very same time as the deportations were proceeding with minimal response from the population, the force of angry and concerned popular opinion was, as we have seen, bringing to a halt the removal of crucifixes from Bavarian schools and — of incomparably greater importance — the gassing of thousands of mentally defective persons in the 'euthanasia

---

[14] BAK, R22/3381, fol. 90v, GenStA Nürnberg, 10 Dec. 1941; StAB, K9/XV, 995, Kriminalpolizei Forchheim, 27 Nov. 1941.

[15] Evidence from regions outside Bavaria is summarized by Stokes, 'The German People', pp. 180 ff.

[16] In: GStA, Reichsstatthalter 823.

action'. Compared with the popular interest in the film *I Accuse*, which attempted a justification of euthanasia, the obnoxious 'documentary' film *The Eternal Jew* was apparently badly attended.[17] A second disguised private survey of opinion by Michael Müller-Claudius in 1942 revealed that whereas just under a third of his selected group of Party members had been indifferent or non-commital about the Jewish Question following the November pogrom of 1938, the figure was now 69 per cent.[18]

Though people often knew about the deportations before they took place, their knowledge of the fate of the Jews in the east has inevitably been the subject of much speculation and debate. Documentary evidence can hardly provide an adequate answer to the question: 'how much did the Germans know?', and given the generally prevailing silence and the difficulties of interpretation only tentative suggestions can be made. Undoubtedly, however, the generalization of one historian that 'people were acquainted with the ultimate fate of the deported Jews' is far too sweeping.[19] Most people in fact probably thought little and asked less about what was happening to the Jews in the east. The Jews were out of sight and literally out of mind for most. But there is incontrovertible evidence that knowledge of atrocities and mass shootings of Jews in the east was fairly widespread, mostly in the nature of rumour brought home by soldiers on leave. If most rumour was unspecific, eye-witness accounts of shootings and also broadcasts from foreign radios provided material which was sufficiently widely circulated for Bormann to feel

[17] Steinert, p. 243, citing a report from KL Kiel from December 1941; cf. also Stokes, 'The German People', p. 183, n. 64. On the other hand, the film did apparently run in sixty-six Berlin cinemas simultaneously in the autumn of 1940 (D. Singleton and A. Weidenfeld, *The Goebbels Experiment*, London, 1942, p. 213), and the anti-Semitic film '*Jud Süß*' was a popular success (R.E. Herzstein, *The War that Hitler Won. Nazi Propaganda*, London, 1979, p. 426).

[18] Müller-Claudius, pp. 167–76.

[19] Kulka, p. XLIV. Contrast Stokes, 'The German People', p. 181 and the sources listed in n. 57. A recent article by H.-H. Wilhelm, 'Wie geheim war die Endlösung?', in Benz (ed.), *Miscellanea*, pp. 131–8, goes even farther than Kulka in arguing that anyone with ears to hear and eyes to read could hardly fail to grasp the broad hints of extermination given in speeches and editorials by Nazi leaders during the war.

obliged in autumn 1942 to give new propaganda directives for countering the rumours of 'very sharp measures' taken against Jews in the east.[20] Concrete details were seldom known, but an awareness that dire things were happening to the Jews was sufficient to make people already worried about possible retaliatory measures of the enemy should Germany lose the war, as the Government President of Swabia pointed out in November 1942 in the light of 'a further rumour about the fate of the Jews taken to the east.'[21] A month later an SD report from Middle Franconia stated:

One of the strongest causes of unease among circles attached to the Church and in the rural population at the present time is formed by news from Russia in which shooting and extermination (*Ausrottung*) of the Jews is spoken about. This communication frequently leaves great anxiety, care, and worry in those sections of the population. According to widely held opinion among the rural population, it is not at all certain now that we will win the war and if the Jews come to Germany again they will exact dreadful revenge on us.[22]

A Catholic priest in the same locality also referred directly to the extermination of the Jews in a sermon in February 1943. He was reported as saying that Jesus was descended from the Jews and that it was therefore 'not right if Jewry was persecuted or exterminated (*ausgerottet*) since the Catholic faith was based upon the same.'[23]

It was, however, above all the attempts by Goebbels to exploit the discovery of mass graves of Polish officers at Katyn in April 1943 which suddenly cast a ray of light on knowledge among the German people of the murder of Jews in the eastern territories. The regional headquarters of the SD in Würzburg reported in mid-April:

The thorough and detailed reportage about the murder of 12,000 Polish officers by the GPU [Soviet secret police] had a mixed reception. Especially among sections of the intelligentsia, the propaganda put out by radio and press was rejected. Such reportage was regarded as exaggerated. Among those associated with the Churches the view was put forward that it could be a matter of mass graves laid out by Germans for the murdered Polish and Russian Jews.[24]

[20] Cited by Steinert, pp. 252 f.
[21] GStA, MA 106684, RPvS, 10 Nov. 1942.
[22] StAN, 212/11/VI, 1792, SD–AS Schwabach, 23 Dec. 1942.
[23] Ibid., 6 Mar. 1943.   [24] StAW, SD/37, HAS Würzburg, 17 Apr. 1943.

The Government President of Swabia also noted that, according to one report he had received, the Katyn propaganda had provoked 'discussion about the treatment of the Jews in Germany and in the eastern territories.'[25] Such comments were typical of remarks being noted in many parts of Germany. According to the SD's central digest, people were saying that Germans 'had no right to get worked up about this action of the Soviets because from the German side Poles and Jews have been done away with in much greater numbers.'[26] Party reports reaching Bormann spoke also of comments of clergy referring to the 'terrible and inhumane treatment meted out to the Jews by the SS' and to the 'blood guilt of the German people'.[27] Similar comments were heard after the uncovering at Winniza in July 1943 of mass graves of Ukrainian victims of the Russian secret police.[28] Soon afterwards, Bormann, commissioned directly by Hitler, provided new directives about treatment of the Jewish Question, stating now that in public 'all discussion of a future complete solution (Gesamtlösung)' had to cease, and it could only be said 'that Jews had been conscripted en bloc for appropriate deployment of labour.'[29] The Nazi leadership was clearly aware that public feeling in Germany was not ready for frank disclosures on the extermination of the Jews.

Recorded comments about the murder of Jews refer almost invariably to mass shootings by the Einsatzgruppen, which in many cases were directly witnessed by members of the Wehrmacht.[30] The gassing, both in mobile gas-units and then in the extermination camps, was carried out much more secretly, and found little echo inside Germany to go by the almost complete absence of documentary sources relating to it.[31] Even so, the silence was not total. Rumours did circulate, as two cases from the Munich 'Special Court' dating from 1943 and 1944 and referring to the gassing of Jews in

[25] GStA, MA 106684, RPvS, 10 May 1943.
[26] Meldungen, p. 383; Stokes, 'The German People', p. 186; Steinert, p. 255; Kulka, pp. 288-9.
[27] Kulka, p. 290, based on reports from North Westphalia.
[28] Stokes, 'The German People', p. 187; Steinert, p. 255.
[29] Cited in Steinert, p. 257.
[30] Cf. Docs. on Nazism, pp. 611 ff.
[31] Cf. Steinert, p. 261; Stokes, 'The German People', pp. 184-5.

mobile gas-vans, prove. In the first case a middle-aged Munich woman admitted having said in autumn 1943: 'Do you think then that nobody listens to the foreign broadcasts? They have loaded Jewish women and children into a wagon, driven out of the town, and exterminated (*vernichtet*) them with gas.' For these remarks, made to her neighbour's mother, and for derogatory comments about Hitler she was sentenced to three years in prison.[32] In the other case, an Augsburg furniture removal man was indicted of having declared in September 1944 that the Führer was a mass-murderer who had Jews loaded into a wagon and exterminated by gas.[33]

These appear to be the only instances in the Munich 'Special Court' files which touch upon the gassing of Jews in the occupied territories. They were presumably the tip of the iceberg, but on the available evidence one can take it no further. Whether there was anything like hard information circulating about the extermination camps in Poland is again a question which cannot be satisfactorily answered on the basis of available sources. The silence of the documents on this point has to be viewed critically. One might assume that knowledge – or at very least highly suggestive rumour – of the systematic extermination of the Jews in the camps was more widely circulating than is apparent from surviving documentation. On the other hand, many people genuinely first learnt about the nature and purpose of the camps in the horrifying disclosures at the Nuremberg Trials. It is quite likely, in fact, that there were differences in the degree of knowledge or surmise between the eastern regions bordering on Poland and areas in the west and south of the Reich. At any rate, according to a report of the *Gauleitung* of Upper Silesia in May 1943, following the Katyn disclosures, the Polish resistance movement had daubed up the slogan 'Russia-Katyn, Germany-Auschwitz' in public places of the industrial region of Upper Silesia. 'The concentration camp Auschwitz, generally known in the east, is meant', added the report.[34]

[32] StAM, SGM 12719.
[33] StAM, SGM 6501. The proceedings were abandoned when it transpired that he had been denounced out of sheer revenge for having denounced his accuser at an earlier date. This does not alter the fact that the case is proof of rumours circulating about gassing of Jews.
[34] Printed in Kulka, p. 289.

An exhaustive search of the extensive Bavarian materials, on the other hand, reveals no mention of the name Auschwitz, or of the name of any other extermination camp in the east. There was some knowledge of the camps among leading members of the group which plotted the attempt on Hitler's life in 1944 and among Church leaders, and the extent of auxiliary services to the camps meant that total secrecy was a practical impossibility.[35] The extent of knowledge will never be known. The judicious, if inconclusive, assessment of one historian that 'it may be doubted . . . whether even rumours of Auschwitz as a Jewish extermination centre had circulated widely throughout Germany — and if they had, whether they were believed', is probably as far as one can take it.[36]

All the evidence points towards the conclusion that for the people of Bavaria, as for the German population as a whole, the Jewish Question was hardly a central topic of concern during the war years. And most of what few comments survive from this period touch mainly upon the imagined connection between the persecution of the Jews and the war itself. A Munich waiter, for instance, was denounced for allegedly having said in May 1940 with typically Bavarian finesse: 'If they had left the Jews here and not chucked them out this bloody war would not have happened.'[37] A hairdresser, also from Munich, sentenced to four years in a penitentiary for repeatedly 'malicious, hateful, agitatory, and base-minded comments' about Führer, Party, and State in spring 1942 was said to have called Hitler 'a crazy massmurderer' and blamed him for the war 'because if he had left the Catholic Church and the Jews alone things would not have come to this pitch.' She added for good measure 'that she preferred Jewish women as customers to the wives of the SS men. In the course of time she had become sick to death of the latter.'[38] A number of comments betray the fact that many people regarded the allied bombing-raids as revenge and relaliation for the treatment of the Jews. A labourer in

[35] Cf. Stokes, 'The German People', p. 184; Steinert, pp. 258–9.
[36] Stokes, 'The German People', p. 185.
[37] StAM, SGM 12539.
[38] StAM, SGM 12573.

Weißenburg was condemned by the Munich 'Special Court' to eighteen months in prison for allegedly saying:

You will see alright. Weißenburg will have to put up with the flyers in good measure. The English haven't forgotten that so many from Weißenburg were in Dachau. In fact there were hardly any others in Dachau apart from those from Weißenburg. If only they had let the Jews go. They don't fly into the bishopric [of Eichstätt] because they [the people of Eichstätt] haven't done anything.[39]

In Lower Franconia, too, comments could be heard in the summer of 1943 relating the allied terror-bombing to retaliation for the November pogrom of 1938. People were asking whether the Jews would return to their former homes if Germany lost the war and pointed to the absence of air-raids on 'outright Jewish cities' like Fürth and Frankfurt.[40] The raids on Schweinfurt gave the inhabitants of Bad Brückenau renewed occasion in May 1944 to relate the bombing to Nazi anti-Jewish policies. Contrasts were drawn with the handling of the Jewish Question in Hungary, whose government had not followed the Nazi pattern of persecution of the Jews until March 1944:

Many national comrades are of the opinion that the Jewish Question has been solved by us in the most clumsy way possible. They say quite openly that Hungary has learnt from our failure in this matter. And certainly our cities would still be intact if we had only brought the Jews together in ghettos. In that way we would have today a very effective means of threat and counter-measure at our disposal.[41]

Similar sentiments also found expression in the files of unbelievably inhumane letters sent to Goebbels from all over Germany, themselves a witness of the success of years of propaganda, suggesting for example that Jews should not be allowed in air-raid shelters but should be herded together in the cities threatened by bombing and the numbers of their dead published immediately after each air-raid; or that the Americans and British should be told that ten Jews would be shot for each civilian killed in a bomb-attack.[42]

[39] StAM, SGM 12520.
[40] StAW, SD/37, HAS Würzburg, 7 Sept. 1943; cf. also SD/22, AS Schweinfurt, 6 Sept. 1943. Fürth and Frankfurt did not escape the bombing for much longer.
[41] StAW, SD/12, AS Bad Brückenau, 8 May 1944.   [42] Steinert, p. 260.

Comments about the relationship between the Jews and the war demonstrate — and we saw in Chapter 6 that this was a feature of the pre-war period too — that the methods of the persecution of the Jews were often criticized at the same time as the basic principles behind the persecution were found acceptable. Furthermore, talk of 'retaliatory' air-raids, or the 'revenge of the Jews' descending upon Germany if the war were lost,[43] all point unmistakably towards the traces of belief in a 'Jewish World Conspiracy' theory, present before the Third Reich and massively boosted by Nazi propaganda.[44]

The last two years of the war saw the 'broad mass' of 'ordinary' Germans preoccupied less than ever with the Jewish Question, despite an unceasing barrage of propaganda on the issue. By mid-1944 there were a mere 1,084 Jews left in Bavaria, in Germany as a whole fewer than 15,000.[45] Though slogans about the Jew being the world enemy continued to be pumped into young Germans, Party propagandists reckoned that hundreds of thousands of them were now hardly in a position to know 'what the Jew is'. Whereas the elder generation knew 'it' from their own experience, the Jew was for the young only a 'museum-piece', something to look at with curiosity, 'a fossil wonder-animal (fossiles Wundertier) with the yellow star on its breast, a witness to bygone times but not belonging to the present', something one had to journey far to see.[46] This remarkable admission is testimony at one and the same time to the progress of abstract anti-Semitism, and to the difficulty of keeping alive the hatred of an abstraction. To be anti-Semitic in Hitler's Germany was so commonplace as to go practically unnoticed.[47] And the hallmarks of anti-Semitic attitudes outlasted the Third Reich, to be detected in varying degrees of intensity in three-fifths of those Germans in the American Zone tested by public opinion researchers of the occupying forces in 1946.[48]

[43] StAM, SGM 12443.

[44] Cf. N. Cohn, *Warrant for Genocide*, London, 1967, for the spread of the 'world conspiracy' theory.

[45] Ophir, *Pinkas*, p. XL; Steinert, p. 259.

[46] Cited in Steinert, p. 259.

[47] Cf. Speer, p. 126.

[48] *Public Opinion in Occupied Germany. The OMGUS Surveys, 1945-1949*,

Very many, probably most, Germans were opposed to the Jews during the Third Reich, welcomed their exclusion from economy and society, saw them as natural outsiders to the German 'National Community', a dangerous minority against whom it was legitimate to discriminate. Most would have drawn the line at physical maltreatment. The Nazi Mayor of Mainstockheim near Kitzingen in Lower Franconia no doubt spoke for many when, in preventing violence and destruction by SA and Party fanatics during the pogrom of November 1938, he reportedly said: 'You don't have to have anything to do with the Jews. But you have got to leave them in peace.'[49] Such an attitude was not violent. But it was discriminatory. And such 'mild' anti-Semitism was clearly quite incapable of containing the progressive radical dynamism of the racial fanatics and the deadly bureaucratization of the doctrine of race-hatred. Our examination of popular opinion on the Jewish Question has shown that in its anti-Jewish policies the Nazi regime acted not in plebiscitary fashion, but with increasing autonomy from popular opinion until the extermination policy in the east was carried out by the SS and SD as a 'never to be written glorious page of our history', as Himmler put it, whose secret it was better to carry to the grave.[50] The very secrecy of the 'Final Solution' demonstrates more clearly than anything else the fact that the Nazi leadership felt it could not rely on popular backing for its extermination policy.

And yet it would be a crass over-simplification to attribute simply and solely to the criminal ideological paranoia of Hitler, Heydrich, and a few other leading personalities of the Third Reich the implementation of policies which led to the death-camps. The 'Final Solution' would not have been possible without the progressive steps to exclude the Jews from German society which took place in full view of the

---

ed. by A.J. Merritt and R.L. Merritt, Urbana, 1970, pp. 146 f.; cf. pp. 239 f. for a second survey in April 1948.

[49] WL, 'Der 10. Nov.', pp. 28 f.

[50] *International Military Tribunal*, xxix, pp. 145 ff (Doc.PS-1919); H. Buchheim, 'Command and Compliance', in H. Krausnick *et al.*, *Anatomy of the SS State*, London, 1968, p. 359.

public, in their legal form met with widespread approval, and resulted in the depersonalization and debasement of the figure of the Jew. It would not have been possible without the apathy and widespread indifference which was the common response to the propaganda of hate. And it would not have been possible, finally, without the silence of the Church hierarchies, who failed to articulate what opposition there was to Nazi racial policies, and without the consent ranging to active complicity of other prominent sections of the German élites — the civil service bureaucracy, the armed forces, and not least leading sectors of industry. Ultimately, therefore, dynamic hatred of the masses was unnecessary. Their latent anti-Semitism and apathy sufficed to allow the increasingly criminal 'dynamic' hatred of the Nazi regime the autonomy it needed to set in motion the holocaust.

Conclusion

We have examined three selected spheres of popular opinion in the Third Reich. The first comprised the subjective perception by differing social groups of their own socio-economic position during the Nazi dictatorship. The evidence we considered suggests strongly that the material conditions directly affecting the everyday lives of the population provided the most continuous, and usually the most dominant, influence upon the formation of political opinion. The acute perception of social injustice, the class-conscious awareness of inequalities, the persistent feelings of exploitation by *'die Großen'* indicate that status awareness — how people saw themselves and others around them — changed less in the Third Reich than is often supposed. We have seen considerable cause to doubt the assertion of the latest biographer of Hitler, that 'one of Hitler's unique tricks was to give the Germans a sense of community, of sacrifice, of joint effort, while in fact he also gave them a better life.'[1] The view that a revolution in status perception amounting to a 'triumph of egalitarianism' took place between 1933 and 1939 also seems hard to accept on the evidence presented here, as does the considered opinion that 'interpreted social reality . . . reflected a society united like no other in recent German history.'[2] The material we have reviewed reveals, in fact, beneath the surface unity of the propaganda image, a remarkably disunited society. Under the propaganda varnish of the 'National Community' old antagonisms continued unabated, heightened even by Nazi social and economic policy, and new ones were added to them. The extent of disillusionment and discontent in almost all sections of the population, rooted in the socio-economic experience of daily life, is remarkable. This 'real world' of the Third Reich, as it affected the everyday lives

---

[1] N. Stone, *Hitler*, London, 1980, p. 55.
[2] Schoenbaum, pp. 272-3, 283, 285-6.

of ordinary people, was one filled with dissension and conflict. It scarcely amounted to a 'wonderland' in which no one was sure 'what was up and what was down'.[3] Most people, as we have seen, were in little doubt about that.

At the same time, the shallowness of much opinion, its lack of political significance, and its frequent susceptibility to the penetration of Nazi ideas has been amply demonstrated. Widespread though the discontent was in all sections of the population with the results of Nazi social and economic policies, it seldom became translated into political opposition. Dissent was overwhelmingly verbal. Frequently it amounted to no more than the traditional grumblings about prices, pay, labour shortages, work conditions, bureaucratic controls, and the many other grievances which people in all societies find to preoccupy them. The difference to most other societies was, however, that these complaints were now politicized by the regime itself and thereby turned into political dissent. The age-old sport of venting spleen on the government, whatever its colour, was turned by the Nazis into punishable crime. The result of this, however, and of the attempted politicization of all spheres of daily life by the regime, meant in practice that the association of economic discontent with aversion to the Nazi form of government was sharpened.[4] Even so, such alienation as took place was for the most part of little moment for the regime. As we saw, observers agreed that criticism of the regime was at its most vehement among the peasantry and the *Mittelstand*. Yet this produced few outward signs of opposition. Despite the obviously massive discontent among the peasantry about the labour shortage and about the intervention of the Reich Food Estate in marketing and production, peasant opposition was minimal compared for instance with that offered by Soviet peasants during Stalin's forced collectivization in the

---

[3] Ibid., pp. 280-1.

[4] For the general theoretical problem of the relationship between economic militancy and anti-State protest, see D. Geary, 'Identifying Militancy: The Assessment of Working-Class Attitudes Towards State and Society', in R.J. Evans (ed.), *The German Working Class*, London, 1981, and cf. also D. Geary, *European Labour Protest, 1848-1939*, London, 1981.

early 1930s.[5] Though disenchanted by Nazi policies, German farmers seldom felt their very existence as a class threatened. From middle-class social groups there was even less active opposition, whatever the undoubted grievances. It is, in fact, in part the very absence of opposition which makes the middle class under Nazism such a difficult subject to analyse. The case of the working class is clearly different. Here the level of repression — far greater than that encountered in the countryside or by the petty bourgeoisie — saw to it that expressions of hostility were voiced less readily·and more carefully. However, the political background, the nature of industrial work, and the existing traditions of class consciousness and solidarity prompted an increase in *active* dissent and opposition in the changing conditions after 1936. Protest was not necessarily politically motivated. But it was evaluated and interpreted as a political act by the regime itself. This had its own logic. The peasantry and the middle-class groups posed no threat to the regime. If disenchanted, querulous, angered, and frustrated, such groups were not totally alienated by Nazism. Their grievances in one direction were so frequently overcome by integration in another. They could identify with and approve of much that Nazism stood for and could offer them. Working-class dissent was of an entirely different order of importance. Quite apart from the activities of the underground illegal organizations, it potentially endangered the stability of the regime and the accomplishment of its aims. Furthermore, the attempt to integrate the industrial working class into the Third Reich was only partially and half-heartedly carried out. The alienation of the majority of industrial workers, who had lost much and gained little through Nazism, ran recognizably deep. And it was a constant source of worry to the Nazi rulers.[6]

The second sphere of popular opinion we examined concerned the impact upon the political attitudes of Catholics and Protestants of the Church–State conflict.

[5] For peasant opposition in the Smolensk area during the collectivization period, see D.R. Brower, 'Collectivized Agriculture in Smolensk: The Party, the Peasantry, and the Crisis of 1932', *Russian Review*, xxxvi (1977), 151–66, and M. Fainsod, *Smolensk under Soviet Rule*, New York, 1963.

[6] Cf. Mason, 'The Workers' Opposition', and Mason, 'Containment', *passim*.

If discontent with the material conditions of everyday life was the most continuous force shaping popular opinion in the Third Reich among all social classes — though resulting, apart from among the working class, in little active opposition — the deepest antagonisms and sharpest forms of dissent and popular opposition which we have encountered in Bavaria were not the product of class relations or economic conditions at all. Among the substantial sections of the population closely attached to the major religious denominations, no single aspect of Nazism created so much hostility or shaped attitudes towards the regime as decisively as the attack on the Christian Churches. While both Churches had much weaker support among the industrial working class than among the peasantry and petty bourgeoisie — the social composition of the Protestant opposition over the Meiser affair in 1934 and of the Catholic defiance of the 'crucifix edict' in 1941 was heavily drawn from the latter two social groups — the 'Church struggle' clearly united widely differing sections of the population in the conservative defence of existing institutions, traditions, and values. The alienation caused by anti-Church measures was, as we saw, taken seriously by the authorities. The opposition broke down, however, at the point where conservative and Nazi values converged. The alienation was seldom total. It amounted for the most part to a realignment of relationships between the churchgoing population and the Nazi regime, but not to a permanent or total disintegration nor to a substantive threat to the stability of the regime.

At the same time, the evidence we considered suggests that Nazi policy failed categorically to break down existing religious allegiances. The view that 'by inroads on religious traditionalism . . . the Nazis won their successes in their struggle against the Churches'[7] accords only in a most superficial sense with the conclusions derived from this study. Arguably, the renewed influence of the Churches in the postwar society of West Germany, especially in predominantly Catholic regions such as Bavaria, where even the denominational primary school — the butt of Nazi ideological

---

[7] Dahrendorf, p. 410.

Gleichschaltung — was restored after 1945,[8] is itself testimony to the limited impact of Nazism on the social position and role of the Churches, and to the ultimate success of especially the Catholic Church's policy of self-preservation during the Third Reich.

The third aspect of popular opinion dealt with in this study relates to the persecution of the Jews. Compared with the simmering unrest and discontent on economic matters and the depth of feeling which gave rise on occasion to explosive and, within a limited framework, often effective outbursts of opposition on Church issues, the detachment and general lack of active interest and involvement when it came to anti-Jewish policies and measures is depressingly striking. The secondary relevance of the Jewish Question as far as popular opinion was concerned stands out in sharp relief from the primary importance attached to it in Nazi ideology and by the leaders of Party and State. This central issue for Hitler and the Nazi leadership was, contrary to what is often thought about the 'scapegoat' value of the Jews, largely unsuccessful as an agent for mobilizing and integrating the masses. On the other hand, the undoubted utility of a whipped-up anti-Jewish campaign for stirring Party activists into motion or allowing them to let off steam seems clear. And the masses, if not galvanized into active demonstrations of hatred, were for the most part sympathetic — increasingly so it seems — towards Nazi aims though not methods. The major barriers to the penetration of Nazi race hatred were provided by adherence to Christian or to liberal humanist values. As the reactions to 'Crystal Night' from Bavaria and other parts of the Reich showed, disgust, anger, and sympathy for the Jews was most prominently forthcoming in Church circles (especially in Catholic areas) and among liberal intellectuals.

The lack of any substantial protest in the Jewish Question may fairly be attributable in good measure to the fear and sense of hopelessness at crossing the Nazis on an issue which

---

[8] Spindler, pp. 985-6. As late as 1964-5 only 3.7 per cent of Bavarian primary schools were 'community schools', 96.3 per cent denominational. In 1968, with the approval of the Churches, a 'uniform Christian primary school' following common tenets of Christianity was introduced throughout Bavaria.

they regarded as of such prime importance. At the same time, the autonomy which the regime developed in its handling of the Jewish Question has also to be seen as a reflection of the fact that, unlike the Church–State conflict or social policy, few strong feelings (other than those of Nazis themselves) existed on the issue. The regime could act, as it were, in a vacuum of opinion and in the certainty that the persecution of such an isolated minority would provoke no significant opposition even if there was little active backing for it. We saw that the Churches preferred silence and non-participation in the Jewish Question. Prominent and influential intellectuals, the other possible opinion-leaders,[9] had silence forced upon them — so far as they had not chosen or been compelled to take the path of emigration — or retired to the passive disapproval of the 'inner emigration'.[10]

Seldom has a government placed so much store on the control and manipulation of opinion as did the Nazi regime. Yet, despite some notable propaganda successes, steerage was incomplete. A 'popular opinion' independent of the Goebbels-directed 'public opinion' continued to exist beneath the monolithic uniformity of the Third Reich's propaganda image.

Seldom has a government sought to delimit so rigidly the terms of politically acceptable behaviour and to punish so remorselessly all dissenting voices as did the Nazi regime. Yet, despite the massively intimidating coercive apparatus of the police State, opposition in a wide variety of forms, even leaving aside the brave few who daily risked their lives in the twilight world of the underground resistance, continued to exist beneath the monolithic image of total consensus and total control.

At the end of this study of popular opinion and political dissent in Nazi Germany, it is reasonable to ask to what extent popular opinion and 'popular opposition' influenced Nazi policy, whether in fact it had any impact at all on the

---

[9] Cf. G. Ionescu and I. de Madariaga, *Opposition, Past and Present of a Political Institution*, London, 1968, pp. 171–8.

[10] For a good example of the dilemmas facing one prominent German intellectual who decided to stay in Germany cf. E. Heisenberg, *Das politische Leben eines Unpolitischen. Erinnerungen an Werner Heisenberg*, Munich, 1980.

Nazi leadership, or whether the regime could ignore it altogether.

In the sphere of social policy, the regime's apprehension about stirring up unrest in the industrial working class, rooted in memories of 1918, certainly limited its manoeuvrability.[11] Contrary to much weighty advice, Hitler was unwilling to depress living standards by cutting spending in the pre-war years, and anxious to avoid imposing too many demands on the civilian population during the war. In 1938 Hitler himself banned any rise in food prices because of its likely effect on morale, and just after the beginning of the war the attempt to reduce wages and abolish various bonuses was abandoned following worker protest and the threat of disruptive unrest in major industrial regions.[12] In the spring of 1940, after a winter of considerable unrest caused by the coal crisis, Goebbels thought the mood regarding food shortages so critical that he ordered the Propaganda Ministry to treat the subject with great caution, adding his own intention of improving food rations in Berlin since in the case of any further fall in rations morale in the city could scarcely be maintained.[13] The reluctance to risk damaging morale and provoking opposition through an unpopular measure was also, it has been argued, at the back of the regime's unwillingness to mobilize female labour during the war.[14] The efforts made by the Nazis to neutralize, contain, and integrate the working class bear witness to their sensitivity towards worker feeling and the growth of industrial unrest in the later 1930s. Though Hitler and his immediate entourage seem to have had no fear of a direct political uprising among the working class, the reluctance to ignore

---

[11] Cf. Mason, 'The Legacy of 1918'.

[12] BAK, R43/II/194, fol. 103; cf. Grundmann, p. 112; Mason, 'The Workers' Opposition', p. 130.

[13] *Kriegspropaganda 1939–1941. Geheime Ministerkonferenzen im Reichspropagandaministerium*, ed. W.A. Boelcke, Stuttgart, 1966, p. 337.

[14] T.W. Mason, 'Women in Germany 1925–1940', *History Workshop Journal*, ii (1976), 19–22; D. Winkler, pp. 113 ff.; Salter, pp. 90–1. As Dörte Winkler points out, however, Hitler's rejection of female conscription before 1943 — and this was decisive in the issue — was overwhelmingly ideologically motivated, and Hitler held stubbornly to his position despite arguments that without female conscription the 'social peace' could not be guaranteed — D. Winkler, pp. 116–17.

worker morale imposed real constraints upon the regime and no doubt helped to persuade Hitler in the process that his original diagnosis was correct, that there was no way out of Germany's increasingly acute economic cul-de-sac except through a war of conquest and plunder.[15]

The sensitivity shown towards the working class was not matched by similar regard for opinion in other social groups. By the mid-1930s Hitler was saying that the peasantry, having benefited disproportionately in the initial years of the Third Reich, had to bear sacrifices along with other classes of society.[16] The clamour of unrest about the labour shortage crisis in the pre-war years made itself felt in all the higher echelons of Party and State. But Hitler remained unmoved. Darré, the Agriculture Minister, could not even get an audience with the Führer. The memoranda he painstakingly and unceasingly compiled went unread, or at least unanswered, by Hitler. When eventually persuaded to comment in October 1940, Hitler's final word on the bitter complaints of the farmers about the labour shortage was that they would be attended to after the war.[17] The petty bourgeoisie, disunited as a class and loosely held together ideologically in accordance with much of what Nazism offered, was devoid of economic or social bargaining power. Discontent in this sector could be ignored with impunity.[18] The chances of petty-bourgeois opinion changing government policy were as good as nil. Where as a class the petty bourgeoisie benefited under Nazism it was because its interests coincided with those of the regime rather than because they were specifically taken up and represented by Nazi policy.

The most clear-cut instances we have seen in the preceding chapters where the regime was influenced by and gave way

[15] Cf. Mason, 'Innere Krise', pp. 182 ff.; W. Carr, *Hitler. A Study in Personality and Politics*, London, 1978, pp. 58-9. Hitler's words to his generals in August 1939 point clearly in this direction: 'It is difficult to take decisions which involve spilling blood but for us it is comparatively easy since for us there is only the choice of going through with it or of losing. We can hold out in the present economic situation and with all our resources under strain for perhaps ten or fifteen years, but no longer. We are therefore compelled to take decisions' – *Docs. on Nazism*, p. 563.

[16] Farquharson, pp. 82-5; cf. also pp. 193-5.

[17] BAK, R43/II/195, fol. 182.

[18] Winkler, 'Der entbehrliche Stand', p. 40.

to the pressure of opinion and 'popular opposition' occurred in the sensitive area of the 'Church struggle', and most notably in the halting of the 'euthanasia action' in 1941. Hitler in particular showed himself acutely aware of the potential damage to popularity, confidence, and morale arising from the conflict with the Churches, intervening, as we saw, to end the Protestant Church dispute in 1934 and castigating *Gauleiter* Wagner for his irresponsibility in inciting the crucifix disturbances of 1941.

Though he claimed in a speech in 1937 to prefer the German people's fear and respect to its love,[19] Hitler was in fact sharply aware of the value of plebiscitary support from all sections of the population. He spoke of the function of the plebiscites which followed major foreign policy successes in terms of their effect at home as much as abroad, and of the need for constantly renewed psychological mobilization of the people. He expressed on more than one occasion his apprehension about a drop in his popularity and about the danger of future instability should the run of successes not be continued.[20]

Yet it was distinctly morale rather than opinion which concerned Hitler and the Nazi leadership. This was shown most clearly in the middle of the war when, at a time that the SD reports were falling into increasing disfavour on account of their negative and defeatist tone, a distinction was demanded by Nazi leaders between comments on the 'mood' (*Stimmung*) of the population and evaluation of the essential 'attitude' or 'bearing' (*Haltung*) of the people.[21] It was claimed that although the 'mood' was obviously depressed

---

[19] In his unpublished speech to Nazi trainee leaders at the Ordensburg in Sonthofen in 1937: 'We want to lead our people to the forefront! Whether they love us is a matter of indifference! Just as long as they respect us! Whether they hate us is unimportant, just so long as they fear us' — *Ausgewählte Dokumente zur Geschichte des Nationalsozialismus 1933–1945*, ed. H.A. Jacobsen and W. Jochmann, Bielefeld, 1961, Bd. ii, Dok. 23. xi. 1937.

[20] Cf. I. Kershaw, 'The Führer Image and Political Integration: the popular conception of Hitler in Bavaria during the Third Reich', in G. Hirschfeld and L. Kettenacker (eds.), *Der 'Führerstaat': Mythos und Realität*, Stuttgart, 1980, pp. 157–8.

[21] E.K. Bramsted, *Goebbels and National Socialist Propaganda 1925–1945*, Michigan, 1965, p. 276.

as a result of bombing raids, rationing, and other privations of war, the basic 'attitude' of the German people remained positive and unwavering. Hitler made his own feelings clear in one of his 'Table Talk' monologues in 1942 when, in the circle of his intimates, he declared: 'If what people always say were decisive, everything would long since have been lost. The true attitude of the people lies, however, much deeper and is based on a very firm inner bearing.'[22] Such views were given support by the very one-sided reports coming in from Party offices.[23] In any case, Bormann shielded Hitler from the negative SD reports, and the Führer seldom received or read opinion reports, except for a few towards the end of the war.[24] Goebbels's own bitter comments show both how unpalatable the reported criticisms of the German people were becoming by the mid-war period, and how little the leadership of the Reich were prepared to heed them:

The leaders of the Reich certainly don't need to know whenever someone living in the back of beyond unburdens his anguished heart. Just as the Führer need not know if somewhere in some company people complain about the way the war is run, it is unnecessary for the political leaders to know if here or there someone damns the war or curses it or vents his spleen.[25]

The increasingly negative tenor of the SD reports was, however, becoming more than Goebbels and other prominent Nazis could stomach: the central digest of reports coming in from all parts of the Reich was halted in July 1944.[26]

Opinion as such, therefore, was unlikely to sway Hitler or the Nazi leadership either where it did not suggest a dangerous

[22] H. Picker, *Hitlers Tischgespräche im Führerhauptquartier 1941 bis 1942*, Stuttgart, 1963, p. 206.

[23] Cf. Unger, ch. 8, esp. p. 242. At the very start of the war, Hitler had made clear that he expected no reports of bad mood from Party functionaries: 'No one should report to me that in his *Gau*, or in his district, or in his group, or in his cell the mood might be bad. You are responsible for the mood!' — *Hitler. Reden und Proklamationen*, p. 1317.

[24] *Meldungen*, p. XVII; Steinert, pp. 20–1; Stokes, 'SD', pp. 223–35; D.H. Kitterman, 'National Diary of German Civilian Life during 1940: the SD Reports', University of Washington, Ph. D. thesis, 1972, pp. 27–8.

[25] *The Goebbels Diaries*, ed. L.P. Lochner, London, 1948, p. 258.

[26] *Meldungen*, pp. XXVI–XXVIII. Though central digests were no longer made, local and regional SD offices continued to send in their reports until the end of the war.

drop in morale, or where it ran counter to fundamentals of
Nazi policy. In two areas, especially, popular opinion was
practically devoid of relevance. These were foreign policy and
the persecution of the Jews, the two areas central to Hitler's
own *Weltanschauung*.

Even in parliamentary democracies foreign affairs are
probably less influenced by public opinion than any other
sphere of politics. Yet, indirect though it was, the impact of
opinion on British and French foreign policy in the 1930s
and on British overseas policy after Suez, or the effect of
popular pressure on the USA to withdraw from Vietnam in
the 1960s was considerable. The overwhelming majority of
Germans in the 1930s dreaded another war, yet by 1939
they were involved in one. By playing on the ready-made
massive support for any *fait accompli* which had the effect
of revising the detested Versailles settlement, and by exploiting the widespread feeling of national insecurity, Hitler
was able to use popular opinion to legitimate his chosen
course of German foreign policy. As one perceptive observer
put it following the Rhineland coup in 1936:

> Hitler can no longer escape from his policy. He has removed the possi-
> bility of that through the dissolution of the Reichstag and the new
> election. With more than 90 per cent of the votes he will get approval
> for this, his policy, on 29 March. Then the ring is sealed and he can no
> longer step out of it. The dictator lets himself be bound by the people
> to the policy which he wanted.[27]

The rapid fall in Hitler's popularity in the later war years was
testimony to the growing recognition that his policies were
responsible for the horrors and miseries of war. By 1944,
perhaps even earlier, a very large number of Germans would
have been prepared to cut their losses and to surrender in
order to bring about an end to the destruction. This had no
impact whatsoever on the regime's leadership, which was
determined to continue the struggle even if this meant the
eventual total destruction of the German nation.

The regime's autonomy in the Jewish Question was equally
clear. The terror, harassment, and hounding of Jews out of
German society was not carried out in response to the

---

[27] ASD, ES/M33/Hans Dill an Otto Wels, 7 Mar. 1936.

demands of popular opinion, though neither was it hindered by any vociferous opposition to the measures. The indifference which characterized popular attitudes towards the Jewish Question, coupled with the plebiscitary backing and wide popular support for the avowed goals of national integration and national revival, provided the void in which vague and loosely formulated anti-Jewish policies, once set in train, could build up their own momentum which led to Auschwitz. That the 'Final Solution' was meant to be a secret which 'it was better to carry to the grave'[28] indicates just how far the Jewish Question had come from populist politics.

Nazism contained something for most Germans; it also contained much that alienated, in different ways, very many Germans. Nazi ideology was so diffuse, and included so many aspects which were largely a recasting of orthodox bourgeois values that, by emphasizing those values, the regime could build upon a considerable consensus already present in wide sections of society. However, Nazism painted over rather than eliminated the divisions within German society, which remained reflected, however darkly, in the formation and expression of opinion. Despite the extravagant claims made by Goebbels and the propagandists, attitudes were formed in the Third Reich as in every society by a multiplicity of factors, only some of which were directly controllable by the regime, and which involved shadings of opinion dictated by class or group allegiance, individual preferment or benefit from the political system, denominational affiliation, geography, type of community relationships, nature of local political leadership, and strength of previous political, ideological, and religious attachment.

Far from a neat division into pro- and anti-Nazi attitudes, an examination of popular opinion during the Third Reich produces a complex mosaic of overlapping but disparate pieces. The verticalization of opinion – the reduction of it into its component parts – was a crucial consequence of *Gleichschaltung* and the elimination of any political apparatus which could build and organize horizontal, cross-sectional opinion. The fracturing or atomization of opinion also

---

[28] Cf. above, Chapter 9 note 50.

accentuated the ambivalence of political views — rejection of parts of Nazism but approval and acclamation of other crucial aspects, and the inability or unwillingness to draw general ideological conclusions from specific instances of antagonism. The important, multifaceted substrata of hostile or antagonistic opinion coexisted therefore with, or were neutralized by, the transcending consensus of support for national policy, the identifying focus of which was Hitler. Significantly, as the 'positive' integration of the population declined sharply from the mid-war onwards, coercion and repression had to be increased proportionately. They were all that was left. In a despairing moment near the end of the war, Hitler himself seems to have come close to accepting the failure of his mission to transform German values, to create a new mentality in the people. He is reputed to have said that he had had no time in which to shape the people to his liking and would have required twenty years to bring to maturity an élite which would have imbibed 'the National Socialist way of thinking' along with its mother's milk.[29]

Popular opinion could make itself felt only in the most muted way during the Third Reich. The autonomy which the Nazi government gained, and which led to war and genocide, arose out of the vacuum created by the German people's abdication, between 1930 and 1933, of its democratic rights. These rights alone are the safeguard of a measure of influence for public opinion, however incomplete or imperfect, in shaping government policy and in controlling those who wield power.

[29] *The Testament of Adolf Hitler*, ed. F. Genoud, London, 1961, pp. 58-9.

List of Abbreviations and Glossary of German Terms and Names used in the Text

AA	*Arbeitsamt* (Employment Office)
Abschn.	*Abschnitt* (SD regional administrative office, equivalent in status to the *Hauptaußenstelle*; administrative subdivision of an NSLB-*Kreiswaltung*)
Alter Kämpfer	'Old Fighter', a Nazi term distinguishing those who had joined the Party before 30 January 1933 from those disparaged as newcomers and opportunists
AS	*Außenstelle* (local SD office)
ASD	Archiv der sozialen Demokratie, Bonn
BA	*Bezirksamt (svorstand)* ((Head of) District Office, the unit of local government administration, from 1939 *Landrat (samt)*)
BAK	Bundesarchiv Koblenz
BA/MA	Bundesarchiv/Militärarchiv, Freiburg im Breisgau
Bayerische Ostmark	'Bavarian Eastern March', name of the *Gau* comprising Upper Franconia, the Upper Palatinate, and Lower Bavaria, adjacent to the Czech and Austrian borders
Bayerischer Wald	'Bavarian Forest', a large tract of the eastern part of Lower Bavaria, extending to the Czech border
Bayern I–IV	*Bayern in der NS-Zeit. Soziale Lage und politisches Verhalten der Bevölkerung im Spiegel vertraulicher Berichte*, ed. M. Broszat, E. Fröhlich and F. Wiesemann, Munich/Vienna, 1977; *Bayern in der NS-Zeit. Herrschaft und Gesellschaft im Konflikt*, vols. ii–iv, ed. M. Broszat, E. Fröhlich, and (for

vols. iii–iv) A. Grossmann, Munich/Vienna, 1979–81

BBB   *Bayerischer Bauernbund* (Bavarian Peasant League)

BdM   *Bund deutscher Mädel* (Hitler Youth girls' organization)

Beamte   Civil servants (including teachers as well as government officials)

Bekenntnisschule   Denominational school

*Bezirksamtsvor-
stand*   See under BA and *Landrat*

Bgm.   *Bürgermeister* (mayor)

*'Bonzen',
'Bonzentum',
'Bonzokratie'*   Term of contempt denoting the 'big-wigs', 'bosses', or 'high-ups' and the implied corrupt nature of their rule

BPP   *Bayerische Politische Polizei* (Bavarian Political Police, after 1936 Gestapo)

BVP   *Bayerische Volkspartei* (Bavarian People's Party)

DAF   *Deutsche Arbeitsfront* (German Labour Front)

DBS   *Deutschland-Berichte der Sopade* (*Germany Reports of the Sopade*)

DDP   *Deutsche Demokratische Partei* (German Democratic Party)

Dienstboten   Agricultural 'servants' — farmhands usually hired on annual contract and normally living on the farm premises

DNVP   *Deutschnationale Volkspartei* (German National People's Party)

DVP   *Deutsche Volkspartei* (German People's Party)

*Erbhof
(Erhöfe)*   Entailed farm(s) under the provisions of the Reich Entailed Law (*Reichserbhofgesetz*) of 1933

Erntedankfest   Nazi harvest thanksgiving festival

ES   *Emigration Sopade* (name of the collection of files in the Archiv der sozialen Demokratie, Bonn)

Gau	Nazi Party administrative region
Gauleiter	Head(s) of Party regional administration
GBF	*Gendarmerie-Bezirksführer* (head of district police)
Gemeinschafts-schule	'Community School', Nazi non-denominational school to replace the *Bekenntnisschule*
Gendarmerie	Police constabulary in non-urban areas
GenStA	*Generalstaatsanwalt* (Chief State Attorney in an OLG region)
Gestapa	*Geheimes Staatspolizeiamt* (Head Office of the Secret State Police)
Gestapo	*Geheime Staatspolizei* (Secret State Police)
GHS	*Gendarmerie-Hauptstation* (District main police station)
GI	*Gendarmerie-Inspektion* (Police inspectorate of a district)
GKF	*Gendarmerie-Kreisführer* (head of district police, change of nomenclature from GBF in 1939)
Gleichschaltung	Nazi term denoting the 'bringing into line' or 'co-ordination', i.e. Nazification, of State and society from 1933
GP	*Gendarmerie-Posten* (local police station, name changed from GS in 1939)
GS	*Gendarmerie-Station* (local police station, name changed to GP in 1939)
GStA	Bayerisches Hauptstaatsarchiv, Abteilung II, Geheimes Staatsarchiv, Munich
GW	*Gauwaltung* (*Gau* administration of NSLB)
HAS	*Hauptaußenstelle* (main SD office of a region)
Heimtückefälle	'Special Court' (cf. SGM) cases dealing with alleged offences under the *'Heimtücke'* ('malicious practices') decree of 21 Mar. 1933 and law of 20 Dec. 1934.
HJ	*Hitlerjugend* (Hitler Youth)
HStA	Bayerisches Hauptstaatsarchiv, Abteilung I, Allgemeines Staatsarchiv, Munich

IfZ	Institut für Zeitgeschichte, Munich
IWM	Imperial War Museum, London
KdF	*Kraft durch Freude* ('Strength through Joy' organization of the DAF)
KL	*Kreisleiter* (Nazi Party District Leader)
KLB	*Die kirchliche Lage in Bayern nach den Regierungspräsidentenberichten 1933–1943*, ed. H. Witetschek and (vol. iv) W. Ziegler: vol. i, *Regierungsbezirk Oberbayern*, Mainz, 1966; vol. ii, *Regierungsbezirk Ober- und Mittelfranken*, Mainz, 1967; vol. iii, *Regierungsbezirk Schwaben*, Mainz, 1971; vol. iv, *Regierungsbezirk Niederbayern und der Oberpfalz*, Mainz, 1973.
KPD	*Kommunistische Partei Deutschlands* (German Communist Party)
KW	*Kreiswaltung* (district administrative unit of NSLB)
Landrat	Head of State administration at District level (known before 1939 as *Bezirksamtsvorstand*)
LB	*Lagebericht* (situation report)
LK	*Landkreis* (government administrative district from 1939, formerly *Amtsbezirk*)
LRA	*Landratsamt* (office of government district administration, before 1939 *Bezirksamt*)
Mainfranken	Main Franconia, Nazi Party *Gau* corresponding to the state administrative region of Lower Franconia
MF	Mittelfranken (Middle Franconia)
Mittelstand	Literally 'middle estate', an archaic status term roughly equivalent to 'lower middle class' or 'petty bourgeoisie'
NB	Niederbayern (Lower Bavaria)
Nbg.-Dok.	Nuremberg Document(s)

NS	*Nationalsozialismus, nationalsozialistisch* (Nazism, Nazi)
NSBO	*Nationalsozialistische Betriebszellenorganisation* (Nazi Factory Cell Organization)
NSDAP	*Nationalsozialistische Deutsche Arbeiterpartei* (Nazi Party)
NS-Hago	*Nationalsozialistische Handwerks-, Handels- und Gewerbeorganisation* (Nazi Craft, Commerce, and Trade Organization)
NSLB	*Nationalsozialistischer Lehrerbund* (Nazi Teachers' Association)
NSV	*Nationalsozialistische Volkswohlfahrt* (Nazi People's Welfare Organization)
OB	Oberbayern (Upper Bavaria)
OF	Oberfranken (Upper Franconia)
Ogrl.	*Ortsgruppenleiter* (Nazi Party local leader)
OLG	*Oberlandesgericht* (Higher Regional Court)
OLGP	*Oberlandesgerichtspräsident* (President of a Higher Regional Court)
OP	Oberpfalz (Upper Palatinate)
Ortsbauernführer	Local peasant leader
Pd	*Polizeidirektion* (City police administration)
Pg	*Parteigenosse* (Nazi 'Party Comrade')
RI	*Rüstungsinspektion* (Armaments Inspectorate)
RP	*Regierungspräsident* (Government President, head of State regional administration, controlling a governmental region (*Regierungsbezirk*))
S	Schwaben (Swabia)
SA	*Sturmabteilung* (Nazi Storm Troop, paramilitary organization)
Schupo	*Schutzpolizei* (municipal police constabulary)
Schutzhaft	'Protective custody', a euphemism for summary arrest and internment, usually in a concentration camp

SD	*Sicherheitsdienst* (Security Service)
SGM	*Sondergericht München* (Munich 'Special Court' dealing mainly with political offences)
Sopade	*Sozialdemokratische Partei Deutschlands* (exiled SPD executive based in Prague (1933–8), Paris (1938–40), and finally, from 1940, in London)
SPD	*Sozialdemokratische Partei Deutschlands* (German Social Democratic Party)
SS	*Schutzstaffeln* (police and security organization run by Himmler)
StAA	Staatsarchiv Amberg
StAB	Staatsarchiv Bamberg
StAL	Staatsarchiv Landshut
StAM	Staatsarchiv München
StANeu	Staatsarchiv Neuburg an der Donau
StAN	Staatsarchiv Nürnberg
StAW	Staatsarchiv Würzburg
StJBB	*Statistisches Jahrbuch für Bayern*
Stpl.	*Stützpunktleiter* (Nazi Party leader of local base)
UF	Unterfranken (Lower Franconia)
uk-Stellung	*'unabkömmliche Stellung'* — wartime reserved occupation, exempt from call-up
VfZ	*Vierteljahrshefte für Zeitgeschichte*
völkisch	racial-nationalist
Volksgemein-schaft	'National Community' — Nazi social concept implying a harmonious society free from class conflict and class divisions
Volksgenosse (n)	'National Comrade(s)', Nazi parlance for ordinary citizens
Wehrkreis	'Defence District', regional unit of *Wehrmacht* administration
WHW	*Winterhilfswerk* (Winter Aid Scheme)
WL	Wiener Library, London (since removed to Tel Aviv, leaving only a microfilm library in London)

WWI	*Wehrwirtschaftsinspektion* (Army Economic Inspectorate)
ZdBSL	*Zeitschrift des Bayerischen Statistischen Landesamts*
Zwangswirt-schaft	State interventionist 'coercive economy', a term deriving from the First World War and encapsulating resentment at State interference in the 'free economy'

Archival Sources

1. *Archiv der sozialen Demokratie (Friedrich-Ebert-Stiftung), Bonn*
ES 31-4, 63-6, 147

2. *Bayerisches Hauptstaatsarchiv, Abt. I, Allgemeines Staatsarchiv, Munich*
MF 66928
MInn 73708, 73725-6
MK 42584
Sonderabgabe 1722, 1725, 1727

3. *Bayerisches Hauptstaatsarchiv, Abt. II, Geheimes Staatsarchiv, Munich*

(i) *Government Presidents' and Police Reports*
Upper Bavaria
MA 102138, MA 106670-1, MA 106691, MA 106695
Lower Bavaria and the Upper Palatinate
MA 102141, MA 102144, MA 106672-4, MA 106691, MA 106696
Upper and Middle Franconia
MA 102154, MA 102155/3, MA 106677-9, MA 106694, MA 106696
Swabia
MA 102149, MA 106682-4, MA 106693, MA 106695
Lower Franconia
MA 102151, MA 106680-1, MA 106694, MA 106696
Polizeidirektion Augsburg
MA 106686, MA 106695, MA 106697
Polizeidirektion München
MA 106685, MA 106697
Bayerische Politische Polizei (from Oct. 1936 Gestapo, Leitstelle München)
MA 106687-90

(ii) *Other Files*

MA 101241/1-2, MA 105248, MA 105257, MA 105618, MA 106311, MA 106410-12, MA 106457, MA 106468, MA 106730-3, MA 106765, MA 106767, MA 107257, MA 107291; Reichsstatthalter 39-40, 112-13, 157, 447, 562-5, 578, 644, 694

4. Berlin Document Centre

Personal File of SS-Oberf. Hermann von Schade (re. Adolf Wagner)

5. Bundesarchiv, Koblenz

NS6/416; NS26/1410; R18/5038, 5350, 5355; R22/3355, R22/3379, R22/3381; R43/II/194-5; R55/443-6; R58/ 717,999, 1094-6; Zsg. 101-2

6. Bundesarchiv/Militärarchiv, Freiburg im Breisgau

RW19/9-34, 38, 41, 48, 57, 67-78; RW20/7/16-17, RW20/ 13/8-9

7. Imperial War Museum, London

FD 847/46; FD 5424/45

8. Institut für Zeitgeschichte, Munich

Db 05.04; Nürnberger Dokumente D-906/5, 9, 14, 17-18, 22; NO-520, 795; PS-843-4, 1969

9. Landratsamt Amberg/Sulzbach (Registratur)

LRA Amberg/Sulzbach P62

10. Landratsamt Friedberg (Registratur)

LRA Friedberg VII/12/6

11. Landratsamt Neumarkt in der Oberpfalz (Registratur)

LRA Neumarkt 1624; LRA Parsberg 939

12. Landratsamt Obernburg am Main (Registratur)

Gruppe XXII/43; Sammelakt 'Kirche und Nationalsozialismus'

13. Landratsamt Schongau (Registratur)

LRA Schongau 201

14. *Landratsamt Traunstein (Registratur)*

LRA Traunstein IV-7-177

15. *Staatsarchiv Amberg*

AG Cham 16/34, 72/35; BA Amberg 2397-9, 2859, 3665, 3736; BA Vohenstrauß 4674

16. *Staatsarchiv Bamberg*

K5/3478; K8I/IV, 1476; K8/III, 18470-5; K9/XV, 280, 995, 1321; K14/VIII/26; M30/173, 731, 780, 1048-9; M33/153-4, 175, 410, 631

17. *Staatsarchiv Landshut*

164/10, 5094-5; 164/14, 5731; 164/19, 3681; 181/9; 181/24

18. *Staatsarchiv München*

Gestapo 17, 58; LRA 5169, 28340, 29130, 29654-6, 30676-8, 31933, 47138, 47140, 48235, 59595, 61611-20, 79887-8, 99497, 99532, 112209, 113813, 116116, 134055-60, 135112-17; NSDAP 126-7, 249, 254, 256, 282, 285, 318, 349, 375-8, 440, 447, 468, 494, 567-8, 617, 654-5, 980, 983; OLG 127; SGM (holding of some 10,000 files of the *Sondergericht München*)

19. *Staatsarchiv Neuburg an der Donau*

NSDAP Mischbestand, Gau Schwaben (not yet catalogued; old file numbers cited)

Sammlung Schumacher LO 47, 51-2, 60, Anhang Nr. 3; LO A5, 15, 18, 30/35, 53, 66

20. *Staatsarchiv Nürnberg*

212/1/III, 2145; 212/8/V, 4237, 4241, 4266, 4346; 212/11/VI, 1530, 1792; 212/12/V, 99; 212/13/II, 654; 212/17/III, 8444; 212/18/VIII, 661; 218/1/1, 357-9, 431

21. *Staatsarchiv Würzburg*

Gauleitung Mainfranken II/5, 41; IV/9, 13; XII/1, 2, 6; Sammlung Schumacher 14, 17, 27, 29, 43-4; SD-Hauptaußenstelle Würzburg 1-59; uncatalogued, provisional file nos. given: BA Alzenau 1936-40; BA Bad Neustadt 125/1-7

22. *Stadtarchiv Coburg*

A7870, A8521

23. *Wiener Library, London*

'B' and 'P' series of Jewish 'Eye-Witness Reports of Nazi Persecution; 'Der 10. November 1938' (typescript of collected short reports by persecuted and émigré Jews, compiled in 1939 and 1940 by S. Brückheimer); Exile Reports on Conditions in Germany: *'Deutsche Informationen'*, 1936-9; *'Deutsche Inlandsberichte'*, 1939-41; *'Deutsche Mitteilungen'*, 1938; *'Deutschland-Berichte der Sopade'*, 1934-40; *'Deutschland-Information des Zentralkomitees der KPD'*, 1935-7 (incomplete)

List of Works Cited

Adam, U.D., *Judenpolitik im Dritten Reich*, Düsseldorf, 1972.

Allen, W.S., *The Nazi Seizure of Power. The Experience of a Single German Town*, Chicago, 1965.

Allen, W.S., 'The Appeal of Fascism and the Problem of National Disintegration', in Turner (ed.), *Reappraisals*.

Allen, W.S., 'Die deutsche Öffentlichkeit und die "Reichskristallnacht" — Konflikte zwischen Werthierarchie und Propaganda im Dritten Reich', in Peukert and Reulecke (eds.), *Die Reihen fast geschlossen*.

Andreas-Friedrich, R., *Der Schattenmann*, Berlin, 1947.

Arndt, I., 'Machtübernahme und Judenboykott in der Sicht evangelischer Sonntagsblätter', in Benz (ed.), *Miscellanea*.

Ausgewählte Dokumente zur Geschichte des Nationalsozialismus 1933-1945, ed. H.A. Jacobsen and W. Jochmann, vol. ii, Bielefeld, 1961.

Ay, K.-L., *Die Entstehung einer Revolution. Die Volksstimmung in Bayern während des Ersten Weltkrieges*, Berlin, 1968.

Ay, K.-L., 'Volksstimmung und Volksmeinung als Voraussetzung der Münchner Revolution von 1918', in Bosl (ed.), *Bayern im Umbruch*.

Baier, H., *Die Deutschen Christen im Rahmen des bayerischen Kirchenkampfes*, Nuremberg, 1968.

Baier, H., *Kirchenkampf in Nürnberg*, Nuremberg, 1973.

Barta, T., 'Living in Dachau, 1900-1950' (unpublished paper).

Bayern in der NS-Zeit (vols. i-iv), ed. M. Broszat, E. Fröhlich, F. Wiesemann (vol. i), and A. Grossman (vols. iii-iv), Munich/Vienna, 1977-1981 (cited in the text as *Bayern I* etc.).

'Bayerns Volk und Wirtschaft nach dem Stand der Jahre 1933 und 1934', *Beiträge zur Statistik Bayerns*, Heft 123, Bayerisches Statistisches Landesamt, Munich, 1935.

LIST OF WORKS CITED

Beer, H., *Widerstand gegen den Nationalsozialismus in Nürnberg 1933-1945*, Nuremberg, 1976.

Behrend-Rosenfeld, E.R., *Ich stand nicht allein. Erlebnisse einer Jüdin in Deutschland 1933-1944*, Hamburg, 1949.

Benz, W. *et al.* (eds.), *Miscellanea. Festschrift für Helmut Krausnick*, Stuttgart, 1980.

Berichte des SD und der Gestapo über Kirchen und Kirchenvolk, ed. H. Boberach, Mainz, 1971.

'Berufsgliederung der bayerischen Bevölkerung 1933', *ZdBSL*, lxvi (1934).

Bessel, R. and Jamin, M., 'Nazis, Workers and the Uses of Quantitative Evidence', *Social History*, iv (1979).

Bessel, R. and Jamin, M., 'Statistics and the Historian: a Rejoinder', *Social History*, v (1980).

Blaich, F., 'Die bayerische Industrie 1933-1939', in *Bayern II*.

Blessing, W.K., 'Umwelt und Mentalität im ländlichen Bayern. Eine Skizze zum Alltagswandel im 19. Jahrhundert', *Archiv für Sozialgeschichte*, xix (1979).

Bosl, K. (ed.), *Bayern im Umbruch. Die Revolution von 1918, ihre Voraussetzungen, ihr Verlauf und ihre Folgen*, Munich/Vienna, 1969.

Bracher, K.D., Schulz, G., and Sauer, W., *Die nationalsozialistische Machtergreifung*, Ullstein edn., 3 vols., Frankfurt am Main, 1974.

Bramsted, E.K., *Goebbels and National Socialist Propaganda 1925-1945*, Michigan, 1965.

Bretschneider, H., *Der Widerstand gegen den Nationalsozialismus in München 1933 bis 1945*, Munich, 1968.

Broszat, M., 'Soziale Motivation und Führer-Bindung des Nationalsozialismus', *VfZ*, xviii (1970).

Broszat, M., *The Hitler State*, London, 1981.

Broszat, M., 'Resistenz und Widerstand', in *Bayern IV*.

Brower, D.R., 'Collectivized Agriculture in Smolensk: The Party, the Peasantry, and the Crisis of 1932', *Russian Review*, xxxvi (1977).

Buchheim, H., 'Command and Compliance', in Krausnick, *Anatomy*.

Caplan, J., 'Theories of Fascism: Nicos Poulantzas as Historian', *History Workshop Journal*, iii (1977).

Caplan, J., 'Recreating the Civil Service: Issues and Ideas in the Nazi Regime', in Noakes (ed.), *Govt., Party and People.*

Carr, W., *Hitler. A Study in Personality and Politics*, London, 1978.

Chronik der Agrarpolitik und Agrarwirtschaft des Deutschen Reiches von 1933-45, ed. W. Tornow, Hamburg/Berlin, 1972.

Cohn, N., *Warrant for Genocide*, London, 1967.

Conway, J.S., *The Nazi Persecution of the Churches, 1933-45*, London, 1968.

Dahrendorf, R., *Society and Democracy in Germany*, London, 1968.

Dawidowicz, L., *The War against the Jews 1933-45*, Harmondsworth, 1977.

De Courcy, J., *Searchlight on Europe*, London, 1940.

Deutschland-Berichte der Sopade 1934-1940 (7 vols.), Frankfurt am Main, 1980 (cited in the text as DBS).

'Die bayerische Bevölkerung nach Wirtschaftsabteilungen und nach der Stellung im Beruf auf Grund der Berufszählung vom 17. Mai 1939', *ZdBSL*, lxxiv (1942).

Dobkowski, M. and Wallimann, I. (eds.), *Towards the Holocaust*, (New York, 1982).

Documents on Nazism, ed. J. Noakes and G. Pridham, London, 1974.

Domarus, W., *Nationalsozialismus, Krieg und Bevölkerung*, Munich, 1977.

Eiber, L., *Arbeiter unter der NS-Herrschaft. Textil- und Porzellanarbeiter im nordöstlichen Oberfranken 1933-1939*, Munich, 1979.

Eilers, R., *Die nationalsozialistische Schulpolitik*, Cologne, 1963.

Eley, G., *Reshaping the German Right. Radical Nationalism and Political Change after Bismarck*, New Haven, 1980.

Evans, R.J. (ed.), *Society and Politics in Wilhelmine Germany*, London, 1978.

Evans, R.J. (ed.), *The German Working Class*, London, 1981.

Fainsod, M., *Smolensk under Soviet Rule*, New York, 1963.

Farquharson, J.E., *The Plough and the Swastika. The NSDAP and Agriculture 1928-45*, London, 1976.

Farr, I., 'Populism in the Countryside: the Peasant Leagues

in Bavaria in the 1890s', in Evans (ed.), *Society and Politics*.

Faulhaber, M., *Judentum, Christentum, Germanentum*, Munich [1934].

Fischer, C., 'The Occupational Background of the SA's Rank and File Membership during the Depression Years, 1929 to Mid-1934', in Stachura (ed.), *The Shaping of the Nazi State*.

Fischer, C. and Hicks, C., 'Statistics and the Historian: the Occupational Profile of the SA', *Social History*, v (1980).

Flannery, H.W., *Assignment to Berlin*, London, 1942.

Forstmeier, F. and Volkmann, H.-E. (eds.), *Wirtschaft und Rüstung am Vorabend des Zweiten Weltkrieges*, Düsseldorf, 1975.

Fröhlich, E. and Broszat, M., 'Politische und soziale Macht auf dem Lande. Die Durchsetzung der NSDAP im Kreis Memmingen', *VfZ*, xxv (1977).

Geary, D., *European Labour Protest, 1848–1939*, London, 1981.

Geary, D., 'Identifying Militancy: The Assessment of Working-Class Attitudes towards State and Society', in Evans (ed.), *The German Working Class*.

Geary, D., 'The Failure of German Labour in the Weimar Republic', in Dobkowski and Wallimann (eds.), *Towards the Holocaust*.

Geiger, T., *Die soziale Schichtung des deutschen Volkes*, Stuttgart, 1932.

Genschel, H., *Die Verdrängung der Juden aus der Wirtschaft im Dritten Reich*, Göttingen, 1966.

Geschichte der deutschen Arbeiterbewegung, ed. W. Ulbricht et al., vols. ix–xi, Berlin, 1968-9.

Gies, H., 'The NSDAP and Agrarian Organizations in the Final Phase of the Weimar Republic', in Turner (ed.), *Nazism and the Third Reich*.

'Glaubensjuden in Bayern auf Grund der Volks- und Berufszählung vom 16. Juni 1933', *ZdBSL*, lxx (1938).

Goebbels Diaries, The, ed. L.P. Lochner, London, 1948.

Gordon, S.A., 'German Opposition to Nazi Anti-Semitic Measures between 1933 and 1945, with particular reference to the Rhine–Ruhr Area', State University New York/Buffalo, Ph.D. thesis, 1979.

402 LIST OF WORKS CITED

Gotto, K. and Repgen, K. (eds.), *Kirche, Katholiken und Nationalsozialismus*, Mainz, 1980.

Graml, H., *Der 9. November 1938. 'Reichskristallnacht'*, Bonn, 1953.

Graml, H. et al., *The German Resistance to Hitler*, London, 1970.

Gritschneder, O., 'Die Akten des Sondergerichts über Pater Ruper Mayer S.J.', *Beiträge zur altbayerischen Kirchengeschichte* (1974).

Gruchmann, L., 'Euthanasie und Justiz im Dritten Reich', *VfZ*, xx (1972).

Grunberger, R., *A Social History of the Third Reich*, London, 1971.

Grundmann, F., *Agrarpolitik im Dritten Reich. Anspruch und Wirklichkeit des Reichserbhofgesetzes*, Hamburg, 1979.

Guillebaud, C.W., *The Social Policy of Nazi Germany*, Cambridge, 1941.

Haffner, S., *Anmerkungen zu Hitler*, Munich, 1978.

Hagmann, M., *Der Weg ins Verhängnis*, Munich, 1946.

Hambrecht, R., *Der Aufstieg der NSDAP in Mittel- und Oberfranken (1925–1933)*, Nuremberg, 1976.

Hanke, P., *Zur Geschichte der Juden in München zwischen 1933 und 1945*, Munich, 1967.

Heiber, H., 'Der Fall Grünspan', *VfZ*, v (1957).

Heisenberg, E., *Das politische Leben eines Unpolitischen. Erinnerungen an Werner Heisenberg*, Munich, 1980.

Helmreich, E.C., 'The Arrest and Freeing of the Protestant Bishops of Württemberg and Bavaria, September–October 1934', *Central European History*, ii (1969).

Henn, E., 'Die bayerische Volksmission im Kirchenkampf', *Zeitschrift für bayerische Kirchengeschichte*, xxxviii (1969).

Hennig, E., *Bürgerliche Gesellschaft und Faschismus in Deutschland. Ein Forschungsbericht*, Frankfurt am Main, 1977.

Herbst, L., 'Die Krise des nationalsozialistischen Regimes am Vorabend des Zweiten Weltkrieges und die forcierte Aufrüstung. Eine Kritik', *VfZ*, xxvi (1978).

Herzstein, R.E., *The War that Hitler Won. Nazi Propaganda*, London, 1979.

Hesse, H., 'Auswirkungen nationalsozialistischer Politik auf die bayerische Wirtschaft (1933-1939)', *Zeitschrift für bayerische Landesgeschichte*, xliii (1980).

Hetzer, G., 'Die Industriestadt Augsburg. Eine Sozialgeschichte der Arbeiteropposition', in *Bayern III*.

Hirschfeld, G. and Kettenacker, L. (eds.), *Der 'Führerstaat': Mythos und Realität*, Stuttgart, 1980.

Hitler. *Reden und Proklamationen 1932-1945*, ed. M. Domarus, 4 vols., Wiesbaden, 1973.

Hitler. *Sämtliche Aufzeichnungen, 1905-1924*, ed. E. Jäckel, Stuttgart, 1980.

Hockerts, H.-G., *Die Sittlichkeitsprozesse gegen katholische Ordensangehörige und Priester 1936/1937*, Mainz, 1971.

Honolka, B., *Die Kreuzelschreiber*, Hamburg, 1961.

'How popular was Streicher?', *Wiener Library Bulletin*, v-vi (1957).

Hüttenberger, P., 'Vorüberlegungen zum "Widerstandsbegriff"', in Kocka (ed.), *Theorien in der Praxis des Historikers*.

Hüttenberger, P., 'Heimtückefälle vor dem Sondergericht München 1933-1939', in *Bayern IV*.

Ionescu, G. and Madariaga, I. de, *Opposition. Past and Present of a Political Institution*, London, 1968.

Jäger, H., and Rumschüttel, H., 'Das Forschungsprojekt "Widerstand und Verfolgung in Bayern 1933-1945"', *Archivalische Zeitschrift*, lxxiii (1977).

'Juden im Deutschen Reich 1816 bis 1933', *Wirtschaft und Statistik*, xv (1935).

Kater, M.H., 'Sozialer Wandel in der NSDAP im Zuge der nationalsozialistischen Machtergreifung', in Schieder (ed.), *Faschismus als soziale Bewegung*.

Katholische Kirche und Nationalsozialismus, ed. H. Müller, Munich, 1965.

Kershaw, I., *Der Hitler-Mythos. Volksmeinung und Propaganda im Dritten Reich*, Stuttgart, 1980.

Kershaw, I., 'The Führer Image and Political Integration: the popular conception of Hitler in Bavaria during the Third Reich', in Hirschfeld and Kettenacker (eds.), *Der 'Führerstaat'*.

Kershaw, I., 'The Persecution of the Jews and German

Popular Opinion in the Third Reich', *Leo Baeck Institute Year Book*, xxvi (1981).

Kirche im Kampf. Dokumente des Widerstands und des Aufbaus in der Evangelischen Kirche Deutschlands von 1933 bis 1945, ed. H. Hermelink, Tübingen, 1950 (cited in the text as Hermelink).

Kirchliche Lage in Bayern nach den Regierungspräsidentenberichten 1933-1943, ed. H. Witetschek and (vol. iv) W. Ziegler, 4 vols., Mainz, 1966, 1967, 1971, 1973, (cited in the text as KLB i, etc.).

Kitterman, D.H., 'National Diary of German Civilian Life during 1940: the SD Reports', Univ. of Washington, Ph. D. thesis, 1972.

Kleinöder, E., 'Verfolgung und Widerstand der Katholischen Jugendvereine. Eine Fallstudie über Eichstätt', in *Bayern II*.

Kleinöder, E., 'Katholische Kirche und Nationalsozialismus im Kampf um die Schule. Antikirchliche Maßnahmen und ihre Folgen untersucht am Beispiel von Eichstätt', *Sammelblatt des Historischen Vereins Eichstätt*, lxxiv (1981).

Kochan, L., *Pogrom. 10 November 1938*, London, 1957.

Kocka, J., 'The First World War and the "Mittelstand": German Artisans and White Collar Workers', *Journal of Contemporary History*, viii (1973).

Kocka, J., *Angestellte zwischen Faschismus und Demokratie*, Göttingen, 1977.

Kocka, J., 'Zur Problematik der deutschen Angestellten 1914-1933', in Mommsen *et al.* (eds.), *Industrielles System*.

Kocka, J. (ed.), *Theorien in der Praxis des Historikers*, Göttingen, 1977.

Krausnick, H., 'The Persecution of the Jews', in Krausnick *et al.*, *Anatomy*.

Krausnick, H., *et al.*, *Anatomy of the SS State*, London, 1968.

Kriegspropaganda 1939-1941. Geheime Ministerkonferenzen im Reichspropagandaministerium, ed. W.A. Boelcke, Stuttgart, 1966.

Krohn, C.-D., and Stegmann, D., 'Kleingewerbe und Nationalsozialismus in einer agrarisch-mittelständischen Region. Das

Beispiel Lüneburg 1930-1939', *Archiv für Sozialgeschichte*, xvii (1977).

Kuczynski, J., *Die Geschichte der Lage der Arbeiter unter dem Kapitalismus*, vol. v, Berlin, 1966.

Kühnl, R. (ed.), *Texte zum Faschismusdiskussion I*, Hamburg, 1974.

Kulka, O.D., ' "Public Opinion" in National Socialist Germany and the "Jewish Question"', *Zion*, xl (1975), text in Hebrew, documentation in German, summary in English.

Larson, C.J. and Wasburn, P.C. (eds.), *Power, Participation and Ideology*, New York, 1969.

Leppert-Fögen, A., *Die deklassierte Klasse*, Frankfurt am Main, 1974.

Lewy, G., *The Catholic Church and Nazi Germany*, London, 1964.

Linn, D., *Das Schicksal der jüdischen Bevölkerung in Memmingen von 1933-1945*, Stuttgart, 1968.

Lovin, C.R., 'German Agricultural Policy 1933-1936', Univ. of California, Ph.D. thesis, 1965.

Mammach, K., *Die deutsche antifaschistische Widerstandsbewegung 1933-1939*, Berlin, 1974.

Mann, R., 'Widerstand gegen den Nationalsozialismus', *Neue Politische Literatur*, xxii (1977).

Mann, R., 'Everyday Life in National Socialist Germany. Popular Protest and Regime Support', unpubl. paper presented to the Social Science History Assocn., Columbus, Ohio, 1978.

Mason, T.W., 'The Legacy of 1918 for National Socialism', in Nicholls and Matthias (eds.), *German Democracy*.

Mason, T.W., *Arbeiterklasse und Volksgemeinschaft*, Opladen, 1975.

Mason, T.W., 'Innere Krise und Angriffskrieg 1938/1939', in Forstmeier and Volkmann (eds.), *Wirtschaft und Rüstung*.

Mason, T.W., 'Women in Germany 1925-1940', *History Workshop Journal*, i and ii (Spring, Autumn, 1976).

Mason, T.W., *Sozialpolitik im Dritten Reich*, Opladen, 1977.

Mason, T.W., 'The Workers' Opposition in Nazi Germany', *History Workshop Journal*, xi (1981).

Mason, T.W., 'The Containment of the Working Class in Nazi Germany', (as yet unpublished paper).

Meldungen aus dem Reich, ed. H. Boberach, Neuwied, 1965.

Merkl, P., *Political Violence under the Swastika. 581 Early Nazis,* Princeton, 1975.

Mitscherlich, A. and Mielke, F., *The Death Doctors,* London, 1962.

Mommsen, H., *Beamtentum im Dritten Reich,* Stuttgart, 1966.

Mommsen, H. *et al.* (eds.), *Industrielles System und politische Entwicklung in der Weimarer Republik,* Düsseldorf, 1977.

Moore, B., *Injustice. The Social Bases of Obedience and Revolt,* London, 1978.

Müller, A., *Geschichte der Juden in Nürnberg 1146–1945,* Nuremberg, 1968.

Müller-Claudius, M., *Der Antisemitismus und das deutsche Verhängnis,* Frankfurt am Main, 1948.

Nadler, F., *Eine Stadt im Schatten Streichers,* Nuremberg, 1969.

Nationalsozialismus im Alltag, ed. F.J. Heyen, Boppard-am-Rhein, 1967.

Nettl, J.P., *Political Mobilization. A Sociological Analysis of Methods and Concepts,* London, 1967.

Neuhäusler, J., *Kreuz und Hakenkreuz,* 2 vols., Munich, 1946.

Nicholls, A.J., 'Hitler and the Bavarian Background to National Socialism', in Nicholls and Matthias (eds.), *German Democracy.*

Nicholls, A.J. and Matthias, E. (eds.), *German Democracy and the Triumph of Hitler,* London, 1971.

Niewyk, D.L., *The Jews in Weimar Germany,* Manchester, 1980.

Noakes, J., 'The Oldenburg Crucifix Struggle of November 1936: a case-study of opposition in the Third Reich', in Stachura (ed.), *The Shaping of the Nazi State.*

Noakes, J. (ed.), *Government, Party, and People in Nazi Germany,* Exeter, 1980.

Ophir, B.Z., *Pinkas Hakehillot. Encyclopedia of Jewish Communities from their Foundation till after the Holocaust. Germany–Bavaria,* Jerusalem, 1972 (in Hebrew with an introduction in English).

Ophir, B.Z. and Wiesemann, F., *Die jüdischen Gemeinden in*

Bayern 1918–1945. Geschichte und Zerstörung, Munich, 1979.

Opitz, R., 'Die faschistische Massenbewegung' in Kühnl (ed.), *Texte zur Faschismusdiskussion I.*

Orlow, D., *The History of the Nazi Party*, vol. ii, *1933–1945*, Newton Abbot, 1973.

Partei-Statistik (*Stand:1935*), ed. Reichsorganisationsleiter der NSDAP, vol. i, Munich, 1935.

Pätzold, K., *Faschismus, Rassenwahn, Judenverfolgung*, Berlin, 1975.

Paucker, A., *Der jüdische Abwehrkampf gegen Antisemitismus und Nationalsozialismus in den letzten Jahren der Weimarer Republik*, 2nd edn., Hamburg, 1969.

Persecution of the Catholic Church in the Third Reich, London, 1942.

Peterson, E.N., *The Limits of Hitler's Power*, Princeton, 1969.

Petzina, D., 'Die Mobilisierung deutscher Arbeitskräfte vor und während des zweiten Weltkrieges', *VfZ*, xviii (1970).

Peukert, D., 'Der deutsche Arbeiterwiderstand 1933–1945', *Aus Politik und Zeitgeschichte* (*Beilage zur Wochenzeitung 'das Parlament'*), 14 July 1979.

Peukert, D. and Reulecke, J. (eds.), *Die Reihen fast geschlossen. Beiträge zur Geschichte des Alltags unterm Nationalsozialismus*, Wuppertal, 1981.

Picker, H., *Hitlers Tischgespräche im Führerhauptquartier 1941 bis 1942*, Stuttgart, 1963.

Pommern 1934/35 im Spiegel von Gestapo Lageberichten und Sachakten, ed. R. Thévoz et al., Cologne/Berlin, 1974.

Poulantzas, N., *Fascism and Dictatorship*, Verso edn., London, 1979.

Preller, L., *Sozialpolitik in der Weimarer Republik*, Düsseldorf, (1949), 1978.

Pridham, G., *Hitler's Rise to Power: the Nazi Movement in Bavaria, 1923–1933*, London, 1973.

Public Opinion in Occupied Germany. The OMGUS Surveys, 1945–1949, ed. A.J. Merritt and R.L. Merritt, Urbana, 1970.

Rauschning, H., *Hitler Speaks*, London, 1939.

Rodrigue, A., 'German Popular Opinion and the Jews under

the Nazi Dictatorship', Univ. of Manchester, undergraduate dissertation, 1978.

Rößler, H., 'Erinnerung an den Kirchenkampf in Coburg', *Jahrbuch der Coburger Landesstiftung* (1975).

Saage, R., *Faschismustheorien. Eine Einführung*, Munich, 1976.

Saldern, A. von, *Mittelstand im 'Dritten Reich'. Handwerker-Einzelhändler-Bauern*, Frankfurt am Main, 1979.

Salter, S., 'Class Harmony or Class Conflict? The Industrial Working Class and the National Socialist Regime 1933–1945', in Noakes (ed.), *Govt., Party, and People*.

Sauer, P., *Württemberg in der Zeit des Nationalsozialismus*, Ulm, 1975.

Schewick, B. van, 'Katholische Kirche und nationalsozialistische Rassenpolitik', in Gotto and Repgen (eds.), *Kirche*.

Schieder, W. (ed.), *Faschismus als soziale Bewegung*, Hamburg, 1976.

Schleunes, K.A., *The Twisted Road to Auschwitz. Nazi Policy towards German Jews 1933–1939*, Chicago, 1970.

Schoenbaum, D., *Hitler's Social Revolution*, Anchor Books edn., New York, 1967.

Scholder, K., *Die Kirchen und das Dritte Reich*, vol. i, Frankfurt am Main, 1977.

Schwarz, S., *Die Juden in Bayern im Wandel der Zeiten*, Munich, 1963.

Sereny, G., *Into that Darkness. From Mercy Killing to Mass Murder*, London, 1974.

Singleton, D. and Weidenfeld, A., *The Goebbels Experiment*, London, 1942.

Sonnenberger, F., 'Der neue "Kulturkampf". Die Gemeinschaftsschule und ihre historischen Voraussetzungen', in *Bayern III*.

Sozialgeschichtliches Arbeitsbuch III. Materialien zur Statistik des Deutschen Reiches 1914–1945, ed. D. Petzina *et al.*, Munich, 1978.

Speer, A., *Erinnerungen*, Frankfurt am Main, 1969.

Spindler, M. (ed.), *Handbuch der bayerischen Geschichte, Band IV, Das Neue Bayern 1800–1970* (in 2 parts), Munich, 1974–5.

Stachura, P.D. (ed.), *The Shaping of the Nazi State*, London, 1978.

Stachura, P.D., 'Who were the Nazis? A Socio-Political Analysis of the National Socialist *Machtübernahme*', *European Studies Review*, xi (1981).

Stand und Problematik der Erforschung des Widerstandes gegen den Nationalsozialismus (*Studien und Berichte aus dem Forschungsinstitut der Friedrich-Ebert-Stiftung*), hectographed, Bad Godesberg, 1965.

Statistisches Jahrbuch für Bayern (*1936*), ed. Bayerisches Statistisches Landesamt, Munich, 1936.

Steinert, M.G., *Hitlers Krieg und die Deutschen*, Düsseldorf, 1970.

Sterling, E.S., *Judenhaß. Die Anfänge des politischen Antisemitismus in Deutschland* (*1815-1850*), Frankfurt am Main, 1969.

Stokes, L.D., 'The *Sicherheitsdienst* (SD) of the *Reichsführer* SS and German Public Opinion, September 1939-June 1941', Johns Hopkins University, Ph. D. thesis, Baltimore, 1972.

Stokes, L.D., 'The German People and the Destruction of the European Jews', *Central European History*, vi (1973).

Stone, N., *Hitler*, London, 1980.

Tenfelde, K., 'Proletarische Provinz. Radikalisierung und Widerstand in Penzberg/Oberbayern 1900 bis 1945', in *Bayern IV*.

Testament of Adolf Hitler, ed. F. Genoud, London, 1961.

Thalmann, R. and Feinermann, E., *Crystal Night: 9-10 November, 1938*, London, 1974.

Thränhardt, D., *Wahlen und politische Strukturen in Bayern 1848-1953*, Düsseldorf, 1973.

Toury, J., *Soziale und politische Geschichte der Juden in Deutschland 1847-1871*, Düsseldorf, 1977.

Troll, H., 'Aktionen zur Kriegsbeendigung im Frühjahr 1945', in *Bayern IV*.

Turner, H.A. (ed.), *Nazism and the Third Reich*, New York, 1972.

Turner, H.A. (ed.), *Reappraisals of Fascism*, New York, 1975.

Unger, A.H., *The Totalitarian Party*, Cambridge, 1974.

Verfolgung und Widerstand unter dem Nationalsozialismus in Baden, ed. J. Schadt, Stuttgart, 1976.

Volk, L., *Der bayerische Episkopat und der Nationalsozialismus 1930-1934*, Mainz, 1965.

Volk, L., 'Kardinal Faulhabers Stellung zur Weimarer Republik und zum NS-Staat', *Stimmen der Zeit*, clxxvii (1966).

Volksopposition im Polizeistaat, ed. B. Vollmer, Stuttgart, 1957.

Wiesemann, F., *Die Vorgeschichte der nationalsozialistischen Machtübernahme in Bayern 1932/1933*, Berlin, 1975.

Wiesemann, F., 'Arbeitskonflikte in der Landwirtschaft während der NS-Zeit in Bayern 1933-1938', *VfZ*, xxv (1977).

Wiesemann, F., 'Juden auf dem Lande: Die wirtschaftliche Ausgrenzung der jüdischen Viehhändler in Bayern', in Peukert and Reulecke (eds.), *Die Reihen fast geschlossen*.

Wilhelm, H.-H., 'Wie geheim war die Endlösung?', in Benz (ed.), *Miscellanea*.

Winkler, D., 'Frauenarbeit versus Frauenideologie', *Archiv für Sozialgeschichte*, xvii (1977).

Winkler, H.A., *Mittelstand, Demokratie und Nationalsozialismus*, Cologne, 1972.

Winkler, H.A., 'From Social Protectionism to National Socialism: the German Small-Business Movement in Comparative Perspective', *Journal of Modern History*, xlviii (1976).

Winkler, H.A., 'German Society, Hitler, and the Illusion of Restoration 1930-33', *Journal of Contemporary History*, xi (1976).

Winkler, H.A., 'Vom Protest zur Panik: Der gewerbliche Mittelstand in der Weimarer Republik', in Mommsen *et al.* (eds.), *Industrielles System*.

Winkler, H.A., 'Der entbehrliche Stand. Zur Mittelstandspolitik im "Dritten Reich"', *Archiv für Sozialgeschichte*, xvii (1977).

Witetschek, H., 'Die bayerischen Regierungspräsidentenberichte 1933-1943 als Geschichtsquelle', *Historisches Jahrbuch*, lxxxvii (1967).

Wolf, E., 'Political and Moral Motives behind the Resistance', in Graml *et al.*, *The German Resistance*.

Wright, J.R.C., *'Above Parties': The Political Attitudes of the German Church Leadership 1918-1933*, Oxford, 1974.

Wunderlich, F., *Farm Labour in Germany 1810-1945*, Princeton, 1961.

Zahn, G.C., *German Catholics and Hitler's War: a study in Political Control*, London, 1963.

Zipfel, F., 'Die Bedeutung der Widerstandsforschung für die allgemeine zeitgeschichtliche Forschung', in *Stand und Problematik der Erforschung des Widerstandes*.

Zofka, Z., *Die Ausbreitung des Nationalsozialismus auf dem Lande. Eine regionale Fallstudie zur politischen Einstellung der Landbevölkerung in der Zeit des Aufstiegs und der Machtergreifung der NSDAP 1928-1936*, Munich, 1979.

Select Bibliography of Relevant Works Published Since the Appearance of the First Edition

I Resistance

Balfour, Michael: *Withstanding Hitler in Germany 1933–45*, London, 1988.

Baranowski, Shelley: *The Confessing Church, Conservative Elites, and the Nazi State*, Lewiston/Queenston, 1986.

Botz, Gerhard: 'Methoden- und Theorieprobleme der historischen Widerstandsforschung', in Helmut Konrad and Wolfgang Neugebauer (eds.), *Arbeiterbewegung-Faschismus-Nationalbewußtsein*, Vienna/Munich/Zurich, 1983, pp. 137–51.

Broszat, Martin: 'Resistenz und Widerstand', in Martin Broszat, *Nach Hitler. Der schwierige Umgang mit unserer Geschichte*, Munich, 1986, pp. 68–91.

Bull, Hedley (ed.): *The Challenge of the Third Reich*, Oxford, 1986.

Graml Hermann: *Widerstand im Dritten Reich. Probleme, Ereignisse, Gestalten*, Frankfurt am Main, 1984.

Hoffmann, Peter: *German Resistance to Hitler*, Cambridge Mass., 1988.

Housden, Martyn: *Resistance and Conformity in the Third Reich*, London, 1997.

Kershaw, Ian: *The Nazi Dictatorship. Problems and Perspectives of Interpretation*, 4th edn., London, 2000, ch.8.

Large, David Clay (ed.): *Contending with Hitler. Varieties of German Resistance in the Third Reich*, Cambridge, 1991.

Löwenthal, Richard and Mühlen, Patrik von zur (eds.): *Widerstand und Verweigerung in Deutschland 1933 bis 1945*, Berlin/Bonn, 1984.

Mason, Tim: 'Arbeiter ohne Gewerkschaften. Massenwiderstand im NS-Deutschland und im faschistischen Italien', *Journal für Geschichte* (Nov.1983), pp. 28–36.

Mehringer, Hartmut: *Widerstand und Emigration. Das NS-Regime und seine Gegner*, Munich, 1997.

Merson, Allan: *Communist Resistance in Nazi Germany*, London, 1985.

Mommsen, Hans: 'Widerstand und Dissens im Dritten Reich', in Klaus-Dietmar Henke and Claudio Natoli (eds.), *Mit dem Pathos der Nüchternheit*, Frankfurt am Main, 1991, pp. 107–18.

Mommsen, Hans: 'German Society and the Resistance against Hitler, 1933–1945', in Christian Leitz (ed.), *The Third Reich*, Oxford/Malden, Mass., 1999, pp. 257–73.

Müller, Klaus-Jürgen (ed.): *Der deutsche Widerstand*, Paderborn, 1986.

Nicosia, Francis R. and Stokes, Lawrence, D. (eds.): *Germans against Nazism*, Oxford, 1990.

Plum, Günter: 'Widerstand und Resistenz', in Martin Broszat and Horst Möller (eds.), *Das Dritte Reich. Herrschaftsstruktur und Geschichte*, Munich, 1983, pp. 248–73.

Schmädeke, Jürgen and Steinbach, Peter (eds.): *Der Widerstand gegen den Nationalsozialismus*, Munich/Zurich, 1985.

Siefken, Hinrich (ed.): *Die Weiße Rose. Student Resistance to National Socialism 1942/1943*, Nottingham, 1991.

Steinbach, Peter and Tuchel, Johannes (eds.): *Widerstand gegen den Nationalsozialismus*, Bonn/Berlin, 1994.

Ueberschär, Gerd R., 'Gegner des Nationalsozialismus', *Militärgeschichtliche Mitteilungen*, 35 (1984), pp. 141–97.

II German Society under Nazi Rule

Abelshauser, Werner and Faust, Anselm: *Wirtschafts- und Sozialpolitik. Eine nationalsozialistische Revolution?*, Nationalsozialismus im Unterricht, Studieneinheit 4, Deutsches Institut für Fernstudien an der Universität Tübingen, Tübingen, 1983.

Albers, Jens: 'Nationalsozialismus und Modernisierung', *Kölner Zeitschrift für Soziologie und Sozialpsychologie*, 41 (1989), pp. 345–65.

Ayçoberry, Pierre: *The Social History of the Third Reich*, New York, 1999.

Baldwin, Peter: 'Social Interpretations of Nazism: Renewing a Tradition', *Journal of Contemporary History*, 25 (1990), pp. 5–37.

Bessel, Richard: 'Living with the Nazis: Some Recent Writing on the Social History of the Third Reich', *European History Quarterly*, 14 (1984), pp. 211–20.

Bessel, Richard (ed.), *Life in the Third Reich*, Oxford, 1987.

Borsdorf, Ulrich and Jamin, Mahilde (eds.): *Über Leben im Krieg. Kriegserfahrungen in einer Industrieregion*, Reinbek bei Hamburg, 1989.

Bridenthal, Renate et al. (eds.): *When Biology became Destiny. Women in Weimar and Nazi Germany*, New York, 1984.

Broszat, Martin, Henke, Klaus-Dietmar, and Woller, Hans (eds.): *Von Stalingrad zur Währungsreform*, Munich, 1988.

Burleigh, Michael and Wippermann, Wolfgang: *The Racial State. Germany, 1933–1945*, Cambridge, 1991.

Burleigh, Michael (ed.): *Confronting the Nazi Past. New Debates on Modern German History*, London, 1996.

Burleigh, Michael: *The Third Reich. A New History*, London, 2000.

Carsten, F.L.: *The German Workers and the Nazis*, London, 1995.

Corni, Gustavo: *Hitler and the Peasants*, New York/Oxford/Munich, 1990.

Crew, David (ed.): *Nazism and German Society, 1933–1945*, London, 1994.

Eitner, *Hans-Jürgen, Hitlers Deutsche: das Ende eines Tabus*, Gernsbach, 1990.

Engelmann, Bernd: *In Hitler's Germany. Everyday Life in the Third Reich*, London, 1988.

Frei, Norbert: *Der Führerstaat. Nationalsozialistische Herrschaft 1933 bis 1945*, 6th revised edn., Munich, 2001 (Engl. *National Socialist Rule in Germany. The Führer State 1933–1945*, Oxford/Cambridge, Mass., 1993).

Frei, Norbert: 'Wie modern war der Nationalsozialismus?' *Geschichte und Gesellschaft*, 19 (1993), pp. 367–87.

Frei, Norbert: 'People's Community and War: Hitler's Popular Support', in Hans Mommsen (ed.), *The Third Reich between Vision and Reality. New Perspectives on German History 1918–1945*, Oxford/New York, 2001, pp. 59–77.

Gellately, Robert: *Backing Hitler. Consent and Coercion in Nazi Germany*, Oxford, 2001.

Haupert, Bernhard and Schäfer, Franz Josef: *Jugend zwischen Kreuz und Hakenkreuz*, Frankfurt am Main, 1991.

Herbert, Ulrich: 'Arbeiterschaft im "Dritten Reich". Zwischenbilanz und offene Fragen', *Geschichte und Gesellschaft*, 15 (1989), pp. 320–60.

Herbert, Ulrich: *Fremdarbeiter. Politik und Praxis des 'Ausländer-Einsatzes' in der Kriegswirtschaft des Dritten Reiches*, Berlin/Bonn, 1985 (Engl. *Hitler's Foreign workers. Enforced Foreign Labor in Germany under the Third Reich*, Cambridge, 1997).

Höhne, Heinz: *Die Zeit der Illusionen*, Düsseldorf/Vienna/New York, 1991.

James, Harold: 'The Prehistory of the Federal Republic', *Journal of Modern History*, 63 (1991), pp. 98–115.

Kershaw, Ian: *The 'Hitler Myth'. Image and Reality in the Third Reich*, Oxford, 1987.

Kirk, Timothy: *Nazism and the Working Class in Austria. Industrial Unrest and Political Dissent in the 'National Community'*, Cambridge, 1996.

Lebor, Adam, and Boyes, Roger: *Surviving Hitler. Choices, Corruption and Compromise in the Third Reich*, London, 2000.

Mai, Gunther: 'Die Nationalsozialistische Betriebszellen-Organisation. Zum Verhältnis von Arbeiterschaft und Nationalsozialismus', *Vierteljahrshefte für Zeitgeschichte*, 31 (1983), pp. 573–613.

Mai, Gunther: '"Warum steht der deutsche Arbeiter zu Hitler?" Zur Rolle der Deutschen Arbeitsfront im Herrschaftssystem des Dritten Reiches', *Geschichte und Gesellschaft*, 12 (1986), pp. 212–34.

Mann, Reinhard: *Protest und Kontrolle im Dritten Reich*, Frankfurt am Main/New York, 1987.

Mason, Tim: *Nazism, Fascism and the Working Class*, ed. Jane Caplan, Cambridge, 1995.

Meier, Kurt: *Kreuz und Hakenkreuz. Die evangelische Kirche im Dritten Reich*, Munich, 1992.

Mommsen, Hans and Willems, Susanne (eds.): *Herrschaftsalltag im Dritten Reich. Studien und Texte*, Düsseldorf, 1988.

Mommsen, Hans: 'Nationalsozialismus als vorgetäuschte Modernisierung', in Walter H. Pehle (ed.), *Der historische Ort des Nationalsozialismus. Annäherungen*, Frankfurt am Main, 1990, pp. 13–46.

Mommsen, Hans: 'Noch einmal: Nationalsozialismus und Modernisierung', *Geschichte und Gesellschaft*, 21 (1995), pp. 391–402.

Mommsen, Hans and Grieger, Manfred: *Das Volkswagenwerk und seine Arbeiter im Dritten Reich*, Düsseldorf, 1996.

Niethammer, Lutz (ed.): *'Die Jahre weiß man nicht, wo man die heute hinsetzen soll'. Faschismuserfahrungen im Ruhrgebiet*, Berlin/Bonn, 1983.

Noakes, Jeremy: 'Nazism and Revolution', in Noel O'Sullivan (ed.), *Revolutionary Theory and Political Reality*, London, 1983, pp. 73–100.

Nolan, Mary: 'Work, Gender and Everyday Life. Reflections on Continuity, Normality and Agency in Twentieth-Century Germany', in Ian Kershaw and Moshe Lewin (eds.), *Stalinism and Nazism. Dictatorships in Comparison*, Cambridge, 1997, pp. 311–42.

Paul, Gerhard and Mallmann, Klaus-Michael (eds.), *Die Gestapo. Mythos und Realität*, Darmstadt, 1995.

Peukert, Detlev J.K.: *Volksgenossen und Gemeinschaftsfremde. Anpassung, Ausmerze und Aufbegehren unter dem Nationalsozialismus*, Cologne, 1982 (Engl. *Inside Nazi Germany. Conformity, Opposition and Racism in Everyday Life*, London, 1987).

Pine, Lisa: *Nazi Family Policy, 1933–1945*, Oxford/New York, 1997.

Prinz, Michael and Zitlemann, Rainer (eds.): *Nationalsozialismus und Modernisierung*, Darmstadt, 1991.

Rauh, Manfred; 'Anti-Modernismus im nationalsozialistischen Staat', *Historisches Jahrbuch*, 108 (1987), pp. 94–121.

Recker, Marie-Louise: *Nationalsozialistische Sozialpolitik im Zweiten Weltkrieg*, Munich, 1985.

Reichel, Peter: *Der schöne Schein des Dritten Reiches. Faszination und Gewalt des Faschismus*, Frankfurt am Main, 1993.

Salter, Stephen: 'Structures of Consensus and Coercion. Workers' Morale and the Maintenance of Work Discipline, 1939–1945', in David Welch (ed.), *Nazi Propaganda* (see below), pp. 88–116.

Salter, Stephen: 'National Socialism, the Nazi Regime and German Society', *The Historical Journal*, 35 (1992), pp. 487–99.

Smelser, Ronald: *Robert Ley. Hitler's Labour Front Leader*, New York/Oxford, 1988.

Stephenson, Jill: 'War and Society in Württemberg, 1939–1945: Beating the System', *German Studies Review*, 8 (1985), pp. 89–105.

Stephenson, Jill: 'Nazism, Modern War and Rural Society in Württemberg', *Journal of Contemporary History*, 32 (1997), pp. 339–56.

Stöver, Bernd: *Volksgemeinschaft im Dritten Reich. Die Konsensbereitschaft der Deutschen aus der Sicht sozialistischer Exilberichte*, Düsseldorf, 1993.

Thamer, Hans-Ulrich: *Verführung und Gewalt. Deutschland 1933–1945*, Berlin, 1986.

Welch, David (ed.): *Nazi Propaganda. The Power and the Limitations*, London, 1983.

Welch, David: 'Propaganda and Indoctrination in the Third Reich: Success or Failure?', *European History Quarterly*, 17 (1987), pp. 403–22.

Welch, David: 'Manufacturing a Consensus: Nazi Propaganda and the Building of a "National Community" (*Volksgemeinschaft*)', *Contemporary European History*, 2 (1993), pp. 1–15.

Welch, David: *The Third Reich. Politics and Propaganda*, London, 1993.

Zitelmann, Rainer: Hitler. *Selbstverständnis eines Revolutionärs*, Hamburg/Leamington Spa/New York, 1987 (Engl. *Hitler. The Politics of Seduction*, London, 1999).

Zitelmann, Rainer: 'Nationalsozialismus und Moderne. Eine Zwischenbilanz', in Werner Süß (ed.), *Übergange. Zeitgeschichte zwischen Utopie und Machbarkeit*, Berlin, 1990, pp. 195–223.

III Reactions to the Persecution of the Jews

Bankier, David: *The Germans and the Final Solution. Public Opinion under Nazism*, Oxford, 1992.

Bankier, David (ed.): *Probing the Depths of German Antisemitism. German Society and the Persecution of the Jews, 1933–1941*, New York/Oxford/ Jerusalem, 2000.

Dipper, Christoph: 'Der deutsche Widerstand und die Juden', *Geschichte und Gesellschaft*, 9 (1983), pp. 349–80.

Eley, Geoff: 'Ordinary Germans, Nazism, and Judeocide', in Geoff Eley (ed.), *The 'Goldhagen Effect'. History, Memory, Nazism - Facing the German Past*, Ann Arbor, Michigan, 2000, pp. 1–31.

Gellately, Robert: *The Gestapo and German Society. Enforcing Racial Policy 1933–1945*, Oxford, 1990.

Goldhagen, Daniel Jonah: *Hitler's Willing Executioners*, New York, 1996.

Gordon, Sarah: *Hitler, Germans, and the 'Jewish Question'*, Princeton, 1984.

Graml, Hermann: *Reichskristallnacht. Antisemitismus und Judenverfolgung im Dritten Reich*, Munich, 1988.

Henry, Frances: *Victims and Neighbors. A Small Town in Nazi Germany Remembered*, South Hadley, Mass., 1984.

Hilberg, Raul: *Perpetrators, Victims, Bystanders. The Jewish Catastrophe 1933–1945*, New York, 1992.

Johnson, Eric A.: *Nazi Terror. The Gestapo, Jews, and Ordinary Germans*, New York, 1999.

Kater, Michael: 'Everyday Anti-Semitism in Prewar Nazi Germany: The Popular Bases', *Yad Vashem Studies*, 16 (1984), pp. 129–59.

Kershaw, Ian: 'Indifferenz des Gewissens. Die deutsche Bevölkerung und die "Reichskristallnacht"', *Blätter für deutsche und internationale Politik*, 33 (1988), pp. 1319–30.

Kershaw, Ian: 'German Popular Opinion during the Final Solution: Information, Comprehension, Reactions', in Asher Cohen, Joav Gelber, and Charlotte Wardi (eds.), *Comprehending the Holocaust*, Frankfurt am Main etc., 1988.

Kershaw, Ian: 'German Popular Opinion and the "Jewish Question", 1939–1943: Some further Reflections', in Arnold Paucker (ed.), *Die Juden im nationalsozialistischen Deutschland 1933–1943*, Tubingen, 1986, pp. 365–86.

Kershaw, Ian: 'Antisemitismus und die NS-Bewegung vor 1933', in Hermann Graml, Angelika Königseder, and Juliane Wetzel (eds.): *Vorurteil und Rassenhaß. Antisemitismus in den faschistischen Bewegungen Europas*, Berlin, 2001, pp. 29–47.

Kulka, Otto Dov: 'Die Nürnberger Rassengesetze und die deutsche Bevölkerung im Lichte geheimer NS-Lage- und Stimmungsberichte', *Vierteljahrshefte für Zeitgeschichte*, 32 (1984), pp. 582–624.

Kulka, Otto Dov and Rodrigue, Aron: 'The German Population and the Jews in the Third Reich', *Yad Vashem Studies*, 16 (1984), pp. 421–35.

Kulka, Otto Dov: 'Popular Christian Attitudes in the Third Reich to National Socialist Policies towards the Jews', in Otto Dov Kulka and Paul R. Mendes-Flohr (eds.): *Judaism and Christianity under the Impact of National Socialism*, Jerusalem, 1987, pp. 251–67.

Kulka, Otto Dov: 'Singularity and its Relativization. Changing Views in German Historiography on National Socialism and the "Final Solution"', *Yad Vashem Studies*, 19 (1988), pp. 151–86.

Kulka, Otto Dov: 'The German Population and the Jews: State of Research and New Perspectives', in David Bankier (ed.), *Probing the Depths of German Antisemitism* (see above), pp. 271–81.

Kwiet, Konrad and Eschwege, Helmut: *Selbstbehauptung und Widerstand. Deutsche Juden im Kampf um Existenz und Menschenwürde, 1933–1945*, Hamburg, 1984.

Marrus, Michael: *The Holocaust in History*, London, 1988.

Michel, Thomas: *Die Juden in Gaukönigshofen / Unterfranken (1550–1942)*, Stuttgart, 1988.

Mommsen, Hans: 'Was haben die Deutschen vom Völkermord an den Juden gewußt?', in Walter H. Pehle (ed.), *Der Judenpogrom 1938. Von der 'Reichskristallnacht' zum Völkermord*, Frankfurt am Main, 1988, pp. 176–200.

Mommsen, Hans and Obst, Dieter: 'Die Reaktion der deutschen Bevölkerung auf die Verfolgung der Juden', in Hans Mommsen and Susanne Willems (eds.): *Herrschaftsalltag im Dritten Reich. Studien und Texte*, Dusseldorf, 1988, pp. 374–485.

Obenaus, Herbert and Sybille (eds.): *'Schreiben, wie es wirklich war!' Aufzeichnungen Karl Dürkefäldens aus den Jahren 1933–1945*, Hanover, 1985.

Strauss, Herbert A, Bergmann, Werner, and Hoffmann, Christhard (eds.): *Lerntag über Gewalt gegen Juden: Die Novemberpogrome von 1938 in historischer Perspektive*, Berlin, 1989.

Walter, Dirk: *Antisemitische Kriminalität und Gewalt. Judenfeindschaft in der Weimarer Republik*, Bonn, 1999.

Wildt, Michael: '"Der muß hinaus! Der muß hinaus!" Antisemitismus in deutschen Nord- und Ostseebädern 1920–1935', *Mittelweg 36*, 10 (2001), pp. 3–25.

Index

Absberg, 338
Africa, 290, 310
'Agrarian Apparatus' of NSDAP, 37
agriculture, 11–13, ch. 1 passim, 33–5,
  66, 282–96; in First World War,
  36; crisis during Depression, 37,
  40; farm production, 40; in-
  come from, 40–1, 63; marketing,
  38, 42, 45, 49, 51–2, 292–3;
  Nazi policies, 40–3, 45, 292–3;
  dairy ordinances, 45–8, 51–2,
  292–3; labour crisis in, 55–63,
  283 ff.; and Four Year Plan, 55,
  62–3; unemployment level in
  (1933), 68; impact of Second
  World War on, 282 ff.
Aichach, 135
Allen, William Sheridan, 231
Alsace-Lorraine, 332
Altbayern, 225
Altenmuhr, 238–9
Altenstadt, 262
Altötting, 145
Alzenau, 47, 241, 258
Amberg, 86, 215, 228, 262, 265
Angestellte, 113 n.4, and see white-
  collar employees
Ansbach, 18, 166, 244, 258–9, 337
Anschluß, 137–8, 258
anti-Bolshevism, 126, 131, 223, 356,
  and see Bolshevism
anti-communism, 21, 64, 96, 126, 131,
  190, 356
anti-Marxism, 18, 70, 112, 189–90,
  223, and see Marxists
anti-Semitism, 5, 96–7, 116, 177, 356,
  370–1, chs. 6 and 9 passim;
  criticized by Cardinal Faulhaber,
  189, 192; spread of racial
  variety, 229–30; limited role in
  Nazi rise to power, 230–1;
  'latent' and 'dynamic', 231, 272,
  372; virulence in Franconia,
  235 ff.; ambivalent attitude of
  Church to, 247; 'objective'
  function of, 275–6; and see
    Jewish Question, Jews
anti-socialism, 66, 70, 112, 185, 187,
  189–90
Armaments Inspectorates, 304
Asbach, 270
Asia, 290
Atzinger, Josef, 253
Aufseß, 289
Augsburg, 15–16, 21, 66, 84–5, 99
  n.91, 101, 105 n.13, 106–7,
  128, 131, 156, 227, 233, 262,
  266, 300 n.58, 309, 358, 361,
  367; Mayor of, 361
Augsburg-Land, District Leader of, 354
Augsburg-Stadt, District Leader of,
  289, 301, 302 and n.64
Auschwitz, 277, 359, 367–8, 384
Austria, 103, 106, 125, 130, 136–7,
  249, 258–9
Autobahnen, 92, 96, and see motor-
  ways

Bad Aibling, 88–90, 130, 138, 233
Bad Brückenau, 322, 369
Baden, 358
Bad Kissingen, 322, 360
Bad Neustadt, 47 and n.52, 48, 240,
  252, 325
Bad Tölz, 207, 233, 263
Bär, Karl, 238
Bär, Kurt, 236, 237 and n.36, 238
Balkan campaign, 289
Baltic, 134
Bamberg, 17, 161, 250–3, 270; Arch-
  bishop of, 215 n.96; Oberlandes-
  gerichtspräsident of, 323 ff.,
  336
Bavaria, features of province on eve of
  Third Reich, 10–29; socio-
  economic structure, 11–16; agri-
  culture in, 11–13, 33–5, ch. 1
  passim; industry in, 11–15; popu-
  lation of, 11–16; administrative
  divisions of, 13; urbanization, 16;

denominational structure, 16-18; political structure, 18-29; growth of Nazism in, 18-17; Nazi takeover of State in, 70; Jewish population of, 225-8; educational structure of, 209; parliament (Landtag) of, 187; Ministry of Education in, 210, 345, 347-8, 353; Ministry of Interior in, 237; Reich Governor of, *see* Epp, Ritter von; *and see* Lower, Upper Bavaria

Bavarian Christian Peasant Association, 38

Bavarian *Ostmark, Gau* of Nazi Party, 27-8, 85, 119

Bavarian People's Party (BVP), 18-21, 23-8, 36 n.8, 64, 116, 124, 157, 187-8, 190, 192, 198, 241 n.50

Bavarian Political Police (BPP), 51-2, 54, 59, 208, 211-12

Bayerische Motorenwerke (BMW), 15, 107

Bayerischer Bauernbund (BBB), 19-20, 23, 36 n.8, 39, 295

Bayerischer Wald, 78-9, 87, 100

Bayreuth, 45, 59, 82, 146, 161, 169, 288; Dean of, 161, 249

Bayrischzell, 103

Beamte, 113 n.4, 115, 118, 132, 140, 142-3, 323, 326, 328, 352, *and see* civil servants

'Beauty of Labour', 95, 122

Belzec, 359

Berchtesgaden, 136-8, 261 n.30, 317, 321, 350; *Landrat* of, 321

Berlin, 159, 170, 273, 290, 362 n.12, 379

Bertram, Cardinal Adolf, 335

'big shots', 'big-wigs', 47, 64, 85, 150, 305-6, 311, *and see Bonzen*

Bischofsheim an der Rhön, 243

black market, 282-3, 294, 307, 321

Bolsheviks, 93, 172, 202, 253, 288, 349, 351, 356

Bolshevism, 64, 94, 96-7, 117, 126, 153, 219, 249, 276, 308, 314, 322, 345, 349, 352, 355-6

bombing, 305, 309-11, 314, 360, 368-70, 382

Bonzen, 85, 96-7, 150, 211, 302 n.64, 323 n.34, *and see* 'big shots'

Bonzentum, 97

'*Bonzokratie'*, 79, 96

Border Secretaries (*Grenzsekretäre*) of the *Sopade*, 9, 74-5, 90, 99, 101, 131

Bormann, Martin, 332, 353, 364, 366, 382

Bruckberg, 337

Brückenau-Hammelburg, 291

Bruckmühl, 90

Brüning, Heinrich, 66, 69, 116, 142, 324

Bund deutscher Mädel (BdM), 195, 200

bureaucracy, expansion of in Third Reich, 113; complaints about excessive, 135, 318 ff.

Bürgerbräukeller, 271

Burglengenfeld, 86, 105 n.14

Burgsinn, 270

butchers, 127-8, 133, 320

call-ups, 283-5, 293, 320

Caritas, 129, 205, 235

Catholic Church, *see* Church

Catholic Press Association for Bavaria, 186

cattle-dealers, 128, 233, 240 ff.

Cattle-Farming Association, 243

Central Association of White Collar Employees, 96

Centre Party (*Zentrum*), 21, 185, 188, 190, 192

Cham, 125, 245, 249

chambers of commerce, 119

China, 106

Church, 2, 5, 96, 134, 145, 289, 375-7, chs. 4, 5, and 8 *passim*; and Jews, 246-57, 272, 275, 368, 372; 'struggle', 3, 5, 8, 50, 65, 161, 182, 193, 289, 331, 376, 381, chs. 4, 5, and 8 *passim*; *and see* clergy

Catholic, chs. 5, 8 *passim*; size of Catholic population, 16-17; political affiliation of Catholic population, 20-1, 23-7; attitude towards Nazism,

Church: Catholic (*cont.*):
27-8; electoral support for NSDAP, 190-1; bishops, 187, 190-1, 212-13, 218-20, 253, 256 n.8, 336 and n.13, 340; hierarchy, 212-13, 218-20, 249, 253, 256, 275, 336, 372; ideological focus of, 185, 189-90, 223, 356; educational demands of, 185, 187, 192, 209 ff., *and see* schools; reaction to 'immorality trials' propaganda, 196-7; incompatibility of *Weltanschauung* with that of Nazism, 203, 210, 332, 353; feast days of, interfered with by Nazis, 208-9, 333-4, 341; schools of, under attack by Nazis, 209 ff.; ideological struggle with Nazism, 203, 222-3, 257; and persecution of Jews, 223, 228-9, 246 ff., 368, 372; subjection to new attacks by Nazi regime (1941), 332 ff.; and 'euthanasia action', 334-40; defence against removal of crucifixes from schools, 340-57
Protestant (evangelical), ch. 4 *passim*; size of Protestant population, 16-17; character of Protestantism in Franconia, 17, 156; political affiliation of Protestants, 20, 23, 26, 158, 162, 172, 182; 'People's Mission', 160-1; Provincial Church Council of, 167-8, 175; Provincial Synod of, 159, 165; attack on independence of in Bavaria, 164 ff.; attempt to set up Reich Church, 159-61, 164 ff.; growing resignation within, 179 ff.; weakening hold over youth, 183-4; and Jews, 246 ff., 368, 372
civil servants, 111-13, 114 n.7, 115-16, 118-19, 121, 140-3, 303, 323-8; denigration by Nazis, 141, 324-8; grievances of, 141-2; in Nazi Party, 142, 143 and n.3, 328; attitudes of during war, 323-9; *and see Beamte*
civil service, 111, 140-3, 323 ff., 372

clergy:
Catholic: chs. 5, 8 *passim*; numbers of in relation to Catholic population, 186; banned from joining NSDAP pre-1933, 190; role in opposition to Nazi measures, 194 ff., 206, 210 ff., 338, 347-8; strength of hold over population, 200-1; alleged criticism of Church leaders, 219-20; and Jews, 228-9, 231, 246-57, 365; and 'euthanasia action', 334-40; and 'crucifix affair', 340-57; *and see* priests
Protestant: ch. 4 *passim*; attitude towards Weimar Republic, 157; signs of early disillusionment in Third Reich, 161-3; support for Bishop Meiser, 165 ff.; numbers in relation to Protestant population, 186; role in organizing opposition (1934), 165 ff., 175-6; and Jews, 228, 231, 246-57
coal shortage (1939-40), 298, 300, 379
Coburg, 156, 158, 162, 175, 235
'coercive economy', ch. 1 *passim*, esp. 36, 42, 50, 52 n.69, 53, 64, 282, 293
Comintern, 84 n.55
Communist Party (KPD), 9, 18-23, 66-7, 70-2, 74, 76, 79, 84 n.55, 88 n.73, 101, 109, 187-8, 193, 241 n.50, 304
Communists, 74-5, 80, 82, 84 n.55, 86, 91, 105 n.13, 118, 174, 211, 236, 302
'Community of Fate' (*Schicksalsgemeinschaft*), 279, 281, 291
'Community Schools', *see* schools
concentration camps, 60, 73-4, 260, 302, 334 n.11
Concordat, Bavarian, 187 and n.7, 188, 209; Reich, 191-2, 201 and n.49, 209, 213-14, 220-1, 223
'Confessing Church', 159, 161, 184 n.77, 250
Congregation of Mary, 200
Corpus Christi Procession, 208
'Council of Trust', 76-7, 86, 100-1
craft guilds, 119

craftsmen, 111, 115, 127, 133–5, 139, 315 ff.
Crucifix issue, 180, 199–200, 205–8, 217, 340–57, 363, 376
Crystal Glass factory, Theresiental, 87
'Crystal Night' (Reichskristallnacht), 236, 253, 257–75, 358, 377, and see pogrom
Czechoslovakia, 78–9, 105–6, 125, 134, 137

Dachau, 31, 73 and n.23, 81–2, 86–8, 355, 369
DAF, see Labour Front
Dahlem, 159
Dairy-farming Associations, 51
Darré, Richard Walther, 37, 40, 45, 380
'Defence Districts' (Wehrkreise), 296–7, 299
Deggendorf, 211, 228, 229 n.14
dentists, 115
denunciation, 6, 238
department stores, 116, 120–1, 123, 133
Depression, 18, 20–1, 67, 70, 98, 136, 158, 162, 235, 277, 315, 324
Deutsche Informationen, 107 and n.23
'Deutschland-Berichte' der Sopade, 9, 94, 99, 105, 148
Deutschland-Informationen der KPD, 88 n.73
Dienstboten, 57–60, and see labour shortage
Dill, Hans, 9, 74
Dinkelsbühl, 244, 262
dissent, definition, 2–4; evaluation, 374 ff.
doctors, 115
domestic service, 13, 68
Düsseldorf, 311 n.94
'Duty Year for Girls', 58

East Elbia, 39
'Eastern Aid', 38–9
Eastern Front, 319–20, 356
Eastern Marches of Bavaria, see Bavarian Ostmark
Ebermannstadt, 53, 130, 169, 205, 242, 289–91, 320
Ebersberg, 353
Eberstein, Friedrich Karl Frhr. von, 149–50

Ebert, Friedrich, 190
Eichstätt, 17, 195, 203–4, 262, 369; Bishop of, 203–4, 340 n.26; diocesan administration of, 215 n.95
Einsatzkommandos, 359
Einzelaktionen, 239–40
elections to Reichstag, 18–27, 190–1, 230
'Emergency Decrees' (1933), 117–18
'Enabling Act' (1933), 191
England, 302 n.64, 303
Epp, Franz Xaver Ritter von, 59, 61, 171, 244, 349, 352–4, 363
Erkersreuth, 49
Erlangen, 21
Eschenbach, 215 n.96
Etsdorf, 215
'euthanasia action', 272, 334–40, 363–4, 381
Evangelical Church, see Church, Protestant
Eyrichshof, 163

'factory assemblies', 77
Fäth, Josef, 199–200
Faulhaber, Cardinal Michael, 187–90, 192, 201–2, 247–8, 335, 348
Feilnbach, 233
female labour, 15–16, 57, 76, 86, 296–9, 307–8, 379 and n.14
Ferstl, Gewerberat, 346 n.40
Films, I Accuse, 340, 364; Jüd Süß, 364 n.17; The Eternal Jew, 364 and n.17
Fischbach, 266
food shortages, 83, 128–9, 298, 301, 304–6
Forchheim, 350, 363
foreign workers (Fremdarbeiter), 58–9, 282 ff., 286–8, 293–5, 296–300, 314 n.99
Förtsch, Father Martin, 252
Four Year Plan, 41, 55, 63, 98, 268
Franconia, 23, 50, 156, 159, 161–2, 167, 169–72, 177–8, 225, 228–9, 232, 235, 244, 248, 254, 265, 286, 336 n.15; Gau of Nazi Party, 27–8, 119, 165–6, 169, 174, 242, 337–8; and see Lower, Middle, Upper Franconia
Frankfurt am Main, 369

Fränkische Schweiz, 125, 317
Fränkische Tageszeitung, 165, 171
Freikorps, 158, 266
Freising, 197
Frick, Wilhelm, 170-3, 239
Friedberg, 309
Frühstockheim, 181
Führer, 135, 138, 146, 149, 168, 172-3, 219, 224, 266, 273, 276, 322, 327, 336, 367-8, 380, 382;
Chancellory of, 338; *and see* Hitler, Adolf
    cult, 75, 78, 96, 121, 127; impact on workers, 75, 94; among petty bourgeoisie, 122-3, 131, 133, 154; in Protestant areas, 172, 177;
    image and Jewish Question, 273, 277
Fulda, Bishops' Conference, 256 n.8, 335
Fürth, 21, 82, 227, 363, 369
Füssen, 266

Galen, Bishop Clemens August Graf von, 339 and n.24, 340 n.26
Garmisch-Partenkirchen, 136-7, 139, 222 n.13, 233, 244, 261, 317-18
Gau Köln-Aachen, 232
Gaukönigshofen, 266
Gau Kurmark, 232
Gendarmerie, 49, 51, 197-8, 207, 263-4, 289, 319, 349
General Trade Association, 117
German Catholic Assembly, 189
'German Christians', 157, 159-61, 174, 179 and n.68, 181-2, 248
German Democratic Party (DDP), 19-20
German National People's Party (DNVP), 19-20
German People's Party (DV), 19-20
Gestapa, 90 n.78, 110 n.31
Gestapo, 80, 90-1, 103, 161, 196, 201, 204, 234 n.27, 243, 246-7, 256, 276, 287, 298-300
Gleichschaltung, 1, 70, 119, 178, 189, 377, 384
Glonn, 212
Goebbels, Joseph, 74, 196, 201 n.49, 257, 260, 263, 267, 271, 326, 339, 365, 369, 378-9, 382, 384

Göring, Hermann, 55
Government President, of Lower Bavaria and the Upper Palatinate, 39, 48, 195, 215 n.95, 217, 222, 269, 346 and n.40, 347; of Lower Franconia, 54, 200, 254 n.7, 332; of Swabia, 46, 60, 90, 245, 268, 365-6; of Upper and Middle Franconia, 142, 165, 177-8, 204, 249, 262, 284, 342; of Upper Bavaria, 39, 50, 54, 89, 106, 129, 136, 197, 222, 233, 239, 254, 263 n.41
Grafeneck, 335
Great Britain, 296, 315
Gressenwöhr, 215
Grohé, Josef, 232
'Grüß Gott' greeting, 196, 221 n.11
'Grumbler' campaign, 46
Grynszpan, Herschel, 258, 260
Guilds, 120 n.26, 127
Günzburg, 245
Gunzenhausen, 166-7, 171, 338; pogrom in, 236-8
Gürtner, Franz, 335
Gustloff, Wilhelm, 239, 259

Hadamar, 335 and n.13
Handwerk, 316, 319-20
Handwerker, 127, 135, *and see* craftsmen
Harvest Thanksgiving (*Erntedankfest*), poor attendance at, 50-1, 54
Haßfurt, 172
Hausham, 21
Heilbrunn, 263
Heinloth, Father, 204
Held, Dr Heinrich, 187-9
Hellmuth, Otto, 323 n.34
Hersbruck, 18, 252, 262
Hess, Rudolf, 239, 271
Hesse, 335, 362 n.12
Heydrich, Reinhard, 371
Hilpoltstein, 17, 28
Himmler, Heinrich, 336, 371
Hindenburg, Paul von, 48
Hitler, Adolf, 1, 4, 26-8, 31, 38-9, 46-7, 64, 71, 73-4, 78, 86-7, 92 and n.81, 94, 96-7, 105, 108, 118, 122-3, 126, 129, 131, 133, 136, 139, 141, 149-50, 152-3, 158 and n.10, 162, 164, 170-1, 173, 177-8, 191-2, 195, 199,

201 n.49, 220, 223-4, 229-31,
239, 271, 273, 277, 279, 300-1,
307 and n.80, 314, 323 and
n.34, 326-7, 330-2, 334, 339,
355, 366-8, 370-1, 373, 377,
379 and n.14, 380 and n.15,
381-3, 385
'Hitler Greeting', 80, 82, 84, 105,
131-2, 168, 177, 196, 221 and
n.11, 317, 328
Hitler Youth (HJ), 50, 129, 146, 162-
3, 199, 205, 207, 236, 244, 252,
355
hoarding, 282
Höchberg, 266
Hof, 13, 86, 162, 304
Hofbräuhaus brewery, Munich, 77
Hofmann, Hans Georg, 237
Holz, Karl, 165, 171
Hop-growing, 134
Horst-Wessel Song, 168, 177
housing shortage, 84, 95, 99 and n.91,
302
Hungary, 369

Ichenhausen, 245
industry, structure in Bavaria, 12-16,
unemployment in (1933), 13,
15, 67-8; conditions in, 76, 78,
80, 86-8, 95, 98; unrest in, 84
n.55, 87-90, ch. 2 passim;
greater surveillance in, 98, 104;
armaments, 85, 91, 95, 98;
during war, 296 ff.; building,
13, 68, 86, 316; ceramics, 15;
porcelain, 13, 76, 78, 86; toy,
15, 125; glass, 79-80, 86; textile,
13, 15, 68, 78, 84-6, 101, 316;
mining, 93, 105 n.14, 109-10
Inheritance Courts, 53
Italy, 153 n.33, 192

Jäger, August, 167-8, 173
Jehovah's Witnesses, 162
Jewish Question, 121, 125, 148, chs.
6 and 9 passim, esp. 224, 226,
228-9, 239, 248-9, 254-6,
271-7, 360-2, 377-8, 383-4;
of little importance in south
Bavaria, 232-3; but of significance in north Bavaria, 235;
Church and, 246 ff., 357;
relative indifference of population towards, 229, 231, 257,
274-5, 359-60, 363-4, 368,
377, 384; 'Final Solution' of,
335, 359, 364 ff., 371, 384;
imagined connection with war,
368-70; and see anti Semitism,
Jews
Jews, 8, 77, 94, 96-7, 124-5, 142-3,
162, 174, chs. 6 and 9 passim,
377, 383; businesses of, 120-1,
231 ff., 240-1, 245; violence
against, 128, 228, 231 ff.,
257-74; boycotts against, 129,
231 ff., 240-1, 244 ff., 259-
60; teachers' discrimination
against in 1938, 147; 'ritual
murder' allegations, 162; Church
and, 223, 228-9, 246-57; distribution of in Bavaria, 225-8;
cattle-dealers, 128, 233, 240 ff.;
'demonstrations' against in 1935,
234-5; emigration of, 259-60,
358; assisted by non-Jews, 269-
70, 361; depersonalization of,
275, 360, 372; increased discrimination against in early war
years, 358-61; deportations,
359, 362-4; extermination of,
359, 364 ff.; introduction of
'Yellow Star' for, 361-2;
rumours about fate of, 364 ff.;
'scapegoat' function of, 377;
and see anti-Semitism, Jewish
Question
Judenedikt, 226
Judges, 327
Jungmädel, 200
Jungvolk, 195, 212
Junker, estates of, 57
justice administration, reports of, 7,
323 ff.; morale during war,
323 ff.

Katyn, 365-7
KdF, see 'Strength through Joy'
Kern, Helmut, 160-1, 167, 175, 251
Kiel, 364 n.17
Kitzingen, 31, 181, 264, 294, 371
Knoeringen, Walter von, 9, 75
Kolbermoor, 88, 90
Königsberg, 158, n.10
Konnersreuth, 207
Kraus, Johann, 203-4, 252

Krauss-Maffei works, Munich, 91-2
and 92 n.81
Kube, Wilhelm, 232, 250
Kulmbach, 102 n.98
Kulturkampf, 185
Kürmreuth, 215

Labour Front (DAF), 80, 84-5, 87-8,
92, 96-7, 100-1, 104, 121-2,
132, 298, 303, 310-11
labour relations, ch. 2 *passim*, esp. 70,
72, 88-90, 98-9, 104, 109, 296,
298-9
Labour Service, 58
labour shortage, in agriculture, 34, 36,
42, 54, 55-63, 282 ff., 285 n.9,
286-91, 293, 380; in industry,
95 ff., 102, 296 ff.; in middle-
class concerns, 132, 135-6, 315,
320
Lageberichte, 7
Lammers, Hans Heinrich, 353
Landsberg am Lech, 134
Landshut, 228, 253
Lateran Agreement (1929), 223
Lauf, 77
Leidersbach, 198-200
Leutershausen, 172, 258
Lewy, Günther, 248
Ley, Robert, 298, 311, 325
Limburg, Bishop of, 335 n.13
living standards, 84, 93, 297-8, 379,
and see housing shortage, prices,
rationing, wages
Lohr, 265
Lower Bavaria, 13-14, 17-18, 20-2,
24-7, 35, 39, 42, 48, 57, 59,
217, 225, 227-8, 232, 253, 262,
269, 284, 286 n.13, 287, 342,
and see Government President
Lower Franconia, 13-14, 17, 22-7, 33-5,
43-4, 47-8, 51, 57, 163, 172,
181, 197-8, 226-7, 235-6, 240-
3, 249, 252, 254 n.7, 258, 259
and n.18, 261 and n.28, 264-5,
269-70, 279, 291, 294, 303,
309, 322, 323 n.34, 332, 342,
369, 371, *and see* Government
President, Main Franconia
lower middle class, *see* middle class,
Mittelstand, petty bourgeoisie
Lower Saxony, 231
Lublin, 359-60

Luther, Martin, 160, 162, 180
Lutheranism, 156-8, 162, 193

Main Franconia, *Gau* of Nazi Party,
27-8, 119, 199, 216
Mainstockheim, 371
'malicious practices', 104-5, 105 n.11,
253
Mann, Reinhard, 311 n.94
'March converts', 27
Marktredwitz, 78
Marxists, 84, 87, 92, 103, 106, 112,
154, 162, 190, 251
Maschinenfabrik Augsburg und
Nürnberg (MAN), 15, 100, 105
n.13, 107
Mason, Tim, 313
Maxhütte iron foundry, Burglengenfeld,
86
May Day celebrations, 86
Mayer, Father Rupert, 201 and n.49,
202-3
Mecklenburg, 11
Meiser, Bishop Hans, 159-61, 163-79,
181, 184 n.77, 217, 376
Memel, 134
Memmingen, 121, 262-4
middle class, ch. 3 *passim*, 281, 315-29,
support for Nazism in 1933,
114-20; growing dissatisfaction
in early years of dictatorship,
120-34; attitude during 'boom'
years, 132 ff., 148-53; morale
on eve of war, 151-3; ideological
affinities with Nazism, 139,
153-5; in war, 315-29; growing
alienation from Nazism, 322-3,
329; absence of opposition in,
375
Middle Franconia, 13-14, 17, 21-6, 33,
35, 43, 57, 81, 103, 124, 147,
156, 158, 172, 227, 235-8,
242 and n.56, 248, 251-2, 254
n.7, 258-9, 262, 305, 320, 338,
365, *and see* Franconia, Government President
Milbertshofen, Jewish settlement in
Munich, 359
Milk Provisioning Associations, 51
Mittelstand, ch. 3 *passim*, 83, 111, 114,
116-17, 120, 122-3, 126, 128,
133-5, 138-9, 153, 229, 315-
16, 319, 329-30, 374; discontent

within, 120 ff.; difficulties of 1937-9, 132 ff.; ideological affinities with Nazism, 139, 153-5; during war, 315 ff.; fears for future of, 319, 321-2; criticism of Nazism, 322-3; *and see* middle class, petty bourgeoisie
Mittenwald, 106, 318-19
Mömlingen, 197-8
monasteries, 129, 185, 338; disappropriation of, 332-3
Moore, Barrington, 312-13
Mosel Valley, 11
motorways, 78, 81-3, 91
Mückermann, Father Hermann, 250
Mühldorf, 128-9, 211 n.81, 353
Müller, Ludwig, Reich Bishop, 159, 164, 167
Müller-Claudius, Michael, 265, 272, 364
Münchberg, 82
Munich, 13, 15-16, 23, 45, 61, 66, 73, 77, 82, 84, 86, 91, 99 and n.91, 107, 117, 120, 122-3, 128, 131, 135-6, 148-9, 157, 166, 168, 170, 173, 189, 201 and n.49, 202, 205-7, 212-14, 216, 221 n.11, 222, 226 n.8, 227, 229, 232-4, 243, 245, 247, 250, 258-9, 261-3, 266-7, 270, 290, 296, 299, 301, 358-9, 366-9
Munich Agreement/Conference, 107, 259
Munich-Freising, Archdiocese of, 187-8, 214, 336, 347-8
Munich-Upper Bavaria, *Gau* of Nazi Party, 28, 62, 118 n.18, 119, 342
Münster, 339
Münsterschwarzach, 332-3
Mussolini, Benito, 192, 223

national community, 2, 5, 29, 31, 54, 72, 85, 116-17, 161, 182, 192, 276, 279, 281, 289, 291, 296, 302-3, 359, 371, 373, ans see *Volksgemeinschaft*
Nationalsozialistische Auslandsorganisation, 239
Nationalsozialistische Betriebszellenorganisation (NSBO), 70, 77, 80
Nationalsozialistische Deutsche Arbeiterpartei (NSDAP), see Nazi Party
Nationalsozialistische Frauenschaft, 346, 355, 362 n.12

Nationalsozialistische Handwerks-, Handels- und Gewerbeorganisation (NS-Hago), 120 and n.26
Nationalsozialistische Volkswohlfahrt (NSV), 85, 101, 144, 328, 333, 341
Nationalsozialistischer Lehrerbund (NSLB), 142-4, 146-7, 213, 216, 269 n.73
Nationalsozialistisches Kraftfahrkorps (NSKK), 143
Nazi Party (NSDAP), reports of on popular opinion, 7; electoral success in Bavaria, 18-20, 23-7; membership, 27-8, 55, 62, 114-19, 132, 134, 140, 142-3, 145, 221; difficulties encountered in penetrating society, 20-5, 28, 48-9, 54-5, 62; attractiveness to peasantry in Depression, 37-8; *Kampfzeit* of, 46, 276; communications difficulties in countryside, 28, 48-9, 62, 285; and worker parties, 66 ff.; social composition of, 67 and n.5, 70; anti-socialism of, 70; support from petty bourgeosie, 114-20; a *Beamtenpartei*, 115; antiChristian ethos of, 115, 162, 182-3, 190, 195, 210; complaints at collections of, 120, 122-3, 133, 221; complaints at corruption in, 122, 123 n.33, 126, 148-50, 196, 303; violence of activists, 129, 205 ff., 234 ff.; image damaged by 'Church struggle', 170 ff., 178-9, 211-12, 345-6; antipathy of Catholic Church towards (pre-1933), 189 ff.; failure to mobilize Catholic population, 195, 221-2; poor attendance at meetings of, 197, 221; antiChurch measures of, 165 ff., 205 ff.; anti-Jewish campaign in 1935, 251 ff.; and pogrom (1938), 257 ff.; anti-Semitism as integrating element with, 275-6; loss of support in middle class, 322-3; and 'euthanasia action', 336-8; and 'crucifix affair', 340 ff.; Chancellory of, 323, 332
Nazism, social aims of, 1-2, 71, 281, 296; growth in Bavaria, 18-27;

Nazism, Social aims of (cont.):
ideology, 1–2, 28–9, 62, 71, 97,
109, 116, 210, 224, 229, 240,
246–7, 256–7, 272, 276, 288–
92, 296, 336, 376–7, 379 n.14,
384; Weltanschauung, 1, 28,
190, 198, 246–7, 256, 383;
attractiveness to youth, 75, 126;
and peasantry, ch. 1 passim,
282–96; and working class, ch. 2
passim, 296–315; and middle
class, ch. 3 passim, 315–30; and
Churches, chs. 4, 5, and 8
passim; impact on Protestantism,
179–84; incompatibility with
Catholicism, 203, 210, 332, 353;
superficiality of hold over
Catholic population, 220; and
Jews, chs. 6 and 9 passim;
difficulties of penetrating on
Jewish Question, 240 ff., 246,
256, 272, 274, 336; loss of
support in middle class, 322–3;
and euthanasia, 334–40
Neu Beginnen, 292 n.30, 303 n.68
Neuendettelsau, 160
Neumarkt in der Oberpfalz, 228, 253,
262, 344 n.38
Neurath, Konstantin von, 173
Neustadt an der Aisch, 18, 252, 262
Neustadt an der Saale, see Bad Neustadt
Neu Ulm, 81, 168
newspapers, 28, 48–9, 62, 93, 117, 162,
165, 171, 186, 196, 201 n.49,
216, 232–3, 243
Niemöller, Martin, 159, 164, 180
Nördlingen, 244, 270
Northeim, 231
Norway, 97
NSBO; NSDAP; NS-Hago; NSLB;
NSKK; NSV: see under
Nationalsozialistische
nuns, 197, 209, 333; dismissed from
teaching posts, 210–12
Nuremberg, 13, 15–16, 21, 66, 82, 86,
99 n.91, 100, 102, 106, 120,
124, 135, 140, 156, 165–6,
169–71, 173–6, 179, 213–14,
216, 227, 229, 234 n.27, 235,
238, 246 n.70, 251, 254, 258,
262, 264, 296–7, 299, 337,
358–9, 363
Nuremberg Laws, 239–40, 268, 272

Nuremberg Party Rally (1935), 239
Nuremberg Trials, 367

Oberammergau, 136, 197, 244, 317
Oberlandesgerichtspräsidenten (OLGP),
Bamberg, 323–8; 336; Munich,
53 n.75, 323; Nuremberg, 323
Ochsenfeld, 204
Ochsenfurt, 266
Oldenburg, 180, 200, 206 and n.62,
207, 217, 340
'Old fighters' of Nazi Party, 27, 121–2,
140–1, 230, 355
opposition, revival of in working class
(1935), 83–4; in Protestant
Church conflict, 166 ff., 174 ff.,
176; in Catholic 'Church struggle',
193 ff., 331 ff., 376; on schools
issue, 209 ff.; of workers to War
Economy Decree, 297–8; to
'euthanasia action', 334–40; to
removal of crucifixes from
schools, 334–40; absence of in
middle class, 375; lack of on
Jewish Question, 377–8; minimal
among peasantry, 374; evaluation of, 374 ff.; influence on
regime, 378 ff.
Ostmark, see Austria
Ottilienheim, 338

Palatinate, 13–14, 16–17, 27, 33–5,
42–3, 88 n.72, 114 n.7, 119,
226–7, 235, 259, 358; Gau of
Nazi Party, 119
Papacy, 249
Papen, Franz von, 69 and n.10
Paris, 9, 50, 53, 99, 258
Parsberg, 343–7
partible inheritance, 34
Passau, 228
'Pastors' Emergency League', 159,
163–4
peasantry, 5, 27, ch. 1 passim, 70,
111–12, 114 n.7, 115 and n.9,
118, 121, 123, 126, 135, 139,
161, 170–2, 195, 241, 243–4,
256, 265–6, 281, 282–96, 341,
351–2, 374–6, 380; structure
of peasant farms in Bavaria,
33–5; in First World War, 34,
36; and appeal of Nazism, 37–
40; mood at 'seizure of power',

38-9; discontent in early years of dictatorship, 41-5, 46-8; and Reich Entailed Farm Law, 42-4, 53; and dairy-farming ordinances, 45-6, 52-3; conservatism of, 48; difficulties of mobilization of, 48-9, 60, 62, 285, 290; impact of labour shortage on, 57-63; low morale in pre-war years, 59-61; low morale during war, 290; attitude towards Nazi State, 59-65, 288 ff., 293-5; indifference towards political events, 39, 48-9, 60-2, 286, 289-90; during war, 282-96; relations with foreign workers, 287-8, 294-5; apathy among, 286, 290; sharpening of discontent in 1941, 288 ff.; limited penetration of Nazi ideology among, 242-4, 246, 256, 265-6, 289-92; and evacuees, 291; and Nazi Party during war, 292, 294
Pegnitz, 102, 262
Penzberg, 21, 105 n.14, 106, 120 n.26, 300 n.58, 314 n.2
'People's Mission', 160-2, 176, 186
petty bourgeoisie, 1-2, 5, 70, ch. 3 passim, 161, 315 ff., 375-6, 380; problems of defining, 111; ideology of, 111-12; difficulties of sources relating to, 112-14; interpretations of position in Third Reich, 113-14; size of, 114 n.7; support for Nazism in 1933, 114 ff.; attractiveness of Nazi ideology to, 116; Führer cult among, 122-3, 131, 133, 154; ideological affinities with Nazism, 139, 153-5; during war, 315 ff.; and see middle class, Mittelstand
Pfaffenhofen, 134
Pfalz, Gau of Nazi Party, 119
Pfarrkirchen, 253
Pirmasens, 88 n.72
plebiscites (1933), 48, 220; (1934), 47-8, 171, 195, 220; (1936), 199, 383; (1938), 217
pogrom, in Gunzenhausen (1934), 236-8; of November 1938, 143, 147, 151, 231, 253-4, 257-75,

358, 364, 371, and see 'Crystal Night'
Poland, 284-5, 332, 359, 367
police, 171, 175, 204, 215, 287, 320; reports of on popular opinion, 7; ordinances on agricultural labourers, 59; of Augsburg, 85; of Hof, 304; of Munich, 82, 201, 203 n.53, 205-6, 234, 245; of Nuremberg, 251; and see Bavarian Political Police, Gestapo
Polish campaign, 284, 360
popular opinion, definition of concept, 4-5; difficulties of evidence, 6-10; reporting by Nazi authorities on, 7-8; reporting by exile organizations on, 7-10; evaluation of significance of, 373 ff.; influence on regime of, 378 ff.
Potsdam, 179-80
Prague, 9, 99
press, Catholic, 185-6; left-wing, 70, 74-5; Nazi, 162, 165, 171, 196, 201 n.49, 232-3, 243, 260 and n.26, 308
prices, agricultural, 36-40, 45, 47 n.52, 49, 52, 54; food, 83, 93, 128, 298, 301, 303-5, 307 n.80, 379
Prichsenstadt, 270
priests, 147, 186, 190, 334; role in shaping opinion and popular opposition, 194 ff.; arrest and punishment of, 196, 201 n.49, 202; and Jewish Question, 229, 246-57; and 'euthanasia action', 338; and 'crucifix affair', 348; and see clergy (Catholic)
Primizfeier, 196-8
prisoners-of-war, 282, 286-7, 297, 300 n.58
'Production Battle', 53, 56-7, 63, 282
propaganda, 4-5, 28, 48, 58, 64, 70-1, 93-4, 95 and n.86, 104, 154, 247, 290-2, 302 n.64, 324, 326, 373, 378, 384; difficulties of among peasantry, 28, 48-9, 290-2; impact on workers, 73-7, 93-4, 95 n.86, 96-7, 309-10; anti-Bolshevik, 96-7, 131; anti-Semitic, 96-7, 230, 243, 272, 274-6, 360, 365-6, 370, 372; appeal to middle class, 116,

propaganda (*cont.*):
150-1, 154; and Catholic
Church, 196, 201 n.49; on
schools issue, 214; on foreign
workers, 288; on civil servants,
324, 326; on euthanasia, 340
Propaganda Ministry, 151, 379
Propoiszk, 291
'protective custody', 52, 71, 103-4,
127, 311 n.94
Protestant Church, *see* Church
Prussia, 11, 21, 36, 47, 144, 146, 157
public opinion, distinguished from
popular opinion, 4

Rackl, Bishop Michael, 203-4, 223
n.18, 340 and n.26
radio, 28, 48, 93, 285, 308, 364
Räterepublik, 18, 157, 229, 266
Rath, Ernst vom, 253, 257-8, 260,
262
rationing, 304, 306-7, 317, 379, 382
raw-material shortages, 120 n.26, 121,
127-8, 132-6, 268, 298, 315-16
rearmament, 15, 55, 95, 98
Reich Bishop, 160, 162-5, 167, *and
see* Müller, Ludwig
Reich Chancellory, 335, 353
Reich Entailed Farm Law (*Reichserbhofgesetz*), 41-5, 48-9,
51-3, 53 n.75, 63
Reich Food Estate (*Reichsnährstand*),
40, 45, 57, 60-1, 63-4, 282,
292, 374
Reich Ministry, of Economics, 244
n.63, 246 n.70, 321; of the
Interior, 239, 335, 337; of
Justice, 335; of Propaganda,
151, 279
Reichstag, elections to, 18-27, 190-1,
230
Reichstag Fire, 117
Regen, 21, 79, 87
Regensburg, 124, 215 n.95, 228, 234
n.27, 262
religious instruction, 147, 182, 210,
216
religious orders, ousted from teaching
posts, 210 ff.
'reserved occupation', 285, 289, 291,
304
resistance, 2-4, 9, 109, 110 n.31, 378;
passive, by peasantry, 46, 49-50,

52; beginnings of by left-wing
underground groups, 72; limited
extent and appeal of among
workers, 74-5, 79; inner, of
workers, 80; inapplicability of
term to Protestant Church con-
flict, 176-7; lack of among
Protestant population in 1939,
181; 'reluctant', within Protest-
ant Church, 184 n.77; difficulties
of in 1940, 304; isolation of,
314
retailers, 111, 317
Revolutionary Trade Union Opposition
(RGO), 70
Revolution of 1918, 18, 69, 156, 185,
189-90, 213, 229
Rhineland, 11, 131, 383
Riga, 359
Röhm, Ernst, 251
Ramantische Straße, 244
Rosenberg, Alfred, 195-6
Rosenheim, 342, 354
Rosenthal porcelain factory, Selb, 86
Rößler, Paster H., 175
Rothenburg ob der Tauber, 18, 172,
244, 262
Ruhpolding, 266
Ruhr, 20, 102 n.98
Rupprecht, ex-Crown Prince of Bavaria,
201
Russia, 63, 93-4, 96-7, 106, 295, 300,
304, 329, 348, 350, 356, 360-1,
365, 367, *and see* Soviet Union,
USSR
Russian campaign, 289-90, 297, 356

SA (*Sturmabteilung*), 50, 67 n.5, 75,
80, 87, 96, 114, 118 n.20, 122,
129-30, 143, 162-3, 172, 198,
205, 236-8, 251, 257-8, 261,
263, 266, 270, 276, 309, 371
Saar, 121
Sandberg, 48
Saxony, 11, 20, 157
Schacht, Hjalmar, 151
Schemm, Hans, 158, 169
Schieder, Julius, 166, 179
Schirach, Baldur von, 146-7
schools, 144-7, 334, 340-57, 376;
convent, 210-13; 'community',
183, 204, 209 ff., 213 ff., 340,
341 n.28, 342, 377 n.8;

denominational, 180, 187, 206, 213 ff., 377 n.8; issue of, 180-3, 201 n.49, 209 ff.
Schulenburg, Fritz-Dietlof, Graf von der, 141
Schwabach, 162, 262, 305-8, 314 n.99
Schwäbische Alb, 335
Schwandorf, 211, 228
Schweinfurt, 172, 267, 270, 309-11, 369
Selb, 13, 86-7
self-employed, 114 n.7, 118-19
service sector, 12, 66, 68
Seugast, 215
Sicherheitsdienst (SD), 7, 56-7, 59-61, 247, 254 n.5, 271, 276, 279, 288, 294, 301-3, 305-11, 320-2, 325, 360, 362, 365-6, 371, 381-2
Sicherheitspolizei, 359
Siebert, Ludwig, 170-3, 352, 356
'Siebert Programme', 58 n.90
Siemens-Schuchert firm, Nuremberg, 100
small businesses, 111, 115-16, 120-1, 127, 134, 137-9, 153, 316 ff.; compulsory closure of, 134, 320-2
Sobibor, 359
Social Democratic Party (SPD), 7, 9, 18-23, 27, 66, 69-76, 79-80, 86, 91-2, 94, 96, 101, 109-10, 157, 187-9, 193, 236, 241 n.50, 304
Sonthofen, 381 n.19
Sopade, 7-9, 44, 46-7, 57, 64, 73-6, 78-80, 83, 85-7, 88 and n.73, 90-5, 99-100, 105 and n.13, 107, 109-10, 120, 122-3, 126-8, 131-2, 137, 139-40, 148-50, 152, 154, 177 and n.61, 178, 219-20, 267, 272-3, 303 and n.68, 315
Soviet Union, 359, and see Russia, USSR; secret police of (GPU), 365-6
Spain, 106
Spanish Civil War, 93
Special Court(s) (Sondergericht(e)), 10, 104-5, 204, 311 n.94; of Munich, 84, 104, 123, 202, 253, 266, 311 n.94, 366-7
Sportpalast, Berlin, 159
SS (Schutzstaffeln) 129-32, 143, 163,
204-5, 207, 222 n.13, 234, 236, 275-6, 366, 368, 371
Staffelstein, 262
Stahlhelm, 80
Stalin, Joseph, 374
Stalingrad, 295, 309-10
Steinbauer, Karl, 252
Stimmungsberichte, 7
Straubing, 228, 262
Streicher, Julius, 162, 169, 172, 228, 229 and n.14, 232, 235-6, 240, 242, 262
'Strength through Joy' (KdF), 76, 80-1, 92, 95-7, 125, 136-8, 306, 313
strikes, 31, 69, 82, 87-8, 90 and n.78, 100, 102-3, 300 and n.58, and see work refusal
Stürmer, Der, 162, 201 n.49, 232-4, 243, 245, 252
Stuttgart, 167
Sudetenland, 9, 58, 103, 137, 152, 213, 258-9
Suez, 383
Swabia, 13-14, 17, 20, 22, 24-5, 33, 35, 52, 57, 59, 75, 81, 115, 134, 225, 227, 233, 245, 262, 266; Gau of Nazi Party, 28, 119; and see Government President
synagogues, desecration and destruction of, 228, 257-9, 261-4, 267, 271

Tatzelwurm, 103
teachers, 113, 115-19, 140, 143-8, 181, 183, 188, 212; in Nazi Party, 143 and n.3, 144-5; grievances of, 144-7; ideological affinities with Nazism, 147-8; opposite pole to priest, 183, 194, 199-200; and crucifix issue, 207, 345, 351, 354-5
Theresienstadt, 359
Theresiental, 87, 90
Thuringia, 11, 156-7, 160
Tittmoning, 222
tourism, 125 and n.44, 130, 134, 136-8, 317-18, 321
trade, 12, 66, 68, 316
tradesmen, 115-16, 120-1, 127, 133-4, 315 ff.
trade unions, 67, 69, 72, 77, 80, 93-4, 96, 98, 315

Traunstein, 134, 142, 351–2
Triumph works, Nuremberg, 86
Trustee of Labour, 89
Tyrol, 103, 137

Uffenheim, 18
Uhlfelder department store, Munich, 120
Ulm, 168, 245
unemployment, 13, 15, 21, 67–9, 71–2, 77–81, 95, 101; relief, 68–9, 71, 78; decline in Third Reich, 77–8, 95, 98, 108 n.25
Unsleben, 240
Unteraltertheim, 270
Upper Bavaria, 13–14, 17, 21–2, 24–5, 33, 35, 42–4, 51, 57, 58 n.90, 61–2, 88, 92, 103, 115, 117, 120 n.26, 125, 130, 134–5, 144, 147, 195, 207, 225, 227, 233, 244, 259, 261, 265, 269 n.73, 293, 342, 351, 353–4, and see Government President, Munich-Upper Bavaria (Gau of Nazi Party)
Upper Franconia, 13–15, 17, 21–7, 35, 43, 49, 53, 57, 78, 82, 85–6, 102–3, 125, 130, 147, 156, 158, 169, 205, 227, 236, 253, 254 n.7, 259, 264, 270, 279, 289, 317, 341, 350, and see Government President
Upper Palatinate, 13–14, 17, 22–5, 27, 35, 42, 47–8, 57, 59, 62, 76, 78–9, 85–6, 106, 125, 161, 207, 211, 215 and n.96, 225, 227–8, 232, 245, 262–3, 265, 269, 286 n.13, 342–3, and see Government President
Upper Silesia, Gauleitung of, 367
USA, 266, 290, 296, 383
USSR, 288, 340 n.26, and see Russia, Soviet Union

Vatican, 188
Veit, Dr Friedrich, 158
Velburg, 345–7
Versailles, settlement of, 383
Vienna, 103
Vietnam, 383
Vilseck, 263
Vohenstrauß, 79
Völkischer Beobachter, 216

Völkischer Block, 19, 187
Völkisch movement, 18, 157–8, 229–30
Volksfront, 50, 53
Volksgemeinschaft, 2, 29, 51, 75, 97, 276, 281, 318, 363, and see national community

Waffen-SS, 130
wages, 58–9, 61, 76, 79–80, 83, 86, 92, 96 ff., 153, 297, 301, 304–5, 307 n.80, 309, 315, 379; reductions in, 69, 80, 87, 95; discontent about, 75, 78–9, 83–5, 87–8, 93, 301, 305–7, 309; increased, 90, 98–9, 102–3; effects of War Economy Decree on, 297
Wagner, Adolf, 147, 173, 216, 234, 341–4, 347–9, 352–6, 381
Wahl, Karl, 234
war, attitudes towards, 93–4, 96–7, 107, 121, 148, 151–2, 286, 290–2, 294, 308, 313; First World, 1–2, 18, 34, 46, 57, 107, 156, 178, 194, 201 n.49, 229, 235, 282, 293–4, 353; Second World, 55, 130, 194; economic effects on Bavarian population, ch. 7 passim; and 'Church struggle', ch. 8 passim; imagined connections with persecution of Jews, 368–70; 'total', 281, 308–9, 326, 329
War Economy Decree, 297
Wasserburg, 49, 122, 140
Weber, Christian, 149–50
Wehrmacht, 58, 142, 152, 283, 289, 293, 295, 304, 310, 316, 320, 348, 366
Wehrmacht Economic Inspectorate, 102, 135, 151
Weiden, 76, 86, 161, 228
Weilheim, 207
Weimar Republic, 18, 21, 28, 36–7, 41, 74, 116–17, 131, 157–8, 185–8, 191, 224, 230, 314
Weiß Ferdl, 148
Weißenburg, 81, 124, 251, 269
Wessel, Horst, 77
western campaign, 286
Westphalia, 323 n.34, 339
Westwall (Siegfried Line), 102 and n.98
Weyarn, 83

white-collar employees, 113 and n.4,
114 n.7, 116, 118-19, 121, 140,
323

Windsheim, 172

Winniza, 366

Winter Aid (WHW), 54, 63, 71, 79-80,
84, 97, 101, 171 and n.52, 172,
214, 342

Wirtschaftspartei, 19

Wittelsbach, house of, 225

work creation, 77-9, 81, 92-3, 96, 108
n.25

workers, ch. 2 *passim*, 64, 139-40, 153,
329, 296-315; and Nazi propaganda, 73-7; 93-4, 96-7; limited
interest in resistance, 74-5, 79,
91, 93, 97, 109; attitude towards
Nazism, 78, 84, 90, 96-7, 303,
305, and ch. 2 *passim*; revival of
opposition (1935), 83-4; before
'Special Court', 84; in armaments
factories, 85, 91, 102, 106-7;
Catholic, 91-2, 96-7; increased
pressure upon in pre-war years,
98-9; absenteeism, 99, 102,
298-9, 302; indiscipline, 99,
102, 110 n.31, 296, 298, 302,
305, 315; sickness, 99, 298-9;
sabotage, 106, 110; growing
bargaining power of, 98 ff.;
relations with foreign workers,
288, 300 and n.58, 314 n.99;
impact of war on, 296-315; low
morale of, 302, 305, 310-11;
bitter complaints of, 305-6;
unrest about ration cuts, 306;
impact of bombing raids on,
309-11; *and see* working class

working class, 5, 8-9, ch. 2 *passim*,
111-12, 123, 161-2, 281, 296-
315, 375-6, 379-80; and Nazi
Party before 1933, 67 and n.5,
70; unemployment in, 67-70;
impact of 'seizure of power'
on, 70-2; militancy in, 83, 85,
90-1, 98, 109, 296, 300-1; unrest in, 83, 84 n.55, 85, 87-90,
303 ff.; growing discontent in,
83, 90, 105; *Sopade*'s estimation
of political attitudes in, 94-5,
96-7; attitudes and behaviour
during war, 296-315; privations
during war, 298, 305-6; resentment at social injustice, 305,
307, 309, 312; neutralization of,
110, 313; alienation of, 375;
regime apprehensive of, 375,
379-80; *and see* workers

work refusal, 81, 99-100, 102 n.98,
300; by foreign workers, 287,
300 and n.58; *and see* strikes

Wunsiedel, 253

Wurm, Bishop Theophil, 164, 167-8,
173, 178, 335

Württemberg, 164, 167-8, 173, 178,
254 and n.5, 335

Würzburg, 16, 227, 266, 270, 302-3,
320, 325, 358-9, 365

'Yellow Star', wearing of imposed on
Jews in 1941, 361-2

Zirndorf, 262

Zündapp-Werke, Nuremberg, 100

Zwiesel, 79-81